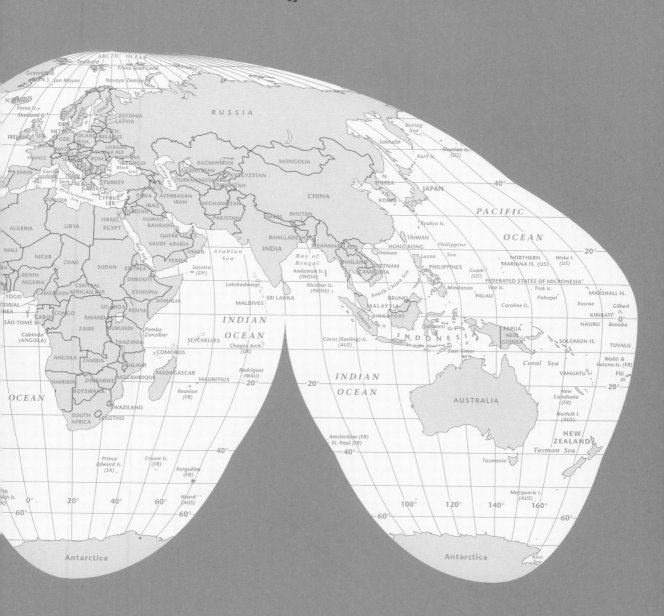

Junior Worldmark Encyclopedia of the Nations

VOLUME 3

Junior Worldmark Encyclopedia of the Nations

An imprint of Gale Research
An ITP Information/Reference Group Company

Changing the Way the World Learns

NEW YORK • LONDON • BONN • BOSTON • DETROIT
MADRID • MELBOURNE • MEXICO CITY • PARIS
SINGAPORE • TOKYO • TORONTO • WASHINGTON
ALBANY NY • BELMONT CA • CINCINNATI OH

VOLUME

Denmark to
Guyana

JUNIOR WORLDMARK ENCYCLOPEDIA OF THE NATIONS

Timothy L. Gall and Susan Bevan Gall, *Editors*
Rosalie Wieder, *Senior Editor*
Deborah Baron and Daniel M. Lucas, *Associate Editors*
Brian Rajewski and Deborah Rutti, *Graphics and Layout*
Cordelia R. Heaney, *Editorial Assistant*
Dianne K. Daeg de Mott, Janet Fenn, Matthew Markovich,
    Ariana Ranson, and Craig Strasshofer, *Copy Editors*
Janet Fenn and Matthew Markovich, *Proofreaders*

U•X•L Staff

Jane Hoehner, *U•X•L Developmental Editor*
Sonia Benson and Rob Nagel, *Contributors*
Thomas L. Romig, *U•X•L Publisher*
Mary Beth Trimper, *Production Director*
Evi Seoud, *Assistant Production Manager*
Shanna Heilveil, *Production Associate*
Cynthia Baldwin, *Product Design Manager*
Barbara J. Yarrow, *Graphic Services Supervisor*
Mary Krzewinski, *Cover Designer*
Margaret McAvoy-Amoto, *Permissions Associate (Pictures)*

Library of Congress Cataloging-in-Publication Data
Junior Worldmark encyclopedia of the nations / edited by Timothy Gall
    and Susan Gall.
        p.   cm.
    Includes bibliographical references and index.
    ISBN 0-7876-0741-X (set)
    1. Geography--Encyclopedias, Juvenile. 2. History--Encyclopedias,
Juvenile. 3. Economics--Juvenile literature. 4. Political science--
Encyclopedia, Juvenile. 5. United Nations--Encyclopedias,
Juvenile. I. Gall, Timothy L. II. Gall, Susan B.
    G63.J86   1995
    910'.3--dc20   95-36739
                                                                    CIP

ISBN 0-7876-0741-X (set)
ISBN 0-7876-0742-8 (vol. 1)   ISBN 0-7876-0743-6 (vol. 2)   ISBN 0-7876-0744-4 (vol. 3)
ISBN 0-7876-0745-2 (vol. 4)   ISBN 0-7876-0746-0 (vol. 5)   ISBN 0-7876-0747-9 (vol. 6)
ISBN 0-7876-0748-7 (vol. 7)   ISBN 0-7876-0749-5 (vol. 8)   ISBN 0-7876-0750-9 (vol. 9)

U•X•L is an imprint of Gale Research Inc.,
an International Thomson Publishing Company.
ITP logo is a trademark under license.

CONTENTS

Guide to Country Articles

Every country profile in this encyclopedia includes the same 35 headings. Also included in every profile is a map (showing the country and its location in the world), the country's flag and seal, and a table of data on the country. The country articles are organized alphabetically in nine volumes. A glossary of terms is included in each of the nine volumes. This glossary defines many of the specialized terms used throughout the encyclopedia. A keyword index to all nine volumes appears at the end of Volume 9.

Flag color symbols

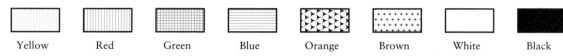

| Yellow | Red | Green | Blue | Orange | Brown | White | Black |

Alphabetical listing of sections

Agriculture	21	Income	18	
Armed Forces	16	Industry	19	
Bibliography	35	Judicial System	15	
Climate	3	Labor	20	
Domesticated Animals	22	Languages	9	
Economy	17	Location and Size	1	
Education	31	Media	32	
Energy and Power	27	Migration	7	
Environment	5	Mining	25	
Ethnic Groups	8	Plants and Animals	4	
Famous People	34	Political Parties	14	
Fishing	23	Population	6	
Foreign Trade	26	Religions	10	
Forestry	24	Social Development	28	
Government	13	Topography	2	
Health	29	Tourism/Recreation	33	
History	12	Transportation	11	
Housing	30			

Sections listed numerically

1	Location and Size	19	Industry
2	Topography	20	Labor
3	Climate	21	Agriculture
4	Plants and Animals	22	Domesticated Animals
5	Environment	23	Fishing
6	Population	24	Forestry
7	Migration	25	Mining
8	Ethnic Groups	26	Foreign Trade
9	Languages	27	Energy and Power
10	Religions	28	Social Development
11	Transportation	29	Health
12	History	30	Housing
13	Government	31	Education
14	Political Parties	32	Media
15	Judicial System	33	Tourism/Recreation
16	Armed Forces	34	Famous People
17	Economy	35	Bibliography
18	Income		

Abbreviations and acronyms to know

GMT= Greenwich mean time. The prime, or Greenwich, meridian passes through Greenwich, England (near London), and marks the center of the initial time zone for the world. The standard time of all 24 time zones relate to Greenwich mean time. Every profile contains a map showing the country and its location in the world.

These abbreviations are used in references to famous people:
b.=born
d.=died
fl.=flourished (lived and worked)
r.=reigned (for kings, queens, and similar monarchs)

A dollar sign ($) stands for US$ unless otherwise indicated.

DENMARK

Kingdom of Denmark

Kongeriget Danmark

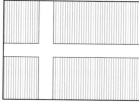

CAPITAL: Copenhagen (København).

FLAG: The Danish national flag, known as the Dannebrog, is one of the oldest national flags in the world, although the concept of a national flag did not develop until the late 18th century when the Dannebrog was already half a millennium old. The design shows a white cross on a field of red.

ANTHEM: There are two national anthems—*Kong Kristian stod ved hojen mast (King Christian Stood by the Lofty Mast)* and *Der er et yndigt land (There Is a Lovely Land)*.

MONETARY UNIT: The krone (Kr) of 100 øre is a commercially convertible paper currency with one basic official exchange rate. There are coins of 25 and 50 øre, and 1, 5, 10, and 20 kroner, and notes of 50, 100, 500, and 1,000 kroner. Kr1 = $0.1515 (or $1 = Kr6.599).

WEIGHTS AND MEASURES: The metric system is the legal standard, but some local units are used for special purposes.

HOLIDAYS: New Year's Day, 1 January; Constitution Day, 5 June; Christmas Day, 25 December; Boxing Day, 26 December. Movable religious holidays include Holy Thursday, Good Friday, Easter Monday, Prayer Day (4th Friday after Easter), Ascension, and Whitmonday.

TIME: 1 PM = noon GMT.

1 LOCATION AND SIZE

Situated in southern Scandinavia, the Kingdom of Denmark consists of Denmark proper, the Faroe Islands, and Greenland. Denmark proper, comprising the peninsula of Jutland (Jylland) and 406 islands, has an area of 43,070 square kilometers (16,629 square miles), slightly more than twice the size of the state of Massachusetts.

The Jutland peninsula accounts for 29,767 square kilometers (11,493 square miles) of the total land area, while the islands have a combined area of 13,317 square kilometers (5,142 square miles).

Except for the southern boundary with Germany, the country is surrounded by water.

Denmark's capital city, Copenhagen, is located on the eastern edge of the country on the island of Sjaelland.

2 TOPOGRAPHY

The average altitude of Denmark is about 30 meters (98 feet). In parts of Jutland, along the southern coast of the island of Lolland, and in a few other areas, the coast is protected by dikes. Almost all of Denmark proper consists of a glacial deposit over a chalk base. The surface is made up of small hills, moors, ridges, hilly islands, raised sea bottoms, and, on the west coast, downs and marshes. There are many small rivers and inland seas.

3 CLIMATE

There is little fluctuation between day and night temperatures, but sudden changes in wind direction cause considerable day-to-day temperature changes. The mean temperature in February, the coldest month, is 0°C (32°F), and in July, the warmest, 17°C (63°F). Rain falls fairly evenly throughout the year, the annual average amounting to approximately 61 centimeters (24 inchs).

4 PLANTS AND ANIMALS

There are many species of ferns, flower, fungi, and mosses; common trees include spruce and beech. Few wild or large animals remain. Birds, however, are abundant; many species breed in Denmark and migrate to warmer countries during the autumn and winter.

5 ENVIRONMENT

Denmark's most basic environmental legislation is the Environmental Protection Act of 1974, which entrusts the Ministry of the Environment, in conjunction with local authorities, with antipollution responsibilities. The quality of the land is endangered by over 3,100 dumping areas for harmful chemicals.

Much of Denmark's industrial and household waste is recycled. In 1985, some 312,000 tons of wastepaper, representing 31% of paper consumed, was collected, and recycled wastepaper accounted for 60% of paper production that year. A special treatment plant on the island of Fyn, handles dangerous chemical and oil wastes.

The waters of the North Sea are contaminated by seepage of industrial pollutants. The nation has 2.6 cubic miles of water. Forty-three percent is used for farming, and 27% for industrial purposes. Remaining environmental problems include air pollution, especially from automobile emissions; excessive noise, especially in the major cities; and the pollution of rivers, lakes, and open sea by raw sewage.

In 1994, Denmark had 23 protected wildlife sites, with an area of 1,631 square miles of about 9.8% of the total land area. As of 1994, one of Denmark's 49 species of mammals and 16 of its 190 bird species were endangered. Seven of the nation's 1,000 bird species were also endangered.

6 POPULATION

At the beginning of 1992, the population of Denmark proper was 5,162,126; the projected population for the year 2000 was 5,245,000. The Faroe Islands had 47,449 people at the end of 1990, and Greenland had 55,117 at the end of 1992.

Excluding the Faroe Islands and Greenland, the population density in 1992 was 120 persons per square kilometer (310 per square mile). The population of Copenhagen, the capital and principal city, was 464,566 at the beginning of 1992 (1,339,395 including suburbs).

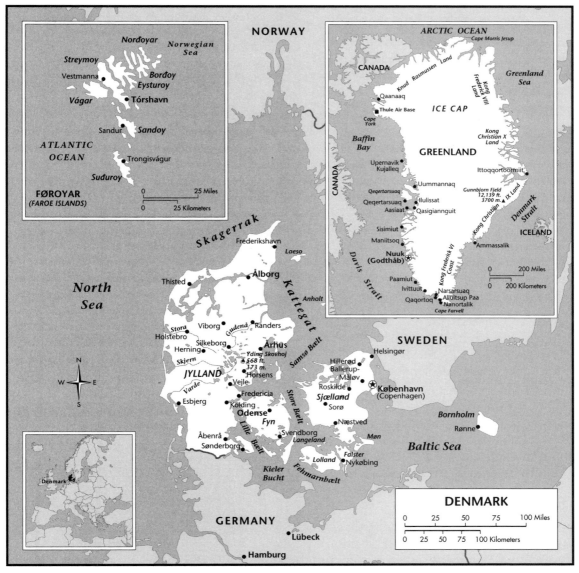

LOCATION: 54°33′31″ to 57°44′55″N; 8°4′36″ to 15°11′59″E. **BOUNDARY LENGTHS:** Germany, 68 kilometers (42 miles); total coastline, 7,314 kilometers (4,545 miles). **TERRITORIAL SEA LIMIT:** 3 miles.

7 MIGRATION

Emigration is limited, owing mainly to the relatively high standard of living in Denmark. Most of the 22,167 Danes who emigrated in 1991 went to the United States (2,317), the United Kingdom (2,715), Germany (2,754), or other Scandinavian and European countries. In the same year,

20,430 immigrants entered Denmark. At the end of 1992, Denmark was harboring 58,300 refugees. The total number of foreigners was 180,103, of whom 33,653 were Turks. Total internal migration was 855,125 in 1991, of which 307,984 was from one municipality to another.

8 ETHNIC GROUPS

The population of Denmark proper is of native northern European stock; the Danes are among the most homogeneous peoples of Europe. There is a small German minority in southern Jutland.

9 LANGUAGES

Danish is the universal language. There are many dialects, but they are gradually being supplanted by standard Danish. Modern Danish has departed further from the ancient Nordic language of the Viking period than have Icelandic, Norwegian, and Swedish (to which Danish is closely related), and there are a substantial number of German and English words. Many Danes can speak English and German, and many more are capable of understanding these languages.

10 RELIGIONS

About 91% of the people adhere to the official religion, the Evangelical Lutheran Church, which is supported by the state and headed by the sovereign. There are small groups of Roman Catholics, Jews, and members of other faiths.

11 TRANSPORTATION

Transportation is highly developed. At the end of 1991 there were 66,482 kilometers

Photo credit: Susan D. Rock.

A pedestrian shopping street in Copenhagen.

(41,312 miles) of public roads, of which 97% were paved. The road system is well engineered and adequately maintained. A new bridge connecting Denmark to Sweden is expected to open by 2000. At the end of 1991, Denmark had 1,593,960 private cars, and 306,456 commercial vehicles. The bicycle is a very popular form of transportation.

The total length of the portion of the railway system owned and operated by the Danish State Railways was 2,120 kilometers (1,317 miles) at the end of 1991; only 555 kilometers (345 miles) of railway were privately operated. In 1990, Danish State Railways performed some 4,851 million passenger-kilometers of service, and transported 7,973,000 tons of freight.

The Danish merchant fleet at the end of 1991 was composed of 296 ships of 5,145,000 gross registered tons. Denmark has many excellent and well-equipped harbors, of which Copenhagen is the most important.

Kastrup Airport near Copenhagen is a center of international air traffic, and accommodated 11,109,000 arriving and departing passengers in 1991. In 1991, Danish airports accommodated 5,028,000 international passengers from 197,501 flights.

12 HISTORY

Although there is evidence of agricultural settlement as early as 4000 BC and of bronze weaponry and jewelry by 1800 BC, Denmark's early history is little known. Tribesmen calling themselves Danes arrived from Sweden around AD 500, and Danish sailors later took part in the Viking raids, especially in those against England. Harald Bluetooth (d.985), first Christian king of Denmark, conquered Norway, and his son Sweyn conquered England.

Denmark, Norway, and England were united until 1042, when the union with England came to an end, and Norway seceded. During the next three centuries, however, Danish control was reestablished over Sweden and Norway, and in the reign of Margrethe (1387–1412) there was a union of the Danish, Norwegian, and Swedish crowns. In 1523, the Scandinavian union was dissolved, but Norway remained united with Denmark until 1814.

The Protestant Reformation was established in Denmark during the reign of Christian III (1534–59). A series of wars with Sweden during the seventeenth and early eighteenth centuries resulted in the loss of Danish territory. Denmark was deprived of Norway by the terms of the Peace of Kiel (1814) and lost its southern provinces of Slesvig, Holstein, and Lauenburg as a result of the Prusso-Danish wars of 1848–49 and 1864.

After this, the Danes concentrated on internal affairs, instituting important economic changes (in particular, specialization in dairy production) that transformed the country from a nation of poor peasants into one of prosperous farmers. Denmark remained neutral in World War I, and after a vote in 1920, North Slesvig was reincorporated into Denmark.

Ignoring the German-Danish nonaggression pact of 1939, Hitler invaded Denmark in April 1940, and the German occupation lasted until 1945. At first, the Danish government continued to function, protecting the nation's Jewish minority and other refugees as long as it could (some 7,200 Jews eventually escaped to neutral Sweden).

However, when a resistance movement developed, destroying factories, railroads, and other targets, the Danish government resigned in August 1943 rather than carry out the German demand for the death sentence against the resistance fighters. Thereafter, Denmark was governed by

Germany directly, and conflict with the resistance grew.

After the war, Denmark became a charter member of the UN and of the North Atlantic Treaty Organization (NATO). In 1952, it joined with the other Scandinavian nations to form the Nordic Council. Having joined European Free Trade Association (EFTA) in 1960, Denmark left that association for the European Community (EC) in 1973. Meanwhile, during the 1950s and 1960s, agricultural and manufacturing production rose impressively, a high level of employment was maintained, and foreign trade grew.

However, the expense of maintaining Denmark's highly developed social security system, persistent inflation, rising unemployment, and increases in the price of imported oil posed political as well as economic problems for Denmark in the 1970s and 1980s, as one weak coalition government followed another.

Economic performance continued to be a major issue in the 1990s. Voters narrowly rejected the Maastricht Treaty on European Union in 1992, but later approved it in 1994 after modifications were made in Denmark's favor.

13 GOVERNMENT

Denmark is a constitutional monarchy. Legislative power is vested jointly in the monarch and in a single-chamber parliament (Folketing). Executive power belongs to the sovereign—through his ministers—and judicial power is exercised by the courts.

The sovereign must belong to the Lutheran Church. The crown is hereditary in the royal house of Lyksborg, which ascended the throne in 1863. On the death of a king, the throne descends to his son or daughter, a son taking precedence.

The single-chamber Folketing is elected every four years (more frequently, if necessary) by direct, secret ballot by Danish subjects 18 years of age and older. There are 179 members, 2 of whom are elected in the Faroe Islands and 2 in Greenland.

Denmark is divided into 14 counties and 275 local units, each governed by an elected council.

14 POLITICAL PARTIES

The major parties support the United Nations and NATO and favor inter-Scandinavian cooperation. Aims of the leading Social Democratic Party are to break up monopolies, redistribute personal incomes by taxation and other measures, divide large farm properties into smaller units, and raise working-class living standards through full employment.

The Conservative Party advocates an economic policy based on the rights of private property and private enterprise. It calls for a national pension system that would encourage personal initiative and savings.

Following the 1990 general election, a new center-right coalition government was formed with Paul Schlüter remaining as prime minister. The coalition was reformed in 1994 composed of the Social Democrats, the Social Liberals, the Centre Democrats, and the Christian People's

Party. Paul Rasmussen (Social Democrat) was appointed prime minister.

15 JUDICIAL SYSTEM

As a rule, cases have their first hearing before the Copenhagen city court, the Aarhus city court, or one of 84 local courts. Certain major cases, however, come under the High Courts *(Landsrettes)* in Copenhagen and Viborg; otherwise these courts function as courts of appeal. The Supreme Court *(Hojesteret),* made up of 15 judges, serves solely as a court of appeal for cases coming from the High Courts.

16 ARMED FORCES

All young men must register for military service at the age of 18 and are subject to 9–12 months service. Women may volunteer for service, including service on combat vessels. The army consists of 17,300 personnel, the navy 4,900, and the air force 7,000. There are also 72,500 members of the reserves and 70,000 in the volunteer home guard. Military expenditures for 1992 amounted to $2.8 billion. Denmark has 1,300 military personnel abroad on peacekeeping assignments.

17 ECONOMY

Denmark is traditionally an agricultural country. Since the end of World War II (1945), however, manufacturing has gained rapidly in importance and now contributes more than agriculture to national income. Denmark has always been a prominent shipping nation.

Danish living standards and purchasing power are relatively high, but because Denmark is a small country, most impor-

Photo credit: Susan D. Rock.

Small craft harbor in Torshavn, Faeroe Islands—a group of islands located in the northern Atlantic.

tant industries must seek foreign markets in order to expand. Natural resources are limited, and therefore Denmark must export in order to pay for the raw materials, feeds, fertilizers, and fuels that must be imported. As a result, the national economy has been greatly influenced by trends and developments abroad.

Since the Danes joined the European Community (EC) on 1 January 1973, their trade position has improved. Economic recessions in 1974–75 and 1980–81 spurred a substantial rise in unemployment. From a rate of 0.9% in 1973, unemployment reached 12.3% in 1993. A trade surplus was registered in 1987 and grew in each of the succeeding five years. The central government deficit declined by two-thirds between 1982 and 1990.

18 INCOME

In 1992, Denmark's gross national product (GNP) was $133,941 million at current prices, or about $26,730 per person. For the period 1985–92 the average inflation rate was 3.4%, resulting in a real growth rate in per person GNP of 1.2%.

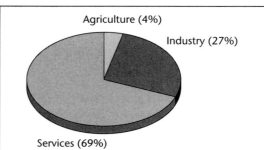

Components of the economy. This pie chart shows how much of the country's economy is devoted to agriculture (includes forestry, hunting, and fishing), industry, or services.

Agriculture (4%)
Industry (27%)
Services (69%)

19 INDUSTRY

Manufacturing has greatly expanded since the end of World War II and now accounts for a far greater share of national income than does agriculture. The chemical, metalworking, and pharmaceutical industries have made notable progress. Handicrafts remain important, and Danish stone, clay, glass, wood, and silver products are world famous.

Machinery, by far the most important industrial export, includes cement-making machinery, dairy machinery, diesel engines, electric motors, machine tools, and refrigeration equipment. Other important exports are canned foods, chemicals and pharmaceuticals, furniture, metal and paper products, ships, and textiles.

20 LABOR

The Danish labor force has grown steadily since World War II. In 1991, it totaled 2,844,000; male participation rates remained stable in the 1980s, while female participation rates went from 51% in 1970 to 75.9% in 1989.

Of those employed in 1990, 31.2% were in public service; 30.1% in trade and services; 20.3% in manufacturing; 6.4% in building and construction; 5.6% in agriculture and fishing; 5.3% in transportation; and 1.1% in other services. Unemployment increased from 1% of the work force in 1970 to 7% in 1980 to an estimated 11% in 1992.

An estimated 80% of all wage-earners, mostly blue-collar workers and government employees, are organized in trade unions. Since 1898, employers have had to insure their staffs against accidents incurred at work. Those disabled by work accidents are entitled to medical attention and compensation. There are also laws protecting women and children, agricultural workers, salaried employees, and seamen.

21 AGRICULTURE

About 60% of the land in 1991 was devoted to agriculture, much of it to natural or planted pastures, most of the cultivated part to feed and root crops. The majority of farms are small and medium-sized. Although the soil is not especially fertile and holdings are kept deliberately small, use of modern farm machinery and widespread use of fertilizers and concentrated feeds result in high yields and excellent quality.

Estimated 1992 yields for the following major crops (in tons) were: barley, 3,022,000; wheat, 3,648,000; rye, 333,000; sugar beets, 3,300,000; potatoes, 1,500,000; and roots and tubers, 1,500,000.

22 DOMESTICATED ANIMALS

Denmark is generally regarded as the world's outstanding example of well-managed animal husbandry. It maintains a uniformly high standard of operations, combining highly skilled labor, scientific experimentation and research, modern installations and machinery, and flexibility in farm management and marketing. Meat, dairy products, and eggs contribute an important share of Danish exports.

The livestock population in 1992 included 2,185,000 head of cattle, 10,345,000 hogs, 160,000 sheep, 32,000 horses, and 15,000,000 fowl. Mink, fox, polecat, finnraccoon, and chinchilla are raised for their pelts.

Production of dairy products for export included 4,600,000 tons of milk, 63,000 tons of butter, and 288,000 tons of cheese. In addition, egg production was 88,000 tons.

23 FISHING

The country's long coastline, located on rich fishing waters, provides Denmark with excellent fishing grounds. Fishing is an important source of domestic food supply, and both fresh and processed fish are important exports. The catch is composed mainly of herring and sprat, cod, mackerel, plaice, salmon, and whiting; but sole and other flatfish, tuna, and other varieties are also caught. Both trout and eel are important. In 1991, the saltwater fishing catch amounted to 1,765,634 tons.

24 FORESTRY

As a result of government policies, Denmark's forests, which were in danger of extinction at the beginning of the nineteenth century, now make up over 11% of the land and are in excellent condition. Spruce and beech are the most important trees. In 1991, approximately 2.3 million cubic meters of broad-leaved trees and conifers were cut. Denmark is a large importer of softwood lumber, especially from the other Scandinavian countries, and is a large particleboard consumer.

25 MINING

In 1991 clay was mined from some 90 pits and used primarily by the cement, brick-making, and ceramic tile industries. The production of sand, gravel, and crushed stone has become important in recent years, to meet domestic demand and also as an export to Germany and other Scandinavian countries. Kaolin is used mostly for coarse earthenware, furnace linings, and as a filler for paper. There are important limestone, chalk, and marl deposits in

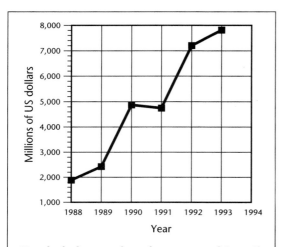

8,000

7,000

6,000

5,000

4,000

3,000

2,000

1,000

Millions of US dollars

1988 1989 1990 1991 1992 1993 1994

Year

Yearly balance of trade measured in millions of US dollars. The balance of trade is the difference between what a country sells to other countries (its exports) and what it buys (its imports). If a country imports more than it exports, it has a negative balance of trade (a trade deficit). If exports exceed imports there is a positive balance of trade (a trade surplus).

Principal exports in 1992 were machinery, meat, transport equipment, fish and shellfish, textiles, and chemical products. Principal imports were food, beverages and tobacco; transport equipment; and petroleum and petroleum products.

In 1992, Denmark's main trade partners were Germany (which accounted for 23.1% of Denmark's total trade), Sweden, the UK, the US, Norway, the Netherlands, France, and Italy.

Denmark terminated its membership in the European Free Trade Association (EFTA) on 1 January 1973 and, along with Ireland and the United Kingdom, became a member of the European Community (EC). Denmark's trade with EC members in 1992 comprised 54.3% of its exports and 53.4% of its imports.

27 ENERGY AND POWER

Denmark has almost no hydropower, and no nuclear power plants; 97.8% of all electric power generation is thermal. Geothermal production accounted for most of the remainder. Some domestic lignite and peat are used, and diesel power is employed in some small energy-generating plants, but the main sources of energy are imported coal and fuel oil. In 1991, 36.3 billion kilowatt hours of electricity were generated.

Production of oil in 1992 totaled 7.8 million tons, at a rate of 160,000 barrels per day, up 11% from 1991.

28 SOCIAL DEVELOPMENT

Denmark was one of the first countries in the world to establish efficient social

Jutland. Limonite (bog ore) is extracted for gas purification and pig iron production. During 1991, some 537,000 tons of salt were mined.

26 FOREIGN TRADE

The Danish economy depends heavily on foreign trade. Raw materials for use in production account for more than half the value of imports. Farm products traditionally comprised the bulk of total Danish exports, but since 1961, industrial exports have exceeded agricultural exports in value. In 1992, industrial products accounted for 70% of Denmark's total commodity exports by value; agricultural and fishing exports accounted for 18%.

Selected Social Indicators

These statistics are estimates for the period 1988 to 1993. For comparison purposes, data for the United States and averages for low-income countries and high-income countries are also given.

Indicator	Denmark	Low-income countries	High-income countries	United States
Per capita gross national product†	$26,730	$380	$23,680	$24,740
Population growth rate	0.2%	1.9%	0.6%	1.0%
Population growth rate in urban areas	0.3%	3.9%	0.8%	1.3%
Population per square kilometer of land	120	78	25	26
Life expectancy in years	75	62	77	76
Number of people per physician	399	>3,300	453	419
Number of pupils per teacher (primary school)	11	39	<18	20
Illiteracy rate (15 years and older)	<1%	41%	<5%	<3%
Energy consumed per capita (kg of oil equivalent)	3,861	364	5,203	7,918

† The gross national product (GNP) is the total dollar value of all goods and services produced by a country in a year. The per capita GNP is calculated by dividing a country's GNP by its population. The World Bank defines low-income countries as those with a per capita GNP of $695 or less. High-income countries have a per capita GNP of $8,626 or more. Less than 14% of the world's 5.5 billion people live in high-income countries, while almost 60% live in low-income countries.

> = greater than   < = less than

Sources: World Bank, Social Indicators of Development 1995, Baltimore: Johns Hopkins University Press, 1995. Central Intelligence Agency, World Fact Book, Washington, D.C.: Government Printing Office, 1994.

services. As of 1988, the nation was ninth in the world in expenditures on social security, and housing, allotting 40.4% of its budget to these areas.

Family allowances are paid to families with incomes below a certain threshold, as are rent subsidies. The 1976 Social Assistance Act provides for an advisory service for persons undergoing social hardship; cash grants in situations not covered by pension law; a home-help service; and assistance in caring for young people experiencing difficulties.

All Danish citizens over 67 years of age may draw old age pensions. Disability pensions are paid to persons with a certain degree of disablement. The state is primarily responsible for the care, education, and support of physically and mentally handicapped persons. There are allowances for unmarried mothers, for the children of widows, and in some cases for the children of widowers.

Laws guarantee equal pay for equal work, and women have and use legal recourse if they encounter discrimination.

There are 34 crisis centers that counsel and shelter victims of domestic violence.

29 HEALTH

Approximately $3,000 is invested in the social and medical well-being of every Dane annually, although health care expenditures have declined over the last decade. Anyone can go to a physician for free, and the public health system entitles each Dane to his/her own doctor. Costs are borne by public authorities, but high taxes help pay these costs.

In 1992 there were 399 people for every physician and a total of 23,000 hospital beds. Total health care expenditures in 1990 were $8,160 million.

Public health authorities have waged large-scale campaigns against tuberculosis, venereal diseases, diphtheria, and poliomyelitis. In 1991, there were 204 AIDS cases. Life expectancy averages 75 years (72 for males and 77 for females).

30 HOUSING

Extensive government support helped to reduce the wartime and immediate post-war housing shortage. The total number of dwellings in 1992 was 2,386,384, of which 635,552 had five or more rooms and a kitchen. In 1991, 20,035 new dwellings were completed, down from 27,237 in 1990. As of 1989, 39% of all housing units were apartments, 41% were detached houses, 11% were un- or semi-detached, 7% were farms, and 1% were youth hostels.

31 EDUCATION

Practically the entire Danish adult population is literate. Primary, secondary, and, in general, university and other higher education are free, and public expenditure on education is therefore high.

Since 1814, education has been compulsory for children aged 7 to 14. The Danish primary school system lasts nine years, and many opt for an additional tenth year. English is included in the curriculum from the fifth grade. After basic schooling, two-thirds of the pupils apply for practical training in a trade or commerce at special schools. The remaining one-third go to secondary schools, which finish after three years with student examination and pave the way for higher education at universities.

Among the 954,073 receiving education in 1990, 655,169 were in public and secondary schools; and 129,503 were in higher educational institutions such as colleges and universities.

There are four universities—the University of Copenhagen, the University of Aarhus, the University of Odense, and the University Center at Roskilde. Many specialized schools and academies of university rank provide instruction in various technical and artistic fields.

32 MEDIA

The radio broadcasting services are operated by the Danish State Radio System. Television broadcasting hours are mainly devoted to current and cultural affairs and to programs for children and young people. There is no commercial advertising on radio or television; owners of sets pay an annual license fee. At the end of 1991 there were 5,310,000 radios and 2,760,000 television sets. In the same year, there were 4,398,000 telephones in Denmark proper, or approximately 856 telephones per 1,000 inhabitants. In 1991, Denmark had 334 movie theaters and produced 11 feature length films.

The 46 daily newspapers in 1991 had an average daily net circulation of 1,842,000. The largest newspapers, with their average daily circulation for 1991, were: *Ekstrabladet* (231,700); *B.T.* (209,380); *Politiken* (156,720); and *Berlingske Tidende* (132,480).

During 1991, book and pamphlet production included 10,198 titles.

33 TOURISM AND RECREATION

Dozens of castles, palaces, mansions, and manor houses, including the castle at Elsinore (Helsingør)—site of Shakespeare's *Hamlet*—are open to the public. Tivoli Gardens, the world-famous amusement park, built in 1843 in the center of Copenhagen, is open from May through mid-September. Copenhagen is an important jazz center and holds a jazz festival in July. The world-famed Royal Danish Ballet, performs in Copenhagen's Royal Theater, which also presents opera and drama.

Greenland, the world's largest island, is part of the Kingdom of Denmark and attracts tourists to its mountains, dog sledges, and midnight sun.

In 1991 there were 37,056 hotel rooms with 92,524 beds in Denmark with a 36%

Photo credit: Susan D. Rock.

Hans Christian Anderson's "Little Mermaid."

occupancy rate. In 1991, an estimated 1,429,000 tourists visited Denmark and spent $3.47 billion.

34 FAMOUS DANES

Denmark's greatest classic writer and the founder of Danish literature is Ludvig Holberg (1684–1754). The two most celebrated 19th-century Danish writers are Hans Christian Andersen (1805–75), whose fairy tales are read and loved all over the world, and the influential philosopher and religious thinker Søren Kierkegaard (1813–55).

Leading novelists include Johannes Vilhelm Jensen (1873–1950), who was awarded the Nobel Prize for literature in 1944 for his series of novels. Isak Dinesen (Karen Blixen, 1887–1962) achieved renown for her volumes of Gothic tales and stories of life in Africa. Famous Danish musicians include the composers Niels Gade (1817–90) and Carl Nielsen (1865–1931), and the tenor Lauritz Melchior (1890–1973).

Notable dancers and choreographers include August Bournonville (1805–79), originator of the Danish ballet style, and Fleming Ole Flindt (b.1936), who has directed the Royal Danish Ballet since 1965. The sculptor Bertel Thorvaldsen (1770–1844) is the artist of widest influence.

Notable scientists include the astronomers Tycho Brahe (1546–1601) and Ole Rømer (1644–1710); the physicist Hans Christian Ørsted (1777–1851), discoverer of electromagnetism; Nobel Prize winners for physics Niels Bohr (1885–1962) in 1922 and his son Aage Niels Bohr (b.1922) and Benjamin Mottelson (b.1926) in 1975. Niels Rybert Finsen (b.Faroe Islands, 1860–1904), August Krogh (1874–1949), and Johannes A. G. Fibiger (1867–1928) were all Nobel Prize-winning 20th-century physicians and physiologists.

Frederik Bajer (1837–1922) was awarded the Nobel Peace Prize. Knud Johan Victor Rasmussen (1879–1933) was an explorer and anthropologist born in Greenland.

Queen Margrethe II (b.1940) became sovereign in 1972.

35 BIBLIOGRAPHY

Jensen, Jorgen. *The Prehistory of Denmark*. New York: Methuen, 1983.

Jones, W. Glyn. *Denmark: A Modern History*. Wolfeboro, N.H.: Longwood, 1986.

Lauring, Palle. *Denmark*. Philadelphia: Nordic Books, 1986.

Lepthien, E. *Greenland*. Chicago: Children's Press, 1989.

MacHaffie, Ingeborg S., and Margaret A. Nielsen. *Of Danish Ways*. New York: Harper & Row, 1984.

Miller, Kenneth E. *Denmark*. Santa Barbara, Calif.: Clio Press, 1987.

Starcke, Viggo. *Denmark in World History*. Philadelphia: University of Pennsylvania Press, 1963.

DJIBOUTI

Republic of Djibouti
République de Djibouti

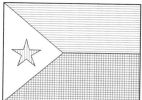

CAPITAL: Djibouti.

FLAG: A white triangle, with a five-pointed red star within, extends from the hoist; the remaining area has a broad light blue band over a broad light green band.

ANTHEM: No information available.

MONETARY UNIT: The Djibouti franc (DFr) of 100 centimes is the national currency. There are coins of 1, 2, 5, 10, 20, 50, 100, and 500 Djibouti francs, and notes of 500, 1000, 5000, and 10,000 Djibouti francs. DFr1 = $0.0056 (or $1 = DFr177.72).

WEIGHTS AND MEASURES: The metric system is in use.

HOLIDAYS: New Year's Day, 1 January; Labor Day, 1 May; Independence Day, 27 June; Christmas Day, 25 December. Movable religious holidays are Milad an-Nabi, Laylat al-Miraj, 'Id al-Fitr, 'Id al-'Adha', and Muslim New Year (1st of Muharram).

TIME: 3 PM = noon GMT.

1 LOCATION AND SIZE

Djibouti (formerly known as French Somaliland and then as the Territory of the Afars and the Issas) is situated on the east coast of Africa along the Bab al-Mandab, the strait that links the Red Sea with the Gulf of Aden. Comparatively, the area occupied by Djibouti is slightly larger than the state of Massachusetts. Djibouti's capital city, Djibouti, is located in the eastern part of the country.

2 TOPOGRAPHY

Djibouti consists of a series of high, arid tablelands surrounding faults, within which are low plains. Many areas exhibit thick layers of lava flow. The saline lake, 'Asal, at 170 meters (558 feet) below sea level, is the lowest point in Africa and the second lowest in the world.

3 CLIMATE

The climate is torrid, and rainfall is sparse and erratic. During the hot season, from May to October, daytime temperatures average 35°C (95°F) and the northeastern monsoon blows. During the warm season, from October to May, average daytime temperatures moderate to 25°C (77°F). Humidity is high all year, but annual rainfall averages less than 13 centimeters (5 inches).

4 PLANTS AND ANIMALS

Most of the vegetation is typical of the desert and semidesert, consisting of thorn scrubs and palm trees. In its animal reserves, Djibouti has antelopes, gazelles, hyenas, and jackals.

5 ENVIRONMENT

Djibouti's most significant environmental problems are deforestation, water pollution, and the protection of its wildlife. The rare trees on the northern mountains are protected within a national park. No hunting of wild animals is permitted, but abuses continue.

6 POPULATION

In 1991, the population was estimated by the government at 542,000, of whom perhaps 317,000 lived in the city of Djibouti, the national capital. However, the United Nations has estimated the 1995 population at only 511,000.

7 MIGRATION

The people of Djibouti are historically nomadic, migrating across borders that now separate nations. The dominant migration in recent years has been from the rural areas of the republic to the capital. At the end of 1992, about 20,000 Somali refugees from southeast Ethiopia were living in Djibouti camps.

8 ETHNIC GROUPS

The Issa branch of the Somali people and related clans constitutes 40–65% of all Djibouti's inhabitants. The Afars, a related people, account for about 25–35%. The remainder consists of Arabs of Yemeni background, French (about 3%), Ethiopians, Somali immigrants, and Italians.

9 LANGUAGES

Although French and Arabic are the official languages, the home languages of the vast majority of Djiboutians are Somali and Afar, both of Cushitic origin.

10 RELIGIONS

At least 94% of all indigenous Djiboutians are Muslims. About 6% of all Djiboutians are Christians.

11 TRANSPORTATION

About 97 kilometers (60 miles) of the single-track, meter-gauge railway linking the capital with Addis Ababa, Ethiopia traverses the Republic of Djibouti. Djibouti had 2,900 kilometers (1,800 miles) of road in 1991, over 280 kilometers (174 miles) of which were paved. In 1991 there were an estimated 13,000 passenger cars and 2,500 commercial trucks, taxis, and buses in Djibouti. A quarter of Ethiopia's imports and half of its exports move through its improved natural harbor. Ambouli Airport, about 6 kilometers (4 miles) from the city of Djibouti, is the country's international air terminal.

12 HISTORY

Somali and Afar herders lived in and around Djibouti for hundreds of years before European explorers came to the area in the nineteenth century. Obock and, later, Djibouti city were recognized as ports of great usefulness on the sea routes to India, Mauritius, and Madagascar. The Italians and British were active colonizers farther south along the Somali coast, and Britain was gaining control in what are now Yemen, the Sudan, and Egypt.

France decided to establish its colonial foothold in 1862 along what is now the northeastern coast of Djibouti. In 1984–85,

France formed the protectorates of Obock and Tadjoura, which were merged to form French Somaliland. In 1896 the boundaries of the colony were officially demarcated between France and Ethiopia.

In 1898, a group of French companies began building a narrow-gauge railway that finally reached Addis Ababa in 1917. The Italians invaded and occupied Ethiopia in the 1930s and during the early part of World War II. During this time there were constant border skirmishes between French and Italian forces. In December 1942, French Somaliland forces joined the Free French under General Charles de Gaulle.

After World War II, French Somaliland gradually gained a measure of local autonomy. In 1957, it obtained a territorial assembly and a local executive council. These bodies were able to advise the French-appointed governor-general. In 1967, French Somaliland joined the French Community as an overseas territory. The territory elected one deputy and one senator to the French National Assembly.

During this period there were ongoing disagreements between the two ethnic groups in the country, the Afars and the Issas. Although the Afars were in the minority, they dominated the government. The Issas complained that the laws unfairly favored the Afars. Consequently, the Issas continued to press the French for full independence. Their movement was opposed by the Afars, who feared Issa domination.

LOCATION: 10°54′ to 12°43′N; 41°45′ and 43°27′E.
BOUNDARY LENGTHS: total coastline, 314 kilometers (196 miles); Somalia, 58 kilometers (36 miles); Ethiopia, 337 kilometers (210 miles); Eritrea, 113 kilometers (70 miles).
TERRITORIAL SEA LIMIT: 12 miles.

Finally, in 1975, the French began to accommodate demands for independence. In a referendum in May 1977, the Issa majority voted decisively for independence, which was officially established on 27 June 1977. Hassan Gouled Aptidon, the territory's premier, was elected the nation's first president and reelected without opposition by universal suffrage in June 1981 and April 1987.

Dissatisfaction with Gouled grew in the late 1980s. This led to uprisings by Afar guerrillas which began in late 1991. Their group was called the Front for the Restoration of Unity and Democracy (FRUD). FRUD gained control of some areas of the north and west. In early 1992, French troops came to the aid of the Djibouti government and the Afars declared a cease-fire. However, fighting continued until mid-1992 when the rebel bases were occupied and their leaders imprisoned.

The military occupation of the north has been expensive for the government. By the end of 1993, about 35% of the government's budget went toward maintaining security in the north. Meanwhile, the economy has suffered markedly as the rebellion has dragged on.

Photo credit: AP/Wide World Photos

Djibouti's flag flutters on the mast of the Presidential palace on the first day of independence of the former French Territory.

13 GOVERNMENT

Djibouti is a parliamentary republic. The president, who according to the constitution must be an Issa, is elected by universal adult suffrage. The prime minister, who heads the cabinet, must be an Afar.

The legislature consists of the unicameral Chamber of Deputies, whose 65 members are elected for five-year terms. Before 1992, candidates came from a single list submitted by the ruling party, the People's Rally for Progress (RPP). In that year, voters approved a new constitution permitting multiparty democracy.

14 POLITICAL PARTIES

Despite the 1992 constitutional changes that legalized opposition party political activity, Djibouti is a de facto one-party system. However, there are also illegal Issa and Afar parties.

The RPP (People's Rally for Progress) holds all seats in the legislature and the presidency. However, two opposition groups, the Democratic Renewal Party (PRD) and the Democratic National Party (PND), function openly.

15 JUDICIAL SYSTEM

The judicial system consists of courts of first instance, a High Court of Appeal, and a Supreme Court. Each of the five administrative districts also has a customary court. The judiciary is not completely independent of the executive branch.

16 ARMED FORCES

About 4,000 French troops are based near the city of Djibouti to deal with threats to French interests in the region. Djibouti's own armed force of 3,800 members is divided into a 3,000-man army, a 100-man navy, and a 100-man air force.

17 ECONOMY

Djibouti has a free-enterprise economy. The country's main economic advantage is its strategic position at the southern entrance to the Red Sea.

The French military base in Djibouti is the country's largest single source of economic activity. The remainder of the economy is centered upon the free port of Djibouti, the railway terminus there, the airport, and government administration.

18 INCOME

Djibouti's gross national product (GNP) is about $1,030 per person.

19 INDUSTRY

Shipbuilding and urban construction are the only major industrial undertakings. Local manufacturing is limited to a mineral-water bottling facility and small plants that produce food, dairy products,

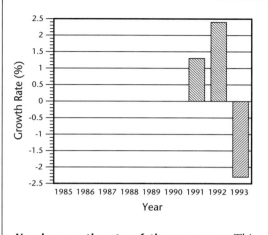

Yearly growth rate of the economy. This economic indicator tells by what percent the economy has increased or decreased when compared with the previous year.

beverages, furniture, building materials, and bottled gas.

20 LABOR

Labor in the cash economy is concentrated in the city of Djibouti, particularly on the docks and in shipbuilding and building construction. The railway is a significant employer, as is the national government. Unemployment and underemployment are widespread.

Under the constitution, workers are free to join unions and strike. However, in 1992, fewer than 20% of workers belonged to unions.

21 AGRICULTURE

Agriculture in Djibouti is very limited. This is due to acute water shortages in rural areas. In 1992, over 22,000 tons of

Selected Social Indicators

These statistics are estimates for the period 1988 to 1993. For comparison purposes, data for the United States and averages for low-income countries and high-income countries are also given.

Indicator	Djibouti	Low-income countries	High-income countries	United States
Per capita gross national product†	$1,030	$380	$23,680	$24,740
Population growth rate	3.1%	1.9%	0.6%	1.0%
Population growth rate in urban areas	3.6%	3.9%	0.8%	1.3%
Population per square kilometer of land	23	78	25	26
Life expectancy in years	49	62	77	76
Number of people per physician	6,155	>3,300	453	419
Number of pupils per teacher (primary school)	42	39	<18	20
Illiteracy rate (15 years and older)	52%	41%	<5%	<3%
Energy consumed per capita (kg of oil equivalent)	975	364	5,203	7,918

† The gross national product (GNP) is the total dollar value of all goods and services produced by a country in a year. The per capita GNP is calculated by dividing a country's GNP by its population. The World Bank defines low-income countries as those with a per capita GNP of $695 or less. High-income countries have a per capita GNP of $8,626 or more. Less than 14% of the world's 5.5 billion people live in high-income countries, while almost 60% live in low-income countries.

> = greater than   < = less than

Sources: World Bank, Social Indicators of Development 1995, Baltimore: Johns Hopkins University Press, 1995. Central Intelligence Agency, World Fact Book, Washington, D.C.: Government Printing Office, 1994.

vegetables were produced. Tomatoes are grown for domestic consumption. Date palms are cultivated along the coastal fringe.

Famine and malnutrition in Djibouti have created a reliance on the distribution of food aid for many of its people.

22 DOMESTICATED ANIMALS

Cattle, fat-tailed sheep, goats, and camels are grazed in the interior; hides and skins are exported. In 1992, Djibouti had an estimated 506,000 goats and 450,000 sheep.

23 FISHING

There is no local tradition of commercial fishing, although the Golfe de Tadjoura, the Gulf of Aden, and the Red Sea are potentially rich sources of commercial and game fish. The catch was 380 tons in 1991.

24 FORESTRY

There are protected forests on the slopes of the mountains north of the Gulf of Tadjoura.

Less than 1% of the country's total land area is forested.

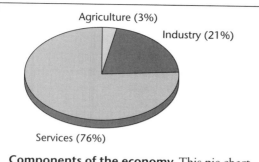

Agriculture (3%)

Industry (21%)

Services (76%)

Components of the economy. This pie chart shows how much of the country's economy is devoted to agriculture (includes forestry, hunting, and fishing), industry, or services.

25 MINING

Salt is extracted from evaporating pans in the marshes of Tadjoura, and lime is produced just west of Djibouti city from an old limestone quarry.

26 FOREIGN TRADE

Imports exceed exports by a large margin. Small amounts of hides and skins and live camels are exported.

In 1991, 57% of exports went to France while 16% went to the Yemen.

Over 26% of Djibouti's imports came from France, while 8.3% came from Ethiopia, 7.2% came from Japan, and 6.5% came from Italy.

27 ENERGY AND POWER

All of Djibouti's electricity is generated from an oil-fired generating station in the capital. Production totaled 178 million kilowatt hours in 1991. One geothermal power station was in operation as of 1991. All petroleum products are imported.

28 SOCIAL DEVELOPMENT

A social service fund covers medical and pension benefits. Although women have the franchise, they do not play a leadership role.

29 HEALTH

Malnutrition is severe, and the incidence of tuberculosis high; malaria is widespread. In 1986 there were 89 physicians. Life expectancy in 1992 was 49 years.

30 HOUSING

Djiboutian nomads generally live in transportable huts *(toukouls)*, which are covered with woven mats or boiled bark pulled into fine strands and plaited. Good-quality urban housing is in short supply.

31 EDUCATION

In 1992 there were 68 primary schools. Secondary schools had a total of 9,740 students. Education is compulsory for six years at the primary level followed by seven years of secondary education. Adult literacy is about 48%.

32 MEDIA

All media are government controlled. Radio and television broadcast in French, Afar, Somali, and Arabic. In 1991 there were 1,385,000 radios and 24,000 television sets. There were 7,500 telephones in 1991.

Djibouti has one daily newspaper, *La Nation de Djibouti,* which had a circulation of 4,000 in 1991.

33 TOURISM AND RECREATION

Tourist attractions include islands in the Golfe de Tadjoura and the Bab al-Mandab. There are a number of active volcanoes near the inland lake, 'Asal. The Forest of the Day is a national park for rare trees of the north.

34 FAMOUS DJIBOUTIANS

Hassan Gouled Aptidon (b.1916) has been president since independence was established.

35 BIBLIOGRAPHY

Schraeder, Peter J. *Djibouti.* Santa Barbara, Calif.: Clio Press, 1991.

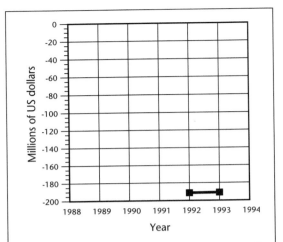

Yearly balance of trade measured in millions of US dollars. The balance of trade is the difference between what a country sells to other countries (its exports) and what it buys (its imports). If a country imports more than it exports, it has a negative balance of trade (a trade deficit). If exports exceed imports there is a positive balance of trade (a trade surplus).

DOMINICA

Commonwealth of Dominica
Dominica

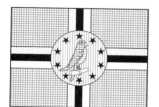

CAPITAL: Roseau.

FLAG: On a green background appears a cross composed of yellow, black, and white stripes; in the center is a red disk with 10 yellow-bordered green stars surrounding a parrot.

ANTHEM: *Isle of Beauty, Isle of Splendor.*

MONETARY UNIT: The East Caribbean dollar (EC$) of 100 cents is the national currency. There are coins of 1, 2, 5, 10, and 25, and 1 dollar, and notes of 5, 10, 20, and 100 East Caribbean dollars. EC$1 = US0.3704 (US$1 = EC$2.70).

WEIGHTS AND MEASURES: The metric system is being introduced, but imperial measures remain in common use.

HOLIDAYS: New Year's Day, 1 January; Labor Day, 1 May; Caricom Day, 2 July; Bank Holiday, 1st Monday in August; National Days, 3–4 November; Christmas, 25 December; Boxing Day, 26 December. Movable religious holidays include Carnival, Good Friday, Easter Monday, and Whitmonday.

TIME: 8 AM = noon GMT.

1 LOCATION AND SIZE

Although usually classified as one of the Windward Islands, Dominica marks the midpoint of the Lesser Antilles in the Caribbean. The island has an area of 750 square kilometers (290 square miles), slightly more than four times the size of Washington, D.C. Its coastline is 148 kilometers (92 miles) long. Dominica's capital city, Roseau, is located on the southwest coast of the island.

2 TOPOGRAPHY

The most rugged island of the Lesser Antilles, Dominica is a mass of peaks, ridges, and ravines. Several mountains are over 1,200 meters (4,000 feet). The whole land mass is of recent volcanic formation.

3 CLIMATE

The temperature averages 25°C (77°F) in winter and 28°C (82°F) in summer. Average yearly rainfall ranges from about 200 centimeters (80 inches) on the drier Caribbean coast to 635 centimeters (250 inches) in mountainous inland areas. Destructive Atlantic hurricanes occur during the late summer months.

4 PLANTS AND ANIMALS

As many as 60 species of trees may be identified on one 4-hectare (10-acre) plot of rainforest, including chataignier, carapite, breadfruit, white cedar, and laurier. There are no large wild animals, but the agouti and manicou can be found, as well as some 135 species of birds.

Photo credit: AP/Wide World Photos

Members of the Carib Indian Tribe watch as a caravan of Freedom Party members passes through the Carib Reservation in Dominica.

5 ENVIRONMENT

Dominica's water supply, already inadequate, is threatened by pollution from untreated sewage and chemicals used in farming. The nation's forests are endangered by the expansion of farming activities. Two large areas have been set aside as nature reserves. The red-necked and imperial parrots are both endangered.

6 POPULATION

In 1991 the population was 71,183. The capital of the island, Roseau, had 15,853 inhabitants. The population density of Dominica in 1991 was 95 persons per square kilometer (245 persons per square mile), one of the lowest in the West Indies.

7 MIGRATION

There are no restrictions on emigration.

8 ETHNIC GROUPS

Current statistics on racial or ethnic origins are not available. In 1981, the vast majority of Dominicans (91%) were black, around 6% of the population was of mixed descent, and a small minority of about 0.5% was of European origin. There were some 3,000 Carib Indians.

9 LANGUAGES

English is the official language of Dominica. Nearly all Dominicans also speak a French patois (dialect), based on a mixture of African and French.

10 RELIGIONS

About 80% of the population is Roman Catholic. There are Anglican and Protestant minorities, as well as Baha'is and some Rastafarians.

11 TRANSPORTATION

A paved road connects the two main towns, Roseau and Portsmouth, with Melville Hall Airport. Much of the road system was severely damaged by the 1979 hurricane. There are 10,200 motor vehicles on the island. A deepwater harbor has been completed near Roseau. Dominica Air Transport and other small airlines connect the island with Martinique, Guadeloupe, Antigua, and Barbados.

12 HISTORY

Dominica was the first island sighted in the New World by Christopher Columbus on his second voyage in 1493. At that time, the island was inhabited by Carib Indians, who resisted conquest.

Strong Indian resistance to further contact prevented either the French or the English from settling there until the eighteenth century. The French took formal possession in 1727 but gave the island to Great Britain in 1763. Coffee plantations were established during the period of French colonization, and sugar was introduced later by the British. However, the

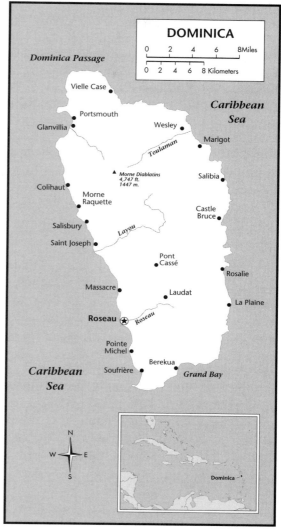

LOCATION: 15°N; 16°W. **TOTAL COASTLINE:** 148 kilometers (92 miles). **TERRITORIAL SEA LIMIT:** 12 miles.

large slave plantations that characterized other West Indian islands never developed on Dominica.

Dominica was governed as part of the Leeward Islands from 1871 until 1939. In

1940 it was transferred to the Windward Islands administration. From 1958 to 1962, the island was a member of the Federation of the West Indies. Dominica became an associated state of the Commonwealth of Nations in 1967 and on 3 November 1978 became an independent republic.

In its first years of independence, Dominica had several problems. Some were brought about by destructive hurricanes, especially Hurricane David in 1979. Others were attributable to the corrupt and tyrannical administration of Premier Patrick John. John was ousted in June 1979, and after a year of interim rule, Mary Eugenia Charles became prime minister in July 1980. She is the first female prime minister in the Caribbean.

13 GOVERNMENT

Under its 1978 constitution, Dominica has a single-chamber parliament, the House of Assembly, with 21 elected and 9 appointed members. Parliament elects a president as head of state, who in turn appoints the prime minister and cabinet.

14 POLITICAL PARTIES

The majority party is the Dominican Freedom Party (DFP), led by the prime minister, Mary Eugenia Charles. The United Workers Party (UWP) and the Democratic Labour Party (DLP) are the other major parties.

15 JUDICIAL SYSTEM

The lowest-level courts are the four magistrates' courts; at the second level is the Court of Summary Jurisdiction. The

Photo credit: AP/Wide World Photos

Supporters of Dominica's Labour Party campaign in the Northeastern region of the country near the town of Atkinson.

highest court is the Eastern Caribbean Supreme Court, based in St. Lucia.

16 ARMED FORCES

There is a police force of 300. Defense from foreign attack would come from the United States or United Kingdom.

17 ECONOMY

Practically the entire economy is based on agriculture, fishing, and forestry. Bananas are the main crop, and coconuts, from which copra is extracted for export, are

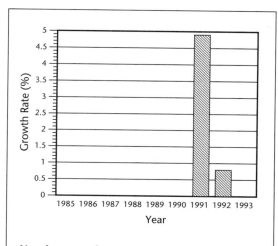

Yearly growth rate of the economy. This economic indicator tells by what percent the economy has increased or decreased when compared with the previous year.

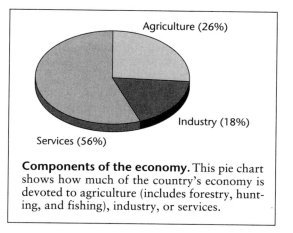

Components of the economy. This pie chart shows how much of the country's economy is devoted to agriculture (includes forestry, hunting, and fishing), industry, or services.

also important. In 1992, unemployment reached 15%; the inflation rate was 5.3%.

18 INCOME

In 1992, Dominica's gross national product (GNP) was $181 million at current prices, or $2,720 per person. For the period 1985–92 the average inflation rate was 5.0%, resulting in a real growth rate in GNP of 5.1% per person.

19 INDUSTRY

Dominica has only light industry, most of it connected with the processing of agricultural products. Soap and toiletries are exported. Home industries produce ceramics, straw products, and some leather work.

20 LABOR

The labor force in 1991 was estimated at 30,600. About 47% of the labor force is employed in agriculture, fishing, and forestry. Only slightly over 10% of the work force is unionized. Unemployment was officially 11% in 1991.

21 AGRICULTURE

The main crop of Dominica is bananas. Production fell after disastrous hurricanes in 1979 and 1980. However, after outside financial support helped the country recover, production rose to 70,000 tons by 1992. Coconuts and citrus fruits are grown in commercial quantities. Agricultural exports amounted to $35 million in 1992.

22 DOMESTICATED ANIMALS

The island does not produce sufficient meat, poultry, or eggs for local consumption. In 1992 there were an estimated 9,000 head of cattle, 5,000 hogs, 10,000 goats, and 8,000 sheep. In 1992,

Selected Social Indicators

These statistics are estimates for the period 1985 to 1993. For comparison purposes, data for the United States and averages for low-income countries and high-income countries are also given.

Indicator	Dominica	Low-income countries	High-income countries	United States
Per capita gross national product†	$2,720	$380	$23,680	$24,740
Population growth rate	0.0%	1.9%	0.6%	1.0%
Population growth rate in urban areas	n.a.	3.9%	0.8%	1.3%
Population per square kilometer of land	95	78	25	26
Life expectancy in years	77	62	77	76
Number of people per physician	2,896	>3,300	453	419
Number of pupils per teacher (primary school)	21	39	<18	20
Illiteracy rate (15 years and older)	6%	41%	<5%	<3%
Energy consumed per capita (kg of oil equivalent)	296	364	5,203	7,918

† The gross national product (GNP) is the total dollar value of all goods and services produced by a country in a year. The per capita GNP is calculated by dividing a country's GNP by its population. The World Bank defines low-income countries as those with a per capita GNP of $695 or less. High-income countries have a per capita GNP of $8,626 or more. Less than 14% of the world's 5.5 billion people live in high-income countries, while almost 60% live in low-income countries.

n.a. = data not available   > = greater than   < = less than

Sources: World Bank, *Social Indicators of Development 1995*, Baltimore: Johns Hopkins University Press, 1995. Central Intelligence Agency, *World Fact Book*, Washington, D.C.: Government Printing Office, 1994.

production of meat totaled 1,000 tons; milk, 5,000 tons; eggs, 158 tons; and cow hides, 40 tons.

23 FISHING

Hurricane David in 1979 destroyed almost all of the island's 470 fishing boats. Since then, the catch has dropped by roughly one-third, totaling only 590 tons in 1991.

24 FORESTRY

Forest and woodland represent 41% of Dominica's total land area. Before Hurricane David, annual output had reached about 265,000 cubic feet of lumber. Commercially valuable woods include mahogany, blue and red mahoe, and teak.

25 MINING

Pumice is the major commodity mined. Limestone, volcanic ash, sand and gravel, and clay deposits have been found.

26 FOREIGN TRADE

In 1991, banana exports accounted for 58.9% of total exports. Dominica's major trading partners were Caribbean Community and Common Market (CARICOM)

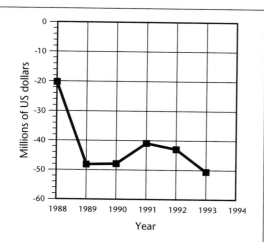

Yearly balance of trade measured in millions of US dollars. The balance of trade is the difference between what a country sells to other countries (its exports) and what it buys (its imports). If a country imports more than it exports, it has a negative balance of trade (a trade deficit). If exports exceed imports there is a positive balance of trade (a trade surplus).

nations, the United States, Canada, and the United Kingdom.

27 ENERGY AND POWER

About 60% of the power supply already comes from hydroelectric sources. The island also has thermal power potential in a volcanic lake. In 1991, 31 million kilowatt hours of electricity were produced.

28 SOCIAL DEVELOPMENT

In 1976, the government established the Social Security Scheme, which covers all workers from 16 to 60 years of age. Benefits include retirement and disability pensions, maternity benefits, and survivors' pensions. Apart from the constitution, there is no specific legislation in force to protect women from sex discrimination.

29 HEALTH

There is one general hospital and 12 health centers. Serious tropical diseases have been eliminated, but due to the high humidity and rainy conditions, tuberculosis and other respiratory diseases continue to be a problem. Average life expectancy was 77 years.

30 HOUSING

Hurricane David destroyed the homes of over four-fifths of the population. Under an emergency housing program, construction supplies were brought into the island, and shelters were built for most of the population.

31 EDUCATION

Much of Dominica's school system had to be rebuilt after the 1979 hurricane. In 1991 there were 65 primary schools, with 605 teachers and 12,100 students enrolled. In the general secondary schools, there were 5,983 students enrolled. Higher educational facilities include a teacher training institute, a technical college, and a nursing school. There were 40 teaching staff and 658 students in higher level institutions in 1991.

32 MEDIA

In 1991 there were 42,000 radios and 5,000 television sets. Two weekly newspapers are published in Roseau, the *New Chronicle* (circulation in 1991, 3,000) and the *Official Gazetts* (600). Dominica had 14,613 telephone lines in operation in

1993. There are 3 AM and 2 FM radio stations and one (cable) television station.

33 TOURISM AND RECREATION

Dominica's principal attraction is the rugged natural beauty of its volcanic peaks, forests, lakes, waterfalls, and over 365 rivers. Day trips to Dominica from Barbados, Guadeloupe, and Martinique have gained increasing popularity. Cricket is the national sport.

In 1991, 46,312 tourists arrived in Dominica, 26,357 from Caribbean countries, followed by 6,898 from the United States and 4,520 from the United Kingdom. Revenues from tourism reached $28 million.

34 FAMOUS DOMINICANS

Maria Eugenia Charles (b.1919), cofounder of the Dominica Freedom Party, became prime minister in 1980.

35 BIBLIOGRAPHY

Booth, Robert. "Dominica, Difficult Paradise." *National Geographic,* June 1990, 100–120.
Caribbean and Central American Databook, 1987. Washington, D.C.: Caribbean/Central American Action, 1986.
Myers, Robert A. *Dominica.* Santa Barbara, Calif.: Clio Press, 1987.

DOMINICAN REPUBLIC

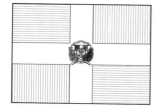

Dominican Republic
Republica Dominicana

CAPITAL: Santo Domingo.

FLAG: The national flag, adopted in 1844, consists of a white cross superimposed on a field of four rectangles, the upper left and lower right in blue, the upper right and lower left in red. The national seal is in the center of the white cross.

ANTHEM: *Himno Nacional,* beginning "Quisqueyanos valientes, alcemos nuestro canto" ("Valiant Dominicans, let us raise our song").

MONETARY UNIT: The Dominican peso (RD$) of 100 centavos is a paper currency. There are coins of 1, 5, 10, 25, and 50 centavos and 1 peso, and notes of 1, 5, 10, 20, 50, 100, 500, and 1,000 pesos. RD$1 = US$0.0766 (US$1 = RD$13.05).

WEIGHTS AND MEASURES: The metric system is the legal standard, but US and Spanish weights are widely used in commercial transactions.

HOLIDAYS: New Year's Day, 1 January; Epiphany, 6 January; Altagracia Day, 21 January; Duarte Day, 26 January; Independence Day, 27 February; Labor Day, 1 May; Restoration of Independence, 16 August; Day of Our Lady of Las Mercedes, 24 September; All Saints' Day, 1 November; Christmas, 25 December. Movable religious holidays include Good Friday and Corpus Christi.

TIME: Eastern Daylight Savings Time is maintained throughout the year; 8 AM = noon GMT.

1 LOCATION AND SIZE

The Dominican Republic occupies the eastern two-thirds of the island of Hispaniola (Haiti occupies the western part) and includes the islands of Beata, Catalina, and Saona, in the Caribbean Sea, and several islets. It has an area of 48,730 square kilometers (18,815 square miles), slightly more than twice the size of the state of New Hampshire. The Dominican Republic has a total boundary length of 1,563 kilometers (969 miles). Its capital city, Santo Domingo, is located on its southern coast.

2 TOPOGRAPHY

The Dominican Republic is generally mountainous, with deserts in the extreme western regions. The principal mountain range is the Cordillera Central, running from east to west. Between the Cordillera Central and the Cordillera Septentriona lies a valley, known for the excellent quality of its soil. The country contains both the highest mountain in the West Indies, Pico Duarte at 3,174 meters (10,414 feet), and the lowest-lying lake, Lago Enriquillo, at 40 meters (131 feet) below sea level.

The Yaque del Norte and the Yaque del Sur are the principal rivers.

3 CLIMATE

Average minimum and maximum temperatures range from 18°C (64°F)–29°C (84°F) in the winter and from 23°C (73°F)–35°C (95°F) in the summer. The coastal plain has an annual mean temperature of 26°C (79°F), while in the Cordillera Central the climate is temperate and the mean is 20°C (68°F). Rainfall varies from 43 centimeters (17 inches) annually in the western areas to 208 centimeters (82 inches) in the northeast.

4 PLANTS AND ANIMALS

Dense rainforests are common in the wetter areas; scrub woodland thrives along the drier slopes; and savanna vegetation is found on the open plains. Dominican mahogany and resinous pine trees grow in the high mountains. The rare hutia (a small rodent) and herds of wild boar are found in the mountainous areas. Lake Enriquillo is the natural habitat of large flocks of flamingos. Spanish mackerel, mullet, bonito, and yellowtail snapper are found in the surrounding waters.

5 ENVIRONMENT

United Nations sources report that, as of 1993, the nation was losing 20,000 hectares per year of its forest lands largely due to commercial development. The problem of deforestation is linked to the nation's decreasing water supply since forests help stop the loss of surface water. As of 1994, the Dominican Republic has an inadequate water supply. The country has 4.8 cubic miles of water with 89% used for farming.

In 1994, one mammal species, five bird species, and four types of reptiles were considered endangered, as were 62 plant species in 1993.

6 POPULATION

The population in mid-1991 was estimated at 7,313,000. For the year 2000, a population of 8,621,000 was projected. The estimated population density in 1991 was 151 persons per square kilometer (391 persons per square mile). Santo Domingo, the capital and largest city, had an estimated population of 2,203,000 in 1990.

7 MIGRATION

The number of Haitians living in the Dominican Republic has been estimated at between 500,000 and 1,000,000. In 1990 there were 357,000 Dominican-born people living in the United States (estimates of the Dominican population in the United States ranged as high as 1,000,000).

8 ETHNIC GROUPS

Ethnic divisions were estimated in 1986 at 16% white, 11% black, and 73% mulatto.

9 LANGUAGES

Spanish is the official language, although some English is spoken in the capital. A Creole dialect is used along the Haitian border.

10 RELIGIONS

In 1993, professing Roman Catholics represented an estimated 91.2% of the

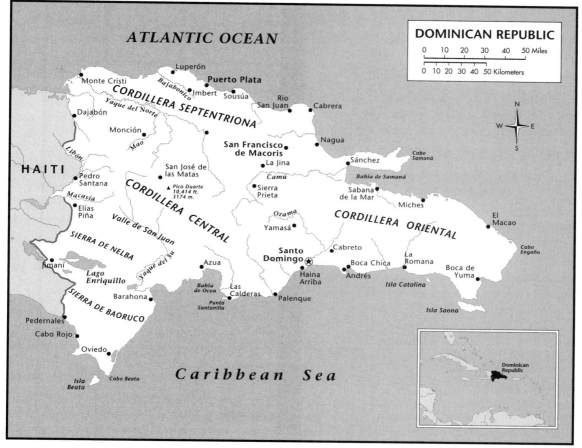

LOCATION: 17°36′22″ to 19°56′9″N; 68°19′24″ to 72°0′48″W. **BOUNDARY LENGTHS:** Total coastline, 1,288 kilometers (799 miles); Haiti, 275 kilometers (170 miles). **TERRITORIAL SEA LIMIT:** 6 miles.

population. Protestants, including Baptists and Seventh-day Adventists, accounted for another 1%. Followers of spirit worship and voodoo number about 60,000.

11 TRANSPORTATION

The national highway system is the dominant means of inland public transportation. In 1991 there were 5,800 kilometers (3,600 miles) of paved roads. In that year, 139,069 passenger cars and 102,969 commercial vehicles were licensed. During the same year, 1,655 kilometers (1,028 miles) of railways were in service.

The Santo Domingo, Andrés, and Haina Arriba harbors handle the vast majority of imports. The Dominican merchant fleet had one ship of 2,000 gross registered tons in 1991. Dominicana de Aviación provides international service from Las Americas International Airport, east of Santo Domingo. There are also international airports at Puerto Plata and La Romana.

12 HISTORY

The island of Hispaniola was first settled by the nomadic and warlike Carib Amerindians and later by the agricultural and peace-loving Arawaks. Christopher Columbus discovered the island and claimed it for Spain in 1492. Santo Domingo, the oldest city in the New World, was founded four years later. By 1517, Hispaniola had become the springboard for Spanish conquest of the Caribbean and the American mainland. The Amerindian population dwindled and was replaced by African slaves.

The importance of Hispaniola declined during the sixteenth and seventeenth centuries. In 1697, Spain recognized French dominion over the western third of the island, now known as Haiti. Nearly one hundred years later, in 1795, Spain ceded the rest of the island—by then called Santo Domingo—to France. Haiti gained its independence from France in 1804, with the rest of the island gaining independence five years later in 1809. However, after a brief attempt at independence, the Dominicans once again fell to Spain, under the Treaty of Paris (1814).

In 1821, the Dominicans, led by José Múñez de Cáceres, again proclaimed their independence. They sought to become part of Simón Bolívar's Republic of Gran Colombia, but in 1822 the Haitians conquered the entire island. The Dominicans withstood 22 years of harsh Haitian rule. Then, taking advantage of a Haitian civil war in 1843, they established the Dominican Republic as an independent state under the leadership of Juan Pablo Duarte.

For the remainder of the nineteenth century, the new republic had a succession of leaders. Each leader sought foreign protection against Haiti. As the twentieth century began, the Dominican Republic entered a stormy period characterized by political instability and increasing debt to the United States. A treaty signed after 1905 provided for repayment of the debt and in 1916 the United States set up a military government on the island. It ruled until 12 July 1924, when sovereignty was restored to the nation.

In 1930, Rafael Leonidas Trujillo Molina was elected president. For the next 31 years, he ruled the Dominican Republic either directly or indirectly. At one point Trujillo arranged for his brother to become president and then, in 1960, installed Joaquín Balaguer as president. However, no matter who was the president, Trujillo was in control. Under Trujillo and his associates, the country achieved some economic progress. However, they brutally suppressed fundamental human rights. Only one party was allowed, the press was totally controlled, and constant purges weeded out all but his most loyal supporters.

Trujillo was assassinated on 30 May 1961. A period of instability followed as various military and political factions competed for power. With anarchy—and rumored communist intervention—threatening, the United States sent 23,000 troops into the Dominican Republic.

Photo credit: AP/Wide World Photos

Wearing a baseball cap emblazoned with the name New York, Raymond Rodriguez, 19, right, dreams of getting on a boat and sailing to Puerto Rico or New York. Rodriguez is shown with two members of his family outside their tin-roof shack in the Dominican Republic town of San Francisco de Macoris.

Balaguer went into exile. Within weeks, the Organization of American States (OAS) had set up an Inter-America Peace Force in the country, and order was restored to the country. After the 1966 elections, all US and OAS troops left the island.

In the 1978 elections, the major opposition parties remained active and vocal. Silvestre Antonio Guzmán Fernández of the PRD (Dominican Revolutionary Party) won with a 158,000-vote plurality, and his party gained a majority in the Chamber of Deputies.

During Guzmán's term, political prisoners were freed, press censorship was practically abolished, and political parties engaged in open activity. At the same time, however, there were mounting economic difficulties. These economic problems were aggravated by two hurricanes in 1979, which together left 1,300 people dead, 500 missing, and 100,000 homeless. In May 1982, a left-wing PRD senator, Salvador Jorge Blanco, was elected president.

President Blanco's administration struggled with the country's growing foreign debt and other economic difficulties.

In May 1986, former president Joaquín Balaguer was returned to office with 41.6% of the vote. Balaguer embarked on an ambitious program of public works that created employment for nearly 100,000 people. But by 1988, inflation was on the rise, and the peso had become unstable.

In 1990, Balaguer won a narrow, hotly contested victory amid claims of fraud by the opposition. His unpopular economic reforms brought national strikes in August and November of 1990, and demands for resignation.

13 GOVERNMENT

The constitution of 28 November 1966 established a republic consisting of 26 provinces and a single National District. The government is controlled by the chief executive, a president directly elected for a four-year term. The National Congress consists of a 30-member Senate and a 120-member Chamber of Deputies.

14 POLITICAL PARTIES

The Dominican Republic's four major parties are all closely linked to specific political leaders. The Social Christian Reform Party (Partido Reformista Social Christiano—PRSC) is led by Trujillo-era politician Joaquín Balaguer.

The Dominican Revolutionary Party (Partido Revolucionario Dominicano—PRD) was founded by Juan Bosch, although he eventually resigned from it to form the Dominican Liberation Party (Partido de la Liberación Dominicana—PLD). The Independent Revolutionary Party (PRI) is the vehicle for Jacobo Majluta Azar, who served as president briefly in 1982.

15 JUDICIAL SYSTEM

The judicial system is headed by a Supreme Court with nine judges, and serves as the highest court of appeals. There are 26 provincial courts.

16 ARMED FORCES

The army of 15,000 is organized into 4 infantry brigades and 4 independent battalions. The air force has 4,200 personnel and is equipped with 10 combat aircraft of United States and United Kingdom origin. The navy of 3,000 mans 18 coastal defense ships and 2 auxiliaries. The national police number 15,000. In 1991, the armed forces budget was $35 million.

17 ECONOMY

As of 1994, agriculture and mining are still the mainstays of the economy. The Dominican Republic has been undergoing rapid modernization, aided by the Caribbean Basin Initiative (CBI).

Light manufacturing is contributing an ever more important share of national production, exports, and employment. Overall economic performance was positive in 1992. A dramatic government program brought the annual inflation rate down from 53.9% in 1992 to only 4.6% in 1993.

18 INCOME

In 1992, the Dominican Republic's gross national product (GNP) was $7,611 million

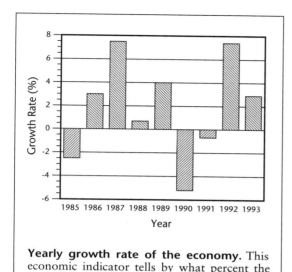

Yearly growth rate of the economy. This economic indicator tells by what percent the economy has increased or decreased when compared with the previous year.

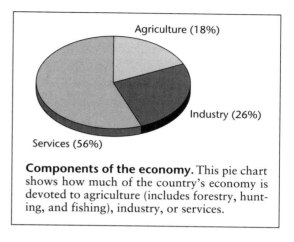

Components of the economy. This pie chart shows how much of the country's economy is devoted to agriculture (includes forestry, hunting, and fishing), industry, or services.

at current prices, or about $1,230 per person. For the period 1985–92 the average inflation rate was 34.4%, resulting in a real growth rate in GNP of 0.3% per person.

19 INDUSTRY

Manufacturing is limited largely to the processing of agricultural and mineral commodities. Including the processing of sugar, food processing represents more than half of total industrial production. Smaller plants, directed mainly toward the local market, produce flour, textiles, powdered and condensed milk, ceramics, aluminum furniture, concrete blocks, earthenware pipes and tiles, air conditioners, barbed wire, and other products.

Manufacturing soared by 12.3% in 1993, aided by an improved electricity supply, which reduced blackouts and boosted production.

20 LABOR

The labor force in 1992 consisted of about 3.24 million persons. In 1989, 18% were engaged in agriculture, 49% in industry, and 33% in services. Unemployment was estimated at 30% of the work force in 1992. In 1992, only 10–15% of the Dominican work force was unionized.

21 AGRICULTURE

After Cuba, the Dominican Republic is the second-largest Caribbean producer of sugarcane, the nation's most important commercial crop. In 1992, sugarcane production was 678 million tons. Another leading cash crop is coffee. Production has averaged about 57,000–59,000 tons annually since the early 1980s.

Cocoa and tobacco are also grown for export. In 1992, production of cocoa was 46,000 tons and of tobacco, 23,000 tons. Production of other crops in that year (in thousands of tons) included rice paddy, 514; tomatoes, 145; beans, 47; and cotton, 2.

22 DOMESTICATED ANIMALS

In 1992, Dominican livestock included 560,000 goats, 122,000 sheep, and 750,000 hogs. In that year, 44,000 tons of beef and about 350,000 tons of milk were produced.

23 FISHING

The fishing industry is relatively undeveloped, and fish for local consumption are imported. In 1991, the total marine catch was 16,098 tons. Marlin, barracuda, kingfish, mackerel, tuna, sailfish, and tarpon are found in the Monte Cristi Bank and Samaná Bay.

24 FORESTRY

Practically all the timber cut is for land clearing and fuel.

25 MINING

The Dominican Republic has a variety of mineral resources. Production, however, has stagnated since the mid-1980s. In 1991 production of bauxite dropped to 7,000 tons, about 29,062 tons of ferronickel were mined, production of gold was 3,160 kilograms, and silver output was 21,954 kilograms.

26 FOREIGN TRADE

The country's trade balance has traditionally been in deficit. The country remains subject to rising and falling export revenues, since the government's efforts to free exports from the ups and downs of the

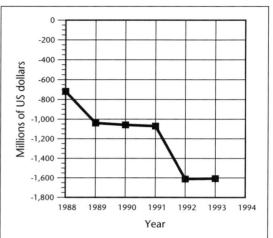

Yearly balance of trade measured in millions of US dollars. The balance of trade is the difference between what a country sells to other countries (its exports) and what it buys (its imports). If a country imports more than it exports, it has a negative balance of trade (a trade deficit). If exports exceed imports there is a positive balance of trade (a trade surplus).

commodities market have not yet succeeded.

27 ENERGY AND POWER

With no coal and little petroleum, the country has depended upon imported diesel oil for its electrical energy. Electricity production in 1991 was 5.3 billion kilowatt hours. Steam thermal units supply about 72% of the nation's energy needs.

28 SOCIAL DEVELOPMENT

Social assistance is administered by the Department of Public Health and Welfare, which administers medical, disability, maternity, old age, and survivors' benefits, as well as workers' compensation. An

Selected Social Indicators

These statistics are estimates for the period 1988 to 1993. For comparison purposes, data for the United States and averages for low-income countries and high-income countries are also given.

Indicator	Dominican Republic	Low-income countries	High-income countries	United States
Per capita gross national product†	$1,230	$380	$23,680	$24,740
Population growth rate	2.1%	1.9%	0.6%	1.0%
Population growth rate in urban areas	3.4%	3.9%	0.8%	1.3%
Population per square kilometer of land	151	78	25	26
Life expectancy in years	70	62	77	76
Number of people per physician	1,754	>3,300	453	419
Number of pupils per teacher (primary school)	47	39	<18	20
Illiteracy rate (15 years and older)	17%	41%	<5%	<3%
Energy consumed per capita (kg of oil equivalent)	340	364	5,203	7,918

† The gross national product (GNP) is the total dollar value of all goods and services produced by a country in a year. The per capita GNP is calculated by dividing a country's GNP by its population. The World Bank defines low-income countries as those with a per capita GNP of $695 or less. High-income countries have a per capita GNP of $8,626 or more. Less than 14% of the world's 5.5 billion people live in high-income countries, while almost 60% live in low-income countries.

> = greater than   < = less than

Sources: World Bank, *Social Indicators of Development 1995*, Baltimore: Johns Hopkins University Press, 1995. Central Intelligence Agency, *World Fact Book*, Washington, D.C.: Government Printing Office, 1994.

Institute for the Development of Women was created in 1975.

29 HEALTH

In 1992, 80% of the population had access to health care services. Total health care expenditures were $263 million. Average life expectancy was 70 years.

30 HOUSING

Rapid population growth and migration to urban areas have combined to create an increasingly serious housing shortage. The 1979 hurricanes prompted a construction boom; not, however, to create new housing but to replace units that had been destroyed by the storms.

31 EDUCATION

The 1990 estimated adult literacy rate was 83%. Eight years of education is compulsory. In 1989 there were 4,854 primary schools with 21,850 teachers and 1,032,055 students. In addition to the state-run Autonomous University of Santo Domingo, there are four private universities.

32 MEDIA

In 1992 there were 130 AM and 40 FM radio stations and 18 television stations.

Photo credit: AP/Wide World Photos

Residents of San Francisco de Macoris, Dominican Republic, walk in the town's street lined with shanties.

In 1992 there were approximately 1,250,000 radios and 615,000 television receivers. In 1993 there were some 350,000 telephones.

The daily newspapers of the Dominican Republic are rated by the Inter-American Press Association as among the freest in Latin America. The leading daily is *El Caribe* (circulation 75,000 in 1991). Two other major newspapers are *El Nacional* (circulation 45,000), and the *Listín Diario* (about 60,000).

33 TOURISM AND RECREATION

The Dominican Republic has more world-class hotels than any other Caribbean nation. The country was estimated to have attracted two million visitors in 1993 and to have generated revenues of approximately $1.3 billion. In 1991, hotel rooms numbered 22,555. Popular resort centers along the coast include La Romana. The Juan Pablo Duarte Olympic Center is one of the best-equipped sports facilities in the Caribbean.

34 FAMOUS DOMINICANS

Juan Pablo Duarte (1813–76) is a hero of the Dominican Republic's fight for independence from Haiti in 1844. Rafael Leonidas Trujillo Molina (1891–1961) was the country's dominant political figure from 1930 until his assassination on 30 May 1961.

Juan Bautista Alfonseca (1810–75), the father of Dominican music, was the first composer to make use of Dominican folklore. Juan Marichal (b.1938) achieved fame in the United States as a baseball pitcher.

35 BIBLIOGRAPHY

Dominican Republic and Haiti: Country Studies. 2d ed. Washington, D.C.: Library of Congress, 1991.

Haverstock, Nathan A. *Dominican Republic in Pictures.* Minneapolis: Lerner Publications Co., 1988.

Schoenhals, Kai P. *Dominican Republic.* Santa Barbara, Calif.: Clio Press, 1990.

ECUADOR

Republic of Ecuador
República del Ecuador

CAPITAL: Quito.

FLAG: The flag consists of three horizontal stripes, the yellow uppermost stripe being equal to the combined widths of the blue center stripe and the red lower stripe; coat of arms superimposed at center of the flag.

ANTHEM: *Salve, O Patria (Hail, O Fatherland)*.

MONETARY UNIT: The sucre (s/) of 100 centavos is a nonconvertible paper currency. There are coins of 10, 20, and 50 centavos and 1 sucre, and notes of 50, 100, 500, 1,500, 5,000, and 10,000 sucres. s/1 = $0.0042 (or $1 = s/238.75).

WEIGHTS AND MEASURES: The metric system is the legal standard, but local and old Spanish units are also used.

HOLIDAYS: New Year's Day, 1 January; Epiphany, 6 January; Labor Day, 1 May; Battle of Pichincha, 24 May; Simón Bolívar's Birthday, 24 July; Quito's Independence Day, 10 August; Guayaquil's Independence Day, 9 October; Columbus Day, 12 October; All Saints' Day, 1 November; All Souls' Day, 2 November; Cuenca's Independence Day, 3 November; Foundation of Quito, 6 December; Christmas Day, 25 December. Movable holidays include Carnival and Holy Week.

TIME: Mainland, 7 AM = noon GMT; Galápagos Islands, 6 AM = noon GMT.

1 LOCATION AND SIZE

The fourth-smallest country in South America, Ecuador is located on the west coast of the continent and crossed by the equator (the country gets its name from the Spanish word for "equator"). It has a total boundary length of 4,247 kilometers (2,653 miles).

The Galápagos Islands, a province of Ecuador, are approximately 1,130 kilometers (700 miles) off the coast. The total area of the republic, including all of its territory, is estimated at 283,560 square kilometers (109,483 square miles), slightly smaller than the state of Nevada.

Ecuador's capital city, Quito, is located in the north central part of the country.

2 TOPOGRAPHY

Ecuador is characterized by three distinct regions: the coast; the highlands, or Sierra; and the eastern interior jungles, or Oriente. The Daule and Guayllabamba rivers form the principal river systems and serve as important arteries of transportation.

The Andes mountains are studded with massive snow-capped volcanoes. Chimborazo, the highest peak, soars 6,310 meters (20,702 feet).

3 CLIMATE

The climate varies with the region. Most of the coast consists of wet, tropical forest, and is increasingly humid toward the north. The Guayaquil area has two seasons: a hot rainy period and a cooler dry season. The tropical jungles east of the Andes, are more humid than the coast; there, temperatures are high, and rain falls all year round.

The capital, Quito, on the central plateau, has perpetual spring, with an average temperature of 13°C (55°F) and about 127 centimeters (50 inches) of rainfall annually. Cold and wind increase as the slopes surrounding the central plateau ascend to form the páramo, or highland meadow.

4 PLANTS AND ANIMALS

The arid strip along half of Ecuador's coast, with occasional low shrubs and isolated ceiba trees, contrasts sharply with the northern coast and the inner portion of the southern coast, where the typical dense growth of the tropical jungle abounds. The high mountain slopes are covered with wiry páramo grass. The highland valleys support temperate-zone plants, including potatoes and corn.

Ecuadoran jungles support smaller mammals, reptiles, and birds. In the highlands, the condor and a few other species of birds are found. There is relatively little wild game because of the density of the population and the intensive use of the land.

Photo credit: Susan D. Rock.

A native woman and her child.

5 ENVIRONMENT

As of 1994, Ecuador's major environmental problems were erosion in the highland areas; deforestation, especially in the rainforest east of the Andes; and water pollution. It is estimated that, at current deforestation rates, coastal forests will be completely eliminated within 15 years and the Amazon forests will be gone within 40 years. Traditional farming practices have been blamed for most of these problems, but oil development has also played a role in the clearing of forests.

The expansion of Ecuador's population centers threatens its wildlife. Twenty-one species of mammals, 64 bird species, and 8 reptile species are currently endangered, as well as 256 plant species.

Endangered species in the Galápagos Islands include the Galápagos giant tortoise.

6 POPULATION

In 1990, the total population was 9,648,189. The projected population for the year 2000 was 13,090,000. Quito, the capital, has 1,100,847 inhabitants.

7 MIGRATION

Within Ecuador, the largest migration is from rural areas to the cities, as urban employment opportunities widen. There is also a growing movement from the over-populated highlands to the virgin lands of the Oriente (eastern region) and the coast.

8 ETHNIC GROUPS

The population of Ecuador is about 40% mestizo (mixed Amerindian and white). Another 40% are Amerindian, 10–15% white, and 5% black. The Amazon Basin, including parts of Ecuador and Peru, is inhabited by many primitive tribes, including the Jívaros, once famous for their shrunken-head war trophies.

9 LANGUAGES

The official language of Ecuador is Spanish, spoken by about 93% of the population. Nearly 7% of the total population speak only Quichua, a dialect of the Quechua language, which originated with the Incas.

LOCATION: 1°26′30″N to 5°1′s; 75°11′44″ to 81°1′w.
BOUNDARY LENGTHS: Colombia, 590 kilometers (368 miles); Peru, 1,420 kilometers (887 miles); Pacific coastline, 2,237 kilometers (1,398 miles). **TERRITORIAL SEA LIMIT:** 200 miles.

10 RELIGIONS

Roman Catholic was introduced by the Spaniards with the conquest in 1540. In 1993, an estimated 93% of the population was Roman Catholic. Protestants, including Anglicans, Baptists, and Methodists, make up less than 2% of the population. Spirit worship survives among the Amerindians of the interior jungles. Freedom of worship is guaranteed by the constitution.

11 TRANSPORTATION

The rugged topography (landscape) and climate of Ecuador have greatly hindered the development of adequate means of land transportation. In 1991 there were 28,000 kilometers (17,399 miles) of highways serving 265,000 passenger cars and 60,000 commercial vehicles. Railways, all government owned, are of decreasing importance because of their poor condition and competition from highways. The three railroad networks total 965 kilometers (600 miles).

Guayaquil has modern port facilities ten kilometers (six miles) from the Daule River. The Daule River basin is important for transportation in the coastal provinces.

Ecuador's rugged terrain has hastened the growth of air travel. There are international airports at Guayaquil and Quito. The government-run Ecuatoriana de Aviación provides service between Ecuador and the rest of Latin America. It carries about 252,300 international and domestic passengers annually.

12 HISTORY

The coastal regions of present-day Ecuador supported corn-cultivating communities as early as 4500 BC. Highland tribes, which had formed a loose federation by AD 1000, were absorbed into the Inca Empire in the late fifteenth century. Spanish forces under Francisco Pizarro conquered Ecuador in 1531. In 1534 the city of San Francisco de Quito, later to become the capital of the republic, was founded. It had been the northern capital of the Inca Empire, and was left in ashes by the retreating Amerindians.

The Spanish governed the region as the Audencia of Quito, part of the Viceroyalty of Peru. The Spanish colonial period was a time of ruthless mistreatment of the Amerindians and bickering and bloodshed among the Spanish in the struggle for power and riches.

After several failed attempts to throw off Spanish rule, a decisive struggle began on 9 October 1820, with the proclamation of an independent Guayaquil. Finally, on 24 May 1822, with the Battle of Pinchincha, the Spanish were defeated. Liberated Ecuador became part of Símon Bolívar's dream, the Republic of Gran Colombia, consisting of modern Ecuador, Colombia, Venezuela, and Panama.

In 1830, when this union collapsed, the traditional name Quito was dropped in favor of La República del Ecuador, "The Republic of the Equator." The Republic's first president, Juan José Flores, claimed the Galápagos Islands for his new nation in 1832.

General Eloy Alfaro ushered in the Radical Liberal era with the revolution of 1895. Under Eloy and the succeeding Liberal presidents, church and state were carefully separated. The Guayaquil-Quito railway was completed, uniting the coast and the highlands commercially.

The Liberal era continued until 1944. During that time it was plagued with numerous periods of violence and crisis. Territory was lost to Brazil in 1904,

Photo credit: Susan D. Rock.

Overview of Old Quito.

Colombia in 1916, and finally Peru in 1942.

From 1944 to 1961, a succession of elected governments held office. In 1961, with Ecuadorian currency in a slump and consumers heavily taxed, the air force revolted and sent president Velasco Ibarra into exile.

After a period of time, which included rule by a four-man military junta, Velasco once again won the presidency in 1968. However, on 22 June 1970, following a fiscal crisis, he suspended the 1967 constitution and assumed dictatorial power. He was overthrown in a bloodless coup in 1972, but military rule continued.

Democracy returned to Ecuador in 1979 with the election of Jaime Roldós Aguilera, and elected governments have run the country since that time.

Ecuador was dealt two staggering blows in the 1980s: the 1986 plunge in world oil prices cut revenues by 30%, and a devastating earthquake in March 1987. The earthquake destroyed a portion of the country's main oil pipeline. Because of the damage, oil exports were cut off for four months. In addition, 20,000 were left homeless and there was more than $1 billion in damage.

In 1992, voters elected a conservative government, headed by President Sixto

Durán-Ballén of the Republican Unity Party (PUR), and Vice President Alberto Dahik of the Conservative Party (CP).

13 GOVERNMENT

Ecuador's Chamber of Representatives consists of 77 provincial and national members. The president and vice-president are elected for four-year terms, and the president cannot be reelected. The president controls the armed forces and can declare a state of siege. Ecuador has 20 continental provinces, plus the Galápagos Islands.

14 POLITICAL PARTIES

There are currently 18 parties active in Ecuadorian politics. Modern parties on the right include the Social Christian Party (PSC), the Republican Unity Party (PUR), and the Conservative Party (CE). On the left are the Democratic Left (ID), the Popular Democracy Party (DP) of former President Hurtado, and the traditional Radical Liberal Party (PLR).

15 JUDICIAL SYSTEM

Traditionally, the judicial function has been carried out by five levels of tribunals. The parochial judge handles only minor civil cases. Cantonal courts try minor civil and criminal actions. Provincial courts handle most criminal cases and serious civil and commercial suits. Superior courts handle appeals from the lower courts. The highest court is the Supreme Court, which has 31 justices and three alternates chosen by the Chamber of Representatives for six-year periods.

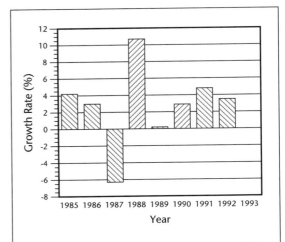

Yearly growth rate of the economy. This economic indicator tells by what percent the economy has increased or decreased when compared with the previous year.

16 ARMED FORCES

The armed forces of 57,500 are designed for internal security more than external defense. In 1991, Ecuador spent $261 million on defense. A one-year draft supports an army of 50,000. The navy numbers 4,500 (including 1,500 marines), and the air force 3,500.

17 ECONOMY

Ecuador's economy grew by 3.5% in 1992, mainly as a result of increased petroleum production and government economic policies. The inflation rate was 60% at the end of 1992; the Ballén administration had set a target of 30% for the following year, but inflation fell only to an estimated 40% in 1993.

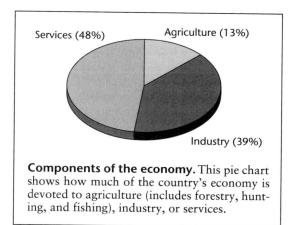

Components of the economy. This pie chart shows how much of the country's economy is devoted to agriculture (includes forestry, hunting, and fishing), industry, or services.

18 INCOME

In 1992, Ecuador's gross national product (GNP) was $11,843 million at current prices, or about $1,200 per person. For the period 1985–92 the average inflation rate was 49.6%, resulting in a real growth rate in GNP of 0.6% per person.

19 INDUSTRY

In 1992, manufacturing output continued the recovery which began in 1991, especially in tobacco products, textiles, wood and paper, chemicals, and metallic minerals. The vast mineral resources of Ecuador also present an opportunity for industrial development.

20 LABOR

In 1991, the civilian labor force numbered 4.4 million. Of that number, 30.8% were engaged in agriculture, 24.9% in services, 11.6% in manufacturing and mining, 14.2% in commerce, 5.9% in construction, 3.9% in transportation, and 8.7% in other activities. The unemployment rate officially stood at 8% in 1991. Only 13.5% of workers belong to labor unions.

21 AGRICULTURE

Traditionally, agricultural products have included bananas, coffee, tea, rice, sugar, beans, corn, potatoes, and tropical fruit. Popular recent export products include roses and carnations, strawberries, melons, asparagus, heart of palm, and tomatoes. The major crops of the highlands are corn, barley, wheat, kidney beans, potatoes, horsebeans, peas, and soybeans, all for domestic consumption.

22 DOMESTICATED ANIMALS

There were 4,665,000 head of cattle in 1992. Nearly all the sheep (1,511,000 in 1992) are in the highlands; most are raised by Amerindians. In 1992 there were an estimated 2,434,000 hogs and 314,000 goats.

23 FISHING

In the waters around the Galápagos Islands, Ecuador has some of the world's richest fishing grounds, particularly for tuna, and the nation is a leading producer of canned tuna. Ecuador also produces more shrimp than any other nation in the Americas, and exports more than 35,000 tons annually, mostly to the United States. The total catch in 1991 was 383,600 tons.

24 FORESTRY

One of Ecuador's vast untapped resources is its forestland. The tropical jungles contain more than 2,240 known species of trees. Ecuador is the world's largest producer and exporter of balsa. Several

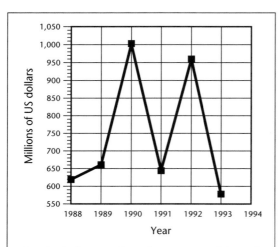

Yearly balance of trade measured in millions of US dollars. The balance of trade is the difference between what a country sells to other countries (its exports) and what it buys (its imports). If a country imports more than it exports, it has a negative balance of trade (a trade deficit). If exports exceed imports there is a positive balance of trade (a trade surplus).

varieties of hardwoods, including species of mahogany, are used in cabinetmaking.

25 MINING

Aside from petroleum, Ecuador's known mineral resources include gold, silver, copper, bismuth, tin, lead, zinc, clays, kaolin, limestone, marble, and sulfur. The total value of mineral output was $1.2 billion in 1991, down from $1.4 billion in 1990.

26 FOREIGN TRADE

In 1992, exports exceeded $3 billion, of which oil contributed 44%; bananas, 22%; and manufactured products, 8%. Imports that year totaled over $2 billion, of which food accounted for 10%; fuel

and energy, 4%; and capital goods, 38%. The United States accounts for about 44% of Ecuador's foreign trade, and the Latin American Free Trade Association for most of the remainder.

27 ENERGY AND POWER

By February 1993, oil production had risen to 330,000 barrels per day. Total production of electric power in 1991 amounted to 6.9 billion kilowatt hours, 72% of it hydroelectric. Electricity prices are the lowest in the Andean region.

28 SOCIAL DEVELOPMENT

The benefits of Ecuador's social security program, for those who fulfill the requirements, consist of health and maternity insurance with free medical service, accident insurance, old age pensions, survivors' pensions, funeral expenses, and unemployment insurance.

Despite equal legal status, women have fewer educational and employment opportunities than men.

29 HEALTH

It is estimated that 88% of the population has access to health care services. There is one doctor for every 957 people in Ecuador. In 1994 the country spent over $440 million on health care.

Malnutrition and infant mortality are the country's two basic health problems. Life expectancy was estimated at 69 years.

30 HOUSING

Almost all rural homes and many city dwellings on the coast are made with split

Selected Social Indicators

These statistics are estimates for the period 1988 to 1993. For comparison purposes, data for the United States and averages for low-income countries and high-income countries are also given.

Indicator	Ecuador	Low-income countries	High-income countries	United States
Per capita gross national product†	**$1,200**	$380	$23,680	$24,740
Population growth rate	**2.3%**	1.9%	0.6%	1.0%
Population growth rate in urban areas	**3.6%**	3.9%	0.8%	1.3%
Population per square kilometer of land	**38**	78	25	26
Life expectancy in years	**69**	62	77	76
Number of people per physician	**957**	>3,300	453	419
Number of pupils per teacher (primary school)	**32**	39	<18	20
Illiteracy rate (15 years and older)	**14%**	41%	<5%	<3%
Energy consumed per capita (kg of oil equivalent)	**561**	364	5,203	7,918

† The gross national product (GNP) is the total dollar value of all goods and services produced by a country in a year. The per capita GNP is calculated by dividing a country's GNP by its population. The World Bank defines low-income countries as those with a per capita GNP of $695 or less. High-income countries have a per capita GNP of $8,626 or more. Less than 14% of the world's 5.5 billion people live in high-income countries, while almost 60% live in low-income countries.

n.a. = data not available   > = greater than   < = less than

Sources: World Bank, *Social Indicators of Development 1995,* Baltimore: Johns Hopkins University Press, 1995. Central Intelligence Agency, *World Fact Book,* Washington, D.C.: Government Printing Office, 1994.

bamboo siding and a palm thatch or corrugated iron roof. A housing development bank, Banco de la Vivienda, was established in 1961.

31 EDUCATION

Literacy for persons 15 years of age and over rose from 56% in 1950 to 86% in 1990 (males, 90.4% and females, 83.9%). At the primary level, there are approximately 32 pupils per teacher, with a total of 1.8 million primary students. The secondary level had 771,928 students in 1987. At the universities and all higher level institutions, there were 206,541 students enrolled and 12,856 teaching staff in 1990. The Central University of Ecuador dates from 1594.

32 MEDIA

In 1991 Ecuador had more than 300 radio stations and 33 television stations, most of them in color. There were 3,420,000 radio receivers and 910,000 television sets in the same year. In 1991 there were 691,460 telephones in use.

In 1991, Ecuador had 26 daily newspapers. The leading newspapers, with their estimated daily circulations in 1991, were *El Universo* (190,000); *El Comercio*

Photo credit: Susan D. Rock.

Mt. Cotopaxi is the world's highest active volcano at 19,347 feet.

(140,000); *Últimas Noticias* (80,000); and *Hoy* (70,000).

33 TOURISM AND RECREATION

Tourist facilities on the coast include modern resort hotels and fine beaches. Ecuador's highlands, reached by air or by the spectacular railroad or highway, are rich in natural beauty. Quito, the second-highest capital in the world, has modern hotels and transportation, together with historic churches and monasteries.

An important part of Ecuador's cultural life is the feria, or market day, which takes place weekly in many towns. The Galápagos Islands, world-famous for their unusual wildlife, have become a popular site for ecotourism.

In 1991, there were 364,585 visitor arrivals in Ecuador, 35% from Colombia, 18% from the United States, and 12% from Peru. Tourism receipts totaled $189 million. There were 29,464 hotel rooms with 58,629 beds.

34 FAMOUS ECUADORANS

Ecuadorans claim Atahualpa (1500?–33), the last emperor of the Incas, as the first renowned figure in their country's history. The sixteenth-century Amerindian general Rumiñahui is remembered for his heroic resistance to Spanish conquest.

Outstanding Ecuadorans of the twentieth century include the poets Gonzalo Escudero (1903–71) and César Dávila Andrade (1918–67); and the painter Oswaldo Guayasamin Calero (b.1919).

35 BIBLIOGRAPHY

Corkill, David. *Ecuador*. Santa Barbara, Calif.: Clio Press, 1989.

Darwin, Charles. *Voyage of the Beagle*. Garden City, N.Y.: Natural History Press, 1962 (orig. 1840).

Ecuador in Pictures. Minneapolis: Lerner Publications Co., 1987.

Hanratty, Dennis M., ed. *Ecuador, a Country Study*. 3d ed. Washington, D.C.: Library of Congress, 1991.

Hassaureck, Friedrich. *Four Years Among the Ecuadorians*. Carbondale: Southern Illinois University Press, 1967.

Lepthien, E. *Ecuador*. Chicago: Children's Press, 1986.

Plage, Dieter and Mary. "Galapagos Wildlife." *National Geographic,* January 1988, 122–145.

EGYPT

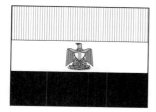

Arab Republic of Egypt

Jumhuriat Misr al-'Arabiyah

NAME: Egypt (Misr) is the name by which this ancient country has been known for more than 6,000 years. In 1958, the nation established by the merger of Egypt and Syria adopted the name United Arab Republic. Egypt retained this name (despite the breakaway of Syria in 1961) until 1971, when under a new constitution it became the Arab Republic of Egypt.

CAPITAL: Cairo (Al-Qahira).

FLAG: The flag is a tricolor of three horizontal stripes—red, white, and black—with the national emblem in the center white stripe.

ANTHEM: *The Arab Republic of Egypt Hymn.*

MONETARY UNIT: The Egyptian pound (E£) is a paper currency of 100 piasters or 1,000 milliemes. There are coins of 1, 5, 10, and 20 piasters and notes of 25 and 50 piasters and 1, 5, 10, 20, 50, and 1000 pounds. E£1 = US$3.38 (or US$1 = E£0.2959).

WEIGHTS AND MEASURES: The metric system is the official standard, but various local units also are used: 1 feddan, consisting of 333.3 kassabah, equals 0.42 hectare (1.038 acres).

HOLIDAYS: New Year's Day, 1 January; Evacuation Day, 18 June; Revolution Day, 23 July; Armed Forces Day, 6 October; Popular Resistance Day, 24 October; Victory Day, 23 December. Movable holidays include Sham an-Nassim (Breath of Spring), of ancient origin, as well as such Muslim religious holidays as 'Id al-Fitr, 'Id al-'Adha', and the 1st of Muharram (Muslim New Year).

TIME: 2 PM = noon GMT.

1 LOCATION AND SIZE

Situated at the northeastern corner of Africa, the Arab Republic of Egypt has an area of 1,001,450 square kilometers (621,900 square miles). The cultivated and settled area (Nile Valley, Delta, and oases) constitutes only about 3.5% of Egypt's land area; the Libyan and Western deserts occupy about 75% of the total. Comparatively, the area occupied by Egypt is slightly more than three times the size of the state of New Mexico. The total boundary length was 5,139 kilometers (3,193 miles) following the 1982 withdrawal by Israel. Egypt's capital city, Cairo, is located in the northeastern part of the country.

2 TOPOGRAPHY

The altitude of Egypt ranges from 133 meters (436 feet) below sea level in the Libyan Plateau to 2,640 meters (8,660 feet) above sea level in the Sinai Peninsula. The bulk of the country is covered by the Sahara Desert, but other areas include the Nile Delta, (sloping to the sea between Alexandria and Port Said), the Nile valley, and the broad elevated plain south of Cairo. East of the Nile, the Arabian Desert extends to the Red Sea. Egypt's outstanding topographic feature is the Nile River.

3 CLIMATE

Most of Egypt is a dry subtropical area. Northern winds temper the climate along the Mediterranean, but the interior areas are very hot. The temperature sinks quickly after sunset because there are no clouds to hold in the heat. Annual rainfall averages 2.5 centimeters (1 inch) south of Cairo and 20 centimeters (8 inches) on the Mediterranean coast, but sudden storms sometimes cause devastating flash floods. Hot, dry sandstorms, known as *khamsins*, come off the Western Desert in the spring. In Cairo, average temperatures range from 7° to 29°C (45° to 84°F) in January, and 22° to 36°C (72° to 97°F) in July.

4 PLANTS AND ANIMALS

Plants are those common in dry subtropical and tropical lands, such as papyrus. Egypt has no forests but does have date palm and citrus groves; eucalyptus and cypress have been introduced. Sheep, goats, and donkeys are found throughout the country, and camels are found in all the deserts. Egypt has some 300 types of birds. There are few wild animals: hyena, jackal, lynx, and mongoose, and wild

Photo credit: Susan D. Rock.
St. Catherine's Monstery at Mt. Sinai.

boars which live in the Nile Delta. The Nile is adequately stocked with fish, but only a few crocodiles remain along the shores of Lake Nasser.

5 ENVIRONMENT

Egypt's environmental problems stem from its aridity (dryness), extremely uneven population distribution, shortage of arable (able to be farmed) land, and pollution. Soil fertility has declined because of overcultivation. Heavy use of pesticides, inadequate sewage disposal, and uncontrolled industrial waste have created a major water pollution problem. The expanded irrigation of desert areas

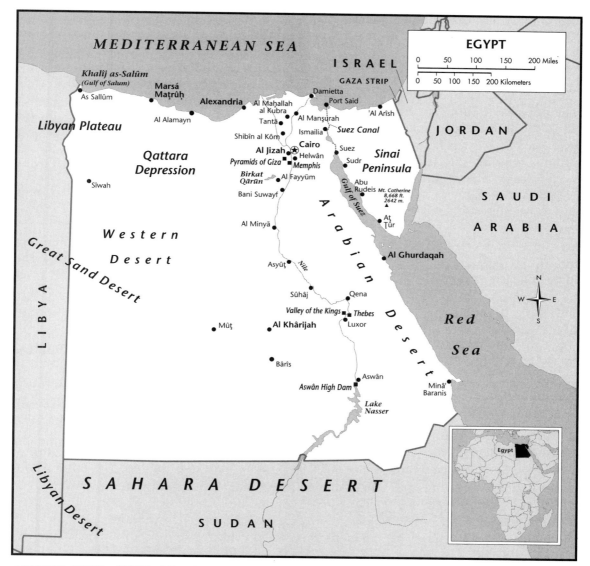

LOCATION: 21°35' to 31°35'N; 25° to 36°E. **BOUNDARY LENGTHS:** Total coastline, 2450 kilometers (1520 miles); Israel, 255 kilometers (160 miles); Gaza strip 11 kilometers (7 miles); Sudan: 1,273 kilometers (790 miles); Libya, 1,150 kilometers (716 miles). **TERRITORIAL SEA LIMIT:** 12 miles.

after completion of the Aswân High Dam in 1970 has increased soil salinity (saltiness) and promoted the spread of waterborne diseases.

The tremendous rise of human population in the Nile Valley over the centuries has crowded out and nearly destroyed Egypt's wildlife in that region. The hunting of any bird has been prohibited by law. Endangered species include the Sinai leopard.

6 POPULATION

The population of Egypt was estimated at 58,274,848 in 1994, an increase of 20.8% over the 1986 census figure of 48,259,238. A population of 64,810,000 was projected for the year 2000. Although the average population density for the whole country is 55 persons per square kilometer (142 per square mile), the average in cultivated areas is close to 1,650 per square kilometer (4,270 per square mile), one of the highest densities in the world. Some 99% of all Egyptians live in the Nile Valley. In 1990, Cairo, the capital, had a population of 6,542,000.

7 MIGRATION

Nearly all Jews, who formed less than 0.3% of the population in 1966, left the country after the 1967 war with Israel. With the completion of the Aswân High Dam in 1970, up to 100,000 Nubian tribesmen were moved from flooded parts of the upper Nile and resettled in the plain downstream. During the 1970s many people moved from rural to urban areas. In the 1970s and first half of the 1980s, more than three million workers took jobs in other countries. In 1992 some 2,850,000 Egyptians were living abroad, including about one million in Libya and 850,000 in Saudi Arabia.

8 ETHNIC GROUPS

Egyptians make up about 97% of the population of Egypt. They are a product of the intermixture of ancient Egyptians with the invaders of many millennia from various parts of Asia and Africa. Minorities are mainly other Arabs, Berbers, Nubians, Armenians, Greeks, Maltese, and Indians, with a few remaining British and French residents. Several tribes of Bedouins live in the deserts and the Sinai Peninsula.

9 LANGUAGES

The language of most of the population is Arabic, a Semitic tongue. The 1971 constitution declares Arabic to be Egypt's official language. English and French are spoken by most educated Egyptians. The Copts, a large Christian sect which dates back to the fifth century AD, still pray in the Hamitic tongue of the ancient Egyptian pharaohs.

10 RELIGIONS

The majority religion is Islam, of which the Sunni Muslims are the largest sect. The 1971 constitution declares Islam to be the state religion. According to the 1986 census, 90% of the population was Muslim and 5.9% was Christian. The latter figure includes Coptic Christians, Roman Catholics, and Orthodox. The religious authorities of those groups say the figure of 5.9% is too small. The Jewish minority has virtually disappeared.

11 TRANSPORTATION

Egypt's transportation system is well developed, with 51,925 kilometers (32,266 miles) of roads in 1991, of which 34% were paved. In 1992, 1,119,727 passenger cars and 466,650 commercial vehicles were registered. In 1982, in an

Photo credit: Susan D. Rock.

Pharoahs, rulers in Egypt around 2500 BC, built great pyramids as royal tombs.

attempt to alleviate Cairo's notorious traffic congestion, work began on a city subway system, the first subway to be built in Africa. Railroad track totaling some 5,110 kilometers (3,175 miles) links all parts of the country. Steamer ship service on the Nile is an important means of domestic transport, as are 3,100 kilometers (1,926 miles) of navigable canals. Alexandria, Port Said, and Suez are the principal ports.

The Suez Canal, about 160 kilometers (100 miles) long, was constructed between 1859 and 1869 under the supervision of the French engineer Ferdinand de Lesseps. In 1956, at Egypt's insistence, the British withdrew from the area, and Egypt nationalized the canal. Cairo International Airport is used by numerous international airlines, including Egypt's own; in 1991 it serviced 5.6 million passengers.

12 HISTORY

Early History

Egypt has the oldest recorded history in Western civilization, dating back 5,000 years. In early times, the desert provided protection against invaders, while the Nile River provided food. Therefore, by 3400 BC the civilization of Egypt was well developed. The country was united about 3100 BC by Menes (or Narmer), king of Upper Egypt. Menes conquered Lower Egypt and established the first of some 30 dynasties that were ruled over by a divine king, or pharaoh. Menes created a centralized state; under his dynastic successors, trade flourished, and the hieroglyphic form of writing was perfected.

During the fourth dynasty (c.2613–2494 BC), the pharaohs (rulers) began to build the great pyramids as royal tombs. The pharaohs of the twelfth dynasty built vast irrigation schemes and developed a thriving civilization at Thebes. It was under their rule that a system of cursive writing was developed. Ancient Egypt attained its apex during the eighteenth dynasty (c.1570–1320 BC), under pharaohs Thutmose III, Amenhotep III, Amenhotep IV, and Tutankhamen.

In subsequent centuries, political instability weakened the kingdom. Egypt was invaded by Assyria (673–663 BC), annexed by Persia (525 BC), and finally, conquered by Alexander the Great (332 BC). Alexander established the Macedonian dynasty, which ruled Egypt from 323 to 30 BC. During this period, the city of Alexandria flourished as the intellectual center of the Hellenistic world. The best-known ruler of this dynasty was Queen Cleopatra. She was defeated at the Battle of Actium in 31 BC by the Roman general Caius Octavius (Augustus), who claimed Egypt for Rome. The Roman Empire was divided into east and west following the death of Theodosius in AD 395. After the split, Egypt became part of the Eastern Roman (Byzantine) Empire.

7th–early 19th Century

Egypt was conquered by the Arab ruler 'Amr ibn-al-'As in 639–42. The Arab conquerors established firm control of the area. From 1250 to 1517, Egypt was ruled by a military caste called the Mamluks. However, the Mamluks were conquered by the Ottoman Turks in 1517. Egypt remained a Turkish territory for four centuries.

In 1805, an Albanian soldier, Muhammad 'Ali, was appointed ruler (wali) of Egypt. He succeeded in establishing his own dynasty which ruled the country, first under nominal Ottoman control, and later as a British protectorate. Muhammad 'Ali and the dynasty that he began destroyed feudalism, stabilized the country, encouraged the planting of cotton, and opened the land to European penetration and development.

The Suez Canal and British Intervention

In 1859, work began on a ship canal which would connect the Mediterranean Sea with the Red Sea. It was to become known as the Suez Canal. The canal, begun under the direction of the French promoter Ferdinank de Lesseps, took ten years to complete.

After the completion of the Suez Canal (1869), Egypt became a world transportation hub and therefore a desirable strategic location. However, financial mismanagement of the building of the canal led to bankruptcy. These developments led to rapid expansion of British and French financial oversight. That, in turn, provoked popular resentment, unrest, and finally, revolt in 1879 among the Egyptions. British forces crushed the revolt in 1882, and England seized control of Egypt's government in 1882. To secure its interests in World War I, Britain declared a formal protectorate over Egypt on 18 December 1914.

After the war, in 1922, England recognized Egypt as an officially sovereign country under King Fuad. Egyptian nationalism gathered momentum in World War II, during which Egypt was used as an Allied base of operations. Many political and social problems motivated a successful coup on 23 July 1952 and in 1954 Lieutenant Colonel Gamal Abdel Nasser, leader of the revolution, came to power.

Nasser and the Aswân Dam

To increase the production in his country, Nasser entered into preliminary agreements with the United States, Britain, and the United Nations to finance a new dam at Aswân. At the same time, he negotiated economic aid and arms shipments from the Soviet Union and its allies in Eastern Europe. This angered the United States. In response, the United States withheld its financial backing for the dam. In retaliation, on 26 July 1956, President Nasser took control of the Suez Canal and announced that he would use the profits from its operations to build the dam. The dam was completed with aid and technical assistance from the Soviet Union.

On 29 October 1956, there was a three-nation plot to bring down Nasser and reassert control over the Canal. Israeli armed forces swept into Egypt's Sinai Peninsula. Britain and France then issued an ultimatum to both sides to cease fire. When Egypt rejected the ultimatum, Britain and France landed troops in the Port Said area and bombed Egyptian cities from the air. The intervention of the United States and the Soviet Union, acting through the United Nations, led to the withdrawal of the British, French, and Israeli forces by March 1957.

Egypt and Syria

On 1 February 1958, Egypt and Syria proclaimed their union in the United Arab Republic (UAR) with Nasser as president. However, differing economic and political conditions prevented a complete fusion of the two regions. On 28 September 1961, the Syrian army revolted, and two days later it proclaimed Syrian independence. Egypt continued to try for Arab unity, signing agreements with Iraq, Yemen, Syria again, and Libya during the 1960s and early 1970s. None of these agreements produced a lasting political union.

On 5 June 1967, Egypt closed the Gulf of Aqaba to Israeli shipping. In what later became known as the "Six-Day War," Israel quickly crippled the Egyptian air force and occupied the Gaza Strip and the Sinai and blocked the Suez Canal. During the years after 1967, a "War of Attrition" was fought along the Canal with each side shelling the other and Israeli planes bombing Egyptian cities.

Nasser Dies and Sadat Takes Over

When Nasser died on 28 September 1970, his vice-president, Anwar al-Sadat, became president. President Sadat firmly established his hold on the government and began to implement pragmatic economic and social policies including improved relations with the United States.

Frustrated in his ambition to recover the Sinai, President Sadat broke the 1967 ceasefire agreement on 6 October 1973, initiating the "Yom Kippur War" He attacked Israeli forces in the Sinai Peninsula while Syria attacked Israeli forces occupying the Syrian Golan Heights. After initial successes, the Egyptian strike forces were defeated by Israeli troops, who then crossed the Canal south of Ismâ'ilîyah. A ceasefire that came into effect on 24 October left Egyptian troops in the Sinai and Israeli troops on the west bank of the Canal. United States Secretary of State Henry Kissinger negotiated an agreement that left Egypt in full control of the Canal and established a UN-supervised buffer zone in the Sinai between the Egyptian and Israeli forces. In November 1975, the Sinai oil fields at Abu Rudeis and Sudr were returned to Egypt.

President Sadat went to Jerusalem in November 1977 and received Israeli Prime Minister Menachem Begin at Ismâ'ilîyah the following month. In September 1978, Sadat entered into negotiations with Begin, mediated by United States President Carter, at Camp David, Maryland. Following further negotiations, Sadat signed the Egyptian-Israeli Peace Treaty in Washington, D.C., on 26 March 1979. For their roles as peacemakers, Sadat and Begin were jointly awarded the 1978 Nobel Peace Prize. But other Arab leaders denounced the accords and sought to isolate Egypt within the Arab world.

Sadat Is Assassinated

In early September 1981, Sadat ordered the arrest of 1,536 Muslims, Christian Copts, leftists, and other persons accused of violent acts. One month later, on 6 October, Sadat was assassinated in Cairo by four Muslim fundamentalists. The vice-president, Muhammad Hosni (Husni) Mubarak, who had been Sadat's closest adviser, succeeded him as president. Mubarak pledged to continue Sadat's policies, particularly the terms of the peace treaty with Israel. Relations with Israel cooled during 1982, however, especially after Israeli troops moved into Lebanon.

Following the Amman Arab summit conference in November 1987, Egypt renewed diplomatic relations with a number of Arab states and in May 1989 rejoined the Arab League. Mubarak continued Sadat's policies of moderation and peacemaking abroad and gradual political liberalization and movement towards the free market at home. In 1990, Egypt played a key role in the coalition to expel Iraq from Kuwait and in 1993 and 1994 was active in promoting the Israeli-Palestinian peace accord.

Mubarak was reelected president in 1987 and 1993. The most serious opposition to the Mubarak government is from outside the political system. Religious parties are banned and, as a consequence, Islamic militants have resorted to violence against the regime. Security forces have cracked down hard, but the militant movement has gathered strength, fueled by discontent with poor economic conditions, corruption, secularism, and Egypt's ties with the United States and Israel.

13 GOVERNMENT

The president of the republic is the head of state and supreme commander of the armed forces. The president's power to declare war and make treaties with foreign countries is subject to the approval of the People's Assembly. The Assembly is a unicameral legislative body consisting (in 1988) of 444 elected and 10 appointed members serving five-year terms. A 210-member advisory body, the Shura Council, was formed in 1980. The People's Assembly nominates the president, who must then be confirmed by plebiscite (popular vote) for a six-year term.

14 POLITICAL PARTIES

The Arab Socialist Union (ASU; founded by President Nasser as the Egyptian National Union in 1957) was the sole legal political party until 1976, when President Sadat allowed three minor parties to participate in parliamentary elections. In 1978, Sadat replaced the ASU with his own organization, the National Democratic Party (NDP), of which he became chairman. In January 1982, President Mubarak was elected without opposition as chairman of the NDP. The New Wafd (Delegation) Party is the middle class successor of the dominant party of the pre-Nasser period, now allied with the Moslem Brotherhood.

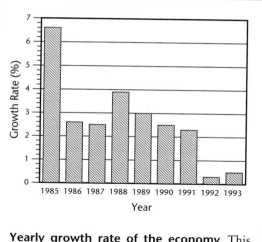

Yearly growth rate of the economy. This economic indicator tells by what percent the economy has increased or decreased when compared with the previous year.

15 JUDICIAL SYSTEM

Simple police offenses, misdemeanors, and civil cases involving small amounts are subject to the jurisdiction of a single-judge. The trial courts of the central tribunals, consisting of three judges each, hear more serious cases and also consider appeals. Traffic in narcotics and press offenses, considered serious crimes, are tried by the courts of appeals. The highest tribunal is the Court of Cassation.

16 ARMED FORCES

Military service is compulsory for all males over eighteen. In 1993, the armed forces consisted of 410,000 men. The army had 290,000 men, organized into 12 combined arms divisions and 39 special brigades. The army reserves totaled about 500,000 men. The air force had 30,000 men and 492 combat aircraft and 74 armed helicopters, plus 70,000 personnel in the air defense command. The navy had 20,000 men, 4 submarines, 1 destroyer, 4 frigates, and about 39 other armed vessels for coast defense.

17 ECONOMY

Historically, the Egyptian economy was mostly agricultural, with cotton as the mainstay. Land prices are extremely high because of the shortage of arable (able to be farmed) land. Not enough food is produced to meet the needs of a rapidly growing population. Although Egypt has expanded its private sector in recent years, industry remains centrally controlled and for the most part government owned. Since the 1950s, the government has developed the petroleum, services, and construction sectors, largely at the expense of agriculture. In 1992–93 tourism plunged an estimated 20% because of attacks by Islamic extremists on tourist groups.

18 INCOME

In 1992, Egypt's gross national product (GNP) was $34,514 million at current prices, or $660 per person. For the period 1985–92 the average inflation rate was 17.1%, resulting in a real growth rate in GNP of 0.8% per person.

19 INDUSTRY

Great achievements have been made in industrial development. Cement, glass, iron and steel products, fertilizers, paper, petroleum refining, electric power, spinning, and sugar are among the industries that have increased production. Newer

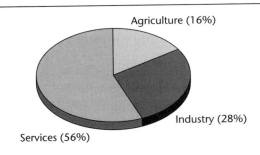

Components of the economy. This pie chart shows how much of the country's economy is devoted to agriculture (includes forestry, hunting, and fishing), industry, or services.

industries include tires, refrigerators, air conditioners, sewing machines, bicycles, electric meters, batteries, wire, and cable. Egypt and the Republic of South Africa are the largest producers of petroleum refinery products in Africa.

20 LABOR

Egypt's civilian labor force (15–64 years) increased from 14.8 million in 1990 to 15.3 million in 1991, when 33.1% of the work force was employed in agriculture, 46% in services, and 20.9% in industry. Unemployment was estimated at 12% in 1992. The most important trade union is the Egyptian Trade Union Federation, which opposes the privatization of profitable state-owned companies, an important part of reforms initiated in 1991 to stabilize the economy.

21 AGRICULTURE

During the 1970s agriculture lost its position as the dominant economic sector. Agricultural exports, which accounted for

87% of all merchandise export value in 1960, fell to 35% in 1974 and to 13% by 1992.

Cotton has been the staple crop, but its importance as an export is declining. Receipts from exported cotton only accounted for 1% of total exports in 1992, down from 11% in 1985. Egypt is also a substantial producer of wheat, corn, sugarcane, fruit and vegetables, fodder, and rice.

22 DOMESTICATED ANIMALS

Little land is available for raising animals, but efforts were made in the 1980s to increase the output of fodder per land unit. In 1992, the estimated livestock population included 36,000,000 chickens, 4,800,000 goats, 4,350,000 sheep, 3,036,000 head of buffalo, 3,016,000 head of cattle, and 115,000 hogs. Livestock products in that year included 2,021,000 tons of cow and buffalo milk, 726,000 tons of meat, and 127,440 tons of eggs.

23 FISHING

Fishing is concentrated in the Nile Delta and River and in the Mediterranean and Red seas. The catch of sea, lake, and river fish amounted to 298,913 tons in 1992. Mullet and eels are caught in the Delta and sardines in the Mediterranean. Despite these native resources, however, Egypt has been a net importer of fish.

24 FORESTRY

There are no forests in Egypt. The construction and furniture-making industries rely on wood imports.

25 MINING

Egypt's mineral resources include phosphates (around the Red Sea, along the Nile, and in the Western Desert), coal (in the Sinai), salt, iron oxides, gold, ocher, sulfate of magnesia, talc, building stone, and nitrate of soda. Iron ore deposits have been developed at Aswân to supply the steel plant at Helwân.

26 FOREIGN TRADE

Leading imports are wheat, chemical and pharmaceutical products, raw materials for industry, machinery, and motor vehicles. Egypt suffers from chronic trade deficits, which have steadily increased from 1987 to 1992.

Egypt's shift in political alliances has affected its trade patterns. Before 1973, when Egypt was linked to the then-Soviet Union, 55% of its exports went to the USSR and other socialist countries, which supplied 30% of its imports. Today, the countries of western Europe supply more than 50% of Egypt's imports, with the United States providing some 25% of all imports.

27 ENERGY AND POWER

The brightest spot in Egypt's economic picture in the early 1980s was the development of the petroleum industry. With the return of the Sinai oil fields to Egypt, usable crude oil reserves were estimated at 6.2 billion barrels as of 1 January 1993. Oil production in 1992 averaged 925,000 barrels per day, up 38% from 1992. Usable reserves of natural gas were estimated at 15.4 trillion cubic feet (436 billion cubic meters) in January 1993.

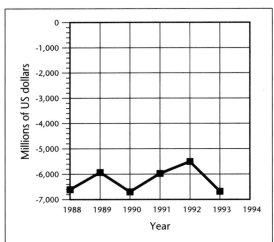

Yearly balance of trade measured in millions of US dollars. The balance of trade is the difference between what a country sells to other countries (its exports) and what it buys (its imports). If a country imports more than it exports, it has a negative balance of trade (a trade deficit). If exports exceed imports there is a positive balance of trade (a trade surplus).

Natural gas production totaled 350 billion cubic feet (9.9 billion cubic meters).

In 1992, electric power output totaled 9.7 billion kilowatt hours. Hydroelectric power provides Egypt with 25% of its electricity production. Egypt's energy needs are estimated to triple by the end of the century. Egypt was the second largest consumer of energy on the African continent in 1992, after South Africa.

28 SOCIAL DEVELOPMENT

Social programs focus on services including health care and family planning. Other social insurance programs include: workers' compensation, old age pensions, and death and disability benefits. Unemployed workers receive 60% of their last monthly wage. Women have won employment opportunities in a number of fields, but Egyptian feminists fear these gains will be lost if Islamic fundamentalists gain control.

29 HEALTH

Serious diseases in Egypt include schistosomiasis, malaria, hookworm, trachoma, tuberculosis, dysentery, beriberi, and typhus. Of children under five years of age in 1990, 13% were considered malnourished. Health care expenditures in 1990 amounted to $921 million.

30 HOUSING

Prior to 1952, most Egyptians lived in mud huts. Postrevolutionary governments, however, have actively concerned themselves with housing. In order to encourage rural housing activities on nonfertile soil, "extension areas" have been allocated for villages, and efforts have been made to provide low-rent housing in towns. Despite these efforts, Egypt's housing shortage remains acute, with about one million units needed in urban areas.

31 EDUCATION

In 1991 there were 6,541,725 students in 15,861 primary schools and 5,300,881 students in secondary schools. Teaching personnel at all levels totaled 566,112 in 1990.

Education is free and compulsory for all children between the ages of six and twelve. Entry to preparatory schools is by competitive examination, which children take at the age of ten. Preparatory schools

Selected Social Indicators

These statistics are estimates for the period 1988 to 1993. For comparison purposes, data for the United States and averages for low-income countries and high-income countries are also given.

Indicator	Egypt	Low-income countries	High-income countries	United States
Per capita gross national product†	$660	$380	$23,680	$24,740
Population growth rate	2.0%	1.9%	0.6%	1.0%
Population growth rate in urban areas	2.4%	3.9%	0.8%	1.3%
Population per square kilometer of land	55	78	25	26
Life expectancy in years	64	62	77	76
Number of people per physician	1,336	>3,300	453	419
Number of pupils per teacher (primary school)	26	39	<18	20
Illiteracy rate (15 years and older)	52%	41%	<5%	<3%
Energy consumed per capita (kg of oil equivalent)	576	364	5,203	7,918

† The gross national product (GNP) is the total dollar value of all goods and services produced by a country in a year. The per capita GNP is calculated by dividing a country's GNP by its population. The World Bank defines low-income countries as those with a per capita GNP of $695 or less. High-income countries have a per capita GNP of $8,626 or more. Less than 14% of the world's 5.5 billion people live in high-income countries, while almost 60% live in low-income countries.

> = greater than   < = less than

Sources: World Bank, *Social Indicators of Development 1995,* Baltimore: Johns Hopkins University Press, 1995. Central Intelligence Agency, *World Fact Book,* Washington, D.C.: Government Printing Office, 1994.

offer four-year courses leading to a certificate. This certificate then allows a student to go on for three-year courses in secondary schools. Here there are a domestic science program for girls, a technical curriculum, and a general curriculum with emphasis on academic studies.

A decree of 23 July 1962 provided free tuition at all Egyptian universities. The traditional center for religious education in the Muslim world is Al-Azhar in Cairo, which in 1983 celebrated 1,000 years of teaching. It is the oldest continuously operating school in the world. All universities and higher level institutions had a total of 708,417 students in 1990. Universities and equivalent institutions had a faculty of 34,553 personnel. The American University in Cairo offers a wide range of undergraduate and graduate courses.

32 MEDIA

The two leading newspapers, with their estimated 1991 daily circulations, were *Al-Ahram (The Pyramid;* 984,800) and *Al-Akhbar (The News;* 741,700). *Al-Jumhuriyah (The Republic;* 850,000) is the official publication of the government; *Al-Ahram* is the unofficial one. The leading evening paper is *Al-Misa'a* (105,000).

There is also an English-language newspaper, the *Egyptian Gazette* (32,000).

Telephone, telegraph, radio, and television services are operated by the state-owned Telecommunication Organization. There are three television channels, broadcasting mostly in Arabic. In 1991 there were 3.9 million licensed television sets. Radios were estimated at 17,500,000 that year. There were an estimated 6,200,000 telephones in use in the same year.

33 TOURISM AND RECREATION

Tourism has been a major foreign exchange earner. In 1991, there were 2,214,277 foreign visitor arrivals. Of those, 40% came from European countries and 42% from Arab countries. However, sporadic attacks by Islamic extremists on tourist groups caused tourism to decline by about 20% in 1992–93.

Principal tourist attractions include the pyramids and Great Sphinx at Giza, the Abu Simbel temples south of Aswân, the Valley of the Kings at Luxor, and the Muhammad 'Ali Mosque in Cairo. Rides are available on *fellucas*, traditional sailing boats of the Nile.

34 FAMOUS EGYPTIANS

Egypt's first recorded ruler, or pharaoh, was Menes (ruled 3100? BC), who united the southern and northern kingdoms and founded the capital at Memphis. Other notable pharaohs included Cheops (ruled 26th century BC), who built the Great Pyramid at Giza, and Tutankhamen (ruled 1361–1352 BC), whose tomb containing valuable treasures was found practically intact in 1922. Cleopatra VII (69–30 BC) was involved in the political conflicts of the Romans.

No one had greater influence on modern Egypt than Gamal Abdel Nasser (Jamal 'Abdel al-Nasir, 1918-70), the leader of the army's revolt against the monarchy in 1952. As prime minister (1954–56) and president (1956–70), Nasser set Egypt on its socialist course and attempted to unify the Arab world.

'Abbas al-Aqqad (1889–1964) has been called the greatest contemporary Arab poet and the most original Arab writer. Taha Husayn (1889–1973), the most widely known modern Egyptian intellectual leader, was minister of education from 1950 to 1952. In 1988, novelist Naguib Mahfouz (b. 1912) won the Nobel Prize for Literature.

35 BIBLIOGRAPHY

Baker, Raymond William. *Sadat and After: Struggles for Egypt's Political Soul.* Cambridge, Mass.: Harvard University Press, 1990.

Botman, Selma. *Egypt from Independence to Revolution, 1919–1952.* Syracuse, N.Y.: Syracuse University Press, 1991.

Cross, W. *Egypt.* Chicago: Children's Press, 1982.

Lehner, Mark. "Computer Rebuilds the Ancient Sphinx." *National Geographic,* April 1991, 32–39.

Metz, Helen Chapin. *Egypt, a Country Study.* 5th ed. Washington, D.C.: Library of Congress, 1991.

Nagel, Rob, and Anne Commire. "Cleopatra VII." In *World Leaders, People Who Shaped the World.* Volume I: Africa and Asia. Detroit: U*X*L, 1994.

EL SALVADOR

Republic of El Salvador
República de El Salvador

CAPITAL: San Salvador.

FLAG: The national flag consists of a white stripe between two horizontal blue stripes. The national coat of arms is centered in the white band.

ANTHEM: *Saludemos la Patria Orgullosos (Let us Proudly Hail the Fatherland).*

MONETARY UNIT: The colón (C), often called the peso, is a paper currency of 100 centavos. There are coins of 1, 2, 3, 5, 10, 25, and 50 centavos and 1 colón, and notes of 1, 2, 5, 10, 25, 50, and 100 colónes. C1 = $0.1147 (or $1 = C8.720).

WEIGHTS AND MEASURES: The metric system is the legal standard, but some old Spanish measures also are used.

HOLIDAYS: New Year's Day, 1 January; Labor Day, 1 May; Independence Day, 15 September; Columbus Day, 12 October; All Souls' Day, 2 November; First Call for Independence, 5 November; Christmas, 25 December. Movable religious holidays include Good Friday, Holy Saturday, Easter Monday, and Corpus Christi; there is a movable secular holiday, the Festival (1st week in August).

TIME: 6 AM = noon GMT.

1 LOCATION AND SIZE

El Salvador, the smallest Central American country, has an area of 21,040 square kilometers (8,124 square miles), slightly smaller than the state of Massachusetts. It has a total boundary length of 852 kilometers (529 miles) and is the only Central American country without a Caribbean coastline. El Salvador's capital city, San Salvador, is located in the west central part of the country.

2 TOPOGRAPHY

El Salvador is a land of mountains and once-fertile upland plains. It is divided into three general topographic regions: the hot, narrow Pacific coastal belt; the central plateau, which is almost surrounded by active volcanoes; and the northern lowlands, formed by the wide Lempa River Valley. El Salvador has several lakes, the largest being Ilopango (Lago de Ilopango), Güija (Lago de Güija), and Coatepeque (Lago de Coatepeque). The Lempa is the most important of some 150 rivers.

3 CLIMATE

Located in the tropical zone, El Salvador has two distinct seasons: the dry season, from November to April, and the wet season, from May to November. The average annual rainfall is 182 centimeters (72 inches). In general, the climate is warm, with an annual average maximum of 32°C

(90°F), and an average minimum of 18°C (64°F).

4 PLANTS AND ANIMALS

Native trees include the mangrove, rubber, dogwood, mahogany, cedar, walnut, pine, and oak. Native wildlife (greatly reduced in recent decades) includes varieties of monkey, jaguar, coyote, tapir, and armadillo, along with several kinds of parrots and various migratory birds.

5 ENVIRONMENT

Peasant farmers burn the small trees and other growth on the hillsides to plant corn and beans, thus hastening the erosion of the topsoil. Pollution is widespread, waste disposal is lax, and water quality is deteriorating. By 1993, 90% of El Salvador's rivers were polluted, and 85% of the people living in rural areas had impure water.

As of 1994, 6 mammal species, 2 types of birds and 1 type of reptile were endangered, as well as 2,500 plant species.

6 POPULATION

As of the 1992 census, the population was 5,047,925. A population of 6,425,000 is projected by the United Nations for the year 2000. El Salvador, with an estimated density in 1992 of 257 persons per square kilometer (665 persons per square mile), is the most densely populated country in Central America. San Salvador had a population in 1992 of 1,522,126.

7 MIGRATION

The civil war in El Salvador has resulted in the emigration of hundreds of thousands of Salvadorans. In mid-1992 there were 4,200 refugees in Mexico, 2,400 in Guatemala, 5,600 in Nicaragua, 5,600 in Costa Rica, 8,800 in Belize, and 400 in Panama. The number of foreign-born Salvadorans in the United States swelled from 94,000 in 1980 to 473,000 in 1990.

8 ETHNIC GROUPS

The population of El Salvador is about 89% mestizo (mixed white and Amerindian), 10% Amerindian (mainly the Pipil tribes), and 1% white.

9 LANGUAGES

The official language of the country is Spanish. A few Amerindians continue to speak Nahuatl.

10 RELIGIONS

About 94% of the population is Roman Catholic and about 3% Protestant. In addition, there are about 7,800 followers of Amerindian tribal religions.

11 TRANSPORTATION

As of 1991 there were 10,000 kilometers (6,200 miles) of roads. In 1991, registered motor vehicles numbered about 160,000, half of which were passenger cars. El Salvador had 602 kilometers (374 miles) of public-service railroad tracks in 1991. The country's three ports—La Unión/Cutuco, La Libertad, and Acajutla—are located on the Pacific coast.

The principal international airport is near San Salvador, and serviced 539,000 international passengers in 1991.

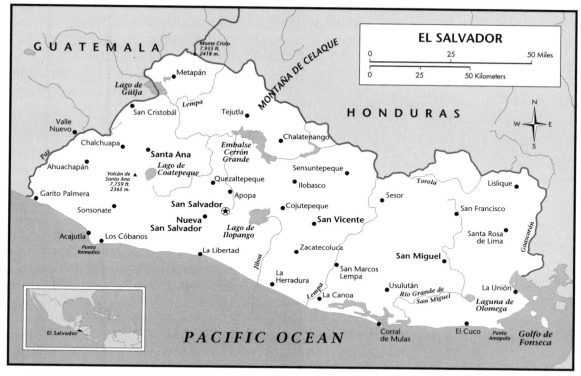

LOCATION: 13°9′ to 14°26′N; 87°41′ to 90°08′W. **BOUNDARY LENGTHS:** Honduras, 342 kilometers (212 miles); Pacific coastline, 307 kilometers (191 miles); Guatemala, 203 kilometers (126 miles). **TERRITORIAL SEA LIMIT:** 200 miles.

12 HISTORY

The Pipil Amerindians were living in the region now known as El Salvador at the time of the Spanish conquest. They were an agricultural people, with a civilization similar to that of the Aztecs.

In 1525, Pedro de Alvarado, a Spanish conquistador (conqueror), defeated the Pipil and founded the cities of Sonsonate and San Salvador. During the Spanish colonial period, San Salvador was one of six administrative regions ruled together with present-day Guatemala.

In 1821, Guatemala led a movement for the independence of all of Central America. El Salvador joined the United Provinces of Central America, which dissolved in 1838-39. The republic of El Salvador was formally proclaimed on 25 January 1859.

During the second half of the nineteenth century, Salvadoran politics were stormy, with frequent presidential changes. The Salvadoran upper class, known as the "14 families," created large coffee plantations, often on the land of displaced Indians.

The period from 1900 to 1930 was fairly stable. However, when General Maximiliano Hernández Martínez seized power in 1931, a 50-year period of military rule began. Hernández ruled for 13 years, brutally suppressing a peasant uprising in 1932, in which 30,000 people were killed. None of the military governments that followed Hernández was able to reduce the economic gap between the landowners and the landless classes.

Landless Salvadorans found land available in neighboring Honduras and migrated there. When the flow of Salvadorans increased during the 1960s, the Honduran government took steps to limit it. Tensions rose between the two nations, and on 14 July 1969, they went to war for four days. A total of 3,000–4,000 people were killed on both sides.

In 1972, José Napoleón Duarte of the Christian Democratic Party (PDC) ran for president against the military candidate. Duarte was denied election by fraud and sent into exile. Armed resistance arose from leftist guerrilla groups, and the right unleashed "death squads" to counter it. By the late 1970s, the situation had escalated into a civil war. In 1979, a coup brought to power a five-member military-civilian junta (a group that controls the government). Attacked by both the left and the right, the junta was unable either to suppress left-wing guerrillas, or to control its own security forces.

In December 1980, Duarte was appointed president by the junta. Following his taking office, a state of siege was proclaimed in an attempt to control widespread violence and human rights violations. It is estimated that at least 62,000 people died between October 1979 and April 1987, most of them civilians murdered by death squads and government security forces.

In 1984, Duarte defeated Roberto D'Aubuisson Arrieta of the National Republican Alliance in a runoff election in May, becoming the first constitutionally elected president in over 50 years. Duarte's regime was a difficult balancing act between right and left, but his overriding problem was the ongoing civil war.

Eventually, El Salvador's economic troubles and charges of government corruption led to the election in 1989 of Alfredo Félix Christiani Burkard of the National Republican Alliance (ARENA). On 31 December 1991 the government and the guerrillas, known as the Farabundo Martí National Liberation Front (Frente Farabundo Martí de Liberación Nacional—FMLN), signed an agreement, the Chapultepec Accord, which ended the civil war.

The accord calls for reforms throughout the military, including the purge of officers linked to human rights abuses, and 50% reduction of the force. In addition, land reforms are to be initiated.

New elections were held in 1994, and voters returned ARENA to power, with Armando Calerón Sol winning the presidential run-off election.

13 GOVERNMENT

The constitution, adopted on 20 November 1983, defines El Salvador as a republic.

It vests executive power in the president, who is to be elected by direct popular vote for a term of five years. Legislative power is exercised by a single-chamber National Assembly composed of 84 deputies.

El Salvador is divided into 14 departments and 262 municipalities.

14 POLITICAL PARTIES

The leading party of the right in El Salvador is the National Republican Alliance (Alianza Republicana Nacionalista—ARENA). The National Conciliation Party (Partido de Conciliación Nacional-PCN), the party of the former military government, is allied with ARENA. Together, the two parties control a majority of seats in the legislature.

The moderate Christian Democratic Party (Partido Demócrata Cristiano—PDC) was founded by former president José Napoleón Duarte. The PDC now makes up the largest opposition party, holding 26 of 84 seats in the National Assembly.

Leftist groups include the Democratic Convergence (CD), a coalition of three leftist parties, and the Farabundo Martí National Liberation Front (Frente Farabundo Martí de Liberación Nacional—FMLN). As part of the peace agreement ending the civil war, FMLN is now a legal party after having ceased its military operations.

15 JUDICIAL SYSTEM

The court system includes justices of the peace, lower-level courts, intermediate level appeals courts, and the Supreme

Photo credit: AP/Wide World Photos

Droves of Salvadorans walk from outlying regions of guerrilla controlled Chalatenango province to vote in municipal elections in 1991. This was the first time many FMLN supporters chose to vote.

Court, made up of 13 justices selected by the National Assembly.

16 ARMED FORCES

All Salvadoran males between 18 and 30 years of age are eligible for military service. In 1993, 43,700 personnel were in service, 40,000 of whom were in the army, 1,300 in the navy and marine corps, and 2,400 in the air force. National police and village militia forces numbered an additional 30,000. In 1991, $220 million was budgeted for national defense. US military

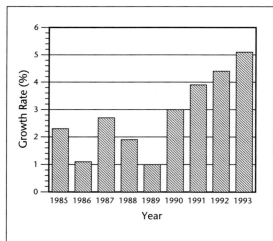

Yearly growth rate of the economy. This economic indicator tells by what percent the economy has increased or decreased when compared with the previous year.

assistance during the civil war (1979–92) reached over $1 billion.

17 ECONOMY

Agriculture is the foundation of El Salvador's economy, providing about two-thirds of the nation's exports and employing one-third of its labor force. In the 1970s, El Salvador was the most industrialized nation in Central America, although a dozen years of civil war have eroded this position.

Recent administrations have carried out a comprehensive economic reform plan oriented toward a free-market economy.

18 INCOME

For the period 1988 to 1993, El Salvador's gross national product (GNP) per person was $1,320. For the period 1985–92 the average inflation rate was 17.7%, resulting in real growth in GNP of 0.9% per person.

19 INDUSTRY

Although industry plays a secondary role in the country's economy, it is the most developed in Central America. In 1992, manufacturing grew by 6%, fueled mainly by clothing production. Other important industries are food and beverages, tobacco, footwear, cement, fertilizers, and petroleum refining.

20 LABOR

The civilian labor force numbered 2.6 million in 1991, of which 604,000 were engaged in agriculture, 680,000 in services, and 227,000 in industry. Unemployment in 1991 was estimated at 10%.

21 AGRICULTURE

Coffee is El Salvador's major crop, accounting for 30% of total agricultural output. Production in 1992 amounted to 147,000 tons. Exports of coffee in 1992 amounted to $150 million.

Cotton production has declined sharply due to the civil war. Production fell from 57,000 tons annually during 1979–81 to four tons in 1992. Sugar production rose to a record 324,257 tons in 1991–93. There were record harvests in 1992 of sugar, beans, and corn. Production amounts in 1992 included 706,000 tons of corn, 214,000 tons of sorghum, 72,000 tons of rice, and 62,000 tons of dry beans.

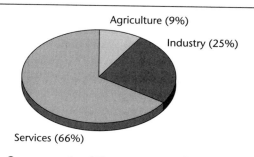

Agriculture (9%)

Industry (25%)

Services (66%)

Components of the economy. This pie chart shows how much of the country's economy is devoted to agriculture (includes forestry, hunting, and fishing), industry, or services.

22 DOMESTICATED ANIMALS

Cattle and hogs are the main livestock in El Salvador. In 1992 there were 1,276,000 head of cattle. The hog population was 310,000 in 1992. Other livestock included 95,000 horses, 23,000 mules, 15,000 goats, and 4,000,000 chickens. In 1992, milk production was 350,000 tons. A total of 47,305 tons of eggs were produced during the same year.

23 FISHING

The fishing industry centers on shrimp. The best coastal fishing grounds are off the southeastern sector. Scaled fish include freshwater robalo, sea bass, mullet, mackerel, swordfish, and redmouth. The total fish catch was 11,341 tons in 1991.

24 FORESTRY

Virgin forests once covered 90% of El Salvador, but in the early 1990s forests and woodlands covered only 5% of the country. Forest products include dyewood (a wood that provides color for dyeing) and lumber, such as mahogany, walnut, and cedar, for furniture and cabinet work.

25 MINING

El Salvador has fewer mineral resources than any other Central American country. In 1991, industrial minerals, especially limestone mined for domestic cement plants, were the primary commodities of the Salvadoran mineral industry.

26 FOREIGN TRADE

In 1992, exports totaled $597.5 million. The country's primary exports were coffee, cotton, sugar, and shellfish (shrimp). Imports increased more substantially, registering a total of $1.6 billion in 1992. Major import items included consumer goods, raw materials, petroleum, food stuffs, capital goods, machinery, construction materials, and fertilizers. El Salvador's major trading partners are the United States, Guatemala, Mexico, Japan, and Germany.

27 ENERGY AND POWER

El Salvador has no exploitable fossil fuels. Electricity production increased to 2.3 million kilowatt hours in 1991. Of that total, hydroelectric sources supplied nearly 60%; petroleum plants contributed 27%; and the remainder was supplied by geothermal resources.

28 SOCIAL DEVELOPMENT

The Salvadoran Social Security Institute provides national insurance for health, accidents, unemployment, invalidism, old age, and death. The Ministry of Public Health and Social Welfare supervises institutions and hospitals for the infirm and aged, as well as child welfare and maternal care services. Women are paid lower wages than men and lack equal access to credit and property ownership.

29 HEALTH

Much of the progress since the 1930s was undermined by the civil war, which over-taxed health care facilities, while shrinking their funding. The National Medical School was shut down in 1980. Between 1985 and 1992, only 56% of the population had access to health care services. Total health care expenditures in 1990 were $317 million.

The principal causes of death remain gastroenteritis (inflammation of lining of stomach or intestines), influenza, malaria, measles, pneumonia, and bronchitis, caused or complicated by malnutrition, bad sanitation, and poor housing. The average life expectancy was 67 years for women and men.

30 HOUSING

Inadequate housing, most critically felt in cities and towns, is widespread throughout El Salvador. In the early 1990s, an estimated 47% of all households did not have easy access to drinking water, and 59% lacked plumbing. Housing problems have been aggravated by the civil war, which has created hundreds of thousands of refugees.

31 EDUCATION

By 1990, illiteracy had been reduced to about 27% (males: 23.8% and females: 30.0%). Primary education is free and

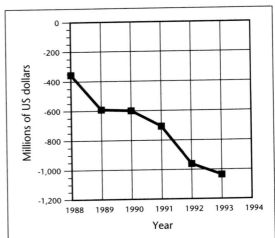

Yearly balance of trade measured in millions of US dollars. The balance of trade is the difference between what a country sells to other countries (its exports) and what it buys (its imports). If a country imports more than it exports, it has a negative balance of trade (a trade deficit). If exports exceed imports there is a positive balance of trade (a trade surplus).

compulsory. Primary education lasts for nine years followed by three years of secondary education.

In 1991 there were 3,516 primary schools. Enrollment in primary schools in 1991 was 1,000,671; in secondary, 94,278. Twelve private and three public universities offer higher education. In 1990, 78,211 students were enrolled at the universities and other higher level institutions.

32 MEDIA

There is an automatic telephone system in San Salvador. In 1993, there was current capacity for 152,546 telephone lines. In 1991 there were 77 AM radio stations,

Selected Social Indicators

These statistics are estimates for the period 1988 to 1993. For comparison purposes, data for the United States and averages for low-income countries and high-income countries are also given.

Indicator	El Salvador	Low-income countries	High-income countries	United States
Per capita gross national product†	$1,320	$380	$23,680	$24,740
Population growth rate	2.1%	1.9%	0.6%	1.0%
Population growth rate in urban areas	2.6%	3.9%	0.8%	1.3%
Population per square kilometer of land	257	78	25	26
Life expectancy in years	67	62	77	76
Number of people per physician	2,822	>3,300	453	419
Number of pupils per teacher (primary school)	44	39	<18	20
Illiteracy rate (15 years and older)	27%	41%	<5%	<3%
Energy consumed per capita (kg of oil equivalent)	222	364	5,203	7,918

† The gross national product (GNP) is the total dollar value of all goods and services produced by a country in a year. The per capita GNP is calculated by dividing a country's GNP by its population. The World Bank defines low-income countries as those with a per capita GNP of $695 or less. High-income countries have a per capita GNP of $8,626 or more. Less than 14% of the world's 5.5 billion people live in high-income countries, while almost 60% live in low-income countries.

> = greater than   < = less than

Sources: World Bank, *Social Indicators of Development 1995,* Baltimore: Johns Hopkins University Press, 1995. Central Intelligence Agency, *World Fact Book,* Washington, D.C.: Government Printing Office, 1994.

including the government-owned Radio Nacional, no FM stations, and 5 commercial television stations. In 1991 there were about 2,175,000 radios in use, and television sets were estimated at 485,000.

The principal newspapers are published in the capital city, but the *Diario de Occidente,* published in Santa Ana, is the oldest daily in the country. The largest San Salvador dailies (with 1991 circulations) are *La Prensa Gráfica,* 95,000; *El Diario de Hoy,* 78,000; *El Mundo,* 40,000; *Diario Latino,* 10,000; and *La Noticia,* 30,000.

33 TOURISM AND RECREATION

Since 1989, tourism has rebounded, rising from 130,602 visitors in 1989 to 198,918 in 1991, of whom 115,230 came from Central America and 62,114 from North America. By that year, El Salvador had 3,185 hotel rooms with a 25.5% occupancy rate, and receipts from tourism totaled $157 million.

One of El Salvador's best-known natural wonders is the volcano Volcán de Santa Ana. Noteworthy are the cathedrals and churches of San Salvador, Santa Ana, and Sonsonate; the parks, gardens, and

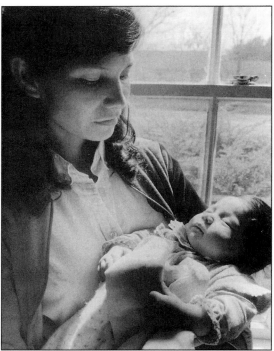

Photo credit: AP/Wide World Photos

A Salvadoran woman and her infant child.

architecture of San Miguel; and the colonial atmosphere of San Vicente. Archaeological ruins of pre-Columbian origin are found in many parts of the country. Among the most striking are those at Tazumal, near Santa Ana, which include large pyramids and buildings with ancient carvings and inscriptions. There are more than 100 pyramid sites in El Salvador; many are still unexcavated. The Pacific coast contains excellent beaches, and there is large-game fishing in the Gulf of Fonseca (Golfo de Fonseca) and in the ocean. Football (soccer) is the national sport.

34 FAMOUS SALVADORANS

The national hero of El Salvador is Father José Matías Delgado (1768–1833), who raised the first call for independence. A renowned political leader was Manuel José Arce (1786–1847), the first president of the United Provinces of Central America. Juan José Cañas (1826–1912) was a poet and diplomat and the author of the Salvadoran national anthem.

Writers of note in the 20th century include Alberto Masferrer (1865–1932), an essayist and poet; and Juan Ramón Uriarte (1875–1927), an essayist and educator. Juan Francisco Cisneros (1823–78) is a nationally recognized painter.

Key figures in Salvadoran politics of the 1970s and 1980s are José Napoleón Duarte (b.1926) and Roberto D'Aubuisson Arrieta (b.1944?). The assassinated Roman Catholic Archbishop Oscar Arnulfo Romero y Galdames (1917–80) was well known as a defender of human rights.

35 BIBLIOGRAPHY

Bachelis, F. *El Salvador*. Chicago: Children's Press, 1990.

Brockman, James R. *The Word Remains: A Life of Oscar Romero*. Maryknoll, N.Y.: Orbis Books, 1982.

Haggerty, Richard A., ed. *El Salvador, a Country Study*. 2d ed. Washington, D.C.: Library of Congress, 1990.

Haverstock, Nathan A. *El Salvador in Pictures*. Minneapolis: Lerner, 1987.

Woodward, Ralph Lee. *El Salvador*. Santa Barbara, Calif.: Clio, 1988.

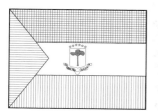

EQUATORIAL GUINEA

Republic of Equatorial Guinea
República de Guinea Ecuatorial

CAPITAL: Malabo (formerly Santa Isabel).

FLAG: The flag is a tricolor of green, white, and red horizontal stripes; a blue triangle joins them at the hoist. The arms in the center of the white stripe hold a cotton tree (the national symbol), six stars—one for each physical division of the country—and the motto "Unidad, Justicia, Paz."

ANTHEM: *Himno Nacional*, beginning "Caminemos pisando la senda de nuestra inmensa felicidad" ("Let us walk on the path of our immense happiness").

MONETARY UNIT: Communauté Financière Africaine franc (CFA Fr), introduced in 1985, is a paper currency tied to the French franc at the rate of CFA Fr 100 = Fr 1. CFA Fr 1 = $0.0018 (or $1 = CFA Fr571). There are coins of 1, 2, 5, 10, 25, 50, 100, and 500 CFA francs and notes of 50, 100, 500, 1,000, 5,000, and 10,000 francs.

WEIGHTS AND MEASURES: The metric system is the legal standard.

HOLIDAYS: New Year's Day, 1 January; Independence Day, 5 March; Labor Day, 1 May; OAU Day, 25 May; President's Birthday, 5 June; Armed Forces Day, 3 August; Human Rights Day, 10 December; Christmas, 25 December. Movable Christian holidays include Good Friday and Easter Monday.

TIME: 1 PM = noon GMT.

1 LOCATION AND SIZE

Located on the west coast of Africa, Equatorial Guinea consists of a mainland enclave, Río Muni, and five inhabited islands: Bioko, Annobón, Corisco, Elobey Chico, and Elobey Grande. Comparatively, the area occupied by Equatorial Guinea is slightly larger than the state of Maryland. The total boundary length of Equatorial Guinea is 835 kilometers (519 miles). The capital city of Equatorial Guinea, Malabo, is located on the island of Bioko.

2 TOPOGRAPHY

Bioko and Annobón are volcanic islands, and Río Muni is a plateau. Most of the country, including the islands, is tropical rain forest.

3 CLIMATE

Equatorial Guinea has a tropical climate with distinct wet and dry seasons. From June to August, Río Muni is dry and Bioko wet; from December to February, the reverse is true. The temperature at Malabo, Bioko, ranges from 16°C to 33°C (61–91°F).

4 PLANTS AND ANIMALS

Dense tropical rainforest vegetation prevails throughout Equatorial Guinea. There are 140 species of trees, especially palms and hardwoods. Yams and bananas were introduced by the early inhabitants and became staples. Monkeys, chimpanzees, elephants, and gray doves are common.

5 ENVIRONMENT

In 1994, Equatorial Guinea's most significant environmental problems were deforestation, water pollution, and the preservation of wildlife. As of 1994, the nation's wildlife was threatened by the expansion of the population centers and resulting damage to the living environment of plants and animals.

6 POPULATION

The population was estimated at 409,425 in 1994, and 452,000 was projected for the year 2000. The principal town is Malabo, on Bioko, with about 31,000 people.

7 MIGRATION

About 100,000 people fled into exile during the regime of Francisco Macías Nguema. About 130,000 were abroad in 1993, including an estimated 80,000 in Gbon and 30,000 in Cameroon.

8 ETHNIC GROUPS

The largest single tribe is the Fang. The Bubi on Bioko are descendants of indigenous Bantu-speaking tribes. Fernandinos—descendants of mainland slaves liberated by the British navy in the 19th century—and Europeans have long dominated commerce and government.

9 LANGUAGES

Spanish is the official language of the government, commerce, and schools. The principal vernacular is Fang, which is a Bantu tongue. Much petty commerce is conducted in pidgin English (Pichinglis).

10 RELIGIONS

Although African traditional religion has left its vestiges among the indigenous tribes, by the mid-1980s about 96% of the population had been converted to Roman Catholicism. As of 1993, Roman Catholics comprised some 98% of the population.

11 TRANSPORTATION

There are 300 kilometers (185 miles) of highways in Bioko and 2,460 kilometers (1,530 miles) in Río Muni. The chief ports are Bata and Mbini in Río Muni and Malabo and Luba on Bioko. Bata's airport was the first major air transport facility.

12 HISTORY

Bioko was apparently uninhabited when the Bubi came by sea from the mainland in the thirteenth century. For the next four centuries, Río Muni seems to have been occupied by the Bantu in a series of waves that superseded the Pygmies. In 1778, Portugal transferred its nominal claims over present-day Equatorial Guinea to Spain in return for Spanish concessions in southern Brazil. The primary Spanish mainland explorations were undertaken between 1875 and 1885. Equatorial Guinea became a province of Spain in 1958.

On 12 October 1968, the colony became the independent Republic of

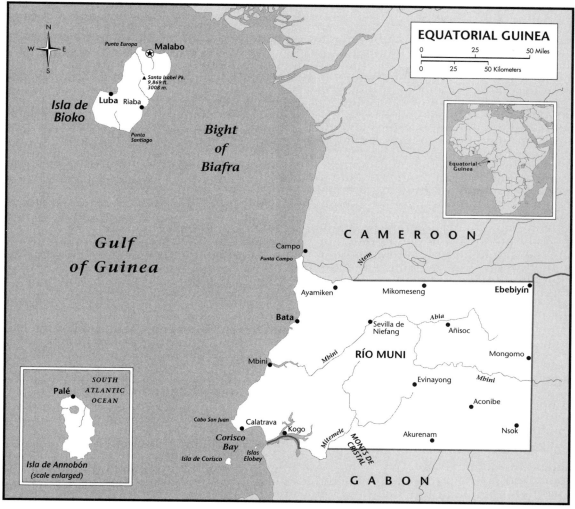

LOCATION: 1°1' to 3°48'N; 8°26' to 11°20'E Annobón at 1°25's and 5°36'E. **BOUNDARY LENGTHS:** Cameroon, 189 kilometers (118 miles); Gabon, 350 kilometers (218 miles); total coastline, 296 kilometers (183 miles). **TERRITORIAL SEA LIMIT:** 12 miles.

Equatorial Guinea. On 23 August 1972, Francisco Macías Nguema was proclaimed president for life. Seven years later, he was overthrown in a military coup. Under the rule of Macías Nguema's nephew, Lieutenant-Colonel Teodoro Obiang Nguema Mbasogo, corruption continued to flourish, with political opponents and others imprisoned or put to death. He was elected head of state without opposition on 25 June 1989. Since 17 November 1991, Equatorial Guinea has officially had a constitutional democracy with multiparty elections. In reality,

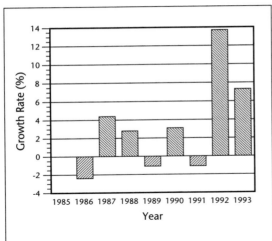

Yearly growth rate of the economy. This economic indicator tells by what percent the economy has increased or decreased when compared with the previous year.

Obiang's Democratic Party of Equatorial Guinea (PDGE) controls the country.

13 GOVERNMENT

On 17 November 1991, a new constitution was adopted, and opposition parties sought official recognition in 1992. In the 21 November 1993 election, the PDGE (the ruling party) won 68 of 80 seats, but the major opposition parties boycotted the election.

14 POLITICAL PARTIES

As of 1992 party membership was restricted to those who had lived continuously in Equatorial Guinea for a number of years. Since most opposition politicians had been in exile since independence, the effect was to prohibit serious opposition.

15 JUDICIAL SYSTEM

The court system includes a Supreme Court, military courts, and customary (traditional) courts. Under the 1991 constitution, the judiciary is not independent of the executive branch.

16 ARMED FORCES

As of 1993, military personnel numbered 1,300—army, 1,100; navy, 120; and air force, 100.

17 ECONOMY

The agricultural sector supports 50% of the population. The country exports cocoa, coffee, and timber, and imports large quantities of foodstuffs. Production of oil began in 1991, and the exploration for additional reserves continues. The arrival of significant oil revenues has caused the economy to be viewed with guarded optimism.

18 INCOME

In 1992 Equatorial Guinea's gross national product (GNP) was $146 million at current prices, or $420 per person.

19 INDUSTRY

Equatorial Guinea's manufacturing sector is small. Two sawmills lead industrial production, followed by cement, bleach, and tuna canning plants.

20 LABOR

Most of the labor force of about 177,000 is employed in subsistence agriculture.

21 AGRICULTURE

Agriculture is the main economic activity, involving about 50% of the population. The main food crop is cassava, of which 47,000 tons were produced in 1992. Sweet potatoes are the second-largest food crop, followed by bananas, cocoa, and coffee.

22 DOMESTICATED ANIMALS

In 1992 there were 36,000 sheep, 8,000 goats, 5,000 hogs, and 5,000 cattle.

23 FISHING

The fishing industry is now almost entirely modernized. Shellfish account for roughly half the catch.

24 FORESTRY

Timber from Río Muni is Equatorial Guinea's leading export. In 1991, round-wood production was estimated at 607,000 cubic meters.

25 MINING

Geological surveys indicate some uranium, iron, gold, and other minerals in Río Muni, but there has been no significant exploitation.

26 FOREIGN TRADE

Spain is Equatorial Guinea's principal trading partner. Exports to Spain represent 86.7% of the total exports. Cocoa and timber represent 93% of total exported products. Major imports were foodstuffs and oil products, with most imports coming from France and Spain.

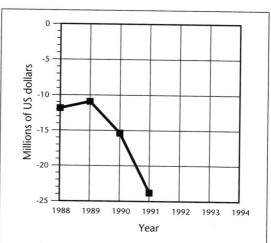

Yearly balance of trade measured in millions of US dollars. The balance of trade is the difference between what a country sells to other countries (its exports) and what it buys (its imports). If a country imports more than it exports, it has a negative balance of trade (a trade deficit). If exports exceed imports there is a positive balance of trade (a trade surplus).

27 ENERGY AND POWER

Power production totaled 18 million kilowatt hours in 1991.

28 SOCIAL DEVELOPMENT

There is little provision for social welfare. The great majority of the population goes without safe drinking water, electricity, basic education, or minimal health care.

29 HEALTH

In 1990, Equatorial Guinea had 99 physicians, and life expectancy was 48 years. Major health problems are preventable diseases (mainly malaria), parasitic disease, upper respiratory infections, gastroenteritis, and complications of pregnancy.

Selected Social Indicators

These statistics are estimates for the period 1988 to 1993. For comparison purposes, data for the United States and averages for low-income countries and high-income countries are also given.

Indicator	Equatorial Guinea	Low-income countries	High-income countries	United States
Per capita gross national product†	$420	$380	$23,680	$24,740
Population growth rate	2.3%	1.9%	0.6%	1.0%
Population growth rate in urban areas	5.6%	3.9%	0.8%	1.3%
Population per square kilometer of land	13	78	25	26
Life expectancy in years	48	62	77	76
Number of people per physician	4,136	>3,300	453	419
Number of pupils per teacher (primary school)	n.a.	39	<18	20
Illiteracy rate (15 years and older)	50%	41%	<5%	<3%
Energy consumed per capita (kg of oil equivalent)	82	364	5,203	7,918

† The gross national product (GNP) is the total dollar value of all goods and services produced by a country in a year. The per capita GNP is calculated by dividing a country's GNP by its population. The World Bank defines low-income countries as those with a per capita GNP of $695 or less. High-income countries have a per capita GNP of $8,626 or more. Less than 14% of the world's 5.5 billion people live in high-income countries, while almost 60% live in low-income countries.   n.a. = data not available.   > = greater than   < = less than
Sources: World Bank, *Social Indicators of Development 1995,* Baltimore: Johns Hopkins University Press, 1995. Central Intelligence Agency, *World Fact Book,* Washington, D.C.: Government Printing Office, 1994.

30 HOUSING

No recent information is available.

31 EDUCATION

Education is free and compulsory from 6 to 14 years of age, and there are four years of secondary education. In 1986, 65,000 pupils attended primary and secondary schools.

32 MEDIA

There were about 2,000 telephones in use in the late 1980s. Equaterial Guinea has three government-owned radio stations and one television station, and two news-papers.

33 TOURISM AND RECREATION

Because Equatorial Guinea has undergone many years of international isolation, its tourism industry is very undeveloped.

34 FAMOUS EQUATORIAL GUINEANS

Francisco Macías Nguema (1924–79) was president until his overthrow and execution. His successor, Lieutenant-Colonel Teodoro Obiang Nguema Mbasogo (b.1946), has ruled since 1979.

35 BIBLIOGRAPHY

Fegley, Randall. *Equatorial Guinea.* Santa Barbara, Calif.: Clio, 1991.

ERITREA

State of Eritrea

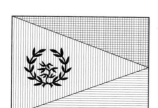

CAPITAL: Asmara (Asmera)

FLAG: A red triangle divides the flag into two right triangles; the upper triangle is green, the lower one is blue. A gold wreath encircling a gold olive branch is centered on the hoist side of the red triangle.

ANTHEM: *Eritrea National Anthem* beginning "Eritrea, Eritrea, Eritrea."

MONETARY UNIT: The birr is the official currency of Eritrea. One birr = US$0.20 as of fall 1994, but the exchange rate is expected to fluctuate.

WEIGHTS AND MEASURES: The metric system is used.

HOLIDAYS: New Year's Day, 1 January; Independence Day, 24 May; Martyrs' Day, 20 June; Anniversary of the Start of the Armed Struggle, 1 September. Movable holidays include 'Id al-Fitr, 'Id al-Adha, and 'Id Milad al-Nabi. Movable Orthodox Christian holidays include Fasika and Meskel.

TIME: 3 PM = noon GMT.

1 LOCATION AND SIZE

Eritrea is located in eastern Africa. Its area is slightly larger than the state of Pennsylvania with a total area of 121,320 square kilometers (46,842 square miles). Total boundary length is 2,781 kilometers (1,728 miles).

2 TOPOGRAPHY

The topography of Eritrea is dominated by the extension of Ethiopia's highlands, descending on the east to a coastal desert plain, on the northeast to hills, and on the southwest to flat-to-rolling plains.

3 CLIMATE

Highs of 60°C (140°F) are not uncommon in Eritrea's southernmost province, reportedly the hottest spot in the world. It is cooler and wetter in the central highlands.

The western hills and lowlands are semiarid. Heavy rainfall occurs during June, July, and August, except in the coastal desert.

4 PLANTS AND ANIMALS

There are populations of lion, leopard, zebra, species of monkey, gazelle, antelope, and elephant. The coastal areas are home to many species of turtle, lobster, and shrimp. Plant life includes acacia, cactus, aloe vera, prickly pear, and olive trees.

5 ENVIRONMENT

No information is available.

6 POPULATION

Non-governmental estimates of the total population in 1992 were 2,650,000 or 2,700,000, excluding refugees abroad; the government of Eritrea reported 3.5 million.

7 MIGRATION

There were believed to be about 750,000 Eritrean refugees, or 20–30% of the total population, abroad in early 1994. Of these, 430,000 were in the Sudan and the rest principally in Ethiopia, Somalia, and Djibouti.

8 ETHNIC GROUPS

Ethnologists classify Eritreans into nine language groups, of which the most populous are believed to be the Tigrinya, Tigre, and Afar.

9 LANGUAGES

No official language has been proclaimed. Arabic and Tigrinya are the working languages of the Eritrean government.

10 RELIGIONS

The population of Eritrea is equally divided between Christians and Muslims, and both Christian and Muslim holidays are observed. The Christian population is mostly Orthodox Christian.

11 TRANSPORTATION

In early 1992, agreements were concluded between the Eritrean and Ethiopian governments to make Assab a free port for Ethiopia. In the summer of 1994, reconstruction began on the railway that extends from Massawa on the Red Sea to Asmara, which had been almost completely destroyed during the war.

12 HISTORY

In April, 1941, British Commonwealth forces captured Eritrea from its Italian colonizers. After a decade of British rule, Eritrea was federated with neighboring Ethiopia in 1952, following a vote in the United Nations. In September 1961, the Eritrean Liberation Front (ELF) launched the armed struggle for Eritrean independence. However, Ethiopia formally annexed Eritrea in 1962. After Emperor Haile Selassie was overthrown in 1974, Ethiopia's Marxist military dictatorship stepped up its campaign against the Eritreans. Between 1978 and 1981, the Eritrean People's Liberation Front (EPLF) fought and defeated the Eritrean Liberation Front (ELF) in a civil war. From 1981 until the end of the war in 1991, the EPLF continued to fight for Eritrean self-determination.

In May 1991, the EPLF captured the last Ethiopian outposts in Eritrea and formed a National Assembly, which elected Isaias Afwerki president of the provisional government. In July the EPLF and the transitional Ethiopian government which had toppled the Mengistu regime issued a charter calling for Eritrean self-determination and mutual accommodation between the two nations. On 23–25 April 1993, 98.5% of the 1,173,000 registered voters participated in a referendum on independence from Ethiopia. The UN certified the results, and on 24 May 1993, Eritrea became Africa's 52nd independent state. Four days later it was admitted to the United Nations and the Organization of African Unity (OAU).

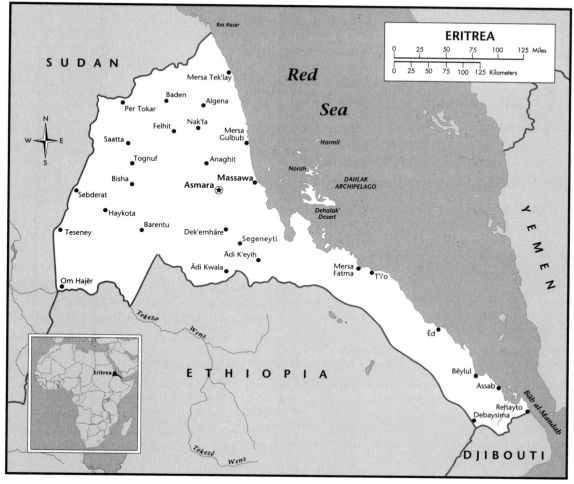

LOCATION: 15°N; 39°E. **BOUNDARY LENGTHS:** Djibouti, 113 kilometers (70 miles); Ethiopia, 912 kilometers (566 miles); Sudan, 605 kilometers (375 miles); coastline, 1,151 kilometers (717 miles). **TERRITORIAL SEA LIMIT:** 12 miles.

13 GOVERNMENT

Upon official independence, a National Assembly was formed, consisting of the Central Committee of the EPLF and 60 other individuals, with ten seats reserved for women. The Constitutional Commission, appointed by the National Assembly in March 1994, has a two-year mandate (until March 1996) to develop a draft constitution. At the time of independence, the National Assembly set a deadline of May 1998 for election of a new government.

14 POLITICAL PARTIES

The Eritrean Liberation Front (ELF) launched the modern phase of Eritrea's war of self-determination in September

1961. In 1970, the Eritrean People's Liberation Front (EPLF) joined the war against Ethiopia. From 1981 to 1991, only the EPLF was operating in Eritrea. At its February 1994 Congress, the EPLF was reformed as the People's Front for Democracy and Justice (PFDJ). The PFDJ elected an Executive Council of 75 members, and called on the government to increase the number of non-PFDJ members in the National Assembly to 75.

15 JUDICIAL SYSTEM

The court system consists of district courts, courts of appeals composed of five judges, and military courts which handle crimes committed by members of the military. Traditional courts play a major role in rural areas, where village elders determine property and family disputes under customary law or in the case of Muslims, the Koran.

16 ARMED FORCES

The process of demobilizing about 50–60% of the army began in July 1993. Following the second phase of demobilization, which began in spring 1994, a total of 47,000 fighters will have been demobilized.

17 ECONOMY

After years of armed struggle against the Ethiopian government Eritrea is still largely dependent on food aid. Reversing the policies of Ethiopia's military regime, the post-independence government has denationalized housing and is committed to denationalization of business and services.

18 INCOME

In 1992 Eritrea's gross domestic product (GDP) was $120–150 per person. In 1992 the GDP was $544 million.

19 INDUSTRY

Ethiopia systematically dismantled the Eritrean industrial sector during the protracted civil war. The government of Eritrea is currently managing industries previously owned by the Ethiopian regime.

20 LABOR

Agriculture is the most important sector and engages an estimated 80% of the population. Unemployment is expected to increase, as an estimated 500,000 refugees return from Sudan.

21 AGRICULTURE

Although farmers have experienced relative peace and good harvests since May 1991, food production has not been able to keep pace with a rapidly expanding population. Principal crops include sorghum, wheat, barley, teff (a grain), millet, legumes, vegetables, fruits, sesame, and linseed.

22 DOMESTICATED ANIMAL

Cattle (especially zebu), sheep, goats, and camels make up the majority of Eritrea's livestock.

23 FISHING

Because Eritrea now controls 1,151 kilometers (717 miles) of Red Sea coastline,

Selected Social Indicators

Statistics for Eritrea are estimates for 1994 only (Eritrea became an independent nation in mid-1993). For comparison purposes data for the United States and averages for low income countries and high income countries for the period 1988–93 are also given.

Indicator	Eritrea	Low-income countries	High-income countries	United States
Per capita gross national product†	**$135**	$380	$23,680	$24,740
Population growth rate	**n.a.**	1.9%	0.6%	1.0%
Population growth rate in urban areas	**n.a.**	3.9%	0.8%	1.3%
Population per square kilometer of land	**22**	78	25	26
Life expectancy in years	**46**	62	77	76
Number of people per physician	**n.a.**	>3,300	453	419
Number of pupils per teacher (primary school)	**37**	39	<18	20
Illiteracy rate (15 years and older)	**80%**	41%	<5%	<3%
Energy consumed per capita (kg of oil equivalent)	**n.a.**	364	5,203	7,918

† The gross national product (GNP) is the total dollar value of all goods and services produced by a country in a year. The per capita GNP is calculated by dividing a country's GNP by its population. The World Bank defines low-income countries as those with a per capita GNP of $695 or less. High-income countries have a per capita GNP of $8,626 or more. Less than 14% of the world's 5.5 billion people live in high-income countries, while almost 60% live in low-income countries.   n.a. = data not available.   > = greater than   < = less than

Sources: World Bank, *Social Indicators of Development 1995,* Baltimore: Johns Hopkins University Press, 1995. Central Intelligence Agency, *World Fact Book,* Washington, D.C.: Government Printing Office, 1994.

long-term prospects for development of offshore fishing and oil are good.

24 FORESTRY

As of late 1993, the Eritrean People's Liberation Front army was involved in tree planting; deforestation has long been a significant problem.

25 MINING

Mineral resources include copper, zinc, lead, gold, silver, marble, granite, barite, feldspar, kaolin, talc, asbestos, and potassium.

26 FOREIGN TRADE

Main exports are raw materials, especially salt, beverages, tobacco, food, and manufactured goods. Imports are mainly manufactured goods, food, and chemicals.

27 ENERGY AND POWER

Operations have resumed at the petroleum refinery at Assab, which produced 3.3 million barrels of refined petroleum products in 1991.

28 SOCIAL DEVELOPMENT

During its struggle for independence, Eritrea created an elaborate and effective system of social services. It launched a literacy program, a health care system (including hospitals), and a food distribution network. The government has allocated a significant budget for construction of housing, schools, and clinics to aid homeless returning refugees.

29 HEALTH

Average life expectancy in 1992 was 46 years. Government estimates report that there is one doctor for every 28,000 people; other estimates are as high as one doctor for every 48,000 people.

30 HOUSING

Thousands of refugees remain homeless after returning to Eritrea, and the government has placed a high priority on providing funding for housing construction.

31 EDUCATION

The adult literacy rate is estimated to be 20%, with literacy for females standing at 10–15%. In 1994, primary school enrollment was reported to be 42% of school-age children, with 68 pupils per textbook, and 37 pupils per teacher.

32 MEDIA

Television broadcasts are Monday, Wednesday, and Saturday evenings in Tigrinya and Arabic languages. *Dimtsi Hafash* radio broadcasts daily in various local languages. The bi-weekly newspaper, *Hadas Eritrea*, appears on Wednesday and Saturday in both a Tigrinya and an Arabic edition. An eight-page weekly newspaper, *Eritrea Profile*, is published on Saturday.

33 TOURISM AND RECREATION

Because Eritrea has inherited the entire coastline of Ethiopia, there is long-term potential for development of tourism.

34 FAMOUS ERITREANS

Isaias Afwerki has been president of Eritrea since its independence from Ethiopia on 24 May 1993.

35 BIBLIOGRAPHY

Birth of a Nation. Asmara, Eritrea: Government of Eritrea, 1993.

Connell, Dan. *Against All Odds*. Trenton, N.J.: Red Sea Press, 1993.

ESTONIA

Republic of Estonia
Eesti Vabariik

CAPITAL: Tallinn.

FLAG: Three equal horizontal bands of blue (top), black, and white.

ANTHEM: *Mu isamaa, mu õnn ja rõõm (My Native Land, My Pride and Joy).*

MONETARY UNIT: The Estonian kroon (EEK) was introduced in August 1992, replacing the Russian rouble.

WEIGHTS AND MEASURES: The metric system is in force.

HOLIDAYS: New Year's Day, 1 January; Independence Day, 24 February; Good Friday, 14 April; Labor Day, 1 May; Victory Day, anniversary of the Battle of Vonnu in 1919, 23 June; Midsummer Day, 24 June; Christmas, 25–26 December.

TIME: 2 PM = noon GMT.

1 LOCATION AND SIZE

Estonia is located in northeastern Europe, bordering the Baltic Sea, between Sweden and Russia. Comparatively, the area occupied by Estonia is slightly larger than the states of New Hampshire and Vermont combined, with a total area of 45,100 square kilometers (17,413 square miles). Estonia's boundary length totals 1,950 kilometers (1,212 miles). Estonia's capital city, Tallinn, is located in the northern part of the country along the Baltic Sea coast.

2 TOPOGRAPHY

The topography of Estonia consists mainly of marshy lowlands.

3 CLIMATE

At the most western point, Vilsandi Saar, the mean temperature is 6°C (42.8°F). At the country's most eastern points, the mean temperature is between 4.2 and 4.5°C (36 to 40°F). Rainfall averages 50 centimeters (20 inches) on the coast and 70 centimeters (28 inches) inland.

4 PLANTS AND ANIMALS

Western Estonia has rich plants and animals. Native plants number 1,500 species. The abundance of woodland and plant species provide a suitable habitat for elk, deer, wild boar, wolf, lynx, bear, and otter.

5 ENVIRONMENT

Sources of air pollution include 300,000 tons of dust from the burning of oil shale within Estonia plus airborne pollutants from industrial centers in Poland and Germany. Estonia's water resources have been affected by industrial and agricul-

Photo credit: Anne Kalosh

A woman wears a traditional Estonian dress at a sidewalk cafe.

tural pollutants. Some rivers and lakes within the country have been found to contain toxic sediments at over ten times the accepted level for safety. Radiation levels from the nuclear accident at Chernobyl, Ukraine, exceed currently accepted safety levels.

As of 1992, 66 types of plants were threatened with extinction.

6 POPULATION

The population of Estonia was estimated at 1,526,177 at the beginning of 1993. A population of 1,576,000 is projected for 2000. The estimated population density at the beginning of 1993 was 35 persons per square kilometer (90 per square mile). Tallinn, the capital, had an estimated population of 452,840.

7 MIGRATION

A 1990 immigration law sets annual quotas. In 1992 there were 3,615 registered immigrants and 37,293 registered emigrants.

8 ETHNIC GROUPS

In 1989, Estonians made up 61.5% of the population; Russians, 30%; Ukrainians, 3%; Belorussians, 2%; and Finns, 1%.

9 LANGUAGES

Estonian is a member of the Finno–Ugric linguistic family. It is closely related to Finnish and distantly related to Hungarian. Standard Estonian is based on the North Estonian dialect. Most borrowed words are from German. The alphabet is Roman.

10 RELIGIONS

Although Estonians are overwhelmingly Lutheran, Seventh-day Adventist, Baptist, and Methodist churches have begun to establish themselves as well. In 1990, 3,500 Jews were living in Estonia.

11 TRANSPORTATION

Some 1,030 kilometers (640 miles) of railroads provide rail access to Russia, Latvia, and the Baltic Sea. Highways in 1990 totaled 30,300 kilometers (18,800 miles). Motor vehicles dominate domestic freight transportation, carrying nearly 75% of all goods.

The Baltic Sea provides Estonia with its main access to international markets. The principal maritime ports are Tallinn and Pärnu. The merchant fleet includes 65 vessels (of which 51 are cargo ships) for a total capacity of 386,634 gross registered tons in 1991. In 1990, a ferry service opened between Tallinn and Stockholm, Sweden.

In 1992, Estonian Air, the principal international airline, carried some 146,300 passengers.

12 HISTORY

What is now Estonia was ruled in turn by the Danes, the Germans, and the Swedes from the Middle Ages until the eighteenth century. Russia annexed the region in 1721. During the nineteenth century, an Estonian nationalist movement arose which by the early twentieth century sought independence.

After the 1917 Bolshevik Revolution and the advance of German troops into Russia, Estonia declared independence on 24 February 1918. After Germany surrendered to the Western powers, ending World War I in November 1918, Russian troops attempted to move back into Estonia. The Estonians, however, pushed them out by April 1919, and the following year Soviet Russia recognized the Republic of Estonia.

The Nazi–Soviet Pact of 1939 assigned Estonia to the Soviet sphere of influence. However, Hitler's forces invaded the USSR in June 1941 and took control of Estonia shortly thereafter. The German

LOCATION: 57°30′ to 59°40′ N; 21°50′ to 28°10′ E.
BOUNDARY LENGTHS: Latvia 267 kilometers (166 miles); Russia, 290 kilometers (180 miles).

Army retreated in 1944 and Soviet forces once again occupied Estonia.

Taking advantage of the greater freedom allowed by Mikhail Gorbachev, an Estonian nationalist movement, the Popular Front, was launched in 1987. Estonia declared its independence from Moscow on 20 August 1991. A new constitution was adopted on 28 June 1992.

13 GOVERNMENT

The 1992 constitution declares Estonia a parliamentary democracy with a single-chamber parliament (the Riigikogu). The president, prime minister, and the cabinet make up the executive branch.

14 POLITICAL PARTIES

The Independent Communist Party of Estonia split from the Soviet Communist Party in January 1991. The Pro Patria Party, the Estonian Social Democratic Party, and the Christian-Democratic Union of Estonia are among the many parties that have emerged in recent years.

15 JUDICIAL SYSTEM

The 1992 constitution established a three-level court system of rural and city courts, district courts, and state courts.

16 ARMED FORCES

Estonia requires 15 months of military service in a border guard, a rapid reaction force, and territorial defense battalions. There were about 2,000 men on duty in 1994. The Russians have 23,000 soldiers, airmen, and air defense troops still in Estonia.

17 ECONOMY

Estonia had one of the strongest economies among the former Soviet republics. However, after the loss of its traditional trading partners with the breakup of the USSR, Estonia's economy began to struggle. By 1992, the growth rate was –25%. Its mineral resources include 60% of former Soviet oil shale deposits.

18 INCOME

In 1992, the gross national product (GNP) was $4,297 million at current prices, or $3,080 per person.

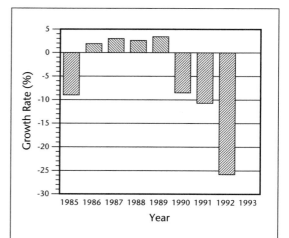

Yearly growth rate of the economy. This economic indicator tells by what percent the economy has increased or decreased when compared with the previous year.

19 INDUSTRY

Industry is the principal sector of Estonia's economy. The textile mills in Narva and Tallinn are the country's largest plants.

20 LABOR

In 1990, the total work force was estimated at 795,500, or 50.5% of the total population. Of the 790,000 employed in 1991, 32.5% were engaged in manufacturing, 25.1% in community, social, and personal services, 12.8% in agriculture, hunting, forestry, and fishing, 9.9% in construction, 8.7% in commerce, 8.5% in transportation and communication, and 2.5% in other areas.

21 AGRICULTURE

Principal crops in 1992 included potatoes,

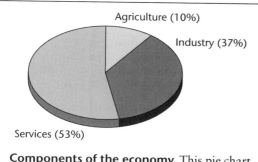

Components of the economy. This pie chart shows how much of the country's economy is devoted to agriculture (includes forestry, hunting, and fishing), industry, or services.

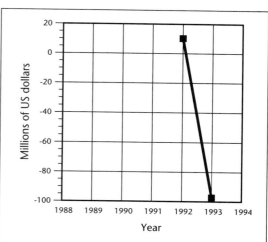

Yearly balance of trade measured in millions of US dollars. The balance of trade is the difference between what a country sells to other countries (its exports) and what it buys (its imports). If a country imports more than it exports, it has a negative balance of trade (a trade deficit). If exports exceed imports there is a positive balance of trade (a trade surplus).

150,000 tons; vegetables and melons, 115,000 tons; wheat, 90,000 tons; and fruit (excluding melons), 24,000 tons.

22 DOMESTICATED ANIMALS

In 1992, there were 799,000 pigs, 708,000 head of cattle, 143,000 sheep, and 5,000,000 chickens. Meat production is well developed and provides a surplus for export. In 1992, 60,000 tons of beef, 90,000 tons of pork, and 23,000 tons of poultry were produced.

23 FISHING

Estonia's Baltic and Atlantic catch is marketed in the former Soviet Union, in spite of its own need for quality fish products.

24 FORESTRY

The production of wood and wood products is the second-largest industry after textiles.

25 MINING

Oil shale is the most important mineral. Phosphate and uranium are also mined.

26 FOREIGN TRADE

In 1992, the majority of exports went to Finland (21%) and Russia (20%), which also supplied most of the imports (23% and 29%, respectively). The main export articles were timber, wood products, and metal.

27 ENERGY AND POWER

Domestic electrical production comes from locally mined oil shale. About 90% of the annual 23–24 million tons mined is burned to produce electricity. In 1991,

Selected Social Indicators

These statistics are estimates for the period 1988 to 1993. For comparison purposes, data for the United States and averages for low-income countries and high-income countries are also given.

Indicator	Estonia	Low-income countries	High-income countries	United States
Per capita gross national product†	$3,080	$380	$23,680	$24,740
Population growth rate	-0.3%	1.9%	0.6%	1.0%
Population growth rate in urban areas	0.1%	3.9%	0.8%	1.3%
Population per square kilometer of land	35	78	25	26
Life expectancy in years	69	62	77	76
Number of people per physician	255	>3,300	453	419
Number of pupils per teacher (primary school)	25	39	<18	20
Illiteracy rate (15 years and older)	<1%	41%	<5%	<3%
Energy consumed per capita (kg of oil equivalent)	0	364	5,203	7,918

† The gross national product (GNP) is the total dollar value of all goods and services produced by a country in a year. The per capita GNP is calculated by dividing a country's GNP by its population. The World Bank defines low-income countries as those with a per capita GNP of $695 or less. High-income countries have a per capita GNP of $8,626 or more. Less than 14% of the world's 5.5 billion people live in high-income countries, while almost 60% live in low-income countries.

> = greater than   < = less than

Sources: World Bank, *Social Indicators of Development 1995*, Baltimore: Johns Hopkins University Press, 1995. Central Intelligence Agency, *World Fact Book*, Washington, D.C.: Government Printing Office, 1994.

Estonia produced 16 billion kilowatt hours of electricity and exported 7.9 billion kilowatt hours.

28 SOCIAL DEVELOPMENT

During 1993, public attention focused increasingly on the welfare of children. Several safe havens for children were established. Discrimination based on race, sex, nationality, or religion is illegal under the constitution. Men and women generally receive equal pay for equal work.

29 HEALTH

In 1990, there were 255 people per physician in the country. In 1992, the infant mortality rate was 20 per 1,000. Life expectancy averages 69 years.

30 HOUSING

On 1 January 1991, 51,000 households (or 12%) were on waiting lists for urban housing. Housing space per person totaled 20.3 square meters at the end of 1991, and 34.3 million square meters altogether, of which 10.1 million were privately owned.

A view of the capital city of Tallinn, Estonia.

Photo credit: Anne Kalosh

32 MEDIA

In 1937, the highest radio tower in Europe (196.7 meters) was built in Türi. Estonian Radio broadcasts in Estonian, Russian, Finnish, and several other languages. Estonian television began broadcasting in 1955, and started color broadcasts in 1972. It broadcasts on four channels in Estonian and Russian.

In 1989, 111 newspapers were officially registered. The most popular daily newspapers (with 1993 circulation figures) are the *Postimees* (73,500) and the *Rahva Hääl* (Voice of the People, 62,600). The most widely read weeklies are the *Maaleht* (Country News, 65,200) and the *Eesti Ekspress* (Estonian Express, 40,000).

33 TOURISM AND RECREATION

After declining under Soviet rule, tourism is becoming one of the major areas of Estonia's economy. Visitors are drawn to the country's scenic landscapes, historic architecture, music and dance festivals, regattas, and beach resorts. The ancient town of Tallinn is a major tourist attraction and is linked by regular ferries to Helsinki, Finland, and Stockholm, Sweden.

34 FAMOUS ESTONIANS

Lennart Meri and Mart Laar have been president and prime minister of Estonia since October 1992, respectively. Writer Friedrich Reinhold Kreutzwald wrote the epic *Kalevipoeg* (Son of Kalev), which marked the beginning of Estonian national literature around 1860.

31 EDUCATION

The country's adult literacy rate in 1990 was 99.7% (men, 99.9%; women, 99.6%).

Estonian-language schools provide nine years of primary and three years of secondary education.

There are two well-known universities: the University of Tartu and the Talliva Technical University. In 1991–92, all higher level institutions had 25,643 pupils.

Photo credit: Anne Kalosh

This outdoor cafe is in the center of Tallinn, the capital of Estonia.

35 BIBLIOGRAPHY

Rank, Gustav. *Old Estonia, the People and Culture.* Bloomington: Indiana University, Research Center for Language and Semiotic Studies, 1976.

Raun, Toivo U. *Estonia and the Estonians.* 2d ed. Stanford, Calif.: Hoover Institution Press, 1991.

Taagepera, Rein. *Estonia: Return to Independence.* Boulder, Colo.: Westview Press, 1993.

Vesilind, Priit J. "The Baltic Nations." *National Geographic,* November 1990, 2–37.

ETHIOPIA

Ethiopia

CAPITAL: Addis Ababa.

FLAG: The national flag is a tricolor of green, yellow, and red horizontal stripes.

ANTHEM: Traditional "Ityopia, Ityopia" is in use at the present time. A new anthem will be designated in the near future.

MONETARY UNIT: The birr (B) is a paper currency of 100 cents. There are coins of 1, 5, 10, 25, and 50 cents, and notes of 1, 5, 10, 50, and 100 birr. B1 = $0.2000 (or $1 = B5.00).

WEIGHTS AND MEASURES: The metric system is used, but some local weights and measures are also employed.

HOLIDAYS: Holidays generally follow the Old Style Coptic Church calendar. National holidays include Christmas, 7 January; Epiphany, 19 January; Victory of Adwa (1896), 2 March; Victory Day, 6 April; May Day, 1 May; New Year's Day, 11 September; Feast of the Holy Cross, 27 September. Movable Muslim holidays include 'Id al-Fitr and 'Id al-'Adha'.

TIME: 3 PM = noon GMT.

1 LOCATION AND SIZE

Situated in eastern Africa, Ethiopia (formerly called Abyssinia) has an area of approximately 1,127,127 square kilometers (435,186 square miles), with a length of 1,639 kilometers (1,018 miles) east to west and a width of 1,577 kilometers (980 miles) north to south. Comparatively, the area occupied by Ethiopia is slightly less than twice the size of the state of Texas. Ethiopia's capital city, Addis Ababa, is located near the center of the country.

2 TOPOGRAPHY

Ethiopia is a country of geographic contrasts, varying from as much as 116 meters (381 feet) below sea level in the Denakil depression to more than 4,600 meters (15,000 feet) above sea level in the mountainous regions. It contains a variety of distinct topographical zones: the Great Rift Valley runs through the entire length of the country northeast-southwest; the Ethiopian Highlands are marked by mountain ranges; the Somali Plateau (Ogaden) covers the entire southeastern section of the country; and the Denakil Desert reaches to the Red Sea and the coastal foothills of Eritrea. Ethiopia's largest lake, Lake T'ana, is the source of the Blue Nile River.

3 CLIMATE

The central plateau has a moderate climate with minimal seasonal temperature variation. The mean minimum during the coldest season is 6°C (43°F), while the mean maximum rarely exceeds 26°C (79°F). Temperature variations in the lowlands are much greater, and the heat in the desert and Red Sea coastal areas is extreme, with occasional highs of 60°C (140°F). Heavy rainfall occurs in most of the country during June, July, and August.

4 PLANTS AND ANIMALS

Ethiopia has a large variety of indigenous plant and animal species. In some areas, the mountains are covered with shrubs such as pyracantha, jasmine, poinsettia, and a varied assortment of evergreens. The lakes in the Great Rift Valley region abound with numerous species of birds, and wild animals are found in every region. Among the latter are the lion, civet and serval cats, elephant, bush pig, gazelle, antelope, ibex, kudu, dik-dik, and oribi.

5 ENVIRONMENT

Overgrazing, deforestation, and poor agricultural practices have contributed to soil erosion so severe that substantial areas of farmland have been lost to cultivation. As of 1994, 600,000 acres of arable land are washed away each year. The combined effects of severe drought and a 17-year civil war have also added to Ethiopia's environmental problems. Ethiopia's forests and water supply are also endangered. Each year, the nation loses 340 square miles of forest land. Endangered species in Ethiopia include the simian fox, African wild ass, Tora hartebeest, and Waliaibex (found only in Ethiopia).

6 POPULATION

The population was estimated at approximately 55,600,000 in 1994. A population of over 64,173,000 was projected for the year 2000. The population of Addis Ababa, the capital and chief city, was estimated at 1,808,000 in 1990.

7 MIGRATION

Somalia has more than one million refugees from Ethiopia of Somali ethnic background. As of 1990, some 586,000 were in refugee camps. At the end of 1992 Ethiopia was harboring 406,100 Somali refugees. About 135,000 Ethiopians left Eritrea in 1991 when a new separatist government took power. There is also internal migration from rural to urban areas.

8 ETHNIC GROUPS

Ethiopia is a composite of more than 70 ethnic groups. The Amhara-Tigray group constitutes approximately 45% of the population and has traditionally been dominant politically. The Oromo (Galla) group represents approximately 40% of the population and is concentrated primarily in the southern half of the nation.

The Falasha (who call themselves Beta Israel, and are popularly known as "black Jews") live in the mountains of Simen. Some 14,000 were secretly flown to Israel via the Sudan in 1984–85, and about 14,000 more were flown out of Addis Ababa in 1991. Another 4,500 are believed to remain.

9 LANGUAGES

At least 70 different languages are spoken in Ethiopia. Amharic, the official national language, is a Semitic tongue, the native language of perhaps 30% of the people. Oromo, a Cushitic tongue, is widely spoken in the south, perhaps by 40% of all

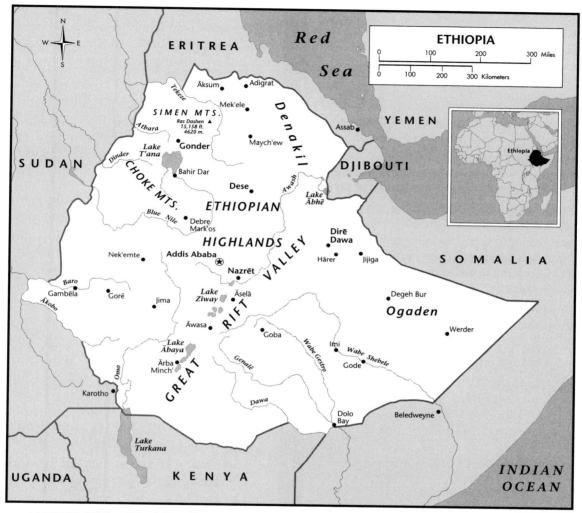

LOCATION: 3°30′ to 18°N; 33° to 48°E. **BOUNDARY LENGTHS:** Eritrea, 912 kilometers (566 miles); Djibouti, 337 kilometers (210 miles); Somalia, 1,626 kilometers (1,016 miles); Kenya, 830 kilometers (518 miles); Sudan, 1,606 kilometers (1,003 miles).

Ethiopians. English is the principal second language taught in schools.

10 RELIGIONS

In 1993 about 40% of Ethiopians were Ethiopian Orthodox Christians. More numerous are the Muslim peoples who inhabit the southwestern, northwestern, and eastern reaches of Ethiopia, amounting to some 45% of the population. There are also followers of African traditional religions, and Falasha who practice an ancient form of Judaism. Few Falasha remain after massive immigration and evacuation to Israel in 1984–85 and 1991.

11 TRANSPORTATION

It is estimated that more than half of Ethiopia's produce is transported by pack animals, reflecting the inadequacy of the country's road network and the rugged terrain. The road system in 1991 (before Eritrean independence), comprised 44,300 kilometers (27,500 miles). The number of passenger cars in use in 1992 was 37,799, and the number of commercial vehicles 20,939. A railway line from Djibouti to Addis Ababa is 880 kilometers (547 miles) long. Only one river, the Baro, is used for transport. The Addis Ababa airport handles international jet transportation.

12 HISTORY

Early History

Humanlike fossils dating back 4.4 million years were found in the Awash River Valley. They are the oldest known fossils of human ancestors. Ethiopia first appears in written history as the Aksumite (or Axumite) Empire. Although it was probably established around the beginning of the Christian era, national tradition attributes the foundation of the empire to Menelik I, the son of King Solomon and the Queen of Sheba.

Christianity was introduced in the fourth century by Frumentius of Tyre. The rise of Islam in the seventh century and the subsequent conquest of Egypt created a crisis for the Coptic Christian communities of northeast Africa. Ethiopia alone

met the challenge, surviving until the 1970s as a Christian island in a Muslim sea.

The Aksumite dynasty suffered a slow decline between the twelfth and sixteenth centuries, as a succession of rulers struggled to resist the growing power of Muslims in various parts of the country. The eighteenth and nineteenth centuries formed a period of political decentralization and incessant civil war. Lij Kassa Haylu was crowned Emperor Tewodros (Theodore II) in 1855 and succeeded in reunifying the empire, but he was defeated and killed by a British expeditionary force under General Robert Napier in 1868.

Italian Occupation

Italy occupied the Eritrean port of Assab (1869) and annexed Eritrea in 1890. The Italian advance was stopped by the defeat and total rout of a large Italian army by the Emperor Menelik II at Adwa (near Adigrat) in 1896. This Ethiopian victory is still commemorated as a national holiday. Italy, however, maintained control of Eritrea and also occupied the coastal region of Banadir (Italian Somaliland—now Somalia) in 1900.

Haile Selassie Becomes Emperor

Menelik died in 1913. Ras Tafari Mekonnen of Shewa was selected as heir apparent to his successor, and head of the government. On 2 November 1930, he was crowned Emperor Haile Selassie I. When Italy invaded and conquered Ethiopia in 1935–36, he was forced to flee the country, but he returned in 1941 (at the start of World War II) with the aid of

British forces. After the war, Eritrea, which had been under British administration since 1941, was federated to Ethiopia in 1952 and was incorporated into the empire 10 years later. By this time, an Eritrean secessionist movement was already stirring.

After an abortive coup in 1960, Selassie's political power began to lessen as political opposition increased. Guerrilla activity in Eritrea increased noticeably and student and labor unrest grew. In 1974 armed forces overthrew the government. The emperor was deposed and the monarchy was abolished. Haile Selassie died on 27 August 1975.

The new Provisional Military Administrative Council, also called the Dergue, came under the leadership of Mengistu Haile Mariam. The economy was extensively nationalized in 1975. Mengistu declared himself a Marxist-Leninist in 1976 and established close relations with Moscow.

The war with Eritrean secessionists continued. In addition, in mid-1977, Somalia invaded the Ogaden area in Ethiopia in order to support the claims of ethnic Somalis in Ogaden for self-determination. The Somali assault was repulsed with the assistance of Soviet arms and Cuban soldiers. Ethiopia signed a 20-year treaty with the USSR, and close links with Libya and the People's Democratic Republic of Yemen were established.

A devastating drought and famine struck northern Ethiopia during 1982–84, taking an unknown toll in lives. Between November 1984 and October 1985 an

Photo credit: AP/Wide World Photos

Children line up to be counted outside their school in Ethiopia.

international relief effort distributed 900,000 tons of food to nearly 8 million people. Food aid continued on a reduced scale, while the government launched massive resettlement programs.

Guerrillas Overthrow the Marxist Regime

Despite mobilizing one million troops and receiving massive Soviet bloc military aid, the government was not able to defeat the Eritrean and Tigrayan insurgencies. The guerrillas finally prevailed, and on 21 May 1991, the Marxist dictator, Mengistu, was forced to resign as president. He fled into exile in Zimbabwe.

In July, delegates from the guerrilla groups agreed to a plan establishing a transitional government and granting Eritrea the right to hold an internationally supervised referendum on independence. The vote, held on 23–25 April 1993, was for Eritrean independence. The United Nations certified the results, and on 24 May 1993, Eritrea became Africa's 52nd independent state.

Ethiopia's new transitional government pledged to oversee the establishment of Ethiopia's first multiparty democracy. The one-party state was disbanded and freedom of the press was permitted. New elections were planned for mid-1995. Although there have been complaints about the government's human rights record, there is a marked improvement over the Mengistu years.

13 GOVERNMENT

After Mengistu's defeat in May 1991, a transitional government was established under the leadership of the Ethiopian People's Revolutionary Democratic Front (EPRDF). New elections were scheduled for mid-1995.

14 POLITICAL PARTIES

There were no established political parties in Ethiopia until the 1970s, when a number of illegal separatist groups became active militarily. The separatists successfully defeated Mengistu's forces, and after Mengistu fled in May 1991, they established a transitional government under their coalition banner, the Ethiopian People's Revolutionary Democratic Front (EPRDF).

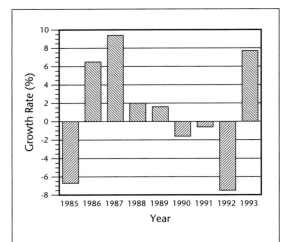

Yearly growth rate of the economy. This economic indicator tells by what percent the economy has increased or decreased when compared with the previous year.

15 JUDICIAL SYSTEM

The Transitional Government of Ethiopia is now putting into place a system of courts consisting of regional and central courts. Each region will have local (*Woreda*), district and Supreme Courts. There are also local Shari'a courts which hear religion and family cases involving Muslims. A federal Supreme Court will have jurisdiction over cases involving federal laws and issues of national import.

16 ARMED FORCES

A new post–civil war military establishment is not yet formed. The two major rebel factions have perhaps 200,000 men armed with Russian weapons and vehicles captured from the Mengistu government in 1991. Soviet aviation and naval equipment also remains, but there is no Ethiopian air force or navy. All Russian and Cuban troops have departed.

17 ECONOMY

Ethiopia's economy has been undergoing major reforms since May 1991, when a market-oriented government came to power. Three major droughts in the past twenty years, civil war, and cross-border conflicts have devastated the economy as much as socialist-style totalitarianism.

18 INCOME

In 1992 Ethiopia's gross national product (GNP) was $6,206 million at current prices, or $100 per person.

19 INDUSTRY

While Ethiopia's industrial sector engages primarily in food processing, it also produces sugar, alcohol and soft drinks, cigarettes, cotton and textiles, footwear, soap, ethyl alcohol, quicklime, and cement. In addition, Ethiopia's petroleum refinery produces some 800,000 tons of petroleum products annually. Since 1991, privatization of Ethiopia's industry has been a major objective of the new government, reversing the policies of its predecessor.

20 LABOR

Government estimates in 1992 indicated that 23,518,000 Ethiopians were economically active. About 80% of the total were engaged in agriculture and livestock raising. In 1992, about 70,860 persons were classified as unemployed. The 1975 Labor Code, which was still in effect in 1992, established an 8-hour workday and a 48-hour workweek.

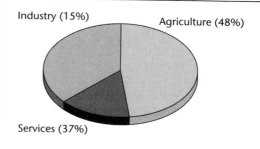

Components of the economy. This pie chart shows how much of the country's economy is devoted to agriculture (includes forestry, hunting, and fishing), industry, or services.

21 AGRICULTURE

Coffee is by far the most valuable cash export crop, accounting for 60% of foreign exchange earnings. The word *coffee* is derived from Kaffa (Kefa), the region around the city of Jima in the southwest that is still the largest coffee-producing area of the country. Coffee production was estimated at 216,000 tons in 1992, second in Africa. Qat, the leaves from a shrub that are used to make tea and which have a mild narcotic effect, is another important cash export crop.

The most commonly produced cereal is teff (*Eragrostis abyssinica*), which is used to make the Ethiopian unleavened bread called injera. Corn and barley are the next most important grains, with an annual gross production of at least one million tons each. Sorghum, wheat, millet, peas, beans, lentils, and oilseeds are produced in substantial quantities; sugarcane and cotton are also grown.

22 DOMESTICATED ANIMALS

Ethiopia has the largest livestock population in Africa. The number of cattle (zebu type) was estimated at 31 million in 1992, about three-fifths of them primarily work animals. Meat production was estimated at 571,000 tons in 1992; milk production was an estimated 774,000 tons. The number of sheep and goats was estimated at 23.2 million and 18.1 million, respectively, but periodic drought may have made the actual number much lower. The number of horses was estimated at 2,750,000, mules at 630,000, donkeys at 5,200,000, and camels at 1,070,000. These were primarily pack animals.

23 FISHING

With the secession of Eritrea, Ethiopia lost access to an estimated 1,151 kilometers (717 miles) of Red Sea coastline. In 1992, the Ethiopian and provisional Eritrean governments agreed to make Assab a free port for Ethiopia. Most Ethiopians do not eat seafood.

24 FORESTRY

Eucalyptus stands, introduced in the nineteenth century, are a valuable source of firewood, furniture, and poles. A species of acacia is a source of gum arabic.

25 MINING

Little of Ethiopia's expected mineral potential has been exploited. Mining and quarrying came to only $6.5 million in 1991. Construction materials, including cement, are the most significant mineral commodity both in value and quantity. Gold is the principal export mineral for

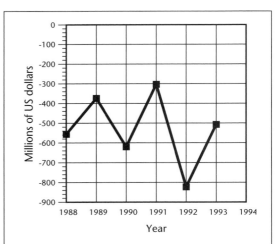

Yearly balance of trade measured in millions of US dollars. The balance of trade is the difference between what a country sells to other countries (its exports) and what it buys (its imports). If a country imports more than it exports, it has a negative balance of trade (a trade deficit). If exports exceed imports there is a positive balance of trade (a trade surplus).

revenue; production amounted to 2,000 kilograms in 1991, up from 848 kilograms in 1990.

26 FOREIGN TRADE

Coffee, tea, cocoa, and spices lead exports, accounting for 65% of the total. Livestock accounted for an additional 18.2%. Ethiopia is heavily dependent on imported manufactured goods. Machinery, petroleum, and petroleum products represent the leading import items. Of Ethiopia's exports, 24% go to Germany and 9.8% to the United States. Of Ethiopia's imports, 17.3% come from Italy, 11.4% from Germany, 11.0% from the former Soviet Union, and 10.9% from the United States.

Selected Social Indicators

These statistics are estimates for the period 1988 to 1993. For comparison purposes, data for the United States and averages for low-income countries and high-income countries are also given.

Indicator	Ethiopia	Low-income countries	High-income countries	United States
Per capita gross national product†	$100	$380	$23,680	$24,740
Population growth rate	3.0%	1.9%	0.6%	1.0%
Population growth rate in urban areas	4.7%	3.9%	0.8%	1.3%
Population per square kilometer of land	41	78	25	26
Life expectancy in years	48	62	77	76
Number of people per physician	30,560	>3,300	453	419
Number of pupils per teacher (primary school)	30	39	<18	20
Illiteracy rate (15 years and older)	38%	41%	<5%	<3%
Energy consumed per capita (kg of oil equivalent)	23	364	5,203	7,918

† The gross national product (GNP) is the total dollar value of all goods and services produced by a country in a year. The per capita GNP is calculated by dividing a country's GNP by its population. The World Bank defines low-income countries as those with a per capita GNP of $695 or less. High-income countries have a per capita GNP of $8,626 or more. Less than 14% of the world's 5.5 billion people live in high-income countries, while almost 60% live in low-income countries.

> = greater than   < = less than

Sources: World Bank, *Social Indicators of Development 1995,* Baltimore: Johns Hopkins University Press, 1995. Central Intelligence Agency, *World Fact Book,* Washington, D.C.: Government Printing Office, 1994.

27 ENERGY AND POWER

Production of electricity totaled 973 million kilowatt hours in 1991, of which the majority was hydroelectric. About 91% of Ethiopia's energy comes from fuel wood and animal wastes, and the rest from petroleum products and electricity.

28 SOCIAL DEVELOPMENT

Other than modest government allocations for pensions, labor and social welfare, and housing and community services, Ethiopia has no public welfare or social security programs. A major effort is being made to achieve widespread literacy among women.

29 HEALTH

The availability of modern health services reaches only a small portion of the population. In 1993 there was only one physician for every 30,560 people.

Between 1974 and 1992, there were 575,000 war-related deaths. Hundreds of thousands of Ethiopians died during a famine in 1973, and as many as one million may have died between 1983 and 1985. Average life expectancy in 1992 was estimated at only 48 years. Widespread diseases include malaria, tuberculosis, syphilis, gonorrhea, leprosy, dysentery, and schistosomiasis.

30 HOUSING

Except in Addis Ababa, Dire Dawa, and a few other urban centers, most houses are built of mud or mortar and have thatched or tin roofs. In the rural areas the traditional thatched hut *(tukul)* is still the most common dwelling.

31 EDUCATION

Compulsory and free public education exists at the primary level. In 1991, elementary schools had a total enrollment of 2,063,636 pupils in 8,434 schools with 68,399 teachers. On average, there are 27 students per teacher in elementary schools. Junior and senior secondary schools had 775,211 pupils with 22,721 teachers. Universities and equivalent institutions had 20,948 pupils with 1,440 teachers.

32 MEDIA

In 1991 there were 153,010 telephones in use. Radio and television stations are run by the government. In 1991 there were an estimated 9.7 million radios and 130,000 television sets in use. The largest daily newspaper is *Addis Zeman* with a circulation of 30,000.

33 TOURISM AND RECREATION

The chief tourist attractions are big-game hunting, early Christian monuments and monasteries, and the ancient capitals of Gonder and Aksum. There are seven national parks. In 1991 there were 81,581 international tourist arrivals, 30% from Africa and 26% from Europe.

34 FAMOUS ETHIOPIANS

The most famous Ethiopian in national legend is Menelik I, the son of the Queen of Sheba and King Solomon, regarded as the founder of the Aksumite Empire. Emperor Menelik II (1844–1913) is considered the founder of modern Ethiopia. Emperor Haile Selassie I (1891–1975) was noted for his statesmanship and his introduction of many political, economic, and social reforms.

35 BIBLIOGRAPHY

Abebe, Daniel. *Ethiopia in Pictures*. Minneapolis: Lerner, 1988.
Beckwith, Carol and Angela Fisher. "The Eloquent Surma of Ethiopia." *National Geographic*, February 1991, 77–102.
Fradin, D. *Ethiopia*. Chicago: Children's Press, 1988.
Nagel, Rob, and Anne Commire. "Haile Selassie I." In *World Leaders, People Who Shaped the World*. Volume I: Africa and Asia. Detroit: U*X*L, 1994.
Ofcansky, Thomas P. and LaVerle Berry (eds.). *Ethiopia, a Country Study*. 4th ed. Washington, D.C.: Library of Congress, 1993.
Wubneh, Mulatu, and Yohannis Abate. *Ethiopia: Transition and Development in the Horn of Africa*. Boulder, Colo.: Westview, 1988.

FIJI

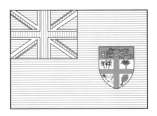

CAPITAL: Suva.

FLAG: The national flag of Fiji consists of the red, white, and blue Union Jack in the upper left corner of a light blue field, with the Fiji shield in the lower right corner.

ANTHEM: *God Bless Fiji.*

MONETARY UNIT: The Fiji dollar (F$) of 100 cents is the national currency. There are coins of 1, 2, 5, 10, 20, and 50 cents, and notes of 1, 2, 5, 10, and 20 Fiji dollars. F$1 = US$0.6642 (or US$1 = F$1.5056).

WEIGHTS AND MEASURES: The metric system is official, but some British weights and measures are still in use.

HOLIDAYS: New Year's Day, 1 January; Constitution Day, 24 July; Independence Day, 10 October; Christmas Day, 25 December; Boxing Day, 26 December. Movable religious holidays include Good Friday, Easter Monday, Dewali, and Milad an-Nabi.

TIME: 12 midnight = noon GMT.

1 LOCATION AND SIZE

Fiji, situated in the South Pacific, is made up of some 850 islands, of which only about 100 are inhabited. The island of Rotuma is geographically separate from the others and has an area of 44 square kilometers (17 square miles). Rotuma lies about 570 kilometers (350 miles) north-northeast. The nation's total area is 18,270 square kilometers (7,054 square miles), slightly smaller than the state of New Jersey. Fiji's coastline is 1,129 kilometers (702 miles) long. Its capital city, Suva, is located on the island of Viti Levu.

2 TOPOGRAPHY

The larger Fiji islands are volcanic, with rugged peaks. Coral reefs surround the islands. Viti Levu's highest point, Mt. Victoria (Tomanivi), is 1,323 meters (4,340 feet) above sea level. Its main river, the Rewa, is navigable by small boats for 113 kilometers (70 miles).

3 CLIMATE

Temperatures at sea level range from 16° to 32°C (61–90°F). Annual rainfall averages 312 centimeters (123 inches) in Suva. At sea level there are well-defined wet and dry seasons, with a mean annual average of 178 centimeters (70 inches) of rain.

4 PLANTS AND ANIMALS

The larger islands have forests on the windward side and grassland on the slopes protected from the wind. Mangroves and coconut plantations rim the coasts. Among native animals are bats, rats, snakes, frogs, lizards, and many species of birds.

Boy transporting firewood via ox sledge.

5 ENVIRONMENT

The main challenges to the environment in Fiji are loss of forests, soil erosion and pollution. Over the last 20 years, 30% of Fiji's forests have been eliminated by commercial interests. Pesticides and chemicals used in the sugar and fish processing industries pollute the land and water supply. The nation has 6.9 cubic miles of water, with 60% used for farming purposes, and 20% used for industrial activity. Its cities produce 100,000 tons of solid waste per year. As of 1994, 1 species of mammal, 5 types of birds, 4 species of reptiles and 1 type of amphibian were considered endangered, as well as 25 of Fiji's 1,500 plant species.

6 POPULATION

Fiji's population at the end of 1992 was estimated at 758,275. The population was projected to be 800,000 in the year 2000. The population density is was estimated at 41 persons per square kilometer (107 per square mile). Suva, the capital, had a population of 71,608 in 1986.

7 MIGRATION

There has been a steady flow of people from rural to urban areas. There was a substantial increase in emigration by Indians in the immediate aftermath of the military takeover of May 1987. Most of the more than 35,000 people who left between 1987 and 1993 were Indian Fijians.

8 ETHNIC GROUPS

The native Fijian population is mostly Melanesian, intermingled with Polynesian. In 1990, the population was estimated to be 46% of Indian origin, 49% native Fijian, and 5% other Pacific races or European.

9 LANGUAGES

English is the official language, but Fijian and Hindi are also used in Parliament. Fijian dialects belong to the Malayo-Polynesian language group. The Bau dialect is used throughout the islands except on Rotuma, where Rotuman is spoken.

10 RELIGIONS

About 53% of Fijians are Christians, primarily Methodist, with 9% Roman Catholic. Among Indian Fijians, 38% are Hindu, 8% Muslim, and 5% Sikh or other.

11 TRANSPORTATION

As of 1991, Fiji had 3,300 kilometers (2,051 miles) of main roads. Registered automobiles numbered about 32,000 and other vehicles, 28,000. A private rail system of about 644 kilometers (400 miles) serves most of the sugar-producing areas. Major ports are Suva and Lautoka. An international airport serves regularly scheduled flights to neighboring Pacific islands, Australia, and New Zealand via Air Pacific.

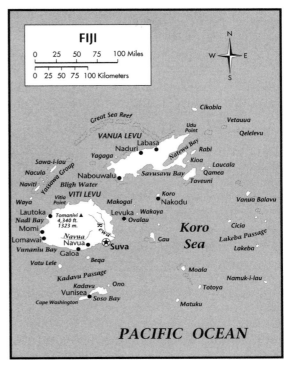

LOCATION: 15°43′ to 21°2′s; 176°54′E to 178°28′w (not including Rotuma, which is at 12°30′s; 177°5′E).
TERRITORIAL SEA LIMIT: 12 miles.

12 HISTORY

Fiji was settled by Polynesian and Melanesian peoples at least 2,500 years ago. Early European explorers in the seventeenth and eighteenth centuries were followed by traders, army deserters, shipwreck survivors, and missionaries in the nineteenth century. On 10 October 1874, Fiji was proclaimed a possession and dependency of the British crown.

From 1870 to 1916, nearly 50,000 Indian contract laborers arrived to work on European-owned sugar plantations. By 1920, they had settled as free farmers. On 10 October 1970, Fiji became a sovereign and independent state within the Commonwealth of Nations, with Kamisese K. T. Mara, head of the Alliance Party, as prime minister. He and his majority party won elections in 1972, 1977, and 1982, but lost the April 1987 elections to an Indian-based coalition. Within a year, Lieutenant Colonel Sitivendi Rabuka led two military takeovers aimed at restoring political leadership to ethnic Fijians. He suspended the constitution, dissolved the parliament, and declared Fiji a republic. Full civilian rule returned in January 1990 when Rabuka gave up his position as minister of home affairs and became head of the armed forces.

The adoption in 1990 of a new constitution which favored rural Melanesian control of Fiji led to heavy Indian emigration causing serious economic difficulties. After elections in February 1994, Major-General Sitiveni Rabuka formed a coalition government.

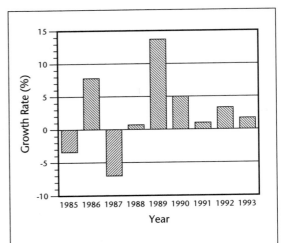

Yearly growth rate of the economy. This economic indicator tells by what percent the economy has increased or decreased when compared with the previous year.

13 GOVERNMENT

Following the 1987 coup, a new Constitution went into effect in July 1990. It established Fiji as a sovereign, democratic republic with a two-chamber legislature. Fiji's president was to be appointed to a five-year term by the Great Council of Chiefs, which would also nominate 24 Melanesians to the 34-member Senate. The 70-member House of Representatives was to be elected by the people every five years.

14 POLITICAL PARTIES

Major political parties include the Fijian Political Party (SVT—primarily Fijian), led by Major General Sitivini Rabuka; the National Federation Party (NFP—primarily Indian); the Christian Fijian Nationalist Party (CFNP); the Fiji Labour Party (FLP); and the General Voters Party (GVP).

15 JUDICIAL SYSTEM

The 1990 Constitution reorganized the judicial system. The courts include the Magistrate Courts, a High Court, and the Court of Appeals. A Supreme Court established by the 1990 Constitution is not yet functioning.

16 ARMED FORCES

Fiji's armed forces in 1993 consisted of 5,000 men, of whom 4,700 were in the army and 300 in the navy. Fiji spends about $25 million a year on defense.

17 ECONOMY

Fiji's economy is mostly based on agriculture and tourism, and is heavily dependent on foreign trade. Since 1989, revenues from tourism have been the country's leading source of income from abroad.

18 INCOME

Fiji's gross national product (GNP) is about $1,510 million at current prices, or $1,900 per person. For the period 1985–92 the average inflation rate was 5.2%, resulting in a real growth rate of 2.6% per person in the GNP.

19 INDUSTRY

Fiji's industry is based primarily on the processing of agricultural products, mainly sugarcane and coconut, and on the mining and processing of minerals. Estimated industrial production in 1993 included 415,000 cubic tons of sugar, 3,650 kilograms of gold, 9,750 tons of coconut oil, and 463,000 cubic meters of timber.

20 LABOR

In March 1992, Fiji had a wage labor force of 91,803 persons. Many more Fijians are farmers. In 1992, the entire labor force was 265,200. The unemployment rate was about 6% in 1992.

In Fiji, children under the age of 12 are not permitted to work. Young people between the ages of 12 and 17 may not be employed in industry or work with machinery. The Ministry of Labour and Industrial Relations enforces child labor

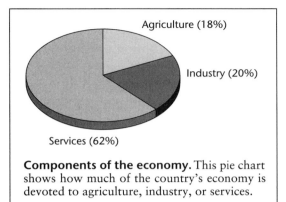

Components of the economy. This pie chart shows how much of the country's economy is devoted to agriculture, industry, or services.

laws, except in cases where young people work on family farms or businesses.

21 AGRICULTURE

Sugarcane production totaled 3,500,000 tons in 1992. In 1992, sugar exports accounted for 90% of agricultural exports. Production of copra (dried coconut meat that yields coconut oil) and coconuts in 1992 was 19,000 tons and 239,000 tons, respectively. Rice output was 33,000 tons.

22 DOMESTICATED ANIMALS

Beef production totaled about 5,000 tons in 1992, and the output of goat meat and pork was about 1,000 tons each.

23 FISHING

The fish catch in 1991 totaled 31,089 tons, over 25% of which was tuna. Mackerel, snapper, grouper, and mullet are other important species caught.

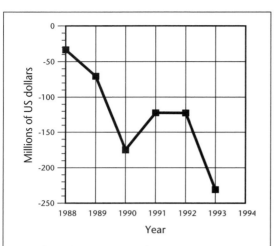

Yearly balance of trade measured in millions of US dollars. The balance of trade is the difference between what a country sells to other countries (its exports) and what it buys (its imports). If a country imports more than it exports, it has a negative balance of trade (a trade deficit). If exports exceed imports there is a positive balance of trade (a trade surplus).

24 FORESTRY

Some 65% of the land area is forested. Output of logs in 1991 totaled 307,000 cubic meters. Exports of sawn timber and other wood products were valued at $47.5 million in 1992.

25 MINING

Production of gold, the country's most important mineral, surged in 1988, when 4,273 kilograms of the refined metal were produced. Large copper deposits have been found on Viti Levu.

26 FOREIGN TRADE

Australia is Fiji's main trading partner, followed by New Zealand, Japan, the United Kingdom, the United States, and Singapore.

27 ENERGY AND POWER

The Monasavu hydroelectric project was completed in 1984. Its output is 525 million kilowatt hours. Exploration for oil and natural gas has taken place, but has been unsuccessful.

28 SOCIAL DEVELOPMENT

General welfare programs include poverty relief, maintenance of homes for the aged, free medical and legal aid to the needy, child care, and social casework to deal with delinquency. Most Fijian women fulfill traditional roles.

29 HEALTH

Fiji's health standards are relatively high. In 1986, there were 385 doctors and a total of 27 hospitals. The main health problem is influenza. Estimated average life expectancy is 72 years.

30 HOUSING

In 1986, housing stock totaled 126,100 units, of which 30% were made of corrugated iron or tin, 30% were concrete, and 26% were wood.

31 EDUCATION

In 1991 there were 144,924 pupils and 4,664 teachers in primary schools and 61,614 secondary school pupils. The University of the South Pacific had over 2,800 students in 1986. In 1991, all higher-level institutions combined had 7,908 students and a faculty of 277. The literacy rate in

Selected Social Indicators

These statistics are estimates for the period 1988 to 1993. For comparison purposes, data for the United States and averages for low-income countries and high-income countries are also given.

Indicator	Fiji	Low-income countries	High-income countries	United States
Per capita gross national product†	**$1,900**	$380	$23,680	$24,740
Population growth rate	**1.4%**	1.9%	0.6%	1.0%
Population growth rate in urban areas	**2.1%**	3.9%	0.8%	1.3%
Population per square kilometer of land	**41**	78	25	26
Life expectancy in years	**72**	62	77	76
Number of people per physician	**1,970**	>3,300	453	419
Number of pupils per teacher (primary school)	**31**	39	<18	20
Illiteracy rate (15 years and older)	**15%**	41%	<5%	<3%
Energy consumed per capita (kg of oil equivalent)	**525**	364	5,203	7,918

† The gross national product (GNP) is the total dollar value of all goods and services produced by a country in a year. The per capita GNP is calculated by dividing a country's GNP by its population. The World Bank defines low-income countries as those with a per capita GNP of $695 or less. High-income countries have a per capita GNP of $8,626 or more. Less than 14% of the world's 5.5 billion people live in high-income countries, while almost 60% live in low-income countries.

> = greater than   < = less than

Sources: World Bank, *Social Indicators of Development 1995,* Baltimore: Johns Hopkins University Press, 1995. Central Intelligence Agency, *World Fact Book,* Washington, D.C.: Government Printing Office, 1994.

1985 was an average of 85%: 90% for males and 81% for females.

32 MEDIA

Suva had 62,373 telephones in 1991. The Fiji Broadcasting Commission offers programs in Fijian, English, and Hindustani over Radio Fiji. There is no television broadcast service. In 1991, Fiji had 448,000 radios and 11,000 television sets. The leading daily newspapers are the English-language *Fiji Times* (with a 1991 circulation of 31,600) and *Daily Post* (10,000), the Fijian *Nai Lalakai* (10,500), and the Hindi *Shanti Dut* (9,187).

33 TOURISM AND RECREATION

In 1991, there were 259,350 tourist arrivals, with 33% from Australia, 12% from the United States, and 12% from New Zealand. There were 4,466 hotel rooms with a 52% occupancy rate. Popular tourist attractions are the beach resorts and traditional Fijian villages. Spectator sports include soccer, cricket, rugby and basketball.

34 FAMOUS FIJIANS

Well-known Fijians include Ratu Sir Lala Sukuna (d.1958), the first speaker of the

Legislative Council in 1954; and Ratu Sir Kamisese K. T. Mara (b.1922), the prime minister since 1970 and president as of 1994.

35 BIBLIOGRAPHY

Lal, Brij V. *Broken Waves: A History of the Fiji Islands in the Twentieth Century*. Honolulu: University of Hawaii Press, 1992.

FINLAND

Republic of Finland
Suomen Tasavalta

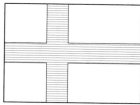

CAPITAL: Helsinki.

FLAG: The civil flag contains an ultramarine cross with an extended right horizontal on a white background. The state flag flown on government buildings is the same but also includes, at the center of the cross, the coat of arms, consisting of a gold lion and nine white roses on a red background.

ANTHEM: *Maammelaulu* (in Swedish, *Vårt land; Our Land).*

MONETARY UNIT: The markkaa (METERS) of 100 penniä is a convertible currency with one official exchange rate. There are coins of 10 and 50 penniä and 1 and 5 markkaa, and notes of 10, 50, 100, 500 and 1,000 markkaa. M1 = $0.1829 (or $1 = M5.4678).

WEIGHTS AND MEASURES: The metric system is the legal standard.

HOLIDAYS: New Year's Day, 1 January; May Day, 1 May; Independence Day, 6 December; Christmas, 25–26 December. Movable holidays include Good Friday, Easter Monday, Whitsun, and Midsummer Day (late June). Epiphany, Ascension, and All Saints' Day are adjusted to fall always on Saturdays.

TIME: 2 PM = noon GMT.

1 LOCATION AND SIZE

Part of Fenno-Scandia (the Scandinavian Peninsula, Finland, Karelia, and the Kola Peninsula), Finland has an area of 337,030 square kilometers (209,260 square miles), slightly smaller than the state of Montana. Its length, one-third of which lies above the Arctic Circle, is 1,160 kilometers (721 miles) from north to south; its width is 540 kilometers (336 miles) from east to west. Finland has a total boundary length of 3,754 kilometers (2,323 miles).

Finland's capital, Helsinki, is located on the country's southern coast.

2 TOPOGRAPHY

Southern and western Finland consists of a coastal plain with a strongly indented coastline and thousands of small islands stretching out to the Åland Islands. Central Finland is a large lake plateau with a majority of the country's 60,000 lakes.

Northern Finland is densely forested. The highest elevations are in the Norwegian border areas. Many interconnected lake and river systems provide important natural waterways.

3 CLIMATE

Because of the warming influence of the Gulf Stream, Finland's climate is quite mild for its high latitude. During the winter, the average temperature ranges from −14°C to −3°C (7–27°F), while summer mean temperatures range from 13°C to 17°C (55–63°F). Average annual precipitation (including both rain and snow) ranges from 40 centimeters (16 inches) in northern Finland to 70 centimeters (28 inches) in southern Finland.

4 PLANTS AND ANIMALS

Finland's forests are mainly pine, spruce, and birch. There are more than 1,200 native species of plants. Of 22,700 species of wildlife, more than 75% are insects. At least 67 species of mammals are native to Finland. Fur-bearing animals (otter, marten, ermine) are declining in number, while elk, fox, and beaver have increased. Of some 370 species of birds, half of which nest in Finland, perhaps the best known is the cuckoo, the sign of spring. Of some 70 species of fish, 33 have some economic importance. In fresh waters, the perch, walleyed pike, great northern pike, and others are plentiful. Salmon remains the favorite of fly fishers.

Photo credit: Matti Tirri.

These Finnish children are gathering mushrooms.

5 ENVIRONMENT

To preserve Finland's shoreline, 30–50% of the shores suitable for recreational use may not be developed. As of mid-1986, 18% of Finland's surface water was considered satisfactory, and 80% was good or outstanding. Nevertheless, industrial pollutants from within the country and from surrounding countries affect the purity of both the nation's air and water supplies. Acid rain from high concentrations of sulphur has damaged the nation's lakes.

Finland's cities produce 2.8 million tons of solid waste per year. By 1986, emissions of sulfur compounds had decreased about one-third from their peak, in the 1970s, of 600,000 tons annually. Lead-free gasoline was introduced in 1985. Finland produces 199.5 tons of hydrocarbon emissions per year.

Care is taken to protect the plants and animals of the forests. Closed hunting seasons, nature protection areas, and other game-management measures are applied to preserve threatened animal species. In 1994, 3 of the nation's 67 mammal species and 12 of its 370 bird species were threatened, as well as 1 type of freshwater fish and 11 plant species out of 1,450.

6 POPULATION

As of the November 1990 census, Finland's population was 4,998,478. The projected population for the year 2000 is 5,113,000. Distribution is uneven, with the density generally increasing from northern and inland regions to the southwestern region. In 1991, Helsinki, the capital, had a population of 497,542.

7 MIGRATION

In 1988, Finland had 9,540 immigrants and 8,318 emigrants, for a net gain of 1,222. The number of foreigners was 34,618 in 1991—only 0.7% of the population. Europeans constituted two-thirds of the total.

There was a heavy migration from rural areas, particularly the east and northeast, to the urban, industrialized south, especially between 1960 and 1975. By 1980, 90% of all Finns lived in the southernmost 41% of Finland.

8 ETHNIC GROUPS

The Finns are thought to be descended from Germanic stock and from tribes that originally inhabited west-central Russia. Excluding the Swedish-speaking minority of about 250,000, there are only two very small non-Finnish ethnic groups: Lapps and Gypsies. In 1990 there were about 4,400 Lapps. The Gypsy population numbers about 5,000 to 6,000.

9 LANGUAGES

Finnish belongs to the Finno-Ugric language group and is closely related to Estonian and remotely to Hungarian. At the end of 1991, 93.3% of the population was primarily Finnish-speaking, and 5.9% was primarily Swedish-speaking. Swedish-speaking Finns make up more than 95%

LOCATION: 59°30′10″ to 70°5′30″N; 19°7′3″ to 31°35′20″E. **BOUNDARY LENGTHS:** Russia, 1,313 kilometers (820 miles); Sweden, 586 kilometers (364 miles); Norway, 729 kilometers (445 miles); total coastline, 1,126 kilometers (694 miles). **TERRITORIAL SEA LIMIT:** 4 miles.

of the population of the Åland Islands, and Swedish-speaking majorities are also found in parts of some western provinces.

In 1990, only 24,783 individuals had another language as the mother tongue, principally Russian, English, or German.

10 RELIGIONS

As of 1990, 87.8% of the inhabitants belonged to the Evangelical Lutheran Church, which enjoys state support. Approximately 1.1% of the inhabitants were members of the Orthodox Church in Finland, which also receives state support. It has three dioceses, and owes allegiance to the Ecumenical Patriarch of Constantinople.

Other religious bodies include the Free Church, Jehovah's Witnesses, Adventists, Roman Catholics, Methodists, Mormons, Baptists, Swedish Lutherans, and Jews. The Civil Register comprises those individuals who prefer not to affiliate with any church (about 9.7% at the end of 1989).

11 TRANSPORTATION

In 1991 there were 103,000 kilometers (64,000 miles) of roads. That same year, registered motor vehicles included 1,922,541 passenger cars, 264,390 trucks, and 8,968 buses. There were 5,924 kilometers (3,681 miles) of railway lines in operation in 1991. They performed 3,230 million passenger-kilometers of service in 1991.

In the same year, the merchant fleet had combined gross registered tons of 609,000. At the end of 1991 there were 160 passenger vessels, 19 tankers, and 268 dry cargo vessels. Import traffic is concentrated at Naantali (near Turku), Helsinki, Kotka, and Turku, while the ports of Kotka, Hamina (northeast of Kotka), Kemi, Oulu, and Rauma handle most exports. In 1990, imports and exports by sea totaled 58,872,000 tons. In addition, over 10,834,000 passengers arrived or departed Finland by sea. In 1991 there were 6,675 kilometers (4,148 miles) of navigable inland waterways.

In 1992, state-run Finnair served 3,247,600 passengers and carried 112,900,000 ton-kilometers of freight.

12 HISTORY

Ancestors of present-day Finns came to Finland by way of the Baltic regions during the first centuries AD. These peoples were mainly hunters, trappers, and farmers. Swedish control was established gradually beginning around 1154. Finland became a province and later a grand duchy of the Swedish kingdom. This relationship was to last until the early 1800s. As a result of over six centuries of attachment to Sweden, Finland's political system, economic life, and social order developed largely along Swedish lines.

After Sweden's military defeat in 1808–09, Finland was transferred to Russia. Alexander I granted Finland a privileged self-ruling status, continuing its status under the Swedes. Toward the end of the nineteenth century, a Russian drive to change this status brought several decades of strained relations. After the Bolshevik seizure of power in Russia in the fall of 1917, Finland declared its independence on 6 December. A short civil war followed (28 January—10 May 1918), with intervention by both the Russian Bolsheviks and Germany.

In July 1919, Finland became a democratic parliamentary republic. Disputes with Sweden (over the Åland Islands) and the former USSR (over East Karelia) were settled. Nearly two decades of peace followed, and there were noteworthy economic and social advances. However, in the 1930s, the country became involved in the worsening relations between the great powers.

Following demands by the former USSR for a defense agreement or territorial concessions, there were two wars between the countries: the Winter War, lasting from 30 November 1939 to 13 March 1940, and the Continuation War, from 26 June 1941 to 19 September 1944 (during World War II). The armistice terms of 1944 required Finland to give up territory and pay reparations to the Soviets, and to expel German troops from its soil.

Postwar Finland's economic recovery has been striking. Since World War II, Finland has followed a policy of neutrality and good relations with its neighbors. Traditional ties with other Nordic countries have been maintained and strengthened. The dominant figure of postwar politics was Urho Kekkonen, the Agrarian (later Center) Party leader who held the presidency from 1956 to 1981, when he resigned because of ill health.

The cornerstone of his policy was maintenance of a center-left coalition that included the Communists and good relations with the former USSR. Social Democratic leader Mauno Koivisto, the prime minister, became acting president in October 1981 and was elected president in January 1982 and reelected in 1988. In the presidential elections of February 1994, Martti Ahtisaari, of the Finnish Social Democratic Party, was elected president, defeating Elisabeth Rehn (Defense Minister) of the Swedish People's Party.

In March 1987, the conservative National Coalition Party made strong gains in parliamentary elections and formed Finland's first conservative-led government since World War II. The conservative trend continued in March 1991 with the Center Party leading a new four-party center-right coalition under Esko Aho.

The collapse of the Soviet Union has led Finland to reassess its relationship with Europe and, in February 1993, Finland applied for membership in the European Communities. Finland officially joined the EC on 1 January 1995.

13 GOVERNMENT

Finland is a parliamentary republic. The constitution of 17 July 1919 vests supreme executive power in a president, who presides over and is assisted by a Council of State (cabinet). The president is elected directly (since 1991) for a six-year term. The president initiates legislation, issues decrees, directs foreign relations, and serves as commander-in-chief of the armed forces as well as appointing the highest civil servants.

The parliament (*Eduskunta*) is a single-chamber legislative body originally set up in 1906. Its 200 members are elected for four-year terms. Finland was the first

Photo credit: Matti Tirri.

A view of Helsinki, Finland's capital, from the sea.

country in Europe to grant suffrage (the right to vote) to women in national elections (1906).

Finland is divided into 12 provinces *(lääni)* and, as of 1994, 460 municipalities.

14 POLITICAL PARTIES

Four major parties have dominated political life in Finland: the moderate Finnish Social Democratic Party (Suomen Sosiali-demokraattinen Puolue—SSDP); the Center Party (Keskusrapuolue—KESK), which represents agricultural interests; the National Coalition Party (Kansallinen Kokoomus—KOK), which is considered "conservative middle-class"; and the Finnish Christian League (Suomen Kristillinen Liitto—SKL), usually found on the political right with the KOK.

The Swedish People's Party (Svenska Folkpartiet—SFP) focuses on protecting the common interests of Finland's Swedish-speaking population. The Finnish People's Democratic League (Suomen Kansan Demokraattinen Liitto—SKDL) represents the extreme left. The Greens, an environmentalist alliance, won four seats in the Eduskunta in 1987, although they were not formally organized as a political party.

Following the general election of March 1991, the Center Party led by Esko Aho emerged as the largest single party in parliament. A new four-party, center-right coalition was formed made up of the Center Party, the National Coalition Party, the Swedish People's Party, and the Finnish Christian League.

15 JUDICIAL SYSTEM

There are three levels of courts: local, appeals, and supreme. In 1986 there were 72 rural district courts, 28 municipal courts, and 6 appeals courts. The final court of appeal, the Supreme Court *(Korkeinoikeus),* sits in Helsinki under a president and 23 justices.

16 ARMED FORCES

In 1993, the army had 27,300 personnel; the navy, 2,500 personnel and 53 vessels of various types; and the air force, 3,000 personnel and 116 combat aircraft. Finland maintains 500,000 reservists, of whom 50,000 receive annual training.

Under the Paris Peace Treaty of 1947, Finland is prohibited from possessing or constructing atomic weapons, submarines, and bombers. There is compulsory military service for all males at age 17. Defense expenditures are around $2 billion a year. Finland provided 1,400 soldiers to seven different peacekeeping operations in 1993.

17 ECONOMY

Handicapped by relatively poor soil, a severe northern climate, and lack of coal, oil, and most other mineral resources necessary for the development of heavy industry, the Finns have still been able to build a productive economy. This was made possible by unrivaled forests (Finland's "green gold") and waterpower resources ("white gold"), as well as by the Finnish disposition toward hard work and ingenuity.

Agriculture, long the traditional calling of the large majority of Finns, has been undergoing continuous improvement, with growing specialization in dairying and cattle breeding. The industries engaged in producing timber, wood products, paper, and pulp are highly developed, and these commodities make up an overwhelming proportion of the country's exports.

Dependent on foreign sources for a considerable portion of its raw materials, fuels, and machinery, and on exports as a source of revenue, the Finnish economy is very sensitive to changes at the international level. Finland's economy was hard hit by the collapse of the former USSR, which had been its chief trading partner. Loss of export sales to the USSR plus high labor costs and excessive borrowing created a deep recession in 1991. The unemployment rate reached 17.9% in 1993.

18 INCOME

In 1992, Finland's gross national product (GNP) was $116,309 million at current prices, or $19,300 per person. For the period 1985–92 the average inflation rate was 5.1%, resulting in a real growth rate in GNP of 0.7% per person.

19 INDUSTRY

Since the end of World War II (1945), industrial progress has been noteworthy. Contributing factors include the pressure of having to make World War II reparation payments; large quantities of available electric power; increased mining operations; development of transportation and communications; and steady foreign demand for Finnish exports.

In terms of value of production and size of labor force, the metals industry is the most important, accounting for 16.6% of the industrial labor force in 1991. Also highly significant are the food, pulp and paper, machinery, chemical, and electrical products and instruments industries.

20 LABOR

In proportion to the total population, the labor force of Finland is large. In 1991, about 66% of the population aged 15–74 years—a total of 2,484,000—participated in the labor force. The percentages of the

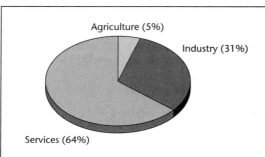

Agriculture (5%)

Industry (31%)

Services (64%)

Components of the economy. This pie chart shows how much of the country's economy is devoted to agriculture (includes forestry, hunting, and fishing), industry, or services.

labor force in the major sectors of the economy in 1991 were public administration, education, medical, social and other personal services, 30.3%; commerce, 15%; industry, 21%; finance and business services, 10.1%; agriculture, forestry and fishing, 8.6%; transport and communications, 7.7%; construction, 7.2%; and unknown, 0.1%.

Since the mid-1960s, the unemployment rate has crept upward, reaching 7.6% in 1991. In 1992, over 80% of both workers and employers were members of trade unions and employers' collective bargaining associations. There were a total of 1,165 industrial disputes involving 102,560 workers.

The minimum age of employment is closely tied with compulsory school requirements. Young people aged 15 may work if they have completed at least 10 years of school, although their work hours are limited to 9 hours per day, or 48 hours per week, and must be between 8:00 a.m. and 10:00 p.m. Young people aged 14

may be employed at light work during school holidays for a maximum of two-thirds of the holiday period. The work hours of a child under age 15 must not exceed 7 hours per day, or 36 hours per week, and must fall between 7:00 a.m. and 7:00 p.m. There must be a 14-hour period without work every day and a 39-hour period without work every week.

21 AGRICULTURE

Agriculture is closely linked to forestry and stock raising. Finnish farmers have a relatively small amount of available land, and climate and soil conditions are often difficult. Farms are generally small in size. The average farm has about 13.5 hectares (33 acres) of land that can be cultivated.

The main crops in 1992 (in tons) were barley, 1,531,000; oats, 998,000; sugar beets, 1,049,000; potatoes, 673,000; and wheat, 212,000. A total of 2,579,000 hectares (6,373,000 acres) were classified as potential farmland in 1991.

22 DOMESTICATED ANIMALS

Livestock production contributes about 70% of total agricultural income. Livestock in 1992 included cattle, 1,263,000 head; hogs, 1,357,000; sheep, 61,000; and horses, 49,000. There were 5,000,000 poultry that same year. Some 350,000 reindeer are used by the Lapps as pack animals and for meat.

Production of meat and dairy products in 1992 included pork, 176,000 tons; beef, 117,000 tons; eggs, 67,500 tons; butter, 56,660 tons; and cheese, 88,321 tons.

Milk production in 1992 was 2,399,000 tons.

23 FISHING

In 1991, some 2,000 people took part in commercial fishing, but only half were full-time professional fishermen. The total catch in that year was about 82,813 tons and fishery exports totaled $10.6 million, or 1.5% of total agricultural exports. The most important catch is Atlantic herring, with 51,546 tons caught in 1991. Other important species are pike, salmon, rainbow trout, and cod.

24 FORESTRY

The forest area covered 23.2 million hectares (57.3 million acres), or about 76% of the total land area in 1991. The most important varieties are pine (45% of the total growing stock), spruce (37%), birch, aspen, and alder. Some 5,000 sawmills were operating in 1992.

In 1991, the total timber felled for sale (chiefly spruce pulpwood, birch pulpwood, pine pulpwood, fuel wood, sawn logs, and veneer logs) was 34 million cubic meters. Forestry employed some 72,000 persons in 1992, including 46,000 in the chemical wood processing industry. In the 1980s, production of paper and paperboard rose significantly, while the mechanical wood processing industry went into decline.

Over 70% of annual Finnish forestry output is exported, including 90% of all printing paper and 35% of all particleboard produced. Over 80% of forestry product exports are sent to Western

Photo credit: Matti Tirri.

Fishing is a popular pastime in Finland.

Europe. In 1992, exports of forestry products accounted for 36% of the total export value.

25 MINING

Overall, mining and metal processing employed about 65,000 persons in Finland as of 1991. Of that total, about 825 were employed in mining and quarrying. A chromium mine on the Gulf of Bothnia near the Swedish border is one of the largest in the world, with estimated reserves of 150 million metric tons.

Zinc metal production in 1991 was 170,400 tons; feldspar came to 53,000 tons; and chromite to 458,000 tons. Other

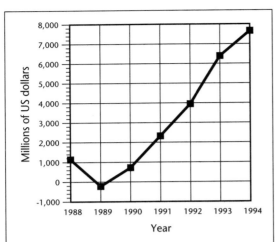

Yearly balance of trade measured in millions of US dollars. The balance of trade is the difference between what a country sells to other countries (its exports) and what it buys (its imports). If a country imports more than it exports, it has a negative balance of trade (a trade deficit). If exports exceed imports there is a positive balance of trade (a trade surplus).

processed minerals were nickel, selenium, cobalt, silver, and gold. Mineral reserves are declining, and many are expected to be soon exhausted due to intense mining activity over the last 400 years.

26 FOREIGN TRADE

Finland is highly dependent on imported energy. Principal merchandise exports in 1992 were paper products, engineering and other metal products, nuclear reactors and parts, and electrical machinery and equipment.

In 1992, European Free Trade Association (EFTA) countries took 19.5% of Finland's exports and supplied 19% of its imports. European Communities countries bought 53.2% of Finnish exports and supplied 47.2% of Finland's imports. The former Soviet bloc accounted for 6.8% of exports. Principal trading partners were Germany, Sweden, and the United Kingdom.

27 ENERGY AND POWER

Production of electric energy rose from 6,600 million kilowatt hours in 1956 to 58,137 million kilowatt hours in 1991 (13,096 million kilowatt hours from water power, 19,502 million kilowatt hours from nuclear power, and 25,539 from thermal power). Finland has four nuclear power plants.

Most of Finland's water power resources are located along the Oulu and Kemi rivers. Oil—all imported—accounted for 35% of the energy used in 1991.

28 SOCIAL DEVELOPMENT

Social welfare legislation in Finland is patterned largely on Scandinavian models. Major benefits include employees' accident insurance, old age and disability insurance, unemployment insurance, sickness insurance, compensation for war invalids, and family and child allowances. Total social and housing expenditure in 1988 was estimated at 36.1% of government outlays.

Some private welfare organizations, like the Mannerheim Child Welfare League, have won widespread recognition. Each city operates a maternal and child-care clinic. There is a maternity allowance, which covered 170 weekdays as of 1 January 1991. The father may share in a por-

Selected Social Indicators

These statistics are estimates for the period 1988 to 1993. For comparison purposes, data for the United States and averages for low-income countries and high-income countries are also given.

Indicator	Finland	Low-income countries	High-income countries	United States
Per capita gross national product†	$19,300	$380	$23,680	$24,740
Population growth rate	0.5%	1.9%	0.6%	1.0%
Population growth rate in urban areas	1.1%	3.9%	0.8%	1.3%
Population per square kilometer of land	15	78	25	26
Life expectancy in years	76	62	77	76
Number of people per physician	370	>3,300	453	419
Number of pupils per teacher (primary school)	18	39	<18	20
Illiteracy rate (15 years and older)	<1%	41%	<5%	<3%
Energy consumed per capita (kg of oil equivalent)	5,635	364	5,203	7,918

† The gross national product (GNP) is the total dollar value of all goods and services produced by a country in a year. The per capita GNP is calculated by dividing a country's GNP by its population. The World Bank defines low-income countries as those with a per capita GNP of $695 or less. High-income countries have a per capita GNP of $8,626 or more. Less than 14% of the world's 5.5 billion people live in high-income countries, while almost 60% live in low-income countries.

> = greater than   < = less than

Sources: World Bank, *Social Indicators of Development 1995,* Baltimore: Johns Hopkins University Press, 1995. Central Intelligence Agency, *World Fact Book,* Washington, D.C.: Government Printing Office, 1994.

tion of this time and also gets a 12-day paternity leave at the time of birth.

Women have a high level of education and hold a large number of elective political posts. However, they seldom hold high-paying management positions and earn on average only 80% of what men do.

29 HEALTH

The entire population is covered by health insurance, which includes compensation for lost earnings and treatment cost. In 1992 Finland had 13,500 physicians (1 physician per 370 people). In 1990, there were an estimated 440 hospitals, with just over 67,000 total beds.

While female health is good by international standards, male mortality in the over-25 age bracket is much higher in Finland than in most industrial countries, due mainly to heart disease. In addition, there has been an increase in suicide and alcohol-related problems among young men.

The major causes of death in 1990 were: cardiovascular diseases (24,589); cancer (10,082); respiratory diseases (3,746); gastrointestinal diseases (1,847); other diseases (5,088); accidents/violence

(4,735); and suicides (1,512). Life expectancy in 1992 was 76 years.

30 HOUSING

From 1974 through 1985, 558,000 new units were added to the housing stock. In 1991, 51,803 new dwellings were completed, down from 65,397 in 1990. The total number of dwellings in 1990 was 2,209,556, of which the greatest number (672,496) had two rooms and a kitchen. The standard of new dwellings is relatively high, and the overall housing stock is young. About 75% of the present stock has been built since 1950. The housing density was about 0.78 persons per room in 1980.

31 EDUCATION

The primary and lower secondary grades form a compulsory nine-year program. The upper secondary school (gymnasium) and vocational schools have both required and elective courses. Practically all adults are literate.

Entrance to the universities is through annual examinations. There were 13 universities and 12 colleges and institutes in 1991, with a total of 173,702 students. Among the best known are the University of Helsinki, Turku University, the Helsinki School of Economics, and the University of Tampere. University study is free of charge.

32 MEDIA

In 1991, 66 daily newspapers with a total circulation of 2,707,000 were published in Finland. Major newspapers and their daily circulation in 1991 were *Helsingen Sanomat* (482,400); *Ilta-Sanomat* (215,300); *Aamulehti* (145,100); *Turun Sanomat* (134,700); and *Maaseudun Tulevaisuus* (124,800). The leading weekly journals in 1991 were *Seura* (circulation 272,300) and *Apu* (279,200).

Broadcasting is run by Yleisradio, of which the government owns over 90%, and MTV, a commercial company. The number of radios was estimated at 4,980,000 in 1991. Regular television transmission began in 1958. The number of television sets was 2,760,000 in 1991. In the same year, there were 3,140,000 telephones in use.

33 TOURISM AND RECREATION

Finland offers natural beauty and tranquility in forest cottages and on the tens of thousands of islands that dot the 60,000 lakes and the Baltic Sea. Winter offers cultural events and cross-country skiing. Finland is the original home of the sauna, a national tradition.

In 1991, tourists spent 2,200,870 nights in hotels and other establishments. There were 47,997 rooms and 100,869 beds in hotels and other facilities, and tourism receipts totaled $1.19 billion. Anticipated European Communities membership in 1995 is expected to boost tourism by making Finland more competitive and accessible to visitors.

From 1906 to 1984, Finns won 128 Olympic gold medals, 118 silver, and 142 bronze. Popular sports include skiing, running, rowing, and wrestling.

Photo credit: Susan D. Rock

Finland's best-known composer, Jean Sibelius, is commemorated with this monument in Sibelius Park.

34 FAMOUS FINNS

Great Finnish literary figures include Elias Lönnrot (1802–84), compiler of the national epic, the *Kalevala,* and Aleksis Kivi (1834–72), the founder of modern Finnish-language literature and author of *The Seven Brothers.* Frans Eemil Sillanpää (1888–1964), a Nobel Prize winner (1939), was known to English-language audiences through his *Meek Heritage* and *The Maid Silja.* Väinö Linna (b.1920) was a Scandinavian Literature Prize winner (1963) and author of *The Unknown Soldier* (1954).

Well-known Finnish architects include Eliel Saarinen (1873–1950) and his son Eero Saarinen (1910–61), whose career was chiefly in the United States. A leading sculptor was Wäinö Aaltonen (1894–1966). Well-known painters include Helena Schjerfbeck (1852–1946), Akseli Gallen-Kalléla (1865–1931), and Tyko Sallinen (1879–1955).

Arts and crafts hold an important place in Finnish culture: leading figures are Tapio Wirkkala (1915–85) and Timo Sarpaneva (b.1926). Finnish music has been dominated by Jean Sibelius (1865–1957). Also notable are the composer of operas and symphonies Aulis Sallinen (b.1935), and opera and concert bass vocalist Martti Talvela (b.1935).

Famous scientists are A. I. Wirtanen (1895–1973), Nobel Prize winner for chemistry in 1945; Rolf Nevanlinna (1895–1980), mathematician; Edward Westermarck (1862–1939), ethnographer and sociologist; and Yrjö Väisälä (1891–1971), astronomer.

Outstanding athletes include Hannes Kolehmainen (1890–1966) and Paavo Nurmi (1897–1973), who between them won 14 Olympic medals in track. Another distance runner, Lasse Viren (b.1949), won gold medals in both the 1972 and 1976 games.

Marshal Carl Gustaf Emil Mannerheim (1867–1951) is a major figure in the creation of an independent Finland. President Juho Kusti Paasikivi (1870–1956) was important to the postwar period. Sakari Tuomioja (1911–64) was prominent in United Nations affairs. President Urho Kekkonen (1900–86) was instrumental in preserving Finland's neutrality.

35 BIBLIOGRAPHY

Engman, Max and David Kirby, eds. *Finland: People, Nation, State.* Bloomington: Indiana University Press, 1989.

Hintz, M. *Finland.* Chicago: Children's Press, 1983.

Irwin, John. *The Finns and the Lapps.* New York: Holt, Rinehart & Winston, 1973.

Jutikkala, Eino. *A History of Finland,* translated by Paul Sjoblom. New York: Dorset Press, 1988.

Kirby, D. G. *Finland in the Twentieth Century.* Minneapolis: University of Minnesota Press, 1980.

Rajenen, Aini. *Of Finnish Ways.* Minneapolis: Dillon, 1981.

Singleton, Frederick Bernard. *A Short History of Finland.* Cambridge; New York: Cambridge University Press, 1989.

Solsten, Eric and Sandra W. Meditz, eds. *Finland, A Country Study.* 2d ed. Washington, D.C.: Library of Congress, 1990.

FRANCE

French Republic

République Française

CAPITAL: Paris.

FLAG: The national flag is a tricolor of blue, white, and red vertical stripes.

ANTHEM: *La Marseillaise.*

MONETARY UNIT: The franc (Fr) is a paper currency of 100 centimes. There are coins of 5, 10, and 20 centimes and ½, 1, 2, 5, 10, and 20 francs, and notes of 20, 50, 100, 200, and 500 francs. Fr1 = $0.1751 (or $1 = Fr5.71).

WEIGHTS AND MEASURES: The metric system is the legal standard.

HOLIDAYS: New Year's Day, 1 January; Labor Day, 1 May; World War II Armistice Day, 8 May; Bastille Day, 14 July; Assumption, 15 August; All Saints' Day, 1 November; World War I Armistice Day, 11 November; Christmas, 25 December. Movable holidays include Easter Monday, Ascension, and Pentecost Monday.

TIME: 1 PM = noon GMT.

1 LOCATION AND SIZE

Situated in Western Europe, France is the second-largest country on the continent, with an area (including the island of Corsica) of 547,030 square kilometers (211,209 square miles). The area occupied by France is slightly more than twice the size of the state of Colorado. France has a total boundary length of 6,315 kilometers (3,926 miles).

France's capital city, Paris, is located in the northcentral part of the country.

2 TOPOGRAPHY

Topographically, France is one of the most varied countries of Europe, with elevations ranging from sea level to the highest peak of the continent, Mont Blanc (4,807 meters/15,771 feet), which is on the border with Italy.

Much of the country is ringed with mountains. In the northeast is the Ardennes Plateau, which extends into Belgium and Luxembourg. To the east are the Vosges, the high Alps, and the Jura Mountains. Along the Spanish border are the Pyrenees, much like the Alps in ruggedness and height.

At the center of France is the Paris Basin. Low hills cover much of Brittany and Normandy. The high land of the Massif Central, topped by extinct volcanoes, occupies the south central area.

The main rivers are the Rhône (812 kilometers/505 miles), between the Paris Basin and the Mediterranean; the Seine (776 kilometers/482 miles), draining into the English Channel; the Loire (1,020 kilometers/634 miles), which flows through central France to the Atlantic; and the

Garonne (575 kilometers/357 miles), which flows across southern France to the Atlantic.

3 CLIMATE

Three types of climate may be found within France: the oceanic climate, prevailing in the western parts of the country; the continental (transition) type of climate, found over much of eastern and central France; and the Mediterranean climate, widespread throughout the south of France, except in the mountainous southwest.

The mean temperature is about 12°C (54°F) at Paris and 15°C (59°F) at Nice. In central and southern France, annual rainfall is light to moderate, ranging from about 68 centimeters (27 inches) at Paris to 100 centimeters (39 inches) at Bordeaux. Rainfall is heavy in Brittany, the northern coastal areas, and the mountainous areas, where it reaches more than 112 centimeters (44 inches).

4 PLANTS AND ANIMALS

France's plants and animals are as varied as its range of topography and climate. It has forests of oak and beech in the north and center, as well as pine, birch, poplar, and willow. The Massif Central has chestnut and beech; the subalpine zone, juniper and dwarf pine. In the south are pine forests and various oaks.

Eucalyptus (imported from Australia) and dwarf pines abound in the southeast area known as Provence. Toward the Mediterranean are olive trees, vines, and mulberry and fig trees, as well as laurel, wild herbs, and the low vegetation known as maquis (from which the French resistance movement in World War II took its name).

The Pyrenees and the Alps are the home of the brown bear, chamois, marmot, and alpine hare. In the forests are polecat and marten, wild boar, and various deer. Hedgehog and shrew are common, as are fox, weasel, bat, squirrel, badger, rabbit, mouse, otter, and beaver.

The birds of France are largely migratory. Warblers, thrushes, magpies, owls, buzzards, and gulls are common. There are storks in the Vosges lowlands and elsewhere, eagles and falcons in the mountains, pheasants and partridge in the south. Flamingos, terns, buntings, herons, and egrets are found in the Mediterranean zone. The rivers hold eels, pike, perch, carp, roach, salmon, and trout. Lobster and crayfish are found in the Mediterranean.

5 ENVIRONMENT

The mid-1970s brought passage of laws governing air pollution, waste disposal, and chemicals. Water pollution is a serious problem in France due to the accumulation of industrial contaminants, agricultural nitrates, and waste from the nation's cities. Only 52% of the population has adequate sewage facilities. France has 40.8 cubic miles of water with 69% used for industrial purposes and 15% used for farming. France's cities produce 18.7 million tons of solid waste per year.

As of 1994, 20% of France's forests were damaged due to acid rain and other contaminants. Air pollution is a significant

FRANCE

LOCATION: 42°20′ to 51°5′N; 4°47′W to 8°15′E. **BOUNDARY LENGTHS:** Belgium, 620 kilometers (387 miles); Luxembourg, 73 kilometers (45 miles); Germany, 451 kilometers (280 miles); Switzerland, 573 kilometers (358 miles); Italy, 488 kilometers (305 miles); Andorra, 60 kilometers (37 miles); Spain, 623 kilometers (389 miles); total coastline (including islands), 3,427 kilometers (2,125 miles). **TERRITORIAL SEA LIMIT:** 12 miles.

Photo credit: Corel Corporation.
A farmer from the Rhone Valley.

environmental problem in France. However, there has been substantial progress in reducing airborne emissions in major cities. The amount of sulfur dioxide in Paris decreased from 122 micrograms per cubic meter of air in 1971 to 54 micrograms in 1985.

In December 1984 there were six national parks, with a total area of 12,279 square kilometers (4,740 square miles). In a total of 113 mammal species, 6 are currently threatened, as are 21 of 342 bird species, 2 of 36 types of reptiles, 1 of 29 types of amphibians, and 3 species of fresh-water fish in a total of 70. Of at least

4,300 known plant species, 143 are currently endangered.

Endangered species in France in 1994 included the Mediterranean monk seal, the gray wolf, and the large blue butterfly.

6 POPULATION

The estimated population as of mid-1994 was 57,289,648. Projected population for the year 2000 was 58,792,000. Average density in 1990 was 104 persons per square kilometer (270 per square mile).

According to the 1990 census, 38 cities had more than 100,000 inhabitants. Paris proper, the capital, is the largest city, with a population in 1990 of 2,175,200. Greater Paris, with some 9,318,821 inhabitants in 1990, remained a heavily populated urban area, with a density of 3,920 people per square kilometer (10,153 per square mile). The next largest cities, with 1990 populations, are Marseille, 807,726; Lyon, 422,444; Toulouse, 365,933; Nice, 345,674; Strasbourg, 255,937; and Nantes, 252,029.

7 MIGRATION

In 1990 there were 3,607,590 recorded foreign residents of France. (Another 200,000 were believed to be in the country illegally.) The largest groups were the Portuguese (645,578), Algerians (619,923), Moroccans (584,708), Italians (253,679), Spaniards (216,015), Tunisians (207,496), and Turks (201,480). The growing presence of foreigners has become a political issue met by crackdowns on illegal immigrants and restrictions on citizenship. At the end of 1992 France was harboring 182,600 refugees.

8 ETHNIC GROUPS

Most citizens are of French ancestry, but there are also small groups of Flemings, Catalans, Germans, Armenians, Gypsies, Russians, Poles, and others. The largest resident alien groups are Algerians, Portuguese, Moroccans, Italians, Spaniards, Tunisians, and Turks.

9 LANGUAGES

Not only is French the national language of France, but it is estimated that more than 300 million people throughout the world have French as their official language or mother tongue. Other languages spoken within France itself include Breton (akin to Welsh) in Brittany; a German dialect in the Vosges region; Flemish in northeastern France; Spanish, Catalan, and Basque in the southwest; Provençal in the southeast, and an Italian dialect on the island of Corsica.

10 RELIGIONS

In 1993, about 83.5% of the population was Roman Catholic and 2% was Protestant, mostly Calvinist or Lutheran. With the increased number of North Africans in metropolitan France, by 1992 the number of Muslims had risen to an estimated 1,900,000. The French Jewish community, estimated at 530,000 in 1990, is the fourth-largest in the world, after the United States, Israel, and the former Soviet Union. More than half are immigrants from North Africa.

11 TRANSPORTATION

France has one of the most highly developed transportation systems in Europe. Its outstanding characteristic has long been the degree to which it is centralized at Paris—plateaus and plains offering easy access radiate from the city in all directions, and rivers with broad valleys converge on it from all sides. In 1991, the road network of 803,000 paved kilometers (499,000 miles) included 33,400 kilometers (20,755 miles) of national highways. By 1992 there were 23.8 million passenger cars and 5 million commercial vehicles.

As of January 1992 there were 36,706 kilometers (22,809 miles) of railway track. As of the end of 1992, France ranked seventh in the world in the number of rail passengers carried, and eighth in tons of freight transported. Le Train à Grande Vitesse (TGV) is the fastest train in the world, averaging 250 kilometers (155 miles) per hour over most of its run. The Paris subway (Métro) has over one million passengers a day. Parisian bus lines carry about 800,000 passengers daily. A 50-kilometer (31-mile) rail tunnel under the English Channel (the "Chunnel") linking France and England was completed in 1993.

France, especially in its northern and northeastern regions, is well provided with navigable rivers and connecting canals, and inland water transportation is of major importance. In 1991 there were about 6,969 kilometers (4,331 miles) of navigable waterways in heavy use. The French merchant marine, as of January

1992, had a total of 102 ships with 2.9 million gross registered tons. The leading ports are Marseille, Le Havre, Dunkerque, Rouen, Bordeaux, and Cherbourg.

France's national airline, Air France, operates regularly scheduled flights to all parts of the world and carries about 79% (1992) of total passenger air traffic by French carriers. In 1992, Air France flew 42,931 million passenger-kilometers and transported 3,731,200 ton-kilometers of freight. The two international airports of Paris, Charles de Gaulle and Orly, lead all others in France in both passenger and freight traffic. Together they handled 44.8 million passengers and 853,000 tons of freight in 1991.

12 HISTORY

Cave paintings and engravings, the most famous of them at Lascaux in the southwest, testify to human habitation in France as early as 30,000 years ago.

Detailed knowledge of French history begins with the conquest of the region (58–51 BC) by Julius Caesar. At that time it was inhabited by Celtic tribes known as the Gauls. Under Roman rule the Gallic provinces were among the most prosperous and civilized of the Roman Empire.

Early in the fifth century, Teutonic tribes—the Visigoths, Burgundians, and Franks (from whom the French take their name)—invaded the region. Charlemagne (r.768–814), was the greatest of the early Frankish rulers. Through wide conquests, he added to the territories under his rule, eventually reigning over an area corresponding to present-day France plus Germany, Belgium, Luxembourg, the Netherlands, and northern Italy.

After the death of Charlemagne, his empire was broken up and weakened. At the end of the tenth century, Hugh Capet (r.987–996) founded the line of French kings that was to rule the country for the next 800 years. Feudalism—the system under which a feudal lord gave his subjects land in exchange for military and other services—was well-established by this time.

Between 1066 and 1070, William II, the duke of Normandy, conquered England in what became known as the Norman Conquest. He became England's king as William I, introducing the French language and culture to that country.

The reign of Philip IV ("the Fair," 1285–1314) marks the height of French royal power in the medieval period. After the death of Pope Boniface VIII, Philip moved the seat of the papacy to Avignon, where the popes resided under French control until 1377.

In 1337 Edward III of England, Philip's grandson, challenged the right of Philip's nephew, Philip VI, to the throne. This set off a series of wars between France and England that lasted from 1337 to 1453 and became known as the Hundred Years' War.

The Hundred Years' War

The first part of the Hundred Years' War was really a struggle between dynasties rather than a national struggle. The English armies themselves were com-

Photo credit: Corel Corporation.

Roman ruins located in the town of Arles in southern France.

manded by French-speaking nobles and a French-speaking king. Modern nationalism came into play with the campaign launched by Henry V, who became an English national hero after his decisive victory at Agincourt in 1415.

French nationalism found an inspiration in the figure of Joan of Arc. Confident that she had a divinely inspired mission to save France, this young woman led the siege of Orléans and had France's prince, called the dauphin, crowned Charles VII. Joan fell into English hands and was burned at the stake in 1431. However, the French armies continued to advance. By 1461 the English had been driven from almost all French territory.

As the Protestant Reformation gained a growing following in France, bitter hostility developed between the Protestants (called Huguenots) and the Catholics. In the 16th century, a series of fierce religious civil wars devastated France. On 23–24 August 1572, thousands of Protestants were slaughtered in the Massacre of St. Bartholomew. When the Protestant Henry of Navarre mounted the throne, he embraced Catholicism and in 1598 signed the Edict of Nantes, which guaranteed religious freedom to the Huguenots.

In the 17th century, Cardinal Richelieu, the minister of Louis XIII, enhanced the king's absolute rule at home and combated the power of the Austrian Habsburgs abroad. He destroyed the political power of the Protestants and led France in 1635 into the Thirty Years' War. The Peace of Westphalia (1648), which ended the Thirty Years' War, and the Peace of the Pyrenees (1659) established France as the dominant power on the European continent.

The reign of Louis XIV (1661-1715) marked the high point of the French monarchy. He transformed the French state into an absolute monarchy based on the so-called divine right of kings. Great overseas colonies were carved out in India, Canada, and Louisiana.

Nevertheless, the Sun King, as he was called, left the country in a weaker position than he had found it. In 1685, he revoked the Edict of Nantes, and an estimated 200,000 Huguenots fled the country to escape persecution. The economy was severely affected by the loss of many skilled workers. Louis undertook a long series of foreign wars that weakened France economically and militarily.

Further wars in the eighteenth century cost France its Indian and Canadian colonies and bankrupted the country. Meanwhile, the center of economic power in the kingdom had shifted to the hands of the middle class, who resented the unproductive ruling class.

The French Revolution

In 1789, Louis XVI convened the Estates-General, the national assembly, made up of representatives from all three "estates" (the nobility, clergy, and commoners). The representatives of the third estate, the Commons, broke away and proclaimed themselves the National Assembly. This action marked the beginning of the French Revolution, although the act that best symbolized the power of the revolution was the storming of the Bastille, a royal prison, by a Paris mob on 14 July—an event still commemorated as a national holiday.

Louis XVI was forced to accept a new constitution providing for a limited monarchy. The Assembly's successor, the National Convention, elected in September 1792, proclaimed the First French Republic. Louis XVI and his queen, Marie Antoinette, were convicted of treason and beheaded. The radical Jacobins under Maximilien Robespierre seized power and instituted a Reign of Terror from 1793 to 1794, executing thousands of people. In 1795, a new, moderate constitution was introduced, and executive power was vested in a Directory of five men.

The Directory fell in 1799, when the military hero Napoleon Bonaparte led a coup d'état and established the Consulate. In 1804, he had himself proclaimed emperor as Napoleon I and ruled France until his downfall in 1814.

Napoleon led his imperial armies to a striking series of victories. By 1808, he was the master of all Europe west of Russia with the exception of the British Isles. Napoleon's ill-fated attempt to conquer Russia in 1812 was followed by the creation of a powerful alliance against him, consisting of Russia, Prussia, Britain, and Sweden. He met his final defeat at the hands of British and Prussian forces at Waterloo (in present-day Belgium) on 18 June 1815.

Charles X, who took over the throne in 1824, tried to restore the absolute powers of the monarchy. He was overthrown in 1830 in the three-day "July revolution." In 1848, the regime of Louis Philippe, who succeeded Charles, was overthrown in the name of the Second Republic. Four years later, however, its first president, Louis Napoleon, the nephew of Napoleon I, had himself proclaimed emperor under the title Napoleon III.

The Second Empire, which lasted from 1852 to 1871, was characterized by colonial expansion and great material prosperity. The emperor's aggressive foreign policy eventually led to the Franco-Prussian War (1870–71), which ended in a crushing defeat for France and in his own

A military cemetery near Arras in northern France. Major battles from both World Wars were fought on French soil.

downfall. Democratic government finally triumphed in France under the Third Republic, whose constitution was adopted in 1875.

The Twentieth Century

During World War I (1914–18), the forces of France, the United Kingdom, Russia, and the United States were locked in an extended struggle with those of Germany, Austria-Hungary, and Turkey. Almost all the bitter fighting in the west was conducted on French soil. Among the Allies, French casualties—including nearly 1,400,000 war dead—were second only to those sustained by Russia.

The heavily industrialized provinces of Alsace and Lorraine, lost to Germany during the war, were restored to France under the Treaty of Versailles (1919). In addition, Germany was ordered to pay heavy war reparations. Nevertheless, the French economy, plagued by recurrent crises, was unable to achieve great prosperity in the 1920s. The worldwide economic depression of the 1930s was accompanied in France by inflation, widespread unemployment, and profound social unrest.

In the meantime, Germany, under Adolph Hitler and his Nazi party, was rearming and threatening war on the European continent.

In a futile attempt to secure peace, the French government went along with British Prime Minister Neville Chamberlain's policy of appeasement toward Hitler. Hitler was not to be appeased, however, and when Germany invaded Poland in September 1939, France joined the United Kingdom in declaring war on Germany.

On 10 May 1940, the Germans invaded western Europe, outflanking the French Maginot Line fortifications and routing the French armies between the Belgian frontier and Paris. Northern France was placed under direct occupation by the Germans. The South was ruled by the Vichy government under the World War I hero, Marshal Pétain, which cooperated closely with the Germans.

French resistance gathered overseas around General Charles de Gaulle, who had escaped to London. De Gaulle organized a provisional government and the Free French forces. Regular French units and resistance fighters alike fought in the 1944 campaign that drove the Germans from France, and shortly after the liberation of Paris, de Gaulle's provisional government moved to Paris. It was officially recognized by the United States, the United Kingdom, and the former USSR in October 1944.

After World War II, France still faced almost continuous fighting overseas. It lost Indochina in 1954. Later Algeria was the scene of a nationalist rebellion by Muslims. After a rebellion by French settlers in Algeria in 1958, General de Gaulle, the only leader who could rally the nation, was installed as premier. He ended the threat peaceably, and in December 1958, he was officially named the first president of the Fifth Republic.

Algeria gained independence on 1 July 1962. Nearly all of France's former African territories were given their independence as well. France has continued to provide economic assistance, and its ties with most of the former colonies have remained close. During the mid-1960s, de Gaulle sought to distance France from the Anglo-American alliance. France developed its own atomic weapons and withdrew its forces from the NATO command.

The political stability of the mid-1960s ended in the spring of 1968, with student riots and a month-long general strike that severely weakened the Gaullist regime. In April 1969, General de Gaulle resigned. In June, Georges Pompidou, a former premier in de Gaulle's government, was elected the second president of the Fifth Republic. In 1974, after President Pompidou died in office, an Independent Republican, Valéry Giscard d'Estaing, became the third president of the Fifth Republic. Giscard strengthened relations with the United States but continued to follow a middle course between the superpowers in world affairs.

A Socialist, François Mitterrand, was elected president in May 1981. Mitterrand launched a program of economic reforms, including government takeover of many industrial companies and most major banks. Mitterrand committed French troops to a peacekeeping force in Lebanon, and aided the Chadian government against domestic rebels and their Libyan backers.

A major scandal was the disclosure in 1985 that French agents were responsible for the destruction in New Zealand of a ship owned by the environmentalist group, Greenpeace, protesting French nuclear tests in the South Pacific.

In March 1986 elections, the Socialists lost their majority in the National Assembly. In order to keep control of the government, Mitterrand had to appoint a conservative prime minister to head a new center-right cabinet. The new prime minister, Jacques Chirac, successfully began a program to denationalize 65 state-owned companies. This plan was opposed by Mitterrand. In 1988, Mitterand won a commanding 54% of the vote and a second seven-year term, and Chirac resigned.

By 1994, however, Mitterrand had grown ill and announced he would retire in May 1995. In the elections that followed, Chirac received 52% of the vote and gained the presidency. In post-election remarks, he made unemployment one of the prime targets for his incoming administration. Joblessness in France stood at 12.2% in May 1995.

13 GOVERNMENT

Under the constitution of the Fifth Republic (1958), as subsequently amended, the president of the republic is elected for a seven-year term by direct universal voting. The president appoints the premier and, on the premier's recommendation, the other members of the cabinet. The president has the power to dissolve the National Assembly, in which event new elections must be held in 20–40 days. The president executes laws approved by the legislature, has the right of pardon, and is commander of the armed forces.

The Parliament consists of two houses, the National Assembly and the Senate. The National Assembly is composed of 577 deputies, each representing an electoral district. The deputies' term of office, unless the Assembly is dissolved, is five years. The Senate consists of 321 members elected to nine-year terms, one-third being chosen every three years. All citizens aged 18 or over are eligible to vote.

To become law, a measure must be passed by Parliament. Bills, which may be initiated by the president, are introduced in either house, except finance bills, which must be introduced in the Assembly.

14 POLITICAL PARTIES

Since the late 1950s, French politics has been dominated by four political groups: the Gaullists; an independent center-right coalition; the Socialists; and the Communists.

The Gaullist party, called the Rally for the Republic (Rassemblement pour la République—RPR) was founded by the current president Jacques Chirac in 1976. In the same year, the centrist parties formed the Union for French Democracy (Union pour la Démocratie Française—UDF).

15 JUDICIAL SYSTEM

There are two types of lower judicial courts in France, the civil courts and the criminal courts. The function of the civil courts is to judge conflicts arising between persons. The function of the criminal courts is to judge violations against the law. The most serious crimes, for which the penalties may range to life imprisonment, are tried in assize courts. Special administrative courts deal with disputes between individuals and government agencies.

From the lower courts, appeals may be taken to appeals courts. Judgments of the appeals courts are final, except that appeals on the interpretation of the may be taken to the highest of the judicial courts, the Court of Cassation in Paris.

The Conseil Constitutionnel rules on whether or not laws are constitutional. The death penalty was abolished in 1981.

16 ARMED FORCES

All French males between the ages of 18 and 45 must perform 10 months of national service. The annual draft intake is around 200,000 a year. Women may volunteer, and 14,000 now serve.

In 1993 there were 431,700 regular personnel in the armed services, including 260,900 in the army, 91,700 in the air force, 64,900 in the navy, 94,600 in the Gendarmerie Nationale, and 14,000 in various other service organizations. Reserves totaled 904,700, including 770,200 army reserves. About one-third of the reserve force is able to be mobilized. In 1992 the military budget was $35 billion.

France's Force Action Rapide (47,300) is an elite five-division force designed for rapid air deployment anywhere in the world. The French army uses weapons and equipment of French manufacture.

France began building its own independent nuclear force during the de Gaulle era and has conducted a number of atmospheric nuclear tests. France maintains substantial forces abroad. It has a composite air squadron in Turkey and almost 6,000 troops deployed on peacekeeping missions to seven different countries, including Croatia.

France is one of the world's leading makers and sellers of armaments, including the Mirage aircraft, Super Étendard fighter-bombers, and Exocet missiles, tanks, and armored vehicles. During 1981–91, French arms exports had a value of around $40 billion.

17 ECONOMY

France is one of the most richly endowed countries of Europe. The favorable climate, extensive areas of rich soil, and long-established tradition of skilled agriculture have created ideal conditions for a thriving farm economy. Large deposits of iron ore, a well-integrated network of power plants, important domestic reserves of natural gas, good transport, and high standards of industrial workmanship have made French industry one of the most modern in Europe.

18 INCOME

In 1992, France's gross national product (GNP) was $1,278,652 million at current prices, or $22,490 per person. For the period 1985–92 the average inflation rate

A vineyard in southern France near the town of Apt.

million tons of crude steel and 12.8 million tons of pig iron. French plants produced 471,800 tons of aluminum.

The French automotive industry, which employed 356,200 workers in 1991, is one of the largest in the world. Some 3,190,000 automobiles were produced in 1991. The French aircraft industry specializes in advanced design and experimental development. Some of its models, such as the Caravelle and the Mirage IV, have been used in over 50 countries.

Chemicals, one of the fastest-growing industries in France, range from perfumes and cosmetics to such industrial materials as sulfuric acid. In 1991, 2,549,000 television sets and 1,865,000 radios were produced. Refineries produced 82.1 million tons of petroleum products in 1991.

Production of textiles (in thousands of tons) in 1991 included cotton yarn, 153,800; wool yarn, 20,200; and synthetic fibers, 496,100. In 1991, France produced 62 million hectoliters of wine, more than any other country.

was 3.1%, resulting in a real growth rate in GNP of 2.2% per person.

19 INDUSTRY

Industry has expanded considerably since World War II, with major progress in the electronics, transport, processing, and construction industries. France is the fourth-leading industrial power, after the United States, Japan, and Germany. In 1992, industry accounted for more than 31% of the labor force and over four-fifths of all exports.

The steel industry suffered from the impact of worldwide recession in the early 1980s. In 1991, production included 18.5

20 LABOR

Of the resident employed population, as of 31 December 1992, 66.4% were employed in trade, transportation, and services, 28.5% in industry, and 5.1% in agriculture.

In January 1982, a 39-hour workweek and a fifth week of paid vacation were introduced. The labor code and other laws provide for work, safety, and health standards. In 1992, there were 1,330 localized strikes involving 16,300 workers.

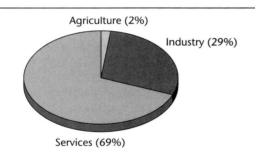

Agriculture (2%)

Industry (29%)

Services (69%)

Components of the economy. This pie chart shows how much of the country's economy is devoted to agriculture (includes forestry, hunting, and fishing), industry, or services.

21 AGRICULTURE

Agriculture, which accounts for about 2% of the gross domestic product, employs about 7% of the labor force. Since the early 1970s, the agricultural labor force has diminished by about 60%. France is the only country in Europe to supply all its own basic food needs. The high quality of the nation's agricultural products contributes to the excellence of its famous cooking.

Among agricultural products, food grains (wheat, barley, oats, corn, and sorghum), industrial crops (sugar beets, flax), root crops (potatoes), and wine are by far the most important. In 1992, the wheat crop totaled 32,600,000 tons and barley, 10,474,000 tons. Other totals (in tons) included oats, 690,000; corn, 14,613,000; sugar beets, 31,334,000; and potatoes, 6,495,000.

Wine production in 1992 came from 6,522,000 tons of crushed grapes (23% of world production). There is large-scale production of fruits, chiefly apples, pears, peaches, and cherries. In 1991, France led the world in wine production, and ranked fifth in the production of wheat and eighth in corn production.

22 DOMESTICATED ANIMALS

In 1992, farm animals included 20,928,000 head of cattle, 10,579,000 sheep, 12,384,000 hogs, 1,221,000 goats, and 340,000 horses. Poultry and rabbits are raised in large numbers, both for farm families and for city markets. Meat production in 1992 included 1,780,000 tons of beef, 1,960,000 tons of pork, and 1,664,000 tons of poultry. In 1991, France ranked thirteenth in beef and veal production in the world.

Dairy farming prospers in the rich grasslands of Normandy. Total cows' milk production in 1992 was 25,341,000 tons. France produces some 300 kinds of cheese. In 1992, cheese production totaled about 1,522,700 tons. Butter production was 470,000 tons.

23 FISHING

France's 3,427 kilometers (2,125 miles) of coastline, dotted with numerous small harbors, have long supported a flourishing coastal and high-seas fishing industry. Total production in 1991 was 812,773 tons, including about 158,000 tons of oysters. Herring, skate, whiting, sole, mackerel, tuna, sardines, lobsters, and mussels make up the principal seafood catch, along with large quantities of cod.

24 FORESTRY

Although many of the original trees were cut in the course of centuries, strict forest management practices and sizable reforestation projects during the last 100 years have restored French forests considerably. Since 1947, the government has subsidized the planting of 2.1 million hectares (5.2 million acres) of forest land.

About 66% of the forestland is covered with oak, beech, and poplar and 34% with resinous trees. There were some 14.8 million hectares (36.5 million acres) of forest in 1991. Production of roundwood in 1991 was 44.7 million cubic meters.

25 MINING

France is among the world's leading producers of coal. It also has sizable deposits of iron ore, antimony, bauxite, magnesium, pyrites, tungsten, and certain radioactive minerals. However, production of some of these resources has declined significantly. France is self-sufficient in salt, potash, and fluorspar. Reserves of lead and zinc are limited. In 1991, France was the fifth largest producer of uranium, at 2,907 metric tons. Due to low market prices, several uranium mines have recently been closed.

Coal production (including lignite) decreased from a post–World War II high of over 60 million tons in 1958 to 12.3 million tons in 1991. Iron ore production fell from 49.7 million tons in 1975 to 29 million tons in 1980 and 7.4 million tons by 1991. France is also a leading producer of bauxite (a mineral named after Les Baux, in the south of France), but produc-

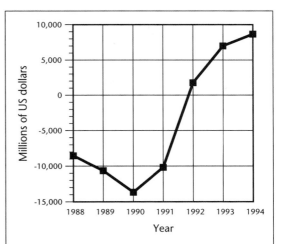

Yearly balance of trade measured in millions of US dollars. The balance of trade is the difference between what a country sells to other countries (its exports) and what it buys (its imports). If a country imports more than it exports, it has a negative balance of trade (a trade deficit). If exports exceed imports there is a positive balance of trade (a trade surplus).

tion declined from 3.3 million tons in 1973 to 400,000 tons in 1991.

26 FOREIGN TRADE

Leading French exports, by major categories, are capital goods (machinery, heavy electrical equipment, transport equipment, and aircraft), consumer goods (autos, textiles, and leather), and semifinished products (mainly chemicals, iron, and steel). Major imports are fuels, machinery and equipment, chemicals and paper goods, and consumer goods.

Germany continues to be France's most important trading partner, accounting for 18.7% of imports and 17.6% of exports in 1992. Other major trading partners are

Italy, Belgium-Luxembourg, and the United Kingdom.

27 ENERGY AND POWER

Petroleum production in 1991 totaled 2.8 million tons, while consumption totaled 94.6 million tons. Production of natural gas in southwestern France totaled 4 million cubic meters in 1991, meeting only a small fraction of domestic requirements.

Primary energy sources in 1991 were oil, which provided 35% of France's power; coal, 9%; natural gas, 13%; nuclear fuels and hydroelectric power, 39%; and other sources (including solar power), 4%. Although France lost ownership of its Saharan oil and natural gas deposits after Algerian independence, arrangements were made with the Algerian government to keep up the flow of oil to France. France now receives most of its liquefied natural gas from Algeria.

The burden of alternatives to fossil fuel falls mainly on nuclear power. A tidal power plant has also been in operation in Brittany since 1967, and the world's first solar furnace was built in 1969. Since 1914, Paris has been burning its garbage to provide heat. By 1981, trash burning was supplying over 30% of the city's heating needs.

Atomic energy is controlled by the state. In 1991, net installed power capacity of nuclear plants amounted to 59.1 million kilowatts. Of the total power production in 1991, 13.3% was produced by conventional thermal means, 13.9% by hydroelectric stations, and 72.8% by nuclear power plants. France was ranked second in 1991, behind the United States, among producers of nuclear power, at 315 billion kilowatt hours.

28 SOCIAL DEVELOPMENT

By the early 1980s, virtually every person living in France was covered by some form of social assistance. As of 1988, France was tenth in the world in percentage of its budget spent on social security and housing (10%).

In addition to providing for the partial reimbursement of medical, pharmaceutical, and hospitalization expenses, health insurance guarantees the payment of cash benefits as partial compensation for loss of earnings during the period of disability. Maternity insurance provides for the payment of pharmaceutical, medical, surgical, and hospitalization expenses incurred during pregnancy, confinement, and postnatal treatment, as well as other benefits.

Unemployed workers receive daily payments not limited in time but reduced by 10% each consecutive year. Disability insurance pays a pension to compensate for the loss of earnings and costs of care. Old age insurance guarantees payment of a pension when the insured reaches age 65, provided his or her contributions have been sufficient. Death insurance provides payment of a lump sum to the dependents of the insured.

Monthly benefits are paid to employed heads of families having at least two dependent children. Maternity and prenatal allowances are also paid. The growth of the feminist movement in the 1970s led to the creation in 1974 of a special cabinet

Selected Social Indicators

These statistics are estimates for the period 1988 to 1993. For comparison purposes, data for the United States and averages for low-income countries and high-income countries are also given.

Indicator	France	Low-income countries	High-income countries	United States
Per capita gross national product†	$22,490	$380	$23,680	$24,740
Population growth rate	0.4%	1.9%	0.6%	1.0%
Population growth rate in urban areas	0.5%	3.9%	0.8%	1.3%
Population per square kilometer of land	104	78	25	26
Life expectancy in years	77	62	77	76
Number of people per physician	461	>3,300	453	419
Number of pupils per teacher (primary school)	12	39	<18	20
Illiteracy rate (15 years and older)	<1%	41%	<5%	<3%
Energy consumed per capita (kg of oil equivalent)	4,031	364	5,203	7,918

† The gross national product (GNP) is the total dollar value of all goods and services produced by a country in a year. The per capita GNP is calculated by dividing a country's GNP by its population. The World Bank defines low-income countries as those with a per capita GNP of $695 or less. High-income countries have a per capita GNP of $8,626 or more. Less than 14% of the world's 5.5 billion people live in high-income countries, while almost 60% live in low-income countries.

> = greater than   < = less than

Sources: World Bank, *Social Indicators of Development 1995,* Baltimore: Johns Hopkins University Press, 1995. Central Intelligence Agency, *World Fact Book,* Washington, D.C.: Government Printing Office, 1994.

office for women's rights. In 1992, the Penal Code was revised to include provisions stipulating up to one year in prison and up to the equivalent of $20,000 in fines for workplace sexual harassment.

29 HEALTH

Patients have the option of seeing a private doctor on a fee basis or going to a state-operated facility. During the 1980s, there was a trend away from inpatient and toward outpatient care, with a growing number of patients receiving care at home.

In 1993, the population per physician was 461. There are over 1,000 public hospitals and 2,700 private hospitals. There are also about 11,000 infants' and children's facilities of various kinds.

Life expectancy in 1992 averaged 77 years for men and women. From 1985 to 1990, major causes of death were: noncommunicable diseases (362 per 100,000); and injuries (76 per 100,000).

30 HOUSING

In 1984 there were over 24,249,000 housing units in France. By 1991, the total number of housing units had risen to 26,080,000. More than six million new dwellings were completed between 1970 and 1986. In 1992 the total number of new dwellings completed was 248,400.

Living standards are high. About 97% of all French households have a refrigerator, over 90% a television set, 84% a washing machine, 73% an automobile, 35% a freezer, and 23% a dishwasher.

31 EDUCATION

Education is compulsory for children from the age of 6 to 16 and is free in all state primary and secondary schools. Higher education is not free, but academic fees are low, and more than half of the students are excused from payment. Practically the entire adult population is literate.

Freedom of education is guaranteed by law, but the state exercises certain controls over private schools, nearly all of which follow a curriculum prescribed by the Ministry of Education. In 1993, there were 6,610,046 pupils in primary schools (ages 6–11); 3,336,599 in secondary schools; and 2,230,512 in high schools. Choice of a lycée (or secondary school) depends on aptitude test results.

University enrollment was 1,756,918 in 1991. There are 70 public universities within 26 académies, which now act as administrative units. The former University of Paris, also referred to as the Sorbonne, was the oldest in France and one of the leading institutions of higher learning in the world. It is now divided into 13 units, only a few of which are at the ancient Left Bank site.

32 MEDIA

Under new government policies, many private radio stations have been established since the 1980s. In 1991 there were about 50.6 million radio receivers. In 1991, television sets numbered about 23.2 million, and there were 34,345,980 telephones.

The number of newspapers has consistently declined in the postwar period. In 1991, there were 96 dailies in the country, and total circulation amounted to 9.3 million copies. The leading Paris newspapers with their estimated average daily circulation in 1991 are: *Le Figaro* (433,500); *Le Monde* (382,000); *Le Parisien* (365,660); *Le Parisien Libéré* (365,660); and *France-Soir* (334,000).

There are some 14,000 periodicals, of which the most widely read is the illustrated *Paris-Match,* with a weekly circulation of about 900,000. Several magazines for women also enjoy wide popularity, including *Elle*, (1991 circulation 360,000).

33 TOURISM AND RECREATION

In 1991, France was the world's top tourist destination with an estimated 54.8 million overnight visitors, 49.8 million of them from other European countries. Receipts from tourism amounted to $21.3 billion.

France has countless tourist attractions, ranging from the museums and monuments of Paris (including the splendid Eiffel Tower, newly renovated with glass elevators) to beaches of the southeast and ski slopes in the Alps. There are more than 547,292 rooms with over one million beds in lodgings ranging from small country inns to deluxe châteaus.

Sophisticated dining, hearty regional specialties, and an extraordinary variety of fine wines attract food and wine lovers the world over. The area between the Rhône River and the Pyrenees contains the largest single stretch of vineyards in the world. In 1992 Euro Disneyland, 20 miles east of Paris, opened with great fanfare.

The most popular French sport is soccer (commonly called "le foot"). Other favorite sports are skiing, tennis, water sports, and bicycling. Paris hosted the Winter Olympics in Albertville in 1992. Le Mans is the site of a world-class auto race.

34 FAMOUS FRENCH

Principal figures of early French history include Charlemagne (742–814), who was crowned emperor of the West on 25 December 800; and William II, Duke of Normandy (1027–87), later William I of England ("the Conqueror," r.1066–87). Joan of Arc (Jeanne d'Arc, 1412–31) was the first to have a vision of France as a single nation. She died a martyr and became a saint and a national heroine.

Henry IV (Henry of Navarre, 1553–1610) proclaimed the Edict of Nantes in 1598, granting religious freedom to his Protestant subjects.

The era of Louis XIV ("le Roi Soleil," or "the Sun King," 1638–1715) was in many respects the golden age of France. Famous literature of the period includes the dramas of Pierre Corneille (1606–84), Molière (Jean-Baptiste Poquelin, 1622–73), and Jean Racine (1639–99). Two

Photo credit: Corel Corporation.

Venus De Milo.

leading French philosophers and mathematicians of the period, René Descartes (1596–1650) and Blaise Pascal (1623–62), left their mark on the whole of European thought.

1700–1900

During the 18th century, France again was a leader in many fields. Jean-Jacques Rousseau (b.Switzerland, 1712–78) was a famous philosopher. In literature, the towering figure was Voltaire (François Marie Arouet, 1694–1778).

The rule of Louis XVI (1754–93) and his queen, Marie Antoinette (1755–93), and the social order they represented, ended with the French Revolution. Outstanding figures of the Revolution included Jean-Paul Marat (1743–93), Maximilien Marie Isidore Robespierre (1758–94), and Georges Jacques Danton (1759–94). Napoleon Bonaparte (1769–1821), a military leader in the Revolution, later became emperor of France.

During the 19th century, French science, literature, and art all but dominated the European scene. Louis Jacques Mendé Daguerre (1789–1851) was the inventor of photography. Other scientists included the zoologist Jean-Baptiste Lamarck (1744–1829) and chemist Louis Pasteur (1822–95). Louis Braille (1809–52) invented the method of writing books for the blind that bears his name. Literary figures included the fiction writers Honoré de Balzac (1799–1850) and Victor Marie Hugo (1802–85). Louis Hector Berlioz (1803–69) was the greatest figure in 19th-century French music. Georges Bizet (1838–75) is renowned for his opera *Carmen*.

In painting, the 19th century produced the impressionists and postimpressionists Camille Pissarro (1830–1903), Édouard Manet (1832–83), Hilaire Germain Edgar Degas (1834–1917), Paul Cézanne (1839–1906), Claude Monet (1840–1926), Pierre Auguste Renoir (1841–1919), Paul Gauguin (1848–1903), Georges Seurat (1859–91), and Henri de Toulouse-Lautrec (1864–1901). Auguste Rodin (1840–1917) was the foremost sculptor.

The Twentieth Century

Albert Schweitzer (1875–1965), musician, philosopher, physician, and humanist, a native of Alsace, received the Nobel Peace Prize in 1952. Famous scientists include the chemist and physicist Pierre Curie (1859–1906) and his wife, Polish-born Marie Sklodowska Curie (1867–1934), who shared the 1903 Nobel Prize for physics with her husband and won a Nobel Prize again, for chemistry, in 1911.

Significant composers include Claude Achille Debussy (1862–1918), Maurice Ravel (1875–1937), Olivier Messiaen (b.1908), and composer-conductor Pierre Boulez (b.1925). The painters Henri Matisse (1869–1954), Spanish-born Pablo Picasso (1881–1973), and Russian-born Marc Chagall (1887–1985) are world famous.

35 BIBLIOGRAPHY

Agulhon, Maurice. *The French Republic, 1879–1992.* Oxford, UK; Cambridge, Mass.: B. Blackwell, 1993.

Aplin, Richard. *A Dictionary of Contemporary France.* London: Hodder & Stoughton, 1993.

Ardagh, John. *Cultural Atlas of France.* New York, NY: Facts on File, 1991.

Chambers, Frances. *France.* Denver, Colo.: Clio Press, 1990.

Cook, Malcolm ed. *French Culture Since 1945.* New York: Longman, 1993.

Corbett, James. *Through French Windows: an Introduction to France in the Nineties.* Ann Arbor, Mich.: University of Michigan Press, 1994.

Gough, Hugh and John Horne. *De Gaulle and Twentieth-century France.* New York: Edward Arnold, 1994.

Morrison, M. *French Guiana.* Chicago: Children's Press, 1994.

Nagel, Rob, and Anne Commire. "Joan of Arc." In *World Leaders, People Who Shaped the World.* Volume II: Europe. Detroit: U*X*L, 1994.

Winchester, Hilary P. M. *Contemporary France.* New York: J. Wiley & Sons, 1993.

GABON

Gabonese Republic
République Gabonaise

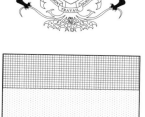

CAPITAL: Libreville.

FLAG: The flag is a tricolor of green, golden yellow, and royal blue horizontal stripes.

ANTHEM: *La Concorde (Harmony)*.

MONETARY UNIT: The Communauté Financière Africaine franc (CFA Fr) is a paper currency. There are coins of 1, 2, 5, 10, 25, 50, 100, and 500 CFA francs, and notes of 50, 100, 500, 1,000, 5,000, and 10,000 CFA francs. CFA Fr1 = $0.0018 (or $1 = CFA Fr571).

WEIGHTS AND MEASURES: The metric system is the legal standard.

HOLIDAYS: New Year's Day, 1 January; Day of Renewal, 12 March; Labor Day, 1 May; Africa Freedom Day, 25 May; Assumption, 15 August; Independence Day, 17 August; All Saints' Day, 1 November; Christmas, 25 December. Movable religious holidays include Easter Monday, Ascension, Pentecost Monday, 'Id al-Fitr, and 'Id al-'Adha'.

TIME: 1 PM = noon GMT.

1 LOCATION AND SIZE

Situated on the west coast of Africa and centered on the Equator, Gabon has an area of 267,670 square kilometers (103,348 square miles), extending 717 kilometers (446 miles) north-northeast to south-southwest and 644 kilometers (400 miles) east southeast to west northwest. Comparatively, the area occupied by Gabon is slightly smaller than the state of Colorado. Gabon's capital city, Libreville, is located on the country's northwestern coast.

2 TOPOGRAPHY

A steep slope rising from the coastal lowlands covers the north and east and most of the south. There are mountains in various parts of Gabon, the highest peak being Mt. Iboundji (1,575 meters/5,167 feet).

Almost the entire territory is contained in the basin of the Ogooué River, which is about 1,100 kilometers (690 miles) long.

3 CLIMATE

Gabon has the moist, hot climate typical of tropical regions. The hottest month is January, with an average high at Libreville of 31°C (88°F) and an average low of 23°C (73°F). From June to September there is almost no rain but high humidity. There is occasional rain in December and January. During the remaining months, rainfall is heavy.

4 PLANTS AND ANIMALS

About 85% of the country is covered by heavy rain forest, with trees towering as high as 60 meters (200 feet) and more than 3,000 species of plants. In the coastal regions, marine plants abound, and wide areas are covered with tall papyrus grass. Most tropical fauna species are found in Gabon. Wildlife includes elephants, buffalo, antelope, situtungas, lions, panthers, crocodiles, and gorillas.

5 ENVIRONMENT

Gabon's environmental problems include deforestation, pollution and wildlife preservation. The forests that cover 85% of the country are threatened by excessive logging activities. Pollution of the land is a problem in Gabon's growing urban centers due to industrial and domestic contaminants. The nation's water is affected by pollutants from the oil industry. The expansion of Gabon's urban population is accompanied by a greater demand for meat. As a result, the nation's wildlife suffers from poaching.

6 POPULATION

The population of Gabon was estimated at 1,375,000 in 1995 by the United Nations. This figure, however, was far higher than the US Census Bureau estimate of 1,126,808 for 1994. Most of the people live on the coast or are concentrated along rivers and roads. Large areas of the interior are sparsely inhabited. Libreville, the capital and principal city, had about 289,000 inhabitants in 1990.

7 MIGRATION

Because of its limited population and booming economy, Gabon relies heavily on laborers from other African nations, including Benin, Cameroon, Equatorial Guinea, Mali, and Senegal. About 100,000–200,000 non-Gabonese Africans are believed to be in Gabon, many of them from Equatorial Guinea or Cameroon. About 122,000 Gabonese live abroad, according to a 1981 government paper.

8 ETHNIC GROUPS

There are at least 40 distinct tribal groups in Gabon, of which the largest is the Fang (about 30% of the population). The Mbédé, Eshira, Bapounou, Batéké, and Bakèlè are other major groups.

9 LANGUAGES

French is the official language of the republic. The Fang language is spoken in the north, and other Bantu languages are spoken elsewhere in the country.

10 RELIGIONS

Christians in Gabon number perhaps 60% of the total population, with 52.7% of the country being Roman Catholic in 1993. There are about 10,000 Muslims. Much of the population practices traditional African religions, both exclusively and in addition to Christianity.

11 TRANSPORTATION

The second stage of the Trans-Gabon Railway, completed in December 1986, links Booué with Franceville (357 kilometers/222 miles) via Moanda, thus allowing exports of manganese from the southeast and forestry exploitation in the same region. Main roads connect virtually all major communities. In 1991, the road network totaled 7,500 kilometers (4,660 miles). In 1991 there were about 23,000 automobiles and 17,000 commercial vehicles in use.

The busiest ports are Port-Gentil, the center for exports of petroleum products and imports of mining equipment, and Owendo, which has timber-handling facilities. Gabon has three international airports—at Libreville, Port-Gentil, and Franceville. Traffic handled in 1991 at the Léon Mba airport at Libreville came to 611,000 passengers and about 10,900 tons of freight.

12 HISTORY

Bantu peoples began to migrate to what is now Gabon from Cameroon and eastern Nigeria at least 2,000 years ago. The Portuguese sighted the coast as early as 1470 and gave Gabon its name because the shape of the Rio de Como estuary reminded them of a "gabao," a Portuguese hooded cloak. After the Portuguese, the region was visited by the English, Dutch, and French. During the seventeenth century, the great French trading companies entered the slave trade. French Jesuit missionaries were active along the coast during this period, and their influence eventually extended to the powerful native kingdoms inland.

In 1839, the French signed a treaty with Denis, the African king whose authority extended over the northern Gabon coast. The treaty granted the kingdom to France in return for French protection. A similar treaty gained much of the southern coast below the Ogooué. Gradually, other coastal chiefs accepted French control. The present capital, Libreville ("place of freedom"), was founded in 1849 by slaves who had been freed from a contraband-slave runner.

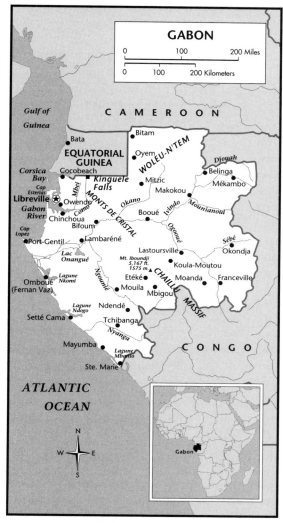

LOCATION: 2°19′N to 3°55′S; 9°18′ to 14°32′E. **BOUNDARY LENGTHS:** Cameroon, 302 kilometers (188 miles); Congo, 1,656 kilometers (1,029 miles); Atlantic coastline, 739 kilometers (459 miles); Equatorial Guinea, 386 kilometers (240 miles). **TERRITORIAL SEA LIMIT:** 12 miles.

French explorers gradually penetrated the interior after 1847, and in 1890 Gabon formally became a part of French Congo. In 1910 it was organized as a separate colony, part of French Equatorial Africa.

On 28 September 1958, the territory of Gabon voted to become a self-governing republic within the French Community. Independence was formally proclaimed on 17 August 1960, and on 12 February 1961, Léon Mba was elected president of the republic, heading a government of national union in which Jean-Hilaire Aubame served as foreign minister. Friction developed between Mba and Aubame, however, and after several years of political maneuvering, Aubame led a successful takeover on 18 February 1964. Mba was reinstated on the very next day through French military intervention, as provided for by a treaty signed between the Mba government and the French in 1960.

Mba created the post of vice-president in February 1967, and at his death on 28 November of that year, power was transferred peacefully to his vice-president, Albert-Bernard Bongo. On 12 March 1968, Bongo announced the formal institution of a one-party system and the creation of the Gabon Democratic Party (PDG) as the country's sole legal political organization. He was reelected without opposition in 1973, 1979, and 1986. (It was announced in 1973 that Bongo had taken the name of Omar and converted to Islam.)

However, depressed oil prices in the late 1980s damaged the economy and caused unrest among the population. After months of prodemocracy rallies and strikes, Bongo ended 22 years of one-party rule in 1990. In January 1991, the Assembly passed by unanimous vote a law legalizing opposition parties. On 5 December 1993, multiparty presidential elections confirmed Bongo, running as an independent, as president with 51% of the vote, against Paul Mba Abessole. Opposition parties protested the result, and Abessole announced the formation of a rival government, dedicated to new presidential elections, restoring peace, and maintaining national unity.

13 GOVERNMENT

In March–April 1990, a national political conference discussed the political system. The conference approved sweeping reforms, including the creation of a national senate, decentralization of the budgetary process, and freedom of assembly and press.

A new constitution came into force in March 1991. It provided for a basic bill of rights and an independent judiciary, but retained a strong presidency. However, opposition parties set up a rival government after losing in the 1993 presidential elections.

14 POLITICAL PARTIES

On 12 March 1968, the Democratic Party of Gabon (Parti Démocratique Gabonais—PDG), headed by Albert-Bernard Bongo, became the sole political party. The Movement for National Reform (Mouvement de Redressement National—MORENA), an opposition group, emerged in 1981 and formed a government in exile in 1985. Emerging since the legalization of opposition party activity in

Photo credit: AP/Wide World Photos

Residents of Libreville, Gabon stand in front of a chicken restaurant. American businesses have replaced many long established French-run stores.

March 1991 are the Association for Socialism in Gabon (APSG), the Gabonese Socialist Union (USG), the Circle for Renewal and Progress (CRP), and the Union for Democracy and Development (UDD).

15 JUDICIAL SYSTEM

The civil court system consists of three tiers: the trial court, the appellate court, and the Supreme Court. The 1991 constitution, which established many basic freedoms and fundamental rights, also created a Constitutional Court, a body which considers only constitutional issues.

16 ARMED FORCES

In 1993, Gabon had an army of 3,250 personnel; a navy of 500, with 7 vessels; and an air force of 1,000, with 20 combat aircraft and 7 armed helicopters. Paramilitary forces of coast guards and police totaled 4,800. France maintains a battalion of 500 marines in Gabon.

17 ECONOMY

Rich in resources, Gabon is a country that, for a period of 15 years, realized a growth rate of 9.5% before succumbing to oil-price instability and the laws of international borrowing. Gabon is not self-sufficient in food although 75.5% of its

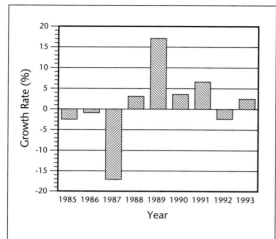

Yearly growth rate of the economy. This economic indicator tells by what percent the economy has increased or decreased when compared with the previous year.

period 1985–92 the average inflation rate was 1.6%, resulting in a real growth rate in GNP of −2.1% per person.

19 INDUSTRY

Gabon's industry is centered on petroleum, mining, and timber processing. Timber-related concerns include five veneer plants and one of the world's largest plywood factories (capacity 85,000 cubic meters), located in Port-Gentil. In 1984, Gabon produced an estimated 97,000 cubic meters of veneers and 74,800 cubic meters of plywood. Other industries include textile plants, cement factories, breweries, shipyards, and cigarette factories. Industrial output in 1985 included 244,678 tons of cement and 1,216,893 hectoliters of beer.

20 LABOR

Owing to a domestic labor shortage, Gabon employed migrant workers (especially from Burkina Faso) to complete the Trans-Gabon Railway. In 1992 there were 87,000 persons in the labor force, down from 105,000 in 1990. Since the 1990 National Conference, many small company-based unions have been started, resulting in sporadic and often disruptive strikes.

21 AGRICULTURE

Since independence, the dominant position of the petroleum sector has greatly reduced the role of agriculture. Gabon relies heavily on other African states and Europe for much of its food and other agricultural needs. There has been an intensive effort to diversify and increase

population (mid-1980s) gain their livelihood in the agricultural sector, where the staple food crops are cassava, plantains, and yams. The coffee sector has been hard hit in recent years by low world prices and lower producer prices. Rubber production has been promoted in recent years, and Gabon now has four rubber plantations.

In the face of dramatically rising prices following France's devaluation of the CFA franc, uncertainty and anger led petroleum workers to strike for a doubling of their wages. France has said it will nearly halve Gabon's debt, a move that has encouraged the international financial community.

18 INCOME

In 1992 Gabon's gross national product (GNP) was $5,341 million at current prices, or $4,960 per person. For the

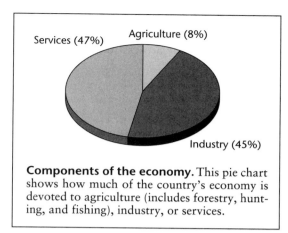

Components of the economy. This pie chart shows how much of the country's economy is devoted to agriculture (includes forestry, hunting, and fishing), industry, or services.

agricultural production. However, agriculture received low priority until the 1976–81 development plan, and laborers prefer to seek employment in urban areas.

In 1992, Gabon produced about 260,000 tons of cassava, 115,000 tons of yams, 72,000 tons of other roots and tubers, 245,000 tons of plantains, 31,000 tons of vegetables, and 24,000 tons of corn. Sugarcane production was about 160,000 tons. Cocoa is the most important cash crop. Cocoa production in 1992 was 2,000 tons. Coffee production totaled 2,000 tons in 1992.

22 DOMESTICATED ANIMALS

Animal farming is limited by the presence of the tsetse fly, though tsetse-resistant cattle have recently been imported from Senegal. In 1992 there were an estimated 164,000 hogs, 252,000 sheep and goats, 29,000 head of cattle, and 2 million chickens. Poultry production satisfies about one-half of Gabon's consumption demand. Typical annual production of poultry amounts to 3,000 tons.

23 FISHING

While there have been recent improvements in the fishing industry, it is still relatively undeveloped. Traditional fishing accounts for two-thirds of total catch. The waters off the Gabonese coast contain large quantities of fish. Gabonese waters are estimated to be able to support an annual catch of 15,000 tons of tuna and 12,000 tons of sardines. The total catch in 1991 was 22,000 tons, almost all from the Atlantic.

24 FORESTRY

Gabon is the largest exporter of raw wood in the region. Its forests contain over 400 species of trees, with about 100 species suitable for industrial use. Gabon supplies 90% of the world's okoumé, which makes excellent plywood, and also produces hardwoods, such as mahogany, kevazingo, and ebony. Other woods are dibetou (tigerwood or African walnut), movingui (Nigerian satinwood), and zingana (zebrano or zebrawood). Roundwood removals were estimated at 4,286,000 cubic meters in 1991, of which 1,633,000 were industrial wood and 2,653,000 fuel wood. Reforestation has been continuously promoted, and selective thinning and clearing have prevented the okoumé from being forced out by other species.

25 MINING

Gabon is the richest of the former French Equatorial African colonies in known mineral deposits. Oil, potash, uranium, manganese, iron, lead, zinc, diamonds, marble, and phosphate have been discov-

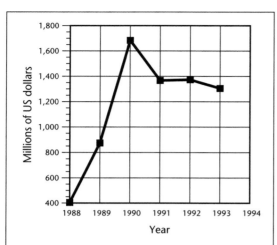

Yearly balance of trade measured in millions of US dollars. The balance of trade is the difference between what a country sells to other countries (its exports) and what it buys (its imports). If a country imports more than it exports, it has a negative balance of trade (a trade deficit). If exports exceed imports there is a positive balance of trade (a trade surplus).

ered, and several deposits are being exploited commercially.

After petroleum, manganese is Gabon's second most important mineral product. The country is the world's fourth leading producer of manganese.

Gold deposits in the Etéké region of southern Gabon yielded 50 kilograms in 1991. The Mékambo and Belinga iron fields in the northeastern corner of Gabon are ranked among the world's richest.

26 FOREIGN TRADE

Gabon has a record of trade surpluses. Forestry is second only to the petroleum sector in export earnings, at 8.8% of total exports. Crude petroleum accounted for 65% of total exports in 1986. Gabon is also a leading exporter of manganese. In 1992, agricultural imports by Gabon accounted for nearly 14% of all imports.

France is Gabon's leading trade partner, accounting for 42.7% of exports, 53.1% of imports, and 49.6% of total trade. Trade with other European Community members made up 19.7% of Gabon's total trade. The United States was Gabon's second leading export customer, taking in 16.9% of exports. Other major trade partners included Spain, the United Kingdom, Italy, Germany, and Japan.

27 ENERGY AND POWER

Gabon's proven petroleum reserves were estimated at 172 million tons in 1973, but by 1992 had fallen to an estimated 100 million tons. Total production of crude oil rose to 10,600,000 tons in 1989 and 14,700,000 tons in 1992. Natural gas reserves had dwindled to an estimated 11.3 billion cubic meters by 1993.

In 1991 there were hydroelectric stations at the Kinguélé and Tchimbélé dams on the Mbei River and at the Petite Poubara Dam on the Ogooué. Thermal installations numbered 24. Production increased from 114 million kilowatt hours in 1971 to 914 million kilowatt hours (77% hydroelectric) in 1991.

28 SOCIAL DEVELOPMENT

Family allowances are paid to all salaried workers. Other benefits include workers' compensation, old age insurance, medicine and hospitalization, and housing assis-

Selected Social Indicators

These statistics are estimates for the period 1988 to 1993. For comparison purposes, data for the United States and averages for low-income countries and high-income countries are also given.

Indicator	Gabon	Low-income countries	High-income countries	United States
Per capita gross national product†	**$4,960**	$380	$23,680	$24,740
Population growth rate	**1.7%**	1.9%	0.6%	1.0%
Population growth rate in urban areas	**3.5%**	3.9%	0.8%	1.3%
Population per square kilometer of land	**4**	78	25	26
Life expectancy in years	**54**	62	77	76
Number of people per physician	**4,279**	>3,300	453	419
Number of pupils per teacher (primary school)	**44**	39	<18	20
Illiteracy rate (15 years and older)	**39%**	41%	<5%	<3%
Energy consumed per capita (kg of oil equivalent)	**953**	364	5,203	7,918

† The gross national product (GNP) is the total dollar value of all goods and services produced by a country in a year. The per capita GNP is calculated by dividing a country's GNP by its population. The World Bank defines low-income countries as those with a per capita GNP of $695 or less. High-income countries have a per capita GNP of $8,626 or more. Less than 14% of the world's 5.5 billion people live in high-income countries, while almost 60% live in low-income countries.

> = greater than   < = less than

Sources: World Bank, *Social Indicators of Development 1995,* Baltimore: Johns Hopkins University Press, 1995. Central Intelligence Agency, *World Fact Book,* Washington, D.C.: Government Printing Office, 1994.

tance. Contributions are made by employers and employees at a fixed percentage of the employee's wage.

29 HEALTH

Most of the health services are public, but there are some private institutions, of which the best known is the hospital established in 1913 in Lambaréné by Albert Schweitzer.

Gabon's medical system is considered one of the best in West Africa. Records indicate that from 1985 to 1992, 90% of the population had access to health care services. A comprehensive government health program treats such diseases as leprosy, sleeping sickness, malaria, filariasis, intestinal worms, and tuberculosis. Life expectancy is 54 years.

30 HOUSING

Credit institutions make small loans for the repair of existing houses and larger loans (amounting to almost the total cost of the house) for the construction of new houses. The government has established a national habitation fund, and there have been a number of urban renewal projects.

31 EDUCATION

Education is free and compulsory between the ages of 6 and 16. In 1991 there were

1,024 primary schools with 210,000 pupils and 4,782 teachers. At the secondary level, general schools had 42,871 pupils and vocational schools had 8,477 pupils. There is also an adult literacy program. The adult literacy rate was estimated at 61% in 1990. About one-half of all schools are private or church-supported.

Omar Bongo University, at Libreville, includes faculties of law, sciences, and letters. At the university and other equivalent institutions, there were 3,000 students in 1991.

32 MEDIA

Radio-Diffusion Télévision Gabonaise (RTG), which is owned and operated by the government, broadcasts in French and native languages. Color television broadcasts have been introduced in major cities. In 1981, a commercial radio station, Africa No. 1, began operations. The most powerful radio station on the continent, it has participation from the French and Gabonese governments and private European media. In 1991 there were 13,800 telephones, 171,000 radios, and 45,000 television sets.

The national press service is the Gabonese Press Agency, which publishes a daily bulletin. *L'Union* in Libreville is the only daily newspaper. It is government-controlled and had an average daily circulation of 15,000 in 1991.

33 TOURISM AND RECREATION

Gabon's tourist attractions include fine beaches, ocean and inland fishing facilities, and scenic sites. Many visitors come to see the hospital founded by Albert Schweitzer at Lambaréné. In addition, there are two national parks and four wildlife reserves. Tourism facilities are limited. Hotel room capacity in 1990 was about 2,799. In 1991, an estimated 128,000 tourists arrived in Gabon, 76% from Europe and 15% from Africa. Tourism receipts totaled $8 million.

34 FAMOUS GABONESE

The best-known Gabonese are Léon Mba (1902–67), the president of the republic from 1960 to 1967, and Omar Bongo (Albert-Bernard Bongo, b.1935), the president of the republic since Mba's death.

35 BIBLIOGRAPHY

Barnes, James Franklin. *Gabon: Beyond the Colonial Legacy.* Boulder, Colo.: Westview Press, 1992.
Cousins, Norman. *Dr. Schweitzer of Lambaréné.* Westport, Conn.: Greenwood, 1973.
Gardinier, David E. *Gabon.* Santa Barbara, Calif.: Clio Press, 1992.

THE GAMBIA

Republic of the Gambia

CAPITAL: Banjul (formerly Bathurst).

FLAG: The flag is a tricolor of red, blue, and green horizontal bands, separated by narrow white stripes.

ANTHEM: *For the Gambia, Our Homeland.*

MONETARY UNIT: In 1971, the dalasi (D), a paper currency of 100 butut, replaced the Gambian pound. There are coins of 1, 5, 10, 25, and 50 butut and 1 dalasi, and notes of 1, 5, 10, 25, and 50 dalasi. D1 = $0.1031 (or $1 = D9.701).

WEIGHTS AND MEASURES: Both British and metric weights and measures are in use.

HOLIDAYS: New Year's Day, 1 January; Confederation Day, 1 February; Independence Day, 18 February; Labor Day, 1 May; Assumption, 15 August; Christmas, 25 December. Movable religious holidays include Good Friday, Easter Monday, 'Id al-Fitr, 'Id al-'Adha', and Milad an-Nabi.

TIME: GMT.

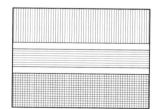

1 LOCATION AND SIZE

Located on the west coast of Africa, the Republic of the Gambia (commonly known as "The Gambia") has an area of 11,300 square kilometers (4,363 square miles), slightly more than twice the size of the state of Delaware.

The Gambia's capital city, Banjul, is located on the Atlantic coast.

2 TOPOGRAPHY

The Gambia River, the country's major waterway, rises in Guinea and flows through the Republic of the Gambia for 470 kilometers (292 miles). The land on either side of the river is generally open savanna, or tropical plains, with wooded areas along the drainage channels.

3 CLIMATE

The Gambia has a subtropical climate with distinct cool and hot seasons. From November to mid-May there is uninterrupted dry weather, with temperatures as low as 16°C (61°F) in Banjul and surrounding areas. Hot, humid weather predominates the rest of the year, with a rainy season from June to October.

4 PLANTS AND ANIMALS

Plants include many flowers, such as yellow cassias and scarlet combretum as well as bougainvillea, oleander, and a dozen varieties of hibiscus. Distinctive animals include several varieties of monkeys.

5 ENVIRONMENT

The Gambia's environmental concerns include deforestation, desertification, and water pollution. Deforestation is the most serious problem, with slash-and-burn agriculture the principal cause. A 30% decrease in rainfall over the last 30 years has increased the rate of desertification for the Gambia's agricultural lands. Water pollution is a significant problem due to lack of adequate sanitation facilities. More and more, the Gambia's wildlife is threatened by changes in their habitat and poaching.

As of 1994, the Gambia's wildlife is threatened by changes in their habitat and poaching. Seven of the nation's 108 mammal species, and one in a total of 489 bird species is threatened. One type of reptile is also endangered.

6 POPULATION

The population of the Gambia at the time of the 1993 census was 1,025,867. The United Nations population projection for the year 2000 was 1,105,000. Banjul, the capital, had about 195,000 residents in 1990. About 75% of the population is rural.

7 MIGRATION

Each year, some 20,000–30,000 migrants from Senegal, Mali, and Guinea come to the Gambia to help harvest the peanut crop. The Gambia was home to 3,300 Senegalese and 300 Liberian refugees at the end of 1992.

8 ETHNIC GROUPS

The Mandingo (Malinké) made up an estimated 42% of the population in 1993. Fulani (16%) predominate in the eastern part of the country. Other major groups

Photo credit: AP/Wide World Photos

A mother and child from a Gambian village.

include the Wolof (15%), Jola (9%), and Serahuli (8%).

9 LANGUAGES

English is the official language, but there are 21 distinct languages spoken throughout the country. The main native languages are Wolof and Mandinka, the latter spoken by the Mandingo.

10 RELIGIONS

About 85% of the population is now Muslim. Christians (3%) are concentrated in the Banjul area. Some Gambians also practice traditional African religions.

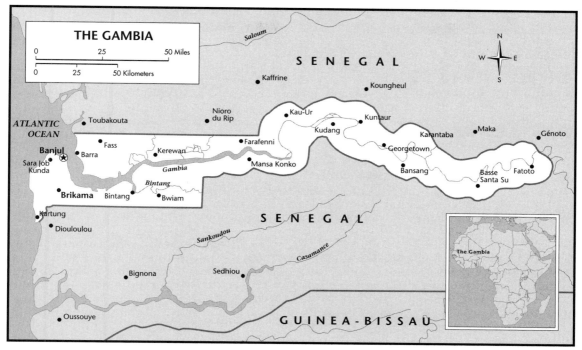

THE GAMBIA

ATLANTIC OCEAN

SENEGAL

SENEGAL

GUINEA-BISSAU

Saloum · Kaffrine · Koungheul · Nioro du Rip · Kau-Ur · Kudang · Kuntaur · Karantaba · Maka · Génoto · Toubakouta · Fass · Kerewan · Farafenni · Georgetown · Mansa Konko · Gambia · Bansang · Basse Santa Su · Fatoto · Banjul · Barra · Sara Job Kunda · Bintang · Brikama · Bintang · Bwiam · Kartung · Diouloulou · Sankoudou · Casamance · Bignona · Sedhiou · Oussouye

The Gambia

LOCATION: 13°10′ to 13°35′36″N; 13°43′5″ to 16°49′31″W. **BOUNDARY LENGTHS:** Senegal, 756 kilometers (470 miles); Atlantic coastline, 71 kilometers (44 miles). **TERRITORIAL SEA LIMIT:** 12 miles.

11 TRANSPORTATION

The Gambia River not only provides important internal transport but also is an international commercial link. Banjul, the principal port, receives about 300 ships annually.

As of 1991 there were 3,083 kilometers (1,916 miles) of roads. About 6,000 passenger cars and 2,500 commercial vehicles were in use.

The Gambia has no railroads. There is an international airport at Yundum, 26 kilometers (16 miles) southwest of Banjul. Air Gambia, 60% state owned, acts as an agent only; foreign air carriers provide international service.

12 HISTORY

A Mali-based Mandingo empire was dominant in the thirteenth and fourteenth centuries. Portuguese sailors discovered the Gambia River in 1455, and in 1587, English merchants began to trade in the area. Between 1765 and 1783, the Gambia formed part of the British colony of Senegambia, with headquarters at Saint-Louis. In 1783, the greater part of Senegambia was handed back to France, and the Gambia section ceased to be a British colony and was returned to the Royal African

Company. In 1888, the Gambia again became a separate British colony

In 1960, universal adult voting was introduced, and a 34-member House of Representatives replaced the Legislative Council. The Gambia attained full internal self-government on 4 October 1963, with Dr. (later Sir) Dawda Kairaba Jawara as prime minister. An independence constitution, which came into force in February 1965, established the Gambia as a constitutional monarchy within the British Commonwealth.

On 23 April 1970, the Gambia became a republic with Jawara as the first president. He and the ruling PPP (People's Progressive Party) remained in power into the 1980s, weathering an attempted left-wing takeover and a rebellion in July 1981. He was reelected in 1982, 1987, and 1992. Jawara was expected to retire in mid-term, but on 22 July, 1994 he was overthrown in a bloodless military takeover led by Lieutenant Yahya Jammeh.

President Jawara took shelter in an American warship which, at the time, had been on a courtesy call. The junta of junior officers and a few civilians suspended the constitution, banned all political activity, detained its superior officers, and placed ministers of the former government under house arrest. The European Union and the United States suspended aid and pressed for a quick return to civilian rule.

13 GOVERNMENT

Under the republican constitution of 24 April 1970, the president, popularly elected for a five-year term, was the head

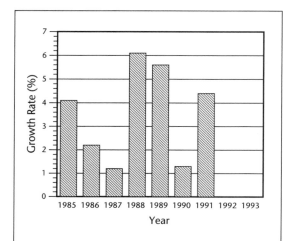

Yearly growth rate of the economy. This economic indicator tells by what percent the economy has increased or decreased when compared with the previous year.

of state. Presidential powers included designating a vice-president, who exercised the functions of a prime minister, and appointing cabinet members. The House of Representatives had 36 members elected by universal adult voting (at age 18). The military government suspended the constitution on 22 July 1994.

14 POLITICAL PARTIES

In April, 1992, The People's Progressive Party (PPP) won 25 seats and the National Convention Party (NCP) won 6. After the 1994 takeover all political parties were banned.

15 JUDICIAL SYSTEM

The Supreme Court, presided over by a chief justice, has both civil and criminal jurisdiction. Appeals from any decision of the Supreme Court go before the Court of Appeals, whose judgments may then be taken to the United Kingdom's Privy Council.

16 ARMED FORCES

The Gambia's armed forces had 800 members in 1993. The 50-member naval patrol had 3 coastal patrol boats. Nigeria provides a 50-man training team, and about 100 Gambian soldiers are serving in a peacekeeping force in Liberia.

17 ECONOMY

The Gambia's light sandy soil is well suited to the cultivation of groundnuts, which is the Gambia's principal agricultural export. However, in 1990, tourism overtook groundnut exports as the nation's number one export earner. Though the Gambian economy is small, its government has been successful in stabilizing external debt and controlling inflation.

18 INCOME

In 1992 the Gambia's gross national product (GNP) was $367 million at current prices, or $350 per person. For the period 1985–92 the average inflation rate was 14.4%.

19 INDUSTRY

Industries include groundnut processing, building and repair of river craft, village handicrafts, and clothing manufacture.

20 LABOR

Most of the population of one million engages in agriculture. Less than 20% of the work force consists of wage earners.

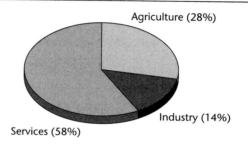

Components of the economy. This pie chart shows how much of the country's economy is devoted to agriculture (includes forestry, hunting, and fishing), industry, or services.

The minimum legal working age is 16. But since most children complete their formal education at age 14, many enter the work force on an informal basis at that time. Employee labor cards include information about workers' ages, but are rarely inspected. Even very young children perform customary chores on family farms or engage in street trading.

21 AGRICULTURE

On upland soils the main food crops, besides peanuts, are millet, manioc, corn, and beans. Inadequate rainfall has adversely affected crop production in recent years. The principal cash crop is peanuts, grown on some 80,000 hectares (198,000 acres). Production totaled 80,000 tons in 1992. That year, the paddy rice crop was estimated at 22,000 tons. Food crops in 1992 included an estimated 24,000 tons of corn and 65,000 tons of millet.

22 DOMESTICATED ANIMALS

The livestock population in 1992 was esti-mated at 400,000 head of cattle, 150,000 goats, 121,000 sheep, and 11,000 hogs.

23 FISHING

In 1991, the catch was 23,743 tons, as compared with 4,100 tons in 1967.

24 FORESTRY

Wood resources are used for fuel (98%), poles, and rural housing construction. Roundwood removals were estimated at 940,000 cubic meters in 1991.

25 MINING

Ilmenite, discovered along the coast in 1953, was mined by British interests until 1959. The Gambia has significant unused glass sand deposits.

26 FOREIGN TRADE

Groundnut products are by far the Gam-bia's leading export. The leading imports are manufactured goods, machinery, transport equipment, and food. The United Kingdom accounted for 57.2% of the Gambia's imports in 1985–86, and Switzerland bought 59.2% of its exports.

27 ENERGY AND POWER

All electric power is produced at thermal stations. Installed capacity in 1985 totaled 13,000 kilowatts, of which about 85% was public. Production amounted to 68 million kilowatt hours.

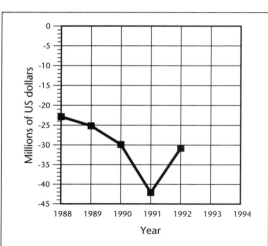

Yearly balance of trade measured in millions of US dollars. The balance of trade is the difference between what a country sells to other countries (its exports) and what it buys (its imports). If a country imports more than it exports, it has a negative balance of trade (a trade deficit). If exports exceed imports there is a positive balance of trade (a trade surplus).

28 SOCIAL DEVELOPMENT

Under tribal organization, the individual's basic welfare needs are traditionally met by the group. Women play little part in the public life of this conservative Islamic country.

29 HEALTH

Health conditions in the Gambia are poor. In 1992, average life expectancy was esti-mated at only 45 years for women and men. Nearly half of all children die by age five, primarily because of malaria and diarrheal diseases. Malaria, tuberculosis, trypanosomiasis, and schistosomiasis are

Selected Social Indicators

These statistics are estimates for the period 1988 to 1993. For comparison purposes, data for the United States and averages for low-income countries and high-income countries are also given.

Indicator	Gambia	Low-income countries	High-income countries	United States
Per capita gross national product†	$350	$380	$23,680	$24,740
Population growth rate	4.5%	1.9%	0.6%	1.0%
Population growth rate in urban areas	6.9%	3.9%	0.8%	1.3%
Population per square kilometer of land	88	78	25	26
Life expectancy in years	45	62	77	76
Number of people per physician	8,333	>3,300	453	419
Number of pupils per teacher (primary school)	30	39	<18	20
Illiteracy rate (15 years and older)	73%	41%	<5%	<3%
Energy consumed per capita (kg of oil equivalent)	57	364	5,203	7,918

† The gross national product (GNP) is the total dollar value of all goods and services produced by a country in a year. The per capita GNP is calculated by dividing a country's GNP by its population. The World Bank defines low-income countries as those with a per capita GNP of $695 or less. High-income countries have a per capita GNP of $8,626 or more. Less than 14% of the world's 5.5 billion people live in high-income countries, while almost 60% live in low-income countries.

> = greater than   < = less than

Sources: World Bank, *Social Indicators of Development 1995,* Baltimore: Johns Hopkins University Press, 1995. Central Intelligence Agency, *World Fact Book,* Washington, D.C.: Government Printing Office, 1994.

widespread. In 1992 there were 12 doctors per 100,000 inhabitants.

30 HOUSING

A Housing Finance Fund provides low-cost housing and related assistance.

31 EDUCATION

Primary school is free but not compulsory and lasts for six years. Secondary schooling is in two stages of five plus two years. In 1991, primary schools had an enrollment of 90,645 students, while secondary schools had 21,786 students. There were nine higher-level schools, including a teachers' training college. The overall adult literacy rate has been estimated at 27%.

32 MEDIA

The *Gambia Weekly* (formerly, *The Gambia News Bulletin*) is issued by the government three times a week. The *Gambia Onward* is also published three times a week, and *The Gambia Times* (1991 circulation 1,000) appears fortnightly. In 1991 there were 9,312 telephones. Radio Gambia is the government noncommercial broadcasting station. There is also a commercial station, Radio Syd. In 1991 there were 150,000 radios.

33 TOURISM AND RECREATION

Tourism has experienced significant growth in recent years. In 1990, 101,419 foreign tourists arrived in the Gambia, 60% from Europe and 38% from Africa. There were 2,553 hotel rooms, and tourism payments reached $26 million.

34 FAMOUS GAMBIANS

The first prime minister of the independent Gambia and the first president of the republic was Alhaji Sir Dawda Kairaba Jawara (b.1924).

35 BIBLIOGRAPHY

Gailey, Harry A. *A History of the Gambia*. New York: Irvington, 1982.

Gamble, David P. *The Gambia*. Santa Barbara, Calif.: Clio Press, 1988.

Zimmermann, R. *The Gambia*. Chicago: Children's Press, 1994.

GEORGIA

Republic of Georgia
Sakartveld Respublika

CAPITAL: T'bilisi (Tbilisi).

FLAG: Maroon field with a small rectangle in the upper hoist side corner. The rectangle is divided horizontally with black on top, white below.

ANTHEM: *National Anthem of the Republic of Georgia.*

MONETARY UNIT: The lari has not yet been issued since the introduction of government coupons began in April 1993. The coupons have replaced the Russian ruble (R) as the official currency.

WEIGHTS AND MEASURES: The metric system is in force.

HOLIDAYS: New Year's Day, 1–2 January; Christmas, 7 January; Independence Day, 26 May; St. George's Day, 22 November.

TIME: 3 PM = noon GMT.

1 LOCATION AND SIZE

Georgia is located in southeastern Europe, bordering the Black Sea, between Turkey and Russia. The area occupied by Georgia is slightly larger than the state of South Carolina, with a total area of 69,700 square kilometers (26,911 square miles). Georgia's boundary length totals 1,461 kilometers (908 miles). Its capital city, T'bilisi, is located in the southeastern part of the country.

2 TOPOGRAPHY

Georgia is mainly mountainous, with the great Caucasus Mountains in the north and lesser Caucasus Mountains in the south. An area known as the Kolkhida Lowland between the two mountain ranges opens to the Black Sea in the west and the Kura River basin lies in the east.

3 CLIMATE

Georgia's climate along the Black Sea coast is Mediterranean, with warm summers and cold winters farther inland. The mean temperature is 23°C (73.8°F) in July and -3°C (27.3°F) in January. Annual rainfall is 51 centimeters (20 inches).

4 PLANTS AND ANIMALS

The Black Sea coast of the Caucasus Mountains contains woods of black alder, oak, elm, and beech with a great number of lianas and some evergreens. Mountain goats, Caucasian goats, Caucasian antelope, European wild boar, porcupine, and leopards inhabit the Caucasus, and reptiles and amphibious creatures abound.

5 ENVIRONMENT

Georgia faces both land and water pollution. In 1994, 70% of the water was

Photo credit: AP/Wide World Photos

An Abkhazian separatist helps a boy to get out of the line of fire during street fighting in Sukhumi when the city was captured by Abkhazian forces in one of the fiercest battles of the conflict.

unsafe. Pesticides from agricultural areas have significantly contaminated the soil.

6 POPULATION

The official population estimate at the beginning of 1991 was 5,471,000. A population of 5,792,000 is forecast for the year 2000. The estimated population density at the beginning of 1991 was 78 persons per square kilometer (203 per square mile). The population of T'bilisi was estimated at 1,268,000 at the start of 1990.

7 MIGRATION

Emigration to other Soviet republics was 39,900 in 1990. As many as 200,000 Georgians may have fled the fighting in Abkhazia in 1993. About 20,000 Georgians also fled the fighting in the autonomous region of South Ossetia in 1992.

8 ETHNIC GROUPS

The population was 70% Georgian in 1989. The leading minorities were Armenian, 8%; Russian, 6%; Azerbaijani, 6%; Ossetian, 3%; Greek, 2%; Abkhazian, 2%; and Ukrainian, 1%.

9 LANGUAGES

Georgian is a South Caucasian language called Kartveli by its speakers. In addition to Georgian, Abkhaz, Ossetian, Armenian, Azari, Russian, and Greek are spoken.

10 RELIGIONS

The majority of the population is Christian (65%), primarily members of the Georgian Orthodox Church. There is also a significant Muslim population (11%), as well as Russian and Armenian Orthodox, Roman Catholic (1%), and, in 1990, some 23,000 Jews.

11 TRANSPORTATION

Railroads in Georgia consist of 1,570 kilometers (975 miles) of track. Railways serve mainly as connections to the Black Sea for inland cities like T'bilisi, Chiat'ura, and Tkvarcheli. Highways in 1990 totaled 33,900 kilometers (21,100 miles). The maritime fleet of 54 ships had a capacity of 715,802 gross registered tons in 1991.

LOCATION: 42°0′N; 44°0′E. **BOUNDARY LENGTHS:** Total boundary lengths, 1,461 kilometers (908 miles); Armenia, 164 kilometers (102 miles); Azerbaijan, 322 kilometers (200 miles); Russia, 723 kilometers (45 miles); Turkey, 252 kilometers (157 miles).

Batumi and Poti are the main Black Sea ports.

12 HISTORY

The first Georgian state can be traced to the fourth century BC. Throughout its history Georgia has been conquered by the Romans, Iranians, Arabs, Turks, and Mongols. Georgia did enjoy independence for short periods of time from the sixth to the twelfth centuries AD. The

Mongols invaded and conquered Georgia by 1236. Later the Ottoman and Persian empires competed for control of the region. Western Georgia became a Russian protectorate in 1783. All of Georgia was absorbed directly into the Russian empire during the nineteenth century.

During the tumult of the Russian revolution, Georgia declared its independence on 26 May 1918. Twenty-two countries recognized this new state, including Soviet

Russia. However, the Red Army invaded in February 1921 and Georgia's brief independence came to an end.

Georgia's first multiparty elections were held in October 1990, during the liberal era of Mikhail Gorbachev's perestroika in the Soviet Union. On 31 March 1991 the people voted for independence from the Soviet Union, and former dissident Zviad Gamsakhurdia was elected president in May 1991. After being removed from office in December 1991, Gamsakhurdia was replaced by former Soviet Foreign Minister Eduard Shevardnadze.

Since the beginning of 1992, Georgia has experienced secessionist movements, civil war, and economic collapse. During the fall of 1993, Georgian forces were forced out of the breakaway region of Abkhazia, whose Muslim minority fought to secede from the country. On 1 December, both sides signed a peace agreement. Georgian forces have also battled separatists in South Ossetia.

After the loss of Abkhazia, civil war broke out again in Georgia itself. During the latter part of 1993, former President Gamsakhurdia and his supporters launched a rebellion in western Georgia. It was defeated when Russia came to Shevardnadze's aid after he agreed to join the Commonwealth of Independent States (CIS).

13 GOVERNMENT

A single-chamber National Parliament with 234 seats was elected in 1992 and chose Eduard Shevardnadze as its chair-

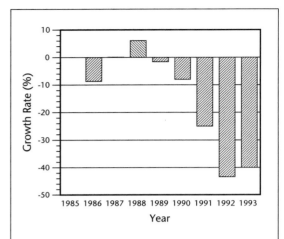

Yearly growth rate of the economy. This economic indicator tells by what percent the economy has increased or decreased when compared with the previous year.

man. The provisional government also has a prime minister and cabinet. A November 1992 law proclaimed the chairman of the parliament also to be president.

14 POLITICAL PARTIES

Some of the most influential parties are the National Democratic Party, the National Independence Party, Charter 91, the All-Georgian Merab Kostava Society, and the Green Party.

15 JUDICIAL SYSTEM

Courts include district courts, a T'bilisi city court, a supreme court in each of the two autonomous republics, and the highest level Supreme Court of the Republic.

The judiciary remains subject to political pressures and other influences.

16 ARMED FORCES

Although there are armed communal militias and over 500,000 men with military experience, Georgia has no national army. It plans to have an army of 20,000, supported by a national guard of 13,000. Russia, however, still has a 20,000-man army corps and tactical air force in Georgia. Only one Russian airborne battalion is officially committed to peacekeeping

17 ECONOMY

Georgia's mild climate makes it an important agricultural producer, raising a growing range of sub-tropical crops (including tea, tobacco, citrus fruits, and flowers) in the coastal region and exporting them to its northern neighbors in return for manufactured goods. Georgia supplied almost all of the former Soviet Union's citrus fruits and tea, and much of its grape crop. The country has deposits of manganese, coal, iron ore, and lead, and a number of oil refineries operate in Batume.

The economy, based largely on the country's mineral deposits and agricultural resources, has been slowed by political unrest.

18 INCOME

In 1992, the gross national product (GNP) was $4,659 million at current prices, or $580 per person. For the period 1985–92 the average inflation rate was 33.7%.

19 INDUSTRY

Heavy industry dominates, and includes metallurgy, construction materials, and machine building. Light industry includes

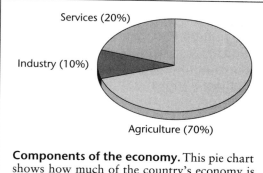

Components of the economy. This pie chart shows how much of the country's economy is devoted to agriculture (includes forestry, hunting, and fishing), industry, or services.

food processing, beverage production, garments, and oil-processing.

20 LABOR

About 30% of the 2.8 million persons in the labor force are engaged in agriculture, with another 18% in industry. Employees have the right to form or join unions freely.

According to the Labor Code, the minimum age for employment is 14. Young people between the ages of 14 and 16 may work no more than 30 hours per week. Although enforcement of the law is left up to labor unions, government officials are confident that the minimum age requirement is widely respected.

21 AGRICULTURE

During the Soviet era, Georgia produced almost the entire citrus and tea crop and most of the grape crop for the entire Soviet Union. In 1992, production levels (in thousands of tons) included cereal grain, 459; tea, 100; vegetables, 820; fruit (excluding grapes), 24; and grapes, 550.

Selected Social Indicators

These statistics are estimates for the period 1988 to 1993. For comparison purposes, data for the United States and averages for low-income countries and high-income countries are also given.

Indicator	Georgia	Low-income countries	High-income countries	United States
Per capita gross national product†	**$580**	$380	$23,680	$24,740
Population growth rate	**0.2%**	1.9%	0.6%	1.0%
Population growth rate in urban areas	**1.1%**	3.9%	0.8%	1.3%
Population per square kilometer of land	**78**	78	25	26
Life expectancy in years	**73**	62	77	76
Number of people per physician	**182**	>3,300	453	419
Number of pupils per teacher (primary school)	**n.a.**	39	<18	20
Illiteracy rate (15 years and older)	**1%**	41%	<5%	<3%
Energy consumed per capita (kg of oil equivalent)	**891**	364	5,203	7,918

† The gross national product (GNP) is the total dollar value of all goods and services produced by a country in a year. The per capita GNP is calculated by dividing a country's GNP by its population. The World Bank defines low-income countries as those with a per capita GNP of $695 or less. High-income countries have a per capita GNP of $8,626 or more. Less than 14% of the world's 5.5 billion people live in high-income countries, while almost 60% live in low-income countries.

> = greater than   < = less than

Sources: World Bank, Social Indicators of Development 1995, Baltimore: Johns Hopkins University Press, 1995. Central Intelligence Agency, World Fact Book, Washington, D.C.: Government Printing Office, 1994.

22 DOMESTICATED ANIMALS

In 1992, the livestock population included sheep, 1,400,000; cattle, 1,100,000; pigs, 850,000; and chickens, 19,000,000. Beef production in 1992 totaled some 45,000 tons; pork, 62,000 tons; and chicken, 20,000 tons. About 500,000 tons of milk were produced in 1992, as were 31,900 tons of eggs.

23 FISHING

The Black Sea and Kura River provide the domestic catch, but are heavily polluted.

24 FORESTRY

Production is primarily for domestic use. In 1990, paper and wood product exports comprised 1.3% of all exports by value in 1990.

25 MINING

Georgia has a number of mineral resources, particularly arsenic, barite, copper, ferroalloys, lead-zinc, and manganese.

26 FOREIGN TRADE

Georgia is heavily dependent on energy imports from other republics, especially

Russia and Turkmenistan. In 1988, total imports were valued at 5,300 million rubles, and exports at 3,400 million rubles.

27 ENERGY AND POWER

In 1992, electricity production amounted to 9.3 billion kilowatt hours. Consumption of electricity in 1992 totaled 11.7 billion kilowatt hours. Oil comes primarily from Azerbaijan, natural gas and electricity from Russia.

28 SOCIAL DEVELOPMENT

Georgians experienced a significant decline in their standard of living in 1992, and unemployment increased sharply due to the republic's industrial slowdown. Women mostly work in low-paying, traditional occupations, often on a part-time basis.

29 HEALTH

In 1990, there was 1 physician per 182 people, and, between 1985 and 1990, there were 11.1 hospital beds per 1,000 people. Total health care expenditures in 1990 were $830 million. Life expectancy in 1992 was an average of 73 years.

30 HOUSING

In 1990, Georgia had 18.8 square meters of housing space per person and, as of 1 January 1991, 128,000 households (or 16%) were on waiting lists for housing in urban areas.

31 EDUCATION

Adult literacy was estimated at 99.0% in 1990, with men estimated at 99.5% and

Photo credit: AP/Wide World Photos

Refugees, who fled the south Ossetian capital during heavy fighting between Georgians and south Ossetian forces, look at the destroyed remains of their home.

women at 98.5%. Georgian students are taught in a number of languages, including Georgian, Russian, Armenian, Azerbaijani, Abkhazian, and Ossetian. Several colleges and universities are located in Georgia.

32 MEDIA

In 1989, Georgia had 149 newspapers. Of these, 128 were published in Georgian, with a combined circulation of 3.2 million. As of January 1992, there were 339,000 telephone applications unfilled.

33 TOURISM AND RECREATION

Bounded by the Black Sea and the Caucasus Mountains, Georgia has been known for its profitable tourist industry, but tourism has stagnated since independence due to political and economic turmoil. The capital, T'bilisi, is over 1,000 years old and offers historic sights as well as warm springs and dramatic mountain views.

34 FAMOUS GEORGIANS

Eduard A. Shevardnadze has been president of Georgia since 1992. Joseph Stalin (1879–1953), longtime leader of the former Soviet Union, was born in Gori, Georgia.

35 BIBLIOGRAPHY

Dolphin, Laurie. *Georgia to Georgia: Making Friends in the U.S.S.R.* New York: Tambourine Books, 1991.
Pitskhelauri, G. Z. *The Longliving of Soviet Georgia.* New York: Human Sciences Press, 1982.

GERMANY

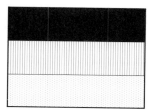

Federal Republic of Germany
Bundesrepublik Deutschland

CAPITAL: Berlin.

FLAG: The flag is a tricolor of black, red, and gold horizontal stripes—the flag of the German (Weimar) Republic from 1919 until 1933.

ANTHEM: *Einigkeit und Recht und Freiheit (Unity and Justice and Liberty).*

MONETARY UNIT: The deutsche mark (DM) is a paper currency of 100 pfennigs. There are coins of 1, 2, 5, 10, and 50 pfennigs and 1, 2, 5, and 10 deutsche marks, and notes of 5, 10, 20, 50, 100, 200, 500, and 1,000 deutsche marks. DM1 = $0.5981 (or $1 = DM1.6720).

WEIGHTS AND MEASURES: The metric system is the legal standard.

HOLIDAYS: New Year's Day, 1 January; Labor Day, 1 May; German Unity Day, 3 October; Repentance Day, Wednesday before the 3rd Sunday in November (except Bavaria); Christmas, 25–26 December. Movable religious holidays include Good Friday, Easter Monday, Ascension, and Whitmonday. In addition, the movable Carnival/Rose Monday holiday and various provincial holidays are also celebrated.

TIME: 1 PM = noon GMT.

1 LOCATION AND SIZE

Germany is located in western Europe, bordering the North Sea between France and Poland. Germany is slightly smaller than the state of Montana with a total area of 356,910 square kilometers (137,804 square miles). Its boundary length totals 6,010 kilometers (3,734 miles). The East Frisian Islands are off the northwest coast. The North Frisian Islands lie along the North Sea coast near Denmark.

Germany's capital city, Berlin, is located in the northeastern part of the country.

2 TOPOGRAPHY

The topography of Germany is varied. The northern lowlands are sandy, with dunes and small hills. The southern limit of the lowland area is formed by a wide zone of fertile soil called loess, reaching from Magdeburg to the central highlands. These highlands include the Harz Mountains, the densely wooded Thuringian Forest, and the Erzgebirge (Ore Mountains).

A group of plateaus and low mountains including the Black Forest and the Swabian Jura form the greater part of southern Germany. They merge gradually with the Bavarian Alps, which form the boundary between Germany, Switzerland, and Austria. The Zugspitze (2,962 meters/9,718 feet), on the Austrian border, is the highest point in Germany.

The only major lake is Lake Constance (the Bodensee), which is shared with Swit-

Photo credit: Courtesy of German Information Center

Bavarian mountain scenery.

zerland and Austria. The Rhine River dominates the western areas. Farther east are the Ems, the Weser, the Elbe, and the Oder. In the South, the Danube flows from west to east.

3 CLIMATE

The climate is temperate. Rapid changes in temperature are rare. Average temperatures in January, the coldest month of the year, range from 1.5°C (35°F) in the lowlands to −6°C (21°F) in the mountains. July is the warmest month of the year, with average temperatures between 18°C (64°F) in low-lying areas to 20°C (68°F) in the sheltered valleys of the south. The upper

valley of the Rhine has an extremely mild climate. The Harz Mountains form their own climatic zone, with cool summers, cold wind, and heavy snowfalls in winter.

Precipitation occurs throughout the year: in the northern lowlands, from 51 to 71 centimeters (20-28 inches); in the central uplands, from 69 to 152 centimeters (27-60 inches); in the Bavarian Alps, to more than 200 centimeters (80 inches). The higher mountains are snow covered from at least January to March.

4 PLANTS AND ANIMALS

Beeches, oaks, and other deciduous trees make up one-third of the forests. Conifers are increasing as a result of reforestation. Spruce and fir trees predominate in the upper mountains, while pine and larch are found in sandy soil. There are many species of ferns, flowers, fungi, and mosses. Fish abound in the rivers and the North Sea. Wild animals include deer, wild boar, mouflon, fox, badger, hare, and small numbers of beaver.

5 ENVIRONMENT

Industrialization has taken its toll on Germany's environment. According to a 1985 United Nations Educational, Scientific, and Cultural Organization (UNESCO) report, Germany had the worst air, water, and ground pollution in Europe. Germany produces 3.6% of the world's total gas emissions, and its particulate emissions total 295 tons per year. By 1994, 50% of Germany's forests had been damaged by acid rain.

GERMANY

LOCATION: 47°16' to 55°4'N; 5°52' to 15°2'E. **BOUNDARY LENGTHS:** Denmark, 68 kilometers (42 miles); Poland, 456 kilometers (285 miles); Czech Republic, 646 kilometers (403 miles); Austria, 784 kilometers (487 miles); Switzerland, 334 kilometers (208 miles); France, 451 kilometers (281 miles); Luxembourg, 138 kilometers (86 miles); Belgium, 167 kilometers (104 miles); Netherlands, 577 kilometers (358 miles); total coastline, 2,389 kilometers (1,480 miles). **TERRITORIAL SEA LIMIT:** 12 miles.

Germany has 23.0 cubic miles of water, of which 69.6% is used for industrial purposes and 19.6% for farming. Water pollution is evident in almost every major river of the Federal Republic of Germany. In the 1980s, the Rhine, from which some 10 million Germans and Dutch draw their drinking water, was 20 times as polluted as in 1949.

Germany produces 21.5 million tons of solid wastes and 15,659 tons of hazardous waste materials per year. Under the nation's basic waste disposal law of 1972, some 50,000 unauthorized dump sites have been closed down and 5,000 regulated sites established.

As of 1986, the Federal Republic of Germany had 67 nature parks and more than 2,000 nature reserves. Of Germany's 94 animal species, 2 are endangered, as are 17 of 305 bird species and 3 freshwater fish species out of 70. In addition, 16 plant species are threatened with extinction.

6 POPULATION

At the end of 1991, the population of Germany totaled 80,274,564. Average population density was 225 persons per square kilometer (582 per square mile). A population of 82,583,000 was projected for the year 2000.

Berlin, the capital, was the largest city in mid-1991, with a population of 3,437,900. Other big cities were Hamburg, 1,660,700; Munich, 1,236,500; Cologne, 955,500; and Frankfurt, 647,200. Bonn, the former capital of West Germany, had a population of 294,300.

7 MIGRATION

It is estimated that about four million people—many of them skilled workers and professionals—crossed from the German Democratic Republic to the Federal Republic of Germany during the 40-year existence of the German Democratic Republic.

The number of foreigners in Germany at the end of 1991 was 5,882,300, or 7.3% of the population. In 1991, 1,182,927 persons immigrated to Germany. A total of 582,240 emigrated from Germany. The 1991 immigrants included 156,299 Germans arriving from the former Soviet Union. There were also 221,024 immigrants from the former Yugoslavia and 128,367 Poles (not counting 17,276 Polish Germans).

Germany is also the most important place in Europe for refugees seeking asylum. In 1992, 438,191 persons received asylum in Germany as refugees. Most of these were Yugoslavs (122,666) or Romanians (103,787).

In 1991 the states of the former German Democratic Republic had a net loss of 172,357 people to the West.

8 ETHNIC GROUPS

The arrival of foreigners as "guest workers" beginning in the late 1950s led to an increase in the number of permanent foreign residents. Of the 5,882,300 foreigners in Germany at the end of 1991, Turks were by far the largest group, numbering 1,779,600. There were 775,100 Yugoslavs, 560,100 Italians, 336,900 Greeks,

271,000 Poles, 186,900 Austrians, 135,200 Spanish, and 93,000 Portuguese.

As joblessness increased in the 1980s and early 1990s, tensions arose between minority residents and young working-class youths influenced by neo-Nazi propaganda.

9 LANGUAGES

German is the official language, and High German is standard. Low German, spoken along the North and Baltic Sea coasts and in the offshore islands, is in some respects as close to Dutch as it is to standard German. Sorbian (also known as Wendish or Lusatian) is a Slavic language spoken by the Sorbian minority of about 50,000–100,000. Many of Germany's sizable foreign-born population still speak their native languages, and there are numerous Turkish-speaking school children.

10 RELIGIONS

In 1993, the Evangelical (Protestant) Church, a federation of several church bodies, comprised some 41% of the population, mostly Lutherans, while Roman Catholics numbered 28,599,000 or 35.6%. A total of some 40,000 Jews lived in Germany in 1990. Other churches include Methodists, Baptists, Mennonites, the Society of Friends, and the Salvation Army. With the arrival of immigrant workers, especially from Turkey, Muslims now make up almost 3% of the entire population.

11 TRANSPORTATION

Although the German transportation network was heavily damaged during World War II, the former Federal Republic of Germany system is now one of the best developed in Europe (although that of the former German Democratic Republic. needs much improvement). Because of the Federal Republic of Germany's central location, almost all continental surface traffic had to cross its territory. In 1991, the railroad system consisted of 45,648 kilometers (28,366 miles) of operational track.

Highways and roads in 1991 totaled 590,909 kilometers (367,191 miles), of which 8,290 kilometers (5,151 miles) were autobahns (highways). As of January 1991 there were 27,483,737 passenger cars, 1,390,052 trucks, and 69,710 buses that had been registered in the West before the reunification with the former German Democratic Republic, which had 6,300,000 passenger cars and 980,000 trucks registered at that time.

The total length of navigable inland waterways and canals was 7,541 kilometers (4,686 miles) in 1991, and there were 31 major ports. The most important inland waterway consists of the Rhine and its tributaries, which carry more freight than any other European waterway. Duisburg is the most important inland port.

Hamburg accounted for 53.8 million tons of overseas traffic in 1989; Wilhelmshaven, 14.5 million tons; Rostock, 20.8 million tons; Bremen, 14.8 million tons; and Bremerhaven, 15 million tons. These five ports handle about 70% of total merchandise traffic.

Lufthansa is the major air carrier. In 1992, it carried 26.9 million passengers.

Photo credit: Courtesy of German Information Center

A sightseeing boat cruises past a German Cathedral.

Major airports are at Hamburg, Hannover, Bremen, Düsseldorf, Cologne-Bonn, Frankfurt, Stuttgart, Nürnberg, Munich, and Berlin.

12 HISTORY

Hunting and gathering peoples roamed the land now known as Germany for thousands of years before the first farmers appeared around 5,000 BC. After the second century BC, Germanic tribes such as the Franks, Vandals, Ostrogoths, and Visigoths gradually emerged. Some of these peoples, whom the Romans called barbarians (from the Latin *barbari*, meaning "foreigners"), overran Italy and helped destroy the Roman Empire. Others settled in Britain, France, and Spain. Charlemagne, king of the Franks (r.768–814), extended his domain to include most of Germany as far as the Elbe. He was crowned emperor at Rome in 800. Charlemagne's empire was eventually divided among his three grandsons, and the German sector itself was divided in the second half of the ninth century.

Otto I, leader of a new Saxon dynasty, united Germany and Italy and was crowned first Holy Roman emperor in 962. Successive generations of Germanic emperors and of various royal families engaged in constant struggles within Germany as well as with various popes. The Holy Roman emperors tended to ally themselves against the nobility and with the prosperous German cities and towns.

The Reformation

During the fifteenth century and part of the sixteenth, Germany was prosperous. Commerce and banking flourished, and great works of art were produced. However, the already weak structure of the empire was further undermined by a great religious division, the Reformation, The Reformation began with Martin Luther in 1517 and ended in the ruinous Thirty Years' War (1618–48), which directly and indirectly (through disease and famine) may have taken the lives of up to two million people.

Afterwards, Germany remained fragmented in more than 300 principalities, bishoprics, and free cities. In the eighteenth century, Prussia rose to first rank among the German states, especially through the military brilliance of Frederick II ("the Great," r.1740–86).

During the French Revolution and the Napoleonic wars, German nationalism asserted itself for the first time since the Reformation. After a series of successful wars with Denmark, Austria, and France, the dynamic Prussian chancellor, Otto von Bismarck, brought about the union of German states (excluding Austria) into the Second Empire, proclaimed in 1871.

The Second German Empire

Germany quickly became the strongest military, industrial, and economic power in Europe and joined other great powers in overseas colonial expansion. While Bismarck governed as chancellor, further wars were avoided and an elaborate system of alliances with other European powers was created. With the advent of Wilhelm II as German emperor (r.1888–1918), the delicate international balance was repeatedly disturbed in a series of crises that led to the outbreak of World War I in 1914.

Despite initial successes, the German armies—allied with Austria-Hungary and Turkey against the United Kingdom, France, Russia, and eventually the United States—were defeated in 1918. As a consequence of the war, in which some 1,600,000 Germans died, the victorious Allies, through the Treaty of Versailles (1919), stripped Germany of its colonies and of the territories won in previous wars, demanded the nation's almost complete disarmament, and imposed strict reparations requirements.

Hitler and World War II

After World War I, Germany became a republic, governed under the liberal Weimar constitution. The serious economic and social problems caused by the military defeat and by the following economic depression, however, brought Adolf Hitler and the National Socialist (Nazi) Party to power in 1933. Hitler converted the republic into a dictatorship and began a military expansion. By 1939, Hitler had brought a great part of Europe under German control, either by military occupation or by alliance.

Germany signed a military alliance with Italy on 22 May 1939 and a non-aggression pact with the former USSR on 23 August. Hitler's army then invaded Poland on 1 September, and France and Britain declared war on Germany two days later. France surrendered on 22 June 1940. The British continued to fight. On 10 December 1941, Germany declared war on the United States, three days after the attack on Pearl Harbor by its ally Japan.

Hitler relied heavily on air power and bombed Britain continuously during 1941–42. But by 1943, German forces were on the defensive. Finally, on 7 May 1945, after Hitler had committed suicide, the Allies received Germany's unconditional surrender. It is estimated that more than 35 million persons were killed during World War II. Of this number, at least 11 million were civilians. Among them were nearly six mil-

Photo credit: Courtesy of German Information Center

These ruins at Dresden show the destruction caused by Allied bombing during World War II.

lion Jews, mostly Eastern Europeans, killed in a deliberate extermination by the Nazi regime known as the Holocaust. There were also nearly five million non-Jewish victims, including Gypsies, homosexuals, political dissidents, and the physically and mentally handicapped.

From Division to Reunification

After the surrender in 1945, Germany was divided into West Germany (controlled by the United Kingdom, France, and the United States) and East Germany (controlled by the Soviet Union). The capital city of Berlin, although totally in East Germany, was also divided in half.

West Germany's first chancellor (1949–63), Konrad Adenauer, the leader of the Christian Democratic Union (CDU), followed a policy of "peace through strength." During his administration, West Germany joined the North Atlantic Treaty Organization (NATO) in 1955 and became a founding member of the European Community in 1957. A treaty of cooperation between France and Germany, signed on 22 January 1963, provided for coordination of policies in foreign affairs, defense, information, and cultural affairs.

The cost of this program of cooperation with the West was further separation from East Germany and abandonment, for the foreseeable future, of the goal of German reunification. During this time, many skilled and highly educated East Germans had been secretly emigrating through Berlin to the West. To stop the flow, East Germany sealed East Berlin off from West Berlin by a wall of concrete and barbed wire. The Western Allies refused to accept the legality of the partition.

Throughout the late 1960s and early 1970s, tensions over the Berlin division generally eased, as did pressures over the issue of reunification. On 21 December 1972, the two Germanys signed a basic treaty and agreed to cooperate culturally and economically.

The economy of Democratic West Germany became one of the strongest in Europe, while that of socialist East Germany failed to live up to western standards.

The mass movement of East Germans through Hungary in the summer of 1989 as well as mass demonstrations in several East German cities led to the collapse of the German Democratic Republic in the fall of 1989 and the fall of the Berlin Wall. Helmut Kohl, who had been West Germany's chancellor since 1983, outlined a ten-point plan for peaceful reunification, including continued membership in NATO and free elections in March 1990. Following these elections, the two Germanys peacefully evolved into a single state.

However, unification has not been easy. Rising unemployment and other problems have raised concerns that the costs of unification were underestimated. Many in the western part of the country resent the costs of absorbing the east, while many in the east are unhappy about the painful change to a market economy.

Berlin has become the new capital of Germany, although the shift from Bonn to Berlin will take place over several years.

13 GOVERNMENT

On 3 October 1990, the Federal Republic of Germany (FRG) and the German Democratic Republic (GDR) were unified in accordance with Article 23 of the Basic Law *(Grundgesetz)* that serves as Germany's constitution.

The two-chamber legislature (the federal parliament) consists of a federal council *(Bundesrat)* and a federal assembly *(Bundestag)*. Following unification, Bundestag membership was raised to 662 deputies. The Bundesrat consists of 68 representatives appointed by the provincial governments.

The chancellor, the leader of the executive branch, is elected by a majority of the Bundestag. The president, who is chief of state, performs largely ceremonial functions.

The reunified Germany consists of 16 states, called *Länder,* which have their own ministerial governments and legislatures.

14 POLITICAL PARTIES

The Social Democratic Party (Sozialdemokratische Partei Deutschlands—SPD) is the oldest and best organized of all German parties. In recent decades it has modified its traditional Marxist program and made an appeal not only to industrial workers but also to farmers, youth, and professional people.

The Christian Democratic Union (Christlich-Demokratische Union—CDU) and its Bavarian affiliate, the Christian Social Union (Christlich-Soziale Union—CSU) emphasize Christian principles but are not linked to specific religious denominations. They favor free enterprise and are supported by small business, professional groups, farmers, and Christian-oriented labor unions.

The Free Democratic Party (Freie Demokratische Partei—FDP) is a more varied organization, consisting of both liberals and strongly nationalistic groups. It rejects socialism in principle.

The Greens (Die Grünen), Germany's newest political party, is a coalition of environmentalists and antinuclear activists.

15 JUDICIAL SYSTEM

Cases receive their first hearing in local, or Landkreis, courts and the superior courts in each of the Länder (states). The Federal Courts of Justice in the cities of Karlsruhe and Berlin are the courts of last resort in regular civil and criminal cases. The Federal Constitutional Court, the highest court in the land, rules on problems concerning the Basic Law and to test the constitutionality of laws.

16 ARMED FORCES

The German armed forces in 1993 numbered 447,000, about half of whom were draftees performing twelve months of required service.

The army is divided into the field army (203,400) and the territorial army (64,000). The navy *(Bundesmarine)* of 35,200 absorbed about 2,000 East German sailors and some of their vessels. The air force *(Luftwaffe)* has 95,000 officers and airmen, including about 9,000 former East Germans. In 1991 Germany spent $39.5 billion for defense.

17 ECONOMY

Germany has the world's third largest economy and the largest in Europe. Germany's unit of currency, the mark, is one of the strongest in the world.

The former German Democratic Republic was the wealthiest nation in the Soviet bloc. However, the unification of Germany in October 1990 proved a heavy economic burden on the West. Subsidies for the East resulted in a large public deficit. Alarmed at the potential for inflation,

Photo credit: Courtesy of German Information Center

An electric furnace in a steel plant. Germany ranked fifth in the world as a steel producer in 1992.

the nation's central bank pursued policies that boosted the value of the mark and had a recessionary effect on the European economy. Consumer prices rose 3.5% in 1991, 4% in 1992, and 4.2% in 1993. The unemployment rate in 1993 was 7.3% in the West, but 15.8% in the East.

18 INCOME

In 1992, Germany's gross national product (GNP) was $1,846,064 million at current prices, or $23,560 per person. For the period 1985–92 the average inflation rate was 2.9%, resulting in a real growth rate in GNP of 2.2% per person.

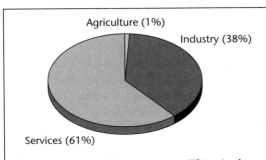

Agriculture (1%)

Industry (38%)

Services (61%)

Components of the economy. This pie chart shows how much of the country's economy is devoted to agriculture (includes forestry, hunting, and fishing), industry, or services.

19 INDUSTRY

The major industrial concentrations of western Germany are the Ruhr-Westphalia complex; the Upper Rhine Valley, Bremen and Hamburg, notable for shipbuilding; the southern region, with such cities as Munich and Augsburg; and the central region, with such industrial cities as Hannover and Braunschweig.

In the East, most of the leading industries are located in the Berlin region or in such cities as Dresden, Leipzig, Halle, and Chemnitz. The main industries in the former German Democratic Republic (GDR) were electrical engineering and electronics, chemicals, glass and ceramics. The optical and precision industries were important producers of export items.

Germany produced 4,227,000 passenger cars, 318,000 trucks and commercial vehicles, and 4,097,000 bicycles in 1992. Germany ranked fifth in the world as a steel producer in 1992, with a crude steel output of 32.6 million tons. Cement pro-

duction totaled 41.7 million tons; motor fuel, 29.2 million tons; and diesel oil, 18.1 million tons.

20 LABOR

With the reunification of the FRG and the GDR on 3 October 1990, the total labor force of the united Germany in 1991–92 numbered 39,011,000. As of September 1991, 1,973,000 were foreign workers, including 632,000 Turks, 325,000 Yugoslavs, and 172,000 Italians.

The right to organize and to join trade unions is guaranteed by the federal and state constitutions. As of 1991–92, 41.7% of the total labor force was unionized.

21 AGRICULTURE

Although 34% of the total area of Germany is devoted to crop production, production falls far short of satisfying industrial and consumer demand.

The states of the former GDR contribute significantly to German agricultural production: grains, 31%; potatoes, 48%; fruits, 43%; and vegetables, 31%. Germany's chief crops in order of yield in 1992 were sugar beets, 27,150,000 tons; wheat, 15,542,000 tons; barley, 12,196,000 tons; and potatoes, 10,975,000 tons. Apples and pears as well as cherries and peaches are significant fruit crops. Germany is a renowned producer of wines for world consumption; 1,340,000 tons of wine were produced in 1992.

22 DOMESTICATED ANIMALS

Germany is the leading meat, milk, and honey producer of Europe. Livestock in

1992 included 17,134,000 head of cattle, 26,063,000 hogs, 2,488,000 sheep, 492,000 horses, 121,000,000 chickens, and 4,000,000 turkeys. Milk production amounted to 28.1 million tons in 1992, and meat production totaled 6.2 million tons. Some 954,000 tons of eggs were produced in 1992.

23 FISHING

The importance of the fishing industry has declined in recent years. The total catch in 1991 amounted to 300,164 tons, including 34,406 tons of cod. The total value of 1991 fishery exports was $715.9 million.

24 FORESTRY

Total forest area amounted in 1991 to over 10,403,000 hectares (25,706,000 acres), more than 29% of the total land area. About two-thirds of the total woodland is coniferous, the remaining third comprising beeches, oaks, and other deciduous trees. A total of 44.9 million cubic meters of timber was cut in 1991. In 1991, Germany was the world's leading producer of particleboard, at over 8.2 million cubic meters, or nearly 17% of world production. Output of paper totaled 13.5 million tons in 1991.

25 MINING

In 1991, Germany was Western Europe's leading producer of alumina, refined copper, refined lead, lignite (of which it was the world's leading producer), pig iron, potash, salt, steel, and refined zinc. Germany ranked second in Western Europe in the production of primary aluminum metal, cadmium, cement, nitrogen in

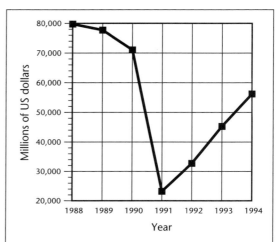

Yearly balance of trade measured in millions of US dollars. The balance of trade is the difference between what a country sells to other countries (its exports) and what it buys (its imports). If a country imports more than it exports, it has a negative balance of trade (a trade deficit). If exports exceed imports there is a positive balance of trade (a trade surplus).

ammonia, elemental sulfur and hard (anthracite) coal.

26 FOREIGN TRADE

Germany is one of the world's great trading nations. In some years—most recently, 1990—it has surpassed the United States as the world's leading exporter. Manufactured products are the leading exports, accounting for 90% of the 1992 total.

In 1992, more than half of Germany's total trade was with European Community countries. Principal trade partners in 1992 were France, the Netherlands, the United States, the United Kingdom, and Italy.

Selected Social Indicators

These statistics are estimates for the period 1988 to 1993. For comparison purposes, data for the United States and averages for low-income countries and high-income countries are also given.

Indicator	Germany	Low-income countries	High-income countries	United States
Per capita gross national product†	$23,560	$380	$23,680	$24,740
Population growth rate	0.6%	1.9%	0.6%	1.0%
Population growth rate in urban areas	0.8%	3.9%	0.8%	1.3%
Population per square kilometer of land	225	78	25	26
Life expectancy in years	76	62	77	76
Number of people per physician	356	>3,300	453	419
Number of pupils per teacher (primary school)	16	39	<18	20
Illiteracy rate (15 years and older)	<1%	41%	<5%	<3%
Energy consumed per capita (kg of oil equivalent)	4,170	364	5,203	7,918

† The gross national product (GNP) is the total dollar value of all goods and services produced by a country in a year. The per capita GNP is calculated by dividing a country's GNP by its population. The World Bank defines low-income countries as those with a per capita GNP of $695 or less. High-income countries have a per capita GNP of $8,626 or more. Less than 14% of the world's 5.5 billion people live in high-income countries, while almost 60% live in low-income countries.

> = greater than   < = less than

Sources: World Bank, Social Indicators of Development 1995, Baltimore: Johns Hopkins University Press, 1995. Central Intelligence Agency, World Fact Book, Washington, D.C.: Government Printing Office, 1994.

27 ENERGY AND POWER

With extensive coal reserves (about 80 billion tons in 1992), Germany is the greatest producer of electric power in Western Europe, and the fifth largest in the world. In 1991, total production of electric power amounted to 573 billion kilowatt hours, of which 68% was produced in conventional thermal plants (mainly fueled by hard coal), 4% in hydroelectric plants, and 28% in nuclear installations. As of 1991, there were 21 nuclear installations operating in the western states.

Natural gas reserves were estimated at 300 billion cubic meters in 1992. Production of crude oil amounted to 3.4 million tons in 1991. Local production is not sufficient to cover consumption, which totaled 134.3 million tons in 1992. Total FRG lignite production in 1991 was 279.4 million tons.

28 SOCIAL DEVELOPMENT

The social security systems of the FRG and the GDR were combined as of 2 January 1992. Unified Germany's social insurance system provides for illness, workers' compensation, unemployment, and old age insurance. Special pension funds provide restitution to Nazi era victims for physical, emotional, and material damage suffered during World War II.

Children's allowances, established in 1955, are granted to all families. Women enjoy full legal equality with men. However, women tend to be concentrated in low-pay and low-status jobs and can have trouble obtaining training in traditionally male fields.

29 HEALTH

In 1993, health insurance in Germany was available to everyone. In 1992, there was one physician for every 356 people. In 1992, the average life expectancy was 76 years.

30 HOUSING

Nearly 2.8 million of the country's 12 million dwellings were destroyed or made uninhabitable as a result of World War II (1939–45). From 1949 to 1972, 12.8 million housing units were built. The reunited Germany had roughly 33,860,000 dwellings in 1992.

Housing in the western states and that in the states of the former East Germany differs considerably. In western Germany, each individual has about 36 square meters of living space, significantly more than is found in the eastern states. About 95% of all homes have a bath and 75% have central heating. Two-thirds of the houses in the east were built before World War II, and many have deteriorated and lack modern sanitary facilities.

31 EDUCATION

Most German schools are state run. Each of the Länder (states), including the six new ones, is responsible for its own system. Attendance at all public schools and universities is free.

Children start school after their sixth birthday and are required to attend until they turn 18 years of age. After four years of primary or elementary school (*Grundschule*), students choose from three types of secondary school: the *gymnasium,* which prepares them for university admissions; the *realschule,* which leads to technical job training and middle management employment; and the *hauptschule,* or general school.

In 1990 there were 8,962,000 pupils in schools of general education and 2,570,000 pupils enrolled in vocational education. There were 1,318,000 students enrolled at universities, 29,000 in colleges of arts, and 373,000 in technical colleges. Teachers at schools of general education numbered 658,000.

32 MEDIA

There are 11 regional broadcasting corporations. In 1991, there were 70 million radios and 44.4 million television sets in Germany. In the same year, Germany had more than 45.7 million telephones. By late 1991, 500,000 new telephone connections had been installed.

Germany has the world's fourth greatest number of newspapers. Daily newspapers numbered 410 per 1,000 inhabitants in 1992, and had a total average circulation of 29,953,000. Of the newspapers sold on the street, the *Bildzeitung* has the largest circulation (4.5 million a day as of 1992). The largest subscription paper is the *Westdeutsche Allgemeine Zeitung* (1992 circulation 700,000).

Major weeklies include *Die Zeit* (490,550), and *Deutsches Allgemeines Sonntagsblatt* (471,700). Over 20,000 periodicals are published in Germany. The best-known internationally is the news magazine *Der Spiegel* (1,101,130), which is modeled after the American *Time* magazine.

33 TOURISM AND RECREATION

In 1991, 15,648,000 foreign tourists visited the newly reunited Germany. Receipts from tourism were $10.9 billion, and there were over a million hotel beds. Germany is famous for its beautiful scenery, particularly the Alps in the south and the river valleys of the Rhine, Main, and Danube. The landscape is dotted with castles and medieval villages. Theater, opera, and orchestral music abound in the major cities. The area that was formerly the GDR offers a number of Baltic beach resorts and scenic Rügen Island.

Facilities for camping, cycling, skiing, and mountain climbing are abundant. Football (soccer) is the favorite sport. Germany hosted and won the World Cup competition in 1974. Tennis has become more popular since Boris Becker won the Wimbledon Championship in 1985.

34 FAMOUS GERMANS

The roster of famous Germans is long in most fields of endeavor. Johann Gutenberg

Photo credit: Courtesy of German Information Center

A picturesque village beneath snow-capped mountains.

(1400?–68?) is generally regarded in the Western world as the inventor of movable metal type, and therefore as the father of modern book printing. Martin Luther (1483–1546), founder of the Reformation, still has a profound influence on German religion, society, music, and language.

The flowering of German literature in the 18th century reached its peak with the greatest German poet, Johann Wolfgang von Goethe (1749–1832), and the greatest German dramatist, Johann Christoph Friedrich von Schiller (1759–1805).

Leading filmmakers include Leni (Helene Bertha Amalie) Riefenstahl. Outstanding performers include Marlene Dietrich (1901–92).

The giants of German Baroque music were Johann Sebastian Bach (1685–1750), and German-born Georg Friedrich Handel (1685–1759), who lived in England. The classical period and all of Western music is dominated by the titanic figure of Ludwig von Beethoven (1770–1827). Outstanding composers of the 19th century were Felix Mendelssohn-Bartholdy (1809–47), Robert Schumann (1810–56), Richard Wagner (1813–83), and Johannes Brahms (1833–97). Major figures of the 20th century are Richard Strauss (1864–1949) and Paul Hindemith (1895–1963).

Outstanding architects include Walter Gropius (1883–1969), leader of the Bauhaus School of Design, and Ludwig Mies van der Rohe (1886–1969).

The 18th and 19th centuries were dominated by the ideas of German thinkers including Immanuel Kant (1724–1804), Georg Wilhelm Friedrich Hegel (1770–1831), Arthur Schopenhauer (1788–1860), Karl Marx (1818–83), Friedrich Engels (1820–95), and Friedrich Wilhelm Nietzsche (1844–1900). In the 20th century, Martin Heidegger (1889–1976) is highly regarded.

Among the most famous German scientists are Nobel Prize winners Max Karl Ernst Ludwig Planck (1858–1947), Albert Einstein (1879–1955), and Werner Heisenberg (1901–76).

Famous figures in German political history include Otto Eduard Leopold von Bismarck (1815–98), the Prussian states-man who made German unity possible and Austrian-born Adolf Hitler (1889–1945), founder of Nazism and dictator of Germany (1933–45).

35 BIBLIOGRAPHY

Carr, William. *A History of Germany, 1815–1985.* 3d ed. London: E. Arnold, 1991.

Childs, David. *Germany in the Twentieth Century.* 3d ed. New York: Icon Editions, 1991.

Ellis, William S. "The Morning After: Germany Reunited." *National Geographic,* September 1991, 2–42.

Gortemaker, Manfred. *Unifying Germany, 1989–1990.* New York: St. Martin's Press, 1994.

Hargrove, J. *Germany.* Chicago: Children's Press, 1991.

McAdams, A. James. *Germany Divided: From the Wall to Reunification.* Princeton, N.J.: Princeton University Press, 1993.

Nagel, Rob, and Anne Commire. "Adolf Hitler." In *World Leaders, People Who Shaped the World.* Volume II: Europe. Detroit: U*X*L, 1994.

———. "Frederick I (Barbarossa)." In *World Leaders, People Who Shaped the World.* Volume II: Europe. Detroit: U*X*L, 1994.

———. "Frederick II, the Great." In *World Leaders, People Who Shaped the World.* Volume II: Europe. Detroit: U*X*L, 1994.

———. "Karl Marx." In *World Leaders, People Who Shaped the World.* Volume II: Europe. Detroit: U*X*L, 1994.

———. "Martin Luther." In *World Leaders, People Who Shaped the World.* Volume II: Europe. Detroit: U*X*L, 1994.

Raff, Diether. *A History of Germany: From the Medieval Empire to the Present.* New York: St. Martin's Press, 1988.

Shirer, William L. *The Rise and Fall of the Third Reich.* New York: Simon & Schuster, 1960.

Vesilind, Priit J. "Berlin's Ode to Joy." *National Geographic,* April 1990, 105–132.

Watson, Alan. *The Germans: Who are They Now?* London: Thames Methuen, 1992.

GHANA

Republic of Ghana

CAPITAL: Accra.

FLAG: The national flag is a tricolor of red, yellow, and green horizontal stripes, with a five-pointed black star in the center of the yellow stripe.

ANTHEM: *Hail the Name of Ghana.*

MONETARY UNIT: The cedi (₵) is a paper currency of 100 pesewas. There are coins of ½, 1, 2½, 5, 10, 20, and 50 pesewas and 1, 5, 10, 20, 50, and 100 cedis, and notes of 1, 2, 5, 10, 20, 50, 100, 200, 500, and 1,000 cedis. ₵1 = $0.0057 (or $1 = ₵176).

WEIGHTS AND MEASURES: The metric system is the legal standard.

HOLIDAYS: New Year's Day, 1 January; Anniversary of the Inauguration of the Fourth Republic, 7 January; Independence Day, 6 March; Labor Day, 1 May; Republic Day, 1 July; Christmas, 25 December; Boxing Day, 26 December; Movable religious holidays include Good Friday and Easter Monday.

TIME: GMT.

1 LOCATION AND SIZE

Situated on the southern coast of the West African bulge, Ghana has an area of 238,540 square kilometers (92,100 square miles), extending 672 kilometers (418 miles) from north to south and 536 kilometers (333 miles) from east to west. Comparatively, the area occupied by Ghana is slightly smaller than the state of Oregon. Ghana's capital city, Accra, is located on the Gulf of Guinea coast.

2 TOPOGRAPHY

The coastline consists mostly of a low sandy shore behind which stretches the coastal plain. There is a forest belt, which extends northward from the western coast, and north of that, tropical plains, drained by the Black Volta and White Volta rivers. Apart from the Volta, only the Pra and the Ankobra rivers permanently pierce the sand dunes, with most of the other rivers terminating in brackish lagoons. There are no natural harbors. Lake Volta is the world's largest man-made lake (8,485 square kilometers/3,276 square miles).

3 CLIMATE

The climate is tropical but relatively mild for the latitude. Except in the north, there are two rainy seasons, from April through June and from September to November. Average temperatures range between 21° and 32°C (70–90°F), with relative humidity between 50% and 80%. Rainfall ranges from 83 to 220 centimeters (33–87 inches) a year. The harmattan, a dry desert wind, blows from the northeast from December to March, lowering the humidity and causing hot days and cool nights in the north.

4 PLANTS AND ANIMALS

Ghana has fewer large and wild mammals than in other parts of Africa. Except for coastal scrub and grassland, the rest of Ghana is tropical plains, or savanna.

5 ENVIRONMENT

Slash-and-burn agriculture and overcultivation of cleared land have resulted in widespread soil erosion and exhaustion. Overgrazing, heavy logging, overcutting of firewood, and mining have taken a toll on forests and woodland. One-third of Ghana's land area is threatened by desertification. Industrial pollutants include arsenic from gold mining and fumes from smelters. Water pollution results from a combination of industrial sources, agricultural chemicals, and inadequate waste treatment facilities. Ghana's cities produce 0.5 million tons of solid waste annually. In 1986, Ghana had five national parks and four other protected areas, with a total area of 1,182,845 hectares (2,922,857 acres). The ban on hunting in closed reserves is only partially enforced.

6 POPULATION

The population in 1994 was estimated at 17,156,376. A population of 20,172,000 was projected for the year 2000. Accra, the capital and principal city, had a population of about 1,405,000 in 1990.

7 MIGRATION

For generations, immigrants from Burkina Faso and Togo have done much of the

Photo credit: Corel Corporation.

Drying groundnuts and other grains, Fihini Village.

manual work, including mining, in Ghana, while immigrant traders from Nigeria have conducted much of the small trade. In 1986, the government estimated that at least 500,000 aliens were residing in Ghana, mostly engaged in trading.

Ghanaians also work abroad, some as fishermen in neighboring coastal countries. At the end of 1992 Ghana was home to 12,000 Liberian refugees. Some 3,200 Ghanaians were refugees in Togo and 200 in Nigeria.

8 ETHNIC GROUPS

Members of the Akan family, who make up more than 40% of the population,

GHANA

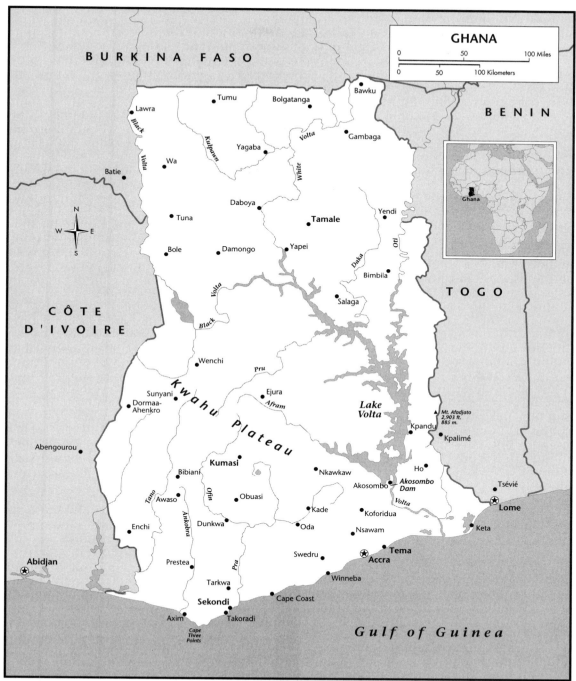

GHANA

Scale: 0 — 50 — 100 Miles / 0 — 50 — 100 Kilometers

BURKINA FASO

BENIN

TOGO

CÔTE D'IVOIRE

Gulf of Guinea

Tumu
Bolgatanga
Bawku
Lawra
Black Volta
Kulpawn
Yagaba
Volta
Gambaga
Wa
White
Batie
Daboya
Tamale
Yendi
Tuna
Oti
Bole
Damongo
Yapei
Daka
Bimbila
Volta
Salaga
Black
Wenchi
Pru
Kwahu Plateau
Sunyani
Ejura
Dormaa-Ahenkro
Afram
Lake Volta
Mt. Afadjato 2,903 ft. 885 m.
Kpandu
Kpalimé
Abengourou
Kumasi
Nkawkaw
Ho
Bibiani
Tsévié
Ofin
Obuasi
Akosombo
Akosombo Dam
Lome
Tano
Awaso
Kade
Koforidua
Volta
Enchi
Ankobra
Dunkwa
Oda
Nsawam
Keta
Swedru
Tema
Prestea
Pra
Accra
Tarkwa
Winneba
Sekondi
Cape Coast
Axim
Takoradi
Cape Three Points

Ghana

LOCATION: 4°45′ to 11°10′N; 1°12′E to 3°15′W. **BOUNDARY LENGTHS:** Togo, 877 kilometers (545 miles); Atlantic coastline, 539 kilometers (335 miles); Côte d'Ivoire, 668 kilometers (415 miles); Burkina Faso, 544 kilometers (338 miles).
TERRITORIAL SEA LIMIT: 12 miles.

include the Twi, or Ashanti, inhabiting northern and central Ghana, and the Fanti, inhabiting the coastal areas. In the southwest, the Nzima, Ahanta, Evalue, and other tribes speak languages related to Twi and Fanti. The Accra plains are inhabited by tribes speaking variants of Ga, while east of the Volta River are the Ewe living in what used to be British-controlled Togoland.

9 LANGUAGES

Of the 56 native languages and dialects spoken in Ghana, 31 are used mainly in the northern part of the country. The languages follow the tribal divisions, with the related languages of Twi and Fanti being most prominent. English is the official language and is the universal medium of instruction in schools.

10 RELIGIONS

In 1993, an estimated 38% of Ghanaians followed traditional African religions. Of the remainder, about 43% belonged to various Christian denominations, mainly Roman Catholic (12.6%), Methodist, and Presbyterian. Approximately 12% were Muslim.

11 TRANSPORTATION

The government's development program has been largely devoted to improving internal communications. Nevertheless, both road and rail systems deteriorated in the 1980s. Rehabilitation began in the late 1980s, with priority being given to the western route, which is the export route for Ghana's manganese and bauxite production and also serves the major gold-

Photo credit: Corel Corporation.

Dancers perform at a festival in the northwest, near Wa.

producing area. Rail lines are the main means of transportation for manganese, bauxite, and gold, as well as products such as cocoa, logs, and sawn timber. They are also widely used for passenger service. There were 953 kilometers (592 miles) of railway in 1991. In 1990, the railways carried 850,000 tons of freight, mostly ore and cement.

Ghana had about 36,000 kilometers (22,370 miles) of roads in 1991. In 1991, Ghana had 82,000 private automobiles and 43,000 commercial vehicles. The government transport department operates a cross-country bus service. In 1991, Ghana had a merchant shipping fleet comprising

8 vessels and 61,000 gross registered tons. Ghana has no natural harbors. The major rivers and Lake Volta provide about 1,400 kilometers (870 miles) of navigable waterways. Accra's international airport serves intercontinental as well as local West African traffic and served 762,000 passengers as of 1990.

12 HISTORY

The recorded history of Ghana began in 1471, when Portuguese traders landed on the coast in search of gold, ivory, and spices. Following the Portuguese came the Dutch, the Danes, the Swedes, the Prussians, and the British. Commerce in gold gave way to the slave trade until the latter was outlawed by Great Britain in 1807. The nineteenth century brought a gradual adjustment to legitimate trade, the withdrawal of all European powers except the British, and many wars involving the Ashanti, who had welded themselves into a powerful military confederacy. Their position as the principal captors of slaves for European traders had brought them into conflict with the coastal tribes. British troops fought seven wars with the Ashanti from 1806 to 1901, when their kingdom was annexed by the British crown.

In 1874, the coastal area settlements had become a crown colony—the Gold Coast Colony—and in 1901 the Northern Territories were declared a British protectorate. In 1922, part of the former German colony of Togoland was placed under British mandate by the League of Nations, and it passed to British trusteeship under the United Nations after World War II. Throughout this period, Togoland was administered as part of the Gold Coast. After a measure of local participation in government was first granted in 1946, the growing demand for self-government eventually led to a resolution calling for independence, and on 6 March 1957 the Gold Coast, including Ashanti, the Northern Territories Protectorate, and the Trust Territory of British Togoland, attained full independent membership in the Commonwealth of Nations under the name of Ghana. The nation became a republic on 1 July 1960.

During the period 1960–65, Ghana's first president, Kwame Nkrumah, steadily gained control over all aspects of Ghana's economic, political, cultural, and military affairs. A referendum in January 1964 established a one-party state and empowered the president to dismiss Supreme Court and High Court judges. In February 1966, Nkrumah was overthrown. A military government calling itself the National Liberation Council (NLC) established rule by decree, dismissing the civilian government and suspending the constitution. A three-year ban on political activities was lifted 1 May 1969, but Ghana's worsening economic condition resulted in another military takeover in January 1972 led by Lieutenant Colonel Ignatius Kutu Acheampong, who formed the National Redemption Council (NRC). Unlike the military rulers who came to power in 1966, however, the NRC made no plans for a rapid return to civilian rule.

The NRC was restructured as the Supreme Military Council in 1976. Two more military takeovers occurred in 1978 and 1979, the second led by a young flight

This typical rural family compound is in the center of the country, near Tamale.

lieutenant, Jerry Rawlings. The new government handed over power to civilians on 24 September 1979, following nationwide elections. The Nkrumah-style People's National Party (PNP) won 71 of 140 parliamentary seats in the balloting, and PNP candidate Hilla Limann was elected president. However, Ghana's economic condition deteriorated, and on 31 December 1981 a new takeover led by Rawlings overthrew the civilian regime. The constitution was suspended, all political parties were banned, and about 100 business leaders and government officials were arrested. Rawlings became chairman of the ruling Provisional National Defense Council. In the following 27 months there were at least five more real or alleged takeover attempts.

A new constitution was approved by referendum on 28 April 1992, and Rawlings was elected in a sharply contested multiparty election on 3 November 1993. On 4 January 1993, the Fourth Republic was proclaimed, and Rawlings was inaugurated as president. Opposition parties, assembled as the Inter-Party Coordinating Committee (ICC), issued a joint statement announcing their acceptance of the "present institutional arrangements" on 7 January, yet still refused to accept the election results.

13 GOVERNMENT

A Consultative Assembly, convened late in 1991 to draw up a new constitution, completed its work in March 1992. In April 1992, the constitution was approved by 92.5% of voters in a low turnout (58% of those eligible). It provides for a presidential system and a legislature (National Assembly) of 200 members. The Cabinet has over 90 officials of ministerial rank, a major contribution to popular unhappiness with government.

14 POLITICAL PARTIES

With the adoption of a new constitution in April 1992, the long-standing ban on political activity was lifted, and Ghanaians prepared for the presidential and legislative elections to be held in November and December. The parties that emerged could be grouped into three clusters. The center-right group was the most cohesive and it consisted of followers of Kofi Busia. They formed the New Patriotic Party (NPP) and chose Adu Boaheu as their presidential candidate. The center-left group was Nkrumahists. Ideological and leadership differences kept them divided into five separate parties, of which the People's National Convention, a party led by ex-President Limann, was best organized. PNDC supporters comprised the third grouping. They favored continuity and, after forming the National Democratic Congress (NDC), were able to draft Rawlings as their candidate.

15 JUDICIAL SYSTEM

The 1993 Constitution established an independent judiciary and a number of institutions such as the Commission for Human Rights to investigate and take actions to remedy alleged violations of human rights. The new court system consists of two levels: superior courts and lower courts. The superior courts include the Supreme Court, the Appeals Court, the High Court, and regional tribunals. Parliament has the authority to create a system of lower courts.

16 ARMED FORCES

In 1993, Ghana's defense forces consisted of units of the army (5,000), navy (1,000), and air force (1,200) as well as a presidential guard of 500 men and the People's Militia (5,000 part-time police). About one-third of the Ghanaian army (2,700) is serving in Liberia and four non-African states on peacekeeping duties.

17 ECONOMY

Ghana's economic history is one of the most interesting of the post-independence period. In a modern-day riches-to-rags story, the cocoa wealth of 1958 gave way to the food crisis of 1983 before Ghanaian leaders turned to the International Monetary Fund (IMF) for advice and financial relief. Since 1983, the economy has made measured progress toward recovery.

Ghana's economy is led by the agricultural sector, which employs two-thirds of the labor force. Cocoa is the dominant export crop. However, 1992 production of 243,000 tons was still well below government targets. Ghana has significant deposits of gold, and important new investments were made in this sector in 1992. In that year, earnings from gold exports exceeded those of cocoa for the first time.

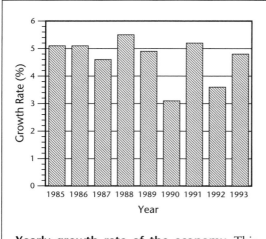

Yearly growth rate of the economy. This economic indicator tells by what percent the economy has increased or decreased when compared with the previous year.

[18] INCOME

In 1992 Ghana's gross national product (GNP) was $7,066 million at current prices, or $430 per person. For the period 1985–92 the average inflation rate was 31.2%, resulting in a real growth rate in GNP of 1.2% per person.

[19] INDUSTRY

Manufacturing represents a small part of the economy (9.3% in 1990). The Tema industrial estate includes the Tema Food Complex, made up of a fish cannery, flour and feed mills, a tin-can factory, and other facilities. The aluminum smelter at Tema is owned by Kaiser Aluminum and is Ghana's largest manufacturing enterprise.

[20] LABOR

In 1989, an estimated 6.5 million Ghanaians were in the labor force, about 55% of them in agriculture. The Ghana Trades Union Congress (TUC), with a total membership of almost 600,000, covers workers and salaried employees in the public and private sectors.

According to law, the minimum age for employment is 15, and night work and hazardous work are prohibited for those under 18. In practice, children are often found working in markets or collecting fares on local buses. Poor economic circumstances often force children to work to help support their families. Inspectors from the Ministry of Labor and Social Welfare inspect workplaces on a yearly basis.

[21] AGRICULTURE

Agriculture, especially cocoa, forms the basis of Ghana's economy. Cocoa exports in 1992 contributed 31% ($304 million) to total exports, down from 35% ($347 million) in 1991. In that year, cocoa production was about 280,000 tons (second highest after Côte d'Ivoire). Cocoa smuggling was made punishable by death in 1982.

Ghana continues to import more food than it exports. The grain harvest in 1992 included corn, 580,000 tons; paddy rice, 100,000 tons; sorghum, 210,000 tons; and millet, 80,000 tons. Other crops were cassava, 400,000 tons; plantains, 1,200,000 tons; coco-yams (taro), 1,200,000 tons; yams, 1,000,000 tons; tomatoes, 100,000 tons; peanuts, 100,000 tons; sugarcane,

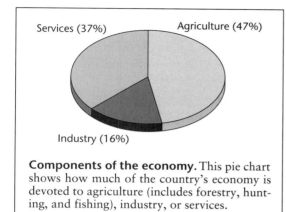

Services (37%)   Agriculture (47%)

Industry (16%)

Components of the economy. This pie chart shows how much of the country's economy is devoted to agriculture (includes forestry, hunting, and fishing), industry, or services.

the roughly 300 timber-producing species are the warwa obech, mahogany, utile, baku, and kokrodua. Species such as avodire, sapale, and makuri are considered the best in Africa. The total production of roundwood in 1991 was 17,122,000 cubic meters. Sawn wood production was 400,000 cubic meters.

110,000 tons; and coconuts, 220,000 tons.

22 DOMESTICATED ANIMALS

Livestock can be raised only in the tsetse-free areas, mainly in the Northern Region and along the coastal plains from Accra to the eastern frontier. Ghana's native West African shorthorn is one of the oldest cattle breeds in Africa. There were 1,400,000 head of cattle in 1992. There were also about 2,600,000 goats, 2,500,000 sheep, 500,000 hogs, and 12,000,000 poultry.

23 FISHING

In 1991, the total marine fish catch was 364,959 tons, and the freshwater catch (not including subsistence fishing) about 57,000 tons. In 1973, an industrial fishing complex at Tema began production of canned pilchards and sardines.

24 FORESTRY

The forest area (primarily in the south) covers about 35% of the country. Among

25 MINING

Gold, the first export of the Gold Coast, is still the most valuable mineral export, although extensive smuggling of gold and diamonds through the years has cut into revenues. Gold production in 1991 was a reported 26,311 kilograms, the highest level since 1964–65. This dramatic production increase was largely the result of the rehabilitation and expansion of the Ashanti mine (near Obuasi), as well as the opening of mines near Tarkwa in 1990. Production of manganese was 319,000 tons in 1991. Diamond production has steadily increased since the early 1980s. In 1991, production amounted to 700,000 carats. Only one relatively small bauxite deposit is worked near Awaso, by Ghana Bauxite Company. In 1991, production amounted to 380,000 tons.

26 FOREIGN TRADE

Although Ghana has historically enjoyed a surplus trade balance, deficits were recorded from 1989 to 1991. Leading exports in 1987 were cocoa, gold, and manganese. Principal imports included machinery and transport equipment, basic manufactures, chemicals, mineral fuels/crude oil, food, and live animals.

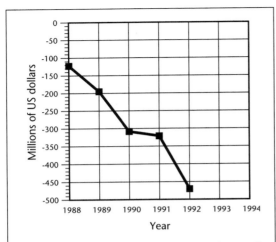

Yearly balance of trade measured in millions of US dollars. The balance of trade is the difference between what a country sells to other countries (its exports) and what it buys (its imports). If a country imports more than it exports, it has a negative balance of trade (a trade deficit). If exports exceed imports there is a positive balance of trade (a trade surplus).

The United Kingdom is Ghana's largest single trade partner, accounting for 26.9% of Ghana's exports and 41.4% of Ghana's imports. The United States (18.6%) and Germany (13.5%) are key export partners. Imports come from Nigeria (13.2%), Germany (11.5%), and the United States (11.1%).

27 ENERGY AND POWER

With the output of the Akosombo hydroelectric plant (912 megawatts) and the newer Kpong facility (160 megawatts), Ghana is largely self-sufficient in electric power and is able to export to Togo and Benin. Output of electricity reached 6,152 million kilowatt hours in 1991. The

Ghana National Petroleum Corporation, which was established in 1984, reported production of oil at the rate of 6,000 barrels per day from an offshore well near Cape Coast in 1991.

28 SOCIAL DEVELOPMENT

The Social Security and National Insurance Trust, established in 1972, covers wage employees. The secretariat of Mobilization and Productivity and the secretariat of Local Government and Rural Development deal with both urban and rural problems, including literacy, child welfare, and occupational safety. Women play a prominent role in agriculture and domestic trade, and are represented at the highest levels of political life.

29 HEALTH

Waterborne parasitic diseases are a widespread health hazard, and the creation of Lake Volta and related irrigation systems has led to an increase in malaria, sleeping sickness, and schistosomiasis. In 1992, Ghana had 4 doctors per 100,000 people, and 60% of the population had access to health care services. In 1990 there were 1.5 hospital beds per 1,000 inhabitants. The average life expectancy is 56 years.

30 HOUSING

Ghana's housing needs have been increasing as the main towns grow in population. In 1982, the government established the State Housing Construction Co. to help supply new low-cost dwelling units. The Cocoa Marketing Board, the Social Security and National Insurance Trust, and other organizations have also invested in

Selected Social Indicators

These statistics are estimates for the period 1988 to 1993. For comparison purposes, data for the United States and averages for low-income countries and high-income countries are also given.

Indicator	Ghana	Low-income countries	High-income countries	United States
Per capita gross national product†	$430	$380	$23,680	$24,740
Population growth rate	3.1%	1.9%	0.6%	1.0%
Population growth rate in urban areas	4.4%	3.9%	0.8%	1.3%
Population per square kilometer of land	67	78	25	26
Life expectancy in years	56	62	77	76
Number of people per physician	25,000	>3,300	453	419
Number of pupils per teacher (primary school)	29	39	<18	20
Illiteracy rate (15 years and older)	40%	41%	<5%	<3%
Energy consumed per capita (kg of oil equivalent)	96	364	5,203	7,918

† The gross national product (GNP) is the total dollar value of all goods and services produced by a country in a year. The per capita GNP is calculated by dividing a country's GNP by its population. The World Bank defines low-income countries as those with a per capita GNP of $695 or less. High-income countries have a per capita GNP of $8,626 or more. Less than 14% of the world's 5.5 billion people live in high-income countries, while almost 60% live in low-income countries.

> = greater than   < = less than

Sources: World Bank, *Social Indicators of Development 1995*, Baltimore: Johns Hopkins University Press, 1995. Central Intelligence Agency, *World Fact Book*, Washington, D.C.: Government Printing Office, 1994.

housing projects. Nevertheless, most houses continue to be built without government assistance.

31 EDUCATION

By 1990, an estimated 60% of the population were literate: 70% of the men and 51% of the women. Primary education has been free since 1952 and compulsory since 1961. Lasting 6 years, it is followed by 7 years of secondary schooling. In 1990, Ghana had 11,165 primary schools with 66,946 teachers and 1,945,422 pupils. General secondary schools had 768,603 pupils and 39,903 teachers.

Ghana has three universities with a combined 1990 enrollment of 9,609: the University of Ghana outside Accra; the University of Science and Technology in Kumasi; and the University of Cape Coast.

32 MEDIA

The government-owned Ghana Broadcasting Corp. makes radio services available throughout the country in English and six other languages. An international telex system was inaugurated in 1962, and a government-owned television service was established in 1965. There were about 4,150,000 radios, 235,000 television sets

Photo credit: International Labour Office

This young woman is studying at the University of Ghana library.

and 77,105 telephones in 1991. The main government-owned newspapers in Accra, with their daily 1991 circulations, are the *Daily Graphic* (100,000) and the *Ghanaian Times* (50,000). The *Pioneer* (100,000) is published in Kumasi.

33 TOURISM AND RECREATION

Ghana has sought to develop a tourist trade. Attractions include casinos, fine beaches, game reserves, and old British, Dutch, and Portuguese trading forts and castles. Native dance forms and folk music thrive in rural areas, and there are many cultural festivals. The National Cultural Center is in Kumasi, the capital of the Ashanti region, an area rich in traditional Ghanaian crafts. There is an Arts Center in Accra, as well as the National Museum, the Alwri Botanical Gardens, and the burial place of American author W.E.B. Du Bois. In 1991, about 172,000 visitors came to Ghana.

34 FAMOUS GHANAIANS

Dr. J. E. K. Wegyir Aggrey (1875–1927), noted educational reformer, played a large part in the development of secondary education. Sir Henley Coussey (1891–1958) and Sir Emmanuel Quist (1882–1959) were distinguished jurists. The writer, sociologist, and civil rights leader W(illiam) E(dward) B(urghardt) Du Bois (b.US, 1868–1963) settled in Ghana in 1961 and is buried in Accra.

Kwame Nkrumah (1909–72), the first president of the republic, served in that capacity until the military takeover of February 1966. He died in exile in Guinea. Kofi Abrefa Busia (1913–78), a noted sociologist, was prime minister from October 1969 to January 1972. Flight-Lieutenant Jerry (John) Rawlings (b.1947), the son of a Scottish father and a Ghanaian mother, led successful military takeovers in 1979 and 1981.

35 BIBLIOGRAPHY

Allman, Jean Marie. *The Quills of the Porcupine: Asante Nationalism in an Emergent Ghana.* Madison: University of Wisconsin Press, 1993.

Beckwith, Carol and Angela Fisher. "Fantasy Coffins of Ghana." *National Geographic,* September 1994, 120–130.

Myers, Robert A. *Ghana.* Santa Barbara, Calif.: Clio Press, 1991.

GREECE

Hellenic Republic

Elliniki Dhimokratia

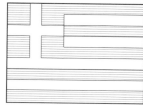

CAPITAL: Athens (Athínai).

FLAG: The national flag consists of nine equal horizontal stripes of royal blue alternating with white and a white cross on a royal-blue square canton.

ANTHEM: *Ethnikos Hymnos (National Hymn)*, beginning "Se gnorizo apo tin kopsi" ("I recognize you by the keenness of your sword").

MONETARY UNIT: The drachma (D) is a paper currency of 100 lepta. There are coins of 50 lepta and 1, 2, 5, 10, 20, and 50 drachmae and notes of 50, 100, 500, 1,000, and 5,000 drachmae. D1 = $0.0041 (or $1 = D246.02).

WEIGHTS AND MEASURES: The metric system is the legal standard.

HOLIDAYS: New Year's Day, 1 January; Epiphany, 6 January; Independence Day, 25 March; Labor Day, 1 May; Assumption, 15 August; National Day (anniversary of successful resistance to Italian attack in 1940), 28 October; Christmas, 25 December; Boxing Day, 26 December. Movable religious holidays include Shrove Monday, Good Friday, and Easter Monday.

TIME: 2 PM = noon GMT.

1 LOCATION AND SIZE

Greece is the southernmost country in the Balkan Peninsula, with a total area of 131,940 square kilometers (50,942 square miles). About a fifth of the area is composed of more than 1,400 islands in the Ionian and Aegean seas. The area occupied by Greece is slightly smaller than the state of Alabama. Continental Greece has a total boundary length of 14,886 kilometers (9,250 miles). The capital city of Greece, Athens, is located along the country's southern coast.

2 TOPOGRAPHY

About four-fifths of Greece is mountainous, including most of the islands. Mt. Olympus (Óros Ólimbos), the legendary home of the ancient gods, is the highest peak (2,917 meters/9,570 feet).

Greece has four geographic regions. The Pindus mountain range divides northern Greece into the damp, mountainous, and isolated Ionian coast in the west and the sunny, dry plains and lesser mountain ranges of the east. The third region, central Greece, is the southeastern finger of the mainland and consists of classical provinces. Southern Greece consists of the mountainous, four-fingered Peloponnesus, separated from the mainland by the Gulf of Corinth (Korinthiakós Kólpos).

3 CLIMATE

The climate in southern Greece and on the islands is Mediterranean, with hot, dry

Photo credit: Susan D. Rock

A town clinging to a volcanic hillside. Most of Greece is covered by mountains.

summers and cool, wet winters. Winters are severe in the northern mountain regions. Average annual rainfall varies from 50 to 121 centimeters (20–48 inches) in the north and from 38 to 81 centimeters (15–32 inches) in the south. The mean temperature of Athens is 17°C (63°F), ranging from a low of 2°C (36°F) in the winter to a high of 37°C (99°F) in the summer.

4 PLANTS AND ANIMALS

Many pharmaceutical plants and other rare plants and flowers considered botani-cal treasures flourish in Greece. Vegetation varies according to altitude. Oranges, olives, dates, almonds, pomegranates, figs, grapes, tobacco, cotton, and rice abound in the lower areas. Forests of oak, chestnut, and pine are found higher up, with beech and fir at the highest altitudes.

Native animals are not plentiful, but bear, wildcat, jackal, fox, and chamois still exist in sparsely populated areas. The wild goat (agrimi) still lives in parts of Greece and on the island of Crete. Migratory and native birds abound, and there are more than 250 species of marine life.

5 ENVIRONMENT

Among Greece's main environmental problems are industrial smog and automobile exhaust fumes in metropolitan Athens. The smog regularly sends hundreds of Greeks to the hospital with respiratory and heart complaints. Hydrocarbon emissions amount to 286.5 tons annually.

Water pollution is also a significant problem due to industrial pollutants, agricultural chemicals such as fertilizers and pesticides, and sewage. The nation's cities produce 3.5 million tons of solid waste per year.

In 1994, 4 of Greece's mammal species and 19 of its bird species were endangered, as well as 3 types of reptiles and 6 types of freshwater fish. Of the nation's 6,000 plant species, 526 were threatened with extinction.

6 POPULATION

The 1991 census reported a total population of 10,269,074. The population for the

GREECE

0 25 50 75 100 Miles

0 25 50 75 100 Kilometers

LOCATION: 34°48′2″ to 41°45′1″N; 19°22′41″ to 29°38′39″E. **BOUNDARY LENGTHS:** Macedonia, 228 kilometers (142 miles); Bulgaria, 494 kilometers (308 miles); Turkey, 206 kilometers (128 miles); Albania, 282 kilometers (176 miles). The total coastline 13,676 kilometers (8,496 miles). **TERRITORIAL SEA LIMIT:** 6 miles.

Photo credit: Greek National Tourist Organization.

A mountain villager wearing traditional Greek dress.

year 2000 was projected at 10,324,000. The 1991 population density was 78 persons per square kilometer (202 per square mile). The greater Athens metropolitan area had 3,096,775 residents in 1991.

7 MIGRATION

Many Greeks leave the country for economic reasons. In 1974, when the Greek military government collapsed, about 60,000 political refugees were living overseas. By the beginning of 1983, about half had returned.

In 1989 there were 225,624 foreigners officially residing in Greece, of whom 52,138 formerly held Greek citizenship. American, British, and German were the leading nationalities. The numbers of illegal aliens in 1993 was estimated at 400,000–600,000, of whom 100,000–200,000 were believed to be Albanians.

8 ETHNIC GROUPS

About 98% of the population was Greek in 1989. Minority groups include Turks, Macedonian Slavs, Albanians, Armenians, Bulgarians, Jews, and Vlachs.

9 LANGUAGES

Modern Greek, the official language, is the first language of about 98% of the population. English and French are widely spoken. Turkish and other minority languages, such as Albanian, Pomakic, Kutzovalachian, and Armenian, also are spoken. The forms of Greek used in everyday speech and popular literature, called demotic *(dimotiki)* differ from the official language *(katharevousa)* generally used by the state, the press, and universities.

10 RELIGIONS

Under the constitution, the Eastern Orthodox Church of Christ is the established religion of Greece, but religious freedom is guaranteed. Members of the Orthodox Church account for about 97% of the population. The remaining 3% are Muslims, Roman Catholics, Protestants, and Jews.

11 TRANSPORTATION

Greek transportation was completely reconstructed and greatly expanded after World War II. The length of roads in 1991 was 38,938 kilometers (24,196 miles). In 1991 there were 2,592,334 motor vehicles, including 1,777,484 cars (more than double the 1980 total), 792,770 trucks, and 22,080 buses.

In 1991 the railroads had a total length of 2,479 kilometers (1,540 miles). Major ports are Thessaloníki, Vólos, Peiraiéfs, and Iráklion. The Greek merchant fleet, the sixth largest in the world, had 914 ships (down from 2,893 in 1982).

Athens Main Airport connects the capital by regular flights to major cities around the world. In 1992, Olympic Airways carried 3,328,400 passengers on domestic flights and 2,137,100 on international flights.

12 HISTORY

Greek civilization first arose on Crete in the third millennium BC—the Minoan civilization (c.3000–c.1100 BC), named after the legendary King Minos. During the second millennium BC, Greece was conquered by Indo-European invaders.

Calling themselves Hellenes, these groups developed what is known as the Mycenaean civilization (c.1600–c.1100 BC) and the characteristic form of ancient Greek political organization, the city-state *(polis)*, laying the foundations of Western civilization. It was they who first tried democratic government; produced the world's first outstanding dramatists, poets, historians, philosophers, and orators; and made the first scientific study of medicine, zoology, botany, physics, geometry, and the social sciences.

By the sixth century BC, the two dominant city-states were Athens and Sparta (Spárti). The fifth century BC, recognized as the golden age of Athenian culture, brought the defeat of Athens by Sparta and its allies in the Peloponnesian War (431–404 BC).

The inability of the Greeks to unite politically led to the takeover of their territories by Philip II of Macedon in 338 BC and by his son Alexander the Great. Through Alexander's ambition for world empire and his admiration of Greek learning, Greek civilization was spread to all the lands he conquered.

Conquered by Rome

The Greeks were defeated by Rome at the close of the Macedonian Wars in 146 BC. Greece was made a Roman province, but Athens remained a center of learning, and the Greek language and culture remained widely influential. Thus, the period between the death of Alexander and the beginning of the Roman Empire is known as the Hellenistic period.

In AD 395, Greece became part of the Eastern Roman Empire, also known as the Byzantine Empire, which lasted for more than a thousand years. During this period, Greek civilization continued to contribute to Byzantine art and culture.

The Ottoman Turks, who conquered Constantinople in 1453 and the Greek peninsula by the end of the decade, gave

Photo credit: Susan D. Rock

The ruins of the Parthenon, built in the fifth century BC, sit atop the Acropolis.

the Greeks a large degree of local independence. Greek merchants ranged throughout the world on their business ventures, but Greece itself was poverty-stricken.

The Struggle for Independence

The Greeks, led by the archbishop of Patras, proclaimed a war of independence against the Turks on 25 March 1821. The revolution, which aroused much sympathy in Europe, succeeded only after Britain, France, and Russia decided to aid the Greeks in 1827. These three nations recognized Greek independence in 1830, and the Ottomans did so later in the year.

During the second half of the nineteenth century and until after World War II, Greece gradually added islands and neighboring territories with Greek-speaking populations.

For Greece, the first half of the twentieth century was a period of wars and rivalries with Turkey. In World War I, Greece had been neutral for three years and had then sided with the Allies. During World War II Greece was occupied by Italy and Germany. After the war, Greece became involved in a five-year civil war (1944–49) between the government and the Communist-supported National Liberation Front. US aid under the Truman Doctrine played a significant role in defeating the rebellion. A new constitution took effect in 1952, the same year Greece joined NATO.

Military Takes Over

On 21 April 1967, a successful takeover of the government was staged by a right-wing military group. This group was to rule Greece for the next eight years. Leftists were rounded up, press censorship was imposed, and political liberties were suspended. Colonel George Papadopoulos was made premier. In 1973, Greece was declared a republic, and Papadopoulos became president, only to be overthrown by a group of officers. The military government fell from power in July 1974. Constantine Karamanlis, a former prime minister and moderate, returned from exile to form a civilian government that effectively ended eight years of dictatorial rule. Prime Minister Karamanlis brought Greece into the European Community in January 1981.

With the victory of the Pan-Hellenic Socialist Movement (Panellinio Socialistikou Kinema—PASOK) in the elections of October 1981, Greece installed its first Socialist government. The new prime minister, Andreas Papandreou, was the son of former Prime Minister George Papandreou.

Tensions arose between Greece and the former Yugoslav republic of Macedonia. After the breakup of Yugoslavia, the territory known within Yugoslavia as Macedonia took steps to declare itself an independent country. However, many Greeks believed the name of the newly independent state implied territorial designs on the northern Greek region which once formed part of historic Macedonia. Greece responded by closing its borders, which left Macedonia without access to the sea.

13 GOVERNMENT

The 1975 constitution abolished the 146-year-old Greek monarchy. The president, who is head of state, appoints the prime minister, who is head of government and requires the support of parliament to remain in power.

Greece is divided into 13 regional governments *(periferiarchis),* which are subdivided into 51 prefectures *(nomoi),* in addition to Greater Athens and the Mt. Áthos region.

14 POLITICAL PARTIES

Postwar political parties in Greece centered more around leaders than issues. On 28 September 1974, Constantine Karamanlis formed the New Democracy Party (Nea Dimokratia—ND), advocating a middle course between left and right, and promoting closer ties with Western Europe. Groups that emerged after 1981 included the Pan-Hellenic Socialist Movement (Panellinio Socialistikou Kinema—PASOK), led by Andreas Papandreou. In May 1986, the Communist Party changed its name to the New Hellenic Left Party.

15 JUDICIAL SYSTEM

The 1975 constitution designates the Supreme Court (Areios Pagos), made up of 11 judges, as the highest court of appeal. It consists of two penal and four civil sections. A Council of State does not hear cases but decides on administrative disputes, administrative violations of laws, and disciplinary procedures affecting civil servants.

16 ARMED FORCES

The Hellenic armed forces belong to NATO. All able-bodied men of 21 years of age are obliged to fulfill 19–23 months of military service, plus reserve service to age 50. The total reserves number 406,000. In 1993, there were 159,300 in the army (including 125,800 male conscripts and 4,200 women volunteers), 19,500 in the navy, and 26,800 in the air force. Two battalions (2,250) serve on Cyprus.

Defense expenditures in 1991 were $3.8 billion.

17 ECONOMY

The Greek economy suffers from a lack of profitable natural resources and a low level of industrial development relative to

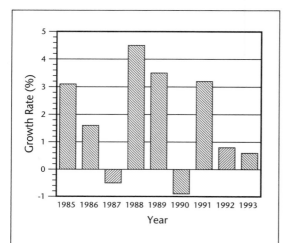

Yearly growth rate of the economy. This economic indicator tells by what percent the economy has increased or decreased when compared with the previous year.

the rest of Western Europe. By 1992, it had fallen behind Portugal to become the poorest European Community member. The country still depends on many imports to meet its food needs.

Greece has stimulated foreign investments in the development of its mineral resources by constitutionally providing guarantees for capital and profits. The government has encouraged tourism, which has developed into a major source of revenue. Greece continues to play a major role in the international shipping industry.

18 INCOME

In 1992, Greece's gross national product (GNP) was $75,106 million at current prices, or $7,390 per person. For the period 1985–92 the average inflation rate was 16.5%, resulting in a real growth rate in GNP of 1.1% per person.

19 INDUSTRY

Manufacturing, which now ranks ahead of agriculture as an income earner, has increased rapidly owing to a strong policy of industrialization. However, Greek industry must rely on imports for its raw materials, machinery, parts, and fuel.

Chief industries in 1991 were food, beverages and tobacco; metals and metal products; machinery and electrical goods; chemicals; textiles; nonmetallic minerals; clothing and footwear; and transport equipment. Selected industrial products in 1990 were sugar, 262,000 tons; wine, 231,000 tons; crude olive oil, 197,000 tons; beer, 3,772,000 hectoliters; and cigarettes, 27.7 million units.

20 LABOR

In 1991, the total civilian labor force was estimated at 3.98 million people. Registered unemployment was 9.0% of the work force in 1991. Females accounted for 37% of the work force in 1990, compared with 23% in 1971. Collective bargaining is provided for by law, and if agreement is not reached, the Ministry of Labor may be called upon to mediate. In 1991 there were 161 strikes resulting in 5,839,650 lost workdays.

The minimum age for employment in industry is 15, with higher limits for certain activities. For work in family businesses, theaters, and the cinema, the minimum age is 12. Family businesses in the areas of farming, food service, or mer-

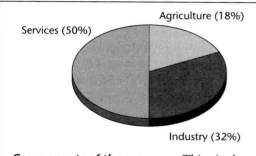

Components of the economy. This pie chart shows how much of the country's economy is devoted to agriculture (includes forestry, hunting, and fishing), industry, or services.

chandising often have younger family members assisting with the work.

21 AGRICULTURE

Agriculture in Greece suffers not only from natural limitations, such as poor soil and droughts, but also from soil erosion, lack of fertilizers, and insufficient investment.

Agricultural production of principal crops in 1992 was estimated as follows (in thousands of tons): wheat, 2,786; corn, 1,955; olives, 1,700; tomatoes, 1,690; grapes, 1,300; potatoes, 965; oranges, 872; barley, 495; olive oil, 330; cotton, 275; tobacco, 182; rice, 95; and oats, 88.

22 DOMESTICATED ANIMALS

In 1992 there were 9,694,000 sheep, 5,832,000 goats, 1,150,000 hogs, 616,000 head of cattle, 165,000 donkeys, 140,000 horses and mules, and 27,000,000 poultry. Although production of milk, meat, and cheese has risen greatly since the end of World War II, Greece still must import large quantities of evaporated and con-

densed milk, cheese, cattle, sheep, hides, and meat. Livestock products in 1992 included (in thousands of tons) milk, 715; meat, 529; cheese, 222; eggs, 142.5; honey, 12; and butter, 5.

23 FISHING

The fishing industry has expanded and been modernized in recent years. The total fish catch was 149,020 tons in 1991. A total of $86 million of fish and fish products were exported in 1992. In the north of Greece, freshwater fisheries have been developed.

24 FORESTRY

Forests cover about one-fifth of the total area. Pine, fir, and oak are the most common trees, and resin (11,879 tons in 1984) and turpentine (1,468 tons) are the principal products. In 1991, 360,000 cubic meters of sawn wood and 1,350,000 tons of firewood were produced. Production of timber is not enough to meet the domestic demand, and many forestry products are imported.

25 MINING

Greece has a wide variety of mineral deposits. Apart from bauxite, however, Greek mines operate far below their productive capacity. Output of bauxite rose to 2,133,521 tons in 1991. Production of iron ore by gross weight has risen to 2,023,678 tons in 1991. Other principal minerals include lignite, magnesite, asbestos, chromite, and nickel.

Other mineral deposits of commercial importance are antimony, gold, asbestos, emery, Santorin earth, pumice, sulfur,

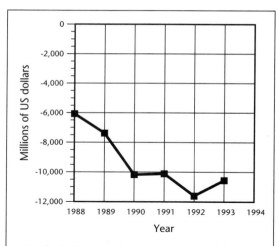

Yearly balance of trade measured in millions of US dollars. The balance of trade is the difference between what a country sells to other countries (its exports) and what it buys (its imports). If a country imports more than it exports, it has a negative balance of trade (a trade deficit). If exports exceed imports there is a positive balance of trade (a trade surplus).

ceramic clay, marble, talc, gypsum, salt, and limestone.

26 FOREIGN TRADE

Main exports in 1992 were manufactured goods, food, live animals, beverages, tobacco, and animal and vegetable oils and fats. Main imports in 1992 included machinery and transport equipment, mineral fuels and lubricants, and inedible crude materials.

About two-thirds of Greece's trade is with other European Community countries. Main suppliers of imports in 1992 included Germany, Italy, and France. Other principal trade partners in 1992 were the Netherlands, Libya, the United States, Belgium-Luxembourg, and the United Kingdom.

27 ENERGY AND POWER

Coal and oil are imported to supply power for the many small generating plants spread over the country. Of generated electricity 91% was provided by thermal power and 9% by hydroelectric stations. Greece has actively explored offshore oil resources. Total production, as of 1991, reached six million barrels.

28 SOCIAL DEVELOPMENT

The Social Insurance Foundation, the national social security system, provides for medical treatment; pays old-age pensions, disability pensions, and benefits to widows, orphans, and parents of deceased pensioners; and offers cash benefits for sickness, tuberculosis, accidents, maternity, and funeral expenses.

In January 1983, Greece's family law was changed by parliament to guarantee equality between marriage partners, make divorce easier, and abolish the traditional dowry as a legal requirement for marriage.

29 HEALTH

In 1985, Greece had 552 hospitals with a total of 54,438 beds. In 1992, there was one doctor for every 578 people. The country spent a total of $3,609 million on health care in 1990.

Pulmonary tuberculosis, dysentery, and malaria, which were once widespread, have been controlled. The incidence of typhoid, which was formerly of epidemic proportions, dropped to only 149 cases in

1985 following the application of US aid to improving sanitary conditions in more than 700 villages. In 1992, life expectancy averaged 78 years.

30 HOUSING

Construction of new dwellings (including repairs and extensions) reached 88,477 units in 1985 and rose to 120,240 in 1990. In 1991, the total number of housing units was 3,428,000. Most new construction is in Athens or Thessaloníki, indicating the emphasis on urban development.

31 EDUCATION

Adult literacy in 1990 was estimated at 93%; 97.6% for men and 89.1% for women. Education is free and compulsory for nine years beginning at age six. In 1989 there were 7,755 primary schools with 834,688 pupils. Secondary schools (gymnasiums) had 843,732 pupils. Technical, vocational, and religious schools had 130,738 pupils.

Greece has several major universities—at Athens, Thessaloníki, Crete, and Pátrai. Together, all institutions of higher education, including technical schools, enrolled 194,419 students in 1989.

32 MEDIA

Radio Athens broadcasts are carried in various parts of the country. Other stations are operated by the Greek armed forces. There are three television channels. There were some 4,270,000 radios in 1991. Television sets numbered 2 million. In the same year, there were 4,522,834 telephones.

The main newspapers and magazines of Athens have nationwide circulation. In 1991 there were 117 daily newspapers. The largest Athenian dailies (with estimated 1991 circulations) were *Ta Nea* (136,500), *Apogevmatini* (71,000), *Ethnos* (76,000), and *Avriani* (44,500).

33 TOURISM AND RECREATION

Tourism has overtaken shipping as the most important element in the Greek economy, with the active encouragement of the Greek National Tourist Organization. The number of foreign tourists visiting Greece in 1991, totaled 8,036,127, of whom 20.8% came from the United Kingdom, 19.4% from Germany, and 5.86% from France. There were 243,950 hotel rooms.

Main tourist sites, in addition to the world-famous Parthenon and Acropolis in Athens, include Mt. Olympus (the home of the gods in ancient mythology), the site of the ancient oracle at Delphi, the Agora at Corinth *(Kórinthos)*, and the Minoan ruins on Crete.

34 FAMOUS GREEKS

The origins of Western literature may be traced to the epics of Homer (c.700 BC), the *Iliad* and the *Odyssey*. Aristophanes (450?–385? BC), the greatest author of comedies, satirized his times in a series of brilliant plays.

Pythagoras (570?–500? BC) was one of the leading philosophers of the period preceding Greece's golden age. Socrates (469?–399 BC) investigated ethics and politics. His greatest pupil, Plato (429?–347

Selected Social Indicators

These statistics are estimates for the period 1988 to 1993. For comparison purposes, data for the United States and averages for low-income countries and high-income countries are also given.

Indicator	Greece	Low-income countries	High-income countries	United States
Per capita gross national product†	**$7,390**	$380	$23,680	$24,740
Population growth rate	**0.4%**	1.9%	0.6%	1.0%
Population growth rate in urban areas	**1.2%**	3.9%	0.8%	1.3%
Population per square kilometer of land	**78**	78	25	26
Life expectancy in years	**78**	62	77	76
Number of people per physician	**578**	>3,300	453	419
Number of pupils per teacher (primary school)	**19**	39	<18	20
Illiteracy rate (15 years and older)	**7%**	41%	<5%	<3%
Energy consumed per capita (kg of oil equivalent)	**2,160**	364	5,203	7,918

† The gross national product (GNP) is the total dollar value of all goods and services produced by a country in a year. The per capita GNP is calculated by dividing a country's GNP by its population. The World Bank defines low-income countries as those with a per capita GNP of $695 or less. High-income countries have a per capita GNP of $8,626 or more. Less than 14% of the world's 5.5 billion people live in high-income countries, while almost 60% live in low-income countries.

> = greater than   < = less than

Sources: World Bank, *Social Indicators of Development 1995,* Baltimore: Johns Hopkins University Press, 1995. Central Intelligence Agency, *World Fact Book,* Washington, D.C.: Government Printing Office, 1994.

BC), used Socrates' question-and-answer method in his famous dialogues. Plato's pupil Aristotle (384–322 BC) established the rules of deductive reasoning. The oath of Hippocrates (460?–377 BC), the father of medicine, is still recited by newly graduating physicians. Euclid (fl.300 BC) evolved the system of geometry that bears his name.

Soon after the decline of Athens, Philip II of Macedon (382–336 BC) and his son Alexander the Great (356–323 BC) gained control over all of Greece and formed a vast empire stretching as far east as India.

The most renowned Greek painter during the Renaissance was El Greco (Domenikos Theotokopoulos, 1541–1614), born on Crete, whose major works, painted in Spain, have influenced many 20th-century artists.

35 BIBLIOGRAPHY

Hadas, Moses. *History of Greek Literature.* New York: Columbia University Press, 1950.

Pettifer, James. *The Greeks: The Land and People Since the War.* London, England; New York: Viking, 1993.

Stein, R. *Greece.* Chicago: Children's Press, 1987.

Stobart, John Clarke. *The Glory That Was Greece: A Survey of Hellenic Cultures and Civilizations.* New York: Grove Press, 1962.

Woodhouse, C. M. *Modern Greece: A Short History.* 4th ed. London: Faber & Faber, 1986.

GRENADA

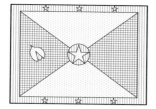

CAPITAL: St. George's.

FLAG: The national flag consists of a red border surrounding a rectangle divided into two gold and two green triangles. There are seven yellow stars—three on the upper and three on the lower red border, and one large star at the apex of the four triangles—representing the six parishes and the island of Carriacou. A yellow nutmeg is represented on the hoist triangle.

ANTHEM: National anthem beginning "Hail Grenada, land of ours, we pledge ourselves to thee."

MONETARY UNIT: The East Caribbean dollar (EC$) is a paper currency of 100 cents. There are coins of 1, 2, 5, 10, 25, and 50 cents, and 1 dollar, and notes of 5, 10, 20, and 100 East Caribbean dollars. EC$1 = US$0.3704 (or US$1 = EC$2.70).

WEIGHTS AND MEASURES: The metric system is in use.

HOLIDAYS: New Year, 1–2 January; Independence Day, 7 February; Labor Day, 1 May; Thanksgiving, 25 October; Christmas, 25 December; Boxing Day, 26 December. Movable holidays include Good Friday, Easter Monday, and Emancipation Day, 1st Monday in August.

TIME: 8 AM = noon GMT.

1 LOCATION AND SIZE

Grenada has an area of 340 square kilometers (131 square miles), slightly less than twice the size of Washington, D.C. Grenada's capital city, St. George's, is located on the island's southwestern coast.

2 TOPOGRAPHY

Volcanic in origin, Grenada is very hilly. The highest peak is Mt. Saint Catherine, at 840 meters (2,756 feet). The coastline has many beaches and small bays.

3 CLIMATE

Temperatures range from 21° to 29°C (70–84°F). Annual rainfall varies from about 150 centimeters (60 inches) to 380 centimeters (150 inches). There is a wet season from June to December.

4 PLANTS AND ANIMALS

The central highlands support a wide variety of forest trees, and many types of tropical flowers and shrubs grow throughout the island. Wildlife includes the hummingbird, egret, dove, and wild pigeon, as well as armadillo, agouti, and monkeys.

5 ENVIRONMENT

Water supply is limited and in some areas is polluted by agricultural chemicals and sewage. Forests are threatened by the expansion of farming activities and the use of wood for fuel. As of 1987, endangered species included the Orinoco crocodile.

6 POPULATION

The population was 99,205 in 1988. Population density is about 267 persons per square kilometer (690 per square mile). St. George's, Grenada's major city and port, had a population estimated at 7,500 in 1995 (35,742 including suburbs).

7 MIGRATION

Grenadians have mainly emigrated to the United Kingdom and Canada. Emigration increased after the 1979 coup by the New Jewel Movement.

8 ETHNIC GROUPS

Blacks, together with those of mixed black and white ancestry, make up about 91% of the population. The remainder consists of small groups of Asian (largely Indian) and European descent.

9 LANGUAGES

English is the official language. A French African patois (dialect) is also spoken.

10 RELIGIONS

As of 1993, an estimated 66% of the population was Roman Catholic. Other main groups are Anglican (20%), Methodist, Seventh-day Adventist, and Presbyterian.

11 TRANSPORTATION

In 1991, Grenada had an extensive road system of 1,000 kilometers (620 miles). In 1984 there were 7,741 registered motor vehicles. The country's major port is St. George's. The international airport at Point Salines served 206,000 arriving and departing passengers in 1991.

12 HISTORY

Grenada was inhabited by Arawak Indians when first discovered on 15 August 1498 by Christopher Columbus, who named it Concepción. By the eighteenth century, the island was known as Grenada. A secure harbor (at St. George's) attracted traders and some French settlers during the sixteenth century. The island alternated between French and British control for about 100 years (from 1674 until the Versailles treaty turned it over to Britain in 1783).

Sugar was Grenada's main product until the nineteenth century, when the development of spices led to a new economic base for the island. During the second half of the nineteenth century, the cultivation of nutmeg, cloves, ginger, and cinnamon earned Grenada the name Isle of Spice.

Grenada's colonial status ended in 1958 when it joined the short-lived Federation of the West Indies. In 1962, the federation dissolved, and in 1967, Grenada became an associated state of the United Kingdom. Independence came on 7 February 1974 in spite of widespread strikes and demonstrations protesting against the secret police of Prime Minister Eric Matthew Gairy.

On 13 March 1979, the opposition party, the New Jewel Movement, seized power, and Maurice Bishop became prime minister of the People's Revolutionary Government (PRG). Bishop suspended the constitution, jailed opposition leaders, and shut down independent newspapers. The PRG was drawn toward Cuba and its allies in the Caribbean region, as relations with the United States and some of Grenada's Caribbean neighbors deteriorated. Cuban advisors and troops supported the PRG in Grenada.

On 19 October 1983, Bishop and several followers were shot to death as the result of a power struggle within the PRG. A hard-line Marxist military council, headed by General Hudson Austin, took over. Six days later, thousands of United States troops, accompanied by token forces from seven other Caribbean nations, invaded the island. Nearly all of the 700 Cubans then in Grenada were captured and expelled. General Austin was placed in detention, and the governor-general, Sir Paul Scoon, formed an interim government that ruled until the 1984 elections.

The elections of 1990 elevated the National Democratic Congress (NDC) to majority status, and Nicholas Brathwaite became prime minister.

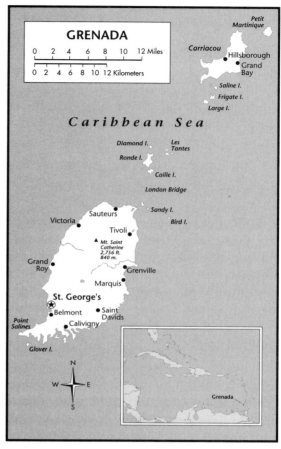

LOCATION: 12°7′N and 61°40′W. **COASTLINE:** 121 kilometers (75 miles). **TERRITORIAL SEA LIMIT:** 12 miles.

13 GOVERNMENT

The constitution provides for a governor-general appointed by the British crown and a parliamentary government with independent executive, legislative, and judicial branches. The bicameral legislature consists of a 13-member Senate and a 15-seat House of Representatives. The main island is divided into six parishes and one dependency.

14 POLITICAL PARTIES

There are six political parties in Grenada. The National Democratic Congress (NDC), a moderate party, gained control of the government in the 1990 elections.

15 JUDICIAL SYSTEM

The Grenada Supreme Court, in St. George's, consists of a High Court of Justice and a two-tier Court of Appeals.

16 ARMED FORCES

The 550-man Royal Grenada Police and Coast Guard provides internal defense.

17 ECONOMY

Since 1983, Grenada's economy has been highly dependent on international trade. Exports of nutmeg, cocoa, spices, and bananas are the main sources of income from abroad. The tourism industry continues to expand. Grenada receives aid from the United States, the European Communities, the United Kingdom, and Canada.

18 INCOME

In 1992, Grenada's gross national product (GNP) was US$210 million at current prices, or US$2,380 per person.

19 INDUSTRY

Industry is small-scale, mainly producing consumer products for local use. Local firms produce beer, oils, soap (from copra), furniture, mattresses, clothing, and a number of other items.

20 LABOR

Grenada's labor force is estimated at 40,000 (1991), including a large supply of unskilled and semiskilled workers. Unemployment was estimated in 1991 at 28% of the labor force.

21 AGRICULTURE

The principal crops for export are nutmeg and mace, bananas, cocoa beans, and other fresh fruits and vegetables. Production in 1992 included bananas, 11,000 tons; cocoa, 2,000 tons; and nutmeg, 1,975 tons. Food crops consist of yams, sweet potatoes, corn, peas, and beans.

22 DOMESTICATED ANIMALS

Most livestock is raised by individuals for their own use. In 1992 there were an estimated 4,000 head of cattle, 23,000 sheep and goats, and 1,000 donkeys.

23 FISHING

The 1991 catch was 1,990 tons, predominantly tuna and scad.

24 FORESTRY

There are approximately 3,000 hectares (7,400 acres) of rainforest. Trees include Honduras mahogany, blue mahoe, and teak.

25 MINING

There is no mining in Grenada except for open-face red gravel deposits.

26 FOREIGN TRADE

In 1992, export of goods reached US$83.3 million. Major export items consisted of nutmeg, cocoa, bananas, mace, and textiles. Grenada exported mainly to Trinidad and Tobago, the United Kingdom, the Netherlands, and Germany.

Total merchandise imports amounted to US$128.2 million. Major import items were foods, machinery and transport equipment, manufactured goods, and fuels. Grenada imported mostly from the United States, United Kingdom, Trinidad and Tobago, Canada, North Korea, and the Netherlands.

Photo credit: Susan D. Rock.

In the capital, St. George's, houses overlook the harbor.

27 ENERGY AND POWER

In 1991, electricity output totaled 52 million kilowatt hours. In 1991, a proposal was put forward to refine Venezuelan crude oil on Grenada by 1996.

28 SOCIAL DEVELOPMENT

A National Insurance Scheme, introduced on 4 April 1983, provides old age, disability, survivor, health, and maternity benefits to workers. There is also a funeral grant. Women's rights advocates claim that many cases of rape and abuse go unreported.

29 HEALTH

Grenada General Hospital and two other general hospitals have a combined total of 360 beds. In 1988, there were 51 doctors. Life expectancy averaged 70 years for both women and men.

30 HOUSING

The Grenada Housing Authority acquires land and constructs low-income housing projects. All main population centers have been supplied with sewerage and piped-water facilities.

31 EDUCATION

Education is free and compulsory for 12 years. In 1989, there were 66 primary schools with 21,616 students and 763 teachers. Postsecondary institutions include the Technical and Vocational Institute and the Teacher Training Col-

Selected Social Indicators

These statistics are estimates for the period 1988 to 1993. For comparison purposes, data for the United States and averages for low-income countries and high-income countries are also given.

Indicator	Grenada	Low-income countries	High-income countries	United States
Per capita gross national product†	**$2,380**	$380	$23,680	$24,740
Population growth rate	**0.7%**	1.9%	0.6%	1.0%
Population growth rate in urban areas	**n.a.**	3.9%	0.8%	1.3%
Population per square kilometer of land	**267**	78	25	26
Life expectancy in years	**70**	62	77	76
Number of people per physician	**1,945**	>3,300	453	419
Number of pupils per teacher (primary school)	**28**	39	<18	20
Illiteracy rate (15 years and older)	**2%**	41%	<5%	<3%
Energy consumed per capita (kg of oil equivalent)	**283**	364	5,203	7,918

† The gross national product (GNP) is the total dollar value of all goods and services produced by a country in a year. The per capita GNP is calculated by dividing a country's GNP by its population. The World Bank defines low-income countries as those with a per capita GNP of $695 or less. High-income countries have a per capita GNP of $8,626 or more. Less than 14% of the world's 5.5 billion people live in high-income countries, while almost 60% live in low-income countries.

n.a. = data not available   > = greater than   < = less than

Sources: World Bank, *Social Indicators of Development 1995,* Baltimore: Johns Hopkins University Press, 1995. Central Intelligence Agency, *World Fact Book,* Washington, D.C.: Government Printing Office, 1994.

lege. The adult literacy rate in the mid-1980s was an estimated 98%.

32 MEDIA

There is 1 AM radio station, no FM stations, and 1 television station. There were some 54,000 radios and 30,000 television sets in 1991. In 1993, there were approximately 20,000 telephone lines. There are five weekly newspapers, published by private companies or political parties.

33 TOURISM AND RECREATION

Grenada offers visitors a wide array of white sand beaches and excellent sailing. Stayover visitors numbered 92,497 in 1991, 49,571 from the Americas and 23,503 from Europe. There were 1,118 hotel rooms with a 65% occupancy rate.

34 FAMOUS GRENADIANS

Eric Matthew Gairy (b.1922), a labor leader, became the first prime minister of independent Grenada in 1974.

35 BIBLIOGRAPHY

Brizan, George. *Grenada, Island of Conflict—From Amerindians to People's Revolution, 1498–1979.* London: Zed Books, 1984.

Schoenhals, Kai P. *Grenada.* Santa Barbara, Calif.: Clio, 1990.

GUATEMALA

Republic of Guatemala
República de Guatemala

CAPITAL: Guatemala City.

FLAG: The national flag consists of a white vertical stripe between two blue vertical stripes with the coat of arms centered in the white band.

ANTHEM: *Himno Nacional,* beginning "Guatemala feliz" ("Happy Guatemala").

MONETARY UNIT: The quetzal (Q) is a paper currency of 100 centavos. There are coins of 1, 5, 10, and 25 centavos, and notes of 50 centavos and 1, 5, 10, 20, 50, and 100 quetzales. Q1 = $0.1720 (or $1 = Q5.8128). US notes are widely accepted.

WEIGHTS AND MEASURES: The metric system is the legal standard, but some imperial and old Spanish units are also used.

HOLIDAYS: New Year's Day, 1 January; Epiphany, 6 January; Labor Day, 1 May; Anniversary of the Revolution of 1871, 30 June; Independence Day, 15 September; Columbus Day, 12 October; Revolution Day, 20 October; All Saints' Day, 1 November; Christmas, 25 December. Movable religious holidays include Holy Thursday, Good Friday, and Holy Saturday.

TIME: 6 AM = noon GMT.

1 LOCATION AND SIZE

Situated in Central America, Guatemala has an area of 108,890 square kilometers (42,043 square miles), slightly smaller than the state of Tennessee. It has a total boundary length of 2,087 kilometers (1,297 miles).

Guatemala's capital city, Guatemala City, is located in the southcentral part of the country.

2 TOPOGRAPHY

A tropical plain parallels the Pacific Ocean, and lowlands lie along the Caribbean coast. Between them, occupying nearly two-thirds of the country, are the Sierra Madre highlands. In the northwest, Guatemala occupies part of the peninsula of Yucatán (the Yucatán peninsula comprises southeast Mexico, parts of Guatemala and Honduras). In this region there is the lowland forest of Petén, once the home of the Mayas. The largest lakes are Izabal (Lago de Izabal), Petén Itzá (Lago Petén Itzá), and Atitlán (Lago de Atitlán).

3 CLIMATE

Because of its consistently temperate climate, Guatemala has been called the "Land of Eternal Spring." The average annual temperature ranges from 25°–30°C (77°–86°F) on the coast to 15°C (59°F) in the higher mountains.

4 PLANTS AND ANIMALS

Flowers of the temperate zone are found in great numbers. Of special interest is the orchid family, which includes the white nun *(monja blanca)*, the national flower. Native animals include the armadillo, bear, coyote, deer, fox, jaguar, monkey, puma, tapir, and manatee. The national bird is the highland quetzal, the symbol of love of liberty, which is said to die in captivity.

5 ENVIRONMENT

Guatemala's main environmental problems are deforestation—over 50% of the nation's forests have been destroyed since 1890—and consequent soil erosion. The nation's water supply is also at risk due to industrial and agricultural pollutants. As of 1994, ten animal species, ten bird species, and four types of reptiles were endangered.

6 POPULATION

The total population was estimated at 9,952,081 in 1994. The projected population for the year 2000 was 12,222,000. The capital and largest city, Guatemala City, had a 1991 estimated population of 1,095,677.

7 MIGRATION

By late 1992, Mexico was harboring an estimated 49,800 Guatemalan refugees. The Guatemalan government estimated that at the end of 1992 there were 222,900 Central Americans from other countries in Guatemala; many were believed to be in transit to Mexico and the United States.

8 ETHNIC GROUPS

Guatemala has a larger proportion of Amerindians in its total population than any other country in Central America. This population is estimated to be more than 50% of the national total. Persons of mixed Amerindian and white ancestry, called mestizos, constitute about 42% of the national total. Blacks and mulattoes (4%) inhabit the Caribbean lowlands. The white population is estimated at about 1% of the total.

9 LANGUAGES

Spanish is the official and commercial language. Amerindians speak some 28 dialects in five main language groups: Quiché, Mam, Pocomam, and Chol—all of the Mayan language family—and Carib.

10 RELIGIONS

Roman Catholicism is the most common religion (70%). In 1986, an estimated 25% of the population combined Christian beliefs with traditional Amerindian rites. About 5,000 follow tribal religions exclusively. There were about 800 Jews in Guatemala in 1990.

Protestant churches were estimated to have fewer than 500,000 followers in 1980, but rapidly growing fundamentalist groups increased the number of Protestants to some 30% in 1991, most of whom are Pentecostals.

11 TRANSPORTATION

In 1991, the total length of Guatemala's road system was 26,429 kilometers

GUATEMALA

0   20   20   75 Miles

0   25   50   75 Kilometers

MEXICO

Paxbán

San Pedro

Usumacinta

La Pava
Nueva

La Libertad

Tikal

Lago
Petén Itzá

Flores

Pasión

San Luis

BELIZE

Caribbean
Sea

Gulf of
Honduras

Sarstún

San Pablo

SIERRA DE LOS CUCHUMATANES

Cobán

Huehuetenango

Negro

Polochic

Fronteras

Livingston

Lago de
Izabal

Puerto
Barrios

Tajumulco Vol.
13,845 ft.
4220 m.

Santa Cruz
del Quiché

Salamá

SIERRA DE LAS MINAS

Motagua

Quetzaltenango

Coatepeque

Mazatenango

Retalhuleu

Champerico

SIERRA

Lago de
Atitlán

Chimaltenango

Antigua
Guatemala

Tiquisate

MADRE

San José

Guatemala City

El Progreso

Jalapa

Escuintla

Jutiapa

Zacapa

Chiquimula

HONDURAS

Paz

EL SALVADOR

PACIFIC   OCEAN

Guatemala

LOCATION: 13°42′ to 18°30′N; 87°30′ to 92°13′W. **BOUNDARY LENGTHS:** Belize, 266 kilometers (166 miles); Honduras, 256 kilometers (160 miles); El Salvador, 203 kilometers (126 miles); total coastline, 400 kilometers (250 miles); Mexico, 962 kilometers (595 miles). **TERRITORIAL SEA LIMIT:** 12 miles.

(16,423 miles) In 1992, about 260,000 motor vehicles were registered. Guatemala Railways operates 90% of the 870 kilometers (541 miles) of narrow-gauge railway.

Puerto Barrios and Livingston on the Caribbean coast are Guatemala's chief ports; the Pacific coast ports are Champerico and San José. In 1991, Guatemala had

Photo credit: Anne Kalosh

A cane cutter on a sugar plantation.

From 1524 until 1821, Guatemala was the center of government for a captaincy-general which extended from Yucatán peninsula to Panama. Spanish political and social institutions were added to Amerindian village life and customs, producing a hybrid culture.

In 1821, the captaincy-general won its independence from Spain and, along with present-day Costa Rica, El Salvador, Honduras, and Nicaragua, formed the United Provinces of Central America in 1824, which lasted until 1838–39. Guatemala proclaimed its independence in 1839.

In the 1950s, the government of president Jacobo Árbenz Guzmán took over the holdings of the United Fruit Co., a United States firm, as part of a land reform program. In the summer of 1954, Colonel Carlos Castillo Armas and an army of Guatemalan exiles, backed by the Central Intelligence Agency (CIA) of the United States, invaded Guatemala from Honduras and toppled the government. Castillo took over, restored the United States properties, and ruled by decree until 1957. General Miguel Ydígoras Fuentes, who became president in 1958, allowed Guatemala to be used as a training area for Cuban exiles in the abortive United States' invasion of the Bay of Pigs in April 1961.

one registered cargo ship of 4,129 gross tons. Aurora Airport at Guatemala City, the first air terminal in Central America, serves aircraft of all sizes, including jumbo jets.

12 HISTORY

The classical Mayan civilization, which began about AD 300, featured highly developed arts and sciences and extensive trade. It collapsed around AD 900 and disintegrated into a number of separate groups. Despite the Amerindians' resistance, they were conquered by the Spanish in 1523–24.

Dr. Julio César Méndez Montenegro, elected in 1966, was the first civilian president since Árbenz and the last for 20 years. After several years of violence between the army and left-wing guerrilla forces, Guatemala returned to military rule with the election of Colonel Carlos

Arana Osorio as president in 1970. Political violence by the military, the left, and right-wing death squads continued for over 20 years, with a succession of governments unable to contain it. In 1993, the military intervened and Ramior de León Carpio was appointed president on 5 June. De León, a human rights advocate, promised to bring to justice those responsible for the dismal state of human rights in Guatemala.

13 GOVERNMENT

In theory, Guatemala is a republic. The president is elected by direct vote for a five-year term and may not be reelected. Each district elects at least two deputies to the single-chamber National Congress. In 1991 there were 116 seats in Congress. Guatemala is divided into 22 departments, plus Guatemala City.

14 POLITICAL PARTIES

Political parties include the Christian Democrats (partido de Democracía Cristiana Guatemalteca—DCG) and the Solidarity Action Movement (Movimiento para Acción y Solidaridad—MAS).

15 JUDICIAL SYSTEM

Courts include the 9-member Supreme Court, 10 courts of appeals, 33 civil courts of first instance, and 10 penal courts.

16 ARMED FORCES

In 1993 the armed forces numbered 42,000 in the army, 1,200 in the navy, and 1,400 in the air force. Defense expenditures amounted to $113 million (1990).

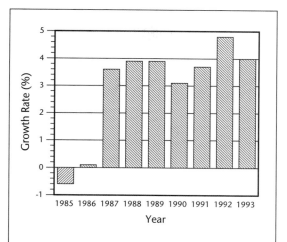

Yearly growth rate of the economy. This economic indicator tells by what percent the economy has increased or decreased when compared with the previous year.

17 ECONOMY

Since the Spanish conquest in the 1500s, the economy of Guatemala has depended on the export of one or two agricultural products. In 1986, the chief exports in order of value were coffee, bananas, sugar, and cotton. In the 1990s the Guatemalan economy—the largest in Central America—has been growing at a healthy pace.

18 INCOME

In 1992, Guatemala's gross national product (GNP) was $9,568 million at current prices, or about $1,100 per person.

19 INDUSTRY

In 1993, manufacturing occupied third place in the country's economy. Most manufacturing is devoted to light assembly and food processing operations. Products include beverages, candles, cigarettes, furniture, matches, rubber goods, and apparel.

20 LABOR

Most of Guatemala's Amerindian population engages in subsistence agriculture and self-employed handicraft activity. In 1990, the number of Guatemalan workers was 2,880,000. Unemployment in 1990 was estimated at 40.7%.

21 AGRICULTURE

The principal cash crops are coffee, sugar, bananas, and cotton, followed by hemp, essential oils, and cacao. Cash crop output in 1992 included 9,788,000 tons of sugarcane, 207,000 tons of coffee, 18,000 tons of cotton, and 465,000 tons of bananas. Production of crops for domestic consumption included 1,250,000 tons of corn and 100,000 tons of dry beans, along with rice, wheat, and fruits and vegetables.

22 DOMESTICATED ANIMALS

The wool industry in the western highlands supplies the famed Guatemalan weavers. In 1992, there were 2,097,000 head of cattle, 1,100,000 hogs, 676,000 sheep, and 114,000 horses.

23 FISHING

Guatemalan waters are rich in fish, including shrimp, snapper, and tuna. The total catch in 1992 was 6,733 tons.

24 FORESTRY

The forests in the northwest region yield cabinet woods, timber, extracts, oils,

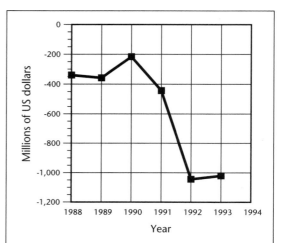

Yearly balance of trade measured in millions of US dollars. The balance of trade is the difference between what a country sells to other countries (its exports) and what it buys (its imports). If a country imports more than it exports, it has a negative balance of trade (a trade deficit). If exports exceed imports there is a positive balance of trade (a trade surplus).

gums, and dyes. Mahogany, cedar, and balsam are important export products, as is chicle for chewing gum.

25 MINING

The principal commercial minerals are antimony, gold, iron ore, and lead. Nickel deposits in the area of Lake Izabal (Lago de Izabal) had an annual production capacity of 9,000 tons in 1991. In 1990, about 60 kilograms of gold was produced.

26 FOREIGN TRADE

Main export items include coffee, sugar, cardamom, bananas, and other non-traditional vegetables, and textiles and apparel. Primary imports are machinery, electronics, petroleum products, chemicals, plastics and paper products. Guatemala's leading trading partners were the United States, Mexico, Japan and Germany.

27 ENERGY AND POWER

In 1991, total electricity production reached 2,330 million kilowatt hours. Guatemala's main petroleum resources lie in the north and around the Gulf of Honduras, where much exploration has taken place. Production averaged 1,352 barrels per day in 1991.

28 SOCIAL DEVELOPMENT

Social security provides maternity benefits, general medical insurance, and pensions for the disabled, aged, widows, and minors. Despite legal equality, women are paid significantly less than their male counterparts.

29 HEALTH

From 1985–92, only 34% of the population had access to health care services. Among the chief causes of death are heart disease, intestinal parasites, bronchitis, influenza, and tuberculosis. Malnutrition, alcoholism, and inadequate sanitation and housing also pose serious health problems. The average life expectancy is 65 years. From 1966–92, there were about 140,000 war-related deaths.

30 HOUSING

Many of the nation's urban housing units and most of its rural dwellings are poorly built and lack electricity and drinkable water. In 1983, only 48% of the urban population and 28% of the rural population had sewer service.

31 EDUCATION

In 1990, the adult literacy rate was estimated at 55% (males: 63% and females: 47%). Elementary education is free and compulsory for six years. In 1991 there were 9,362 primary schools with 1,249,413 pupils and 36,757 teachers. The general secondary schools had 294,907 pupils. The University of San Carlos of Guatemala, in Guatemala City, is the most important center of higher learning.

32 MEDIA

In 1992 there were 91 AM radio stations, and 25 television stations. In 1991 there were an estimated 625,000 radios and 490,000 television sets. In 1993 there were 190,218 telephones.

The leading daily newspapers published in Guatemala City (with 1991 circulations) are *Prensa Libre* (72,000); *El Gráfico* (60,000); and *Diario la Hora* (17,000).

33 TOURISM AND RECREATION

Tourism has rebounded since Guatemala's return to civilian rule in 1986. In 1991, a record 513,620 foreign visitors entered the country; 406,595 from the Americas and 93,630 from Europe. There were 23,022 rooms with an 83.5% occupancy rate. Tourist expenditure in 1993 increased to $275 million. Guatemala's main tourist attractions are Mayan ruins, such as Tikal; colonial churches in Guatemala City,

Selected Social Indicators

These statistics are estimates for the period 1988 to 1993. For comparison purposes, data for the United States and averages for low-income countries and high-income countries are also given.

Indicator	Guatemala	Low-income countries	High-income countries	United States
Per capita gross national product†	**$1,100**	$380	$23,680	$24,740
Population growth rate	**2.9%**	1.9%	0.6%	1.0%
Population growth rate in urban areas	**3.9%**	3.9%	0.8%	1.3%
Population per square kilometer of land	**89**	78	25	26
Life expectancy in years	**65**	62	77	76
Number of people per physician	**2,185**	>3,300	453	419
Number of pupils per teacher (primary school)	**34**	39	<18	20
Illiteracy rate (15 years and older)	**45%**	41%	<5%	<3%
Energy consumed per capita (kg of oil equivalent)	**159**	364	5,203	7,918

† The gross national product (GNP) is the total dollar value of all goods and services produced by a country in a year. The per capita GNP is calculated by dividing a country's GNP by its population. The World Bank defines low-income countries as those with a per capita GNP of $695 or less. High-income countries have a per capita GNP of $8,626 or more. Less than 14% of the world's 5.5 billion people live in high-income countries, while almost 60% live in low-income countries.

> = greater than   < = less than

Sources: World Bank, *Social Indicators of Development 1995,* Baltimore: Johns Hopkins University Press, 1995. Central Intelligence Agency, *World Fact Book,* Washington, D.C.: Government Printing Office, 1994.

Antigua Guatemala, and other towns and villages; and the colorful markets and fiestas.

34 FAMOUS GUATEMALANS

Well-known 20th-century Guatemalan political personalities are Colonel Jácobo Árbenz Guzmán (1913–71), president during 1951–54, and General Miguel Ydígoras Fuentes (1896–1982), president during 1958–63. The novelist Miguel Ángel Asturias (1899–1974) was awarded the Nobel Prize for literature in 1967.

35 BIBLIOGRAPHY

American University. *Guatemala: A Country Study.* Washington, D.C.: Government Printing Office, 1983.

Brill, M. and H. Targ. *Guatemala.* Chicago: Children's Press, 1993.

Guatemala in Pictures. Minneapolis: Lerner, 1987.

Sexton, James D. *Campesino: The Diary of a Guatemalan Indian.* Tempe: University of Arizona Press, 1985.

Smith, Griffin, Jr. "Guatemala: A Fragile Democracy." *National Geographic,* June 1988, 768–803.

Stuart, George E. "Maya Heartland Under Siege." *National Geographic,* November 1992, 94–107.

Woodward, Ralph Lee. *Guatemala.* Santa Barbara, Calif.: Clio, 1992.

GUINEA

Republic of Guinea
République de Guinée

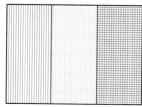

CAPITAL: Conakry.

FLAG: The national flag is a tricolor of red, yellow, and green vertical stripes.

ANTHEM: *Liberté (Liberty)*.

MONETARY UNIT: A new currency, the syli (s), of 100 cauris, was introduced in October 1972; s1 = 10 old Guinea francs. The Guinea franc (GFr) of 100 centimes was restored in January 1986 on a one-to-one basis with the syli. There are notes of 25, 50, 100, 500, 1,000, and 5,000 GFr. GFr1 = $0.0023 (or $1 = GFr440).

WEIGHTS AND MEASURES: The metric system is the legal standard.

HOLIDAYS: New Year's Day, 1 January; Labor Day, 1 May; Anniversary of Women's Revolt, 27 August; Referendum Day, 28 September; Independence Day, 2 October; Armed Forces Day, 1 November; Day of 1970 Invasion, 22 November; Christmas, 25 December. Movable religious holidays include 'Id al-Fitr, 'Id al-'Adha', and Easter Monday.

TIME: GMT.

1 LOCATION AND SIZE

Guinea, on the west coast of Africa, has an area of 245,860 square kilometers (94,927 square miles), extending 831 kilometers (516 miles) southeast–northwest and 493 kilometers (306 miles) northeast–southwest. Comparatively, the area occupied by Guinea is slightly smaller than the state of Oregon.

Guinea's capital city, Conakry, is located on the country's Atlantic coast.

2 TOPOGRAPHY

The country can be divided into four regions: Lower Guinea (Guinée Maritime), the coastal plain; Middle Guinea, a plateau region deeply cut in many places by narrow valleys; Upper Guinea (Haute Guinée), a gently rolling plain; and the forested Guinea Highlands (Guinée Forestière), which include Mt. Nimba (1,752 meters/5,747 feet), the highest peak in the country, at the juncture of Guinea, Liberia, and Côte d'Ivoire.

The Niger River and its important tributary the Milo have their source in the Guinea Highlands.

3 CLIMATE

The coastal region and much of the inland area have a tropical climate with a long rainy season of six months, a relatively high and uniform annual temperature, and high humidity. Conakry's year-round average high is 29°C (84°F), and the low is 23°C (73°F). Its average rainfall is 430 centimeters (169 inches) per year. April is the hottest month. July and August are the wettest.

4 PLANTS AND ANIMALS

Dense mangrove forests grow along the river mouths. Farther inland, the typical vegetation of Lower Guinea is woodland, with many woody vines and bushes below. The higher plateaus and peaks have dense forest, and some plants found nowhere else in the world have been reported there. Large areas of Upper Guinea have only tall grass. Trees include the shea nut, tamarind, and locust bean. There is rain forest along the border with Liberia.

The elephant, hippopotamus, buffalo, lion, leopard, and many kinds of antelope and monkey are to be found in Guinea, as well as crocodiles and several species of venomous snakes. Birds are plentiful and diverse.

5 ENVIRONMENT

Centuries of slash-and-burn agriculture have caused forested areas to be replaced by grassland or brush. Mining, the expansion of hydroelectric facilities, and pollution contribute to the erosion of the country's soils and desertification. Water pollution and improper waste disposal are major environmental problems in Guinea. Nearly two-thirds of the people living in rural areas do not have pure water. Guinea's cities produce 300,000 tons of solid waste per year. Human activity and hunting have reduced Guinea's wildlife, especially its large mammals. A nature reserve has been established on Mt. Nimba.

6 POPULATION

A 1992 census reported the population at about 5,040,000. This was admittedly an undercount and did not include refugees, either. A 1995 population of 6,700,000 was estimated by the United Nations, which has projected a population of 7,759,000 for the year 2000. Conakry, the capital and largest city, had an estimated population of 1,127,000 in 1990.

7 MIGRATION

After independence, Guineans left the country in increasing numbers, mostly for Senegal and Côte d'Ivoire. In the early and mid-1980s, probably two million Guineans were living abroad, perhaps half of them in Senegal and Côte d'Ivoire. Many of them returned after the end of the Sékou Touré government in 1984. At the end of 1992, Guinea was accommodating 478,500 refugees fleeing the Liberian civil war. There were also about 120,000 refugees from Sierra Leone who were escaping the spillover from the Liberian fighting.

8 ETHNIC GROUPS

Of Guinea's two dozen ethnic groups, three predominate: the Fulani, Malinké, and Susu. Notable among the 3,500 or so non-Africans in the mid-1980s were Lebanese and Syrians.

9 LANGUAGES

French is the official language and the language of government business. A literacy program begun in 1968 sought eventually to teach all citizens to speak and write one of the eight main local languages: Malinké (Maninkakan), Fulani (Poular), Susu,

LOCATION: 8° to 15°w; 7°35' to 12°30'N. BOUNDARY LENGTHS: Senegal, 330 kilometers (205 miles); Mali, 932 kilometers (579 miles); Côte d'Ivoire, 605 kilometers (376 miles); Liberia, 563 kilometers (350 miles); Sierra Leone, 652 kilometers (405 miles); Atlantic coastline, 352 kilometers (219 miles); Guinea-Bissau, 386 kilometers (240 miles). TERRITORIAL SEA LIMIT: 12 miles.

Kpelle (Guerzé), Loma (Toma), Kissi, Coniagui, and Bassari, all of which belong to the Niger-Congo language group.

10 RELIGIONS

More than 90% of all Guineans, particularly the Fulani and Malinké, are Muslims. Most of the remainder practice traditional African religions. Less than 2% of the population is Christian. In May 1967, President Sékou Touré ordered that only Guinean nationals be allowed to serve in the country's Roman Catholic priesthood.

Photo credit: AP/Wide World Photos

Guinean students held a silent protest in Conakry during a youth rally the Pope attended on his visit to Guinea. The banner reads, "Stop the repression. Yes to peace. For dialogue. Peace to the soul of our martyrs."

11 TRANSPORTATION

Lack of an adequate transportation network has slowed the country's development. As of 1991, the railway was being improved with French assistance. A standard-gauge track of about 112 kilometers (70 miles) along this line, between Conakry and Kindia, links the port and the OBK bauxite mine. Of 30,100 kilometers (18,700 miles) of roads, only some 1,145 kilometers (711 miles) were paved in 1987. There were 23,155 automobiles and 13,000 commercial vehicles in 1992. Conakry has a natural deepwater harbor that handles foreign cargo (mostly bauxite and alumina). Conakry's airport handles international jet traffic.

12 HISTORY

The Malinké people did not begin arriving in Guinea until the thirteenth century, nor did the Fulani come in considerable numbers until the seventeenth century. In 1725, a holy war *(jihad)* was declared in the northwest by Muslim Fulani. The onslaught, directed against the Malinké, was ultimately successful in establishing the independence of the Fulani of the northwest and uniting them under the Almany (or head chief) Alfa of Timbo.

Meanwhile, European exploration of the Guinea coast was begun by the Portuguese in the middle of the fifteenth century. By the seventeenth century, French, British, and Portuguese traders and slavers were competing with one another. When the slave trade was prohibited during the first half of the nineteenth century, Guinea's creeks provided secluded hiding places for slavers pursued by the ships of the British Royal Navy. French rights along the coast were expressly preserved by the Peace of Paris (1814), and French—as well as British and Portuguese—trading activities expanded in the middle years of the nineteenth century, when trade in peanuts, palm oil, hides, and rubber replaced that in slaves. A French protectorate was established over the region in 1881, but France did not gain a secure hold on the area for another 15 years. The capture in 1898 of Samory Touré, a Malinké who had led resistance to the French, marked the end of local resistance to France's occupation of Guinea, Ivory Coast (now Côte d'Ivoire), and southern Mali.

In 1891, Guinea was declared a French territory separate from Senegal, of which it had been a part. Four years later, the French territories in West Africa were united under a governor-general, an arrangement that remained substantially unchanged until Guinea attained independence. In 1946, Africans in Guinea became French citizens, but citizenship was at first restricted to certain groups and was not replaced by universal adult voting rights until 1957.

The End of Colonial Rule

Guinea became an independent state on 2 October 1958, with Ahmed Sékou Touré, leader of Guinea's strongest labor union, as president. During its first three decades of independence, Guinea developed into a militantly Socialist state, with nearly complete government control over the country's economic and political life. Guinea expelled the US Peace Corps in 1966 because of supposed involvement in a plot to overthrow President Touré. Similar charges were directed against France. Diplomatic relations were ended in 1965 and did not resume until 1975. An ongoing source of tension between Guinea and its French-speaking neighbors was the estimated half-million Guineans in Senegal and Côte d'Ivoire, some of them active dissidents who, in 1966, formed the National Liberation Front of Guinea (Front de Libération Nationale de Guinée—FLNG). Between 1969 and

1976, according to Amnesty International, Guinea detained 4,000 persons for political reasons, with the fate of 2,900 unknown.

In 1977, protests against the government's economic policy led to riots in which three regional governors were killed. Touré responded by relaxing restrictions, offering amnesty to exiles (thousands of whom returned), and releasing hundreds of political prisoners. Ties were loosened with the Soviet bloc, as Touré sought increased Western aid and private investment for Guinea's sagging economy. Touré was elected unopposed to a fourth 7-year term as president on 9 May 1982. According to the government radio, he received 100% of the vote. A new constitution was adopted that month, and during the summer Touré visited the United States as part of an economic policy reversal that found Guinea seeking Western investment to develop its huge mineral reserves. Measures announced in 1983 brought further economic liberalization.

Military Takes Over

Touré died on 26 March 1984 while undergoing cardiac treatment at the Cleveland Clinic, where he had been rushed after being stricken in Sa'udi Arabia the previous day. On 3 April, however, just as the Political Bureau of the ruling Guinea Democratic Party (PDG) was about to name its choice as Touré's successor, the armed forces seized power, denouncing the last years of Touré's rule as a "bloody and ruthless dictatorship." The constitution was suspended, the National Assembly dissolved, and the PDG abolished. The leader of the takeover, Colonel Lansana Conté, assumed the presidency on 5 April, heading the Military Committee for National Recovery (Comité Militaire de Redressement National—CMRN). About 1,000 political prisoners were freed.

Conté suppressed an attempted military takeover led by Colonel Diarra Traoré on 4 July 1985. Almost two years later, it was announced that 58 persons, including both takeover leaders and members of Toure's government, had been sentenced to death. However, it was believed that many of them, as well as Traoré, had actually been shot days after the takeover attempt. All were identified with the Malinké, who were closely identified with the Touré regime. The military government adopted free-market policies in an effort to revive the economy. Under pressure locally and from abroad, Guinea embarked on a transition to multiparty democracy. The military-dominated government has not been entirely supportive of the process. It legalized parties in April 1992, but did not really allow them to function freely. It postponed presidential elections for over a year (until 19 December 1993) and then verified the results (Conté was elected by a narrow margin) after international monitors had rejected them as fraudulent. The legislative elections were delayed even longer. The military leadership continues to govern in the face of growing unpopularity.

13 GOVERNMENT

In practice, under the Touré regime, the legislature, the cabinet, and the national administration were subordinate to the PDG (the ruling party) in the direction and control of the nation. The Assembly and the cabinet (appointed by Touré) carried out the decisions and orders of the party arrived at by the party congress, national conference, and the Political Bureau.

The armed forces leaders who seized power after Touré's death have ruled Guinea first through the Military Committee for National Recovery (CMRN), followed by a transitional Committee of National Recovery (CTRN) set up in February 1991. Although two-thirds of the cabinet members are civilians, military leaders still control the government.

14 POLITICAL PARTIES

Political parties were legalized in April 1992. By late 1993, over 40 political parties were legally registered. Some were allied with the military government (e.g., the Party for Unity and Progress) and others were identifiably ethnic-based. The most significant national opposition parties are the Rally for the Guinean People (RPG), the Union for a New Republic (UNR), and the Party for Renewal and Progress.

15 JUDICIAL SYSTEM

There are district courts, two Courts of Appeal (in Kankan and in Conakry), and a Supreme Court. There is also a State Security Court and a military tribunal, which handles criminal cases involving military personnel. A traditional system of dispute resolution exists alongside the court system at the village and neighborhood level.

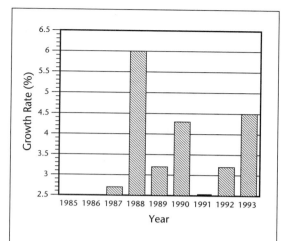

Yearly growth rate of the economy. This economic indicator tells by what percent the economy has increased or decreased when compared with the previous year.

16 ARMED FORCES

The armed forces numbered about 9,700 in 1993, including 8,500 in the army, 400 in the navy, and 800 in the air force. The army had 11 battalions with 53 T-34 and T-54 tanks among its predominantly Soviet-made equipment. The navy had 9 craft, and the air force 12 combat aircraft, including 8 Soviet-made MiG-21 fighters. There was a People's Militia of 7,000 and 2,600 in the police force and Republican Guard. Defense spending in 1989 was estimated at $27 million.

17 ECONOMY

After two decades of socialist-style economic management, a major reform movement gained political power in 1984. Of the more than 100 state enterprises, most were closed. Food prices were decontrolled, private trade reestablished, and the government began actively to seek foreign investment for sectors other than mining and energy. Monetary reform was enacted in early 1986, with a 93% currency devaluation.

18 INCOME

In 1992 Guinea's gross national product (GNP) was $3,103 million at current prices, or $500 per person. For the period 1985–92 the average inflation rate was 23.1%, resulting in a real growth rate in GNP of 0.8% per person.

19 INDUSTRY

Shortages of raw materials, technical experience, and adequate markets are common. While the alumina smelter at Fria operates at over 90% capacity, other industrial plants operate at closer to 10% capacity. Among Guinea's other plants are a fruit cannery at Mamou, a fruit juice factory at Kankan, a tea factory at Macenta, and a palm oil works at Kassa. During the socialist years, a sizeable state-owned industrial sector emerged. Guinea had 135 state-run industries in 1985. All but 24 had been sold or dissolved by mid-1992.

20 LABOR

Over 80% of Guinea's population relies on subsistence agriculture and livestock raising. Most of the wage and salary earners work for the government. Mining is the other major source of salaried employment. The work week for industry is 40 hours. Salaried workers, including public sector civilian employees, have the right to strike.

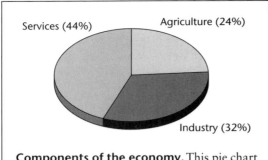

Services (44%)   Agriculture (24%)

Industry (32%)

Components of the economy. This pie chart shows how much of the country's economy is devoted to agriculture (includes forestry, hunting, and fishing), industry, or services.

21 AGRICULTURE

Guinea publishes no production statistics, so hard data on agricultural output are unavailable. The principal subsistence crops (with estimated 1992 production) are manioc, 660,000 tons; rice, 757,000 tons; sweet potatoes, 100,000 tons; yams, 100,000 tons; and corn, 94,000 tons. Cash crops are peanuts, palm kernels, bananas, pineapples, coffee, coconuts, sugarcane, and citrus fruits.

22 DOMESTICATED ANIMALS

In 1992 there were an estimated 1,900,000 head of cattle, 510,000 sheep, 460,000 goats, 33,000 hogs, and 13,000,000 chickens. Almost all the cattle are the small humpless Ndama variety kept by the Fulani in the northwest and Upper Guinea, where sheep and goats also are herded.

23 FISHING

Guinea's annual ocean fisheries potential exceeds 200,000 tons, according to World Bank estimates. Tuna is the most important catch. Several small scale fishing ventures have been established, including a shrimp farming project financed by the African Development Bank.

24 FORESTRY

Forests and woodland make up almost two-thirds of Guinea's land area. The nation's forest resources offer great promise, the major constraint on development being lack of adequate transportation. Removal of roundwood was estimated at 3,988,000 cubic meters in 1991.

25 MINING

Mining is the most active sector of the Guinean economy. As of 1991, Guinea was second only to Australia in the production of bauxite. Peak production was 17.5 million tons in 1990, up from 9 million tons in 1986. However, declining prices have led the Guinean mineral industry to diversify into gold and diamond production.

26 FOREIGN TRADE

Export estimates for 1988 show bauxite and alumina as the export leaders, at 78% of total earnings. Diamonds and gold accounted for an additional 15%. Coffee and other products represented another 7% of the total. Semi-manufactured goods topped the list of imports at 44% of the total. Making up the other 56% were food products (13%), consumer goods (13%), petroleum products (14%), and capital goods (16%).

Guinea's exports (1986) went primarily to the United States (23%), Germany

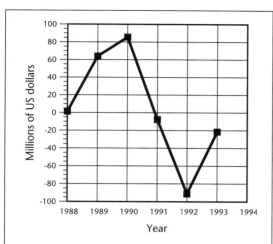

Yearly balance of trade measured in millions of US dollars. The balance of trade is the difference between what a country sells to other countries (its exports) and what it buys (its imports). If a country imports more than it exports, it has a negative balance of trade (a trade deficit). If exports exceed imports there is a positive balance of trade (a trade surplus).

(14%), and Spain (13%). The biggest share of imports came from France (37%).

27 ENERGY AND POWER

In 1991, a total of about 521 million kilowatt hours was produced, much of it consumed by the Boké bauxite-processing complex. In 1991, wood accounted for 70% of the total energy requirement.

28 SOCIAL DEVELOPMENT

There was a decline in social services during the Touré years (1958–84). Although officially free medical treatment is available, as well as free care for pregnant women and for infants, in reality, health service is poor. Life expectancy is 45 years; 41 years for males and 46 years for females, among the lowest in the world.

29 HEALTH

In 1992 there were 773 physicians, or 13 per 100,000 people. It is estimated that 75% of the population had access to health care services. Malaria, yaws, leprosy, and sleeping sickness (in the forest areas in the Guinea Highlands) have been the major tropical diseases. Also widespread are schistosomiasis, tuberculosis, and venereal diseases.

30 HOUSING

The most common rural dwelling is round, windowless, and made of wattle and daub or sun-dried mud bricks, with a floor of packed earth and a conical thatched roof. Urban dwellings are usually one-story rectangular frame or mud-brick buildings, generally without electricity or indoor plumbing.

31 EDUCATION

Education is free and compulsory between the ages of 7 and 13. In 1990, the estimated adult literacy rate was 24.0%, for males 34.9% and 13.4% for females. Children go through 6 years of primary and 7 years of secondary school.

In 1991 there were 359,406 primary-level pupils. Secondary schools, general, vocational and teachers' training served 768,603 pupils. The Gamal Abdel Nasser Polytechnic Institute, established at Conakry in 1963, enrolled about 120 students in 1986. The Valéry Giscard d'Estaing Institute of Agro-Zootechnical Sciences had 1,003 students in 1986. The Univer-

Selected Social Indicators

These statistics are estimates for the period 1988 to 1993. For comparison purposes, data for the United States and averages for low-income countries and high-income countries are also given.

Indicator	Guinea	Low-income countries	High-income countries	United States
Per capita gross national product†	$500	$380	$23,680	$24,740
Population growth rate	3.1%	1.9%	0.6%	1.0%
Population growth rate in urban areas	5.8%	3.9%	0.8%	1.3%
Population per square kilometer of land	25	78	25	26
Life expectancy in years	45	62	77	76
Number of people per physician	7,692	>3,300	453	419
Number of pupils per teacher (primary school)	49	39	<18	20
Illiteracy rate (15 years and older)	76%	41%	<5%	<3%
Energy consumed per capita (kg of oil equivalent)	66	364	5,203	7,918

† The gross national product (GNP) is the total dollar value of all goods and services produced by a country in a year. The per capita GNP is calculated by dividing a country's GNP by its population. The World Bank defines low-income countries as those with a per capita GNP of $695 or less. High-income countries have a per capita GNP of $8,626 or more. Less than 14% of the world's 5.5 billion people live in high-income countries, while almost 60% live in low-income countries.   > = greater than   < = less than

Sources: World Bank, Social Indicators of Development 1995, Baltimore: Johns Hopkins University Press, 1995. Central Intelligence Agency, World Fact Book, Washington, D.C.: Government Printing Office, 1994.

sity of Conakry, founded in 1984, was in the process of formation in 1987.

32 MEDIA

All media are owned or controlled by the government, and censorship is strict. Telephone, telegraph, and postal services are also government-owned. In 1991 there were about 248,000 radio receivers and 42,000 television sets in use.

33 TOURISM AND RECREATION

An annual cultural festival that includes theatrical and dance groups is held in October.

34 FAMOUS GUINEANS

Samory Touré (1830?–1900), a Malinké born in Upper Guinea, conquered large areas and resisted French military forces until 1898. The founder of modern Guinea was his alleged great-grandson Ahmed Sékou Touré (1922–84), a prominent labor leader and political figure who became Guinea's first president in 1958.

35 BIBLIOGRAPHY

Adamolekun, Lapido. Sékou Touré's Guinea: An Exercise in Nation Building. New York: Methuen, 1976.

Nkrumah, Kwame. Kwame Nkrumah: The Conakry Years, His Life and Letters. Atlantic Highlands, N.J.: PANAF, 1990.

Rivière, Claude. Guinea: The Mobilization of a People. Ithaca, N.Y.: Cornell University Press, 1977.

GUINEA-BISSAU

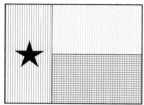

Republic of Guinea-Bissau
República da Guiné-Bissau

CAPITAL: Bissau.

FLAG: The flag has equal horizontal stripes of yellow over green, with a red vertical stripe at the hoist bearing a black star.

ANTHEM: *Esta é a Nossa Pátria Bem Amada (This Is Our Well-Beloved Land).*

MONETARY UNIT: The Guinean peso (PG) of 100 centavos replaced the Guinean escudo (GE) on 2 February 1976. There are coins of 50 centavos and 1, 2½, 5, and 20 pesos, and notes of 50, 100, 500, and 1,000 pesos. PG1 = $0.0808 (or $1 = PG12.369).

WEIGHTS AND MEASURES: The metric system is used.

HOLIDAYS: New Year's Day, 1 January; Death of Amilcar Cabral, 20 January; Labor Day, 1 May; Anniversary of the Killing of Pidjiguiti, 3 August; National Day, 24 September; Anniversary of the Movement of Readjustment, 14 November; Christmas Day, 25 December. Movable religious holidays include Korité (end of Ramadan) and Tabaski (Feast of the Sacrifice).

TIME: 11 AM = noon GMT.

1 LOCATION AND SIZE

Situated on the west coast of Africa, Guinea-Bissau, formerly Portuguese Guinea, has a total area of 36,120 square kilometers (13,946 square miles). Comparatively, the area occupied by Guinea-Bissau is slightly less than three times the size of the state of Connecticut.Besides its mainland territory, it includes the Bijagós Archipelago (Archipélago dos Bijagós) and various coastal islands.

The capital city, Bissau, is located on the country's Atlantic coast.

2 TOPOGRAPHY

The country is swampy at the coast and low-lying inland, except in the northeast. There are no major mountains. The most important rivers include the Cacheu, Géba, and Corubal.

3 CLIMATE

Guinea-Bissau has a hot, humid climate, with a rainy season from mid-May to mid-November and a cooler dry season the rest of the year. During the dry season, the harmattan (dust-laden wind) blows from the Sahara.

4 PLANTS AND ANIMALS

There are thick jungles in the interior plains, rice and mangrove fields along the coastal plains and swamps, and tropical grasslands in the north. Parts of Guinea-Bissau are rich in game, big and small. Several species of antelope, buffalo, monkeys, and snakes are found.

5 ENVIRONMENT

One of the most significant environmental problems in Guinea-Bissau is fire, which destroys 40,000 hectares (99,000 acres) of land per year and accelerates the loss of the nation's forests. Another environmental issue is soil damage.

6 POPULATION

The population of Guinea-Bissau was 767,739 according to the 1979 census, and was estimated at 1,099,676 in 1994. Bissau, the capital city, had an estimated population of 71,000 in 1990.

7 MIGRATION

In 1975, after the settlement of a war against the Portuguese colonial administration, approximately 100,000 refugees returned from neighboring Senegal and Guinea. At the end of 1992, there were still 5,000 in Senegal, and 12,200 Senagalese in Guinea-Bissau.

8 ETHNIC GROUPS

The principal African ethnic groups are the Balante (an estimated 30% of the African population); the Fulani (20%); the Malinké (13%); and the Mandyako (14%) and Pepel (7%). The Cape Verdean mulatto (mixed-race) community accounts for about 2% of the total population.

9 LANGUAGES

Each tribe has its own language, subdivided into numerous dialects. A Guinean "crioulo," or Africanized Portuguese patois, is the national language, while Portuguese is the official language.

10 RELIGIONS

Most of the population (54%) has retained traditional African religious beliefs, even the minority who have formally adopted Islam or Christianity. As of 1993, an estimated 38% of the population adhered to the Islamic faith, while about 8% was Christian.

11 TRANSPORTATION

There is no rail line in Guinea-Bissau. In 1991, the country had an estimated 3,218 kilometers (2,000 miles) of roads. In the same year, there were some 5,700 motorized vehicles, mostly in the city of Bissau. Bissau is the main port and the site of a modern international airport.

12 HISTORY

The earliest inhabitants, hunters and fishermen, were replaced by the Baga and other peoples who came from the east. The Portuguese explorer Nuno Tristão arrived in the region in June 1446 and established the first trading posts. The slave trade developed during the seventeenth century, centering around the port of Bissau. In 1879, the area was made a separate Portuguese dependency.

In 1951, Guinea-Bissau was made a Portuguese overseas province. In September 1956, a group of dissatisfied Cape Verdeans founded an underground movement aimed at achieving independence from Portugal. It was named the African Party for the Independence of Guinea and Cape Verde (Partido Africano de Independência da Guiné e Cabo Verde—PAIGC), and Amilcar Cabral became its secretary-general. By 1963, large-scale guerrilla warfare had broken out in the territory.

During the following years, PAIGC soldiers, fighting a Portuguese force of about 30,000, increased their hold on the countryside. When Cabral was assassinated on 20 January 1973, Aristides Pereira took over the leadership of the movement, which on 24 September 1973 proclaimed the independence of the Republic of Guinea-Bissau. On 26 August 1974, the Portuguese government (under new leadership following a takeover earlier that year) and the PAIGC signed an agreement in Algiers providing for the independence of Guinea-Bissau effective 10 September.

The new government, under President Luis de Almeida Cabral, had to deal with extensive economic turmoil brought about by the war. On 14 November 1980, President Cabral, who was of mixed European and American Indian ancestry with close ties to Cape Verde, was overthrown by a group of Guinean blacks under João Bernando Vieira's command. Vieira and the PAIGC ruled Guinea-Bissau as a one-party state for ten years. However, in 1990, he denounced single-party rule, and in April 1991, Guinea-Bissau formally began a multiparty system and adopted a new constitution.

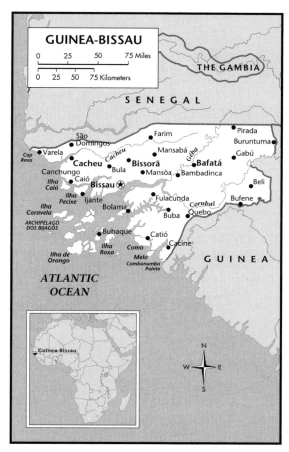

LOCATION: 10°52′ to 12°42′N; 13°38′ to 16°43′W.
BOUNDARY LENGTHS: Senegal, 338 kilometers (210 miles); Guinea, 386 kilometers (240 miles); Atlantic coastline, 398 kilometers (247 miles). **TERRITORIAL SEA LIMIT:** 12 miles.

13 GOVERNMENT

A new constitution was adopted in April 1991, and opposition political parties were permitted. Government continues to control the pace of political reform, which remains very slow. In 1993, it formed a National Elections Commission charged with organizing legislative and presidential elections for March 1994.

14 POLITICAL PARTIES

Formerly, the ruling African Party for the Independence of Guinea and Cape Verde (Partido Africano de Independência da Guiné e Cabo Verde—PAIGC) was the sole legal party. However, opposition parties were legalized by a new constitution adopted in April 1991. The most important opposition party is Bafata, the Guinea-Bissau Resistance-Bafata Movement.

15 JUDICIAL SYSTEM

The Supreme Court has jurisdiction over serious crimes and serves as an appeals court for the regional military courts. In rural areas, persons are often tried outside the formal system by traditional law.

16 ARMED FORCES

The People's Revolutionary Armed Forces (FARP) in 1993 numbered 9,200, of whom 6,800 were soldiers, 300 sailors, and 100 airmen, all considered part of a single service army.

17 ECONOMY

Guinea-Bissau's economy is mainly agricultural. The government is firmly committed to market-style economic policies after an initial decade of socialist central planning.

18 INCOME

In 1992 Guinea-Bissau's gross national product (GNP) was $217 million at current prices, or $240 per person. Inflation jumped from 17% in 1988 to 110% in 1992.

19 INDUSTRY

Manufacturing constitutes a very minor part of Guinea-Bissau's economy. Industries include a sugar refinery, and a rice and groundnut processing plant. Brewing,

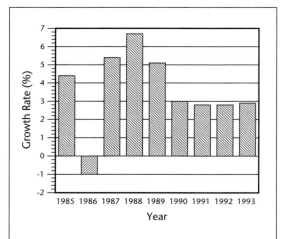

Yearly growth rate of the economy. This economic indicator tells by what percent the economy has increased or decreased when compared with the previous year.

urban construction, and vehicle assembly are also represented.

20 LABOR

Subsistence agriculture sustained about 85% of the population of one million in 1992. The constitution grants workers the freedom to join and form trade unions.

21 AGRICULTURE

Rice is the major staple crop. Corn, millet, and sorghum are also produced and consumed very widely. In 1992, Guinea-Bissau produced 123,000 tons of rice, 25,000 tons of millet, 20,000 tons of peanuts, 25,000 tons of coconuts, 30,000 tons of cashew nuts, and 8,000 tons of palm kernels. Palm kernels, cashew nuts, and peanuts are the most important export crops.

22 DOMESTICATED ANIMALS

In 1992, there were an estimated 450,000 head of cattle and 300,000 hogs, as well as 250,000 sheep and 250,000 goats.

23 FISHING

Guinea-Bissau's total catch was an estimated 5,000 tons in 1991.

24 FORESTRY

Guinean forests and tropical grasslands supply wood and timber for domestic consumption and fuel and construction material. Roundwood production was about 569,000 cubic meters in 1991.

25 MINING

Mineral production in 1991 was limited to crude construction materials, worth about $6 million.

26 FOREIGN TRADE

Cashew nuts have led all exports in terms of revenue, followed by groundnuts, shrimp and fish, sawn wood, cotton and palm kernels. Imports, which were estimated at $54.9 million in 1988, include industrial and commercial supplies, fuels and lubricants, and transport equipment, as well as imported foods, beverages, and tobacco. In 1985, most of Guinea-Bissau's exports went to Romania (44.6%) and France (18.3%). Of Bissau's imports, 20.1% came from Portugal, while 6.0% came from France and 5.8% came from the Netherlands.

27 ENERGY AND POWER

In 1991 hydroelectric power production was 41 million kilowatt hours and crude oil production totaled 4,000 barrels.

28 SOCIAL DEVELOPMENT

Provision of health services, sanitation, and basic education is the principal social goal of the Guinea-Bissau government. Women play an active part in government at all levels.

29 HEALTH

The health care system is inadequate. In 1992, there were an estimated 12 physicians per 100,000 people. The average life expectancy is 47 years: 45 years for males and 49 years for females.

30 HOUSING

As of 1979, 44% of all housing units were adobe, 32% were mud, and 20% were mud and/or quirinton, a combination of woven branches and straw.

31 EDUCATION

In 1988 there were 79,035 primary pupils and 6,630 students enrolled in secondary schools. Education is compulsory between the ages of 7 and 13, but only about 55% of all children in this age group actually attend school. In 1990, 36% of the adult population was estimated to be literate.

32 MEDIA

The Guinea-Bissau's government-owned newspaper, *No Pintcha,* had an estimated circulation of 1,500 in 1991. There are

Selected Social Indicators

These statistics are estimates for the period 1988 to 1993. For comparison purposes, data for the United States and averages for low-income countries and high-income countries are also given.

Indicator	Guinea-Bissau	Low-income countries	High-income countries	United States
Per capita gross national product†	$240	$380	$23,680	$24,740
Population growth rate	2.1%	1.9%	0.6%	1.0%
Population growth rate in urban areas	4.3%	3.9%	0.8%	1.3%
Population per square kilometer of land	28	78	25	26
Life expectancy in years	47	62	77	76
Number of people per physician	8,333	>3,300	453	419
Number of pupils per teacher (primary school)	25	39	<18	20
Illiteracy rate (15 years and older)	64%	41%	<5%	<3%
Energy consumed per capita (kg of oil equivalent)	37	364	5,203	7,918

† The gross national product (GNP) is the total dollar value of all goods and services produced by a country in a year. The per capita GNP is calculated by dividing a country's GNP by its population. The World Bank defines low-income countries as those with a per capita GNP of $695 or less. High-income countries have a per capita GNP of $8,626 or more. Less than 14% of the world's 5.5 billion people live in high-income countries, while almost 60% live in low-income countries.

> = greater than   < = less than

Sources: World Bank, *Social Indicators of Development 1995,* Baltimore: Johns Hopkins University Press, 1995. Central Intelligence Agency, *World Fact Book,* Washington, D.C.: Government Printing Office, 1994.

two radio networks and one television network. In 1991 there were 39,000 radios in the country. An estimated 3,000 telephones were in use in the late 1980s.

33 TOURISM AND RECREATION

Game shooting, a major attraction for many travelers in Africa, is popular in Guinea-Bissau. The island of Bubaque and the town of Bolama are cited for their charm and beauty.

34 FAMOUS GUINEANS

The best-known Guinean of recent years was Amilcar Cabral (1921–73), a key figure in the war for independence. Luis de Almeida Cabral (b.1931), his younger brother, subsequently became the first president of Guinea-Bissau.

35 BIBLIOGRAPHY

Forrest, Joshua. *Guinea-Bissau: Power, Conflict, and Renewal in a West African Nation.* Boulder, Colo.: Westview Press, 1992.
Galli, Rosemary. *Guinea-Bissau.* Santa Barbara, Calif.: Clio, 1990.

GUYANA

Cooperative Republic of Guyana

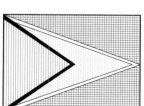

CAPITAL: Georgetown.

FLAG: A red triangle at the hoist extending to the flag's midpoint is bordered on two sides by a narrow black stripe; extending from this is a golden arrowhead pointing toward the fly and bordered on two sides by a narrow white stripe. Two green triangles make up the rest of the flag.

ANTHEM: Begins "Dear land of Guyana, of rivers and plains."

MONETARY UNIT: The Guyanese dollar (G$) of 100 cents is a paper currency tied to the US dollar. There are coins of 1, 5, 10, 25, 50, and 100 cents, and notes of 1, 5, 10, 20, and 100 Guyanese dollars. G$1 = US$0.0075 (or US$1 = G$132.80).

WEIGHTS AND MEASURES: Guyana officially converted to the metric system in 1982, but imperial weights and measures are still in general use.

HOLIDAYS: New Year's Day, 1 January; Republic Day, 23 February; Labor Day, 1 May; Caribbean Day, 26 June; Freedom Day, 7 August; Christmas, 25 December; Boxing Day, 26 December. Movable religious holidays include Good Friday, Easter Monday, Phagwah, 'Id al-'Adha, Yaou-Mun-Nabi, and Dewali.

TIME: 9 AM = noon GMT.

1 LOCATION AND SIZE

Situated on the northeast coast of South America, Guyana is the third-smallest country on the continent, with an area of 214,970 square kilometers (83,000 square miles), slightly smaller than the state of Idaho. Guyana has a total boundary length of 2,921 kilometers (1,815 miles).

Guyana's capital city, Georgetown, is located on the country's Atlantic coast.

2 TOPOGRAPHY

Guyana has three main natural regions: a low-lying coastal plain; a region of heavily forested, hilly land, which comprises almost five-sixths of Guyana's land area; and a region of mountains and savannas in the south and west. There are several large rivers, including the Essequibo, Demerara, and Berbice.

3 CLIMATE

The average temperature at Georgetown is 27°C (81°F). There is little seasonal variation in temperature or in humidity, which averages 80–85%. Rainfall averages 230 centimeters (91 inches) a year along the coast and 150 centimeters (59 inches) in the southwest.

4 PLANTS AND ANIMALS

In inland areas there are extensive equatorial forests, with green-heart a major species. Varieties of trees may number as many as 1,000. Local animals include locusts, moth borers, acoushi ants, bats, and other small mammals. There may be more than 728 species of birds.

5 ENVIRONMENT

Because at least 85% of Guyana is still wilderness, the environment has so far sustained little serious damage. The air is clean, but water supplies are threatened by sewage and by agricultural and industrial chemicals. The nation's cities produce 100,000 tons of solid waste per year.

Kaieteur National Park is the only specifically designated conservation area. In 1994, 12 mammal species, 9 bird species, 3 types of reptiles, and 1 freshwater fish were endangered, as well as 68 of Guyana's 6,000 to 8,000 plant species.

6 POPULATION

Guyana's population (758,619 at the 1980 census) was estimated by the United Nations at 808,000 in 1992. A population of 1,883,000 is projected for the year 2000. The capital and chief port, Georgetown, had a population estimated at 195,000 in 1985.

7 MIGRATION

There was significant emigration in the 1980s, creating shortages of skilled workers and managers. Unofficial estimates put the number at 10,000 to 30,000 a year in the late 1980s. Their destinations were chiefly the United States and Canada. In 1990 there were 123,000 Guyanese-born people in the United States.

8 ETHNIC GROUPS

An estimated 51% of the population is of Asian Indian descent and 43% of African descent. There are also Amerindians, Chinese, Portuguese, and other Europeans, together constituting the remaining 6%.

9 LANGUAGES

English is the official language. Also spoken are Chinese, Portuguese, Amerindian languages, and a patois (dialect) used mainly by those of African descent.

10 RELIGIONS

There are Christian (estimated at 50% in 1993), Hindu (33%), and Muslim (9%) communities. The major Christian denominations include Anglican, Roman Catholic (8%), Methodist, Presbyterian, and Lutheran.

11 TRANSPORTATION

About 187 kilometers (116 miles) of rail track are in service. Georgetown is the main port. Waterfalls and rapids near the coast have prevented the development of river transportation to the interior.

Roadways measured 7,665 kilometers (4,763 miles) in 1991, mostly gravel or dirt. That year, Guyana had about 24,000 passenger cars, and 9,000 commercial taxis, trucks and buses. Georgetown's Timehri International Airport is served by several international carriers. Guyana Airways Corporation, a government company, operates domestic and international air service.

12 HISTORY

The coastline was first charted by Spanish sailors in 1499, at which time the area was inhabited by Amerindians of the Arawak, Carib, and Warrau groups. By 1746, the Dutch had established settlements on the Essequibo, Demerara, and Berbice rivers. The English gained formal possession of them at the Congress of Vienna in 1815, and they were united into the Colony of British Guiana in 1831.

British imperial policy changed after World War II, and British Guiana received a new constitution providing for a two-chamber legislature and universal adult vote. The colony was granted full internal self-government in 1961 and became a sovereign and independent nation on 26 May 1966.

Guyana was proclaimed a cooperative republic on 23 February 1970, the 207th anniversary of a Guyanese slave revolt. The People's National Congress (PNC) ruled as the majority party between 1968–92.

Guyana became known to the United States public in 1978 in the wake of the Jonestown massacre. The previous year, the Government of Guyana had allowed an American, James Warren "Jim" Jones, to establish the People's Temple commune at what became known as Jonestown, in the northwest. After several commune members murdered a group of United States investigators at a nearby airstrip, Jones and more than 900 of his followers committed suicide by drinking poisoned punch on 18 November 1978.

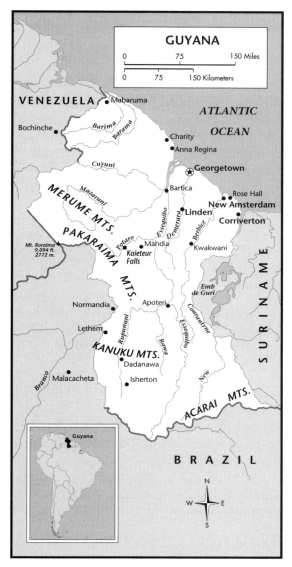

LOCATION: 1°12′ to 8°34′N; 56°29′ to 61°23′W.
BOUNDARY LENGTHS: Atlantic coastline, 459 kilometers (285 miles); Suriname, 600 kilometers (372 miles); Brazil, 1,119 kilometers (694 miles); Venezuela, 743 kilometers (461 miles). **TERRITORIAL SEA LIMIT:** 12 miles.

Desmond Hoyte, president from 1985–92, sought to improve Guyana's relations with non-Socialist nations. By 1992 the country had grown tired of the PNC, and elected Cheddi Jagan of the People's Progressive Party to the presidency.

13 GOVERNMENT

As of 23 February 1970, Guyana became a cooperative republic. Under a new constitution approved in 1980, the single-chamber National Assembly consisted of 53 members. The office of executive president, created by the 1980 constitution, is filled by the leader of the majority party as both chief of state and head of government. The president appoints a cabinet, including a prime minister, who also holds the title of first vice-president. Guyana is divided into ten regions.

14 POLITICAL PARTIES

The People's National Congress (PNC) dominated Guyana's politics from independence in 1968 until 1992. It draws its members primarily from urban blacks. Guyana's other major party is the People's Progressive Party (PPP), which gained the majority position in 1992. Appealing to Asian Indian rice farmers and sugar workers, the PPP has usually taken a traditional socialist position along the lines of international Communism.

15 JUDICIAL SYSTEM

The Supreme Court has two divisions: the high court and the court of appeal. Magistrates' courts have jurisdiction over less serious civil and criminal matters.

16 ARMED FORCES

The Combined Guyana Defense Force numbered 2,000 full-time officers and

Photo credit: AP/Wide World Photos

Members of a special police corps patrol downtown streets in Georgetown after national elections led to disturbances and lootings.

troops (including a women's army corps) in 1993. Reserves and paramilitary forces numbered 2,000. Defense expenditures in 1988 were US$14.4 million.

17 ECONOMY

The bulk of the population is engaged in agriculture, either as laborers on sugar plantations, or as peasant cultivators of rice. Although sugar and rice continued to be important export earners, bauxite's share of national exports grew from 25% in 1970 to 48% in 1985.

In recent years, Guyana's economy has improved dramatically under the Economic

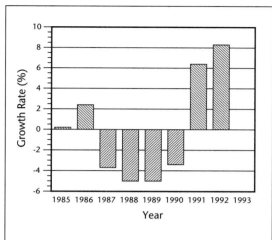

Yearly growth rate of the economy. This economic indicator tells by what percent the economy has increased or decreased when compared with the previous year.

Recovery Program (ERP) launched by the government in April 1989 to steer the country towards a more open free market system. Inflation has dropped from a 1989–91 annual average of 60–100% to only 14% in 1992.

18 INCOME

In 1992, Guyana's gross national product (GNP) was US$268 million at current prices, or US$350 per person. For the period 1985–92 the average inflation rate was 67.3%, resulting in a real growth rate in GNP of −5.4% per person.

19 INDUSTRY

Industry is limited chiefly to processing bauxite, sugar, and rice for export and food and beverages for the local market. Industrial products in 1983 included wheat flour, 10,000 tons; rum, 133,000 hectoliters; and cigarettes, 408 million.

20 LABOR

The total work force in 1992 was about 250,000; unemployment reached 12.9% during the same year. The Trades Union Congress is the national labor federation.

21 AGRICULTURE

The rebound of the Guyanese economy in 1992 was primarily due to increased sugar and rice production. Increased cultivation, replanting schemes, and favorable weather, helped stimulate a 40% increase in sugar production, which was estimated at 3,081,000 tons in 1992. Rice production in 1992 was 274,000 tons. Agricultural exports in 1992 totaled US$175.7 million, up from US$127 million in 1991. Other crops, grown for domestic consumption, include bananas, citrus, cassava, and yams.

22 DOMESTICATED ANIMALS

Livestock in 1992 included 225,000 head of cattle, 60,000 hogs, 130,000 sheep, and 13,000,000 chickens. Other important domestic animals are goats, horses, mules, and donkeys.

23 FISHING

Efforts are being made to increase the fish catch in order to improve the local diet and reduce imports of fish. The catch was 40,756 tons in 1991. About 3,653 tons of shrimp were harvested.

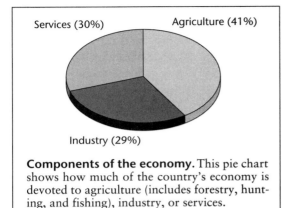

Services (30%)   Agriculture (41%)

Industry (29%)

Components of the economy. This pie chart shows how much of the country's economy is devoted to agriculture (includes forestry, hunting, and fishing), industry, or services.

24 FORESTRY

Forests cover about 16,369,000 hectares (40,448,000 acres), but commercial exploitation has been confined to a relatively small section in the northeast. Green-heart is the most important timber produced and exported. Timber production was about 175,000 cubic meters in 1991.

25 MINING

Mineral production is second only to agriculture in importance. Guyana is the 11th largest producer of bauxite in the world; in 1991, over 2.2 million tons were produced. Gold, diamonds, and crushed stone also are mined. In 1991, gold mine output was 11,000 kilograms, and 18,189 metric carats of diamonds were mined. Bauxite and gold account for almost 40% of the country's exports.

26 FOREIGN TRADE

In 1991, merchandise imports were US$252 million. Fuel from Venezuela accounted for about 25% of Guyana's merchandise imports, and imports from the United States, primarily industrial equipment and unprocessed food, accounted for about 33%. In recent years, seafood has accounted for over US$15 million a year in foreign exchange earnings. Guyana's timber exports are expected to reach US$60 million a year.

27 ENERGY AND POWER

Total electric energy produced was 500 million kilowatt hours in 1991. Frequent power failures have hampered production, and thus impeded economic growth.

28 SOCIAL DEVELOPMENT

Social welfare benefits include workers' compensation, maternity and health insurance, death benefits, disability, and old age pensions.

The 1990 Equal Rights Act, which was intended to end sex discrimination, has been difficult to enforce.

29 HEALTH

In 1990, there were 200 doctors, and 96% of the population had access to health care services. In 1993 the average life expectancy was 65 years. Public health measures had virtually eliminated malaria as a major problem. Filariasis, enteric fever, helminthiasis, nutritional deficiencies, and venereal diseases all still pose significant health risks. Yellow fever remains a constant threat.

Selected Social Indicators

These statistics are estimates for the period 1988 to 1993. For comparison purposes, data for the United States and averages for low-income countries and high-income countries are also given.

Indicator	Guyana	Low-income countries	High-income countries	United States
Per capita gross national product†	$350	$380	$23,680	$24,740
Population growth rate	0.6%	1.9%	0.6%	1.0%
Population growth rate in urban areas	2.1%	3.9%	0.8%	1.3%
Population per square kilometer of land	4	78	25	26
Life expectancy in years	65	62	77	76
Number of people per physician	4,040	>3,300	453	419
Number of pupils per teacher (primary school)	29	39	<18	20
Illiteracy rate (15 years and older)	4%	41%	<5%	<3%
Energy consumed per capita (kg of oil equivalent)	349	364	5,203	7,918

† The gross national product (GNP) is the total dollar value of all goods and services produced by a country in a year. The per capita GNP is calculated by dividing a country's GNP by its population. The World Bank defines low-income countries as those with a per capita GNP of $695 or less. High-income countries have a per capita GNP of $8,626 or more. Less than 14% of the world's 5.5 billion people live in high-income countries, while almost 60% live in low-income countries.

> = greater than   < = less than

Sources: World Bank, *Social Indicators of Development 1995,* Baltimore: Johns Hopkins University Press, 1995. Central Intelligence Agency, *World Fact Book,* Washington, D.C.: Government Printing Office, 1994.

30 HOUSING

Housing is a critical problem, as is the lack of adequate water supplies and of effective waste disposal and sewage systems. Urban development plans have been prepared for Georgetown and New Amsterdam.

31 EDUCATION

The adult literacy rate in 1990 was 96% (with males reported at 97.5% and females at 95.4%), among the highest in South America. School attendance is free and compulsory for children between the ages of 6 and 14. In 1988, there were 414 schools at the primary level with 118,015 students enrolled. The University of Guyana was established in 1963. In 1989, there were 450 teachers and 4,665 students enrolled at universities and all higher level institutions.

32 MEDIA

Broadcasting is carried on by the government-owned Guyana Broadcasting Corp. There were an estimated 392,000 radios and 31,000 TV sets in use in 1991. In that year there were 33,000 telephones in use.

In 1991 there were two daily newspapers in Guyana, the state-owned *Guyana*

Chronicle (circulation 14,000) and the *Mirror* (20,000).

33 TOURISM AND RECREATION

Guyana's scenery varies from the flat marshy coastal plain to the savannas, plateaus, and mountains of the interior; the 226-meter (740-foot) Kaieteur Falls, four times as high as Niagara Falls, is the country's most outstanding scenic attraction. Riding, hunting, fishing, and swimming are available in the southern savanna of the Rupununi. Cricket is the national sport.

34 FAMOUS GUYANESE

Citizens of Guyana who have established literary reputations abroad include the novelist Edward Ricardo Braithwaite (b.1912), and the poet and novelist Jan Carew (b.1925). Linden Forbes Sampson Burnham (1923–85), former leader of the PNC, dominated Guyanese politics from 1964 until his death. Cheddi Berret Jagan, Jr. (b.1918), has been the main opposition leader since 1964, returning to office in 1992. Hugh Desmond Hoyte (b.1930) served as president from 1985–92.

35 BIBLIOGRAPHY

Brill, M. *Guyana*. Chicago: Children's Press, 1994.

Chambers, Frances. *Guyana*. Santa Barbara: Clio, 1989.

Daly, Vere T. *A Short History of the Guyanese People*. London: Macmillan Education, 1975.

Guyana in Pictures. Minneapolis: Lerner, 1988.

Merrill, Tim, ed. *Guyana and Belize: Country Studies*. 2d ed. Washington, D.C.: Library of Congress, 1993.

GLOSSARY

aboriginal: The first known inhabitants of a country. A species of animals or plants which originated within a given area.

acid rain: Rain (or snow) that has become slightly acid by mixing with industrial air pollution.

adobe: A brick made from sun-dried heavy clay mixed with straw, used in building houses. A house made of adobe bricks.

adult literacy: The ability of adults to read and write.

afforestation: The act of turning arable land into forest or woodland.

agrarian economy: An economy where agriculture is the dominant form of economic activity. A society where agriculture dominates the day-to-day activities of the population is called an agrarian society.

air link: Refers to scheduled air service that allows people and goods to travel between two places on a regular basis.

airborne industrial pollutant: Pollution caused by industry that is supported or carried by the air.

allies: Groups or persons who are united in a common purpose. Typically used to describe nations that have joined together to fight a common enemy in war.

In World War I, the term Allies described the nations that fought against Germany and its allies. In World War II, Allies described the United Kingdom, United States, the USSR and their allies, who fought against the Axis Powers of Germany, Italy, and Japan.

aloe: A plant particularly abundant in the southern part of Africa, where leaves of some species are made into ropes, fishing lines, bow strings, and hammocks. It is also a symbolic plant in the Islamic world; anyone who returns from a pilgrimage to Mecca (Mekkah) hangs aloe over his door as a token that he has performed the journey.

Altaic language family: A family of languages spoken in portions of northern and eastern Europe, and nearly the whole of northern and central Asia, together with some other regions. The family is divided into five branches: the Ugrian or Finno-Hungarian, Smoyed, Turkish, Mongolian, and Tunguse.

althing: A legislative assembly.

amendment: A change or addition to a document.

Amerindian: A contraction of the two words, American Indian. It describes native peoples of North, South, or Central America.

amnesty: An act of forgiveness or pardon, usually taken by a government, toward persons for crimes they may have committed.

Anglican: Pertaining to or connected with the Church of England.

animism: The belief that natural objects and phenomena have souls or innate spiritual powers.

annual growth rate: The rate at which something grows over a period of 12 months.

annual inflation rate: The rate of inflation in prices over the course of a year.

anthracite coal: Also called hard coal, it is usually 90 to 95 percent carbon, and burns cleanly, almost without a flame.

anti-Semitism: Agitation, persecution, or discrimination (physical, emotional, economic, political, or otherwise) directed against the Jews.

apartheid: The past governmental policy in the Republic of South Africa of separating the races in society.

appeasement: To bring to a state of peace.

appellate: Refers to an appeal of a court decision to a high authority.

applied science: Scientific techniques employed to achieve results that solve practical problems.

aquaculture: The culture or "farming" of aquatic plants or other natural produce, as in the raising of catfish in "farms."

aquatic resources: Resources that come from, grow in, or live in water, including fish and plants.

aquifer: An underground layer of porous rock, sand, or gravel that holds water.

arable land: Land that can be cultivated by plowing and used for growing crops.

arbitration: A process whereby disputes are settled by a designated person, called the arbitrator, instead of by a court of law.

archipelago: Any body of water abounding with islands, or the islands themselves collectively.

archives: A place where records or a collection of important documents are kept.

arctic climate: Cold, frigid weather similar to that experienced at or near the north pole.

aristocracy: A small minority that controls the government of a nation, typically on the basis of inherited wealth.

armistice: An agreement or truce which ends military conflict in anticipation of a peace treaty.

artesian well: A type of well where the water rises to the surface and overflows.

ASEAN *see* Association of Southeast Asian Nations

Association of Southeast Asian Nations: ASEAN was established in 1967 to promote political, economic, and social cooperation among its six member countries: Indonesia, Malaysia, the Philippines, Singapore, Thailand, and Brunei. ASEAN headquarters are in Jakarta, Indonesia. In January 1992, ASEAN agreed to create the ASEAN Free Trade Area (AFTA).

atheist: A person who denies the existence of God or of a supreme intelligent being.

atoll: A coral island, consisting of a strip or ring of coral surrounding a central lagoon.

atomic weapons: Weapons whose extremely violent explosive power comes from the splitting of the nuclei of atoms (usually uranium or plutonium) by neutrons in a rapid chain reaction. These weapons may be referred to as atom bombs, hydrogen bombs, or H-bombs.

austerity measures: Steps taken by a government to conserve money or resources during an economically difficult time, such as cutting back on federally funded programs.

Australoid: Pertains to the type of aborigines, or earliest inhabitants, of Australia.

Austronesian language: A family of languages which includes practically all the languages of the Pacific Islands—Indonesian, Melanesian, Polynesian, and Micronesian sub-families. Does not include Australian or Papuan languages.

authoritarianism: A form of government in which a person or group attempts to rule with absolute authority without the representation of the citizens.

autonomous state: A country which is completely self-governing, as opposed to being a dependency or part of another country.

autonomy: The state of existing as a self-governing entity. For instance, when a country gains its independence from another country, it gains autonomy.

average inflation rate: The average rate at which the general prices of goods and services increase over the period of a year.

average life expectancy: In any given society, the average age attained by persons at the time of death.

Axis Powers: The countries aligned against the Allied Nations in World War II, originally applied to Nazi Germany and Fascist Italy (Rome-Berlin Axis), and later extended to include Japan.

bagasse: Plant residue left after a product, such as juice, has been extracted.

Baha'i: The follower of a religious sect founded by Mirza Husayn Ali in Iran in 1863.

Baltic states: The three formerly communist countries of Estonia, Latvia, and Lithuania that border on the Baltic Sea.

Bantu language group: A name applied to the languages spoken in central and south Africa.

banyan tree: An East Indian fig tree. Individual trees develop roots from the branches that descend to the ground and become trunks. These roots support and nourish the crown of the tree.

Baptist: A member of a Protestant denomination that practices adult baptism by complete immersion in water.

barren land: Unproductive land, partly or entirely treeless.

barter: Trade practice where merchandise is exchanged directly for other merchandise or services without use of money.

bedrock: Solid rock lying under loose earth.

bicameral legislature: A legislative body consisting of two chambers, such as the U.S. House of Representatives and the U.S. Senate.

bill of rights: A written statement containing the list of privileges and powers to be granted to a body of people, usually introduced when a government or other organization is forming.

bituminous coal: Soft coal; coal which burns with a bright-yellow flame.

black market: A system of trade where goods are sold illegally, often for excessively inflated prices. This type of trade usually develops to avoid paying taxes or tariffs levied by the government, or to get around import or export restrictions on products.

bloodless coup: The sudden takeover of a country's government by hostile means but without killing anyone in the process.

boat people: Used to describe individuals (refugees) who attempt to flee their country by boat.

bog: Wet, soft, and spongy ground where the soil is composed mainly of decayed or decaying vegetable matter.

Bolshevik Revolution. A revolution in 1917 in Russia when a wing of the Russian Social Democratic party seized power. The Bolsheviks advocated the violent overthrow of capitalism.

bonded labor: Workers bound to service without pay; slaves.

border dispute: A disagreement between two countries as to the exact location or length of the dividing line between them.

Brahman: A member (by heredity) of the highest caste among the Hindus, usually assigned to the priesthood.

broadleaf forest: A forest composed mainly of broadleaf (deciduous) trees.

Buddhism: A religious system common in India and eastern Asia. Founded by and based upon the teachings of Siddhartha Gautama, Buddhism asserts that suffering is an inescapable part of life. Deliverance can only be achieved through the practice of charity, temperance, justice, honesty, and truth.

buffer state: A small country that lies between two larger, possibly hostile countries, considered to be a neutralizing force between them.

bureaucracy: A system of government that is characterized by division into bureaus of administration with their own divisional heads. Also refers to the inflexible procedures of such a system that often result in delay.

Byzantine Empire: An empire centered in the city of Byzantium, now Istanbul in present-day Turkey.

CACM *see* Central American Common Market.

candlewood: A name given to several species of trees and shrubs found in the British West Indies, northern Mexico, and the southwestern United States. The plants are characterized by a very resinous wood.

canton: A territory or small division or state within a country.

capital punishment: The ultimate act of punishment for a crime, the death penalty.

capitalism: An economic system in which goods and services and the means to produce and sell them are privately owned, and prices and wages are determined by market forces.

Caribbean Community and Common Market (CARICOM): Founded in 1973 and with its headquarters in Georgetown, Guyana, CARICOM seeks the establishment of a common trade policy and increased cooperation in the Caribbean region. Includes 13 English-speaking Caribbean nations: Antigua and Barbuda, the Bahamas, Barbados, Belize, Dominica, Grenada, Guyana, Jamaica, Montserrat, Saint Kitts-Nevis, Saint Lucia, St. Vincent/Grenadines, and Trinidad and Tobago.

CARICOM *see* Caribbean Community and Common Market.

carnivore: Flesh-eating animal or plant.

carob: The common English name for a plant that is similar to and sometimes used as a substitute for chocolate.

cartel: An organization of independent producers formed to regulate the production, pricing, or marketing practices of its members in order to limit competition and maximize their market power.

cash crop: A crop that is grown to be sold rather than kept for private use.

cassation: The reversal or annulling of a final judgment by the supreme authority.

cassava: The name of several species of stout herbs, extensively cultivated for food.

caste system: One of the artificial divisions or social classes into which the Hindus are rigidly separated according to the religious law of Brahmanism. Membership in a caste is hereditary, and the privileges and disabilities of each caste are transmitted by inheritance.

Caucasian: The white race of human beings, as determined by genealogy and physical features.

Caucasoid: Belonging to the racial group characterized by light skin pigmentation. Commonly called the "white race."

cease-fire: An official declaration of the end to the use of military force or active hostilities, even if only temporary.

CEMA *see* Council for Mutual Economic Assistance.

censorship: The practice of withholding certain items of news that may cast a country in an unfavorable light or give away secrets to the enemy.

census: An official counting of the inhabitants of a state or country with details of sex and age, family, occupation, possessions, etc.

Central American Common Market (CACM): Established in 1962, a trade alliance of five Central American nations. Participating are Costa Rica, El Salvador, Guatemala, Honduras, and Nicaragua.

Central Powers: In World War I, Germany and Austria-Hungary, and their allies, Turkey and Bulgaria.

centrally planned economy: An economic system all aspects of which are supervised and regulated by the government.

centrist position: Refers to opinions held by members of a moderate political group; that is, views that are somewhere in the middle of popular thought between conservative and liberal.

cession: Withdrawal from or yielding to physical force.

chancellor: A high-ranking government official. In some countries it is the prime minister.

cholera: An acute infectious disease characterized by severe diarrhea, vomiting, and, often, death.

Christianity: The religion founded by Jesus Christ, based on the Bible as holy scripture.

Church of England: The national and established church in England. The Church of England claims continuity with the branch of the Catholic Church that existed in England before the Reformation. Under Henry VIII, the spiritual supremacy and jurisdiction of the Pope were abolished, and the sovereign (king or queen) was declared head of the church.

circuit court: A court that convenes in two or more locations within its appointed district.

CIS *see* Commonwealth of Independent States

city-state: An independent state consisting of a city and its surrounding territory.

civil court: A court whose proceedings include determinations of rights of individual citizens, in contrast to criminal proceedings regarding individuals or the public.

civil jurisdiction: The authority to enforce the laws in civil matters brought before the court.

civil law: The law developed by a nation or state for the conduct of daily life of its own people.

civil rights: The privileges of all individuals to be treated as equals under the laws of their country; specifically, the rights given by certain amendments to the U.S. Constitution.

civil unrest: The feeling of uneasiness due to an unstable political climate, or actions taken as a result of it.

civil war: A war between groups of citizens of the same country who have different opinions or agendas. The Civil War of the United States was the conflict between the states of the North and South from 1861 to 1865.

climatic belt: A region or zone where a particular type of climate prevails.

Club du Sahel: The Club du Sahel is an informal coalition which seeks to reverse the effects of drought and the desertification in the eight Sahelian zone countries: Burkina Faso, Chad, Gambia, Mali, Mauritania, Niger, Senegal, and the Cape Verde Islands. Headquarters are in Ouagadougou, Burkina Faso.

CMEA *see* Council for Mutual Economic Assistance.

coalition government: A government combining differing factions within a country, usually temporary.

coastal belt: A coastal plain area of lowlands and somewhat higher ridges that run parallel to the coast.

coastal plain: A fairly level area of land along the coast of a land mass.

coca: A shrub native to South America, the leaves of which produce organic compounds that are used in the production of cocaine.

coke: The solid product of the carbonization of coal, bearing the same relation to coal that charcoal does to wood.

cold war: Refers to conflict over ideological differences that is carried on by words and diplomatic actions, not by military action. The term is usually used to refer to the tension that existed between the United States and the USSR from the 1950s until the breakup of the USSR in 1991.

collective bargaining: The negotiations between workers who are members of a union and their employer for the purpose of deciding work rules and policies regarding wages, hours, etc.

collective farm: A large farm formed from many small farms and supervised by the government; usually found in communist countries.

collective farming: The system of farming on a collective where all workers share in the income of the farm.

colloquial: Belonging to ordinary, everyday speech: often especially applied to common words and phrases which are not used in formal speech.

colonial period: The period of time when a country forms colonies in and extends control over a foreign area.

colonist: Any member of a colony or one who helps settle a new colony.

colony: A group of people who settle in a new area far from their original country, but still under the jurisdiction of that country. Also refers to the newly settled area itself.

COMECON *see* Council for Mutual Economic Assistance.

commerce: The trading of goods (buying and selling), especially on a large scale, between cities, states, and countries.

commercial catch: The amount of marketable fish, usually measured in tons, caught in a particular period of time.

commercial crop: Any marketable agricultural crop.

commission: A group of people designated to collectively do a job, including a government agency with certain law-making powers. Also, the power given to an individual or group to perform certain duties.

commodity: Any items, such as goods or services, that are bought or sold, or agricultural products that are traded or marketed.

common law: A legal system based on custom and decisions and opinions of the law courts. The basic system of law of England and the United States.

common market: An economic union among countries that is formed to remove trade barriers (tariffs) among those countries, increasing economic cooperation. The European Community is a notable example of a common market.

commonwealth: A commonwealth is a free association of sovereign independent states that has no charter, treaty, or constitution. The association promotes cooperation, consultation, and mutual assistance among members.

Commonwealth of Independent States: The CIS was established in December 1991 as an association of 11 republics of the former Soviet Union. The members include: Russia, Ukraine, Belarus (formerly Byelorussia), Moldova (formerly Moldavia), Armenia, Azerbaijan, Uzbekistan, Turkmenistan, Tajikistan, Kazakhstan, and Kirgizstan (formerly Kirghiziya). The Baltic states—Estonia, Latvia, and Lithuania—did not join. Georgia maintained observer status before joining the CIS in November 1993.

Commonwealth of Nations: Voluntary association of the United Kingdom and its present dependencies and associated states, as well as certain former dependencies and their dependent territories. The term was first used officially in 1926 and is embodied in the Statute of Westminster (1931). Within the Commonwealth, whose secretariat (established in 1965) is located in London, England, are numerous subgroups devoted to economic and technical cooperation.

commune: An organization of people living together in a community who share the ownership and use of property. Also refers to a small governmental district of a country, especially in Europe.

communism: A form of government whose system requires common ownership of property for the use of all citizens. All profits are to be equally distributed and prices on goods and services are usually set by the state. Also, communism refers directly to the official doctrine of the former U.S.S.R.

compulsory: Required by law or other regulation.

compulsory education: The mandatory requirement for children to attend school until they have reached a certain age or grade level.

conciliation: A process of bringing together opposing sides of a disagreement for the purpose of compromise. Or, a way of settling an international dispute in which the disagreement is submitted to an independent committee that will examine the facts and advise the participants of a possible solution.

concordat: An agreement, compact, or convention, especially between church and state.

confederation: An alliance or league formed for the purpose of promoting the common interests of its members.

Confucianism: The system of ethics and politics taught by the Chinese philosopher Confucius.

coniferous forest: A forest consisting mainly of pine, fir, and cypress trees.

conifers: Cone-bearing plants. Mostly evergreen trees and shrubs which produce cones.

conscription: To be required to join the military by law. Also known as the draft. Service personnel who join the military because of the legal requirement are called conscripts or draftees.

conservative party: A political group whose philosophy tends to be based on established traditions and not supportive of rapid change.

constituency: The registered voters in a governmental district, or a group of people that supports a position or a candidate.

constituent assembly: A group of people that has the power to determine the election of a political representative or create a constitution.

constitution: The written laws and basic rights of citizens of a country or members of an organized group.

constitutional monarchy: A system of government in which the hereditary sovereign (king or queen, usually) rules according to a written constitution.

constitutional republic: A system of government with an elected chief of state and elected representation, with a written constitution containing its governing principles. The United States is a constitutional republic.

consumer goods: Items that are bought to satisfy personal needs or wants of individuals.

continental climate: The climate of a part of the continent; the characteristics and peculiarities of the climate are a result of the land itself and its location.

continental shelf: A plain extending from the continental coast and varying in width that typically ends in a steep slope to the ocean floor.

copra: The dried meat of the coconut; it is frequently used as an ingredient of curry, and to produce coconut oil. Also written *cobra, coprah,* and *copperah.*

Coptic Christians: Members of the Coptic Church of Egypt, formerly of Ethiopia.

cordillera: A continuous ridge, range, or chain of mountains.

corvette: A small warship that is often used as an escort ship because it is easier to maneuver than larger ships like destroyers.

Council for Mutual Economic Assistance (CMEA): Also known as Comecon, the alliance of socialist economies was established on 25 January 1949 and abolished 1 January 1991. It included Afghanistan*, Albania, Angola*, Bulgaria, Cuba, Czechoslovakia, Ethiopia*, East Germany, Hungary, Laos*, Mongolia, Mozambique*, Nicaragua*, Poland, Romania, USSR, Vietnam, Yemen*, and Yugoslavia. Nations marked with an asterisk were observers only.

counterinsurgency operations: Organized military activity designed to stop rebellion against an established government.

county: A territorial division or administrative unit within a state or country.

coup d'ètat or coup: A sudden, violent overthrow of a government or its leader.

court of appeal: An appellate court, having the power of review after a case has been decided in a lower court.

court of first appeal: The next highest court to the court which has decided a case, to which that case may be presented for review.

court of last appeal: The highest court, in which a decision is not subject to review by any higher court. In the United States, it could be the Supreme Court of an individual state or the U.S. Supreme Court.

cricket (sport): A game played by two teams with a ball and bat, with two wickets (staked target) being defended by a batsman. Common in the United Kingdom and Commonwealth of Nations countries.

criminal law: The branch of law that deals primarily with crimes and their punishments.

crown colony: A colony established by a commonwealth over which the monarch has some control, as in colonies established by the United Kingdom's Commonwealth of Nations.

Crusades: Military expeditions by European Christian armies in the eleventh, twelfth, and thirteenth centuries to win land controlled by the Muslims in the middle east.

cultivable land: Land that can be prepared for the production of crops.

Cultural Revolution: An extreme reform movement in China from 1966 to 1976; its goal was to combat liberalization by restoring the ideas of Mao Zedong.

Cushitic language group: A group of Hamitic languages that are spoken in Ethiopia and other areas of eastern Africa.

customs union: An agreement between two or more countries to remove trade barriers with each other and to establish common tariff and nontariff policies with respect to imports from countries outside of the agreement.

cyclone: Any atmospheric movement, general or local, in which the wind blows spirally around and in towards a center. In the northern hemisphere, the cyclonic movement is usually counter-clockwise, and in the southern hemisphere, it is clockwise.

Cyrillic alphabet: An alphabet adopted by the Slavic people and invented by Cyril and Methodius in the ninth century as an alphabet that was easier for the copyist to write. The Russian alphabet is a slight modification of it.

decentralization: The redistribution of power in a government from one large central authority to a wider range of smaller local authorities.

deciduous species: Any species that sheds or casts off a part of itself after a definite period of time. More commonly used in reference to plants that shed their leaves on a yearly basis as opposed to those (evergreens) that retain them.

declaration of independence: A formal written document stating the intent of a group of persons to become fully self-governing.

deficit: The amount of money that is in excess between spending and income.

deficit spending: The process in which a government spends money on goods and services in excess of its income.

deforestation: The removal or clearing of a forest.

deity: A being with the attributes, nature, and essence of a god; a divinity.

delta: Triangular-shaped deposits of soil formed at the mouths of large rivers.

demarcate: To mark off from adjoining land or territory; set the limits or boundaries of.

demilitarized zone (DMZ): An area surrounded by a combat zone that has had military troops and weapons removed.

demobilize: To disband or discharge military troops.

democracy: A form of government in which the power lies in the hands of the people, who can govern directly, or can be governed indirectly by representatives elected by its citizens.

denationalize: To remove from government ownership or control.

deportation: To carry away or remove from one country to another, or to a distant place.

depression: A hollow; a surface that has sunken or fallen in.

deregulation: The act of reversing controls and restrictions on prices of goods, bank interest, and the like.

desalinization plant: A facility that produces freshwater by removing the salt from saltwater.

desegregation: The act of removing restrictions on people of a particular race that keep them socially, economically, and, sometimes, physically, separate from other groups.

desertification: The process of becoming a desert as a result of climatic changes, land mismanagement, or both.

détente: The official lessening of tension between countries in conflict.

devaluation: The official lowering of the value of a country's currency in relation to the value of gold or the currencies of other countries.

developed countries: Countries which have a high standard of living and a well-developed industrial base.

development assistance: Government programs intended to finance and promote the growth of new industries.

dialect: One of a number of regional or related modes of speech regarded as descending from a common origin.

dictatorship: A form of government in which all the power is retained by an absolute leader or tyrant. There are no rights granted to the people to elect their own representatives.

diplomatic relations: The relationship between countries as conducted by representatives of each government.

direct election: The process of selecting a representative to the government by balloting of the voting public, in contrast to selection by an elected representative of the people.

disarmament: The reduction or depletion of the number of weapons or the size of armed forces.

dissident: A person whose political opinions differ from the majority to the point of rejection.

dogma: A principle, maxim, or tenet held as being firmly established.

domain: The area of land governed by a particular ruler or government, sometimes referring to the ultimate control of that territory.

domestic spending: Money spent by a country's government on goods used, investments, running of the government, and exports and imports.

dominion: A self-governing nation that recognizes the British monarch as chief of state.

dormant volcano: A volcano that has not exhibited any signs of activity for an extended period of time.

dowry: The sum of the property or money that a bride brings to her groom at their marriage.

draft constitution: The preliminary written plans for the new constitution of a country forming a new government.

Druze: A member of a Muslim sect based in Syria, living chiefly in the mountain regions of Lebanon.

dual nationality: The status of an individual who can claim citizenship in two or more countries.

duchy: Any territory under the rule of a duke or duchess.

due process: In law, the application of the legal process to which every citizen has a right, which cannot be denied.

durable goods: Goods or products which are expected to last and perform for several years, such as cars and washing machines.

duty: A tax imposed on imports by the customs authority of a country. Duties are generally based on the value of the goods (*ad valorem* duties), some other factors such as weight or quantity (specific duties), or a combination of value and other factors (compound duties).

dyewoods: Any wood from which dye is extracted.

dynasty: A family line of sovereigns who rule in succession, and the time during which they reign.

earned income: The money paid to an individual in wages or salary.

Eastern Orthodox: The outgrowth of the original Eastern Church of the Eastern Roman Empire, consisting of eastern Europe, western Asia, and Egypt.

EC *see* European Community

ecclesiastical: Pertaining or relating to the church.

echidna: A spiny, toothless anteater of Australia, Tasmania, and New Guinea.

ecological balance: The condition of a healthy, well-functioning ecosystem, which includes all the plants and animals in a natural community together with their environment.

ecology: The branch of science that studies organisms in relationship to other organisms and to their environment.

economic depression: A prolonged period in which there is high unemployment, low production, falling prices, and general business failure.

economically active population: That portion of the people who are employed for wages and are consumers of goods and services.

ecotourism: Broad term that encompasses nature, adventure, and ethnic tourism; responsible or wilderness-sensitive tourism; soft-path or small-scale tourism; low-impact tourism; and sustainable tourism. Scientific, educational, or academic tourism (such as biotourism, archetourism, and geotourism) are also forms of ecotourism.

elected assembly: The persons that comprise a legislative body of a government who received their positions by direct election.

electoral system: A system of choosing government officials by votes cast by qualified citizens.

electoral vote: The votes of the members of the electoral college.

electorate: The people who are qualified to vote in an election.

emancipation: The freeing of persons from any kind of bondage or slavery.

embargo: A legal restriction on commercial ships to enter a country's ports, or any legal restriction of trade.

emigration: Moving from one country or region to another for the purpose of residence.

empire: A group of territories ruled by one sovereign or supreme ruler. Also, the period of time under that rule.

enclave: A territory belonging to one nation that is surrounded by that of another nation.

encroachment: The act of intruding, trespassing, or entering on the rights or possessions of another.

endangered species: A plant or animal species whose existence as a whole is threatened with extinction.

endemic: Anything that is peculiar to and characteristic of a locality or region.

Enlightenment: An intellectual movement of the late seventeenth and eighteenth centuries in which scientific thinking gained a strong foothold and old beliefs were challenged. The idea of absolute monarchy was questioned and people were gradually given more individual rights.

enteric disease: An intestinal disease.

epidemic: As applied to disease, any disease that is temporarily prevalent among people in one place at the same time.

Episcopal: Belonging to or vested in bishops or prelates; characteristic of or pertaining to a bishop or bishops.

ethnolinguistic group: A classification of related languages based on common ethnic origin.

EU *see* European Union

European Community: A regional organization created in 1958. Its purpose is to eliminate customs duties and other trade barriers in Europe. It promotes a common external tariff against other countries, a Common Agricultural Policy (CAP), and guarantees of free movement of labor and capital. The original six members were Belgium, France, West Germany, Italy, Luxembourg, and the Netherlands. Denmark, Ireland, and the United Kingdom became members in 1973; Greece joined in 1981; Spain and Portugal in 1986. Other nations continue to join.

European Union: The EU is an umbrella reference to the European Community (EC) and to two European integration efforts introduced by the Maastricht Treaty: Common Foreign and Security Policy (including defense) and Justice and Home Affairs (principally cooperation between police and other authorities on crime, terrorism, and immigration issues).

exports: Goods sold to foreign buyers.

external migration: The movement of people from their native country to another country, as opposed to internal migration, which is the movement of people from one area of a country to another in the same country.

fallout: The precipitation of particles from the atmosphere, often the result of a ground disturbance by volcanic activity or a nuclear explosion.

family planning: The use of birth control to determine the number of children a married couple will have.

Fascism: A political philosophy that holds the good of the nation as more important than the needs of the individual. Fascism also stands for a dictatorial leader and strong oppression of opposition or dissent.

federal: Pertaining to a union of states whose governments are subordinate to a central government.

federation: A union of states or other groups under the authority of a central government.

fetishism: The practice of worshipping a material object that is believed to have mysterious powers residing in it, or is the representation of a deity to which worship may be paid and from which supernatural aid is expected.

feudal estate: The property owned by a lord in medieval Europe under the feudal system.

feudal society: In medieval times, an economic and social structure in which persons could hold land given to them by a lord (nobleman) in return for service to that lord.

final jurisdiction: The final authority in the decision of a legal matter. In the United States, the Supreme Court would have final jurisdiction.

Finno-Ugric language group: A subfamily of languages spoken in northeastern Europe, including Finnish, Hungarian, Estonian, and Lapp.

fiscal year: The twelve months between the settling of financial accounts, not necessarily corresponding to a calendar year beginning on January 1.

fjord: A deep indentation of the land forming a comparatively narrow arm of the sea with more or less steep slopes or cliffs on each side.

fly: The part of a flag opposite and parallel to the one nearest the flagpole.

fodder: Food for cattle, horses, and sheep, such as hay, straw, and other kinds of vegetables.

folk religion: A religion with origins and traditions among the common people of a nation or region that is relevant to their particular life-style.

foreign exchange: Foreign currency that allows foreign countries to conduct financial transactions or settle debts with one another.

foreign policy: The course of action that one government chooses to adopt in relation to a foreign country.

Former Soviet Union: The FSU is a collective reference to republics comprising the former Soviet Union. The term, which has been used as both including and excluding the Baltic republics (Estonia, Latvia, and Lithuania), includes the other 12 republics: Russia, Ukraine, Belarus, Moldova, Armenia, Azerbaijan, Uzbekistan, Turkmenistan, Tajikistan, Kazakhstan, Kyrgizstan, and Georgia.

fossil fuels: Any mineral or mineral substance formed by the decomposition of organic matter buried beneath the earth's surface and used as a fuel.

free enterprise: The system of economics in which private business may be conducted with minimum interference by the government.

free-market economy: An economic system that relies on the market, as opposed to government planners, to set the prices for wages and products.

frigate. A medium-sized warship.

fundamentalist: A person who holds religious beliefs based on the complete acceptance of the words of the Bible or other holy scripture as the truth. For instance, a fundamentalist would believe the story of creation exactly as it is told in the Bible and would reject the idea of evolution.

game reserve: An area of land reserved for wild animals that are hunted for sport or for food.

GDP *see* gross domestic product.

Germanic language group: A large branch of the Indo-European family of languages including German itself, the Scandinavian languages, Dutch, Yiddish, Modern English, Modern Scottish, Afrikaans, and others. The group also includes extinct languages such as Gothic, Old High German, Old Saxon, Old English, Middle English, and the like.

glasnost: President Mikhail Gorbachev's frank revelations in the 1980s about the state of the economy and politics in the Soviet Union; his policy of openness.

global greenhouse gas emissions: Gases released into the atmosphere that contribute to the greenhouse effect, a condition in which the earth's excess heat cannot escape.

global warming: Also called the greenhouse effect. The theorized gradual warming of the earth's climate as a result of the burning of fossil fuels, the use of man-made chemicals, deforestation, etc.

GMT *see* Greenwich Mean Time.

GNP *see* gross national product.

grand duchy: A territory ruled by a nobleman, called a grand duke, who ranks just below a king.

Greek Catholic: A person who is a member of an Orthodox Eastern Church.

Greek Orthodox: The official church of Greece, a self-governing branch of the Orthodox Eastern Church.

Greenwich (Mean) Time: Mean solar time of the meridian at Greenwich, England, used as the basis for standard time throughout most of the world. The world is divided into 24 time zones, and all are related to the prime, or Greenwich mean, zone.

gross domestic product: A measure of the market value of all goods and services produced within the boundaries of a nation, regardless of asset ownership. Unlike gross national product, GDP excludes receipts from that nation's business operations in foreign countries.

gross national product: A measure of the market value of goods and services produced by the labor and property of a nation. Includes receipts from that nation's business operation in foreign countries

groundwater: Water located below the earth's surface, the source from which wells and springs draw their water.

guano: The excrement of seabirds and bats found in various areas around the world. Gathered commercially and sold as a fertilizer.

guerrilla: A member of a small radical military organization that uses unconventional tactics to take their enemies by surprise.

gymnasium: A secondary school, primarily in Europe, that prepares students for university.

hardwoods: The name given to deciduous trees, such as cherry, oak, maple, and mahogany.

harem: In a Muslim household, refers to the women (wives, concubines, and servants in ancient times) who live there and also to the area of the home they live in.

harmattan: An intensely dry, dusty wind felt along the coast of Africa between Cape Verde and Cape Lopez. It prevails at intervals during the months of December, January, and February.

heavy industry: Industries that use heavy or large machinery to produce goods, such as automobile manufacturing.

hoist: The part of a flag nearest the flagpole.

Holocaust: The mass slaughter of European civilians, the vast majority Jews, by the Nazis during World War II.

Holy Roman Empire: A kingdom consisting of a loose union of German and Italian territories that existed from around the ninth century until 1806.

home rule: The governing of a territory by the citizens who inhabit it.

homeland: A region or area set aside to be a state for a people of a particular national, cultural, or racial origin.

homogeneous: Of the same kind or nature, often used in reference to a whole.

Horn of Africa: The Horn of Africa comprises Djibouti, Eritrea, Ethiopia, Somalia, and Sudan.

housing starts: The initiation of new housing construction.

human rights activist: A person who vigorously pursues the attainment of basic rights for all people.

human rights issues: Any matters involving people's basic rights which are in question or thought to be abused.

humanist: A person who centers on human needs and values, and stresses dignity of the individual.

humanitarian aid: Money or supplies given to a persecuted group or people of a country at war, or those devastated by a natural disaster, to provide for basic human needs.

hydrocarbon: A compound of hydrogen and carbon, often occurring in organic substances or derivatives of organic substances such as coal, petroleum, natural gas, etc.

hydrocarbon emissions: Organic compounds containing only carbon and hydrogen, often occurring in petroleum, natural gas, coal, and bitumens, and which contribute to the greenhouse effect.

hydroelectric potential: The potential amount of electricity that can be produced hydroelectrically. Usually used in reference to a given area and how many hydroelectric power plants that area can sustain.

hydroelectric power plant: A factory that produces electrical power through the application of waterpower.

IBRD *see* World Bank.

illegal alien: Any foreign-born individual who has unlawfully entered another country.

immigration: The act or process of passing or entering into another country for the purpose of permanent residence.

imports: Goods purchased from foreign suppliers.

indigenous: Born or originating in a particular place or country; native to a particular region or area.

Indo-Aryan language group: The group that includes the languages of India; also called Indo-European language group.

Indo-European language family: The group that includes the languages of India and much of Europe and southwestern Asia.

industrialized nation: A nation whose economy is based on industry.

infanticide: The act of murdering a baby.

infidel: One who is without faith or belief; particularly, one who rejects the distinctive doctrines of a particular religion.

inflation: The general rise of prices, as measured by a consumer price index. Results in a fall in value of currency.

installed capacity: The maximum possible output of electric power at any given time.

insurgency: The state or condition in which one rises against lawful authority or established government; rebellion.

insurrectionist: One who participates in an unorganized revolt against an authority.

interim government: A temporary or provisional government.

interim president: One who is appointed to perform temporarily the duties of president during a transitional period in a government.

internal migration: Term used to describe the relocation of individuals from one region to another without leaving the confines of the country or of a specified area.

International Date Line: An arbitrary line at about the 180th meridian that designates where one day begins and another ends.

Islam: The religious system of Mohammed, practiced by Moslims and based on a belief in Allah as the supreme being and Mohammed as his prophet. The spelling variations, Muslim and Muhammed, are also used, primarily by Islamic people. Islam also refers to those nations in which it is the primary religion.

isthmus: A narrow strip of land bordered by water and connecting two larger bodies of land, such as two continents, a continent and a peninsula, or two parts of an island.

Judaism: The religious system of the Jews, based on the Old Testament as revealed to Moses and characterized by a belief in one God and adherence to the laws of scripture and rabbinic traditions.

Judeo-Christian: The dominant traditional religious makeup of the United States and other countries based on the worship of the Old and New Testaments of the Bible.

junta: A small military group in power of a country, especially after a coup.

khan: A sovereign, or ruler, in central Asia.

khanate: A kingdom ruled by a khan, or man of rank.

kwashiorkor: Severe malnutrition in infants and children caused by a diet high in carbohydrates and lacking in protein.

kwh: The abbreviation for kilowatt-hour.

labor force: The number of people in a population available for work, whether actually employed or not.

labor movement: A movement in the early to mid-1800s to organize workers in groups according to profession to give them certain rights as a group, including bargaining power for better wages, working conditions, and benefits.

land reforms: Steps taken to create a fair distribution of farmland, especially by governmental action.

landlocked country: A country that does not have direct access to the sea; it is completely surrounded by other countries.

least developed countries: A subgroup of the United Nations designation of "less developed countries;" these countries generally have no significant economic growth, low literacy rates, and per person gross national product of less than $500. Also known as undeveloped countries.

leeward: The direction identical to that of the wind. For example, a *leeward tide* is a tide that runs in the same direction that the wind blows.

leftist: A person with a liberal or radical political affiliation.

legislative branch: The branch of government which makes or enacts the laws.

leprosy: A disease that can effect the skin and/or the nerves and can cause ulcers of the skin, loss of feeling, or loss of fingers and toes.

less developed countries (LDC): Designated by the United Nations to include countries with low levels of output, living standards, and per person gross national product generally below $5,000.

literacy: The ability to read and write.

Maastricht Treaty: The Maastricht Treaty (named for the Dutch town in which the treaty was signed) is also known as the Treaty of European Union. The treaty creates a European Union by: (a) committing the member states of the European Economic Community to both European Monetary Union (EMU) and political union; (b) introducing a single currency (European Currency Unit, ECU); (c) establishing a European System of Central Banks (ESCB); (d) creating a European Central Bank (ECB); and (e) broadening EC integration by including both a common foreign and security policy (CFSP) and cooperation in justice and home affairs (CJHA). The treaty entered into force on November 1, 1993.

Maghreb states: The Maghreb states include the three nations of Algeria, Morocco, and Tunisia; sometimes includes Libya and Mauritania.

maize: Another name (Spanish or British) for corn or the color of ripe corn.

majority party: The party with the largest number of votes and the controlling political party in a government.

mangrove: A tree which abounds on tropical shores in both hemispheres. Characterized by its numerous roots which arch out from its trunk and descend from its branches, mangroves form thick, dense growths along the tidal muds, reaching lengths hundreds of miles long.

manioc: The cassava plant or its product. Manioc is a very important food-staple in tropical America.

maquis. Scrubby, thick underbrush found along the coast of the Mediterranean Sea.

marginal land: Land that could produce an economic profit, but is so poor that it is only used when better land is no longer available.

marine life: The life that exists in, or is formed by the sea.

maritime climate: The climate and weather conditions typical of areas bordering the sea.

maritime rights: The rights that protect navigation and shipping.

market access: Market access refers to the openness of a national market to foreign products. Market access reflects a government's willingness to permit imports to compete relatively unimpeded with similar domestically produced goods.

market economy: A form of society which runs by the law of supply and demand. Goods are produced by firms to be sold to consumers, who determine the demand for them. Price levels vary according to the demand for certain goods and how much of them is produced.

market price: The price a commodity will bring when sold on the open market. The price is determined by the amount of demand for the commodity by buyers.

Marshall Plan: Formally known as the European Recovery Program, a joint project between the United States and most Western European nations under which $12.5 billion in U.S. loans and grants was expended to aid European recovery after World War II.

Marxism *see* Marxist-Leninist principles.

Marxist-Leninist principles: The doctrines of Karl Marx, built upon by Nikolai Lenin, on which communism was founded. They predicted the fall of capitalism, due to its own internal faults and the resulting oppression of workers.

Marxist: A follower of Karl Marx, a German socialist and revolutionary leader of the late 1800s, who contributed to Marxist-Leninist principles.

massif: A central mountain-mass or the dominant part of a range of mountains.

matrilineal (descent): Descending from, or tracing descent through, the maternal, or mother's, family line.

Mayan language family: The languages of the Central American Indians, further divided into two subgroups: the Maya and the Huastek.

mean temperature: The air temperature unit measured by the National Weather Service by adding the maximum and minimum daily temperatures together and diving the sum by 2.

Mecca (Mekkah): A city in Saudi Arabia; a destination of pilgrims in the Islamic world.

Mediterranean climate: A wet-winter, dry-summer climate with a moderate annual temperature range.

mestizo: The offspring of a person of mixed blood; especially, a person of mixed Spanish and American Indian parentage.

migratory birds: Those birds whose instincts prompt them to move from one place to another at the regularly recurring changes of season.

migratory workers: Usually agricultural workers who move from place to place for employment depending on the growing and harvesting seasons of various crops.

military coup: A sudden, violent overthrow of a government by military forces.

military junta: The small military group in power in a country, especially after a coup.

military regime: Government conducted by a military force.

military takeover: The seizure of control of a government by the military forces.

militia: The group of citizens of a country who are either serving in the reserve military forces or are eligible to be called up in time of emergency.

millet: A cereal grass whose small grain is used for food in Europe and Asia.

minority party: The political group that comprises the smaller part of the large overall group it belongs to; the party that is not in control.

missionary: A person sent by authority of a church or religious organization to spread his religious faith in a community where his church has no self-supporting organization.

Mohammed (or Muhammedor Mahomet): An Arabian prophet, known as the "Prophet of Allah" who founded the religion of Islam in 622, and wrote *The Koran,* the scripture of Islam. Also commonly spelled Muhammed, especially by Islamic people.

monarchy: Government by a sovereign, such as a king or queen.

money economy: A system or stage of economic development in which money replaces barter in the exchange of goods and services.

Mongol: One of an Asiatic race chiefly resident in Mongolia, a region north of China proper and south of Siberia.

Mongoloid: Having physical characteristics like those of the typical Mongols (Chinese, Japanese, Turks, Eskimos, etc.).

Moors: One of the Arab tribes that conquered Spain in the eighth century.

Moslem (Muslim): A follower of Mohammed (spelled Muhammed by many Islamic people), in the religion of Islam.

mosque: An Islam place of worship and the organization with which it is connected.

mouflon: A type of wild sheep characterized by curling horns.

mujahideen (mujahedin or mujahedeen): Rebel fighters in Islamic countries, especially those supporting the cause of Islam.

mulatto: One who is the offspring of parents one of whom is white and the other is black.

municipality: A district such as a city or town having its own incorporated government.

Muslim: A frequently used variation of the spelling of Moslem, to describe a follower of the prophet Mohammed (also spelled Muhammed), the founder of the religion of Islam.

Muslim New Year: A Muslim holiday. Although in some countries 1 Muharram, which is the first month of the Islamic year, is observed as a holiday, in other places the new year is observed on Sha'ban, the eighth month of the year. This practice apparently stems from pagan Arab times. Shab-i-Bharat, a national holiday in Bangladesh on this day, is held by many to be the occasion when God ordains all actions in the coming year.

NAFTA (North American Free Trade Agreement): NAFTA, which entered into force in January 1994, is a free trade agreement between Canada, the United States, and Mexico. The agreement progressively eliminates almost all U.S.-Mexico tariffs over a 10–15 year period.

nationalism: National spirit or aspirations; desire for national unity, independence, or prosperity.

nationalization: To transfer the control or ownership of land or industries to the nation from private owners.

native tongue: One's natural language. The language that is indigenous to an area.

NATO *see* North Atlantic Treaty Organization

natural gas: A combustible gas formed naturally in the earth and generally obtained by boring a well. The chemical makeup of natural gas is principally methane, hydrogen, ethylene compounds, and nitrogen.

natural harbor: A protected portion of a sea or lake along the shore resulting from the natural formations of the land.

naturalize: To confer the rights and privileges of a native-born subject or citizen upon someone who lives in the country by choice.

nature preserve: An area where one or more species of plant and/or animal are protected from harm, injury, or destruction.

neutrality: The policy of not taking sides with any countries during a war or dispute among them.

Newly Independent States: The NIS is a collective reference to 12 republics of the former Soviet Union: Russia, Ukraine, Belarus (formerly Byelorussia), Moldova (formerly Moldavia), Armenia, Azerbaijan, Uzbekistan, Turkmenistan, Tajikistan, Kazakhstan, and Kirgizstan (formerly Kirghiziya), and Georgia. Following dissolution of the Soviet Union, the distinction between the NIS and the Commonwealth of Independent States (CIS) was that Georgia was not a member of the CIS. That distinction dissolved when Georgia joined the CIS in November 1993.

news censorship *see* censorship

Nonaligned Movement: The NAM is an alliance of third world states that aims to promote the political and economic interests of developing countries. NAM interests have included ending colonialism/neo-colonialism, supporting the integrity of independent countries, and seeking a new international economic order.

Nordic Council: The Nordic Council, established in 1952, is directed toward supporting cooperation among Nordic countries. Members include Denmark, Finland, Iceland, Norway, and Sweden. Headquarters are in Stockholm, Sweden.

North Atlantic Treaty Organization (NATO): A mutual defense organization. Members include Belgium, Canada, Denmark, France (which has only partial membership), Greece, Iceland, Italy, Luxembourg, Netherlands, Norway, Portugal, Spain, Turkey, United Kingdom, United States, and Germany.

nuclear power plant: A factory that produces electrical power through the application of the nuclear reaction known as nuclear fission.

nuclear reactor: A device used to control the rate of nuclear fission in uranium. Used in commercial applications, nuclear reactors can maintain temperatures high enough to generate sufficient quantities of steam which can then be used to produce electricity.

OAPEC (Organization of Arab Petroleum Exporting countries): OAPEC was created in 1968; members include: Algeria, Bahrain, Egypt, Iraq, Kuwait, Libya, Qatar, Saudi Arabia, Syria, and the United Arab Emirates. Headquarters are in Cairo, Egypt.

OAS (Organization of American States): The OAS (Spanish: Organizaciûn de los Estados Americanos, OEA), or the Pan American Union, is a regional organization which promotes Latin American economic and social development. Members include the United States, Mexico, and most Central American, South American, and Caribbean nations.

OAS *see* Organization of American States

oasis: Originally, a fertile spot in the Libyan desert where there is a natural spring or well and vegetation; now refers to any fertile tract in the midst of a wasteland.

occupied territory: A territory that has an enemy's military forces present.

official language: The language in which the business of a country and its government is conducted.

oligarchy: A form of government in which a few people possess the power to rule as opposed to a monarchy which is ruled by one.

OPEC *see* OAPEC

open economy: An economy that imports and exports goods.

open market: Open market operations are the actions of the central bank to influence or control the money supply by buying or selling government bonds.

opposition party: A minority political party that is opposed to the party in power.

Organization of Arab Petroleum Exporting Countries *see* OAPEC

organized labor: The body of workers who belong to labor unions.

Ottoman Empire: An Turkish empire founded by Osman I in about 1603, that variously controlled large areas of land around the Mediterranean, Black, and Caspian Seas until it was dissolved in 1918.

overfishing: To deplete the quantity of fish in an area by removing more fish than can be naturally replaced.

overgrazing: Allowing animals to graze in an area to the point that the ground vegetation is damaged or destroyed.

overseas dependencies: A distant and physically separate territory that belongs to another country and is subject to its laws and government.

Pacific Rim: The Pacific Rim, referring to countries and economies bordering the Pacific Ocean.

pact: An international agreement.

Paleolithic: The early period of the Stone Age, when rough, chipped stone implements were used.

panhandle: A long narrow strip of land projecting like the handle of a frying pan.

papyrus: The paper-reed or -rush which grows on marshy river banks in the southeastern area of the Mediterranean, but more notably in the Nile valley.

paramilitary group: A supplementary organization to the military.

parasitic diseases: A group of diseases caused by parasitic organisms which feed off the host organism.

parliamentary republic: A system of government in which a president and prime minister, plus other ministers of departments, constitute the executive branch of the government and the parliament constitutes the legislative branch.

parliamentary rule: Government by a legislative body similar to that of Great Britain, which is composed of two houses—one elected and one hereditary.

parochial: Refers to matters of a church parish or something within narrow limits.

patriarchal system: A social system in which the head of the family or tribe is the father or oldest male. Kinship is determined and traced through the male members of the tribe.

patrilineal (descent): Descending from, or tracing descent through, the paternal or father's line.

pellagra: A disease marked by skin, intestinal, and central nervous system disorders, caused by a diet deficient in niacin, one of the B vitamins.

per capita: Literally, per person; for each person counted.

perestroika: The reorganization of the political and economic structures of the Soviet Union by president Mikhail Gorbachev.

periodical: A publication whose issues appear at regular intervals, such as weekly, monthly, or yearly.

petrochemical: A chemical derived from petroleum or from natural gas.

pharmaceutical plants: Any plant that is used in the preparation of medicinal drugs.

plantain: The name of a common weed that has often been used for medicinal purposes, as a folk remedy and in modern medicine. *Plaintain* is also the name of a tropical plant producing a type of banana.

poaching: To intrude or encroach upon another's preserves for the purpose of stealing animals, especially wild game.

polar climate: Also called tundra climate. A humid, severely cold climate controlled by arctic air masses, with no warm or summer season.

political climate: The prevailing political attitude of a particular time or place.

political refugee: A person forced to flee his or her native country for political reasons.

potable water: Water that is safe for drinking.

pound sterling: The monetary unit of Great Britain, otherwise known as the pound.

prefect: An administrative official; in France, the head of a particular department.

prefecture: The territory over which a prefect has authority.

prime meridian: Zero degrees in longitude that runs through Greenwich, England, site of the Royal Observatory. All other longitudes are measured from this point.

prime minister: The premier or chief administrative official in certain countries.

private sector: The division of an economy in which production of goods and services is privately owned.

privatization: To change from public to private control or ownership.

protectorate: A state or territory controlled by a stronger state, or the relationship of the stronger country toward the lesser one it protects.

Protestant Reformation: In 1529, a Christian religious movement begun in Germany to deny the universal authority of the Pope, and to establish the Bible as the only source of truth. (*Also see* Protestant)

Protestant: A member or an adherent of one of those Christian bodies which descended from the Reformation of the sixteenth century. Originally applied to those who opposed or protested the Roman Catholic Church.

proved reserves: The quantity of a recoverable mineral resource (such as oil or natural gas) that is still in the ground.

province: An administrative territory of a country.

provisional government: A temporary government set up during time of unrest or transition in a country.

pulses: Beans, peas, or lentils.

purge: The act of ridding a society of "undesirable" or unloyal persons by banishment or murder.

Rastafarian: A member of a Jamaican cult begun in 1930 as a semi-religious, semi-political movement.

rate of literacy: The percentage of people in a society who can read and write.

recession. A period of reduced economic activity in a country or region.

referendum: The practice of submitting legislation directly to the people for a popular vote.

Reformation *see* Protestant Reformation.

refugee: One who flees to a refuge or shelter or place of safety. One who in times of persecution or political commotion flees to a foreign country for safety.

revolution: A complete change in a government or society, such as in an overthrow of the government by the people.

right-wing party: The more conservative political party.

Roman alphabet: The alphabet of the ancient Romans from which the alphabets of most modern western European languages, including English, are derived.

Roman Catholic Church: The designation of the church of which the pope or Bishop of Rome is the head, and that holds him as the successor of St. Peter and heir of his spiritual authority, privileges, and gifts.

romance language: The group of languages derived from Latin: French, Spanish, Italian, Portuguese, and other related languages.

roundwood: Timber used as poles or in similar ways without being sawn or shaped.

runoff election: A deciding election put to the voters in case of a tie between candidates.

Russian Orthodox: The arm of the Orthodox Eastern Church that was the official church of Russia under the czars.

sack: To strip of valuables, especially after capture.

Sahelian zone: Eight countries make up this dry desert zone in Africa: Burkina Faso, Chad, Gambia, Mali, Mauritania, Niger, Senegal, and the Cape Verde Islands. *Also see* Club du Sahel.

salinization: An accumulation of soluble salts in soil. This condition is common in desert climates, where water evaporates quickly in poorly drained soil due to high temperatures.

Samaritans: A native or an inhabitant of Samaria; specifically, one of a race settled in the cities of Samaria by the king of Assyria after the removal of the Israelites from the country.

savanna: A treeless or near treeless plain of a tropical or subtropical region dominated by drought-resistant grasses.

schistosomiasis: A tropical disease that is chronic and characterized by disorders of the liver, urinary bladder, lungs, or central nervous system.

secession: The act of withdrawal, such as a state withdrawing from the Union in the Civil War in the United States.

sect: A religious denomination or group, often a dissenting one with extreme views.

segregation: The enforced separation of a racial or religious group from other groups, compelling them to live and go to school separately from the rest of society.

seismic activity: Relating to or connected with an earthquake or earthquakes in general.

self-sufficient: Able to function alone without help.

separation of power: The division of power in the government among the executive, legislative, and judicial branches and the checks and balances employed to keep them separate and independent of each other.

separatism: The policy of dissenters withdrawing from a larger political or religious group.

serfdom: In the feudal system of the Middle Ages, the condition of being attached to the land owned by a lord and being transferable to a new owner.

Seventh-day Adventist: One who believes in the second coming of Christ to establish a personal reign upon the earth.

shamanism: A religion of some Asians and Amerindians in which shamans, who are priests or medicine men, are believed to influence good and evil spirits.

shantytown: An urban settlement of people in flimsy, inadequate houses.

Shia Muslim: Members of one of two great sects of Islam. Shia Muslims believe that Ali and the Imams are the rightful successors of Mohammed (also commonly spelled Muhammed). They also believe that the last recognized Imam will return as a messiah. Also known as Shiites. (*Also see* Sunnis.)

Shiites *see* Shia Muslims.

Shintoism: The system of nature- and hero-worship which forms the indigenous religion of Japan.

shoal: A place where the water of a stream, lake, or sea is of little depth. Especially, a sand-bank which shows at low water.

sierra: A chain of hills or mountains.

Sikh: A member of a politico-religious community of India, founded as a sect around 1500 and based on the principles of monotheism (belief in one god) and human brotherhood.

Sino-Tibetan language family: The family of languages spoken in eastern Asia, including China, Thailand, Tibet, and Burma.

slash-and-burn agriculture: A hasty and sometimes temporary way of clearing land to make it available for agriculture by cutting down trees and burning them.

slave trade: The transportation of black Africans beginning in the 1700s to other countries to be sold as slaves—people owned as property and compelled to work for their owners at no pay.

Slavic languages: A major subgroup of the Indo-European language family. It is further subdivided into West Slavic (including Polish, Czech, Slovak and Serbian), South Slavic (including Bulgarian, Serbo-Croatian, Slovene, and Old Church Slavonic), and East Slavic (including Russian Ukrainian and Byelorussian).

social insurance: A government plan to protect low-income people, such as health and accident insurance, pension plans, etc.

social security: A form of social insurance, including life, disability, and old-age pension for workers. It is paid for by employers, employees, and the government.

socialism: An economic system in which ownership of land and other property is distributed among the community as a whole, and every member of the community shares in the work and products of the work.

socialist: A person who advocates socialism.

softwoods: The coniferous trees, whose wood density as a whole is relatively softer than the wood of those trees referred to as hardwoods.

sorghum (also known as Syrian Grass): Plant grown in various parts of the world for its valuable uses, such as for grain, syrup, or fodder.

Southeast Asia: The region in Asia that consists of the Malay Archipelago, the Malay Peninsula, and Indochina.

staple crop: A crop that is the chief commodity or product of a place, and which has widespread and constant use or value.

state: The politically organized body of people living under one government or one of the territorial units that make up a federal government, such as in the United States.

steppe: A level tract of land more or less devoid of trees, in certain parts of European and Asiatic Russia.

student demonstration: A public gathering of students to express strong feelings about a certain situation, usually taking place near the location of the people in power to change the situation.

subarctic climate: A high latitude climate of two types: *continental subarctic*, which has very cold winters, short, cool summers, light precipitation and moist air; and *marine subarctic*, a coastal and island climate with polar air masses causing large precipitation and extreme cold.

subcontinent: A land mass of great size, but smaller than any of the continents; a large subdivision of a continent.

subsistence economy: The part of a national economy in which money plays little or no role, trade is by barter, and living standards are minimal.

subsistence farming: Farming that provides the minimum food goods necessary for the continuation of the farm family.

subtropical climate: A middle latitude climate dominated by humid, warm temperatures and heavy rainfall in summer, with cool winters and frequent cyclonic storms.

subversion: The act of attempting to overthrow or ruin a government or organization by stealthy or deceitful means.

Sudanic language group: A related group of languages spoken in various areas of northern Africa, including Yoruba, Mandingo, and Tshi.

suffrage: The right to vote.

Sufi: A Muslim mystic who believes that God alone exists, there can be no real difference between good and evil, that the soul exists within the body as in a cage, so death should be the chief object of desire, and sufism is the only true philosophy.

sultan: A king of a Muslim state.

Sunni Muslim: Members of one of two major sects of the religion of Islam. Sunni Muslims adhere to strict orthodox traditions, and believe that the four caliphs are the rightful successors to Mohammed, founder of Islam. (Mohammed is commonly spelled Muhammed, especially by Islamic people.) (*Also see* Shia Muslim.)

Taoism: The doctrine of Lao-Tzu, an ancient Chinese philosopher (about 500 B.C.) as laid down by him in the *Tao-te-ching*.

tariff: A tax assessed by a government on goods as they enter (or leave) a country. May be imposed to protect domestic industries from imported goods and/or to generate revenue.

temperate zone: The parts of the earth lying between the tropics and the polar circles. The *northern temperate zone* is the area between the tropic of Cancer and the Arctic Circle. The *southern temperate zone* is the area between the tropic of Capricorn and the Antarctic Circle.

terracing: A form of agriculture that involves cultivating crops in raised banks of earth.

terrorism: Systematic acts of violence designed to frighten or intimidate.

thermal power plant: A facility that produces electric energy from heat energy released by combustion of fuel or nuclear reactions.

Third World: A term used to describe less developed countries; as of the mid-1990s, it is being replaced by the United Nations designation Less Developed Countries, or LDC.

topography: The physical or natural features of the land.

torrid zone: The part of the earth's surface that lies between the tropics, so named for the character of its climate.

totalitarian party: The single political party in complete authoritarian control of a government or state.

trachoma: A contagious bacterial disease that affects the eye.

treaty: A negotiated agreement between two governments.

tribal system: A social community in which people are organized into groups or clans descended from common ancestors and sharing customs and languages.

tropical monsoon climate: One of the tropical rainy climates; it is sufficiently warm and rainy to produce tropical rainforest vegetation, but also has a winter dry season.

tsetse fly: Any of the several African insects which can transmit a variety of parasitic organisms through its bite. Some of these organisms can prove fatal to both human and animal victims.

tundra: A nearly level treeless area whose climate and vegetation are characteristically arctic due to its northern position; the subsoil is permanently frozen.

undeveloped countries *see* least developed countries.

unemployment rate: The overall unemployment rate is the percentage of the work force (both employed and unemployed) who claim to be unemployed.

UNICEF: An international fund set-up for children's emergency relief: United Nations Children's Fund (formerly United Nations International Children's Emergency Fund).

universal adult suffrage: The policy of giving every adult in a nation the right to vote.

untouchables: In India, members of the lowest caste in the caste system, a hereditary social class system. They were considered unworthy to touch members of higher castes.

urban guerrilla: A rebel fighter operating in an urban area.

urbanization: The process of changing from country to city.

USSR: An abbreviation of Union of Soviet Socialist Republics.

veldt: In South Africa, an unforested or thinly forested tract of land or region, a grassland.

Warsaw Pact: Agreement made 14 May 1955 (and dissolved 1 July 1991) to promote mutual defense between Albania, Bulgaria, Czechoslovakia, East Germany, Hungary, Poland, Romania, and the USSR.

Western nations: Blanket term used to describe mostly democratic, capitalist countries, including the United States, Canada, and western European countries.

wildlife sanctuary: An area of land set aside for the protection and preservation of animals and plants.

workers' compensation: A series of regular payments by an employer to a person injured on the job.

World Bank: The World Bank is a group of international institutions which provides financial and technical assistance to developing countries.

world oil crisis: The severe shortage of oil in the 1970s precipitated by the Arab oil embargo.

wormwood: A woody perennial herb native to Europe and Asiatic Russia, valued for its medicinal uses.

yaws: A tropical disease caused by a bacteria which produces raspberry-like sores on the skin.

yellow fever: A tropical viral disease caused by the bite of an infected mosquito, characterized by jaundice.

Zoroastrianism: The system of religious doctrine taught by Zoroaster and his followers in the Avesta; the religion prevalent in Persia until its overthrow by the Muslims in the seventh century.

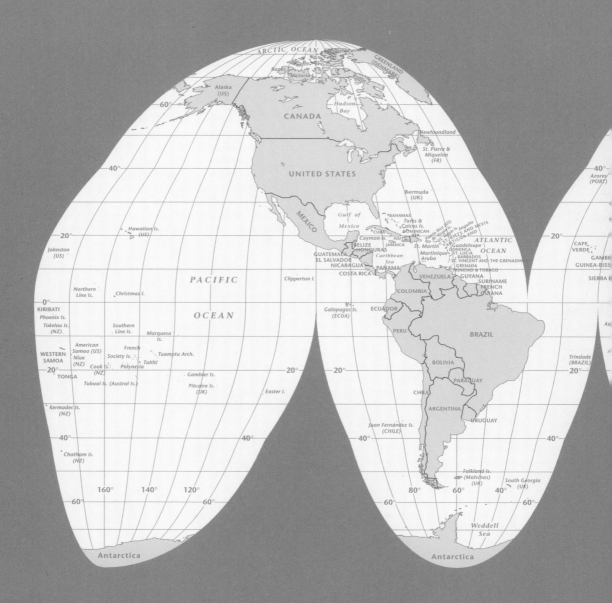

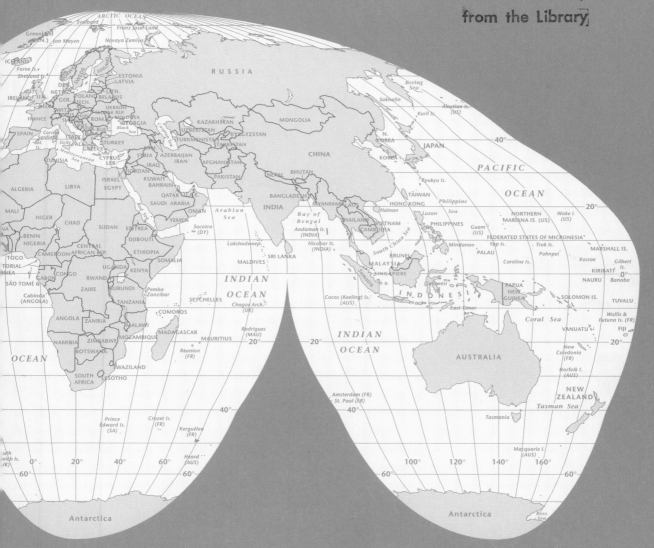

Junior
Worldmark
Encyclopedia
of the

Nations

VOLUME **4**

Junior Worldmark Encyclopedia of the

Nations

VOLUME 4

Haiti to
Kyrgyzstan

An imprint of Gale Research
An ITP Information/Reference Group Company

Changing the Way the World Learns

NEW YORK • LONDON • BONN • BOSTON • DETROIT
MADRID • MELBOURNE • MEXICO CITY • PARIS
SINGAPORE • TOKYO • TORONTO • WASHINGTON
ALBANY NY • BELMONT CA • CINCINNATI OH

JUNIOR WORLDMARK ENCYCLOPEDIA OF THE NATIONS

Timothy L. Gall and Susan Bevan Gall, *Editors*
Rosalie Wieder, *Senior Editor*
Deborah Baron and Daniel M. Lucas, *Associate Editors*
Brian Rajewski and Deborah Rutti, *Graphics and Layout*
Cordelia R. Heaney, *Editorial Assistant*
Dianne K. Daeg de Mott, Janet Fenn, Matthew Markovich,
    Ariana Ranson, and Craig Strasshofer, *Copy Editors*
Janet Fenn and Matthew Markovich, *Proofreaders*

U•X•L Staff

Jane Hoehner, *U•X•L Developmental Editor*
Sonia Benson and Rob Nagel, *Contributors*
Thomas L. Romig, *U•X•L Publisher*
Mary Beth Trimper, *Production Director*
Evi Seoud, *Assistant Production Manager*
Shanna Heilveil, *Production Associate*
Cynthia Baldwin, *Product Design Manager*
Barbara J. Yarrow, *Graphic Services Supervisor*
Mary Krzewinski, *Cover Designer*
Margaret McAvoy-Amoto, *Permissions Associate (Pictures)*

Library of Congress Cataloging-in-Publication Data
Junior Worldmark encyclopedia of the nations / edited by Timothy Gall
    and Susan Gall.
        p.   cm.
    Includes bibliographical references and index.
    ISBN 0-7876-0741-X (set)
    1. Geography--Encyclopedias, Juvenile. 2. History--Encyclopedias,
Juvenile. 3. Economics--Juvenile literature. 4. Political science--
Encyclopedia, Juvenile. 5. United Nations--Encyclopedias,
Juvenile. I. Gall, Timothy L. II. Gall, Susan B.
G63.J86   1995
910'.3--dc20   95-36739
                                                        CIP

ISBN 0-7876-0741-X (set)
ISBN 0-7876-0742-8 (vol. 1)   ISBN 0-7876-0743-6 (vol. 2)   ISBN 0-7876-0744-4 (vol. 3)
ISBN 0-7876-0745-2 (vol. 4)   ISBN 0-7876-0746-0 (vol. 5)   ISBN 0-7876-0747-9 (vol. 6)
ISBN 0-7876-0748-7 (vol. 7)   ISBN 0-7876-0749-5 (vol. 8)   ISBN 0-7876-0750-9 (vol. 9)

U•X•L is an imprint of Gale Research Inc.,
an International Thomson Publishing Company.
ITP logo is a trademark under license.

CONTENTS

Guide to Country Articles

Every country profile in this encyclopedia includes the same 35 headings. Also included in every profile is a map (showing the country and its location in the world), the country's flag and seal, and a table of data on the country. The country articles are organized alphabetically in nine volumes. A glossary of terms is included in each of the nine volumes. This glossary defines many of the specialized terms used throughout the encyclopedia. A keyword index to all nine volumes appears at the end of Volume 9.

Flag color symbols

Yellow   Red   Green   Blue   Orange   Brown   White   Black

Alphabetical listing of sections

Section	No.	Section	No.
Agriculture	21	Income	18
Armed Forces	16	Industry	19
Bibliography	35	Judicial System	15
Climate	3	Labor	20
Domesticated Animals	22	Languages	9
Economy	17	Location and Size	1
Education	31	Media	32
Energy and Power	27	Migration	7
Environment	5	Mining	25
Ethnic Groups	8	Plants and Animals	4
Famous People	34	Political Parties	14
Fishing	23	Population	6
Foreign Trade	26	Religions	10
Forestry	24	Social Development	28
Government	13	Topography	2
Health	29	Tourism/Recreation	33
History	12	Transportation	11
Housing	30		

Sections listed numerically

No.	Section	No.	Section
1	Location and Size	19	Industry
2	Topography	20	Labor
3	Climate	21	Agriculture
4	Plants and Animals	22	Domesticated Animals
5	Environment	23	Fishing
6	Population	24	Forestry
7	Migration	25	Mining
8	Ethnic Groups	26	Foreign Trade
9	Languages	27	Energy and Power
10	Religions	28	Social Development
11	Transportation	29	Health
12	History	30	Housing
13	Government	31	Education
14	Political Parties	32	Media
15	Judicial System	33	Tourism/Recreation
16	Armed Forces	34	Famous People
17	Economy	35	Bibliography
18	Income		

Abbreviations and acronyms to know

GMT= Greenwich mean time. The prime, or Greenwich, meridian passes through Greenwich, England (near London), and marks the center of the initial time zone for the world. The standard time of all 24 time zones relate to Greenwich mean time. Every profile contains a map showing the country and its location in the world.

These abbreviations are used in references to famous people:
b.=born
d.=died
fl.=flourished (lived and worked)
r.=reigned (for kings, queens, and similar monarchs)

A dollar sign ($) stands for US$ unless otherwise indicated.

HAITI

Republic of Haiti
République d'Haïti

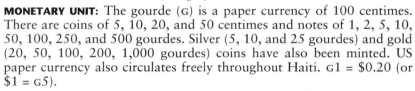

CAPITAL: Port-au-Prince.

FLAG: The upper half is blue, the lower half red; superimposed in the center is the national coat of arms with the motto *L'Union Fait la Force* ("Union makes strength").

ANTHEM: *La Dessalinienne (Song of Dessalines).*

MONETARY UNIT: The gourde (G) is a paper currency of 100 centimes. There are coins of 5, 10, 20, and 50 centimes and notes of 1, 2, 5, 10, 50, 100, 250, and 500 gourdes. Silver (5, 10, and 25 gourdes) and gold (20, 50, 100, 200, 1,000 gourdes) coins have also been minted. US paper currency also circulates freely throughout Haiti. G1 = $0.20 (or $1 = G5).

WEIGHTS AND MEASURES: The metric system is official for customs purposes, but French colonial units and US weights are also used.

HOLIDAYS: Independence and New Year's Day, 1 January; Forefathers Day, 2 January; Pan American Day, 14 April; Labor Day, 1 May; Flag and University Day, 18 May; National Sovereignty Day, 22 May; Assumption, 15 August; Anniversary of the Death of Dessalines, 17 October; UN Day, 24 October; All Saints' Day, 1 November; Commemoration of the Battle of Vertières and Armed Forces Day, 18 November; Discovery of Haiti, 5 December; Christmas, 25 December. Movable religious holidays include Carnival (three days before Ash Wednesday) and Good Friday.

TIME: 7 AM = noon GMT.

1 LOCATION AND SIZE

Haiti occupies the western third of the island of Hispaniola (the Dominican Republic occupies the eastern two thirds). Haiti has an area of 27,750 square kilometers (10,714 square miles) including the islands of Tortuga, Gonâve (Ile de la Gonâve), Les Cayemites, and Vache (Ile Á Vache). The area occupied by Haiti is slightly larger than the state of Maryland. Haiti has a total boundary length of 2,046 kilometers (1,269 miles). Haiti's capital city, Port-au-Prince, is located on Hispaniola's west coast.

2 TOPOGRAPHY

The coastline of Haiti is irregular and forms a long southern peninsula and a shorter northern one, between which lies the Gulf of Gonâve (Golfe de la Gonâve). Three principal mountain ranges—separated by open plains—stretch across the country.

3 CLIMATE

The climate is tropical, with some variation depending on altitude. Temperatures in Port-au-Prince range from 23°–31°C (73°–88°F) in January to an average maximum of 25–35°C (77–95°F) in July. Port-au-Prince receives an average annual rainfall of 137 centimeters (54 inches).

4 PLANTS AND ANIMALS

In the rainforest of the upper mountain ranges, pine and ferns, as well as mahogany, cedar, rosewood, and sapin are found. Coffee, cacao, coconut trees, and native tropical fruits such as avocado, orange, lime, and mango grow wild. Ducks and guinea hens are plentiful, and egrets and flamingos live on the inland lakes. Reptile life includes three varieties of crocodile, numerous small lizards, and the rose boa. Tarpon, barracuda, kingfish, jack, and red snapper abound in the coastal waters.

5 ENVIRONMENT

The virgin forests that once covered the entire country have now been reduced to less than 2% of the total land area. Agricultural chemicals, such as DDT, are widely used in Haiti. These pollutants plus the use of oil with high lead content are a significant source of pollution. Forty-four percent of the nation's city dwellers and 65% of the rural people do not have pure water.

As of 1994, six species of mammals, one bird species, and four types of reptiles were endangered.

6 POPULATION

Haiti, the most densely populated country in the Western Hemisphere, had a 1982 census population of 5,053,189. The 1992 population was estimated to be 6,764,000. The projected population for the year 2000 is 7,959,000. The estimated population density in 1992 was 244 persons per square kilometer (631 per square mile). The district population of Port-au-Prince, the capital and largest city, was estimated as 1,143,626 in 1988.

7 MIGRATION

Emigration from Haiti has been mainly to Cuba, other Caribbean states, Canada, and the United States; illegal emigration to the United States has been substantial since the 1960s. Between 1972 and 1981 more than 55,000 Haitian "boat people," perhaps over 100,000, arrived in Florida. The 1990 census found 290,000 people in the United States of Haitian origin, compared to only 90,000 in 1980.

Several thousand Haitian workers migrate seasonally or permanently to the Dominican Republic each year. In 1986, the Haitian community in the Dominican Republic was estimated to be as many as 500,000 people.

8 ETHNIC GROUPS

About 95% of the inhabitants are pure black, and 5% are mulatto.

9 LANGUAGES

The official languages of Haiti are French and Creole. Nearly all the people speak Creole, a mixture of early seventeenth-century provincial French and African tongues, with English, Spanish, and Amerindian words. Only about 20% speak French. English is used in the capital and to a lesser extent in the provincial cities, and along the Dominican border a Spanish Creole is spoken.

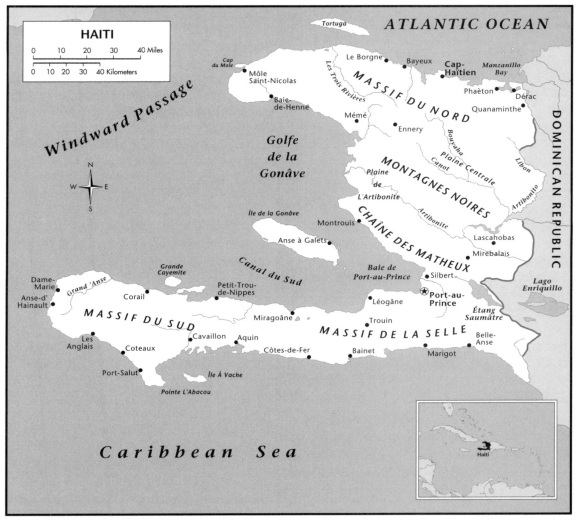

LOCATION: 18°1′42″ to 20°5′44″N; 71°38′ to 74°28′45″W. **BOUNDARY LENGTHS:** Dominican Republic, 275 kilometers (171 miles); total coastline, 1,771 kilometers (1,098 miles). **TERRITORIAL SEA LIMIT:** 12 miles.

10 RELIGIONS

In 1993, Roman Catholics represented an estimated 90% of the population, and Protestants 10%. However, voodoo is still widely practiced, often together with Christianity. In the mid-1980s there were an estimated 60,000 voodoo priests (*houngans*) in Haiti, compared with 427 Roman Catholic priests.

11 TRANSPORTATION

In 1991, Haiti had 4,000 kilometers (2,400 miles) of roads. There were some

3

33,000 passenger cars and 22,000 commercial vehicles in 1992. By 1982, however, most of the railroad system had been closed down; the 40 kilometers (25 miles) of lines that remained in 1991 were being used only for sugarcane transport.

Air Haiti connects principal cities and also serves as an international carrier. A jet airport at Port-au-Prince opened in 1965, and serviced 545,000 passengers in 1991.

12 HISTORY

In 1492, Christopher Columbus made the European discovery of the island of Hispaniola and established a settlement near the present city of Cap-Haïtien. Within 25 years, the native Arawak Amerindians, a peace-loving agricultural people, were virtually wiped out by the Spanish settlers. Some time after 1517, a forced migration of Africans for plantation labor gave Haiti its black population.

The French soon established a colonial presence on nearby mainland coasts and competed with the Spaniards. In 1697, Spain ceded Haiti to the French. Under French rule it became one of the wealthiest Caribbean communities. However, this prosperity, stemming from forestry and sugar, came at a heavy cost in human misery and environmental destruction.

Slavery Revolt

The French Revolution in 1789 outlawed slavery in France, which inspired Haiti's nearly half million black slaves to revolt under the leadership of Toussaint L'Ouverture, an ex-slave who had risen to the rank of general in the French army. By 1801 Toussaint controlled the entire island, and adopted a constitution that abolished slavery. The French emperor Napoleon Bonaparte sent 70 warships and 25,000 men to suppress the Haitians. Toussaint was captured, and died in a French prison.

The Haitians continued to fight under Jean Jacques Dessalines, another black general, and proclaimed their independence in 1804. After being divided for a time into a northern monarchy and a southern republic, Haiti was reunited by Jean Pierre Boyer in 1820, and in 1822 the Haitian army conquered Santo Domingo (now the Dominican Republic). For 22 years there was one republic for the entire island. In 1844, however, one year after Boyer was overthrown, the Dominican Republic proclaimed its independence from Haiti.

Haiti endured a long period of political instability between 1843 and 1915, during which time there were 22 dictators. This era climaxed in the assassination of President Vilbrun Guillaume Sam and was followed by United States military occupation. The occupation ended in 1934 during the administration of President Sténio Vincent (1930–41), who in 1935 proclaimed a new constitution.

After World War II (1939–1945), another period of instability led to a coup d'etat in 1950 that brought General Paul Magloire to power. Magloire's economic policies led to a serious depression, and he was forced from office in 1956.

Reign of Papa Doc

In a September 1957 election François Duvalier, a middle-class black physician known to his followers as Papa Doc, became president. He began to rule by decree in 1958, and on 22 June 1964, he had himself formally elected president for life. Despite several attempted revolts, he strengthened his position, ruling largely through his security force, the Tontons Macoutes.

Political opposition was ruthlessly suppressed, and thousands of suspected dissidents "disappeared." Opposition leaders went into hiding or exile. Haitian exiles in New York, Montreal, Chicago, and Washington mounted an anti-Duvalier campaign during the 1960s. However, invasions in 1964, 1969, and 1970 met with no success.

Papa Doc died on 21 April 1971, and his son Jean-Claude Duvalier, at the age of 19, became president for life the following day. The younger Duvalier (known as Baby Doc) tried to ease political tensions and contributed to the beginnings of an economic revival. However, political arrests did not wholly cease, and there were severe economic problems in the mid- and late 1970s.

Tensions mounted as the economy stagnated after 1980, and civil disorder broke out in the mid-1980s. In February 1986, Jean-Claude and his family fled to France, and the National Governing Council (Conseil National de Gouvernement—CNG), led by Lieutenant-General Henri Namphy, seized power.

Photo credit: AP/Wide World Photos

Haitians crowd around a water truck spraying drinking water in the impoverished Cite Soleil section of Port-au-Prince. Much of Haiti's infrastructure remains in tatters after years of neglect by a military regime that ruled the country while Haitian President Jean-Bertrand Aristide was exiled to the U. S.

Political prisoners were released, and the dreaded Tontons Macoute, Duvalier's clandestine secret police, were disbanded. A national assembly convened in October 1986 and drafted a new constitution that was approved by referendum (direct popular vote) in March 1987. In December 1990, a Roman Catholic priest, Jean-Bertrand Aristide, was elected president with 67.5% of the votes cast.

Upset by Aristide's popularity and his foreign policy, the military, under General

Raoul Cédras, ousted him in October 1991. The United Nations and the Organization of American States (OAS) forged an agreement between Cédras and Aristide that was to return Aristide to the presidency in October 1993, but the military stalled and remained in power. Aristide appealed to the United States, and the administration of President Bill Clinton responded with sanctions against the Haitian regime in May and June of 1994.

In September 1994, as a last resort, the Clinton administration secured international support for a military invasion of Haiti to force Cédras from power. A United States invasion force was assembled and war seemed imminent. However, at the eleventh hour, Clinton sent a special delegation, headed by former United States president Jimmy Carter, to negotiate a peaceful solution to the crisis.

As United States fighter planes were about to take off for Haiti, the Carter team reached an agreement with Cédras and war was averted. American forces peacefully took control of the country and, in October 1994, restored Aristide to power. He subsequently won the election held in September 1995.

13 GOVERNMENT

The constitution adopted in March 1987 established a president elected to a five-year term as head of state. The legislature is made up of a Senate and a House of Representatives. As of 1986, Haiti was divided into 9 departments, 41 arrondissements, and 130 communes.

14 POLITICAL PARTIES

Dozens of parties emerged after the National Governing Council (Conseil National de Gouvernement—CNG) ousted Jean-Claude Duvalier in February 1986. The most prominent has been the National Front for Change and Democracy (FNCD) led by Jean-Bertrand Aristide, a political coalition of 15 parties including the National Cooperative Action Movement (MKN) and the National Congress of Democratic Movements (CONACOM).

15 JUDICIAL SYSTEM

The judiciary consists of four levels: the Court of Cassation, courts of appeal, civil courts, and magistrates' courts. There are also land, labor, and children's courts.

16 ARMED FORCES

In 1993, the Haitian armed forces consisted of about 7,400 personnel in the unified army, navy (coast guard), air force, and police. The air corps consisted of 150 personnel and 7 aircraft, while the naval section had about 250 personnel and only small patrol boats. Defense expenditures were budgeted at $29 million in 1991.

17 ECONOMY

Haiti is one of the world's poorest countries. The economy is basically agricultural: coffee, sugar, sisal, cotton, castor beans, cacao, plantains, and essential oils are the main products.

The trade embargo imposed on Haiti after the 1991 military coup, headed by General Cédras, had a serious effect on the

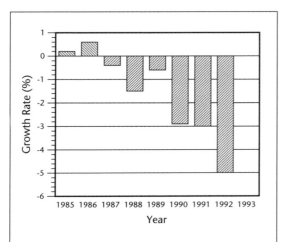

Yearly growth rate of the economy. This economic indicator tells by what percent the economy has increased or decreased when compared with the previous year.

Haitian economy. Prior to the embargo in 1991, the United States alone supplied over 60% of Haiti's total legal imports and purchased over 85% of its exports.

18 INCOME

In 1992, Haiti's gross national product (GNP) was $2,479 million at current prices, or about $340 per person. For the period 1985–92 the average inflation rate was 7.7%, resulting in a real growth rate in GNP of –2.9% per person.

19 INDUSTRY

Industry is primarily devoted to the processing of agricultural and forestry products. Other industries produce aluminum, enamelware, garments and hats, essential oils, plastics, soap, pharmaceuticals, and paint. The trade embargo imposed in 1991 reduced domestic and foreign demand and

created a serious shortage of energy and spare parts.

Products of light industry in 1986 included 846 million cigarettes, 210,500 tons of essential oils, 127,600 tons of flour, 1,373,300 tons of detergents, 1,059,000 tons of toilet soap, and 646,700 yards of synthetic fibers.

20 LABOR

In 1990, the labor force was estimated at 2.9 million. Agriculture employed 75%; industry and commerce, 18%; and services, 7%. The official 1990 unemployment rate was 14%, or 339,680 persons. Unofficially, however, the unemployment rate in 1991 was put at 25–50%.

21 AGRICULTURE

With three-quarters of the laboring population deriving its living exclusively from the soil, farming is the mainstay of the Haitian economy.

The most important commercial product is coffee, which accounts for 22% of Haitian exports. Other important crops include sugarcane, bananas, corn, rice, sorghum, beans, and cocoa beans.

22 DOMESTICATED ANIMALS

In 1992 there were 1,300,000 head of cattle, 880,000 hogs, 1,150,000 goats, 296,000 mules and burros, 90,000 sheep, and 13,000,000 poultry. Livestock products in 1992 included 67,000 tons of meat, 26,000 tons of goat's milk, 16,000 tons of cow's milk, and 3,300 tons of eggs.

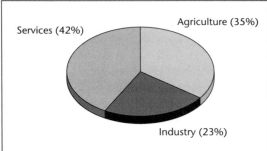

Services (42%) Agriculture (35%)

Industry (23%)

Components of the economy. This pie chart shows how much of the country's economy is devoted to agriculture (includes forestry, hunting, and fishing), industry, or services.

23 FISHING

The commercial fishing industry is not well developed. Reef fish, including giant grouper and rock lobster, are important as food sources because deep-sea fishing is limited. Carp and tertar, a native fish, are abundant, but lack of transport facilities limits this important food source. The catch was estimated at 5,150 tons in 1991.

24 FORESTRY

The intensive use of the forests for fuel, both in colonial times and in the modern era, and the clearing of woodlands for agriculture resulted in a decline of Haiti's forestland from over 2.7 million hectares (6.7 million acres) in the 1400s to no more than 36,000 hectares (133,000 acres) by 1991. Of the estimated 5,957,000 cubic meters of wood cut in 1991, almost 96% was used for fuel.

25 MINING

Haiti possesses undeveloped resources of lignite, copper, gold, silver, antimony, tin, sulfur, coal, nickel, gypsum, and porphyry. Mining is limited, and mineral exploration has generally been conducted by foreign companies. The Haitian marble industry is being developed for export possibilities; clay, limestone, gravel, salt, and stone are also produced for the domestic market.

26 FOREIGN TRADE

Haiti's major export trading partners are the United States, France, Japan, Italy, Belgium, and the Dominican Republic. Its major import partners include the United States, Japan, France, Canada, the Netherlands Antilles, and Venezuela.

Primary exports include textiles, electronics, toys and sporting goods, coffee, mangoes, sisal, essential oils, and cocoa. Primary imports include machine and manufacturing products, food and beverages, oils, and chemicals.

27 ENERGY AND POWER

Electrical power output increased to 475 million kilowatt hours in 1991. More than half of the nation's electricity was generated by petroleum-burning plants in 1991. As of 1990, only 10% of the population had access to electricity. During the trade embargo placed on Haiti from 1991 to 1994, gasoline and other petroleum products were regularly smuggled through the Dominican Republic to Haiti.

28 SOCIAL DEVELOPMENT

Public social insurance programs are limited, but there is a widespread tradition of self-help and personal charity. The national lottery is the principal source of

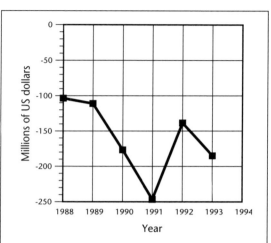

Yearly balance of trade measured in millions of US dollars. The balance of trade is the difference between what a country sells to other countries (its exports) and what it buys (its imports). If a country imports more than it exports, it has a negative balance of trade (a trade deficit). If exports exceed imports there is a positive balance of trade (a trade surplus).

1990, there were about 333 reported cases of tuberculosis per 100,000 inhabitants. Malnutrition and gastrointestinal diseases are responsible for more than half of all deaths. In the early 1980s, Haitians were named among the groups that had high risk factors for contracting acquired immune deficiency syndrome (AIDS).

30 HOUSING

Although housing projects have been constructed in cities such as Port-au-Prince and in Cap-Haïtien, there is an increasing shortage of low-cost housing. Outside the capital and some other cities, housing facilities are generally primitive and almost universally without sanitation.

31 EDUCATION

The adult literacy rate was estimated at 53% in 1990 (males: 59% and females: 47%). In 1990, Haiti had 7,306 primary schools, with 555,433 pupils and 26,208 teachers. In general secondary schools there were 184,968 students and 9,470 teachers. The sole university, the Université d'État d'Haïti (Port-au-Prince) had an enrollment of 4,600 in 1986. There are also five colleges.

32 MEDIA

In 1993 there were 33 radio stations and 4 TV stations, providing commercial and government broadcast services; 310,000 radios and 31,000 television sets were in use. In 1993 there were 50,000 telephone lines. The principal Haitian newspaper is *Le Matin,* with a circulation of 10,500.

welfare funds, while an employer tax provides workers' compensation for occupational accidents to the relatively small number of industrial workers. Old age, disability, and survivor benefits are funded by taxes on employees and employers.

29 HEALTH

In general, sanitation facilities in Haiti are among the poorest in Latin America. In 1991, only 24% of Haiti's population had access to adequate sanitation. Only half the population had access to health care services in 1992. Total health care expenditures for 1990 were $193 million.

The average life expectancy is 57 years for women and men. Tuberculosis has long been a serious health problem, and in

Selected Social Indicators

These statistics are estimates for the period 1988 to 1993. For comparison purposes, data for the United States and averages for low-income countries and high-income countries are also given.

Indicator	Haiti	Low-income countries	High-income countries	United States
Per capita gross national product†	$340	$380	$23,680	$24,740
Population growth rate	2.0%	1.9%	0.6%	1.0%
Population growth rate in urban areas	4.0%	3.9%	0.8%	1.3%
Population per square kilometer of land	244	78	25	26
Life expectancy in years	57	62	77	76
Number of people per physician	7,304	>3,300	453	419
Number of pupils per teacher (primary school)	21	39	<18	20
Illiteracy rate (15 years and older)	47%	41%	<5%	<3%
Energy consumed per capita (kg of oil equivalent)	47	364	5,203	7,918

† The gross national product (GNP) is the total dollar value of all goods and services produced by a country in a year. The per capita GNP is calculated by dividing a country's GNP by its population. The World Bank defines low-income countries as those with a per capita GNP of $695 or less. High-income countries have a per capita GNP of $8,626 or more. Less than 14% of the world's 5.5 billion people live in high-income countries, while almost 60% live in low-income countries.   > = greater than   < = less than

Sources: World Bank, *Social Indicators of Development 1995,* Baltimore: Johns Hopkins University Press, 1995. Central Intelligence Agency, *World Fact Book,* Washington, D.C.: Government Printing Office, 1994.

33 TOURISM AND RECREATION

In the 1980s, tourism was weakened by the island's depressed economy, political turbulence, and by the alleged link between Haitians and acquired immune deficiency syndrome (AIDS). In 1991, tourist arrivals totaled 119,000 (103,000 from North America), down from 158,000 in 1981. There were 1,500 hotel rooms, and tourists spent $46 million in that year.

34 FAMOUS HAITIANS

The national heroes of Haiti include Pierre Dominique Toussaint L'Ouverture (1743–1803), leader of its first independence movement, and Jean Jacques Dessalines (1758–1806), who defeated Napoleon's army.

John James Audubon (1785–1851), an artist and ornithologist, was born in Haiti. The primitive painter Héctor Hippolyte (1890–1948) was the leader of the Afro-Art Renaissance in the Caribbean. Ludovic Lamothe (1882–1953) used voo-doo music in his compositions.

35 BIBLIOGRAPHY

Abbott, Elizabeth. *Haiti: The Duvaliers and their Legacy.* New York: Simon and Schuster, 1991.

Haggerty, Richard A. (ed.) *Dominican Republic and Haiti: Country Studies.* 2d ed. Washington, D.C.: Library of Congress, 1991.

HONDURAS

Republic of Honduras
República de Honduras

CAPITAL: Tegucigalpa.

FLAG: The national flag consists of a white horizontal stripe between two blue horizontal stripes, with five blue stars on the white stripe representing the five members of the former union of Central American provinces.

ANTHEM: *Himno Nacional,* beginning "Tu bandera es un lampo de cielo" ("Thy flag is a heavenly light").

MONETARY UNIT: The lempira (L), also known as the peso, is a paper currency of 100 centavos. There are coins of 1, 2, 5, 10, 20, and 50 centavos, and notes of 1, 2, 5, 10, 20, 50, and 100 lempiras. L1 = $0.50 (or $1 = L2).

WEIGHTS AND MEASURES: The metric system is the legal standard; some old Spanish measures are still used.

HOLIDAYS: New Year's Day, 1 January; Day of the Americas, 14 April; Labor Day, 1 May; Independence Day, 15 September; Birthday of Francisco Morazán, 3 October; Columbus Day, 12 October; Army Day, 21 October; Christmas, 25 December. Movable religious holidays include Holy Thursday, Good Friday, and Holy Saturday.

TIME: 6 AM = noon GMT.

1 LOCATION AND SIZE

Situated in Central America, Honduras has a total area of 112,090 square kilometers (43,278 square miles), slightly larger than the state of Tennessee. It has a total boundary length of 2,170 kilometers (1,349 miles).

The capital city of Honduras, Tegucigalpa, is located in the south central part of the country.

2 TOPOGRAPHY

Honduras is mountainous, with the exception of the northern Ulúa and Aguán river valleys on the Caribbean Sea and the southern coastal area. There are four main topographic regions: the eastern lowlands; the northern coastal plains; the central highlands; and the Pacific lowlands.

There are two large rivers in the north, the Patuca and the Ulúa. Other important features include the Choluteca and Nacaome rivers in the south, Lake Yojoa (Largo de Yojoa) in the west, and Caratasca Lagoon (Laguna de Caratasa) in the northeast.

3 CLIMATE

The northern Caribbean area and the southern coastal plain have a wet, tropical climate, but the interior is drier and cooler. Temperatures vary from a mean of

31°C (88°F) in the coastal lowlands to 23°C (73°F) at the highest altitudes. Average annual rainfall varies from over 240 centimeters (95 inches) along the northern coast to about 84 centimeters (33 inches) in the south. The northwest coast is vulnerable to hurricanes.

4 PLANTS AND ANIMALS

Tropical trees, ferns, moss, and orchids abound, especially in the rainforest areas. Mammal life includes the anteater, armadillo, coyote, deer, and fox. Birds include the black robin, hummingbird, macaw, nightingale, thrush, and many others.

5 ENVIRONMENT

The major environmental problems are loss of soil fertility, erosion, and destruction of forests for lumber, firewood, and land cultivation. According to the World Environment Center, Honduras could be completely deforested by the year 2000.

Rivers and streams in Honduras are threatened by pollution from mining chemicals. Honduras' cities produce 0.5 million tons of solid waste per year. Air pollution results from a lack of pollution control equipment for industries and automobiles.

One species of mammal, 11 bird species, and 3 reptiles are threatened, and 43 plant species are endangered.

6 POPULATION

In mid-1994, the population was estimated at 5,380,341, and the projected population for the year 2000 is 6,846,000. The estimated population density was 46 per square kilometers (124 per square miles) in 1994. Tegucigalpa, the capital and principal city, had 576,661 residents in 1988, including suburbs.

7 MIGRATION

When the Sandinistas (a military and political group) took over in Nicaragua in 1979, former National Guard members began to arrive in Honduras, and by 1983 there were 5,000–10,000 of them along the border. In addition, at least 25,000 Miskito Amerindians from Nicaragua and about 21,000 Salvadorans had fled to Honduras by the end of 1986. Many of them later returned, but by the end of 1992 about 100,000 citizens of Central American nations had taken refuge in Honduras.

8 ETHNIC GROUPS

The vast majority (90–92%) of the Honduran people are mestizo, a mixture of white and Amerindian. About 5–7% of the population is Amerindian. Blacks comprise 2% of the population. Approximately 1% of the population is white, chiefly of Spanish origin.

9 LANGUAGES

The official language is Spanish. However, English is used widely, especially in northern Honduras. The more important Amerindian languages include Miskito, Zambo, Paya, and Xicaque.

10 RELIGIONS

In 1993, an estimated 93.5% of the population was Roman Catholic. The Protestant population accounted for another

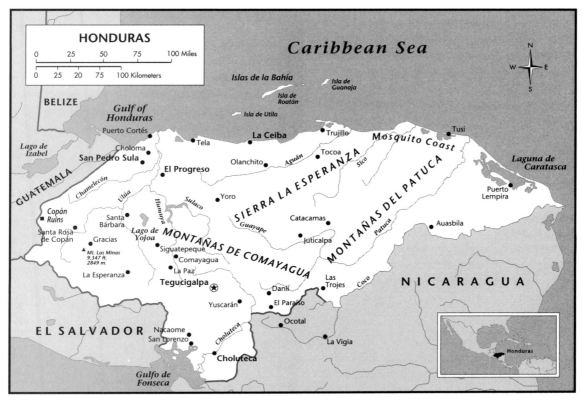

HONDURAS

0	25	50	75	100 Miles
0	25	20	75	100 Kilometers

LOCATION: 13° to 16°N; 83°10′ to 89°20′w. **BOUNDARY LENGTHS:** Caribbean coastline, 591 kilometers (367 miles); Nicaragua, 922 kilometers (573 miles); Gulf of Fonseca coastline, 74 kilometers (46 miles); El Salvador, 335 kilometers (208 miles); Guatemala, 248 kilometers (154 miles). **TERRITORIAL SEA LIMIT:** 12 miles.

3%, and there were also small numbers of spirit worshippers, Amerindian tribal religionists, Muslims, Buddhists, Baha'is, and Jews.

11 TRANSPORTATION

In 1991 there were 8,950 kilometers (5,562 miles) of highways. In 1992 there were 140,000 motor vehicles, of which 45,000 were passenger vehicles. Rail service exists only in the north, connecting the industrial and banana-growing northeastern coastal zone with the principal ports and cities. There are 785 kilometers (488 miles) of track.

Principal ports—Puerto Cortés, Tela, and La Ceiba—serve the country on the Caribbean side.

There are more than 30 landing fields in Honduras, including three international airports. Transportes Aéros Nacionales de Honduras/Servicio Aéreo de Honduras (TAN/SAHSA) flies to the United States, Mexico, and other Central American countries and also provides domestic passenger service, carrying some 357,600 passengers in 1991.

12 HISTORY

The Mayan ceremonial center at Copán in western Honduras flourished in the eighth century AD, but was in ruins when Columbus reached the mainland on his fourth voyage in 1502. He named the region Honduras, meaning "depths."

Colonization began in 1524 under Gil González de Ávila. In 1539, Honduras was made part of the captaincy-general of Guatemala, and for most of the period until 1821, it was divided into two provinces, Comayagua and Tegucigalpa. Some silver was mined in Tegucigalpa.

Honduras joined other provinces of Central America in declaring independence from Spain in 1821. After coming briefly under the Mexican empire of Agustín de Iturbide in 1822–23, Honduras was a member of the United Provinces of Central America from 1824 to 1838.

United States corporate interests, especially the United Fruit Co. (now United Brands), and military dictators dominated Honduran political and economic life during the first half of the 20th century. Elected politics was dominated by the conservative General Tiburcio Carías Andino (1932–48). In the 1950s and early 60s there were several different governments, with military coups in 1956 and 1963, when power was seized by a conservative coalition of military, Nationalist Party, and Liberal Party leaders under an air force officer, Colonel Oswaldo López Arellano.

This government was legalized almost two years later by an elected national assembly, which adopted a new constitution and proclaimed López president in June 1965. During López's second term, a bitter and destructive four-day war broke out in July 1969 between Honduras and El Salvador.

Although the immediate cause of the war was hostility arising from a World Cup elimination-round soccer match between the two countries, the underlying causes were a long-standing border dispute and the long-term migration of some 300,000 Salvadorans in search of land, which the Honduran government made it illegal for Salvadoran immigrants to own. With the help of the OAS, a compromise ceasefire was arranged. In June 1970, the two nations accepted a seven-point peace plan, creating a demilitarized zone along their common frontier.

López and the military continued to dominate Honduran politics until López was overthrown in April 1974 by a group of lieutenant colonels. Two more military governments followed between 1975 and 1983. This period saw strong economic growth and, at the same time, a gradual movement toward democracy.

Under a new constitution in 1982, Roberto Suazo Córdova of the Liberal Party became president, and the military continued to grow in response to domestic unrest and the fighting in neighboring Nicaragua and El Salvador.

By 1983, several thousand anti-Sandinista guerrillas (popularly known as "contras") in Honduras were working for the overthrow of Nicaragua's Sandinista government, while the Honduran army, backed by the United States, was helping Salvadoran government forces in their fight against leftist guerrillas. The CIA used Honduras during that time as a base for covert activities against the Sandinista regime. In exchange, the United States sent large amounts of economic aid to Honduras.

In November 1985, Hondurans elected José Simón Azcona Hoyo to the presidency in the first peaceful transfer of power between elected executives in half a century. Azcona signed the Central American peace plan outlined by President Oscar Arias Sánchez of Costa Rica, but did not move to close down contra bases as promised.

In 1989, Rafael Leonardo Callejas of the National (conservative) Party was elected. Callejas focused on domestic issues, especially reducing the deficit. Significantly, he maintained good relations with the military, which sat on the sidelines as voters went to the polls in November 1993, when the Liberal Party returned to power in the person of Carlos Roberto Reina.

Photo credit: AP/Wide World Photos

An old woman holds a piece of her pottery in a small Honduran village near the Nicaraguan border. Years of war and political upheaval in Central America have left thousands homeless, resources untapped, and have caused a slow movement for reforms to ease the plight of the area's poor.

13 GOVERNMENT

The constitution of 1982 defines Honduras as a democratic republic headed by a president who must be a native-born civilian. The president is elected by direct popular vote for a four-year term. The executive branch also includes a cabinet of 12 ministers. The 1982 constitution provides for the popular election of deputies to the single-chamber National Assembly, consisting of 128 deputies. All men and women 18 years of age and older are eligible to vote.

Honduras is divided into 18 departments, which are further divided into municipalities (284 in 1986).

14 POLITICAL PARTIES

The two major parties in Honduras are the Liberal Party (Partido Liberal—PL) and the National Party (Partido Nacional—PN). The National Party is generally the more conservative of the two.

Two minor parties occupy mildly leftist positions: the Christian Democratic Party, under Efraín Díaz, and the National Innovation and Unity Party, led by Germán Leitzelar. Neither takes more than a couple of seats in the Assembly.

15 JUDICIAL SYSTEM

Judicial power is exercised by the nine-member Supreme Court and five courts of appeal, as well as by lower-level courts and local judges. The Supreme Court has the power to declare laws unconstitutional.

16 ARMED FORCES

The regular forces consisted of 16,800 personnel in 1993; there were 14,000 in the army, 1,800 in the air force, and 1,000 in the navy. Police forces numbered 5,500 personnel. Two years of compulsory peacetime military service may be required of all males between the ages of 18 and 55. The defense budget in 1992 was $43.4 million.

17 ECONOMY

Honduras is one of the three largest exporters of bananas in the world. It is, nevertheless, by most measures, the poorest nation on the mainland of the Americas. Income per person is one of the lowest in Latin America, although it has been improving moderately since 1990.

With its economy heavily dependent on banana production, the country is vulnerable to crop and world market price varia-

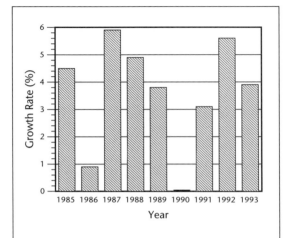

Yearly growth rate of the economy. This economic indicator tells by what percent the economy has increased or decreased when compared with the previous year.

tions. The vast majority of banana holdings are controlled by two United States companies—United Brands and Standard Fruit.

Shortly after taking office in January 1990, President Rafael Leonardo Callejas announced a major market-oriented economic reform package. The success of the program has led to a marked improvement in the country's economic performance.

18 INCOME

Honduras' gross national product (GNP) was $3,142 million at current prices, or about $600 per person. For the period 1985–92, the average inflation rate was 11.3%, resulting in a real growth rate in GNP of 0.5% per person.

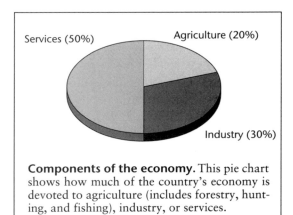

Components of the economy. This pie chart shows how much of the country's economy is devoted to agriculture (includes forestry, hunting, and fishing), industry, or services.

19 INDUSTRY

The largest firms are found in the cement, cotton, sugar, and wood products industries, and these companies are also active exporters. Small to mid-size industrial enterprises have sprung up in textiles, household preparations, light metals, and food products.

Manufacturing grew by 8.6% in 1992. Growth was greatest among food and tobacco products, wood and paper products, and basic metalworking and metal products. The country has a well-established clothing assembly industry. Total apparel exports to the United States exceeded $200 million in 1992.

20 LABOR

In 1992, the economically active population totaled 1,728,599, of whom agriculture engaged 37%; services, 19.3%; manufacturing, 14.5%; commerce, 16.3%; construction, 4.2%; and other sectors, 8.7%. The unemployment rate by the end of 1991 was 15%. About 20% of the labor force was unionized in 1991.

21 AGRICULTURE

Agriculture is the most important part of the economy, accounting for almost 40% of employment in 1992. However, farming methods are inefficient, and crop yields and qualities are low. The principal export crops are bananas and coffee; the major subsistence crops are corn, sorghum, beans, and rice. Crop production for 1992 included sugarcane, 3,004,000 tons; bananas, 1,086,000 tons; sorghum, 69,000 tons; beans, 46,000 tons; and rice, 41,000 tons.

22 DOMESTICATED ANIMALS

Honduran consumption of milk and meat is traditionally low. However, pastures remain the largest category of land in Honduras and, in 1992, accounted for 25% of the total land area. In 1992, the cattle population numbered 2,351,000 head; hogs, 750,000; horses and mules, 241,000; and chickens, 8,000,000. That year, 380,000 tons of milk and 31,000 tons of eggs were produced.

23 FISHING

There is commercial fishing in Puerto Cortés, and other areas are served by local fishermen. In 1991, the total catch was 20,989 tons. In 1992, the fisheries' sector grew by 14.7% due to investment in southern shrimp farms.

24 FORESTRY

In 1991, about 28% of Honduras was covered by forests, including stands of longleaf pine and such valuable hardwoods as cedar, ebony, mahogany, and walnut. Total roundwood production in 1991 amounted to 6.2 million cubic meters, and forest products exports were valued at $29.1 million.

25 MINING

Lead and zinc, as well as small amounts of cadmium, copper, silver, and gold are commercially important. The nonmetallic minerals extracted in Honduras are cement, marble, and salt. Inadequate transportation continues to hamper full development of mineral resources.

In 1992, the significant growth of construction activity boosted demand for gravel and iron, which caused the mining industry to grow by 33% that year. In 1991, production of zinc was 38,280 tons; lead, 8,719 tons; silver, 39,359 kilograms; and gold, 179 kilograms.

26 FOREIGN TRADE

Honduras exports a limited range of agricultural commodities, with bananas, coffee, and shrimp and lobster accounting for two-thirds of total exports. Important import categories are industrial raw materials and intermediate products, nondurable consumer goods, and industrial capital goods.

As of 1992, the United States continued to be Honduras's chief trading partner, supplying approximately 60% of its imports and purchasing over half of its exports. Other main partners in the 1990s include Japan, Mexico, and Venezuela. Total exports rose to $900 million in

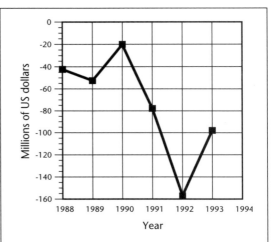

Yearly balance of trade measured in millions of US dollars. The balance of trade is the difference between what a country sells to other countries (its exports) and what it buys (its imports). If a country imports more than it exports, it has a negative balance of trade (a trade deficit). If exports exceed imports there is a positive balance of trade (a trade surplus).

1993; total imports grew to $1,000 million in 1993.

27 ENERGY AND POWER

Much of Honduras's energy is derived from the burning of wood; about 25% is provided by imported crude oil and petroleum products, supplied mainly by Mexico and Venezuela. Hydroelectricity and geothermal energy provided 10% and 3%, respectively, of Honduras's energy needs in 1991. Electrical power production in 1991 was 1,105 million kilowatt hours.

28 SOCIAL DEVELOPMENT

The present Honduran Social Insurance Law covers accidents, illness, maternity,

---

Selected Social Indicators

These statistics are estimates for the period 1988 to 1993. For comparison purposes, data for the United States and averages for low-income countries and high-income countries are also given.

Indicator	Honduras	Low-income countries	High-income countries	United States
Per capita gross national product†	**$600**	$380	$23,680	$24,740
Population growth rate	**3.0%**	1.9%	0.6%	1.0%
Population growth rate in urban areas	**4.6%**	3.9%	0.8%	1.3%
Population per square kilometer of land	**46**	78	25	26
Life expectancy in years	**68**	62	77	76
Number of people per physician	**2,326**	>3,300	453	419
Number of pupils per teacher (primary school)	**38**	39	<18	20
Illiteracy rate (15 years and older)	**27%**	41%	<5%	<3%
Energy consumed per capita (kg of oil equivalent)	**180**	364	5,203	7,918

† The gross national product (GNP) is the total dollar value of all goods and services produced by a country in a year. The per capita GNP is calculated by dividing a country's GNP by its population. The World Bank defines low-income countries as those with a per capita GNP of $695 or less. High-income countries have a per capita GNP of $8,626 or more. Less than 14% of the world's 5.5 billion people live in high-income countries, while almost 60% live in low-income countries.

> = greater than   < = less than

Sources: World Bank, *Social Indicators of Development 1995,* Baltimore: Johns Hopkins University Press, 1995. Central Intelligence Agency, *World Fact Book,* Washington, D.C.: Government Printing Office, 1994.

---

old age, occupational disease, unemployment, disability, death, and other circumstances affecting the capacity to work and maintain oneself and one's family. Actual coverage, however, has been limited mainly to maternity, sickness, and workers' compensation.

Women represented 26.3% of the labor force in 1986. In that year, seven women were serving in the National Assembly.

29 HEALTH

Health conditions in Honduras are among the worst in the Western Hemisphere, and health care remains inadequate. In 1992 there were 2,326 people per physician. In 1992, 66% of the population had access to health care services. Total health care spending in 1990 was $134 million.

Major causes of illness are diseases of the digestive tract, intestinal parasites, influenza, pneumonia, cancer, and infant diseases. Malnutrition, impure water, poor sewage disposal, and inadequate housing are the major causes of health problems. Life expectancy is an average of 68 years.

30 HOUSING

Many urban dwellings and most rural dwellings lack running water, electricity, and indoor plumbing. Estimates of the shortage in housing units grew to 500,000 in 1985. Projects underway during the early 1980s included a $30-million low-cost housing program sponsored by the Housing Finance Corporation.

31 EDUCATION

The rate of illiteracy among adults in 1990 was estimated at 27% (males, 24.5% and females, 29.4%). Public education is free and compulsory for children between the ages of 7 and 15. In 1985, 82.6% of primary-school-age children were actually in school. As of 1990 there were 7,593 primary and elementary schools, with 908,446 students and 23,872 teachers. Secondary and normal schools had 194,083 pupils and 8,507 teachers.

In 1990, total university enrollment was 39,324, with 3,258 teaching staff. The major university is the National Autonomous University of Honduras, founded at Tegucigalpa in 1847.

32 MEDIA

During 1993, Honduras had 182 radio stations and 28 television stations. There were 2,045,000 radios, 385,000 television sets, and 2,300,000 telephones.

There is no press censorship. Of four daily newspapers in the republic in 1991, two were in Tegucigalpa and two in San Pedro Sula. The country's principal newspapers (with 1991 circulation) were *La Tribuna* (50,000), *El Tiempo (30,000),* and *El Heraldo* (31,000), all published in Tegucigalpa, and *La Prensa,* published in San Pedro Sula.

33 TOURISM AND RECREATION

Honduran governments have attempted to attract foreign visitors. After a period of stagnation, tourism experienced modest growth in the late 1980s. In 1991, there were an estimated 198,000 tourist arrivals, mostly from the Americas. There were 6,739 hotel rooms and 11,946 beds, and tourists spent $31 million. The main tourist attraction is the restoration at Copán, the second-largest city of the ancient Mayan Empire. There are also beaches on the northern coast and good fishing in Trujillo Bay and Lake Yojoa.

34 FAMOUS HONDURANS

José Cecilio del Valle (1780–1834), a member of the French Academy of Sciences, was an intellectual and political leader, and the author of the Central American declaration of independence. Outstanding literary figures include Marco Aurelio Soto (1846–1908), an essayist and liberal president, and Froilán Turcios (1875–1943).

35 BIBLIOGRAPHY

Barry, Tom. *Honduras: A Country Guide.* Albuquerque, N.M.: Inter-Hemispheric Education Resource Center, 1990.

Fasquelle, Ricardo Agurcia and William L. Fash, Jr. "Maya Artistry Unearthed." *National Geographic,* September 1991, 94–105.

Honduras in Pictures. Minneapolis, Minnesota: Lerner Publications Company, 1987.

Howard-Reguindin, Pamela F. *Honduras.* Santa Barbara, Calif.: Clio, 1992.

Targ, H. and M. Brill. *Honduras.* Chicago: Children's Press, 1995.

HUNGARY

Republic of Hungary

Magyar Népköztársaság

CAPITAL: Budapest.

FLAG: The national flag, adopted in 1957, is a tricolor of red, white, and green horizontal stripes.

ANTHEM: *Isten áldd meg a magyart (God Bless the Hungarians).*

MONETARY UNIT: The forint (Ft) of 100 fillérs is a paper currency with flexible rates of exchange. There are coins of 10, 20, and 50 fillérs and 1, 2, 5, 10, 20, 100, and 200 forints, and notes of 50, 100, 500, 1,000, and 5,000 forints. Ft1 = $0.0098 (or $1 = Ft102.041).

WEIGHTS AND MEASURES: The metric system is the legal standard.

HOLIDAYS: New Year's Day, 1 January; Anniversary of 1848 uprising against Austrian rule, 15 March; Labor Day, 1 May; Constitution Day, 20 August; Day of the Proclamation of the Republic, 23 October; Christmas, 25–26 December. Easter Monday is a movable holiday.

TIME: 1 PM = noon GMT.

1 LOCATION AND SIZE

Hungary is a landlocked country in Central Europe, with an area of 93,030 square kilometers (35,919 square miles), slightly smaller than the state of Indiana. It has a total boundary length of 2,242 kilometers (1,393miles).

Hungary's capital city, Budapest, is located in the north central part of the country.

2 TOPOGRAPHY

The country has four chief geographic regions: the Danube (Duna) River valley, the Great Plain (Alföld), the Balaton region, and the Northern Mountains. Hungary's river valleys and its highest mountains are in the northeast. The chief rivers are the Danube (Duna) and Tisza. The largest lake is Balaton. Hungary's highest point is Mt. Kékes at 1,015 meters (3,330 feet) in the Mátra Mountains, northeast of Budapest.

3 CLIMATE

Hungary lies at the meeting point of three climatic zones: the continental, Mediterranean, and oceanic. Yearly temperatures vary from a minimum of –14°C (7°F) to a maximum of 36°C (97°F). Rainfall varies, but the annual average is approximately 63 centimeters (25 inches)—more in the west and less in the east—with maximum rainfall during the summer months. Severe droughts often occur in the summers.

4 PLANTS AND ANIMALS

Oak is the predominant deciduous tree. Various conifers are located in the mountains. Among the abundant wildlife are deer, boar, hare, and mouflon (wild sheep). The Great Plain (Alföld) is a breeding ground and a migration center for a variety of birds. Fish are plentiful in rivers and lakes.

5 ENVIRONMENT

Chemical pollution of the air and water is extensive, but resources to combat pollution are scarce. Pollution from sulphur and nitrogen oxides affects 41% of the population of Hungary. One hundred percent of the city dwellers and 95% of people living in rural areas have pure water. The nation's cities produce 1.9 million tons of solid waste.

Protected areas in 1984 included national parks, 141,000 hectares (348,417 acres); conservation districts and reservations, 330,800 hectares (817,400 acres); and urban parks and greenbelts, 8,029 hectares (19,840 acres). As of 1994, two of Hungary's mammal species, 16 of its bird species, and 21 plant species are endangered.

6 POPULATION

According to the census of 1 January 1990, the population totaled 10,374,823. As of 1 January 1992, it was estimated at 10,337,200. Average density in 1990 was 110 persons per square kilometer (289 per square mile). A population of 10,507,000 is forecast by the United Nations for the year 2000. But Hungary's own forecast for the year 2000 is no higher than 10,216,700. Budapest, the capital and principal city, had a population of 2,015,955 at the beginning of 1992. Eight other cities had populations exceeding 100,000.

7 MIGRATION

Sizable population migration during the two world wars resulted from military operations, territorial changes, and population transfers. Emigration totaled 42,700 between 1981 and 1989. It is now practically nonexistent. Only 778 persons left in 1991, according to official statistics.

At the end of 1992 Hungary was harboring 32,000 refugees, of whom 29,000 were from the former Yugoslavia. There were 54,693 registered asylum seekers in 1991.

8 ETHNIC GROUPS

Ethnically, Hungarians are of Magyar descent. According to the 1990 census, the ethnic composition in 1985 was as follows: Hungarians, 97.8%; Gypsies, 1.4%; Germans, 0.3%; Slovaks, 0.1%; Croats, 0.1%; Romanians, 0.1%; and others, 0.2%. An independent study in the 1980s found about 500,000 Gypsies, about 230,000 Germans, about 100,000 Slovaks, about 100,000 Yugoslavs, and about 30,000 Romanians.

Between 1.7 million and 2.5 million Magyars live in Romania, where they have reportedly been victims of ethnic discrimination. Another 600,000 Magyars live in Slovakia, 400,000 in the former Yugoslavia, and 180,000 in Ukraine.

9 LANGUAGES

Magyar is the universal language. Written in Latin characters, Magyar belongs to the Finno-Ugric family, a branch of the Ural-Altaic language group. Magyar is also characterized by the presence of Turkish,

HUNGARY

0	25	50 Miles
0	25	50 Kilometers

SLOVAKIA

UKRAINE

Rimayská
Sobota

Berehove

Vienna

Bratislava

Nové
Zámky

Ipoly

CSERHÁT

BUKK

Miskolc

Salgótarján

MÁTRA

Tiszaújváros

Nyíregyháza

Neusiedler
See

Sopron

Győr

Dorog

Gyöngyös

▲ *Kékes*
3,327 ft.
1,014 m.

Eger

Tisza

Satu
Mare

AUSTRIA

Rába

Tatabánya

Százhalombatta

Budapest

Kiskörei-
víztároló

Debrecen

Szombathely

BAKONY

Várpalota

Albertirsa

D

ROMANIA

Veszprem

Székesfehérvár

Szolnok

Oradea

Ajka

Zala

Sió

Dunaujváros

Duna

Kecskemét

Ö

L

Körös

N

SLOVENIA

Balaton

F

Békéscsaba

W   E

Nagykanizsa

A

Hódmezővásárhely

L

S

Kaposvár

Szekszárd

Szeged

Maros

Arad

Zagreb

Drava

MECSEK MTS.

Pécs

Mohács

Bjelovar

Novi Sad

Hungary

CROATIA

Osijek

SERBIA

Sava

Belgrade

LOCATION: 45°48′ to 48°35′N; 16°5′ to 22°58′E. **BOUNDARY LENGTHS:** Slovakia, 608 kilometers (378 miles); Ukraine, 215 kilometers (134 miles); Romania, 432 kilometers (268 miles); Croatia and Serbia, 631 kilometers (392 miles); Austria, 356 kilometers (221 miles).

Slavic, German, Latin, and French words. In addition to their native language, many Hungarians speak English, German, French, or (since World War II) Russian.

10 RELIGIONS

As of 1993, an estimated 63% of the people were Roman Catholics, with some two million Reformed Calvinists, members of the Hungarian Reformed Church. There were 100,000 Jews in 1991. Most of the

remainder were nonreligious or atheistic. State relations with the Roman Catholic Church, hostile under the former Hungarian People's Republic, improved considerably in 1990 after Hungary reestablished diplomatic relations with the Vatican.

11 TRANSPORTATION

Transportation facilities have improved steadily since the 1960s. Budapest is the transportation center. In 1991, roads totaled 130,000 kilometers (80,800 miles). In 1991, Hungary had 2,015,455 passenger cars and 201,039 trucks.

As of 1991, Hungary had 7,779 kilometers (4,834 miles) of track, of which 97% was standard gauge. Most freight is carried by trucks. Pipeline transport is of lesser importance, accounting for 40% of fuel transport in 1990.

Navigable waterways totaled 1,622 kilometers (1,008 miles) in 1988, of which the Danube (Duna) and Tisza rivers made up over half. In 1991, the merchant marine fleet consisted of 14 cargo ships and one bulk vessel.

Ferihegy Airport in Budapest, the most important center for domestic and international flights, handled 50,900 aircraft landings and takeoffs and 1,763,000 arriving and departing passengers in 1991. All domestic traffic is handled by the Hungarian Air Transportation Enterprise (Magyar Légiközlekedési Vallalat—MALÉV), which carried 910,700 passengers in 1991, but only 181,600 in 1992.

12 HISTORY

The Roman Emperor Augustus conquered the western part of present-day Hungary—called Pannonia—in 9 BC. The following centuries saw invasions by the Huns, Goths, and other groups. The Avars ruled for 250 years and, like the Huns, established a khanate (kingdom) in the Hungarian plain.

The Magyars (Hungarians) invaded the plains of present-day Hungary in AD 896 and were conquered by Otto the Great, king of Germany and Holy Roman emperor, in 955. They were converted to Christianity under King Stephen I (r.1001–38), who was canonized in 1083. The Holy Crown of St. Stephen became the national symbol, and a constitution was gradually developed. However, the Mongols devastated the country in 1241–42.

Medieval Hungary was famous for its gold mines. It prospered during the reign of Matthias Corvinus (1458–90), the son of the famous military hero János Hunyadi. However, Turkish armies had begun to threaten the region during the fifteenth century, and Hungary's golden age ended with their defeat by the Turks in 1526.

With the defeat of the Turks at Vienna in 1683, Turkish power ended and that of the Habsburg kings of Austria became stronger. In 1713, after many unsuccessful uprisings against the Habsburgs, the Hungarian national assembly accepted the Pragmatic Sanction, an agreement binding Hungary to Austria.

During the first half of the nineteenth century, Hungary experienced a rise in Magyar nationalism. The revolt of 1848 established a short-lived Hungarian republic. Eventually Austria, weakened by its war with Prussia, was forced to compromise. In 1867 a dual monarchy of Austria and Hungary was established, with a degree of self-government for the Magyars.

After World War I (1914–1918), in which Austria-Hungary was defeated, the dual monarchy collapsed, and a democratic republic was established under Count Mihály Károlyi. This was replaced in March 1919 by a Communist government led by Béla Kun, but Romanian troops invaded Hungary and helped overcome it.

The Treaty of Trianon in 1920 left large numbers of Magyars in Romania and elsewhere beyond Hungary's borders. In the hope of recovering its "lost" territories, Hungary formed alliances with the Axis powers and sided with them during World War II (1939–1945). In March 1944, the German army occupied Hungary, but Soviet troops invaded the country later that year and liberated it by April 1945.

Under Communist Rule

In 1946, a republican constitution was adopted, and a coalition government was established. The Hungarian Workers (Communist) Party seized power in 1948. Hungarian foreign trade was oriented toward the Soviet bloc, and industry and land were taken over by the government. Resentment to Soviet influence led to a popular uprising in October 1956 that was quickly put down by Soviet military force after a few days' success. Many people fled the country, and many others were executed.

From 1956, Hungary was a firm ally of the USSR. In 1968, the New Economic Mechanism was introduced in order to make the economy more competitive and open to market forces. Reform measures beginning in 1979 further encouraged private enterprise. The movement toward relaxation of tensions in Europe in the 1970s was reflected in the improvement of

Photo credit: AP/Wide World Photos

A child carries a poster that reads: "Justice to 1956" during a mass demonstration staged by independent groups in downtown Budapest in 1989. About 100,000 people joined this rally as Hungary celebrated the 1956 popular uprising against Soviet influence.

Hungary's relations with Western countries, including reestablishment of diplomatic relations with the Federal Republic of Germany in 1973.

The energy crisis of the late 1970s, aggravated by the abandonment of the New Economic Mechanism at Soviet insistence, led to growing foreign debt. By the late 1980s the country owed $18 billion, the highest rate of debt in Europe.

This debt and other social factors spurred political change. In October 1989 the state constitution was amended to create a multiparty political system. After the 1990 general election, the first major free election to be held in more than four decades, a coalition government was formed.

Under prime minister Jozsef Antall, Hungary began to transform its economy with the goal of transferring 30–35% of state assets to private control by the end of 1993. Hungary's liberal investment laws and comparatively well-developed industries permitted the nation to become an early leader in attracting Western investors. However, many found the pace of transition too slow, especially since the government did not keep to its own time schedule.

In addition, right-wing elements in society began to preach nationalistic intolerance of Hungary's ethnic minorities. Approximately 10% of the Hungarian population is non-Hungarian, including large populations of Jews and Gypsies.

In the parliamentary elections of May 1994, voters turned overwhelmingly to the Hungarian Socialist Party (the former Communist party), giving it an absolute majority of 54%.

Hungary's international debt remains very high—the country ran a $936 million trade deficit for the first two months of 1994 alone—forcing new Prime Minister Gyula Horn to continue most of the same economic reform programs which the previous government began. There is concern, however, that the Socialists' victory could lead to reversal of some of the important democratic gains of the recent past.

13 GOVERNMENT

Hungary's present constitution remains based upon the 1949 Soviet-style constitution, with major changes made in 1972 and 1988. The lack of a new constitution has left Hungary with a number of remnants of the Communist era. This has been most noticeable in regards to the media, which have no constitutional guarantee of freedom.

The present system is a multiparty republic, with a parliamentary government. There is one legislative house, with 386 seats. The head of state is the President, who is elected by the Parliament, for a five-year term. The head of the government is the prime minister, leader of the largest party seated in the Parliament.

Hungary is divided into 19 districts, and the capital city, Budapest, is considered an independent district.

14 POLITICAL PARTIES

Each of the last two parliaments has seated representatives of the same six political parties. However, the relative numbers of seats shifted dramatically between 1990 and 1994.

The dominant party is the Hungarian Socialist Party (HSP) (the former Communist Party), which took 209 of the legislature's 386 seats in the 1994 elections. Although it supports a market economy system, the HSP, like the Communists of the past, stresses party unity and discipline.

The Alliance of Free Democrats (AFD) favors closer integration with Europe and cooperation with Hungary's neighbors. With its right wing purged in 1993, the Hungarian Democratic Forum (HDF) is a party of strong support for the ethnic minorities within Hungary. The Independent Smallholders' Party (ISP) is a center-right party which seeks to ensure Hungarian interests in the context of European integration.

The Christian Democratic People's Party (CDPP) is a center-right group with a religious dimension. The Alliance of Young Democrats (AYD) is similar in program to the AFD, but with narrower appeal. The final parliamentary party is the Agrarian Alliance, which is primarily concerned with issues affecting the nation's farmers.

Hungary also has a noticeable "skinhead" movement, which has provoked fights and other disturbances, especially with Gypsies.

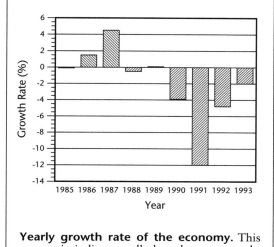

Yearly growth rate of the economy. This economic indicator tells by what percent the economy has increased or decreased when compared with the previous year.

15 JUDICIAL SYSTEM

Cases usually receive their first hearing before provincial city courts or Budapest district courts. Appeals can be submitted to county courts or the Budapest Metropolitan Court. The Supreme Court is basically a court of appeal, although it may also hear important cases in the first instance. A Constitutional Law Council was established in April 1984 to verify the constitutionality of proposed laws.

16 ARMED FORCES

Military service is compulsory. All males aged 18 to 55 are eligible for induction for 12 months' service. In 1993, Hungary had an army of 63,500 men in four mixed divisions; an air force of 17,300 men and 91 combat aircraft; and a rivercraft brigade with 51 small craft. Security forces, consisting of frontier and border guards under the direction of the Ministry of the Interior, number about 20,000. The defense budget was estimated at $1.16 billion in 1992.

17 ECONOMY

Since 1949, industry has expanded rapidly, and it now contributes a larger share than agriculture to the national income. However, industrial growth was slow in the 1980s. The government participates in limited economic activities in developing countries. Hungary's gross debt to the West rose to about $24.5 billion as of

December 1993, the largest rate of debt of all European countries.

After the fall of Communism in 1989, Hungary began a painful transition to a market economy. Freed to reach their own level, consumer prices rose 162% between 1989 and 1993. The rate of unemployment was 12.2% at the end of 1992. Hungary became an associate member of the European Union (EU) in 1994.

18 INCOME

In 1992, the gross national product (GNP) was $30,671 million, or $3,350 per person. For the period 1985–92 the average inflation rate was 18.5%, resulting in a growth rate in GNP of –1.5% per person.

19 INDUSTRY

Industry, only partially developed before World War II, has expanded rapidly since 1948 and provides the bulk of exports. In 1993, industrial production was only two-thirds of the 1985 level.

The 1993 output of steel was 1,836,000 tons; crude aluminum, 27,879 tons; nitrogenous fertilizers, 220,574 tons (in terms of nitrogen); superphosphates, 424,563 tons (phosphoric acid); footwear, 11,963,000 pairs; and buses, 3,211. Other products, with 1993 output totals, include cement, 2,532,000 tons; television receivers, 188,021; television sets, 185,000; washing machines, 34,258; refrigerators, 482,952; fluorescent tubes, 39,253,000; and cotton and woolen fabrics, 97.5 million square meters.

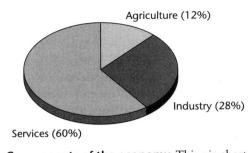

Components of the economy. This pie chart shows how much of the country's economy is devoted to agriculture (includes forestry, hunting, and fishing), industry, or services.

Agriculture (12%)
Industry (28%)
Services (60%)

20 LABOR

Of the total of 4,710,000 workers in 1991, 29.6% were in industry; 19.3% in agriculture; 12.8% in trade; 8.7% in transportation; 6.5% in construction; and 23.1% in other branches of the economy, including administration, health, and education. Women constituted 52% of the civilian labor force. In 1991, unemployment was at 8.4%, up from 1.6% in 1990.

The five-day week is typical, but many Hungarians have second or third jobs.

21 AGRICULTURE

More than half of Hungary's area lies in the Great Plain (*Alföld*). Although the soil is fertile, most of the region lacks adequate rainfall and is subject to droughts, requiring extensive irrigation. In 1991, some 145,000 hectares (358,300 acres) of land were irrigated.

The traditional agricultural crops have been food grains, with wheat, corn (maize), and rye grown on more than half the total planted area. In recent years, much progress has been made in industrial crops, especially oilseeds and sugar beets. Fruit production (especially for preserves) and wine production are also significant. The wine output in 1992 was 500,000 tons. That year, over 800,000 tons of grapes were produced on 135,000 hectares (333,600 acres).

22 DOMESTICATED ANIMALS

The number and quality of animals are much lower than in neighboring countries, due in large part to an inadequate supply of animal feed. At the end of 1992 there were 5,993,000 hogs, 1,808,000 sheep, 1,420,000 head of cattle, and 75,000 horses. Poultry numbered 36,000,000. The 1992 output of livestock products was 1,214,000 tons (live weight) of meat, 2,370,000 tons of milk, and 5,740 tons of wool. Egg production was 228,000 tons.

23 FISHING

Fishing was unimportant before World War II, but production has increased in recent years. The catch is composed mainly of carp, catfish, and perch. The 1991 catch was 29,378 tons.

24 FORESTRY

Forests totaled 1,701,000 hectares (4,203,000 acres), or 18.4% of Hungary's total area, in 1991. Oak, ash, and beech are the most important tree varieties. Because of the relatively small forest area and the high rate of use, Hungary traditionally has had to import timber. Production rose from 3.5 million cubic meters in 1960 to 6 million cubic meters in 1991.

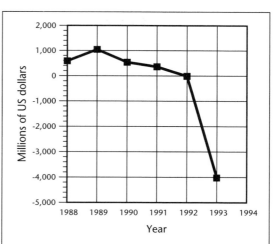

Yearly balance of trade measured in millions of US dollars. The balance of trade is the difference between what a country sells to other countries (its exports) and what it buys (its imports). If a country imports more than it exports, it has a negative balance of trade (a trade deficit). If exports exceed imports there is a positive balance of trade (a trade surplus).

25 MINING

In 1991 the country's mineral industry was still state-owned. Mineral reserves are small. Bauxite, which is found in various parts of western Hungary, has been among the most important minerals. Bauxite production in 1991 was 2,037,000 tons. Hungary produced 54,783 tons of manganese ore during the same year.

26 FOREIGN TRADE

Hungary's total trade volume increased in 1993. Hungary imports raw materials and semifinished products and exports finished products. While agricultural products made up 57% of total exports before

World War II, they stood at 21.4% in 1993.

Other exports in 1993 were industrial consumer goods (25.2%), and raw materials and semifinished products (36.2%). Industrial consumer goods made up 21.2% of total imports in 1993; raw materials and semifinished products, 33.4%; machinery and equipment, 26.9%; and fuels and electric energy, 12.6%.

The USSR used to be by far Hungary's most important supplier and customer. Germany has become the chief customer, with the former USSR second and (in 1993) still its chief supplier. Austria ranks third in both respects and Italy fourth. The European Community countries took half of Hungary's exports in 1992.

27 ENERGY AND POWER

All natural sources of power are state property, and all electric power plants are under state supervision. In 1990, installed capacity was 6.96 million kilowatts, of which thermal electric generating plants accounted for 68%; nuclear power plants, 25%; and hydroelectric power facilities, 7%. Oil and natural gas are rapidly replacing coal as the major energy source.

Increased energy production has not kept up with consumption, and reliance on foreign power sources has been increasing. In 1991, imports accounted for about 50% of Hungary's total energy requirements and nearly 80% of its crude oil consumption.

28 SOCIAL DEVELOPMENT

By 1974, 99% of the population enjoyed the benefits of social insurance. Coverage includes relief for sickness, accidents, unemployment, and old age and incapacity, and provides maternity allowances for working women, allowances for children, and payment of funeral expenses.

Women receive their monthly average earnings during maternity leave, which lasts 24 weeks. An employed woman or a father raising his child alone is entitled to unpaid leave until the child is 3 years old.

Women have the same legal rights as men, including inheritance and property rights. They hold a large number of the positions in teaching, medicine, and the judiciary, which are all relatively low-paid professions.

29 HEALTH

By the end of 1974, 99% of the population was covered by social insurance and enjoyed free medical services. Free professional assistance is given to insured pregnant women and to the mothers of newborn children. Limited private medical practice is permitted. Total health care spending in 1990 came to $1,958 million. In 1991, there were 335 people for each doctor.

Hungary has a declining population which is aging rapidly. Arteriosclerosis is a major cause of death, and there is a high incidence of cardiovascular disease. Contributing factors include work-related stress, together with smoking and dietary factors. Average life expectancy was 69 years in 1992.

Selected Social Indicators

These statistics are estimates for the period 1988 to 1993. For comparison purposes, data for the United States and averages for low income countries and high income countries are also given.

Indicator	Hungary	Low-income countries	High-income countries	United States
Per capita gross national product†	**$3,350**	$380	$23,680	$24,740
Population growth rate	**-0.5%**	1.9%	0.6%	1.0%
Population growth rate in urban areas	**0.3%**	3.9%	0.8%	1.3%
Population per square kilometer of land	**110**	78	25	26
Life expectancy in years	**69**	62	77	76
Number of people per physician	**335**	>3,300	453	419
Number of pupils per teacher (primary school)	**12**	39	<18	20
Illiteracy rate (15 years and older)	**1%**	41%	<5%	<3%
Energy consumed per capita (kg of oil equivalent)	**105**	364	5,203	7,918

† The gross national product (GNP) is the total dollar value of all goods and services produced by a country in a year. The per capita GNP is calculated by dividing a country's GNP by its population. The World Bank defines low-income countries as those with a per capita GNP of $695 or less. High-income countries have a per capita GNP of $8,626 or more. Less than 14% of the world's 5.5 billion people live in high-income countries, while almost 60% live in low-income countries.   > = greater than   < = less than

Sources: World Bank, *Social Indicators of Development 1995,* Baltimore: Johns Hopkins University Press, 1995. Central Intelligence Agency, *World Fact Book,* Washington, D.C.: Government Printing Office, 1994.

30 HOUSING

Although the housing stock increased from 3,122,000 units in 1970 to 3,846,000 in 1986, construction has not kept pace with the needs of Hungary's growing urban population. The construction rate for new dwellings has been greater in smaller cities and towns than in Budapest.

31 EDUCATION

Practically the entire adult population is literate. Eight years of primary and four years of secondary education are free. The state also pays most of the costs for higher education.

In 1991 there were 3,641 general elementary schools, with 89,276 teachers and 1,081,213 pupils, and general secondary schools, with 10,732 teachers and 130,378 students. The same year, 3,865 students were in teacher training and 390,908 were in vocational courses. Institutions of higher education had 107,079 students and 17,477 professors and lecturers in 1991. Although there are university fees, many students are excused from payment or pay reduced fees.

32 MEDIA

In 1990 Hungary had 47 radio stations and 41 television stations. By early 1985, cable television was operating in 12 cities.

In 1991, Hungary had 6,280,000 radios, 4,340,000 television sets, and 1,770,000 telephones.

In 1991 there were 28 daily newspapers, with an average combined daily circulation of 2.9 million. Budapest has always been Hungary's publishing center. The larger Budapest dailies as of 1991, with circulation figures, were Népszabadság, 327,000; Népszava, 181,000; Kurir, 134,000; Magyar Nemzet, 121,000; and Esti Hírlap, 93,000.

33 TOURISM AND RECREATION

Hungary, at the crossroads of Central Europe, had the world's fifth-highest number of tourist arrivals (21.8 million) in 1991. Of Hungary's visitors, 26.2% came from Romania, 15.9% from Germany, 13.9% from Austria, and 8.6% from the former Yugoslavia. There were 25,549 hotel rooms with a 48.2% occupancy rate, and tourism receipts totaled $1.03 billion.

Among Hungary's diverse tourist attractions are Turkish and Roman ruins, medieval towns and castles, more than 500 thermal springs (some with resort facilities), and Lake Balaton, the largest freshwater lake in Europe. Budapest, a city of over two million people, is a major tourist attraction and cultural capital, with two opera houses and several annual arts festivals. The Budapest Grand Prix, the only Formula-1 motor race in Eastern Europe, was inaugurated in August 1986.

34 FAMOUS HUNGARIANS

The Hungarians were converted to Christianity under King Stephen I (r.1001–38), who was canonized in 1083. The Holy Crown of St. Stephen became the national symbol.

The Hungarian-born Joseph Pulitzer (1847–1911) was a noted journalist and publisher in the United States. Hungarian musicians include the composers Franz Liszt (1811–86), and Béla Bartók (1881–1945). Renowned Hungarian-born conductors who became famous worldwide include Fritz Reiner (1888–1963), George Széll (1897–1970), and Eugene Ormándy (1899–1985). Béla Lugosi (Blasko, 1882–1956) and Peter Lorre (Laszlo Loewenstein, 1904–64) were famous actors.

Budapest-born Edward Teller (b.1908) contributed to atomic research in the United States.

35 BIBLIOGRAPHY

Burant, Stephen R. (ed.). *Hungary: A Country Study.* 2d ed. Washington, D.C.: Government Printing Office, 1990.

Hintz, M. *Hungary.* Chicago: Children's Press, 1988.

Hoensch, Jorg K. *A History of Modern Hungary, 1867–1986.* New York: Longman, 1988.

Lasky, Melvin J. (ed.). *The Hungarian Revolution: The Story of the October Uprising.* New York: Praeger, 1957.

Nagel, Rob, and Anne Commire. "Stephen I." In *World Leaders, People Who Shaped the World.* Volume II: Europe. Detroit: U*X*L, 1994.

Sugar, Peter F. (ed.). *A History of Hungary.* Bloomington: Indiana University Press, 1990.

ICELAND

Republic of Iceland
Lýðveldið Ísland

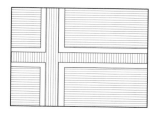

CAPITAL: Reykjavík.

FLAG: The national flag, introduced in 1916, consists of a red cross (with an extended right horizontal), bordered in white, on a blue field.

ANTHEM: *O Guð vors lands (O God of Our Land).*

MONETARY UNIT: The new króna (κ), introduced 1 January 1981 and equivalent to 100 old krónur, is a paper currency of 100 aurar. There are coins of 5, 10, and 50 aurar and 1, 10 and 50 krónur, and notes of 10, 50, 100, 500, 1,000 and 5,000 krónur. sκ1 = $0.0139 (or $1 = κ71.690).

WEIGHTS AND MEASURES: The metric system is used.

HOLIDAYS: New Year's Day, 1 January; First Day of Summer, April; Labor Day, 1 May; National Holiday, 17 June; Bank Holiday, August; Christmas, 25–26 December. Movable religious holidays include Holy Thursday, Good Friday, Easter Monday, Ascension, and Whitmonday. Half-holidays are observed on Christmas Eve, 24 December, and New Year's Eve, 31 December.

TIME: GMT.

1 LOCATION AND SIZE

Iceland, the westernmost country of Europe, is an island in the North Atlantic Ocean, just below the Arctic Circle. It has an area of 103,000 square kilometers (39,769 square miles), slightly smaller than the state of Kentucky. The total length of its coastline is about 4,970 kilometers (3,090 miles). The republic includes many smaller islands, of which the chief are the Westman Islands (Vestmannaeyjar) off the southern coast.

Iceland's capital city, Reykjavík, is located on the country's southwest coast.

2 TOPOGRAPHY

Iceland consists mainly of a central volcanic plateau ringed by mountains, the high-est of which is Hvannadalshnúkur (2,119 meters/6,953 feet). Among the many active volcanoes, there is an average of about one eruption every five years.

There are also many lakes, snowfields, hot springs, and geysers (the word "geyser" itself is of Icelandic origin). The longest river is the Thjórsá in southern Iceland. Most rivers are short and none are navigable. Good natural harbors are provided by fjords on the north, east, and west coasts.

3 CLIMATE

Despite Iceland's northern latitude, its climate is fairly mild because of the Gulf Stream. Temperatures at Reykjavík average from 11°C (52°F) in July to −1°C (30°F) in January, with an annual mean of about 4°C (39°F). Humidity is high, and there is much fog in the east. Annual rainfall in the north ranges from 30 to 70 centimeters (12–28 inches); in the south, 80–130 centimeters (31–51 inches); and in the mountains, up to 225 centimeters (89 inches).

4 PLANTS AND ANIMALS

Although there are a few small trees (ash, aspen, birch, and willow), the chief forms of vegetation are grass, mosses, and small shrubs (heather, willow, dwarf birch). Some 400 different species of flowers have been listed, but most of these are scarce.

The fox, the chief native animal, is common. Wild reindeer, once abundant, were almost exterminated and therefore have been protected in recent years. The waters around Iceland abound in whales and many types of seals and fish. Dolphin, grampus, and porpoise are numerous. Salmon are found in many rivers, and trout in rivers and lakes. There are about 100 species of birds, both resident and migratory. Most of them are aquatic. The chief resident birds are eiderduck (raised commercially for their down) and ptarmigan. Iceland has no reptiles or frogs, and little insect life.

5 ENVIRONMENT

Because of Iceland's sparing use of hydrocarbon fuels, its air is cleaner than that of most industrialized nations. However, its water supply is polluted by excessive use of fertilizers. Population increases in the cities also contribute to water pollution. The nation's cities produce 0.1 million tons of solid waste annually.

At the end of 1985 there were four national parks, 27 nature reserves, and 34 other protected areas. As of 1994, one mammal species and two bird species were endangered, as well as two plant species.

6 POPULATION

Total population as of 1 December 1991 was estimated at 259,577. A population of 283,000 was projected for the year 2000. The average density as of December 1991 was 3 people per square kilometer (7.7 per square mile). Reykjavík, the capital, had a population of 99,623 in 1991.

7 MIGRATION

Little immigration has occurred since the original settlement in the ninth and tenth centuries. In 1991, the number of emigrants was 2,982. Among the 15,745 emigrating during 1986–90, 4,147 went to Denmark, 4,506 to Sweden, 2,228 to Norway, and 1,473 to the United States. Most of the 3,989 immigrants in 1991 (a record) were from Nordic countries or the United States.

8 ETHNIC GROUPS

The population is almost entirely Icelandic, descended from the original settlers, who came chiefly from Norway (with a mixture of Scots and Irish) in the late ninth and early tenth centuries. In 1991 there were 5,395 foreigners, of whom 1,095 were Danish.

9 LANGUAGES

Icelandic, the national language, derives from the Old Norse language that was spoken throughout Scandinavia at the

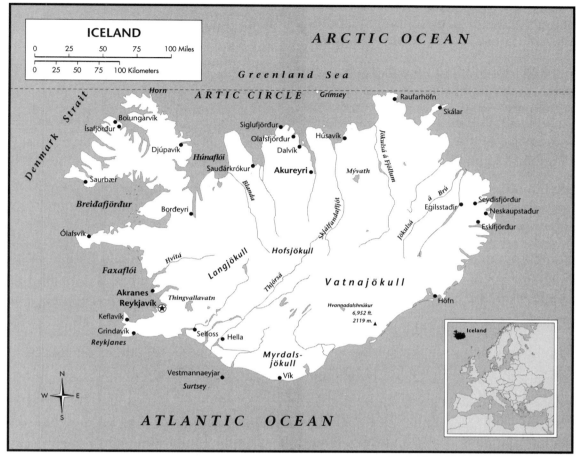

LOCATION: 63°19′ to 67°7′5″N; 13°16′7″ to 24°32′3″W. **BOUNDARY LENGTHS:** Total coastline, 4,970 kilometers (3,090 miles). **TERRITORIAL SEA LIMIT:** 12 miles.

time of settlement. It has changed little through the centuries, partly because of the country's isolation. To this day, Icelanders are able to read the great thirteenth-century sagas without special study.

10 RELIGIONS

The Evangelical Lutheran Church, the national church, is endowed by the state, but there is complete freedom for all faiths, without discrimination. All of Ice-

land constitutes a single diocese of the national church, headed by a bishop with his seat at Reykjavík. There are 281 parishes. About 93% of the people belong to the established church. Of the remainder, 3.7% belong to other Lutheran denominations, and 1% are Roman Catholics.

11 TRANSPORTATION

There are no railways or navigable inland waters. All important towns and districts

Photo credit: Susan D. Rock

A scenic valley in Iceland.

can be reached by bus and truck via interurban roads (12,343 kilometers/7,670 miles in 1991), but 88% are dirt roads of poor quality. Registered passenger cars in 1991 numbered 120,862 and there were 16,012 commercial vehicles.

Icelandair operates domestic routes as well as international flights to the UK, Scandinavia, and Germany, and transatlantic flights with stopovers at Reykjavík. In 1992, it carried 510,000 passengers on international routes and 257,100 on domestic routes.

12 HISTORY

Iceland's first known settler, Ingólfur Arnarson, sailed from his native Norway to Iceland and settled at what is now Reykjavík in 874. During the late ninth and early tenth centuries, the island was settled by other Norwegians fleeing the oppressive rule of their king and by smaller groups of Scottish and Irish emigrants. In 930, a central legislative and judicial assembly, the *Althing,* was established, and a uniform code of laws for the entire country was compiled.

Christianity was introduced in the year 1000, but the memory of the old pagan religion was preserved in twelfth- and thirteenth-century Icelandic literature. Many of the early settlers were great seafarers and continued their westward voyages of discovery and exploration from Iceland.

Most famous of these were Eric the Red (Eiríkur Thorvaldsson), who discovered and settled in Greenland in 982, and his son Leif Ericsson (Leifur Eiríksson), who around the year 1000 discovered the North American continent.

When all the Scandinavian countries came under the rule of Denmark at the end of the fourteenth century, Iceland became a Danish dominion. Lutheranism was introduced in the 1540s. Danes had a complete monopoly of trade with Iceland until 1786.

The last decades of the 18th century were a period of economic ruin for Iceland, compounded by poor harvests, epidemics, and volcanic eruptions (notably that of 1783, the worst in Iceland's history). The population dwindled to 38,000 by 1800, less than half the number in the period of independence before Danish rule. In that year, the king abolished the Althing, long since reduced in power.

Within a few decades, however, a nationalist movement had gained strength. After a long constitutional struggle—led by a national hero, Jón Sigurðsson, who was both statesman and scholar—limited home rule was granted in 1874, and almost complete home rule in 1903.

By agreement with Denmark in 1918, Iceland was declared a free and independent state. The Danish king continued to function as king of Iceland, and Denmark conducted Iceland's foreign affairs. But Iceland had the right to end this arrangement after 25 years.

Cut off from Denmark during World War II (1939–45) by the German occupation of that country, Iceland established diplomatic relations with the United Kingdom and the United States. British forces, who took over the protection of the island in 1940, were replaced the following year by United States troops, who remained until early 1947. In May 1944, more than 97% of those participating voted to end the union with the king of Denmark and, on 17 June 1944, Iceland became an independent republic.

In 1946, Iceland was admitted to United Nations membership and three years later it became a party to the North Atlantic Treaty Organization (NATO). In March 1970, Iceland joined the European Free Trade Association (EFTA), and a trade agreement was reached with the European Community in February 1973. To protect its fishing industry, Iceland extended its fishing zone in 1958, 1972, and 1975, provoking conflict with the UK and other countries.

Depressed world fish prices continued to weaken the economy in the early 1990s. The government launched a program including devaluation of the króna in an attempt to reduce inflation.

13 GOVERNMENT

Iceland is an independent republic. Executive power is vested in the president and the government, legislative power in the president and the legislative assembly (Althing). The president is elected by universal voting for a four-year term. Executive power is exercised by a prime minister selected by the president.

Iceland is divided into 23 counties (sýslur) and 14 independent towns (kaup-staðir).

14 POLITICAL PARTIES

No one major party in recent years has been able to command a majority of the votes, and coalition governments have been the rule. The general election of April 1991 resulted in a new center-right coalition led by David Oddsson of the Independence Party and members of the Social Democratic People's Party.

15 JUDICIAL SYSTEM

The district magistrates (sýslumenn) and the town magistrates (bæjarfógetar) administer justice on a local level in 26 lower courts. Appeals are heard by the Supreme Court, consisting of eight justices (all appointed for life by the president), who elect one of their number as chief justice for a two-year term. There are special courts for maritime cases, labor disputes, and other types of cases.

16 ARMED FORCES

Iceland is the only NATO member with no military force of its own, although the government does maintain armed fishery protection vessels and planes manned by 130 personnel. United States forces (3,000) and Dutch (30) are stationed at Keflavík for air and anti-submarine defense.

17 ECONOMY

Iceland's economy, once primarily agricultural, is now based overwhelmingly on fishing. Crop raising plays a small role,

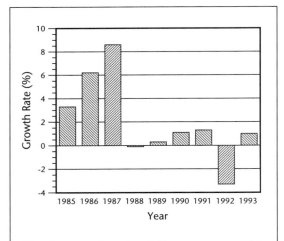

Yearly growth rate of the economy. This economic indicator tells by what percent the economy has increased or decreased when compared with the previous year.

since most of the land is unsuitable for cultivation and the growing season is short. Sheep raising and dairying are the chief agricultural activities, with horse breeding also substantial. Since Iceland has almost no known mineral resources and has had no concentrations of population until recent decades, industry is small-scale and local, depending heavily on imported raw and semimanufactured materials.

18 INCOME

In 1992, Iceland's gross national product (GNP) was $6,177 million at current prices, or $24,950 per person.

19 INDUSTRY

Fish processing is the most important industry. Facilities for freezing, salting, sun-curing, and reducing fish to oil or fish meal are flexible enough to allow shifting from one process to another based on demand. By-products include fish meal and cod-liver oil.

Other industry is small-scale and designed to meet local needs. Chief manufactured items include fishing equipment, electric stoves and cookers, paints, clothing, soaps, candles, cosmetics, dairy products, confectionery, and beer.

20 LABOR

In 1990, 18.4% of employment in Iceland was in fish processing or other manufacturing, 14.4% in commerce, 0.8% in electricity and steam production, 7.2% in community, social, and personal services, 8% in business services, 9.6% in construction, 6.4% in transportation and communications, 4.8% in agriculture, 5.6% in fishing, 18.4% in government, and 6.4% in other areas.

About 76% of all workers belong to trade unions. Unemployment is very low by international standards, averaging 1.5% in 1991. Emigration for employment is common, and Icelanders can be found working all over the world, especially in the other Nordic countries, Europe, and the United States. The customary workweek is 46 hours.

21 AGRICULTURE

In the nineteenth century and earlier, agriculture was the chief occupation, but by 1930, fewer than 36% of the people devoted their energies to farming, and that number has continued to fall. Hay is the principal crop. Other crops are potatoes,

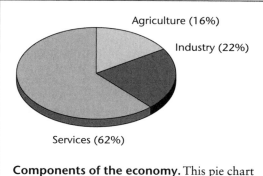

Agriculture (16%)

Industry (22%)

Services (62%)

Components of the economy. This pie chart shows how much of the country's economy is devoted to agriculture (includes forestry, hunting, and fishing), industry, or services.

turnips, oats, and garden vegetables. In hot-spring areas, vegetables, flowers and even tropical fruits are increasingly being cultivated in greenhouses heated with hot water from the springs.

22 DOMESTICATED ANIMALS

Animal farming is a highly mechanized industry carried out by well-educated farmers. Mutton and lamb are the primary meat products. Cattle are raised mainly for dairy products, and their number has been rising steadily. Beef production is insignificant. Sheep at the end of 1992 numbered an estimated 487,300; cattle, 76,000 head; horses, 75,200; and poultry, 179,000.

Estimated livestock products in 1992 included milk, 110,000 tons; mutton and lamb, 11,000 tons; and eggs, 3,900 tons. Iceland provides its own meat, dairy products, and eggs. Horse-breeding is also a growing branch of animal husbandry in Iceland, as the popularity of the Iceland horse (which has five gaits) grows at home and abroad.

23 FISHING

Accounting for about 17% of Iceland's employment, fishing and fish processing provide the main source of foreign exchange, accounting for 82% (or $1,252.7 million) of total exports. Icelanders consume more fish per person annually (over 90 kilograms/198 pounds live weight equivalent) than any other people in Europe.

24 FORESTRY

There are no forests of commercial value, and the existing trees (ash, birch, aspen, and willow) are small. In recent years, the remaining woods have been protected and reforestation has begun.

25 MINING

Mineral resources are few. Sulfur and lignite are now being processed experimentally. Diatomite mining is underway near Lake Mývath. In 1991 aluminum production was 88,768 tons and ferro-silicon production was 50,299 tons.

26 FOREIGN TRADE

Imports include almost all Icelandic requirements except fish, meats, dairy products, and some agricultural products. Leading imports are machinery and transport equipment, manufactures, mineral fuels and lubricants, and chemicals. Fish and fish products make up nearly 80% of total exports. The remainder consists of aluminum, ferro-silicon, meat, wool, sheepskins, and other material. Iceland is a

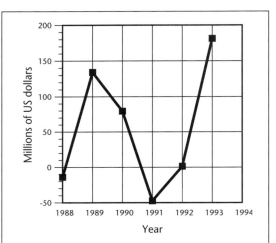

Yearly balance of trade measured in millions of US dollars. The balance of trade is the difference between what a country sells to other countries (its exports) and what it buys (its imports). If a country imports more than it exports, it has a negative balance of trade (a trade deficit). If exports exceed imports there is a positive balance of trade (a trade surplus).

member of the European Free Trade Association (EFTA).

The United States, the United Kingdom, and Germany are Iceland's major trade partners. In 1993, trade with European Free Trade Association (EFTA) nations accounted for 9% of Iceland's exports and 23.7% of its imports; with the United States, for 16% of exports and 9.3% of imports; and with the European Community, 59.8% of exports and 48.4% of imports.

27 ENERGY AND POWER

Hydroelectric power potential from Iceland's many swift rivers and waterfalls is high. An estimated 45 billion kilowatt hours per year can be had from the five principal glacial rivers. Electric energy output in that year was 4,494 million kilowatt hours, with hydroelectric output accounting for 94%.

In 1992, some 85% of the population heated their houses with geothermal power. In recent years, however, a significant decline in flow from geothermal drill holes has raised concern that this energy resource may not be so boundless as was once thought.

28 SOCIAL DEVELOPMENT

The national health insurance scheme includes insurance against sickness, accident, and unemployment; pensions for the aged and disabled; and a health service that provides treatment and care of the sick.

Studies show that women earn about 40% less than men in comparable jobs.

29 HEALTH

The incidence of tuberculosis, once widespread, has been greatly reduced. Leprosy, also common in earlier times, has been practically eliminated, with no new cases reported in recent decades. There were three reported cases of AIDS in 1990. Life expectancy for 1992 was 78 years (80 years for women and 76 for men), among the highest in the world and highest among the Nordic countries. Iceland spent $26,618,000 on health care in 1991.

30 HOUSING

The total number of dwellings at the end of 1985 was 84,821. In 1991, 1,490 dwellings were completed, of which 795 were one- or two-family houses. In the towns, traditional turf houses long ago gave way to wooden ones, but for some decades most new housing has been concrete. Virtually all dwellings have electricity, piped water, and central heating.

31 EDUCATION

There is practically no adult illiteracy. Education is compulsory for children aged 7 to 15. In 1991 there were 214 public schools and five universities and colleges. The University of Iceland in Reykjavík was founded in 1911.

32 MEDIA

Icelandic radio broadcasts via numerous public and private stations. Two television stations broadcast seven days a week. In 1991 there were approximately 202,000 radios, 80,000 television sets, and 124,951 telephones.

The three daily newspapers published in Reykjavík, with their average daily circulation in 1991, were *Morgunblaðid,* 45,000; *Timinn,* 14,000; and *Pjóðviljinn,* 13,000.

33 TOURISM AND RECREATION

Iceland offers such diverse and unusual natural attractions as active volcanoes, glaciers, and hot springs. Among popular recreational sports are swimming (possible year-round in geothermal pools), salmon fishing, pony trekking, and golf. The approximate number of foreign visitors to Iceland in 1991 was 143,000, of whom 116,000 were from Europe.

Selected Social Indicators

These statistics are estimates for the period 1988 to 1993. For comparison purposes, data for the United States and averages for low income countries and high income countries are also given.

Indicator	Iceland	Low-income countries	High-income countries	United States
Per capita gross national product†	**$24,950**	$380	$23,680	$24,740
Population growth rate	**1.1%**	1.9%	0.6%	1.0%
Population growth rate in urban areas	**1.3%**	3.9%	0.8%	1.3%
Population per square kilometer of land	**3**	78	25	26
Life expectancy in years	**78**	62	77	76
Number of people per physician	**357**	>3,300	453	419
Number of pupils per teacher (primary school)	**n.a.**	39	<18	20
Illiteracy rate (15 years and older)	**<1%**	41%	<5%	<3%
Energy consumed per capita (kg of oil equivalent)	**5,025**	364	5,203	7,918

† The gross national product (GNP) is the total dollar value of all goods and services produced by a country in a year. The per capita GNP is calculated by dividing a country's GNP by its population. The World Bank defines low-income countries as those with a per capita GNP of $695 or less. High-income countries have a per capita GNP of $8,626 or more. Less than 14% of the world's 5.5 billion people live in high-income countries, while almost 60% live in low-income countries.

n.a. = data not available.   > = greater than   < = less than

Sources: World Bank, *Social Indicators of Development 1995,* Baltimore: Johns Hopkins University Press, 1995. Central Intelligence Agency, *World Fact Book,* Washington, D.C.: Government Printing Office, 1994.

34 FAMOUS ICELANDERS

Two famous early Icelanders were Eric the Red (Eiríkur Thorvaldsson), who discovered and colonized Greenland in 982, and his son Leif Ericsson (Leifur Eiríksson, b.970), who introduced Christianity to Greenland and discovered the North American continent (c.1000). Jón Sigurðsson (1811–79), Iceland's national hero, was a champion of the fight for independence.

Snorri Sturluson (1178–1241) was the author of the famous *Prose Edda*, a collection of Norse myths. The novelist Halldór Kiljan Laxness (b.1902) received the Nobel Prize for literature in 1955. Einar Jónsson (1874–1954), Iceland's greatest sculptor, is represented in European and American museums.

35 BIBLIOGRAPHY

Auden, Wystan Hugh, and Louis MacNeice. *Letters from Iceland.* London: Faber & Faber, 1937.

Byock, Jesse L. *Medieval Iceland: Society, Sagas, and Power.* Berkeley: University of California Press, 1988.

Lepthien, E. *Iceland.* Chicago: Children's Press, 1987.

Levathes, Louise E. "Iceland: Life Under the Glaciers." *National Geographic,* February 1987, 184–215.

Roberts, David. *Iceland.* New York: H.N. Abrams, 1990.

Scherman, Katherine. *Daughter of Fire: A Portrait of Iceland.* Boston: Little, Brown, 1976.

INDIA

Republic of India
Bharat Ganarajya

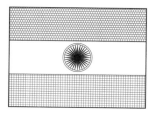

CAPITAL: New Delhi.

FLAG: The national flag, adopted in 1947, is a tricolor of deep saffron, white, and green horizontal stripes. In the center of the white stripe is a blue wheel representing the wheel (chakra) that appears on the abacus of Asoka's lion capital (c.250 BC) at Sarnath, Uttar Pradesh.

ANTHEM: *Jana gana mana (Thou Art the Ruler of the Minds of All People)*. A national song of equal status is *Vande Mataram (I Bow to Thee, Mother)*.

MONETARY UNIT: The rupee (R) is a paper currency of 100 paise. There are coins of 5, 10, 20, 25, and 50 paise, and 1, 2, and 5 rupees, and notes of 2, 5, 10, 20, 50, 100, and 500 rupees. R1 = 0.0319 (or $1 = R31.370).

WEIGHTS AND MEASURES: Metric weights and measures, introduced in 1958, replaced the British and local systems. Indian numerical units still in use include the lakh (equal to 100,000) and the crore (equal to 10 million).

HOLIDAYS: Republic Day, 26 January; Independence Day, 15 August; Gandhi Jayanti, 2 October. Annual events—some national, others purely local, and each associated with one or more religious communities—number in the hundreds. The more important include Shivarati in February; and Raksha Bandhan in August. Movable religious holidays include Holi, Ganesh Chaturthi, Durga Puja, Dussehra, 'Id al-Fitr, Dewali; and Christmas, 25 December.

TIME: 5:30 PM = noon GMT.

1 LOCATION AND SIZE

The Republic of India, Asia's second-largest country after China, fills the major part of the South Asian subcontinent (which it shares with Pakistan, Nepal, Bhutan, and Bangladesh) and includes the Andaman and Nicobar Islands in the Bay of Bengal and Lakshadweep in the Arabian Sea. India's total area is 3,287,590 square kilometers (1,269,345 square miles), slightly more than one-third the size of the United States. The total boundary length is 21,103 kilometers (13,113 miles).

India's capital city, New Delhi, is located in the north central part of the country.

2 TOPOGRAPHY

Three major features fill the Indian landscape: (1) the Himalayas, which mark the nation's northern boundary; (2) the Peninsula, which holds the bulk of India's mineral wealth, and through which many of its great rivers—the Narmada, Mahanadi, Godavari, Krishna, and Cauvery—flow to the sea; and (3) the Ganges-Brahmaputra Lowland. These three features, plus a narrow coastal plain along the Arabian Sea and a wider one along the Bay of Bengal, establish five major physical-economic zones in India.

Some of the world's highest peaks are found in the northern mountains: Kanchenjunga (8,598 meters/28,208 feet), the third-highest mountain in the world, is on the border with Nepal. The Ganges, Brahmaputra, Son, Yamuna, Chambal, Ghogra, and many other major rivers flow along the great plain of the Ganges-Brahmaputra Lowland, providing India with its richest agricultural land.

3 CLIMATE

The monsoon is the dominant feature of India's climate and helps to divide the year into four seasons: rainy (June–September); moist (October–November); dry cool (December–March); and hot (April–May).

India's weather varies widely. Villages in the Great Indian Desert may experience less than 13 centimeters (5 inches) of rainfall yearly, while some areas near Bangladesh average about 1,140 centimeters (450 inches) yearly. Winter snowfall is normal for the northern mountains and valleys, but for most of India, scorching spring dust storms and severe hailstorms are more common.

The northern half of the country is subject to frost from November through February, but by May a temperature as high

as 49°C (120°F) in the shade may be recorded.

4 PLANTS AND ANIMALS

Almost one-fourth of the land is forested. Pine, oak, bamboo, juniper, deodar, and sal are important species of the Himalayas. Sandalwood, teak, rosewood, mango, and Indian mahogany are found in the southern peninsula. Some 15,000 varieties of flowers abound in India's diverse climatic zones.

India has over 500 species of mammals, 2,100 species of birds, 30,000 species of insects, and a great diversity of fish and reptiles. Wild mammals, including deer, Indian bison, monkeys, and bears, live in the Himalayan foothills and the hilly section of Assam and the plateau.

5 ENVIRONMENT

Among India's most serious environmental problems are land damage, water shortages, and air and water pollution. Despite three decades of flood-control programs, floods in 1980 alone claimed nearly 2,000 lives, killed tens of thousands of cattle, and affected 55 million people on 11.3 million hectares (28 million acres) of land. As of 1994, 60% of the land where crops could be grown had been damaged by grazing, the timber industry, and misuse of agricultural chemicals.

Due to uncontrolled dumping of chemical and industrial waste, fertilizers, and pesticides, 70% of the surface water in India is polluted. Air pollution is most severe in urban centers, but even in rural areas, the burning of wood, charcoal, and dung for fuel, coupled with dust from

INDIA

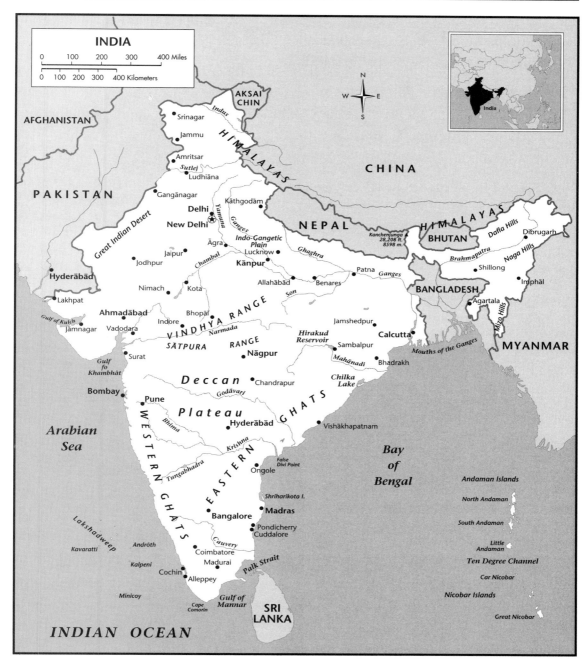

LOCATION: 8°4′ to 37°6′N; 68°7′ to 97°25′E. **BOUNDARY LENGTHS:** 3,380 kilometers (2,100 miles); Nepal, 1,690 kilometers (1,050 miles); Bhutan, 605 kilometers (373 miles); Myanmar, 1,463 kilometers (910 miles); Bangladesh, 4,053 kilometers (2,520 miles); total coastline, 7,000 kilometers (4,360 miles); Pakistan, 2,912 kilometers (1,800 miles). **TERRITORIAL SEA LIMIT:** 12 miles.

wind erosion during the dry season, poses a big problem. Industrial air pollution threatens some of India's architectural treasures, including the Taj Mahal in Agra, part of the exterior of which has been damaged by airborne acids.

In what was probably the worst industrial disaster of all time, a toxic gas leak from a Union Carbide pesticide plant in Bhopal killed more than 1,500 people and injured tens of thousands of others in December 1985.

The Wildlife Act of 1972 prohibits killing and selling of threatened animals. In 1985 there were 20 national parks and more than 200 wildlife sanctuaries. In addition to 39 mammals, 72 birds are endangered, as well as 1,336 plant species.

6 POPULATION

India, the second most populous country in the world, had a population of 843,930,861 in 1991. The July 1994 population estimate by the US Bureau of the Census was 919,923,712, with a UN projection of 1,018,673,000 for the year 2000. The US Census Bureau expects India's population to surpass China's by 2035. The key to India's rapid population growth since the 1920s has been a sharp decline in the death rate because of improvements in health care, nutrition, and sanitation.

India is one of the very few countries of the world where men outnumber women (by 437,597,929 to 406,332,932 in the 1991 census). In 1991, the average population density was 267 persons per square kilometer (691 per square mile).

Cities with more than 1.5 million inhabitants each at the 1991 census included Calcutta (4,399,819), Bombay (9,925,891), Delhi (7,206,704), Madras (3,841,396), and Bangalore (3,302,296).

7 MIGRATION

The partitioning of the South Asian subcontinent to create India and Pakistan in 1947 produced one of the great mass migrations in human history, involving some 20 million people. The number of Bangladeshis illegally in India was estimated at anywhere from 2 to 15 million in 1993. Some 53,733 were caught at the border in 1991 and turned back.

Indians living in foreign countries generally do not become mixed with the local population, but live as separate groups, marry among themselves, and keep their own distinctive culture even after several generations. An estimated 11,644,000 persons of Indian origin were living abroad in 1994.

In 1993 India was harboring nearly 200,000 Tamils from Sri Lanka, including 88,000 in 131 government-run camps, and over 100,000 Tibetan refugees.

8 ETHNIC GROUPS

India's ethnic history is extremely complex, and distinct racial divisions between peoples generally cannot be drawn clearly. However, Negroid, Australoid, Mongoloid, and Caucasoid stocks are discernible. The first three are represented mainly by tribal peoples in the southern hills, the plateau, the Brahmaputra Valley, the Himalayas, and the Andaman Islands. The main

Caucasoid elements are the Mediterranean, including groups dominant in much of the north, and the Nordic or Indo-Aryan, a taller, fairer-skinned strain dominant in the northwest. The dark-complexioned Dravidians of the south have a mixture of Mediterranean and Australoid features.

9 LANGUAGES

The 1961 census recorded 1,652 different languages and dialects in India. One state alone, Madhya Pradesh, had 377. There are officially 211 separate, distinct languages, of which Hindi, English, and 17 regional languages are officially recognized by the constitution.

Hindi is spoken as the mother tongue by about 240 million people (30% of the total population). English is spoken as the native tongue by an estimated 10–15 million Indians and is widely employed in government, education, science, communications, and industry.

10 RELIGIONS

India is the cradle of two of the world's great religions, Hinduism and Buddhism. An estimated 83.5% of the population follows Hinduism. Other religious groups include Muslims (11%) and Christians (2.6%).

The Sikh religion began in the fifteenth century as an attempt to reconcile Muslim and Hindu doctrine, but the Sikhs soon became a warrior sect. Sikhs (about 0.7% of population) are concentrated in the state of Punjab, which since 1980 has been the site of violent acts by Sikh activists demanding greater independence from the Hindu-dominated central government. The remaining 2.3% of the population consisted of Buddhists, Jains, followers of tribal religions, and other groups. (Jainism, a religion that developed at the same time as Buddhism, has largely been confined to India.)

The caste system is a distinct feature of Hinduism, in which every person either is born into one of four groups—*Brahmans* (priests and scholars), *Kshatriyas* (warriors and rulers), *Vaisyas* (shopkeepers, artisans, and farmers), and *Sudras* (farm laborers and menial workers)—or is casteless and thus "untouchable" (now known as *Harijan*).

11 TRANSPORTATION

The railway system is highly developed and is the major means of long-distance internal transport. In 1991, the railways spanned some 61,850 kilometers (38,430 miles), forming the largest system in Asia and the fourth largest in the world. Indian railways operated about 11,000 trains per day, connecting 7,021 stations. Passenger traffic increased to 3,700 million in 1991/92, and freight traffic to 330 million tons.

The national and state road network in 1991 was about 1,120,000 kilometers (695,970 miles), of which 515,000 kilometers (320,020 miles) were hard-surfaced. In 1991 there were 4,667,749 motor vehicles, including 2,490,805 automobiles and taxis; 1,845,377 trucks and jeeps; and 331,567 buses.

India has about 16,200 kilometers (10,070 miles) of inland waterways, with

3,630 kilometers (2,250 miles) navigable by large vessels. The leading port for international shipping is Bombay.

International airports are at Bombay, Calcutta, Delhi, and Madras. The Indian Airlines Corp. operates all internal flights and services to neighboring countries with daily flights to 60 cities. Air-India operates long-distance services to foreign countries on five continents. During 1992, Indian Airlines and Air-India carried an estimated 10.9 million passengers.

12 HISTORY

India is one of the oldest continuously inhabited regions in the world. An early civilization first appeared in the Indus River Valley between 3000 and 2000 BC. It waned around 1500–1200 BC, probably due to the arrival of Aryan (Indo-European-speaking) invaders, who began pouring through Afghanistan into northern India. Then came over a thousand years of instability, as one invading group after another contended for power. During this period, Indian village and family patterns, along with Brahmanism—the ancient form of Hinduism—and its caste system, became well established.

In the eighth century, the first of several waves of Islamic invaders appeared in the northwest, and Islam gradually spread eastward and southward, reaching its territorial and cultural peak under the Mughal (or Mogul) dynasty. ("Mughal" comes from a traditional word for Mongol. The Mughals were descendants of the great fourteenth-century Mongol conqueror Timur, a descendant of Genghis Khan.)

Babur (r.1526–30) was the first of the Mughals to proclaim himself emperor of India. Akbar (r.1556–1605), Babur's grandson, first attempted to establish a national state by teaming with Hindu rajahs (kings). His successors Shah Jahan and Aurangzeb left their memory in massive palaces and mosques, superb fortresses, and dazzling mausoleums (like the Taj Mahal at Agra).

Vasco da Gama reached India's southwest coast by sea in 1498, and for a century the Portuguese had total control over Indian sea trade. Portugal lost its dominant position around 1612, when forces controlled by the British East India Company defeated the Portuguese. The Company, which had been established in 1600, had permanent trading settlements in Madras, Bombay, and Calcutta by 1690.

The British Government took direct control of the British East India Company's Indian domain during the Sepoy Mutiny (1857–59), a widespread rebellion by Indian soldiers in the company's service. In 1859, Queen Victoria was proclaimed Empress of India. The following decades were characterized by significant economic and political development, but also by a growing cultural and political gap between Indians and British.

Nationalism and Independence

In the twentieth century, British power was increasingly challenged by the rise of local independence movements. Among them was the Indian National Congress (INC). Under the leadership of Mohandas Karamchand Gandhi (called the

Photo credit: Cynthia Bassett.

In Varanasi (Banares) along the banks of the holy Ganges River, Hindus bathe facing the sun to the east, with the belief one can be reincarnated into a better life.

Mahatma, or Great Soul) and other nationalist leaders, such as Jawaharlal Nehru, the INC began to attract mass support in the 1930s. Its tactics included noncooperation campaigns and non-violent struggle. The INC strongly believed in education, self-help, and an end to the caste system.

However, as the movement evolved under Gandhi, its leadership style appeared—to Muslims—uniquely Hindu. This led Indian Muslims to form their own organization, the All-India Muslim League (ML). The ML argued that Muslims and Hindus were separate nations and that Muslims required the creation of an independent Islamic state for their protection and fulfillment.

Meanwhile, Mahatma Gandhi's campaigns of nonviolent noncooperation and civil disobedience electrified the countryside. In 1942, Gandhi rejected a British appeal to postpone further talks on Indian self-rule until the end of World War II. Declining to support the British (and Allied) war effort and demanding immediate British withdrawal from India, he launched a "Quit India" campaign. In return, Gandhi and most of India's nationalist leaders were jailed.

The end of World War II in 1945 led to renewed negotiations on independence between Britain and the Hindu and Muslim leaders. In mid-August 1947, with Hindu-Muslim tensions rising, British India was divided into the two self-governing dominions of India and Pakistan. Known as Partition, this division caused a mass movement of Hindus, Muslims, and Sikhs who found themselves on the "wrong" side of new international boundaries. As many as twenty million people moved, and up to three million of these were killed in bloodletting on both sides of the new international frontier. Gandhi, who opposed Partition and worked untiringly for Hindu-Muslim cooperation, became a casualty of the inflamed feelings of the period. He was assassinated by a Hindu extremist five months after Partition.

Among the unresolved legacies of Partition was the fate of the independent state of Jammu and Kashmir, bordering both new nations. A Muslim-majority state with a Hindu maharaja, Kashmir has been the site of periodic Indian-Pakistani clashes since 1948. While Pakistan governs its portion of the former princely state as Azad ("free") Kashmir and as the Northern Areas, the Indian portion is governed as Jammu and Kashmir, a state in the Indian Union.

In the late 1980s, India's cancellation of election results and dismissal of the state government led to the start of an armed rebellion by Muslim militants. Indian repression and Pakistan's undeclared support of the militants have threatened to spark renewed warfare and keep the issue unresolved.

India and China have been at odds over their Himalayan border since the Chinese occupation of Tibet in 1959, leading to clashes between Indian and Chinese troops at a number of locations along the disputed border. The border dispute with China remains unresolved, although tensions have been eased by a stand-still accord signed by the two countries in September 1993.

Nehru's Successors

After the death of India's first prime minister, Jawaharlal Nehru, on 27 May 1964, his successor, Lal Bahadur Shastri, led India in dealing with Hindu-Muslim violence in Kashmir. Shastri died of a heart attack while at Tashkent, Uzbekistan to sign a peace agreement. His successor, Indira Gandhi (Nehru's daughter), pledged to honor the accords. India again went to war with Pakistan in December 1971, this time to support East Pakistan in its civil war with West Pakistan. Indian forces tipped the balance in favor of the separatists, which ultimately led to the creation of Bangladesh from the former East Pakistan.

In June 1975, Gandhi's conviction on minor election law violations in the 1972 polls required her to resign. She continued in power by proclaiming a state of emergency. She imposed press censorship, arrested opposition political leaders, and sponsored legislation that cleared her of the election law violations. These actions, although later upheld by the Supreme Court, resulted in widespread public disapproval.

Two boys on a crowded city street smile for the camera. The United Nations predicts that the population of India will exceed one billion people by the year 2000. The current population is 919 million, or more than three times that of the United States.

Two years later, she was defeated in parliamentary elections, forcing her Congress Party into the parliamentary opposition for the first time. Morarji Desai, of the winning five-party Janata coalition, became prime minister. But Janata, formed solely to oppose Mrs. Gandhi, had no unity or agreed program, and it soon collapsed. Mrs. Gandhi's newly reorganized Congress Party/I ("I" for Indira) gained Hindu votes to win a huge election victory in January 1980, and she regained office.

In October 1983, Sikh discontent led to widespread violence by Sikh separatist militants in Punjab and to the imposition of direct rule in that state. A year later, with the Sikh separatist violence unchecked, Gandhi herself became one of its victims—assassinated by Sikh members of her own guard.

Rajiv Gandhi immediately followed his mother as prime minister. However, during the next two years his popularity declined quickly as the public reacted to government-imposed price increases for basic commodities, his inability to stem rising ethnic violence, and charges of military kickbacks and other scandals.

After a rise in Indo-Pakistan tensions in 1986–87, Rajiv Gandhi and Prime Minister Benazir Bhutto of Pakistan signed an agreement by which both nations agreed not to attack the nuclear facilities of the other in 1988. And in September 1989, Gandhi agreed with Sri Lanka's request to pull his 100,000 troops out of their bloody stand-off with Tamil separatists by the end of the year.

During the election campaign in the spring of 1991, Rajiv Gandhi was assassinated by a disgruntled Sri Lankan Tamil. P.V. Narasimha Rao, a former minister under both Rajiv and Indira Gandhi, formed a minority government that as of fall 1994 continues in office. As prime minister, Rao introduced new economic reforms, opening India to foreign investors and market economics. And despite frail health and advancing years, he brought new vigor to India's post–Cold War foreign policy.

13 GOVERNMENT

India is an independent socialist democratic republic, with no religious ties to the government. Its constitution, which became effective 26 January 1950, provides for a parliamentary form of government. The constitution also contains an extensive set of guidelines similar to the United States Bill of Rights. The right to vote is granted to all at age 21.

India consists of 14 states and 5 union territories, organized, where possible, according to the language spoken. The states and territories are administered as districts and subdivisions.

14 POLITICAL PARTIES

In various forms, the Indian National Congress has controlled the government for most of the years since independence in 1947. Founded in 1885, the Indian National Congress, known after 1947 as the Congress Party (CP), was the most powerful mass movement fighting for independence in British India. It became the ruling party of free India due to its national popularity and because most leaders of the independence movement were among its members, including India's first prime minister, Jawaharlal Nehru.

With the decline of the Congress Party as a national party, there has been a rise in the number of single state, linguistic, ethnic, and regional parties capable of governing only at the state level but available for coalition building at the national level.

15 JUDICIAL SYSTEM

The laws and judicial system of British India were continued after independence with only slight modifications. The Supreme Court consists of a chief justice and up to 17 judges. The Court's duties include interpreting the constitution, handling disputes between the states, and judging appeals from lower courts.

In addition, each state's judicial system is headed by a high court. Judgments from these courts may be appealed to the Supreme Court.

Islamic law (Shari'a) governs many noncriminal matters involving Muslims, including family law, inheritance, and divorce.

16 ARMED FORCES

In 1993 armed forces members totaled 1,265,000. The army had 1,100,000 members, organized into 2 armored divisions, 1 mechanized division, 22 infantry divisions, 10 mountain divisions, 5 independent armored brigades, 8 independent infantry brigades, 3 independent artillery brigades, 6 air defense brigades, 4 engineer brigades, and 1 parachute brigade. Armaments included 3,800 main battle tanks and 100 light tanks.

The navy (including the naval air force) had 55,000 members. Naval vessels included 15 submarines, 2 aircraft carriers, 5 destroyers, 21 frigates, 14 corvettes, 25 patrol boats, and 20 mine warfare ships. The naval air force had 5,000 members, with 46 combat aircraft and 75 armed helicopters. The air force had 110,000 members and 674 combat aircraft. There was 1 light bomber squadron, 28 fighter and ground attack squadrons, 17 interceptor squadrons, 3 reconnaissance squadrons, and 11 helicopter squadrons. There is a coast guard of 3,000 members, 20 aircraft, and 37 patrol craft.

Budgeted defense expenditures in 1991 were around $8 billion. India provides about 500 personnel to five peacekeeping operations. Although India has exploded a nuclear device, it has no operational, readied nuclear forces.

17 ECONOMY

Agriculture makes up the largest segment of the Indian economy. It provides the livelihood for 67% of the population. The

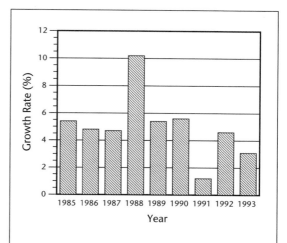

Yearly growth rate of the economy. This economic indicator tells by what percent the economy has increased or decreased when compared with the previous year.

country is rich in mineral, forest, and power resources, and its ample reserves of iron ore and coal provide a substantial base for heavy industry.

Under a planned development program since independence, the government was the driving force behind the nation's industries. In recent years, and especially since 1991, India has placed greater emphasis on private enterprise to stimulate growth and modernization.

Political instability in the late 1980s and oil price shocks resulting from the Gulf War led to an economic crisis in early 1991, but swift reform measures taken by the newly elected government proved highly successful. Inflation declined from 13.1% in 1991/92 to 8.6% in 1993/94.

18 INCOME

In 1992, India's gross national product (GNP) was $271,638 million at current prices, or $300 per person.

19 INDUSTRY

Textile production dominates the industrial field. Millions of cottage workers throughout the country handloom cotton, wool, silk, and rayon. Powerlooms accounted for an increasingly large share of production during the 1980s. Bombay, Ahmadabad, and the provincial cities in southern India led in cotton milling. Total mill-based textile production in 1992 included 1,572 million meters of cotton fabrics and 1,448,000 tons of cotton yarn. Jute manufactures for 1991 amounted to 1,430,000 million tons. Wool, silk, coir, and a growing rayon textile industry are also important.

In 1992, six integrated and 180 small steel plants produced 14.3 million tons of finished steel. Other outputs from the metallurgical sector included 55 million tons of iron ore, 514,000 tons of aluminum ingots, and 1,205,000 tons of pipes and metal tubes. Mechanical engineering industries produced 192 thousand passenger vehicles. The electrical engineering industry produced 360 thousand radio receivers.

The production of computers and a wide range of consumer electronics (color televisions, VCRs, and electronic watches) has been boosted by the recent liberalization of imports of component parts.

The oil-refining industry yielded 48 million tons of refined petroleum prod-

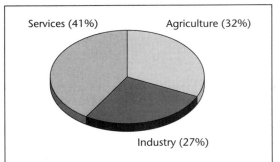

Components of the economy. This pie chart shows how much of the country's economy is devoted to agriculture (includes forestry, hunting, and fishing), industry, or services.

Services (41%) Agriculture (32%) Industry (27%)

ucts. Nitrogen fertilizer production grew from 5,745,000 tons in 1986 to 7,564,000 in 1992, and cement production from 32 million tons to 52 million tons. Refined sugar production, a major agricultural processing industry, totaled 13.3 million tons in 1992.

20 LABOR

In 1991, India's labor force totaled 345 million, of whom 67% were employed in agriculture and 20% were unemployed. The female labor force comprised one-quarter of the total in 1992. Employment in the iron and steel industry in 1991 totaled 286,000, more than any other country except Japan.

Working hours are limited by law to 48 per week for adults. Factory employment of children under 14 years of age is prohibited, even though the government estimates the existence of 17 million child laborers, many of them working in the hand-knotted carpet industry. By law, earned income also includes a cost-of-living allowance and an annual bonus (applicable to factories and all other establishments with 20 employees). In 1992, an estimated 10 million workers belonged to unions.

21 AGRICULTURE

The "green revolution" made India basically self-sufficient in grain output through the use of improved hybrid seeds, irrigation, and fertilizers. In 1992, cereal grain production totaled 101 million tons. Rice leads all crops and, except in the northwest, is generally grown wherever the conditions are suitable. In 1992, 109.5 million tons of rice were produced on 42 million hectares (103.8 million acres). The combined acreage and production of other cereals, mostly grown for human consumption, considerably exceed those of rice. These include jowar, a rich grain sorghum grown especially in the Deccan; wheat, grown in the northwest; and bajra, another grain sorghum grown in the drier areas of western India and the far south. A wheat crop of 55 million tons was harvested on 22.9 million hectares (56.5 million acres) in 1992. Vegetables, pulses (peas, beans, or lentils), and oilseeds are the other main food crops.

Oilseed production in 1993 was a record 24.3 million tons. Nonfood crops are mainly linseed, cotton, jute, and tobacco. The cotton crop in 1993 totaled 10.3 million bales and was large enough to both supply the increasing demands of the domestic textile industry and provide export income. Since World War II, India has been the world's largest producer of black pepper (65,000 tons in 1985/86). It also handles about 70% of the world trade in cardamom, of which 4,400 tons were produced in 1985/86.

India was the world's second-leading producer (after Brazil) of sugarcane in 1992, with an output of 249.3 million tons. Tea, coffee, and rubber plantations contribute significantly to the economy and are the largest agricultural enterprises in India. Tea, the most important plantation crop, is a large foreign exchange earner, with an export value of $554 million in 1992, based on production of 703,000 tons, the highest in the world. Coffee (200,000 tons in 1992) is produced in southern India, and rubber (350,000 tons) in the southwest. Leaf tobacco production totaled 538,000 tons.

22 DOMESTICATED ANIMALS

The livestock population of India is huge and animals as a whole play an important role in the agricultural economy. Since Hindus believe that cows and other animals may contain reincarnated human souls, they do not eat beef and generally do not eat any kind of meat. However, many millions of Muslims, Christians, and Sikhs do.

In 1992 there were an estimated 192.6 million head of cattle—about 15% of the world's total and more than in any other country, 117 million goats, 44.4 million sheep, 10.5 million hogs, 78.5 million water buffalo, 1.5 million camels, 1.5 million asses, 970,000 horses, and 410 million poultry.

Dairy farming has made India self-sufficient in butter and powdered milk. To improve milk production, a dairy development program was begun in 1978 to build up the milking herd to 150 million cross-bred cows. Milk output in 1992 was 29.4 million tons. Estimated egg production was 1,434,000 tons. The production of cattle and buffalo hides and goat- and sheepskins is a major industry. About 54,500 tons of wool were produced in 1992.

23 FISHING

Fishing is an important secondary source of income to some farmers and a primary occupation in small fishing villages. Almost three-fifths of the catch consists of sea fish. Deep-sea fishing is not done on a large scale. In recent years, the government has been encouraging ocean fishing through the establishment of processing plants and the introduction of deep-sea craft.

The total fish catch in 1991 was estimated at 4,036,931 tons, of which marine fish accounted for 2,336,101 tons and inland sources for 1,700,830 tons.

24 FORESTRY

India's forests are mostly broad-leaved. Less than 10% are coniferous. In 1991 there were 66,950,000 hectares (165,433,000 acres) of forestland, about half of which was reserved for the production of timber and other forest products, such as firewood, charcoal, and lac (for shellac). About 138,000 hectares (341,000 acres) were planted annually during the 1980s under government programs. Most forests are owned by state governments and are reserved or protected for the maintenance of permanent timber and water supplies.

Forest products in 1991 included about 279.8 million cubic meters of roundwood and 17.4 million cubic meters of sawn wood, as well as bamboos, canes, fibers, flosses, gums and resins, medicinal herbs, tanning barks, and lac (for shellac).

25 MINING

India is well endowed with industrial minerals. Iron ore reserves, estimated at 11 billion tons of hematite ore containing at least 55% iron, are among the largest in the world. India produced 3,607 tons of crude mica in 1991. Manganese deposits are estimated at 154 million tons. Bauxite deposits, estimated at 2.3 billion tons, slightly exceed those of Jamaica. However, India's output of 4,835,000 tons in 1991 was much less than Jamaica's.

Iron content in mined ore output totaled 35.6 billion tons in 1991. Content of manganese in mined ore produced was 630,450 in 1991. Gold and silver come largely from the far southeastern region, where the gold mines have reached a depth of more than 3.2 kilometers (2 miles) and contain reserves to produce about 55,000 kilograms of gold. Diamonds and emeralds also are mined. In 1991, 1,973 kilograms of gold and 19,000 carats of diamonds were produced.

Coal reserves, scattered through the central peninsula and the northeast, are estimated at 191,857 million tons (97% bituminous, 3% lignite). Coal is among India's most important natural resources and has been the basis of the power, railway, and steel industries. Coal output was about 239.8 million tons in 1991.

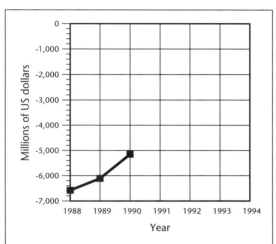

Yearly balance of trade measured in millions of US dollars. The balance of trade is the difference between what a country sells to other countries (its exports) and what it buys (its imports). If a country imports more than it exports, it has a negative balance of trade (a trade deficit). If exports exceed imports there is a positive balance of trade (a trade surplus).

Estimated mineral production in 1991 also included 55,380 tons of mined copper ore, 994,674 tons of chromite, 163,474 tons of zinc concentrates, 1,563,056 tons of gypsum, and 25,000 tons of lead concentrates.

26 FOREIGN TRADE

Given the country's relatively well-developed manufacturing base, items like machine tools, industrial equipment, jewelry, chemicals, garments, and processed food (especially fish) now comprise the country's leading exported items, replacing jute, tea, and other food products that dominated exports in the 1960s and early 1970s.

With a population size second only to China, and a per-person income of $1,250 measured in purchasing power terms, India potentially represents one of the world's important trading partners. The United States remains India's largest partner, while Japan has replaced the former USSR in second place, followed by Germany and the United Kingdom. Leading purchasers of Indian exports in 1990/91 were the United States and Japan. Leading import suppliers were the United States, Japan, and Germany.

27 ENERGY AND POWER

Petroleum reserves were estimated at 600 million tons in 1992. Crude oil production was 28.7 million tons in 1992. As of 1992, 2,800 wells were in operation. Extraction of natural gas increased from 920 million cubic meters in 1973 to 14,900 million cubic meters in 1992. Pipelines consisted of 3,497 kilometers (2,173 miles) for crude oil, 1,703 kilometers (1,058 miles) for refined products, and 902 kilometers (561 miles) for natural gas in 1991.

India supplied 82% of its own power requirements in 1992. Total installed electric capacity, which was 18,500 Megawatts in 1974, rose to 65,000 Megawatts in 1991. An additional generating capacity of 10,000 Megawatts is a goal by the year 2000.

As of 1991, nuclear power accounted for about 5.2 billion kilowatt hours of electricity, or less than 2% of India's total of 294.3 billion kilowatt hours. Conventional thermal plants produced about three-quarters, and hydroelectric facilities about 23%.

Selected Social Indicators

These statistics are estimates for the period 1988 to 1993. For comparison purposes, data for the United States and averages for low income countries and high income countries are also given.

Indicator	India	Low-income countries	High-income countries	United States
Per capita gross national product†	$300	$380	$23,680	$24,740
Population growth rate	2.0%	1.9%	0.6%	1.0%
Population growth rate in urban areas	3.0%	3.9%	0.8%	1.3%
Population per square kilometer of land	267	78	25	26
Life expectancy in years	61	62	77	76
Number of people per physician	250	>3,300	453	419
Number of pupils per teacher (primary school)	61	39	<18	20
Illiteracy rate (15 years and older)	52%	41%	<5%	<3%
Energy consumed per capita (kg of oil equivalent)	243	364	5,203	7,918

† The gross national product (GNP) is the total dollar value of all goods and services produced by a country in a year. The per capita GNP is calculated by dividing a country's GNP by its population. The World Bank defines low-income countries as those with a per capita GNP of $695 or less. High-income countries have a per capita GNP of $8,626 or more. Less than 14% of the world's 5.5 billion people live in high-income countries, while almost 60% live in low-income countries.

> = greater than   < = less than

Sources: World Bank, *Social Indicators of Development 1995*, Baltimore: Johns Hopkins University Press, 1995. Central Intelligence Agency, *World Fact Book*, Washington, D.C.: Government Printing Office, 1994.

28 SOCIAL DEVELOPMENT

India's governments have established an extensive social welfare system. Programs for children include supplementary nutrition for expectant mothers and for children under seven years of age, immunization and health programs, vacation camps for low-income families, and prevocational training for adolescents. Programs for women include welfare grants, women's adult education, and working women's hostels. There are also services for the blind, deaf, mentally retarded, and orthopedically handicapped.

Special measures are aimed at rehabilitating juvenile delinquents, prostitutes, and convicts. Begging in public places is forbidden by law in most states and localities. Other social welfare programs cover displaced persons; family planning and maternity care; rural community development; emergency relief programs for drought, flood, earthquake, and other disasters; untouchability (the *Harijans*); and underdeveloped tribal peoples.

Below the highest political levels, and especially in rural India, the position of women remains inferior to that of men. Laws aimed at preventing employment discrimination, female bondage and prostitution, and the *Sati* (the burning of widows) are often not enforced. A National Commission for Women was established in 1992 to investigate abuses against women. Despite laws against it, child marriages are still arranged in many parts of India.

In 1952, India became the first country in the world to start a nationwide population control program. In 1985–90, India's fertility rate was down 11.2% from the previous five-year period.

29 HEALTH

The government is committed to a goal of "Health for All" by the year 2000 (implementing its eighth five-year plan from 1990 to 1995). The plan includes elimination of malaria, and control of leprosy, tuberculosis, and cataracts. In 1991, there were a total of 39,026 hospitals and dispensaries. There were 637,604 hospital beds (0.76 per 1,000 people). In the same year, India had 331,630 physicians (4 per 1,000 people). There are also some 278,000 registered health care providers following the Ayurvedic (ancient Hindu) and Unani systems.

Primary health care is being provided to the rural population through a network of over 150,000 primary health centers and sub-centers by 586,000 trained midwives and 410,000 health guides (1992 data). Total health care expenditures in 1990 were $17,740,000.

Average life expectancy has increased from 48 years in 1971 to 61 in 1992. However, many diseases remain, especially deficiency diseases such as goiter, malnutrition (due to lack of protein), rickets, and beriberi. In 1994, there was a serious outbreak of pneumonic plague in western India which spread to other parts of the country, killing thousands. India has 106 colleges that teach modern medicine, more than 100 colleges and schools that teach the traditional Ayurvedic and Unani systems of medicine, and 74 that teach homeopathy.

30 HOUSING

Progress has been made toward improving the generally primitive housing in which most Indians live. By 1992, total housing stock numbered 120,746,000 units. The eighth five-year plan (1990–95) called for an investment of $40 billion in housing, with 90% of this sum reserved for private housing. The government's goal is to provide eight million new housing units between 1990 and the year 2000, two million to meet the existing need and six million to meet the needs that will be created by population growth.

31 EDUCATION

According to the 1990 census, the population of India was 48% literate. In 1988, a national literacy mission was begun, following which some states achieved 100% literacy. In 1992, the second program of action on education was introduced to reaffirm the 1986 policy with plans to achieve total literacy and free education for all children up to grade eight by the year 2000.

Free and compulsory elementary education is a guiding principle of the consti-

Photo credit: Cynthia Bassett.

Men bargain for vegetables at the floating market on Dal Lake in Srinagar.

tution. The percentage of the school-age population actually enrolled in primary school increased from 62.4% in 1960 to an estimated 91.8% in 1985. In 1990, there were 558,392 primary level schools with 1,636,898 teachers and 99,118,320 pupils. In general secondary schools, there were 54,180,391 pupils the same year.

India's system of higher education is still basically British in structure and approach. The university system is second only to that of the United States in size with 150 universities and over 5,000 colleges and higher level institutions. The older universities are in Calcutta, Bombay, and Madras, all established in 1857.

32 MEDIA

At the end of March 1991 there were 148,719 post offices in operation. At the same time there were 39,906 telegraph offices. As of 1991 there were 4,420,107 telephones.

Government owned All-India Radio (AIR) operates short- and medium-wave transmission through 148 stations and broadcasts in all major languages and dialects. The number of radios totaled about 68.5 million in 1991. In 1959, India's first television station was inaugurated in Delhi, and color television broadcasting began in 1982. By the end of 1985, the government's Doordarshan television network operated 22 broadcasting centers. In 1991, there were 30 million television sets in the country. India has a thriving film industry, centered at Bombay, Madras, Calcutta, and Bangalore. The output of feature films in 1991 totaled 910, and Indians are frequent filmgoers and users of videocassettes.

In 1989 there were 30,153 newspapers published in some 85 languages, led by Hindi, English, Bengali, Urdu, and Marathi. The majority of Indian newspapers are under individual ownership and have small circulations. About 30% are published in Delhi, Bombay, Calcutta, and Madras.

The principal national English-language newspapers are the *Indian Express* (1992 circulation 646,307), the *Times of India* (538,132), and the *Hindustan Times* (273,628). The largest Hindi daily (with estimated 1992 circulation) is the *Navbharat Times* (450,000).

33 TOURISM AND RECREATION

The national Department of Tourism maintains tourist information offices at home and abroad. It has constructed many facilities for viewing wildlife in forest regions (by minibus, boat, or elephant) and operates tourist lodges in wildlife sanctuaries. All major cities have comfortable Western-style hotels for tourists.

In 1991 there were 44,495 hotel rooms with a 64.9 percent occupancy rate. Tourist arrivals numbered 1,677,508, of whom 591,210 came from southern Asia and 562,731 from Europe. Earnings from tourism totaled $1.31 billion in 1991.

The main tourist attractions are the great cities of Calcutta, Bombay, and Madras. Tourists also visit such monuments as the Red Fort and Jama Masjid mosque in Delhi, the Taj Mahal at Agra, and the Amber Palace in Jaipur. Also popular is the temple at Bodhgaya (about 100 kilometers south of Patna) where the Buddha is said to have achieved enlightenment.

Cricket, field hockey, polo, football (soccer), volleyball, and basketball are all popular pastimes, as are pony-trekking in the hill stations and skiing in northern India.

34 FAMOUS INDIANS

One of the greatest Indians was Siddartha Gautama (624–544 BC according to Sinhalese tradition; 563?–483? BC according to most modern scholars), later known as the Buddha ("the enlightened one").

Contemporary with the Buddha was Vardhamana (599?–527 BC), also known as Mahavira ("great hero"), a saintly thinker of Bihar from whose teachings Jainism evolved. Akbar (1542–1605) greatly expanded the Mughal Empire, which reached its height under Shah Jahan (1592–1666), builder of the Taj Mahal.

Mother Teresa (Agnes Gonxha Bojaxhiu, b.1910, in what is now Yugoslavia) won the Nobel Peace Prize in 1979 for her 30 years of work among Calcutta's poor.

In modern times no Indian so completely captured the Indian masses and had such a deep spiritual effect on so many throughout the world as Mohandas Karamchand Gandhi (1869–1948). Reverently referred to by millions of Indians as the Mahatma ("Great Soul"), Gandhi is considered the greatest Indian since the Buddha. His unusual methods of nonviolent resistance contributed greatly to the liberation of India in 1947.

Gandhi's political heir, Jawaharlal Nehru (1889–1964), had a hold on the Indian people almost equal to that of the Mahatma. Affectionately known as Chacha (Uncle) Nehru, he steered India through its first 17 years of independence. Indira Gandhi (1917–84), the daughter of Nehru and prime minister from 1966 to 1977 and again from 1980 to 1984, continued her father's work in modernizing India. Her son Rajiv (1944–91) succeeded her as prime minister and, in 1985, won for his party the largest parliamentary victory since India became independent.

Modern interpreters of the rich Indian musical tradition include the composer and performer Ravi Shankar (b.1920). Zubin Mehta (b.1936) is an orchestral conductor of international renown.

35 BIBLIOGRAPHY

Brown, Judith M. *Modern India: The Origins of an Asian Democracy.* 2nd ed. New York: Oxford University Press, 1994.

Dash, Narendra Kumar. *An Encyclopaedic Dictionary of Indian Culture.* Delhi: Agam Kala Prakashan, 1992.

Davidson, Robyn. "Wandering With India's Rabari." *National Geographic,* September 1993, 64–93.

Heiderer, Tony. "Sacred Space, Sacred Time: India's Maha Kumbh Mela." *National Geographic,* May 1990, 106–117.

India in Pictures. Minneapolis: Lerner, 1989.

Jha, Shiva C., ed.. *The New Cambridge History of India.* New York: Cambridge University Press, 1987–1993.

McCarry, John. "Bombay." *National Geographic,* March 1995, 42–67.

McNair, S. *India.* Chicago: Children's Press, 1990.

Miller, Peter. "India's Unpredictable Kerala, Jewel of the Malabar Coast." *National Geographic,* May 1988, 592–617.

Nagel, Rob, and Anne Commire. "Akbar.." In *World Leaders, People Who Shaped the World.* Volume I: Africa and Asia. Detroit: U*X*L, 1994.

———. "Jawaharlal Nehru." In *World Leaders, People Who Shaped the World.* Volume I: Africa and Asia. Detroit: U*X*L, 1994.

———. "Mohandas Gandhi." In *World Leaders, People Who Shaped the World.* Volume I: Africa and Asia. Detroit: U*X*L, 1994.

———. "Mother Teresa." In *World Leaders, People Who Shaped the World.* Volume I: Africa and Asia. Detroit: U*X*L, 1994.

Wolpert, Stanley A. *A New History of India.* 4th ed. New York: Oxford University Press, 1993.

INDONESIA

Republic of Indonesia

Republik Indonesia

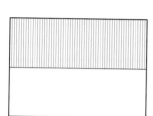

CAPITAL: Jakarta.

FLAG: The national flag, adopted in 1949, consists of a red horizontal stripe above a white stripe.

ANTHEM: *Indonesia Raya (Great Indonesia).*

MONETARY UNIT: The rupiah (Rp) consists of 100 sen. There are coins of 1, 2, 5, 10, 25, 50, and 100 rupiahs, and notes of 100, 500, 1,000, 5,000, and 10,000 rupiahs. Rp1 = $0.0005 (or $1 = Rp2096).

WEIGHTS AND MEASURES: The metric system is standard.

HOLIDAYS: New Year's Day, 1 January; Independence Day, 17 August; Christmas, 25 December. Movable religious holidays include the Prophet's Birthday, Ascension of Muhammad, Good Friday, Ascension Day of Jesus Christ, the end of Ramadan, 'Id al-Fitr, 'Id al-'Adha', and the 1st of Muharram (Muslim New Year).

TIME: Western, 7 PM = noon GMT; Central, 8 PM = noon GMT; Eastern, 9 PM = noon GMT.

1 LOCATION AND SIZE

The Republic of Indonesia consists of five large islands and 13,677 smaller islands (about 6,000 of which are inhabited) forming an arc between Asia and Australia. With a total area of 1,919,440 square kilometers (741,100 square miles), Indonesia is the fourth-largest Asian country, after China, India, and Sa'udi Arabia. Comparatively, the area occupied by Indonesia is almost three times the size of the state of Texas.

The five principal islands are Sumatra, 473,606 square kilometers (182,860 square miles); Java, with an area of 132,600 square kilometers (51,200 square miles); Borneo, of which the 72% belonging to Indonesia is known as Kalimantan, 539,460 square kilometers (208,286 square miles); Sulawesi, formerly called Celebes, 189,216 square kilometers (73,056 square miles); and Irian Jaya (West Irian), the western portion of the island of New Guinea, 421,981 square kilometers (162,927 square miles). Indonesia's total boundary length is 57,318 kilometers (35,616 miles).

Indonesia's capital city, Jakarta, is located on the island of Java.

2 TOPOGRAPHY

The Indonesian island chain consists of three main regions. One of the regions is made up of Sumatra, Java, Kalimantan, and the islands that lie between them. Another region consists of Irian Jaya and extends to Halmahera. Between these two areas is the remaining region, consisting of the Lesser Sunda Islands, the Maluku Islands (Moluccas), and Sulawesi. The large islands have central mountain ranges rising from lowlands and coastal plains.

Many inactive and active volcanoes dot the islands, accounting for the rich volcanic soil that is carried down by the rivers to the plains and lowlands. Peaks rise to 3,650 meters (12,000 feet) in Java and Sumatra. Java, Bali, and Lombok have extensive lowland plains and gently sloping cultivatable mountainsides.

3 CLIMATE

Stretching across the Equator, Indonesia has a tropical climate characterized by heavy rainfall, high humidity, high temperature, and low winds. Rainfall in lowland areas averages 180–320 centimeters (70–125 inches) annually, increasing to an average of 610 centimeters (240 inches) in some mountain areas. Average humidity is 82%. Altitude rather than season affects the temperature in Indonesia. At sea level, the mean annual temperature is about 25–27°C (77–81°F).

4 PLANTS AND ANIMALS

Vegetation ranges from that of the tropical rainforest to that of hill and mountain forests, to the shrub vegetation of mountain areas. The bridge between Asia and Australia formed by the island chain is reflected in the varieties of animal life. The native animals of Sumatra, Kalimantan, and Java are similar to that of Peninsular Malaysia, but each island has its peculiar types. The orangutan is found in Sumatra and Kalimantan but not in Java, the siamang only in Sumatra, the proboscis monkey only in Kalimantan, the elephant and tapir only in Sumatra, and the wild ox in Java and Kalimantan but not in Sumatra. In Sulawesi (Celebes), the Maluku Islands, and Timor, Australian types begin to occur. The bandicoot, a marsupial, is found in Timor. All the islands, especially the Malukus, abound in great varieties of bird life, reptiles, and amphibians. The rich marine life of Indonesia's extensive territorial waters includes a rich variety of corals.

5 ENVIRONMENT

Estimates show that the loss of forest land in Indonesia has increased from 300,000 to 1 million hectares per year over the past 20 years. Flood-control programs involve river dredging, dike strengthening, construction of new dams, and sandbagging of river banks at critical points. The burning of oil and coal along with the abuse of fertilizers and pesticides results in significant damage to the environment.

As of 1986 there were 146 parks and nature reserves, with more in the planning stage. The government's goal was to allocate 10% of the nation's land area to reserves. As of 1994, 49 of Indonesia's mammal species were endangered, and 135 bird species were threatened with extinction.

6 POPULATION

Indonesia is the fourth most populous country in the world. As of the 1990 census, the population (including East Timor) was 179,378,946. The estimated population in 1994 was 203,750,000 according to the United States Bureau of the Census. A population of 217,998,000 is projected by the UN for the year 2000. The growth

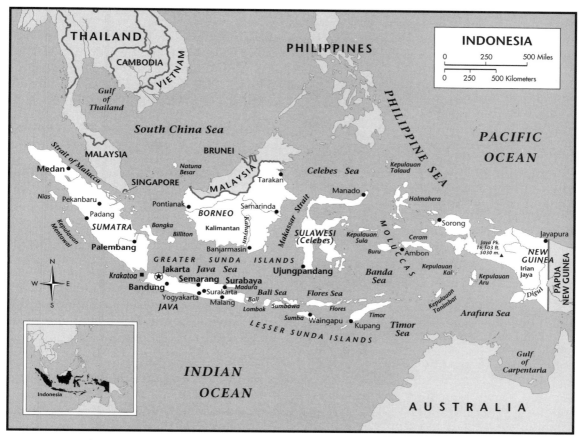

LOCATION: 95°1′ to 141°2′E; 6°5′N to 11°S. **BOUNDARY LENGTHS:** Malaysia, 1,782 kilometers (1,110 miles); Papua New Guinea, 820 kilometers (510 miles); total coastline, 54,716 kilometers (33,996 miles). **TERRITORIAL SEA LIMIT:** 12 miles.

rate is high, estimated to be about 1.7% annually.

Of the 1990 population, 60% (107,513,798) was concentrated around Java. The estimated population of the other major regions in 1989 was Sumatra, 36,881,990 (including nearby islands); Sulawesi (Celebes), 12,507,650; Kalimantan, 8,677,459; and Bali, 2,782,038. Overall population density in 1990 was 96 persons per square kilometer (243 per square mile). Jakarta's population in 1990 was 8,254,000.

7 MIGRATION

Historically, there has been considerable migration from and to China. Migration between the Netherlands and Indonesia has been greatly reduced since independence. In 1990 there were 288,508 registered foreigners in Indonesia (91% Asian),

Photo credit: Corel Corporation.

Children in a village, Sumatra, Indonesia.

and 251,389 Indonesian citizens were listed as being abroad.

Resettlement of people from crowded areas to the less populous outer islands is official government policy. The 1979–84 National Economic Plan had as a target the "transmigration" of 500,000 families from Java, Bali, and Madura to Sumatra, Kalimantan, Sulawesi (Celebes), Maluku Province, and Irian Jaya. Under the 1987–91 plan, 338,433 families were resettled.

Asylum was granted to over 145,000 Indochinese refugees between 1975 and 1993.

8 ETHNIC GROUPS

The native peoples, referred to as Malays or Indonesians, also are found on the neighboring islands of the Philippines, in Peninsular Malaysia, and even as far away as Taiwan and Madagascar.

The population is officially classified into four main ethnic groups: Melanesians, who constitute the majority; Proto-Austronesians, including the Wajaks and the Irianese; Polynesians; and Micronesians.

Ethnic Chinese, the principal minority, were the target of riots in 1974 and 1980. Active mainly in business in the major cities, they are relatively prosperous and widely resented by ethnic Indonesians. In 1992 all but about 300,000 of an estimated five million ethnic Chinese held Indonesian citizenship.

9 LANGUAGES

Bahasa Indonesia, a product of the nationalist movement, is the official language, serving as a common vehicle of communication for the various language groups. It is based primarily on Malay and is similar to the official language of Malaysia. It also contains many words from other Indonesian languages and dialects, as well as from Dutch, English, Arabic, Sanskrit, and other languages. In 1973, Indonesia and Malaysia adopted similar systems of spelling. Outside of Jakarta, only 10–15% of the population speaks the language in the home, but more than half the population uses it as a secondary language.

Use of some 669 local languages persists, including Javanese, Sundanese, and

Malay. English is widely used in industry and commerce.

10 RELIGIONS

An estimated 87% of the inhabitants are followers of Islam, 10% are Christians, 2% are Hindus, 1% are Buddhists or Confucianists, and 1% follow tribal religions. Among Christians, an estimated 2.6% were Roman Catholics in 1993.

Freedom of religion is guaranteed by the constitution, but the government actively supports Islamic religious schools and pays for a number of annual pilgrimages to Mecca. Three million Indonesians on Bali and elsewhere are Hindu in religion and culture. The religious faith of the Chinese in Indonesia may be characterized as Christian or Buddhist-Confucianist.

11 TRANSPORTATION

Transportation facilities suffered greatly from destruction and neglect during World War II and immediately afterwards. The revived and rebuilt system suffered an additional setback during 1957–58 as a result of the withdrawal of the Dutch.

Of the 119,500 kilometers (74,257 miles) of public motor roads in 1991, most were under local jurisdiction. In the same year, Indonesia had 1,416,157 passenger cars, 1,080,936 trucks, and 504,415 buses. Railways connect the main cities in Java and parts of Sumatra. The state owns all of the 6,964 kilometers (4,327 miles) of railroad track in service.

About 21,600 kilometers (13,420 miles) of inland waterways form the most important means of transportation in Kalimantan and in parts of Sumatra. The principal ports of international trade are Tanjungpriok (for Jakarta) and Tanjungperak (for Surabaya) in Java, and Belawan (near Medan) and Padang in Sumatra.

The center of international air traffic is Jakarta's Sukarno-Hatta International Airport, which served some 7.5 million arriving and departing passengers in 1990. As of 1992, the three airlines together carried 2,771,900 international and 7,553,100 domestic passengers.

12 HISTORY

Fossil remains of so-called Java man (*Pithecanthropus erectus*) date from the Pleistocene period, when Indonesia was linked with the Asian mainland. Indian influences permeated Java and Sumatra from the first to the seventh century AD. During this period and extending into the fifteenth century, local Buddhist and Hindu rulers established a number of powerful kingdoms. The last of these, the Hindu kingdom of Majapahit, was at the height of its power during the thirteenth century, when the explorer Marco Polo visited Java and northern Sumatra.

From Colonial Rule to Independence

The Portuguese captured Malacca (Melaka), on the west coast of the Malay Peninsula, in 1511 and established control over the archipelago. The Dutch soon drove the Portuguese out of the islands (except for the eastern half of the island of Timor), beginning nearly 350 years of colonial rule.

Photo credit: Susan D. Rock.

Temple of Borobudur, Java.

With the adoption of what colonial administrators called the "ethical policy" at the beginning of the twentieth century, the first steps were taken to give Indonesians participation in government. A representative body, the Volksraad, was formed and given limited legislative powers.

Following the formation of the Volkstraad, an Indonesian nationalist movement began to develop that steadily gained strength. Nationalists under the leadership of Sukarno and Mohammad Hatta proclaimed an independent republic on 17 August 1945. After four years of fighting and negotiations, the Dutch recognized the independence of all the former Dutch East Indies (except West New Guinea) as the Republic of the United States of Indonesia on 27 December 1949.

Sukarno became the first president of the new nation, and Hatta the vice-president. Eventually, longstanding tensions between Java and the other islands erupted in violence. In response, the Sukarno regime turned to an increasingly authoritarian, anti-Western policy of "guided democracy." In March 1967, following a 1965 communist-led takeover attempt and widespread military action against hundreds of thousands of Indonesian Chinese, the People's Consultative Assembly (Majetis Permusyawaratan Rakyat—MPR) voted unanimously to withdraw all Sukarno's governmental power and appoint the commander of the army, General Suharto, acting president. One year later, it conferred full presidential powers on Suharto, and he was sworn in as president for a five-year term.

Suharto Gains Control

Under Suharto's "New Order," Indonesia turned to the West and began following a conservative economic course stressing private investment. In foreign affairs, Suharto's government achieved closer ties with the United States, Japan, and Western Europe while maintaining links with the USSR.

Following Portugal's withdrawal from East Timor in December 1975, Indonesia sent troops into the former Portuguese colony and gained full control of the territory, which it incorporated as an Indonesian Province. This action was opposed by both the UN and the military group that was then in control of the island. The military and diplomatic struggle over East Timor has continued into the 1990s unresolved.

To strengthen the government in the face of rising Muslim militancy in the late 1970s, Suharto began to reestablish Sukarno as a national hero eight years after his death. The war against Fretilin continued into the 1980s, with reports of massacres by government troops and severe economic hardship among the Timorese.

Between 1969 and 1992, the Transmigration Program, a policy aimed at overcoming uneven population distribution in Indonesia by moving families from the inner islands to the outer islands, moved 1,488,000 families. The program suffered from land disputes with local residents and environmental concerns over loss of forest land. In 1989 tension from land disputes in Java and the outer islands produced social unrest that resulted in clashes between villagers and the armed forces.

On 12 November 1991, during a funeral for a young Timorese killed in demonstrations against Indonesia's rule of East Timor, soldiers opened fire on the defenseless mourners in a massacre that received worldwide attention. Western governments threatened to halt aid, and by 1993 United States policy toward Indonesia shifted toward criticism of Indonesia's rule in East Timor, and a threat to revoke trade privileges. A UN resolution on Indonesia's human rights violations placed the country on a rights "watch" list in 1993.

In December 1992 the island of Flores suffered Indonesia's worst earthquake in modern times. The quake, which registered 6.8 on the Richter scale, killed up to 2,500 people and destroyed 18,000 homes. In March 1993 Suharto was elected to a sixth term as president.

13 GOVERNMENT

In 1967, Sukarno formally relinquished power to Suharto, who had become Indonesia's effective ruler in March 1966. Suharto reorganized the cabinet, making all of its 12 ministers responsible to him. In 1987, memberships in the House of representatives, or DPR, and the People's Consultative Assembly (MPR) were increased to 500 and 1,000, respectively. Under the new system, legislative responsibility rests with the DPR, which consists of 400 elected members and 100 members appointed by the president from the military and other groups. Under the Suharto government, the MPR has acted as a consultative body, setting guidelines for national policy. Its main legislative task is to approve the Broad Outlines of State Policy. In 1993, the MPR elected President Suharto to a sixth term.

Indonesia is divided into 27 provinces and 241 districts (kabupatens).

14 POLITICAL PARTIES

Before the 1971 elections, the government formed a mass organization, known as Golkar (Golongan Karya), as the political vanguard for its "New Order" program. An act of 1975 provided for the fusion of the major political organizations into two parties—the United Development Party (Partai Persuatan Pembangunan—PPP) and the Indonesian Democratic Party (Partai DemoKrasi Indonesia—PDI). The PPP, Golkar's chief opposition, is a fusion of Muslim groups, while the PDI represents the merger of the Indonesian Nationalist Party (PNI), the Christian Party, the Roman Catholic Party, and smaller groups. In the 1992 elections, Golkar won 68% of the popular vote. The PPP took 17%, and the PDI took 15%.

15 JUDICIAL SYSTEM

Government courts, each with a single judge, have jurisdiction in original civil and criminal cases. The High Court hears appeals in civil cases and reviews criminal cases. The Supreme Court is the highest court in the country. Its primary function is judicial review. Judgment in civil cases involving Muslims is based on the principles of Muslim law. Judges are appointed by the central government. In the villages, customary law (adat) continues unchanged.

Islamic law (Shari'a) governs many noncriminal matters involving Muslims, including family law, inheritance and divorce. A civil code based on Roman law is applied to Europeans. A combination of codes is applied to other groups such as ethnic Chinese and Indians.

16 ARMED FORCES

The Indonesian armed forces consist of an army, a navy, and an air force, numbering 283,000 in 1993. The army of 215,000 is divided into a combined arms "Strategic reserve" of 30 battalions and 10 territorial commands that control 90 battalions (mostly infantry). It is manned through a two-year draft law, and it is armed with United States and NATO equipment. There are four special forces battalions.

The air force, with a total membership of 24,000, has 81 combat aircraft, largely of United States origin. The navy, with 44,000 personnel (including naval aviators and marines), had two submarines, 17 frigates, and 48 large patrol craft. Naval forces include a naval air division and a 12,000-man marine brigade. Paramilitary forces include a 180,000-man police force and three other armed security forces, including a trained People's Security force of 300,000.

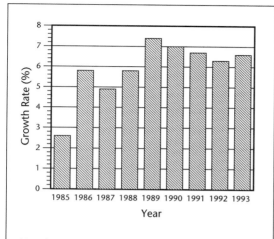

Yearly growth rate of the economy. This economic indicator tells by what percent the economy has increased or decreased when compared with the previous year.

Indonesia spent $1.7 billion for defense in 1991.

17 ECONOMY

In the twentieth century, production of oil, tin, timber, and rubber has become central to the economy. However, agriculture, with rice as the chief crop, remains the main occupation of the vast majority of Indonesians, and standards of living are low, but improving. Indonesia is exceptionally rich in coal, oil, and other industrial raw materials.

In the 1980s policies were designed to reduce restrictions on imports and to encourage foreign investment. Government policies have held the inflation rate at under 10%. Export performance has remained strong, although in 1994 non-oil export growth showed signs of slowing down. An increasingly important element of national income and foreign exchange earnings is tourism with over 3 million visitors to Indonesia annually.

18 INCOME

In 1992, Indonesia's gross national product was $122,825 million at current prices, or $740 per person. For the period 1985–92 the average inflation rate was 8.8%, resulting in a real growth rate in gross national product of 4.7% per person.

19 INDUSTRY

Despite new industries, overall industrial growth has been small since World War II with agriculture foremost in the Indonesian economy. However, in 1991 manufacturing took over as the dominant area. In that year textiles were the key industrial export, accounting for 47% of the total. In 1992 Indonesia's six oil refineries, all owned by Pertamina, produced 572.8 million barrels of refined petroleum.

Steel billet production totaled 560,000 tons in 1992, and Indonesia also produced 6.5 million tons of fertilizer, 16.3 million tons of cement, 1.65 million tons of paper, 5.2 billion meters of cloth, 4.1 million bales of yarn, and 8.5 million cubic meters of plywood. Indonesia is preparing to become a major chemical producer in Asia. The chemicals industry experienced an annual growth rate of 13% over the last several years prior to 1993.

20 LABOR

In 1992, the total employment including armed forces was 78,104,000. Of this

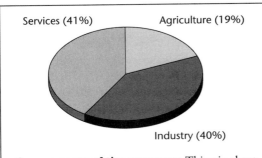

Services (41%)   Agriculture (19%)

Industry (40%)

Components of the economy. This pie chart shows how much of the country's economy is devoted to agriculture (includes forestry, hunting, and fishing), industry, or services.

their families, and so has legalized the employment of children under age 14 with strict limitations: parental consent is required; dangerous or difficult work is prohibited; hours are limited to 4 per day; and employers must report the number of children they employ. There is no legal minimum age for children in this category. Sadly, the law is not enforced. No employers have been punished for violating the restrictions, and employer reports on children in their employ are not collected.

21 AGRICULTURE

About 55% of Indonesian workers are engaged in agriculture. Approximately 22.2 million hectares (54.9 million acres) are under cultivation, and some 60% of the country's cultivated land is in Java. Production of rice, the staple food, has been gradually increasing (47.7 million tons in 1992, as compared with 12.6 million tons in 1964), and now comes close to meeting domestic requirements. This increase has resulted mainly from expanded use of irrigation, fertilizers, and pesticides and cultivation of high-yielding rice, especially insect-resistant types.

total, 42.8 million (55%) were engaged in agriculture; 10.5 million (14%) in community and other services; 7.8 million (10%) in manufacturing; 11.1 million (14%) in commerce; and 5.9 million (7%) in other sectors. The present labor force was estimated at 84 million in 1993, with over 50% between the ages of 15 and 34. Women make up about 40% of the work force.

The number of strikes increased in 1990 to 61 involving 30,706 workers, up from only 20 strikes involving 4,245 employees the year before. In 1991, the general minimum wage increased by 6.3% from the previous year. As of December 1990, there were 655 minimum wage rates in place, set by the different regions and localities. The highest at that time was about $2.12, and the lowest was about $0.42. The 40-hour work week and a basic 7-hour day are standard throughout Indonesia.

Child labor is a serious problem in Indonesia. The government recognizes that some children must work to assist

Other important food crops are corn, which replaces wheat as a staple food on the drier islands; cassavas, which are widely used as a second crop in the dry season; and sweet potatoes, peanuts, and soybeans. Production figures for 1992 included cassava (1,333,000 tons), corn (7,987,000 tons), and sweet potato (2,172,000 tons).

Sugar is the largest commercial crop, with production reaching 23,121,000 tons in 1992. About 1,300,000 tons of rubber

Photo credit: Susan D. Rock.

Woman sorting peanuts, Bali.

and 760,000 horses. There are also about 3,400,000 buffalo in the country. The production of meat (about 1,155,000 tons in 1992) and milk (330,000 tons) is secondary to the raising of animals for farm work and transport. The government has established cattle-breeding stations to improve cattle quality. There were an estimated 600 million chickens and 30 million ducks in 1992, when some 414,000 tons of eggs were produced.

23 FISHING

As Indonesia is the world's largest island group (13,667 islands), fish is a readily-available source of animal protein for domestic consumption. In 1991, the total catch was 3.1 million tons, or 3.3% of the world catch. Commercial fishing is confined to a narrow band of inshore waters, especially off northern Java, but other fishing also takes place along the coast, as well as in the rivers, lakes, coastal swamps, artificial ponds, and flooded rice fields. The government has stocked the inland waters, introduced improved fishing methods, provided for the use of motorized fishing boats and improved tackle, and built or repaired piers. Fish and fish product exports had a value of $1.2 billion in 1991.

24 FORESTRY

Forests represent a potentially vast source of wealth in Indonesia. Of the 109.2 million hectares (269.8 million acres) of forests, nearly three-fourths are in Kalimantan and eastern Indonesia. The more accessible forest areas of Sumatra and Kalimantan furnish the commercially

were produced in 1991/92. In 1992, Indonesia was the world's third largest producer of coffee (after Brazil and Colombia). Some 421,000 tons of coffee were grown that year. Indonesia is the world's second-largest producer of palm oil (after Malaysia); 3,162,228 tons were produced in 1992. Tobacco (84,000 tons in 1992) and copra (1,135,000 tons) are also important export crops.

22 DOMESTICATED ANIMALS

In 1992, the livestock population was 11,000,000 head of cattle, 11,400,000 goats, 5,900,000 sheep, 7,000,00 hogs cut timber for domestic consumption and export. In Java, excessive cutting has caused soil erosion, aggravated floods, created water shortages, and damaged some irrigation facilities. Replanting and rehabilitation of the Javanese forests and reforestation in the Outer Islands are promoted as part of the nation's "regreening program." Teak and other tropical hardwoods are the most valuable species, but there is hope of obtaining wood pulp from pine and bamboo and commercial timber from new plantings of fir and pine.

Sawn wood production in 1991 totaled 9.1 million cubic meters. About two-thirds of the timber output is exported. Indonesia was the world's leading producer of plywood in 1991, at 9,227,000 cubic meters. In 1990, Indonesia accounted for over 29.6% of the world's exports of veneers and plywood (valued at over $2.5 billion), which comprised 10.8% of Indonesia's total exports that year. Indonesia is the world's second largest producer of tropical hardwood logs and lumber, after Malaysia.

25 MINING

In addition to oil, of which Indonesia is one of the world's leading suppliers, the economically important mineral industry produces large quantities of tin and bauxite. Indonesia is the world's second-largest producer of tin (after China). The chief deposits of tin are in three islands off the east coast of Sumatra. Indonesia has 10.5% of the known world tin reserves. Indonesia possesses large deposits of high-grade bauxite. Bauxite production, 648,000 tons in 1964, rose to 1,242,000

tons in 1991. The bauxite is produced at five mining localities on Sumatra.

The railroads use much of the low-grade coal mined in Indonesia. Coal production reached 13,600,000 tons in 1991. Iron ore is found in sizable quantities but is not commercially mined except in central Java. Nickel is produced on Sulawesi and in the Maluku islands, with some of the largest reserves in the world. Copper production began on Irian Jaya in 1974 and amounted to 267,401 tons by 1991. There are fair to good reserves of manganese, small amounts of gold and silver, numerous minor metals in small quantities, iodine, diamonds, phosphates, and considerable supplies of limestone, asphalt, clay, and kaolin.

26 FOREIGN TRADE

Indonesia has run a positive balance of trade throughout the 1990s, with the surplus reaching a record $8.25 billion in 1993. Principal commodities exported are petroleum and petroleum products, rubber, and coffee. The non-oil exports have grown in importance. In 1991–92 they accounted for 64% of Indonesia's total export earnings. The manufacturing sector accounted for 45% of export earnings in 1991–92. Imports consisted mainly of machinery and raw materials (65% in 1991–92).

In the 1970s, Japan became Indonesia's main trade partner, It accounted for 41.7% of Indonesia's exports (mainly petroleum) in 1988 and supplied 25.4% of its imports. Although Japan remains the main trade partner, in 1992 its share of exports was reduced to 37.7%. Other

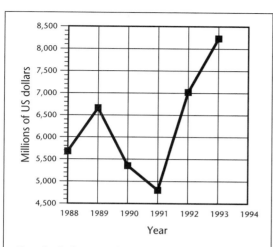

Yearly balance of trade measured in millions of US dollars. The balance of trade is the difference between what a country sells to other countries (its exports) and what it buys (its imports). If a country imports more than it exports, it has a negative balance of trade (a trade deficit). If exports exceed imports there is a positive balance of trade (a trade surplus).

leading trade partners are the United States, Singapore, and Germany.

27 ENERGY AND POWER

Indonesia ranked twelfth among petroleum-producing countries in 1992. Known reserves in 1993 were put at 5.8 billion barrels, and since most of the potential sources have not been surveyed, resources may be much larger. Sumatra, the richest oil area, produces about 70% of Indonesian oil. Kalimantan is the second-leading producer. Java and Madura have a scattering of smaller producing wells. Lesser amounts are also produced in Irian Jaya. Domestic energy consumption is expected to grow 8% per year until the year 2000.

Natural gas production increased rapidly in the 1970s and 1980s, with output totaling 54 billion cubic meters by 1992. Part of production goes for industrial and domestic use, but large amounts are exported in the form of liquefied natural gas (LNG). About 25 million tons of LNG per year are exported to Japan, the Republic of Korea, and Taiwan. Indonesia is the world's largest producer of LNG, providing about 39% of the world's supply.

Power facilities are overburdened, despite heavy government investment in electrical installations. Production totaled 44,660 million kilowatt hours in 1991.

28 SOCIAL DEVELOPMENT

In 1981, the nation's per person income rose for the first time above the $500 level, leading the World Bank to reclassify Indonesia from a low- to a middle-income developing country. Much of this improvement, however, has not filtered down to the rural family, which typically maintains three or four children at a survival level on a small patch of farmland. Most such families depend on income from family members working away from home. Millions of these jobholders or job-seeking migrants inhabit the large and fast-growing slums surrounding Jakarta and other large cities. A family-planning campaign was initiated in the 1970s. By 1985 there were 7,509 family-planning clinics.

Women in Indonesia enjoy a more favorable position than is customary in Muslim societies. This situation is largely the result of the work of Princess Raden Ajeng Kartini at the turn of the century in promoting the development of Javanese women. The movement for the emancipation of women preceded the nationalist movement by at least 10 years. Improvement of the status of women was specifically included in the guidelines for the 1979–84 national economic plan. Under the plan, a woman was appointed to the new cabinet post of associate minister for the role of women. In spite of women's official equality, in practice they often find it hard to exercise their legal rights. Although they constitute roughly one quarter of the civil service, they occupy very few of its top posts.

There is nothing similar to a welfare program in the Western sense, but the society is one in which family and clan relationships run strong. In addition, many orphanages, homes for the aged, youth activities, and private volunteer organizations meet special needs, in some cases receiving government subsidies.

29 HEALTH

National health programs, of which family planning is an important part, stress the building of small and healthy families. Elimination of contagious diseases focuses on malaria, rabies, elephantiasis, tuberculosis, cholera, and leprosy. Overcrowded cities, poor sanitation, impure water supplies, substandard urban housing, and dietary deficiencies are contributing factors to health problems. In 1991, only 51% of the population had access to safe water and 44% had adequate sanitation. Average life expectancy in 1992 was 62 years for men and women. In 1990,

14% of children under 5 years old were considered malnourished.

Indonesia has received much help from the UN, particularly through World Health Organization and UNICEF, in solving health problems. More than one-third of the country's doctors practice in Jakarta and other big cities. In 1992, 80% of the population had access to health care services. In 1991, Indonesia had 1,552 hospitals, with about 120,711 beds. In addition, there were 5,656 public health centers.

30 HOUSING

Housing is a serious problem in both urban and rural areas. In 1989, 55% of all households received their drinking water from wells, 13% from springs, and only 13% from pipes. Lighting was provided to 45% of all households by kerosene lamps, and only 43% of dwellings had private toilet facilities.

The 1975–79 and 1979–84 development plans included government construction of housing. The 1984–89 plan had a target of 300,000 units, of which 140,000 were to be provided by the government and 160,000 by private sources. In 1990 alone, 210,000 new housing units were completed and the total number of dwellings stood at 44,855,000 in 1992.

31 EDUCATION

Under the constitution, six years of primary education are free and compulsory. In practice, however, the supply of schools and teachers is inadequate to meet the

Selected Social Indicators

These statistics are estimates for the period 1988 to 1993. For comparison purposes, data for the United States, and averages for low income countries and high income countries are also given.

Indicator	Indonesia	Low-income countries	High-income countries	United States
Per capita gross national product†	$740	$380	$23,680	$24,740
Population growth rate	1.7%	1.9%	0.6%	1.0%
Population growth rate in urban areas	4.6%	3.9%	0.8%	1.3%
Population per square kilometer of land	96	78	25	26
Life expectancy in years	63	62	77	76
Number of people per physician	7,143	>3,300	453	419
Number of pupils per teacher (primary school)	14.5	39	<18	20
Illiteracy rate (15 years and older)	19%	41%	<5%	<3%
Energy consumed per capita (kg of oil equivalent)	330	364	5,203	7,918

† The gross national product (GNP) is the total dollar value of all goods and services produced by a country in a year. The per capita GNP is calculated by dividing a country's GNP by its population. The World Bank defines low-income countries as those with a per capita GNP of $695 or less. High-income countries have a per capita GNP of $8,626 or more. Less than 14% of the world's 5.5 billion people live in high-income countries, while almost 60% live in low-income countries.

> = greater than   < = less than

Sources: World Bank, *Social Indicators of Development 1995*, Baltimore: Johns Hopkins University Press, 1995. Central Intelligence Agency, *World Fact Book*, Washington, D.C.: Government Printing Office, 1994.

needs of the fast-growing under-15 age group.

The school system includes a six-year primary or elementary school, a three-year junior secondary school, a three-year senior secondary school, and higher education in universities, teacher-training colleges, and academies. Junior and senior technical schools have been brought into line with junior and senior secondary schools.

There are 51 universities, the largest of which are the University of Indonesia (in Jakarta) and the University of Gajah Mada (in Yogyakarta).

32 MEDIA

The government owns and operates postal services and telecommunications facilities through Perumtel, a state enterprise. In 1991 there were 1,015,275 telephones in Indonesia. Programs originating in Jakarta are in Bahasa Indonesia. Programs from regional stations are usually in local languages or dialects. In 1991 there were about 27,500,000 radios.

Television service was inaugurated in 1962. In 1991 there were three television networks, TV-Indonesia (TVRI), Rejawali Citra TV, and an educational network in

Jakarta. In 1991 there were some 11,000,000 television sets.

The government censors foreign films and publications, and Indonesian newspapers have been temporarily closed down for violating news guidelines. In 1982, a new press law established a Press Council of government officials, journalists, and scholars empowered to decide what news may be printed. The government banned three weekly newspapers in June 1994.

Most newspapers are published in Bahasa Indonesia, with a small number appearing in local dialects, English, and Chinese. The leading dailies published in Jakarta (with their estimated 1991 circulations) are *Kompas* (500,000); *Pos Kota* (250,000); *Berita Buana* (150,000); and *Merdeka* (140,000). Other major dailies are *Pikiran Rakyat* (135,000); *Suara Merdeka* (125,000); and the *Surabaya Post* (105,000).

33 TOURISM AND RECREATION

An estimated 2,569,870 foreign tourists visited Indonesia in 1991, of whom 1,926,663 came from Eastern Asia and 481,684 from Europe. There were 123,902 hotel rooms, and tourist expenditures amounted to $2.5 billion.

Among the most popular tourist destinations are Bali, the restored Borobudur Buddhist temple in Java, and historic Yogyakarta. Cultural attractions include traditional Balinese dancing, the mystical sounds of the Indonesian orchestra (gamelan), the shadow puppet (wayang kulit) theater, and the famous Indonesian rijsttafel, a banquet of rice and savories.

34 FAMOUS INDONESIANS

Gajah Mada, prime minister under King Hayam Wuruk (r.1350–89), brought many of the islands under the rule of the Majapahit Empire. Indonesia's only internationally known artist is the painter Affandi (b.1910).

Sukarno (1901–70), a founder and leader of the nationalist movement, is the best-known figure of modern Indonesia. President Suharto (b.1921), leader of Indonesia since Sukarno's overthrow, has dominated Indonesia's political and economic life since 1968.

35 BIBLIOGRAPHY

Cribb, R. B. *Historical Dictionary of Indonesia.* Metuchen, N.J.: Scarecrow Press, 1992.

Frederick, William H. *Visions and Heat: the Making of the Indonesian Revolution.* Athens: Ohio University Press, 1989.

———. and Robert L. Worden (eds.). *Indonesia: A Country Study.* 5th ed. Washington, D.C.: Library of Congress, 1993.

Lubis, Mochtar. *Indonesia: Land under the Rainbow.* New York: Oxford University Press, 1990.

McNair, S. *Indonesia.* Chicago: Children's Press,1993.

Palmier, Leslie (ed.). *Understanding Indonesia.* Brookfield, Vt.: Gower, 1985.

Ricklefs, M. C. *A History of Modern Indonesia since c. 1300.* 2nd ed. Stanford, Calif.: Stanford University Press, 1993.

Zich, Arthur. "Indonesia: Two Worlds, Time Apart." *National Geographic,* January 1989, 96–128.

IRAN

Islamic Republic of Iran

Jomhuri-ye Eslami-ye Iran

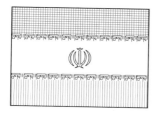

CAPITAL: Tehran.

FLAG: The national flag is a tricolor of green, white, and red horizontal stripes, the top and bottom stripes having the Arabic inscription *Allah Akbar* ("God Is Great") written along the edge nearest the white stripe. In the center, in red, is the coat of arms, consisting of a stylized representation of the word *Allah*.

MONETARY UNIT: The rial (R) is a paper currency of 100 dinars. There are coins of 1, 5, 10, 20, and 50 rials, and notes of 100, 200, 500, 1,000, 2,000, 5,000, and 10,000 rials. R1 = $0.0006 (or $1 = R1,745.47).

WEIGHTS AND MEASURES: The metric system is the legal standard, but local units are widely used.

HOLIDAYS: National Day, 11 February; Oil Nationalization Day, 20 March; No Ruz (New Year), 21–24 March; Islamic Republic Day, 1 April; 13th Day of No Ruz (Revolution Day), 2 April. Religious holidays (according to the lunar calendar) include Birthday of Imam Husayn; Birthday of the Twelfth Imam; Martyrdom of Imam 'Ali; Death of Imam Ja'afar Sadiq; 'Id al-Fitr; Birthday of Imam Reza; 'Id-i-Qurban; 'Id-i-Qadir; Shab-i-Miraj; Martyrdom of Imam Husayn; 40th Day after the Death of Imam Husayn; Birthday of the Prophet; Birthday of Imam 'Ali.

TIME: 3:30 PM = noon GMT.

1 LOCATION AND SIZE

Located in southwestern Asia, Iran covers an area of 1,648,000 square kilometers (636,296 square miles), slightly larger than the state of Alaska. It has a total boundary length of 8,620 kilometers (5,356 miles), and its territory includes several islands in the Persian Gulf.

Iran's capital city, Tehran, is located in the northwestern part of the country.

2 TOPOGRAPHY

Most of the land area consists of a plateau some 1,200 meters (4,000 feet) above sea level with scattered mountains. The Zagros (Kuhha-ye Zagros) and Elburz *(Reshteh-ye Alborz)* mountain ranges form a "V" upon the plateau, enclosing long valleys that provide most of the country's agricultural land. Only the Karun River, emptying into the Persian Gulf, is navigable for any distance, but other rivers, rushing down from high altitudes, offer fine sources of power.

Iran is geologically unstable: an earthquake that struck eastern Iran on 16 September 1978 resulted in at least 25,000 deaths.

3 CLIMATE

Cold winters and hot summers are prevalent across the plateau. On the plateau, the annual rainfall does not exceed 30 centimeters (12 inches), with the deserts and the Persian Gulf area receiving less than 13 centimeters (5 inches). Snow falls heavily on the mountain peaks and is the principal source of water for irrigation in spring and early summer.

The Caspian Sea coastal region is warm and humid throughout the year, with annual rainfall about 100 to 150 centimeters (40–60 inches). Clear days are the rule, for the skies are cloudless more than half the days of each year. The Tehran temperature ranges from an average low of −3°C (27°F) in January to an average high of 37°C (99°F) in July.

4 PLANTS AND ANIMALS

More than one-tenth of the country is forested. Oak, ash, elm, and cypress are found on the mountain slopes rising from the Caspian Sea. On the plateau, areas of scrub oak appear on the best-watered mountain slopes, and villagers cultivate orchards and grow the plane tree, poplar, willow, walnut, beech, maple, and mulberry. Bears in the mountains, wild sheep and goats, gazelles, wild asses, wild pigs, panthers, and foxes abound. Domestic animals include sheep, goats, cattle, horses, water buffalo, donkeys, and camels. The pheasant, partridge, stork, and falcon are native to Iran.

5 ENVIRONMENT

Iran's high grasslands have been eroded for centuries by the overgrazing of livestock. Loss of forest land on the high plateau has been going on for centuries, as nomads and villagers devastate wide areas, and herds of goats swarm over new shoots of grass. United Nations sources estimate that 1 to 1.5 million hectares (2.5 to 3.7 million acres) per year become desert land.

Air and water pollution is a significant problem in Iran due to the aftermath of the Persian Gulf War in 1991. Significant air pollution resulted from the burning of Kuwaiti oil wells. Twenty-five percent of the rural people do not have pure water.

Thirty of Iran's mammal species and 20 bird species are endangered. More than 300 plant species are also threatened.

6 POPULATION

According to the 1991 census, the total population was 55,837,163. The United Nations projected a population of 77,929,000 for the year 2000. Population density was 38 per square kilometer (98 per square mile) in 1991. In 1995, 60% of the population was urban. The rural population in 1987 included 1,152,099 nomads. Tehran, the capital, had a population of 6,042,584 in 1986.

7 MIGRATION

Traditionally, there has been little immigration to Iran, with the exception of Shi'ite Muslims coming from Iraq. There has been some emigration to Europe and the US, particularly by Iranians who were studying overseas at the time of the revolution of 1979. Between 1980 and 1990, however, an increased number of Shi'ite

IRAN

LOCATION: 25° to 40°N; 44° to 63°E. **BOUNDARY LENGTHS:** Afghanistan, 936 kilometers (582 miles); Armenia 35 kilometers (22 miles); Azerbaijan (N) 432 kilometers (268 miles); Azerbaijan (NW) 179 kilometers (111 miles); Caspian Sea coastline, 740 kilometers (460 miles); Gulf of Oman and Persian Gulf coastlines, 2,440 kilometers (1,516 miles); Iraq, 1,458 kilometers (906 miles); Pakistan, 909 kilometers (565 miles); Turkey, 499 kilometers (310 miles); Turkmenistan, 992 kilometers (616 miles). **TERRITORIAL SEA LIMIT:** 12 miles.

Muslims fled Iraq because of the Iran-Iraq and Gulf wars. At the end of 1992, 1,250,100 were refugees in Iran. Perhaps 2.8 million Afghan refugees moved to Iran after the Soviet invasion of Afghanistan in 1979. About 200,000 returned in 1992, and about 2.1 million remained in mid-1993. At least 50,000 refugees from Azerbaijan fled to Iran in 1993 to escape Armenian occupation.

8 ETHNIC GROUPS

Ethnic Iranians, or Persians, number nearly half the total population. In the Zagros range and its extensions are to be found the Kurds (about 9% of the population), Lurs, Bakhtiari, Qashqa'i, and Qajars. Turkish-speaking groups are found in several parts of the country, and there are sizable groups of Azerbaijanis in major cities, including Tehran. Arabs can be found in the south and southwest and in scattered colonies elsewhere.

Nomadic tribal groups migrate in spring and fall between high mountain valleys and hot, lowland plains. The important migratory groups include the Qashqai, Qajars, Bakhtiari, Baluchi, and Turkomans.

9 LANGUAGES

Farsi, commonly called Persian in the West, is the official language of Iran. It is taught in all schools and was spoken by 83% of the population in 1986. An estimated 50–60% spoke it as their native language. An Indo-European language, Farsi derives from ancient Persian, with added Arabic words. Arabic characters and script are used in writing modern Persian.

Dialects of Turkish, or Turki—especially Azari, the language of the Azerbaijanis—are spoken throughout northwestern Iran and in parts of the northeast. The Lurs, Kurds, and Bakhtiari have languages and dialects of their own, and the Baluchi language spoken in southeastern Iran also is of Indo-European origin. A small number of Brahui in the southeast speak a Dravidian language.

10 RELIGIONS

As of 1990, 93.8% of the people were Muslims, members of the Shi'ite sect. Iran is the only Islamic country where Shi'ite Muslims hold the reins of power. Shi'ite Islam is the official religion of the country, and the president, prime minister, and cabinet ministers must be Muslims. Sunni Muslims constitute only about 6%. The Christian population (about 333,000) includes Armenians and, in the northwest area, Nestorian Christians (Assyrians).

Colonies of Parsis, or Zoroastrians, number about 30,000. The Baha'is number about 340,000. The Baha'is have been severely persecuted by the Shi'ite government since the 1979 revolution, and many of their religious leaders have been executed. The Jewish community had dwindled to no more than 14,000 by 1990 and may have declined still further since then under the impact of persecution.

11 TRANSPORTATION

Iran had 140,072 kilometers (87,041 miles) of roads in 1991. The 42,694 kilometers (26,530 miles) of freeway, highway, by-roads, and access roads were asphalted; 96,306 kilometers (59,845 miles) were dirt and gravel roads. In 1991 there were over 1.6 million passenger cars and 600,000 commercial vehicles.

The state-owned Iranian State Railway has 4,850 kilometers (3,013 miles) of track. Iran's main port at Khorramshahr on the Persian Gulf, as well as the port at

Photo credit: Cynthia Bassett.

The Friday Mosque, built over 1,000 year ago, is situated in the old section Esfahān. Almost 94% of the people in Iran are members of the Muslim Shi'ite sect.

Abadan, were largely destroyed in fighting during the 1980–88 war with Iraq. On the Caspian Sea, there is a port near Rasht. In addition, there are the oil shipment ports of Khark Island (a principal target in the war with Iraq) and Abadan. The principal inland waterways are Lake Orumieh (Daryacheh-ye Orumiyeh) and the Karun River.

The state-owned Iran Air maintains frequent service to 15 cities in Iran and is an international carrier. There are international airports at Tehran, Bandar 'Abbas, and Abadan. In 1992, Iran Air carried 4,475,600 international and domestic passengers.

12 HISTORY

As early as 6000 BC, communities on the Iranian plateau were carrying on agriculture, raising domestic animals, and producing pottery and polished stone implements. About 1500 BC, masses of Indo-Europeans, or Aryans, began to cross the plateau of Iran, each group forming its own kingdom in a different part of the region. In 550 BC, Cyrus the Great united the Medes and Persians to establish the Achaemenid Empire.

In his eastward sweep (334–330 BC), the Greek conqueror Alexander the Great defeated vast Achaemenid forces, capturing one of their capitals and burning the other. Later rulers moved west to come in contact with and then to fight the Roman Empire. Wars with Rome were followed by a struggle with the Byzantine Empire.

The Spread of Islam

During the first half of the seventh century AD, Arab warriors burst out of the Arabian Peninsula to spread the teachings of the prophet Muhammad, embodied in Islam. By the opening of the ninth century, Islamic doctrine and ideas had spread over the Iranian plateau, and local dynasties faithful to Islam emerged.

In 1219, Mongol hordes under Genghis Khan (Temujin) began to move into Iran. Successive waves subdued and devastated the country. In 1380, Timur ("Timur the Lame" Nor, in the west called Tamerlane) began to move into the Iranian plateau from the east. Within a decade, the entire area was in his power, bringing a rebirth of culture, but later rulers lacked the force and ability to hold the empire together. Early in the sixteenth century a number of smaller, local dynasties emerged throughout Iran.

In 1722, invading forces from Afghanistan overthrew the Safavids, ending a period of military power and prosperity under the first truly native Iranian dynasty in many centuries. At the end of the eighteenth century, Zand rulers, dominant in the south, were replaced by the Qajars, a Turkish tribe.

The Twentieth Century

By the turn of the twentieth century, the British and Russians controlled areas in the south and north of Iran. The British arranged for a Persian Cossack officer, Reza Rhan, to come to power in 1925 as Reza Shah, the first sovereign of the Pahlavi dynasty. With ruthless authority, he sought to modernize the country. In 1941, suspecting him of pro-German sympathies, the British forced Reza Shah to resign in favor of his 21-year-old son, Muhammad Reza. In April 1946, the British left Iran, and, under pressure from the United Nations and the United States, Soviet troops eventually withdrew in December of that year.

Oil, the source of nearly all Iran's national wealth, quickly came to dominate postwar politics. Between 1947 and 1953, there were conflicts over nationalizing Iran's oil industry, still dominated by British interests in the form of the Anglo-Iranian Oil Co. (AIOC). After 1953, the shah began to increase his power. New arrangements between the National Iranian Oil Co. and a group of United States, United Kingdom, and Dutch oil companies were negotiated during April–September 1954. Iran joined the Western alliance through the Baghdad Pact in 1955, later the Central Treaty Organization.

United States assistance and goodwill were plainly essential for the Shah. In 1961, President John F. Kennedy urged him to undertake a more liberal program. Under the "white revolution" of 1962–63, the Shah initiated land reform, political changes (including, for the first time, the right of women to hold and vote for public office), and broad economic development.

The Shah's dictatorial methods, his use of the secret police (known as SAVAK), his program of rapid Westernization (at the expense of Islamic tradition), his emphasis on lavish display and costly arms imports, and his perceived tolerance of corruption and of United States domination fed opposition in the late 1970s. The economic boom of the previous 15 years also came to an end. Practically the entire population turned against the Shah. Following nine months of demonstrations and violent army reactions, martial law was declared in Iran's major cities in September 1978, but antigovernment strikes and massive marches could not be stopped. The leader of the Islamic opposition, Ayatollah Ruhollah Khomeini (the term *ayatollah* is the highest rank of the Shi'ite Muslim clergy), had spent 15 years in exile, first in Iraq and briefly in France. On 1 February 1979 the Ayatollah returned to an enthusiastic welcome in Tehran. He quickly asserted control and appointed a provisional government, which took power after the final collapse of the Shah's regime on 11 February.

Khomeini Takes Charge

On 1 April Khomeini declared Iran an Islamic Republic. Revolutionary groups made random arrests and illegal executions of political opponents. On 4 November 1979, 53 US hostages (50 of them in the United States embassy compound in Tehran) were seized by militant Iranian students who demanded the return of the Shah from the United States (where he was receiving medical treatment) to stand trial in Iran. Despite vigorous protests by the United States government, the hostages were held for 444 days. A US attempt to free them by military force failed, and the Shah died in Egypt on 27 July 1980. The crisis was finally resolved on 20 January 1981, in an agreement providing for release of the prisoners.

However, conflict between rival political groups within Iran continued, accompanied by repeated bombings and assassinations. By 1982, at least 4,500 people had been killed in political violence, and some estimates placed the total much higher. In September 1982, Sadegh Ghotbzadeh, who had been foreign minister during the hostage crisis, was executed on charges of plotting to kill Khomeini and establish a secular government.

Iraq, meanwhile, had taken advantage of Iran's political chaos and economic disorder to revive an old border dispute, and full-scale war erupted in September 1980, when Iraqi forces invaded Khuzistan in the southwest, and captured the town of Khorramshahr and the oil refinery center of Abadan. Iran then launched its own offensive, invading Iraq but failing to make significant gains. The land war became stalemated, and in 1983 Iraq broadened the war zone to include oil-tanker traffic in the northern Persian Gulf.

Hostilities continued until 1988, when Iran finally yielded to terms for a cease-fire. On 3 June 1989, a few months after calling for the death of novelist Salman Rushdie for blasphemy, Khomeini died of a heart attack. Over three million people attended his funeral. He was succeeded as spiritual guide by President Ali Khamenei.

Iran remained neutral during the Gulf War, receiving (and retaining) Iraqi planes that were flown across the border for safe-keeping. Iran also accepted thousands of Kurdish refugees from Iraq to add to its heavy burden of Afghan refugees from the civil war in that country. Inflation, shortages, and unemployment—the products of revolution, war, and mismanagement—continue to generate widespread popular discontent, fueled also by dissatisfaction with the closed and repressive political system.

13 GOVERNMENT

The constitution of December 1979 established an Islamic republic in conformity with the principles of the Shi'ite faith. Guidance of the republic is entrusted to the country's spiritual leader *(faqih)* or to a council of religious leaders. An appointed Council of Guardians consists of six religious leaders, who consider all legislation for conformity to Islamic principles, and six Muslim lawyers appointed by the Supreme Judicial Council, who rule on limited questions of constitutionality.

The executive branch consists of a president and Council of Ministers. The president is elected by popular vote to a four-year term and supervises government administration. The Majlis consists of 270 members elected directly to four-year terms. Voting is universal for those over age 15. Iran is divided into 24 *ostans* (provinces), each subdivided into 195 *sharestans* (counties) and 500 *bakhsh* (districts).

14 POLITICAL PARTIES

After the overthrow of the shah's regime in February 1979, new political parties were formed. In elections to the Majlis (parliament) in March and May 1980, the Islamic Republican Party (IRP), which was closely identified with Ayatollah Khomeini, emerged as the dominant group.

All parties found not to be acceptable by Islamic standards have been banned. Some operate outside the country. These include the Mujahedeen al Khalq (a left-wing Shi'ite Muslim group with a military branch supported by Iraq) and royalist parties backing the son of the late shah. Only the Liberation Movement of Mehdi Bazargan has been allowed limited participation in politics. The IRP was abolished in 1987, but religious groups maintain political power. Three other parties—a radical group, a pragmatic party, and a conservative faction—regularly compete for seats in the Parliament.

15 JUDICIAL SYSTEM

In August 1982, the Supreme Court invalidated all previous laws that did not conform with the dictates of Islam, and all courts set up before the 1979 revolution were abolished in October 1982. An Islamic system of punishment, introduced in 1983, included flogging, stoning, and amputation for various crimes. There are two different court systems: civil courts and revolutionary courts.

The judicial system is under the authority of the religious leader *(faqih)*. A Supreme Judicial Council responsible to the faqih oversees the Supreme Court, which has 16 branches. The Ministry of Justice oversees law courts in the provinces. The revolutionary courts try cases involving political offenses, narcotics trafficking, and "crimes against God." The trials in revolutionary courts are rarely held in public and there is no guarantee of access to an attorney.

16 ARMED FORCES

Two years' military service is required for all males at age 18. In 1993, the army had 305,000 soldiers (200,000 draftees). Their equipment included 700 main battle tanks, 750 armored fighting vehicles, and 1,300 artillery pieces. The air force had 35,000 men and 262 combat aircraft. Iran also now holds 112 planes of the Iraqi air force. The navy of 18,000 men had 3 destroyers, 5 frigates, and 33 smaller patrol and coastal combatants.

The Revolutionary Guards unit *(Pasdaran)* has an estimated 150,000-man army and 20,000 sailors and marines. Complementing the *Pasdaran* are the *baseej,* radical young volunteers devoted to an Islamic Iran. Membership has been as high as 500,000. The police force numbers 45,000. The official military budget in 1991 was $13 billion.

17 ECONOMY

Iran witnessed rapid economic growth during the reign of Shah Muhammad Reza Pahlavi. With the astonishing growth of its oil revenues, Iran became a major world economic power. Development of its extensive agricultural, mineral, and

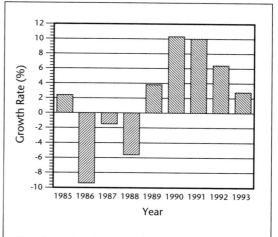

Yearly growth rate of the economy. This economic indicator tells by what percent the economy has increased or decreased when compared with the previous year.

power resources was financed through oil revenues.

The economy has changed drastically since 1979. The war with Iraq, which reduced oil exports, coupled with the decrease in the price of oil, especially in 1986, sent oil revenues downward from $20.5 billion in 1979 to an estimated $5.3 billion in 1986. The war's drain on the state budget, the drop in oil prices, poor economic management, declining agricultural output, and an estimated 1987 inflation rate of 30–50% combined to put serious strains on the economy.

Government economic reforms begun after Iran accepted a UN ceasefire resolution in 1988 led to economic growth and lowered budget deficits and inflation, which dropped from 29% in 1988 to around 10% in 1990. Since then, however, it has edged up to an estimated 20% in 1991 and 1992.

18 INCOME

In 1992, Iran's gross national product (GNP) was $130,910 million at current prices, or $2,120 per person. For the period 1985–92 the average inflation rate was 21.0%, resulting in a real growth rate in GNP of –1.4% per person.

19 INDUSTRY

Iran's industrialization program was set back by the political turmoil and labor disruptions of the late 1970s and by the revolutionary government's takeover of industries in the summer of 1979, causing a loss of investment money and trained managers. A recent development plan (1989/90–1993/94) has increased funding to develop heavy industry.

Main industries are oil refining, petrochemicals, steel, and copper. In 1987, there were several primary refineries—at Abadan, Tehran, Shiraz, Esfahan, and Tabriz—with a capacity of 950,000 barrels per day. Major refinery products are motor fuel, distillate fuel oil, and residual fuel oil.

The textile industry has prospered in recent years with increased production of cotton, woolen, and synthetic fabrics. The making of handwoven carpets is a traditional industry in Iran that flourishes despite competition from machine-made products. However, carpet exports declined throughout the war years. To promote self-sufficiency, Iran has encouraged development of the food-processing,

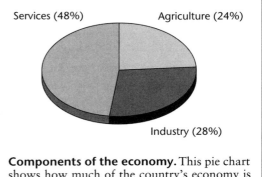

Services (48%) Agriculture (24%)

Industry (28%)

Components of the economy. This pie chart shows how much of the country's economy is devoted to agriculture (includes forestry, hunting, and fishing), industry, or services.

shoemaking, paper and paper products, rubber, pharmaceutical, aircraft, and shipbuilding industries. Other industrial products include cement, nitrogenous fertilizer, phosphate fertilizers, and refined sugar.

20 LABOR

The total labor force was estimated at around 27.5 million in 1990. According to official figures, 30% of the employed work force was in agriculture, 25% was in manufacturing, mining, construction, and utilities, and 45% was in the service industry. Unemployment continues to be a problem. In 1982/83, it was 19%, and by the end of the 1980s it was an estimated 30%.

Article 131 of the Labor Code grants workers the right to form and join their own organizations. Iranian labor law forbids employment of minors under 12 years, but agriculture, domestic service, family businesses, and some other small businesses are exempt from this restriction. Women and minors are prohibited from engaging in hard labor or night work.

21 AGRICULTURE

About one-third of the labor force is employed in agriculture. In 1987, the total land area under cultivation was estimated at 19 million hectares (47 million acres). With a rapidly increasing population and a sharply rising standard of living, Iran no longer produces enough food to meet its needs, and food imports have risen steadily in recent years.

In 1992, Iranian agricultural production (in thousands of tons) included wheat, 10,200; sugar beets, 6,000; barley, 3,700; rice, 2,500; grapes, 1,650; apples, 1,520; oranges, 1,300; dates, 635; cotton, 400; tea, 45; and tobacco, 22. Almonds and pistachios are grown primarily for export. In 1992, Iran was the largest producer of pistachios in the world (170,000 tons, or 59% of global production), and the third largest producer of almonds (after Spain and Italy), at 66,000 tons.

22 DOMESTICATED ANIMALS

Animal farming is the major occupation of nomadic tribes scattered over Iran, and each farming village also keeps flocks that graze on the less productive areas. In 1992 there were 45,000,050 sheep, 23,500,000 goats, 6,900,000 head of cattle, 300,000 water buffalo, 130,000 camels, and 170,000,000 chickens. Cattle are raised as draft animals and for milk and are not fattened for beef. Sheep produce many staple items: milk and butter, animal fat for cooking, meat, wool for making carpets, and skins and hides.

Photo credit: International Labour Office.

A young boy on an Iranian government research station examines the irrigation system.

23 FISHING

The Caspian Sea provides a seemingly endless source of sturgeon, salmon, and other species of fish, some of which breed in the chilly streams that flow into this sea from the high Elburz Mountains (Reshteh-ye Alborz). In 1991, the total fish catch was 277,444 tons. Caviar of unrivaled quality is produced by the Iranian Fisheries Company. About 200,000 kilograms of caviar are sold per year, most of which is exported, providing a large share of the world's supply. The Iran-Iraq war and the resulting environmental damage slowed the development of fisheries in this region.

Total marine catch has more than doubled from 1982–84 levels.

24 FORESTRY

About 18 million hectares (44.4 million acres) are covered by forest and woodland. An estimated 6.7 million cubic meters of roundwood were produced in 1991, about 36% of which was used for fuel. Oak, ash, elm, beech, ironwood, cypress, walnut, and a number of other varieties are found along the northern slopes of the Elburz Mountains (Reshteh-ye Alborz). The high plateau forests of the east contain scrub oak, ash, maple, cedar, wild almond, and pistachio. Date palms, acacias, and tamarisks grow in the Persian Gulf area. The deciduous forests on the Caspian coastal region are among the best in the world. The timber industry has a potential annual capacity of three million cubic meters.

25 MINING

Major iron and copper ore deposits are found near Kerman. Iran also has deposits of antimony, chromite, lead, zinc, manganese, sulfur, salt, mica, silica, limestone, and granite.

Production of primary aluminum in 1991 was 80,000 tons; chromite, 44,000 tons; copper, 80,700 tons; lead, 16,000 tons; manganese, 16,000 tons; molybdenum, 400 tons; and zinc, 70,000 tons. Production of hard coal in 1991 was 1,480,000 metric tons; iron ore, 2,100,000 tons; sulfur, 700,000 tons; and unrefined salt, 900,965 tons. Mineral exports include chromite, refined sulfur, lead, zinc, copper, and decorative stone.

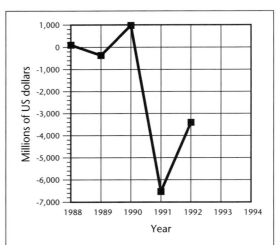

Yearly balance of trade measured in millions of US dollars. The balance of trade is the difference between what a country sells to other countries (its exports) and what it buys (its imports). If a country imports more than it exports, it has a negative balance of trade (a trade deficit). If exports exceed imports there is a positive balance of trade (a trade surplus).

26 FOREIGN TRADE

Since 1984 the trade balance has varied widely, mainly reflecting the volume of oil exports as well as changes in oil prices. Food imports rose rapidly throughout the early 1980s despite the government's emphasis on agricultural development.

The United States was a leading customer for Iran's oil exports during the 1970s, but trade between the two countries has been cut off since the United States ended diplomatic relations in April 1980 during the hostage crisis. In January 1985, Iran, Pakistan, and Turkey formed a new regional trade group, the Economic Cooperation Organization. Trade among the three countries was expected to total

$3 billion a year. Trade with Japan is substantial. International Monetary Fund (IMF) figures indicate that in 1991, Iran exported 15.9% of its goods (mostly petroleum) to Japan, receiving 12.6% of its imports from Japan. That year, Italy bought 9.4% of Iran's exports and shipped Iran 8.9% of its imports. Germany sent Iran 20.6% of its imports.

27 ENERGY AND POWER

Iran's oil reserves, estimated at 92.9 billion barrels (12.7 billion tons) at the end of 1992, constituted 9.2% of the world's known reserves and were exceeded only by those of Sa'udi Arabia, Iraq, United Arab Emirates, and Kuwait. Iran was the second-largest oil producer among OPEC countries in 1992.

In 1980, the revolutionary government ended joint-venture operations with Western oil companies and regrouped them under the Iranian Offshore Oil Company of the Islamic Republic. Despite an OPEC-imposed production ceiling for Iran of 3,184,000 barrels per day, petroleum production reached 3,455,000 barrels per day in 1992 and was scheduled to increase to about four million and five million barrels per day in 1993 and 1994, respectively.

In 1992, Iran's natural gas reserves were estimated at 19.8 trillion cubic meters (699.2 trillion cubic feet). Only Russia possesses larger natural gas reserves. Iran's output climbed to 26,600 million cubic meters in 1992. In 1991, hydroelectric power plants generated 6,600,000 megawatt hours, compared with 50,300,000 megawatt hours in conventional thermal facilities. In 1991, the total electricity output was 56,900,000 megawatt hours.

28 SOCIAL DEVELOPMENT

Traditionally, the family and the tribe were supplemented by Islamic *waqf* (obligatory charity) institutions for the care of the infirm and the indigent. In 1974, the Ministry of Social Welfare was created. At that time, it was anticipated that by the end of the fifth plan (1973–78), some 50% of the urban population would enjoy insurance coverage, but coverage for the whole country was not expected until the end of the 1980s. The 1979 constitution provided for health, unemployment, and old age insurance.

The revolutionary government has been accused of using torture in interrogating political prisoners, and of persecuting such religious minorities as Baha'is and Jews (at least 200 Baha'is had been executed and 767 imprisoned at the end of 1985). The imposition of Islamic fundamentalism brought with it censorship of all media and the undoing, in large part, of the emancipation of women achieved during the previous government.

29 HEALTH

In 1990, there were 83 reported cases of tuberculosis per 1,000 people. One quarter of visits to health centers have been attributed to respiratory disease. National campaigns against such major diseases as malaria and smallpox have been undertaken. Average life expectancy in 1992 was estimated at 68 years for both women and men. In 1992, 80% of the population had access to health care services.

Selected Social Indicators

These statistics are estimates for the period 1988 to 1993. For comparison purposes, data for the United States and averages for low income countries and high income countries are also given.

Indicator	Iran	Low-income countries	High-income countries	United States
Per capita gross national product†	**$2,120**	$380	$23,680	$24,740
Population growth rate	**3.2%**	1.9%	0.6%	1.0%
Population growth rate in urban areas	**4.1%**	3.9%	0.8%	1.3%
Population per square kilometer of land	**38**	78	25	26
Life expectancy in years	**68**	62	77	76
Number of people per physician	**3,333**	>3,300	453	419
Number of pupils per teacher (primary school)	**32**	39	<18	20
Illiteracy rate (15 years and older)	**46%**	41%	<5%	<3%
Energy consumed per capita (kg of oil equivalent)	**1,235**	364	5,203	7,918

† The gross national product (GNP) is the total dollar value of all goods and services produced by a country in a year. The per capita GNP is calculated by dividing a country's GNP by its population. The World Bank defines low-income countries as those with a per capita GNP of $695 or less. High-income countries have a per capita GNP of $8,626 or more. Less than 14% of the world's 5.5 billion people live in high-income countries, while almost 60% live in low-income countries.

> = greater than   < = less than

Sources: World Bank, *Social Indicators of Development 1995,* Baltimore: Johns Hopkins University Press, 1995. Central Intelligence Agency, *World Fact Book,* Washington, D.C.: Government Printing Office, 1994.

The Islamic republic has continued to provide health care programs to the rural areas. In 1992, there were about 3,333 people per each physician. As of 1990, Iran had 1.5 hospital beds per 1,000 people and total health care expenditures of over $3 billion.

30 HOUSING

Housing starts fell sharply after the 1979 revolution, as construction dropped sharply because of lack of funding. In 1983/84, government figures showed that 104,698 residential units were completed in Tehran and other large cities through-out the country. In 1986, 43% of all housing units were constructed of brick with iron beams, 19% were adobe and wood, and 16% were brick with wooden beams. Electricity was available in 84% of all housing units, 95% had a water toilet, 75% had piped water, 54% had a kitchen, and 47% had a bath.

31 EDUCATION

Literacy training has been a prime concern in Iran. In 1990, the literacy rate was estimated at 54.0%, 64.5% for males and 43.3% for females. In 1991, there were 9,787,593 elementary-school pupils, and

5,619,057 total secondary-school students.

Education is basically free in Iran at all levels, from elementary school through university. At university level, however, every student is required to commit himself to serve the government for a number of years equivalent to those spent at the university.

After the 1979 revolution, Khomeini's government carried out the Islamization of the education system. All students were segregated by sex. The Center for Textbooks produced 3,000 new college-level textbooks reflecting Islamic views by 1983. Teaching materials based on Islam were introduced into the primary grades within six months of the revolution.

The country's 16 universities were closed after the 1979 revolution and then reopened gradually between 1982 and 1983 with Islamic curriculums. In 1991, all higher level institutions had 25,208 teachers and 636,255 students. The University of Tehran was founded in 1934. Other major universities are at Tabriz, Mashhad, Ahvaz, Shiraz, and Esfahan.

32 MEDIA

In 1991 there were 2,103,830 telephones in service. In 1991 there were over 13,860,000 radios. The national radio organization and the government television network were merged in 1971 to form National Iranian Radio and Television (NIRT). After 1979, it became the Islamic Republic of Iran Broadcasting Company. There were an estimated 3,750,000 television sets in 1991.

The constitution of 1979 strictly limited freedom of the press. A new press law required publications to be licensed, and their editors were subject to imprisonment. Newspapers that had favored the shah were closed down, and others considered unsympathetic to the ruling IRP were banned. In 1991 there were 11 "authorized" daily newspapers. The major Persian-language dailies were *Kayhan* (circulation 350,000) and *Ettal'at (250,000)*, both in Tehran.

33 TOURISM AND RECREATION

Tourism, which had been low since the 1979 revolution, has begun to grow since the death of Ayatollah Khomeini and the government's attempts to establish closer ties with the West. In 1991, 212,096 tourists visited Iran, 46% from southern Asia, 29% from Europe, and 17% from the Middle East. In 1989, there were 15,584 rooms in hotels and other facilities, with a 68% occupancy rate, and tourism receipts totaled $62 million in 1990. Principal tourist attractions include historic and beautifully decorated mosques, mausoleums, and minarets. There are many sports and physical culture societies in Tehran and the provinces. Emphasis is upon skiing and weight lifting.

34 FAMOUS IRANIANS

Zoroaster (Zarathushtra), who probably lived in the sixth century BC, founded the religion known as Zoroastrianism or Mazdaism. Great Persian rulers of the pre-Christian era include Cyrus ("the Great"; Kurush, r.550–529 BC) and Darius I (Darayavaush, r.521–486 BC). Prominent political figures of modern times are Reza Shah Pahlavi (1877–1944), who reigned from 1925 to his abdication in 1941; and his son, Muhammad Reza Pahlavi (1919–80), who was shah from 1941 until his abdication in 1979. Until his death in 1989, Iran was under the leadership of Ayatollah Ruhollah Khomeini (1900–89).

Omar Khayyam (d.1123?), astronomer and poet, is known in the Western world for his *Rubáiyât,* a collection of verses freely translated by Edward FitzGerald. In the 13th century, Sa'di (Muslih ud-Din, 1184?–1291), possibly the most renowned Iranian poet within or outside of Iran, composed his *Gulistan (Rose Garden)* and *Bustan (Orchard).* Poets of the modern period include the poet laureate Behar (Malik ash-Shuara Bahar, d.1951). Famous among prose writers was Sadeq Hedayat (1903–51), author of the novel *Buf i kur (The Blind Owl).*

35 BIBLIOGRAPHY

Fox, M. *Iran.* Chicago: Children's Press, 1991.

Iran in Pictures. Minneapolis: Lerner, 1988.

Metz, Helen Chapin (ed.). *Iran, a Country Study.* 4th ed. Washington, D.C.: Library of Congress, 1989.

Nagel, Rob, and Anne Commire. "Abbas I." In *World Leaders, People Who Shaped the World.* Volume I: Africa and Asia. Detroit: U*X*L, 1994.

———. "Ruhollah Khomeini." In *World Leaders, People Who Shaped the World.* Volume I: Africa and Asia. Detroit: U*X*L, 1994.

———. "Zoroaster." In *World Leaders, People Who Shaped the World.* Volume I: Africa and Asia. Detroit: U*X*L, 1994.

Wilber, Donald Newton. *Iran, Past and Present: From Monarchy to Islamic Republic.* Princeton, N.J.: Princeton University Press, 1981.

IRAQ

Republic of Iraq
Al-Jumhuriyah al-'Iraqiyah

CAPITAL: Baghdād.

FLAG: The national flag is a tricolor of red, white, and black horizontal stripes, with three five-pointed stars in green in the center of the white stripe.

ANTHEM: *Al-Salaam al-Jumhuri (Salute of the Republic).*

MONETARY UNIT: The Iraqi dinar (ID) is a paper currency of 1,000 fils. There are coins of 1, 5, 10, 25, 50, 100, and 250 fils, and notes of 250 and 500 fils and 1, 5, 10, 50, and 100 dinars. ID1 = $3.2169 (or $1 = ID0.3109).

WEIGHTS AND MEASURES: The metric system is the legal standard, but weights and measures in general use vary, especially in domestic transactions. The unit of land is the dunam, which is equivalent to approximately 0.25 hectare (0.62 acre).

HOLIDAYS: New Year's Day, 1 January; Army Day, 6 January; 14th Ramadan Revolution Day, 8 February; Declaration of the Republic, 14 July; and Peaceful Revolution Day, 17 July. Muslim religious holidays include 'Id al-Fitr, 'Id al-'Adha', Milad an-Nabi, and Islamic New Year.

TIME: 3 PM = noon GMT.

1 LOCATION AND SIZE

Iraq comprises an area of 437,072 square kilometers (168,754 square miles), slightly more than twice the size of the state of Idaho. It has a total boundary length of 3,681 kilometers (2,288 miles). Iraq's capital city, Baghdād, is located in the east central part of the country.

2 TOPOGRAPHY

Iraq is divided into three distinct zones: the desert in the west and southwest; the plains, dominated by the river systems of the Tigris and Euphrates; and the highlands in the northeast, which rise to 3,000 meters (10,000 feet) or more. The sources of the Euphrates and Tigris are in the Armenian Plateau.

3 CLIMATE

Summers are intensely hot and dry, and during the hottest time of the day—often reaching 49°C (120°F) in the shade—people take refuge in underground shelters. Winters are damp and comparatively cold, with temperatures averaging about 10°C (50°F). With annual rainfall of less than 38 centimeters (15 inches), agriculture is dependent on irrigation.

4 PLANTS AND ANIMALS

In the lower regions of the Euphrates and Tigris rivers, papyrus, lotus, and tall reeds form a thick underbrush. Willow, poplar, and alder trees abound. On the upper and middle Euphrates, the licorice bush yields a juice that is extracted for commercial purposes. In the higher Zagros Mountains grows the valonia oak, the bark of which is used for tanning leather. About 30 million date palms produce one of Iraq's most important exports.

Wild animals include the hyena, jackal, fox, gazelle, antelope, jerboa, mole, porcupine, desert hare, and bat. Wild ducks, geese, and partridge are the game birds. Vultures, owls, and ravens live near the Euphrates.

5 ENVIRONMENT

United Nations reports in 1992 stated that Iraq's natural environment "underwent the worst destruction ever possible" during the 1991 Persian Gulf War. The major sources of environmental damage are discharges from oil refineries, factory and sewage discharges into rivers, fertilizer and chemical contamination of the soil, and industrial air pollution in urban areas.

As a result of war damage, water pollution has increased, made worse by toxic chemicals from damaged oil facilities. As of 1994, nine of Iraq's mammal species and 17 of its bird species are endangered. One plant species is threatened with extinction.

6 POPULATION

In mid-1991, the population was officially estimated at 17,903,000. The population for the year 2000 was projected at 24,779,000. The estimated average population density in 1991 was 43 persons per square kilometer (107 per square mile). As of 1987, Baghdād, the capital, had 3,844,608 inhabitants.

7 MIGRATION

To weaken local support in the north for Kurdish rebels, the government forced tens of thousands of Kurds to resettle in the south. In September 1987, a Western diplomat in Baghdād claimed that at least 500 Kurdish villages had been destroyed and 100,000 to 500,000 Kurds relocated. In 1991 some 1.5 million Iraqis fled the country for Turkey or Iran to escape Saddam Hussein's increasingly repressive rule, but fewer than 100,000 remained abroad.

8 ETHNIC GROUPS

Arabs constitute about 76% of the total population. The Kurds, an Islamic non-Arab people, are the largest and most important minority group, constituting about 19%. Other minorities include Turkomans (1.5–2%), Yazidis, Assyrians, and Armenians.

9 LANGUAGES

Arabic is the national language and is the mother tongue of an estimated 79% of the population. Kurdish (16%), or a dialect of it, is spoken by the Kurds and Yazidis. Aranaic, the ancient Syriac dialect, is spoken by the Assyrians. Another Syriac dialect, Mandaean, is the language of worship of the Sabaeans. The Turkomans speak a Turkic dialect.

IRAQ

LOCATION: 29° to 37°30′N; 39° to 48°E. **BOUNDARY LENGTHS:** Turkey, 305 kilometers (190 miles); Iran, 1,458 kilometers (906 miles); Persian Gulf coastline, 19 kilometers (12 miles); Kuwait, 254 kilometers (158 miles); Sa'udi Arabia, 895 kilometers (556 miles); Jordan, 147 kilometers (91 miles); Syria, 603 kilometers (375 miles). **TERRITORIAL SEA LIMIT:** 12 miles.

10 RELIGIONS

Islam is the national religion of Iraq, followed by over 95% of the population in 1993. A slight majority of Muslims belong to the Shi'ite sect and a minority to the Sunni sect. There are also some unorthodox Muslim groups, such as the Yazidis, who consider Satan a fallen angel who will one day be reconciled with God.

In 1991, Christianity claimed some 1 million followers, of whom over 500,000 were Roman Catholic and nearly all the remainder belonged to various branches of Oriental Christianity. Iraq's Jewish community dwindled from about 90,000 in 1948 to 200 in 1990, virtually all Iraqi Jews having emigrated to Israel by the early 1950s.

11 TRANSPORTATION

Major cities, towns, and villages are connected by a modern network of highways and roads which have made old caravan routes extinct. By 1991, Iraq had 34,700 kilometers (21,563 miles) of roads. In 1991 there were some 650,000 cars and 350,000 commercial vehicles in use. In 1991 there were about 2,457 kilometers (1,527 miles) of railway lines.

Baghdād, Al Baṣrah, and Al Mawṣil have international airports. The Iraqi-Iranian war practically closed Iraq's main port of Al Baṣrah and the new port of Umm Qasr (near the Kuwaiti border) on the Persian Gulf. By the beginning of 1992, the merchant marine totaled only 32 ships with 796,000 gross registered tons.

12 HISTORY

Some of the earliest known human settlements have been found in present-day Iraq. Homes, shrines, tools, and pottery found on various sites can be dated as early as 4000 BC. Recorded history in Mesopotamia (the ancient name of Iraq) begins with the Sumerians, who by 3000 BC had established city-states. Beginning with the Babylonians in about 1900 BC, a series of ancient civilizations gained control of the area, including Assyrians (1350 BC); Chaldeans and Medes (612 BC); the Persians, led by Cyrus the Great (539 BC); the Greeks, led by Alexander the Great (327 BC); and the Parthians (138 BC).

The Arabs conquered Iraq in AD 637, and from 750 to 1258, Baghdād thrived as the capital of the 'Abbasids. However, Mongol invasions in the thirteenth and fourteenth centuries ended Iraq's flourishing economy and culture. In 1534, Süleyman the Magnificent conquered Baghdād and, except for a short period of Persian control in the seventeenth century, Iraq remained a province of the Ottoman Turks until World War I (1914–18), when it fell under British military occupation.

The collapse of the Ottoman Empire stimulated Iraqi hopes for freedom and independence. After a period of rule by a provisional government under King Faisal I, Iraq gained independence in 1932 and was admitted to membership in the League of Nations.

Becomes a Republic

On 14 July 1958, a military takeover led by General 'Abd al-Karim al-Qasim

Babylon Wall. The ancient Babylonians ruled Mesopotamia (the ancient name of Iraq) until 1550BC when Babylon was destroyed.

(Kassim) abolished the monarchy and established a republic in its place. Iraq left the anti-communist Baghdād Pact, which the monarchy had joined in 1955. A farm reform law broke up the great landholdings of feudal leaders, and a new economic development program emphasized industrialization. Qasim continued to rule Iraq for four and a half years. On 9 February 1963, however, another military takeover, led by Colonel 'Abd as-Salam Muhammad 'Arif, overthrew his government and executed him.

In July 1968, General (later Marshal) Ahmad Hasan al-Bakr, heading a section of the Ba'th Party, staged a takeover and established a new government with him-

self as president. In July 1970, the Bakr government granted limited political, economic, and cultural independence to Iraq's Kurdish minority. But in March 1974, Kurdish rebels revolted, with Iranian military support, and the Iraqi army replied with a major offensive. On 6 March 1975, Iraq and Iran concluded an agreement by which Iran gave up support for the Kurds.

Hussein Takes Power

Bakr ruled until July 1979, when he was followed as president by his chosen successor, Saddam Hussein (Husayn) al-Takriti. Tensions between Iraq and Iran rose after the Iranian revolution of 1979 and the coming to power of Saddam Hussein. In

September 1980, Iraq mounted a full-scale invasion of Iran. Iranian forces launched a slow but successful counterattack and major offensives aimed at the Iraqi oil port of Al Başrah. Iraqi soldiers repelled the attacks, and the war came to a stalemate, with tens of thousands of casualties on each side.

Attempts by the UN and by other Arab states to resolve the conflict were unsuccessful. In the latter stages of the war, Iraq accepted but Iran regularly rejected proposals for a compromise peace. The war eventually spread to Persian Gulf shipping, as both sides attacked oil tankers and ships transporting oil, goods, and arms. It ended on 20 August 1988 after Iran accepted a UN cease-fire proposal. Having suffered enormous casualties and physical damage, Baghdād began the postwar process of reconstruction.

When Iraq's wartime allies seemed unwilling to help or critical of Iraqi policies, Saddam Hussein turned bitterly against them. Kuwait was the principal target. After threats and troop movements, Iraq invaded and occupied it on 2 August 1990. Saddam Hussein was stubborn in the face of various peace proposals, economic sanctions, and the threatening buildup of coalition forces led by the United States.

A devastating air war began on 17 January 1991 followed by ground attack on 24 February. Iraq was defeated, but not occupied. Despite vast destruction and several hundred thousand casualties, Saddam's government remained firmly in control. The United States continued in 1994 to maintain tight economic sanctions and a ban on oil sales and to require that Iraq submit its nonconventional weapons centers to inspection and monitoring.

13 GOVERNMENT

Since the 1968 takeover, the Ba'th Party has ruled Iraq by means of the Revolutionary Command Council which selects the president and a cabinet composed of military and civilian leaders. The president (Saddam Hussein since 1979) serves as chairman of the Revolutionary Command Council, which exercises both executive and legislative powers. He is also prime minister, commander-in-chief of the armed forces, and secretary-general of the Ba'th Party. A National Assembly of 250 members has little real power. Most senior officials are relatives or close associates of Saddam Hussein.

Iraq is divided into 18 provinces, 3 of which are self-governing Kurdish regions. Provinces are divided into districts, which, in turn, consist of counties.

14 POLITICAL PARTIES

Since the 1968 takeover, the Ba'thists, organized as the Arab Ba'th Socialist Party, have been the ruling political group in Iraq. Other parties are allowed in order to give the appearance of political tolerance. Outside of Iraq, ethnic, religious, and political opposition groups have come together to organize a common front against Saddam Hussein, but they have achieved little. The Shia al Dawa Party was brutally suppressed by Saddam before the Iran-Iraq war. Its remnants are now based in the Iranian city of Tehran.

15 JUDICIAL SYSTEM

The court system is made up of two distinct branches: security courts and a more conventional court system to handle other charges. The security courts have jurisdiction in all cases involving spying, treason, political dissent, smuggling and currency exchange violations, and drug trafficking. The ordinary civil courts have jurisdiction over civil, commercial, and criminal cases except for those that fall under the jurisdiction of the religious courts.

Although there are no Shari'a (Islamic) courts, family courts may administer Shari'a law according to Iraqi custom.

16 ARMED FORCES

Damaged by its defeat in the Gulf War of 1990–91, the Iraqi armed forces are estimated at 382,500 men, half their prewar strength. The army has a strength of 350,000 men (100,000 recalled reservists) and 2,300 tanks; the navy has 1,000 men; and the air force has 30,000 men with perhaps 300 combat aircraft.

During 1981–90, Iraq purchased some $45 billion in arms from the USSR, France, and China. It was the world's principal arms importer for this period. During the war with Iran, Iraq's defense budget averaged more than $13 billion a year.

17 ECONOMY

Oil is the most important sector of the economy. Petroleum production was badly hurt by the war with Iran, however, and the economy was in serious trouble in 1987. In response to the Iraqi invasion of Kuwait on 2 August 1990, the United Nations (UN) imposed comprehensive economic, financial, and military sanctions, totally isolating the Iraqi economy. However, UN Security Council resolutions authorized the export of Iraqi crude oil worth up to $1.6 billion over a limited time to finance humanitarian imports for the Iraqi people.

18 INCOME

In 1992, Iraq's gross national product (GNP) was $35 billion at current prices, or $1,940 per person. In 1992 the inflation rate of consumer prices was 200%.

19 INDUSTRY

Main industries are oil refining, food processing, textiles, leather goods, cement and other building materials, tobacco, paper, and sulfur extraction. The Iraq-Iran and Gulf wars seriously affected Iraqi refining. Refining capacity was restored to 460,000 barrels per day in 1991, and 550,00 barrels per day in 1992.

20 LABOR

Just before the Persian Gulf War in 1990, the total labor force was estimated at 4.4 million. Of the active labor force, agriculture employed 30%; services, 48%; and industry, 22%. In July 1990, Iraqi workers living abroad totaled some 1.6 million.

21 AGRICULTURE

Agricultural production in Iraq has declined due to the war with Iran and the Persian Gulf War. In 1992, wheat production was estimated at 600,000 tons compared with 965,000 tons in 1982. The comparable figures for barley were 400,000 tons and 902,000 tons; for cotton, 5,000 tons and 8,000 tons. Dates, Iraq's most important agricultural export, increased from 374,000 tons in 1982 to an estimated 580,000 in 1992. Crops grown for domestic consumption include millet, lentils, beans, cucumbers, melons, figs, potatoes, corn, sugarcane, tobacco, and mulberries.

22 DOMESTICATED ANIMALS

Sheep raising is important, with wool used domestically for weaving carpets and cloaks. In 1992, Iraq had an estimated 9 million sheep; 1.5 million goats; 1.4 million head of cattle, and numerous donkeys, camels, mules, buffaloes, and poultry. In 1992, of the 530,000 tons of milk produced by all livestock, 52% came from cows, 30% from sheep, 13% from goats, and 5% from buffaloes.

23 FISHING

The 1991 fish catch (including salmon and, especially in the Tigris, carp) was 12,000 tons. Since the war, and the closure of Iraq's ports because of fighting, the Iraqi fishing fleet has been dispersed around the world and does not operate in the Persian Gulf.

24 FORESTRY

The national forestry research center has established tree nurseries and conducted reforestation programs. Output of round-wood was estimated at 155,000 cubic meters in 1991.

25 MINING

Iraq's mineral resources other than oil are limited. Geological surveys have indicated usable deposits of iron ore, copper, gypsum, bitumen, dolomite, and marble. However, these resources have remained largely unmined. Production of all mineral commodities fell since international trade was halted by the embargo.

26 FOREIGN TRADE

Iraq's most valuable export is oil, which has accounted for up to 99% of total export value. Iraq is traditionally the world's largest exporter of dates, with its better varieties going to Western Europe, Australia, and North America. Like oil exports, date exports were drastically reduced due to the war with Iran.

Non-oil exports (often illegal) were estimated at $2 billion for the 12 months following the March 1991 ceasefire. During 1992 Iraq exported 50,000 barrels per day of crude oil and products to Jordan and 20,000 barrels per day of products to Turkey. Iraq's regular trading partners include Brazil, Turkey, and Romania. The US, Japan, and Germany topped the list of two-way trade, while the United Kingdom was an important importer to Iraq.

27 ENERGY AND POWER

Iraq has the second-largest petroleum reserves in the Middle East (after Sa'udi Arabia), with proved deposits estimated at 100 billion barrels in 1992. Because of the war with Iran and the Gulf War, crude oil production fell drastically, from 2,897,000 barrels per day in 1989 to an estimated 450,000 barrels per day in 1992. In 1984,

Selected Social Indicators

These statistics are estimates for the period 1988 to 1993. For comparison purposes, data for the United States and averages for low-income countries and high-income countries are also given.

Indicator	Iraq	Low-income countries	High-income countries	United States
Per capita gross national product†	$1,940	$380	$23,680	$24,740
Population growth rate	2.5%	1.9%	0.6%	1.0%
Population growth rate in urban areas	3.2%	3.9%	0.8%	1.3%
Population per square kilometer of land	43	78	25	26
Life expectancy in years	66	62	77	76
Number of people per physician	1,724	>3,300	453	419
Number of pupils per teacher (primary school)	22	39	<18	20
Illiteracy rate (15 years and older)	40%	41%	<5%	<3%
Energy consumed per capita (kg of oil equivalent)	1,103	364	5,203	7,918

† The gross national product (GNP) is the total dollar value of all goods and services produced by a country in a year. The per capita GNP is calculated by dividing a country's GNP by its population. The World Bank defines low-income countries as those with a per capita GNP of $695 or less. High-income countries have a per capita GNP of $8,626 or more. Less than 14% of the world's 5.5 billion people live in high-income countries, while almost 60% live in low-income countries.

> = greater than   < = less than

Sources: World Bank, *Social Indicators of Development 1995*, Baltimore: Johns Hopkins University Press, 1995. Central Intelligence Agency, *World Fact Book*, Washington, D.C.: Government Printing Office, 1994.

Iraq produced and marketed 28 billion cubic feet of natural gas.

Total electricity production in 1991 was 20,810 million kilowatt hours. The country's generating capacity was about 9,000 megawatts in 1991. Iraq's power installations were repeated targets of Iranian air attacks in the 1980s, and were badly damaged during the conflict in the Persian Gulf in 1990.

28 SOCIAL DEVELOPMENT

A social security law passed in 1971 provides benefits or payments for disability, maternity, old age, unemployment, sickness, and funerals. Although Iraq's constitution guarantees individual rights, the government sharply limits political freedoms and tolerates little public expression of dissent. The government supports equality for women, who make up about 20% of the work force.

29 HEALTH

In 1992, 93% of the population had access to health care services. Considerable effort has been made to expand medical facilities to small towns and more remote areas of the country. In 1992, Iraq had 58 doctors per 100,000 people. In 1990, there were 1.6 hospital beds per 1,000 inhabitants. Life expectancy in 1992 averaged 66 years.

30 HOUSING

In the last 20 years, living conditions for the vast majority of the population have improved greatly. Electricity and running water are normal features of all Iraqi villages in rural areas. Mud huts in remote places are rapidly being replaced by brick dwellings. Traditionally, Iraqis have lived in single-family dwellings, but in the last 15 years, the government has built a number of high-rise apartments, especially in Baghdād, to control urban sprawl. According to the latest available information, total housing units numbered 2,478,000 with 6.5 people per dwelling.

31 EDUCATION

An estimated 60% of adults were literate in 1990, 69.8% of men and 49.3% of women. In 1990, 3,328,212 students attended 8,917 primary schools and 1,166,859 attended secondary schools. Primary schools provide a six-year course, and secondary schools have a three-year intermediate course, followed by a two-year course in preparation for entrance to college. There are seven universities in Iraq, the most important being the University of Baghdād.

32 MEDIA

All communications media are owned and controlled by the government, and criticism of government policies is not permitted. The two leading Arabic newspapers in 1991 were *Al-Thawra* (circulation 200,000) and *Al-Jumhuriyah* (35,000).

The government's Radio Baghdād transmits in Arabic and also has English, Kurdish, and some other foreign-language broadcasts. In 1991 there were two government-operated stations. In the same year, there were about 4,020,000 radios, 1,380,000 television sets, and 886,133 telephones in use in Iraq.

33 TOURISM AND RECREATION

Tourism declined sharply during Iraq's occupation of Kuwait and the Gulf War. In 1991, 267,743 visitors arrived in Iraq, 73% from the Middle East. Many visitors from other Arab states are pilgrims to Islamic shrines. The other main tourist attraction is visiting the varied archeological sites. Popular forms of recreation include tennis, cricket, swimming, and squash.

34 FAMOUS IRAQIS

The most famous kings in ancient times were the Babylonian rulers Hammurabi (r.1792?–1750? BC), and Nebuchadnezzar II (Nabu-kadurri-utsur, r.605?–560? BC). The best-known contemporary Iraqi political leader is General Saddam Hussein (Husayn) al-Takriti (b. 1937), who has served as president of the country since 1979.

35 BIBLIOGRAPHY

Bulloch, John. *Saddam's War: The Origins of the Kuwait Conflict and the International Response.* Boston: Faber and Faber, 1991.

Foster, L. *Iraq.* Chicago: Children's Press, 1991.

Gunter, Michael M. *The Kurds of Iraq: Tragedy and Hope.* New York: St. Martin's Press, 1992.

Hitchens, Christopher. "Struggle of the Kurds." *National Geographic*, August 1992, 32–62.

Severy, Merle. "Iraq: Crucible of Civilization." *National Geographic*, May 1991, 102–115.

Simons, G. L. *Iraq: From Sumer to Saddam.* New York: St. Martin's Press, 1994.

IRELAND

Éire

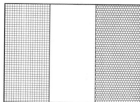

CAPITAL: Dublin (Baile Átha Cliath).

FLAG: The national flag is a tricolor of green, white, and orange vertical stripes.

ANTHEM: *Amhrán na bhFiann (The Soldier's Song).*

MONETARY UNIT: The Irish pound (£) of 100 pence, formerly exchangeable at par with the pound sterling, has floated within the European Monetary System since 1979. Decimal coinage was introduced in February 1971 to replace the former duodecimal system, in which the Irish pound had been divided into 20 shillings of 12 pence each. There are coins of 1, 2, 5, 10, 20, and 50 pence and notes of 1, 5, 10, 20, 50, and 100 pounds. £1 = $0.6970 (or $1 = £1.4347).

WEIGHTS AND MEASURES: As of 1988, Ireland has largely converted from the British system of weights and measures to the metric system.

HOLIDAYS: New Year's Day, 1 January; St. Patrick's Day, 17 March; Bank Holidays, 1st Monday in June, 1st Monday in August, and last Monday in October; Christmas Day, 25 December; St. Stephen's Day, 26 December. Movable religious holidays include Good Friday and Easter Monday.

TIME: GMT.

1 LOCATION AND SIZE

Ireland is an island in the eastern part of the North Atlantic Ocean, west of Britain and northwest of continental Europe. It covers an area of 84,421 square kilometers (32,595 square miles), of which 70,282 square kilometers (27,136 square miles) are in the Irish Republic (Ireland) and the remainder in Northern Ireland, a part of the United Kingdom. Comparatively, Ireland is slightly larger than the state of West Virginia.

2 TOPOGRAPHY

Ireland is a limestone plateau rimmed by coastal highlands. The central plain area, characterized by many lakes, bogs, and scattered low ridges, averages about 90 meters (300 feet) above sea level. Principal mountain ranges include the Wicklow Mountains in the east and Macgillycuddy's Reeks in the southwest. The highest peaks are Carrantuohill (1,041 meters/3,414 feet) and Mt. Brandon (953 meters/3,127 feet), near Killarney, and Lugnaquillia (926 meters/3,039 feet), 64 kilometers (40 miles) south of Dublin.

The coastline, 3,169 kilometers (1,969 miles) long, is heavily indented along the south and west coasts. On the southern coast, river channels have created deep natural harbors. The east coast has few good harbors. Most important of the many rivers is the Shannon, which rises in the mountains along the Ulster border and drains the central plain as it flows 370 kilometers (230 miles) to the Atlantic.

3 CLIMATE

Because of its location in the Atlantic Ocean, Ireland is warmer in winter and cooler in summer than continental Europe. The mean annual temperature is 10°C (50°F), and mean monthly temperatures range from a mild 4°C (39°F) in January to 15°C (59°F) in July. Average yearly rainfall ranges from less than 76 centimeters (30 inches) in places near Dublin on the Irish Sea coast to more than 254 centimeters (100 inches) in some mountainous regions. The sunniest area is the extreme southeast, with an annual average of 1,700 hours of bright sunshine. Winds are strongest near the west coast, where the average speed is about 26 kilometers per hour (16 miles per hour).

4 PLANTS AND ANIMALS

Ireland, once connected to Britain by land, was completely covered by ice sheets during the most recent Ice Age. Consequently, all plant and animal life originated from the natural migration of species, chiefly from other parts of Europe and especially from Britain. However, by 6000 BC the sea had flowed over the land and left Ireland a separate island. With the land bridge gone, the natural migration of plants and animals stopped.

Forest is the natural dominant vegetation, but the total forest area is now only 6% of the total area. The wildlife of Ireland is basically similar to that of Britain and includes foxes, hares, rabbits, and mice, but there are some notable gaps. Among those absent are weasel, polecat, wildcat, most shrews, moles, roe deer, snakes, and common toads. There are also fewer bird and insect species. Among the common domestic animals, Ireland is particularly noted for the Connemara pony, Irish wolfhound, and the Kerry blue terrier.

5 ENVIRONMENT

Industry is a significant source of pollution in Ireland. Ireland produces 1.5 million tons of solid waste and 56,000 tons of hazardous wastes per year. The nation produces 70.5 tons of hydrocarbon emissions and 128.9 tons of particulate emissions per year. However, Ireland enjoys the benefits of a climate in which calms are rare and the winds sufficiently strong to disperse atmospheric pollution. As of 1994, none of Ireland's mammal species were endangered, but 10 of its bird species and 4 plant species were threatened with extinction.

6 POPULATION

According to the official 1991 census, the population was 3,523,401. The United Nations has projected a population of 3,436,000 for the year 2000. About two-fifths of the inhabitants live in rural areas. The largest urban center (excluding suburbs) is Dublin with a population of 477,675. The population density was 50 persons per square kilometers (130 persons per square miles) in 1991.

7 MIGRATION

The great famine in the late 1840s inaugurated the wave of Irish emigrants to the

US, Canada, Argentina, and other countries. By 1851 over 550,000 people had left Ireland. Since then, emigration has been a traditional feature of Irish life. Emigration slowed after World War II but picked up again early in the 1980s when Ireland's economy fell into a deep recession. With unemployment at record highs, it was estimated that up to 7% of the population left the country. As the economy improved emigration slowed and in 1992 Ireland recorded a net gain from migration.

8 ETHNIC GROUPS

Within historic times, Ireland has been inhabited by Celts, Norsemen, French Normans, and English. Through the centuries, the racial strains represented by these groups have been so intermingled that no purely ethnic divisions remain.

9 LANGUAGES

Two languages are spoken, English and Irish (Gaelic). Although Gaelic is taught as a compulsory subject in schools, English remains the language in common use. Only in a few areas (the Gaeltacht), mostly along the western seaboard, is Irish in everyday use.

10 RELIGIONS

There is no established church, but in 1993, about 95% of the population was Roman Catholic. Members of the Church of Ireland were estimated at 4%, other Protestants 1%, and Jews 0.07%.

LOCATION: 51°30′ to 55°30′N; 6° to 10°30′W. **BOUNDARY LENGTHS:** Northern Ireland, 434 kilometers (270 miles); total coastline, 3,169 kilometers (1,969 miles). **TERRITORIAL SEA LIMIT:** 3 miles.

11 TRANSPORTATION

A network of good main roads extends throughout the country and bus routes connect all the major population centers. In 1991 there were 92,294 kilometers

(57,351 miles) of roads, of which 87,422 kilometers (54,324 miles) were surfaced and 4,872 kilometers (3,027 miles) were gravel or crushed stone. Automobiles numbered 828,225; trucks, 148,882; motorcycles, 24,465; and public service vehicles, 9,731. Ireland's railroads, like those of many other European countries, have become increasingly unprofitable because of competition from trucks. There were 1,947 kilometers (1,210 miles) of track in 1991.

There are deepwater ports at Cork and Dublin. Dublin is the main port. Aer Lingus, the Irish national airline, operates services between Ireland and the rest of the world. It carried 2,318,700 passengers in 1992. A domestic airline, Aer Árann Teo, connects Galway with the Aran Islands and Dublin. The three state airports are located at Dublin, Shannon, and Cork.

Photo credit: Irish Tourist Board.

Cobh, near Cork, County Cork.

12 HISTORY

The pre-Christian era in Ireland is known chiefly through legend, although there is archaeological evidence that humans inhabited the region during the Stone and Bronze ages. In about the fourth century BC, the tall, red-haired Celts from Gaul or Galicia arrived, bringing with them the Iron Age. They subdued the native peoples, the Picts in the north and the Érainn tribe in the south, then settled down to establish a Gaelic civilization, absorbing many of the traditions of the previous inhabitants. By the third century AD, the Gaels had established five permanent kingdoms—Ulster, Connacht, Leinster, Meath (North Leinster), and Munster. The kings of these five kingdoms were themselves ruled by a high king at Tara, although his position was primarily ceremonial. After St. Patrick's arrival in AD 432, Christian Ireland rapidly became a center of Latin and Gaelic learning. Irish monasteries drew not only the pious but also the intellectuals of the day, and sent out missionaries to many parts of Europe.

Toward the end of the eighth century, the Vikings began their invasions, destroying monasteries and wreaking havoc on the land, but also intermarrying, adopting Irish customs, and establishing coastal settlements from which have grown Ireland's chief cities. Viking power was finally broken at the Battle of Clontarf in 1014.

About 150 years later, the Anglo-Norman invasions began. Gradually, the invaders gained control of the whole country. Many of them intermarried, adopted the Irish language, customs, and traditions, and became more Irish than the Gaels. But the political attachment to the English crown instituted by the Norman invasion caused almost 800 years of strife, as successive English monarchs sought to subdue Gaels and Norman-Irish alike. Wholesale confiscations of land by the English began under England's Queen Mary I (Mary Tudor) in the 1550s and continued under Elizabeth I, Cromwell, and William III. Treatment of the Irish reached a brutal climax in the eighteenth century with the Penal Laws, which deprived Catholics and Dissenters (those opposed to English rule: the majority of the population) of all legal rights.

By the end of the eighteenth century, many of the English colonists had come to regard themselves as Irish and, like the English colonists in America, resented the domination of London and their own lack of power to rule themselves. In 1783, they forced the establishment of an independent Irish parliament, but it was abolished by the Act of Union (1800), which gave Ireland direct representation in the English parliament. Catholic emancipation was finally achieved in 1829 through the efforts of Daniel O'Connell, but the great famine of the 1840s, when millions died or emigrated for lack of potatoes while landlords continued to export other crops to England, emphasized the tragic condition of the Irish peasant and the need for land reform.

The desire for independence from England continued to grow and after a sometimes bloody struggle, the Anglo-Irish Treaty was signed in 1921. The treaty did not give Ireland complete independence but did established an Irish Free State with dominion status in the British Commonwealth. Dominion status gave Ireland more control over its affairs, but forced Ireland to accept the British monarch as its chief-of-state. The treaty also split Ireland along religious lines. Unlike the rest of Ireland, Protestant-dominated Northern Ireland remained a part of the UK. Violent opposition to dominion status and to a separate government in Northern Ireland precipitated a civil war that lasted almost a year (1922–23). Pro-treaty forces won the war and the Irish Free State was officially proclaimed. In 1937 a new Irish constitution was enacted and the name of the country was officially changed to Ireland (Éire in Irish).

Dominion status proved to be short-lived and in 1948 Ireland voted itself out of the Commonwealth of Nations. On 18 April 1949, it declared itself a republic. Ireland was admitted to the UN in 1955 and became a member of the European Community (EC) in 1973.

Even after independence, sentiment in favor of a reunified Irish Republic remained strong, represented at its extreme by the terrorist activities of the Irish Republican Army (IRA). During the civil violence that disrupted Northern Ireland from the late 1960s on, the Irish government attempted to curb the "provisional wing" of the IRA. This part of the

Scene along the Irish coast.

IRA tried to intimidate the government through ongoing bombings, assasinations, and other types of terrorist means, often using Ireland as a base for attacks in the north. Despite all government efforts, terrorist acts continued.

Over the past 25 years, blodshed over Northern Ireland has left more than 3,000 people dead. Although progress has been made in ending discrimination against Catholics in housing and employment, they are twice as likely as Protestants to be unemployed.

On 22 February 1995, Britain and Ireland issued a set of proposals aimed at bringing peace to Northern Ireland. Both parties agreed to allow Northern Ireland to decide its own fate without interference from either country.

13 GOVERNMENT

Under the Irish constitution legislative power is vested in the national parliament (*Oireachtas*), which consists of the president and two houses—House of Representatives (*Dáil Éireann*) and Senate (*Seanad Éireann*). The parliament sits in Dublin, the capital city. The president is elected by popular vote for seven years. The Dáil consists of 166 seats and the Seanad 60. Suffrage, the right to vote, is universal at age 18.

14 POLITICAL PARTIES

The major political parties are Fianna Fáil, Fine Gael, the Progressive Democrats, the Democratic Left, and the Labour Party.

Fianna Fáil, the Republican party, was in power for all but 6 years during the period from 1932 to 1973, when it lost its majority to a Fine Gael–Labour coalition. In recent years both Fine Gael and Fianna Fáil have lost seats to the Labour Party, which is now the third largest political party in Ireland.

15 JUDICIAL SYSTEM

Justice is administered by a Supreme Court, a high court with full original jurisdiction, and circuit and district courts with local and limited jurisdiction. Individual liberties are protected by the 1937 Constitution and by Supreme Court decisions.

16 ARMED FORCES

The army and its reserves, the air corps, and the naval service are small but well-trained. The army (11,200 regulars, 15,000 reserves) is supplied with British and European weapons and equipment. A navy of 1,000 mans 7 patrol craft. The air force (800) has 16 combat aircraft and 15 armed helicopters.

17 ECONOMY

Until the 1950s, Ireland had a predominantly agricultural economy. However, liberal trade policies and the drive for industrialization have stimulated economic expansion. Now agriculture accounts for only 10.5% of the gross national product (GNP), down from 21%

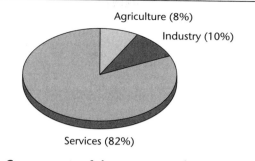

Components of the economy. This pie chart shows how much of the country's economy is devoted to agriculture (includes forestry, hunting, and fishing), industry, or services.

in 1958. Industry, on the other hand, went from 23.5% to 44.5%.

During the early 1980s, Ireland suffered from the worldwide recession, experiencing double-digit inflation and high unemployment. The economy continued to lag through 1986 when unemployment soared to 18% (from 10% in 1981). Although the economy subsequently grew 30% between 1987 and 1992, unemployment remained high; the rate was 16.8% in 1993. Inflation, however, was reduced from 20.4% in 1981 to 1.4% in 1993, its lowest level in 25 years. Today, Ireland is among the least developed countries in the EC and economic growth continues to be hampered by a large public debt and high unemployment.

18 INCOME

In 1992, Ireland's gross national product (GNP) was $42,798 million, or about $13,000 per person.

19 INDUSTRY

Today, the most important products of manufacturing are food, metal and engineering goods, electronics and data processing (including computer programing), engineering, chemicals and chemical products, nonmetallic minerals, and paper and printing.

20 LABOR

In 1992, the total civilian work force was estimated at 1,350,000, of whom 16.1% were unemployed. Of those employed in 1992, 13% were in agriculture, forestry, and fishing (down from 16% in 1986); 28% in industry (unchanged from 1986); and 59% in services (56% in 1986).

About 58% of the labor force is organized into 70 trade unions (1992), affiliated with the Irish Congress of Trade Unions, formed in 1959 by the merger of the Irish Trade Union Congress and the Congress of Irish Unions. The standard workweek is 40 hours, based on 5 days at 8 hours a day. In 1992, there were 38 strikes involving 13,107 workers resulting in 190,609 lost workdays.

21 AGRICULTURE

About 5.6 million hectares (13.9 million acres), or 82% of the total land area, are devoted to agricultural activities. Most of the farmland is used to support livestock, the leading source of Ireland's exports. Most farms are small, although there has been a trend toward consolidation. Principal crops (with their estimated 1992 production) include barley, 1,300,000 tons; sugar beets, 1,380,000 tons; potatoes, 620,000 tons; wheat, 680,000 tons; and oats, 100,000 tons.

22 DOMESTICATED ANIMALS

The main activity of the farming community is the production of grazing animals and other livestock. The estimated livestock population in December 1992 was 6,073,000 head of cattle, 6,187,000 sheep, 1,134,000 hogs, and 9,000,000 poultry. In 1992, butter production totaled about 137,000 tons; cheese, 85,250 tons; and wool (greasy), 19,000 tons. Milk production in 1992 was 5,494,000 tons.

23 FISHING

The total volume of all fish caught in 1991 was 240,703 tons, including 75,256 tons of Atlantic mackerel. Leading varieties of saltwater fish are mackerel, herring, cod, whiting, plaice, ray, skate, and haddock. Lobsters, crawfish, and Dublin Bay prawns are also important. Salmon is Ireland's most important inland species.

24 FORESTRY

Once well forested, Ireland was stripped of timber in the seventeenth and eighteenth centuries by absentee landlords, who converted the forests into farms and grazing lands. In an effort to restore part of the woodland areas, a state forestry program was inaugurated in 1903. By 1991, about 6% of Ireland was forested, up from 5% in 1980. About 95% of the trees planted are evergreens.

25 MINING

Mineral production in 1991 included 429,000 tons of gypsum, 8,500,000 tons

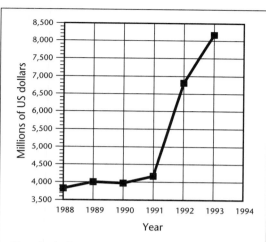

Yearly balance of trade measured in millions of US dollars. The balance of trade is the difference between what a country sells to other countries (its exports) and what it buys (its imports). If a country imports more than it exports, it has a negative balance of trade (a trade deficit). If exports exceed imports there is a positive balance of trade (a trade surplus).

of limestone, and 80,000 tons of barites. Other commercially exploited minerals include lead, zinc, copper, gypsum, salt, clays and shales, dolomite, diatomite, building stone, and aggregate building materials.

In 1989, gold was discovered in County Mayo, with an estimated 498,000 tons of ore with at least 1.5 grams of gold per ton of ore. In 1990, Ireland mined an estimated 45,000 tons of coal which was used for electricity production.

26 FOREIGN TRADE

Ireland's primary exports include computer equipment, chemicals, meat, dairy products, and machinery. In 1992, 31.5% of total Irish exports went to Great Britain and Northern Ireland, 8.2% went to the US. Primary imports include grains, petroleum products, machinery, transport equipment, chemicals, and textile yarns. Major suppliers of imports are Great Britain (38%), other EC countries (28%), and the US (12%).

27 ENERGY AND POWER

Government policy has been to provide adequate energy to meet industrial, commercial, and private domestic needs from native resources. Still, of all EC members, Ireland is the most dependent on imported oil for its energy needs. Hydroelectric plants have been built on the Shannon, Lee, Liffey, and Erne rivers. Natural gas fields exist in the Atlantic Ocean and in fields south of Cork, but reserves are quickly being exhausted. Turf or peat from the extensive Irish bogs supplies the staple fuel for many homes and is utilized as intermediate fuel for electricity production. In 1991, over 6.2 million tons of peat were processed for fuel.

28 SOCIAL DEVELOPMENT

Since 1 April 1974, all wage and salary earners between the ages of 16 and 68 have been covered by a compulsory social insurance program, including unemployment insurance, disability benefits, retirement and old age pensions, widows' pensions, maternity benefits, and a death grant. The predominance of the Roman Catholic Church has had a significant impact on social legislation. Both divorce and abortion are illegal in Ireland. Although a 1986 referendum to pave the way for legalization of divorce under certain circumstances was defeated by a large margin, the measuse is sure to be placed on the ballot again in the future. Contraceptives, the sale of which had been entirely prohibited, became available to married couples by prescription in the early 1980s; the need for a prescription was abolished in 1985. Also in 1985, the minimum age for marriage was raised from 14 to 18 for girls and from 16 to 18 for boys. Since then, Ireland's birth rate has plummeted and now is in line with those of most other European countries.

In 1990, the government established the Second Commission on the Status of Women, to help bring about the participation of women in all aspects of Irish society. Although the number of married women who hold paying jobs has increased in recent years, only a third of Irish women work outside the home.

Photo credit: Irish Tourist Board.

Faces of the Irish.

29 HEALTH

Health services are provided by the Department of Health. A comprehensive health service, with free hospitalization, treatment, and medication, is provided for low-income groups. A somewhat reduced list of services is offered free to the rest of the population. In 1992 there were 4 hospital beds per 1,000 people and 1 physician for every 633 people.

Infant mortality has been reduced from 50.3 per 1,000 live births in 1948 to 18 in 1972 and 5 in 1992. Tuberculosis, long a major cause of adult deaths, declined from 3,700 cases in 1947 to only 18 per 100,000 in 1990. Average life expectancy at birth in 1992 was 75 years.

30 HOUSING

Government subsidies are given to encourage home ownership, and local authorities provide housing for those unable to house themselves adequately. In 1992, over 20,600 new private dwellings were completed.

31 EDUCATION

Education is compulsory for nine years. In 1990, there were 416,747 pupils in 3,320 primary schools; 345,941 in postprimary schools; and 90,296 students in higher

Selected Social Indicators

These statistics are estimates for the period 1988 to 1993. For comparison purposes, data for the United States and averages for low-income countries and high-income countries are also given.

Indicator	Ireland	Low-income countries	High-income countries	United States
Per capita gross national product†	**$13,000**	$380	$23,680	$24,740
Population growth rate	**0.3%**	1.9%	0.6%	1.0%
Population growth rate in urban areas	**0.5%**	3.9%	0.8%	1.3%
Population per square kilometer of land	**50**	78	25	26
Life expectancy in years	**75**	62	77	76
Number of people per physician	**633**	>3,300	453	419
Number of pupils per teacher (primary school)	**25**	39	<18	20
Illiteracy rate (15 years and older)	**2%**	41%	<5%	<3%
Energy consumed per capita (kg of oil equivalent)	**3,016**	364	5,203	7,918

† The gross national product (GNP) is the total dollar value of all goods and services produced by a country in a year. The per capita GNP is calculated by dividing a country's GNP by its population. The World Bank defines low-income countries as those with a per capita GNP of $695 or less. High-income countries have a per capita GNP of $8,626 or more. Less than 14% of the world's 5.5 billion people live in high-income countries, while almost 60% live in low-income countries.

> = greater than   < = less than

Sources: World Bank, *Social Indicators of Development 1995,* Baltimore: Johns Hopkins University Press, 1995. Central Intelligence Agency, *World Fact Book,* Washington, D.C.: Government Printing Office, 1994.

level schools. There were 15,614 teachers at the primary level; 20,830 at the general secondary level; and 5,598 at higher level institutions. Ireland has two universities, the University of Dublin (Trinity College) and the National University of Ireland, and various colleges of education, home economics, technology, and the arts.

32 MEDIA

All postal, telegraph, telex, and telephone services are controlled and operated by the government. In 1991 there were approximately 942,000 telephones in use. Radio Telefís Éireann is the Irish national broadcasting organization. In addition to a radio broadcasting it runs two color television stations. Ireland's second radio service, Radio na Gaeltachta, broadcasting in Irish, was inaugurated in 1972. There were some 2,200,000 radios and 829,000 television sets in 1991.

Four daily newspapers and three Sunday papers issued in Dublin (including the *Sunday World* with a circulation of 255,000) circulate throughout the country, while two dailies and one weekly published in Cork are read widely in the southern half of the country. Smaller cities and towns have their own newspapers, most of them weeklies.

[33] TOURISM AND RECREATION

A total of 3,535,000 tourists entered Ireland in 1991, of whom 86% were from Europe and 10% from North America. Among Ireland's numerous ancient and prehistoric sights are a restored Bronze Age lake dwelling (crannog) near Quin in County Clare, burial mounds at Newgrange and Knowth along the Boyne, and the palace at the Hill of Tara, the seat of government up to the Middle Ages. Numerous castles may be visited, including Blarney Castle in County Cork, where visitors kiss the famous Blarney Stone.

Other popular attractions include Trinity College Library, with its 8th-century illuminated *Book of Kells;* and literary landmarks associated with such writers as William Butler Yeats, James Joyce, Jonathan Swift, and Oscar Wilde.

Ireland has numerous golf courses, some of worldwide reputation. Fishing, sailing, horseback riding, hunting, horse racing, and greyhound racing are other popular sports. The traditional sports of Gaelic football, hurling, and camogie (the women's version of hurling) were revived in the 19th century and have become increasingly popular.

[34] FAMOUS IRISH

A list of famous Irish must begin with St. Patrick (c.385–461), who, though not born in Ireland, represents Ireland to the rest of the world.

Famous warriors include Brian Boru (c.962–1014), who temporarily united the kings of Ireland and defeated the Vikings.

More recently, Éamon de Valera (b. US, 1882–1975), fought Ireland's political battles for Irish independence and became the first president of Ireland. Maud Gonne (c.1865–1953), called the "Irish Joan of Arc," not only inspired much of William Butler Yeats poetry, but also was instrumental in Ireland's independence movement.

Outstanding scientists include Robert Boyle (1627–91), the physicist who defined Boyle's law relating to pressure and volume of gas.

Ireland is particularly proud of its writers. After the Restoration, many brilliant satirists in English literature were born in Ireland, among them Jonathan Swift (1667–1745), dean of St. Patrick's Cathedral in Dublin and creator of *Gulliver's Travels.* More recently Nobel Prize-winning poet-dramatist William Butler Yeats (1865–1939) led a great literary revival that produced a succession of famous playwrights, poets, novelists, and short-story writers.

[35] BIBLIOGRAPHY

A New History of Ireland. Oxford: Clarendon Press, 1993.

Conniff, Richard. "Ireland on Fast-Forward." *National Geographic,* September 1994, 2–36.

Foster, R. F. (ed.). *The Oxford Illustrated History of Ireland.* New York: Oxford University Press, 1989.

Fradin, D. *The Republic of Ireland.* Chicago: Children's Press, 1984.

Nagel, Rob, and Anne Commire. "Saint Patrick." In *World Leaders, People Who Shaped the World.* Volume II: Europe. Detroit: U*X*L, 1994.

ISRAEL

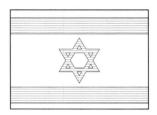

State of Israel

[Arabic:] *Dawlat Israel* [Hebrew:] *Medinat Yisrael*

CAPITAL: Jerusalem (Yerushalayim, Al-Quds).

FLAG: The flag, which was adopted at the First Zionist Congress in 1897, consists of a blue six-pointed Shield of David (Magen David) centered between two blue horizontal stripes on a white field.

ANTHEM: *Hatikvah (The Hope).*

MONETARY UNIT: The new Israeli shekel (NIS), a paper currency of 100 new agorot, replaced the shekel (IS) at a rate of 1,000 to 1 in 1985; the shekel replaced the Israeli pound (IL) in 1980 at the rate of 10 pounds per shekel. There are coins of 5, 10, and 50 agora, 1 and 5 shekels and notes of 10, 50, 100, and 200 shekels. NIS1 = $0.3368 (or $1 = NIS2.9690).

WEIGHTS AND MEASURES: The metric system is the legal standard, but some local units are used, notably the dunam (equivalent to 1,000 square meters, or about 0.25 acre).

HOLIDAYS: Israel officially uses both the Gregorian and the complex Jewish lunisolar calendars, but the latter determines the occurrence of national holidays: Rosh Hashanah (New Year), September or October; Yom Kippur (Day of Atonement), September or October; Sukkot (Tabernacles), September or October; Simhat Torah (Rejoicing in the Law), September or October; Pesach (Passover), March or April; Independence Day, April or May; and Shavuot (Pentecost), May or June. All Jewish holidays, as well as the Jewish Sabbath (Friday/ Saturday), begin just before sundown and end at nightfall 24 hours later. Muslim, Christian, and Druze holidays are observed by the respective minorities.

TIME: 2 PM = noon GMT.

1 LOCATION AND SIZE

Situated in southwestern Asia along the eastern end of the Mediterranean Sea, Israel claims an area of 20,770 square kilometers (8,019 square miles), slightly larger than the state of New Jersey. This total includes the Golan Heights area (1,176 square kilometers/454 square miles), part of the territory captured from Syria during the Six-Day War in 1967. Other territories captured in 1967 and classified as administered territories were the West Bank (also known as Judea and Samaria), 5,878 square kilometers (2,270 square miles); and the Gaza Strip, 362 square kilometers (140 square miles). Israel's total boundary length was 1,102 kilometers (684 miles) in 1988, including the administered areas.

Israel's capital city, Jerusalem, is located near the center of the country.

2 TOPOGRAPHY

The country is divided into three major longitudinal strips: the coastal plain; the hill region, stretching from the hills in the north through Samaria and Judea (also called the West Bank) in the center to the Negev in the south; and the Jordan Valley. The Jordan River, forming the border between Israel (including the West Bank) and Jordan, links the only bodies of water in the country: the Sea of Galilee (Yam Kinneret) and the very salty Dead Sea (Yam ha-Melah). The Dead Sea is the lowest point on the earth's surface, at 393 meters (1,290 feet) below sea level.

3 CLIMATE

Although climatic conditions are varied across the country, the climate is generally temperate. The coldest month is January; the hottest, August. Temperatures range from between 4° and 10°C (40°–50°F) in the hills in January to as high as 49°C (120°F) in August in Elat, in the south. The rainy season lasts from November until April, with rainfall averaging 108 centimeters (43 inches) annually near the Sea of Galilee and only 2 centimeters (0.8 inches) at Elat.

4 PLANTS AND ANIMALS

The Bible (Deuteronomy 8:8) describes the country as "a land of wheat and barley, of vines and fig trees and pomegranates, a land of olive trees and honey." The original forests, evergreen and maquis (scrubby underbrush), have largely been destroyed, but some 200 million new trees have been planted during this century in a major reforestation program. Citrus fruit can be grown in the coastal plain and tropical fruit near the Jordan River.

Surviving animals include jackals, hyenas, and wild boar. With the increase in vegetation and water supplies, bird life and deer have increased.

5 ENVIRONMENT

In 1994, water pollution from industrial and agricultural chemicals and adequate water supply were major environmental issues in Israel. Israel has only 0.4 cubic miles of water with 79% used for farming activity and 5% used for industrial purposes. Ninety-seven percent of the people living in rural areas have pure water. Air pollution from industrial sources, oil facilities, and vehicles is another serious environmental problem.

The planting of new trees, especially since 1948, has helped to conserve the country's water resources and prevent soil erosion. Israel has reclaimed much of the Negev for farming by means of large irrigation projects.

As of 1994, 8 mammal species and 15 bird species are endangered. Three species of plants are threatened with extinction.

6 POPULATION

The population was estimated at 5,195,000 at the end of 1992. A population of 6,023,200 was projected for the year 2000. The estimated population density for the period of 1988–93 was 239 persons per square kilometer (618 per square mile). Tel Aviv-Yafo had a metropolitan population of 356,900 in 1992. The population of Jerusalem, the capital, was 556,500. In the same year, 1,051,500 persons lived on the West Bank (also called Judea and Samaria), and 716,800 in the Gaza Strip.

7 MIGRATION

In 1948, 65% of Israel's Jewish population consisted of immigrants. Many had fled from persecution in Russia. Others came from Central and Eastern Europe, especially during the Nazi period. Israel's declaration of independence publicly opened the state "to the immigration of Jews from all countries of their dispersion," and the 1950 Law of Return granted every returning Jew the right to automatic citizenship. In the years 1948–92, Israel took in 2,242,500 Jewish immigrants.

In 1984–85, some 10,000 Ethiopian Jews, victims of famine, were airlifted to Israel via Sudan. The fall of communism in the former Soviet Union allowed a new exodus of Jews. Some 199,516 immigrants arrived in 1990; 176,100 in 1991; and 77,057 in 1992.

As of March 1993 there were 476,236 Palestinian refugees in the West Bank who had registered with a United Nations relief agency. The registered number in the Gaza Strip was 528,684 in mid-1991. There are also Palestinians in Jordan, Syria, and Lebanon.

8 ETHNIC GROUPS

Of the estimated population of 5,195,900 at the end of 1992, 4,242,500 (81.7%) were Jews, and 953,400 (18.3%) were non-Jews. Of the latter, 76.1% were Muslims, 14.8% were Christians, and 9.1%

LOCATION: 29°29' to 33°17'N; 34°16' to 35°41'E.
TERRITORIAL SEA LIMIT: 6 miles.

were Druzes or members of other ethnic groups. Of the Jewish population, 61.6% had been born in Israel, 25% in Europe or the Americas, and 14.4% in Asia or Africa.

Jews have traditionally been divided into Ashkenazim (Central and East Europeans) and Sephardim (Iberian Jews and their descendants). A more meaningful current division would be that between Occidentals (Jews from Europe and the United States) and Orientals (Jews from the Middle East and Africa). Oriental Jews, who are in the majority, generally believe themselves to be educationally, economically, and socially worse off in comparison to the Occidentals.

Israel's minorities are divided into a number of religious groups and include several small non-Arab national groups, such as Armenians and Circassians.

Photo credit: Susan D. Rock

Western Wall and Dome of the Rock Mosque in the Old City of Jerusalem.

9 LANGUAGES

The official languages are Hebrew and Arabic, with Hebrew being dominant. Hebrew is the language of most of the Old Testament; modern Hebrew is the biblical language as changed by development over the years. Arabic is used by Arabs in parliamentary meetings, in court cases, and in dealings with governmental departments. It is also used in schools for Arab children. English is taught in all secondary schools and, along with Hebrew, is commonly used in foreign business correspondence and in advertising and labeling.

10 RELIGIONS

The land that is now Israel (which the Romans called Judea and then Palestine) is the cradle of two religions: Judaism and Christianity. Jerusalem is the historical site of the First and Second Temples. The First Temple was built by Solomon in the tenth century BC and destroyed by the Babylonians in 586 BC. The Second Temple was built about 70 years later and sacked by the Romans in AD 70. According to the Christian Scriptures, Jesus preached in the Second Temple. Jerusalem is also holy to Islam: the Dome of the Rock marks the site where Mohammed rose into heaven.

Present-day Israel is the only country where Judaism is the majority religion, professed by more than 82% of the population. Over one-fourth of all the world's Jews live there. Most Arabs in Israel are Sunni Muslims (14%). Christians are largely Greek Catholic or Greek Orthodox, but there are also Roman Catholics, Armenians, and Protestants. The Druzes, who split away from Islam in the eleventh century, are considered a separate religious community. The Baha'i world faith is centered in Haifa (Hefa).

11 TRANSPORTATION

In 1991, there were 4,750 miles (2,952 kilometers) of highways, mostly paved. Tracks of the state-owned railway covered 594 kilometers (369 miles) in 1991. Private car ownership nearly tripled during the 1970s. In 1991 there were 1,012,639 motor vehicles, including 848,554 private cars and 164,085 trucks, taxis, and buses.

At the end of 1991, Israel had 31 merchant vessels, with a capacity of 545,000 gross registered tons. Haifa (Hefa) and Ashdod (south of Tel Aviv-Yafo) are the main ports.

Israel Airlines (El Al) operates international flights from Ben-Gurion International airport near Tel Aviv-Yafo. In 1991, the airport had 3.4 million passenger arrivals and departures. Israel Inland Airlines (Arkia) provides domestic service.

12 HISTORY

Origins

Archaeologists believe that the world's earliest known city was Jericho, on the present-day West Bank, built about 7000 BC. Israel's formative period began in approximately 1800 BC, when the Hebrews entered Canaan, the Biblical Promised Land. After a period in Egypt, they returned to Canaan in approximately 1200 BC. The land was then conquered by Assyrians, Babylonians (or Chaldeans), Persians, and Greeks. The Romans conquered Jerusalem and destroyed the Temple in AD 70. The ancient period ended in AD 135, when the Roman Empire exiled most Jews and renamed the region Syria Palaestina, which eventually became Palestine.

During the next 2,000 years, there were successive waves of foreign conquerors—Byzantines, Persians, Arabs, Crusaders, Mongols, Turks, and Britons. Most Jews remained scattered throughout the world (or dispersed, hence the name "diaspora" for this period). Many hoped for an eventual return to their homeland, also called Zion.

Zionism

Modern Zionism, the movement for the reestablishment of a Jewish state, dates from the late nineteenth century. The World Zionist Organization was founded in Basel, Switzerland, in 1897, under the leadership of Theodor Herzl. The British government pledged its support in 1917, in the Balfour Declaration. In 1922, the League of Nations awarded Britain the right to rule over Palestine. Under British rule, the Jewish community grew from 85,000 to 650,000, largely through immigration, on lands purchased from Arab owners. The Arab community began to feel threatened by the inpouring of Jews. In 1939 the British authorities, bowing to Arab pressure, issued a White Paper that placed severe restrictions on Jewish immigration and settlement.

Jews took up arms to resist this policy. After World War II (1939–45), other nations began to support the establishment of a Jewish state as a haven for the survivors of the Nazi Holocaust. The British government finally decided to give up their rule over Palestine. On 29 November 1947, the United Nations General Assembly adopted a plan for the division of Palestine into two economically united but politically independent states, one Jewish and the other Arab.

The Arabs of Palestine at once rose up against this division. The Jews accepted the plan. On 14 May 1948 they proclaimed the formation of the State of Israel. The next day, the Arab League states—Egypt, Iraq, Jordan, Lebanon, Sa'udi Arabia, and Syria—launched a joint armed attack. Hundreds of thousands of Palestinian Arabs fled abroad.

Arab-Israeli Conflict

The war left Israel in possession of a much larger territory than that awarded the Jews under the United Nations plan. The Arab state failed to take shape, as Jordan annexed the West Bank. Meanwhile, Palestinian refugees were resettled in camps on both banks of the Jordan River, in the Gaza Strip, in southern Lebanon, and in Syria.

Arabs periodically raided the borders, and the Israelis fought back. Tensions rose as Arab countries declared economic boycotts and Egypt nationalized the Suez Canal on 26 July 1956. On 29 October 1956, Israel (with British and French support) invaded Egypt and gained control of the Gaza Strip and the Sinai Peninsula. Fighting ended on 4 November and Israel (under pressure from the United States) withdrew from the occupied areas in March 1957.

The Six-Day War

Violations of the truce by both sides continued, and on 5 June 1967, Israel attacked Egypt and its allies, Syria and Jordan. By 11 June, Israel had scored a decisive victory in the conflict, since termed the Six-Day War. Israel took control of the Sinai Peninsula, the Gaza Strip, the Golan Heights, and the West Bank (including Jordanian-ruled East Jerusalem).

The United Nations Security Council unanimously adopted Resolution 242, calling for withdrawal of Israeli armed forces from territories occupied during the war. Israel said that return of the captured territories would have to be part of a general agreement guaranteeing peace. In 1967, the Israeli government began Jewish settlement in these areas. By 1994 there were some 120,000 settlers in the occupied territories.

In 1969 the government of neighboring Lebanon signed an agreement with the organization made up of Palestinian guerrillas known as the Palestine Liberation Organization (PLO). Lebanon agreed to allow the PLO to operate within its borders. A ceasefire between Israel and the PLO took effect in August 1970, but the PLO continued an international campaign of terrorism, highlighted in September 1972 by the kidnap and murder of Israeli athletes at the Olympic Games in Munich, Germany.

On 6 October 1973, during the Jewish high holiday of Yom Kippur, Egypt and Syria attacked Israeli-held territory in the Sinai Peninsula and the Golan Heights at the same time. The Arabs won initial victories, but by 24 October, when a United Nations ceasefire took effect, the Israelis had beaten back their attackers. Although victorious, Israel gave up some territory in the Sinai in return for concessions from Egypt.

A First Try at Peace

The 30-year cycle of Egyptian-Israeli hostilities was broken in September 1978. Israeli Prime Minister Menachem Begin and Egyptian President Anwar al-Sadat agreed on the general framework for a peace treaty which they signed in Washington, D.C., on 26 March 1979. However, the two countries failed to reach agreement on Palestinian self-rule in the West Bank and the Gaza Strip, and Israel continued to establish Jewish settlements in the West Bank despite Egyptian protests.

Other Arab countries condemned Egypt for signing the peace accord, and their relations with Israel remained tense. Hostilities between Israel and the PLO and Syria reached a climax in early June 1982. Israel launched a full-scale invasion of southern Lebanon, aimed at destroying bases from which the PLO had shelled northern Israel and initiated terrorist attacks. A negotiated ceasefire was arranged by US envoy Philip Habib on 25 June, and a multinational peacekeeping force was stationed in the Beirut area.

Israeli feelings about the Lebanese war were divided. Ariel Sharon resigned as defense minister. In 1985, Israel withdrew from southern Lebanon. In December 1987, unarmed Palestinians in Gaza began what became a long series of stone-throwing riots against Israeli troops in the occupied territories. In this uprising (or *intifada* in Arabic), over 1,000 Palestinians were killed as well as several hundred Israelis and Palestinian collaborators.

A Second Try at Peace

During the Gulf War of 1991, Israel was hit by Iraqi missile attacks, convincing some Israelis of the need to move toward peace with the Arabs. Israeli and Palestinian representatives met secretly in Oslo, Norway to work out a peace agreement involving the transfer of authority in the Gaza Strip and the West Bank city of Jericho to interim Palestinian rule. The final form of Palestinian independence was to be resolved in five years. The agreement was signed at the White House in Washington, D.C., on 13 September 1993.

The agreement was opposed by extremists on both sides and was set back by a massacre of 30 Muslims at prayer in the Al Khalil (Hebron) mosque on 25 February 1994 by a militant Israeli settler. Finally, delayed by several months, the

Photo credit: Susan D. Rock

A young boy plays on a military monument outside of Jerusalem.

withdrawal of Israeli forces and establishment of Palestinian self-rule in Gaza and Jericho took place on 18 May 1994.

On 24 September 1995, Israel and the PLO reached a further agreement that would transfer control of much of the rest of the occupied West Bank to its Arab residents. The agreement called for internationally monitored elections, an Israeli release of Palestinian prisoners, further withdrawal of Israeli troops, cooperation in efforts to find new sources of water, and guaranteed freedom of access to sacred sites by both parties. The agreement was denounced by militant Palestinian groups and by Libya.

13 GOVERNMENT

Israel is a democratic republic, with no written constitution. Legislative power resides in the single-chamber Knesset (parliament), whose 120 members are elected for four-year terms by secret vote of all citizens 18 years of age and over. The head of state is the president, who appoints the prime minister and performs ceremonial duties. The cabinet, headed by the prime minister, is collectively responsible to the Knesset.

Israel is divided into six administrative districts, each governed by a commissioner appointed by the central government.

14 POLITICAL PARTIES

Israel's multiparty system reflects the diverse origins of the people and their long practice of party politics in Zionist organizations. The Mapai (Israel Workers Party) led the first coalition governments to rule Israel after independence. It also formed the nucleus of the present socialist Israel Labor Party, which controlled Israel's governments under prime ministers Golda Meir (1969–74) and Yitzhak Rabin (1974–77).

In September 1973, four right-wing nationalist parties combined to form the Likud, which thus became the major opposition bloc in the Knesset (parliament). The Likud became the largest party in the Knesset by winning 43 seats in the May 1977 elections, and its leader Menachem Begin became prime minister. The Likud and Labor parties have been Israel's two main political groupings since that time.

15 JUDICIAL SYSTEM

Magistrates' courts in all towns are the first to hear most cases and settle petty property claims and lesser criminal charges. Three district courts, serving mainly as courts of appeal, have jurisdiction over all other actions except marriage and divorce cases. These are heard, along with other personal and religious matters, in the religious courts of the Jewish (rabbinical), Muslim (Shari'ah), Druze, and Christian communities. The 11-member Supreme Court is the court of last appeal. There is no jury system.

16 ARMED FORCES

Jewish and Druze men between the ages of 18 and 26 are drafted. Drafted Jewish women are trained for noncombat duties. Christians and Muslims may serve on a voluntary basis, but Muslims are rarely allowed to bear arms.

In 1993, the Israeli army had 134,000 active duty soldiers (114,700 draftees) and could mobilize as many as 600,000 more soldiers. There were 3 armored divisions, 4 mechanized infantry brigades, and 1 artillery brigade in the combat-ready force. The navy had 7,000 regulars, 3,300 draftees, and 10,000 reservists.

The air force had 11,000 regulars, 21,800 draftees, and 5,000 reserves. There were 662 functional combat aircraft, with 102 aircraft in reserve, and 93 armed helicopters. The reserve force (430,000) can be effectively mobilized in 48–72 hours. There are 6,000 paramilitary border police.

The Ministry of Defense's expenditure was $7.5 billion in 1992.

17 ECONOMY

The government is obliged to spend a large part of its income on defense. In addition, traditional Middle Eastern sources of supply (oil and wheat) and nearby markets for goods and services have been closed off. Israel must export on a large scale to maintain its relatively high standard of living.

Inflation, a chronic problem, became much worse in the early 1980s. By early 1983, Israel's 130% rate of consumer price inflation was the second-highest in the world. However, in 1985 and 1986, through a new economic program that included strict wage and price controls as well as an 18.8% devaluation of the shekel, Israel's economy seemed to stabilize. The triple-digit inflation had receded to 20.8% in 1989, and 9.4% by 1992.

The administered territories have expanded Israel's economic base, but living standards in these areas are much lower than in Israel proper. Agriculture dominates the economies of these regions.

18 INCOME

For the period 1988–93, Israel's gross national product (GNP) was $68 billion, or about $13,920 per person.

19 INDUSTRY

Major expansion has taken place in textiles, machinery and transport equipment, metallurgy, mineral processing, electrical products, precision instruments, and

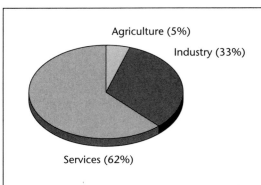

Agriculture (5%)

Industry (33%)

Services (62%)

Components of the economy. This pie chart shows how much of the country's economy is devoted to agriculture (includes forestry, hunting, and fishing), industry, or services.

chemicals. However, industry remains handicapped by reliance on imported raw materials, relatively high wage costs, and inflation.

The chief branches of industry contributing to 1990 output included food, beverages, and tobacco, $3,878 million; metal products, $2,046 million; electrical and electronic equipment, $3,173 million; chemical and oil products, $2,405 million; and transportation equipment, $1,191 million. Israel also produced about 2.5 million tons of phosphate rock and 2.1 million tons of potash in 1990.

20 LABOR

In 1992 there were 1,650,000 employed civilians in Israel, of whom 36.7% were employed in public services; 28.2% in industry, construction, and utilities; 13.9% in commerce; 10.4% in finance and business services; 6.3% in transportation; 3.5% in agriculture; and 1% in other sectors. The unemployment rate in 1991

was 11.2%. The minimum age by law for employment is 15, but the law is not strictly enforced. The majority of Israeli workers, including those in agriculture, are union members.

21 AGRICULTURE

Between 1948 and 1991, the cultivated area was expanded from 165,000 to 436,000 hectares (from 408,000 to 1,077,000 acres). Israeli agriculture emphasizes maximum use of irrigation and modern techniques to increase yields.

Principal crops and 1992 production totals (in tons) were vegetables, 1,270,000; oranges, 513,000; grapefruit, 345,000; wheat, 260,000; potatoes, 215,000; cotton, 31,000; barley, 10,000; and almonds, 3,300.

Israel's distinctive agricultural settlement is the *kibbutz*, a communal farm in which all property is owned jointly by the settlement. The land is leased from the Jewish National Fund, and work assignments, services, and social activities are determined by elected officers.

22 DOMESTICATED ANIMALS

There is little natural grazing land in most areas, and livestock is fed mainly on imported and specially grown feeds. In 1992 there were 23,000,000 chickens, 4,000,000 turkeys, 471,000 sheep and goats, 349,000 cattle, 70,000 pigs, 11,000 horses, and 10,000 camels. About 998,000 tons of milk, 198,000 tons of poultry meat, 108,600 tons of eggs, 37,000 tons of beef, and 2,200 tons of honey were produced.

23 FISHING

Jewish settlers introduced the breeding of fish (mostly carp) into Palestine. The total fish catch was 20,723 tons in 1991. In addition to carp, important freshwater fish include catfish, barbel, and trout. The marine (ocean) catch consists mainly of gray and red mullet, rainbow trout, and grouper.

24 FORESTRY

Natural forests and woodlands cover about 120,000 hectares (297,000 acres), mostly in the north. Forestry products in 1991 included 109,000 cubic meters of plywood and 200,000 tons of paper, newsprint, and cardboard.

25 MINING

The Dead Sea is one of the world's richest sources of potassium chloride (potash), magnesium bromide, and other salt. Israel is the seventh largest producer of phosphate rock, accounting for 2% of world production; the third largest potash producer, with 5% of world production; and the second largest producer of bromine and bromine compounds, accounting for more than 31% of total world production in 1991. Israel's mineral production in 1991 (in thousands of tons) included phosphate rock, 3,370; potash, 1,320; clays, 86; and glass sand, 60.

26 FOREIGN TRADE

Israel's trade deficit increased to about $6.1 billion in 1994. United States exports of nonmilitary goods to Israel amounted to $3.34 billion in 1992. Israel must

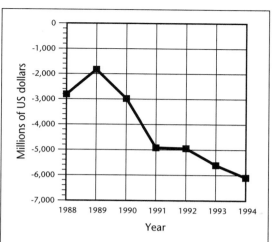

Yearly balance of trade measured in millions of US dollars. The balance of trade is the difference between what a country sells to other countries (its exports) and what it buys (its imports). If a country imports more than it exports, it has a negative balance of trade (a trade deficit). If exports exceed imports there is a positive balance of trade (a trade surplus).

import nearly all of its petroleum and most of its raw materials for industry.

Polished diamonds, chemicals, machinery, transport equipment, and various other manufactures make up about 94% of Israel's exports. Agricultural products, particularly fruits and vegetables, are also significant. Machinery and precious stones and metals were Israel's leading imports in 1991, accounting for 39% of total import value.

In 1991, Israel's chief trading partners were the United States, Germany, Belgium, and Luxembourg. In that year, the United States provided 19% of Israel's imports and took 30% of its exports.

27 ENERGY AND POWER

Israel's production of crude petroleum fell sharply after the Sinai oil fields that Israel had held since the 1967 war were returned to Egypt in 1980. In 1991, Israel produced only 82,000 barrels of crude petroleum, compared with 131,000 barrels in 1988. Domestic output of natural gas in 1991 totaled 32.2 million cubic meters.

Nearly all electricity is supplied by the government-owned Israel Electric Corporation, which uses imported oil and coal. Electricity is generated principally by thermal power stations. Generating capacity has nearly quadrupled since 1970, reaching 4,135 megawatts at the end of 1991. Total production that year amounted to some 21,320 million kilowatt hours.

28 SOCIAL DEVELOPMENT

A national insurance law, which came into force in April 1954, provides insurance for the disabled and for survivors. It also grants maternity benefits and monthly allowances for large families. Workers' compensation provisions cover employees, members of rural cooperatives, and since 1957, all of the self-employed.

Women's rights are protected by the Equal Rights for Women Law (1951) and the Employment of Women Law (1954), which requires equal pay for equal work. In 1993, a new law barred discrimination in unemployment compensation for elderly female citizens.

29 HEALTH

National expenditure on health services totaled $2,301 million in 1990. Estimated life expectancy is 77 years for both men and women. In 1988, there were 161 hospitals, 30 of which were government-operated. The Ministry of Health also operates infant welfare clinics, nursing schools, and laboratories.

30 HOUSING

From 1960 to 1985, a total of 943,350 housing units were constructed. In 1986, 94% of all housing units had piped water, 58.2% had flush toilets, and 99% had electric lighting. Between 1989 and 1991, a sudden rise in immigration from the former Soviet Union and Ethiopia resulted in a dramatic increase in housing demand. Housing starts (the number of new houses that were started to be built) increased 28% in 1991 compared to 1990. As of 1992, the total number of dwellings in Israel was 1,488,000.

31 EDUCATION

Education is compulsory for 11 years and free for all children between 5 and 16 years of age. Primary education is for 8 years followed by 4 years of secondary education. The language of instruction in Jewish schools is Hebrew; in Arab schools it is Arabic. In the period of 1988–93 the estimated literacy rate among Israelis aged 15 and over was 95% total: 97% for men and 93% for women. There were an estimated 16 pupils per teacher in primary schools for the same period. In 1990 secondary level schools had 309,098 students and 46,473 teachers.

Israel had seven institutions of higher learning in 1986/87. The two most outstanding are the Hebrew University

Selected Social Indicators

These statistics are estimates for the period 1988 to 1993. For comparison purposes, data for the United States and averages for low-income countries and high-income countries are also given.

Indicator	Israel	Low-income countries	High-income countries	United States
Per capita gross national product†	**$13,920**	$380	$23,680	$24,740
Population growth rate	**3.8%**	1.9%	0.6%	1.0%
Population growth rate in urban areas	**3.8%**	3.9%	0.8%	1.3%
Population per square kilometer of land	**239**	78	25	26
Life expectancy in years	**77**	62	77	76
Number of people per physician	**344**	>3,300	453	419
Number of pupils per teacher (primary school)	**16**	39	<18	20
Illiteracy rate (15 years and older)	**5%**	41%	<5%	<3%
Energy consumed per capita (kg of oil equivalent)	**2,607**	364	5,203	7,918

† The gross national product (GNP) is the total dollar value of all goods and services produced by a country in a year. The per capita GNP is calculated by dividing a country's GNP by its population. The World Bank defines low-income countries as those with a per capita GNP of $695 or less. High-income countries have a per capita GNP of $8,626 or more. Less than 14% of the world's 5.5 billion people live in high-income countries, while almost 60% live in low-income countries.

> = greater than   < = less than

Sources: World Bank, *Social Indicators of Development 1995,* Baltimore: Johns Hopkins University Press, 1995. Central Intelligence Agency, *World Fact Book,* Washington, D.C.: Government Printing Office, 1994.

(founded in 1918) in Jerusalem and the Israel Institute of Technology (Technion, founded in 1912) in Haifa (Hefa). In 1990, the total number of students in all higher level institutions of Israel was 119,124.

32 MEDIA

The state radio stations include the government's Israel Broadcasting Authority (Shidurei Israel), the army's Defense Forces Waves (Galei Zahal), and the Jewish Agency's Zion's Voice to the Diaspora (Kol Zion la-Gola), aimed mostly at Jewish communities in Europe and the United States. In 1991, there were 2,285,000 tele-phones, 2,290,000 radios, and 1,310,000 television sets in use.

In 1991, 30 daily newspapers and numerous periodicals were published in Hebrew, English, and other languages. The largest national daily Hebrew newspapers (with their average 1991 circulations) are *Yediot Achronot* (280,000), *Ma'ariv* (220,000), *Hadashot* (100,000), and *Ha'aretz* (70,000), all published in Tel Aviv-Yafo.

33 TOURISM AND RECREATION

In 1991, 943,259 tourists visited Israel, 24% from the United States, 12% from

France, and 8% from Germany. Tourism receipts totaled $1.3 billion. There were 28,515 rooms in hotels.

Principal tourist attractions are the many holy and historic places which include sites sacred to three religions: Judaism, Islam, and Christianity. In particular, the Old City of Jerusalem contains the Western ("Wailing") Wall, the Dome of the Rock, and the Church of the Holy Sepulchre. Nearby are the Mount of Olives and Garden of Gethsemane. Another holy place is Bethlehem (Bayt Lahm), the birthplace of both King David and Jesus.

34 FAMOUS ISRAELITES AND ISRAELIS

The State of Israel traces its ancestry to the settlement of the Hebrews in Canaan under Abraham (b. Babylonia, fl.18th century BC), the return of the Israelite tribes to Canaan under Moses (b. Egypt, fl.13th century BC), and the ancient kingdom of Israel, which was united by David (r.1000?–960? BC). During the period of Roman rule, important roles in Jewish life and learning were played by the sage Hillel (b. Babylonia, fl.30 BC–AD 9) and by Simon Bar-Kokhba (bar Kosiba, d.AD 135), leader of an unsuccessful revolt against Roman rule.

Unquestionably, the most famous Jew born in Roman Judea was Jesus (Jeshua) of Nazareth (4? BC–AD 29?), the Christ, or Messiah ("anointed one"), of Christian belief. Peter (Simon, d.AD 67?) was the first leader of the Christian Church, and Paul (Saul, b. Asia Minor, d.AD 67?) was principally responsible for the spread of Christianity.

The emergence of Israel as a modern Jewish state is due in large part to Chaim Weizmann (b. Russia, 1874–1952), the leader of the Zionist movement for 25 years. David Ben-Gurion (Gruen; b. Poland, 1886–1973) served as Israel's first prime minister.

Israel's foremost philosopher was Martin Buber (b. Vienna, 1878–1965), author of *I and Thou*. Famous musicians include Daniel Barenboim (b. Argentina, 1942), Itzhak Perlman (b. 1945), and Pinchas Zukerman (b. 1948).

35 BIBLIOGRAPHY

Belt, Don. "Israel's Galilee." *National Geographic,* June 1995, 62–87.

Bickerton, Ian J. and Carla L. Klausner. *A Concise History of the Arab-Israeli Conflict.* Englewood Cliffs, N.J.: Prentice Hall, 1991.

Feinstein, Steve. *Israel in Pictures.* Minneapolis: Lerner, 1988.

Jones, H. *Israel.* Chicago: Children's Press, 1986.

Meir, Golda. *My Life.* New York: Putnam, 1975.

Nagel, Rob, and Anne Commire. "David Ben Gurion." In *World Leaders, People Who Shaped the World.* Volume I: Africa and Asia. Detroit: U*X*L, 1994.

———. "King David." In *World Leaders, People Who Shaped the World.* Volume I: Africa and Asia. Detroit: U*X*L, 1994.

Reich, Bernard and Gershon R. Kieval. *Israel: Land of Tradition and Conflict.* 2d ed. Boulder, Colo.: Westview Press, 1993.

Sachar, Howard Morley. *A History of Israel: From the Rise of Zionism to Our Time.* New York: Knopf, 1979.

Szulc, Tad. "Who Are the Palestinians?" *National Geographic,* June 1992, 84–113.

ITALY

Italian Republic
Repubblica Italiana

CAPITAL: Rome (Roma).

FLAG: The national flag is a tricolor of green, white, and red vertical stripes.

ANTHEM: *Fratelli d'Italia (Brothers of Italy)*.

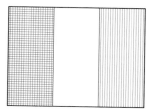

MONETARY UNIT: The lira (L) is a paper currency of 100 centesimi. There are coins of 5, 10, 20, 50, 100, 200, 500, and 1,000 lire, and notes of 1,000, 2,000, 5,000, 10,000, 50,000, and 100,000 lire. The lira has floated freely since February 1973. L1 = $0.0006 (or $1 = L1,611.3).

WEIGHTS AND MEASURES: The metric system is the legal standard.

HOLIDAYS: New Year's Day, 1 January; Epiphany, 6 January; Liberation Day, 25 April; Labor Day, 1 May; Assumption, 15 August; All Saints' Day, 1 November; National Unity Day, 5 November; Immaculate Conception, 8 December; Christmas, 25 December; St. Stephen's Day, 26 December. Easter Monday is a movable holiday. In addition, each town has a holiday on its Saint's Day.

TIME: 1 PM = noon GMT.

1 LOCATION AND SIZE

Situated in southern Europe, the Italian Republic, including the major islands of Sicily and Sardinia, covers a land area of 301,230 square kilometers (116,306 square miles), slightly larger than the state of Arizona. Within the frontiers of Italy are the sovereign Republic of San Marino and the sovereign state of Vatican City.

Italy's capital city, Rome, is located in the west central part of the country.

2 TOPOGRAPHY

Except for the fertile Po River Valley in the north and the narrow coastal belts farther south, Italy's mainland is generally mountainous, with considerable seismic activity. The Alpine mountain area in the north along the French and Swiss borders gives rise to six small rivers that flow southward into the Po. Italy's highest peaks are found in the northwest.

The Po River, the only large river in Italy, flows from west to east at the foot of the Alps. The Apennines, the rugged backbone of peninsular Italy, rise to form the southern border of the Po Plain. Vesuvius, near Naples, is the only active volcano on the European mainland.

While altitudes are lower in southern Italy, the coast is still rugged. The mountainous western coastline forms natural harbors at Naples, Livorno, La Spezia, and Genoa. The low Adriatic coast permits natural ports at Venice (Venezia), Bari, and Taranto.

Sicily, separated from the mainland by the narrow Strait of Messina, has the mountainous continuation of the Apennines. Mount Etna, 3,369 meters, (11,053 feet) is an isolated and active volcano in the northeast between Catania and Messina.

Sardinia, in the Tyrrhenian Sea, is generally mountainous. Its highest peak is 1,834 meters (6,017 feet).

3 CLIMATE

Climate varies with elevation and region. The coldest period occurs in December and January; the hottest in July and August. In the Po Plain, the average annual temperature is about 13°C (55°F); in Sicily, about 18°C (64°F); and in the coastal lowlands, about 14°C (57°F).

4 PLANTS AND ANIMALS

Plants and animals vary with area and altitude. The highest forest belt consists of conifers; beech, oak, and chestnut trees grow on lower mountain slopes. Poplar and willow thrive in the Po Plain. On the peninsula and on the larger islands, Mediterranean vegetation predominates: evergreens, holm oak, cork, juniper, bramble, laurel, myrtle, and dwarf palm.

Although larger mammals are scarce, chamois, ibex, and roe deer are found in the Alps, and bears, chamois, and otters inhabit the Apennines. Ravens and swallows are characteristic birds of Italy. Abundant marine life inhabits the surrounding seas.

5 ENVIRONMENT

Air pollution is a significant problem in Italy. In 1994, Italy produced 911.4 tons of hydrocarbon emissions and 498.1 tons of particulate emissions. The nation's rivers and coasts are polluted by industrial and agricultural contaminants. The island city of Venice faces long-term threats from flooding, pollution, erosion, and sinkage.

Of Italy's mammal species, three are endangered, as well as 19 bird species and 210 plant species.

6 POPULATION

The census of 20 October 1991 recorded a population of 56,411,290. A population of 58,148,000 has been projected for the year 2000. The average population density in 1991 was 190 persons per square kilometer (492 persons per square mile). Rome, the capital and largest city, had an estimated 2,791,354 inhabitants at the end of 1990.

7 MIGRATION

Of the 65,647 Italians who emigrated in 1989, 26,098 went to Germany; 16,347 to Switzerland; 5,277 to France; 4,076 to the United States; and 23,849 to other countries. Immigration in 1989 totaled approximately 81,201 people, of whom Germans accounted for 13,198. In 1990, 781,100 immigrants lived in Italy. This figure did not include some 600,000 who were believed to be illegal immigrants.

Germany had 560,100 Italian residents at the end of 1991, and France had 253,679 in 1990.

ITALY

LOCATION: 47°05′ to 36°38′N; 6°37′ to 18°31′E. **BOUNDARY LENGTHS:** Switzerland, 744 kilometers (462 miles); Austria, 430 kilometers (267 miles); Slovenia, 209 kilometers (130 miles); total coastline including islands of Sicily and Sardinia, 7,458 kilometers (4,634 miles); France, 514 kilometers (320 miles). **TERRITORIAL SEA LIMIT:** 12 miles.

8 ETHNIC GROUPS

For centuries, the majority of Italy's people came from similar ethnic backgrounds. The chief minority groups are the German-speaking people in the Alto Adige (South Tyrol) region and the Slavs of the Trieste area.

9 LANGUAGES

Italian, the official language, is spoken by the vast majority of people. While each region has its own dialect, Tuscan, the dialect of Tuscany (the region around Livorno and Florence) is the standard dialect for Italian. Other languages spoken, mostly in particular regions, include French, Fruilian (related to Romansch of Switzerland), Slovene, and German.

10 RELIGIONS

In 1990, the overwhelming majority (97.6%) of Italians belonged to the Roman Catholic faith. The Federation of the Protestant Churches had about 50,000 members in 1993, the two major denominations being the Lutheran Church and the Waldensians. There were also approximately 45,000 Muslims and 32,000 Jews.

11 TRANSPORTATION

In 1991 Italy's highway system, one of the world's best, totaled 294,410 kilometers (182,946 miles) of roads. A major highway runs through the Mont Blanc Tunnel, connecting France and Italy. In 1991 there were an estimated 28,200,000 passenger cars, 2,443,000 trucks, and 78,000 buses.

In 1991, Italy maintained a total railway trackage of 20,085 kilometers (12,473 miles). The government owns and operates 80% of the rail system, including the principal lines. The navigable inland waterway system, totaling about 2,400 kilometers (1,490 miles), is mainly in the north and consists of the Po River, the Italian lakes, and the network of Venetian and Po River Valley canals.

As of the beginning of 1992, Italy had the twelfth largest merchant fleet in the world, with 493 vessels totaling 6,826,000 gross registered tons. The ports of Genoa and Venice handle the major share of oceangoing traffic to and from the northern industrial centers. Naples, second only to Genoa, is the principal port for central and southern Italy.

Italy's one national airline, Alitalia, maintains a wide-ranging domestic and international network of air routes; in 1992, it transported 13,037,800 passengers. Rome's Fiumicino and Milan's Malpensa and Linate are among the most important airports.

12 HISTORY

The Italian heritage is the oldest in Europe, next to Greece's. The Etruscan civilization, a great seafaring, commercial, and artistic culture, reached its peak in about the seventh century. By 350 BC, after a series of wars with both Greeks and Etruscans, the Latins, with Rome as their capital, gained supremacy, and by 272 BC, they managed to unite the entire Italian peninsula.

This period of unification was followed by one of conquest in the Mediterranean. In the course of a century-long struggle against Carthage, the Romans conquered Sicily, Sardinia, and Corsica. Finally, in 146 BC, at the conclusion of the Third Punic War, Rome became the dominant power in the Mediterranean. From its beginnings, Rome was a republican city-state, but a series of struggles between powerful political figures destroyed the republic.

Roman Empire

Octavian, the final victor (31 BC), was given the title of Augustus ("exalted") by the Senate and became the first Roman emperor. Under imperial rule, Rome undertook a series of conquests that brought Roman law, Roman administration, and "Roman peace" (Pax Romana) to an area extending from the Atlantic to the Rhine River, to the British Isles, to the Iberian Peninsula and large parts of North Africa, and to the Middle East as far as the Euphrates River.

Photo credit: Susan D. Rock

Fountain and ruins of the ancient city of Pompeii.

In AD 313, Emperor Constantine accepted Christianity and moved his capital from Rome to Constantinople. From the fourth to the fifth century, the Western Roman Empire disintegrated under the blows of barbarian invasions, finally falling in 476, and the unity of Italy came to an end.

From the sixth to the thirteenth centuries, Italy suffered a variety of invaders, including the Lombards, Franks, Saracens, and Germans. From the tenth to the fourteenth centuries, Italy was divided into several, often hostile, territories and a number of large and small city-states, such as Venice, Milan, Florence, and Bologna.

By the thirteenth century, the city-states had emerged as centers of commerce and of the arts and sciences. They served as a catalyst for the developing Renaissance, which between the thirteenth and sixteenth centuries led to an unparalleled flowering of the arts, literature, music, and science. However, the emergence of Portugal and Spain as great seagoing nations at the end of the fifteenth century undercut Italian prosperity, and Spain emerged as the dominant force in the region. However, Venice, Milan, and other city-states retained at least some of their former glory.

The French Revolution brought the concept of nationalism to the Italian peninsula. Short-lived republics and even a Kingdom of Italy (under Napoleon's stepson Eugene) were formed. But with the Congress of Vienna (1815), after Napoleon's defeat, many of the old rulers and systems were restored under Austrian domination. However, sporadic revolts led by such figures as Giuseppe Mazzini and Giuseppe Garibaldi, grew into the Risorgimento (national rebirth) movement. It was brought to a successful conclusion with most of Italy united under Victor Emmanuel II of the House of Savoy. On 17 March 1861, the Kingdom of Italy was proclaimed. Italian troops occupied Rome in 1870, and in July 1871, it formally became the capital of the kingdom.

The Twentieth Century

Political reforms introduced by Premier Giovanni Giolitti in the first decade of the twentieth century improved Italy's status among Western powers, but failed to overcome such basic problems as poverty and illiteracy. During World War I (1914–18), Italy, originally an ally of the Central Powers, declared itself neutral in 1914 and a year later joined the British and French. At the Versailles Peace Conference, Italy, which had suffered heavy losses on the Alpine front and felt slighted by its Western allies, failed to obtain all of the territories that it claimed.

This disappointment, coupled with the severe economic depression of the postwar period, created great social unrest and led eventually to the rise of Benito Mussolini, who, after leading his fascist followers in a mass march on Rome, became premier in 1922. (In fascism, a dictatorial leader heads a strong, centralized government. The needs of the nation are valued above the needs of any individual citizen.) Mussolini's fascist dictatorship scored early successes in social welfare, employment, and transportation. The military conquest of Ethiopia (1935–36) added to Italy's colonial strength.

Italy joined Germany against the United States and its allies in World War II. Defeats in Greece and North Africa and the Allied invasion of Sicily toppled Mussolini's regime on 25 July 1943. Soon Italy was divided into two warring zones, one controlled by the Allies in the south and the other held by the Germans. When German power collapsed, Mussolini was captured and executed by Italian partisans.

In 1946, Italy became a republic by popular referendum; the following year, a new constitution was drafted. The conclusion of the war left Italy poverty-stricken and in political chaos. By the early 1950s, however, with foreign assistance (including $1,516.7 million from the United States under the Marshall Plan), Italy managed to restore its economy to prewar levels. From this point, the Italian economy experienced strong development into the 1990s.

13 GOVERNMENT

The head of the Italian Republic is the president, who is elected for a seven-year term by Parliament. Presidential powers and duties include nomination of the prime minister, who, in turn, chooses a Council of Ministers (cabinet) with the approval of Parliament. Legislative power is vested in the two-chamber Parliament, consisting of the 630-member Chamber of Deputies and the 315-member Senate. Parliament is elected by universal direct vote.

Italy is divided into 20 regions, which are further subdivided into 94 provinces.

14 POLITICAL PARTIES

The Christian Democratic Party (Partito Democrazia Cristiana—DC) dominated the government from 1948–81. The DC is referred to as the Popular Party and was part of the Pact for Italy coalition in the 1994 election.

To the right and the left of the DC stand a wide range of parties. The most important of these has traditionally been the Italian Communist Party (Partito Comunista Italiano—PCI), which is now split into two parties: Communist Refounding and the Democratic Party.

15 JUDICIAL SYSTEM

Civil cases and lesser criminal cases are tried before judges called *pretori*. There are 159 tribunals, each with jurisdiction over its own district; 90 assize courts, where cases are heard by juries; and 26 assize courts of appeal. The Court of Cassation in Rome acts as the highest level of appeal in all cases except those involving constitutional matters, which are brought before the special Constitutional Court. For many years, the number of civil and criminal cases has been increasing more rapidly than the judicial resources to deal with them.

16 ARMED FORCES

Since 1949 Italy, as a member of the North Atlantic Treaty Organization (NATO), has maintained large and balanced modern forces. The total strength in 1993 was 354,000 (211,000 draftees), not including 111,400 *carabinieri*, or paramilitary national police. The total reserve strength was 584,000. Mandatory military service is for 12 months for all services.

Army personnel numbered 230,000, including 167,000 draftees. Navy personnel totaled 48,000, including 19,000 draftees and 800 marines, and 600 naval commandos. The air force had a total strength of 76,000 personnel, including 25,000 draftees, and 449 combat aircraft. Italy's military budget for 1991 was $22.7 billion.

17 ECONOMY

As the Italian economy has expanded since the 1950s, its structure has changed markedly. The role of agriculture has declined, while the importance of industry has increased dramatically. Industrial output almost tripled between 1953–68 and generally showed steady growth during the 1970s. Precision machinery and motor vehicles have led the surge in manufacturing, and Italy has generally been a leader in European industrial design and fashion in recent decades. By 1989, Italy had the fifth largest Organization for Economic Cooperation and Development (OECD) economy. The 1993 rate of inflation was 4.2%. Unemployment rose to 11.5% in 1992 and 13.8% in 1993.

Photo credit: Susan D. Rock

Gondolas near Bridge of Sighs, Venice.

18 INCOME

In 1992, Italy's gross national product (GNP) was $1,186,568 million, or about $19,840 per person.

19 INDUSTRY

Italian industry expanded rapidly in the postwar period. Industrial production almost tripled between 1955 and 1968, and has generally showed continued growth. The auto industry, which registered major gains during the 1960s and early 1970s, peaked in 1989, when 1,970,686 passenger cars were produced; in 1992, the production was 1,475,109 cars.

Chemical industry output in 1992 included sulfuric acid, 2,773,478 tons; nitric acid, 1,773,741 tons; and caustic soda, 964,834 tons. The textile industry in 1992 produced 245,055 tons of cotton yarn. In 1992, steel production was 24,792,886 tons, and pig iron production totaled 10,432,447 tons.

20 LABOR

Unemployment increased to 2,713,000 (11.3%) in January 1992. Overall employment rose only to 21,366,000 in 1992. Employment in agriculture declined from 26.9% of the active labor force in 1963 to 7.9% in 1992. Employment in industry was 31.6% (including construction) in 1992. In recent years, employment in services has increased rapidly, accounting for 60.5% of total employment in 1992.

21 AGRICULTURE

Despite government efforts, the agricultural sector has shown little growth in recent decades. Production of major agricultural products in 1992 (in millions of tons) included sugar beets, 14.3; wheat, 8.9; corn, 7.17; tomatoes, 5.49; potatoes, 2.49; oranges, 1.8; and lemons and limes, 0.73.

In 1992, Italy produced 6.38 million tons of wine (second only to France) and 436,000 tons of olive oil. In 1992, tobacco production was 143,000 tons. In 1991, Italy had 1,459,000 tractors (fifth in the world) and 47,000 harvester-threshers.

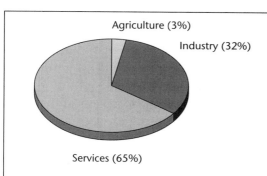

Agriculture (3%)

Industry (32%)

Services (65%)

Components of the economy. This pie chart shows how much of the country's economy is devoted to agriculture (includes forestry, hunting, and fishing), industry, or services.

22 DOMESTICATED ANIMALS

In 1991, 4,880,000 hectares (12,058,000 acres) were being used as meadows and pastures. In 1992, the country had 10,435,000 sheep; 8,549,000 hogs; 1,314,000 goats; 384,000 horses, mules, and asses; and an estimated 139,000,000 chickens. That year, total meat production from hogs, cattle, sheep, and goats was 3,923,000 tons. Meat production falls short of domestic requirements, and about half of all meat consumed must be imported.

23 FISHING

Although coastal and deep-sea fishing in the Mediterranean engage a sizable number of ships and men, the fishing industry is unable to meet domestic needs. The total catch in 1991 was 548,242 tons.

24 FORESTRY

In 1991, a total of 8,393,000 cubic meters of roundwood were produced, with 51% used for fuel. Italy is a major importer of hardwood and softwood lumber, since its rugged terrain and the layout of its forest-land restrict domestic production.

25 MINING

Italy is relatively poor in mineral resources. Nevertheless, domestic production continues to supply a large portion of Italy's need for some minerals, while enough mercury to export is produced. In 1991, 1,726,400 tons of low-grade coal were mined. Alumina production rose to 804,596 tons in 1991. Production of other minerals in 1991 (in tons) included feldspar, 1,304,203 (world's leading producer); barite, 88,426; fluorspar, 98,518; and pumice and pozzolan, 5,200,000.

26 FOREIGN TRADE

Industrial products, textiles and apparel, and foodstuffs are Italy's most important exports. Fuels, meat, grain products, and various raw materials are among the major imports. The bulk of manufactured imports come from European Communities (EC) countries and the United States, which are also the leading customers for Italian exports. In 1992, over 58% of Italy's total trade was with other EC countries.

Germany is Italy's single most active trading partner, accounting for 21% of total trade in 1992. France was next, with 14.5% in 1992. The United States share of Italy's exports in 1992 was 7%, and the share of imports 5.2%.

27 ENERGY AND POWER

In 1992, oil accounted for 61.7% of primary energy consumption; natural gas,

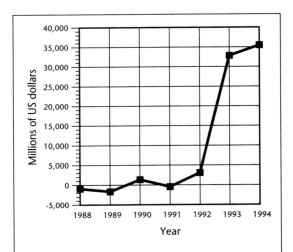

Yearly balance of trade measured in millions of US dollars. The balance of trade is the difference between what a country sells to other countries (its exports) and what it buys (its imports). If a country imports more than it exports, it has a negative balance of trade (a trade deficit). If exports exceed imports there is a positive balance of trade (a trade surplus).

26.9%; coal, 8.9%; and hydroelectricity, 2.5%. Italy imports about 75% of its energy.

28 SOCIAL DEVELOPMENT

Under current social insurance, all workers and their families are covered and receive old-age, disability, and survivor pensions, unemployment and injury benefits, health and maternity coverage, and family allowances.

Women fill only about 10% of managerial positions and are not well represented in the professions.

29 HEALTH

A national health plan, begun in 1980, seeks to provide free health care for all citizens, but certain minimum charges remain. The shortage of medical personnel and hospital facilities in Italy's rural areas remains serious. Total health care expenditures in 1990 were $82,214,000. In 1990, there were 481,000 hospital beds (7.5 per 1,000 people). Average life expectancy was estimated to be 77 years for women and men in 1992.

30 HOUSING

Italy's housing and public building program was a major item in the general program of postwar reconstruction. Between 1940–45, almost 20% of the habitable rooms in the country were destroyed. In 1985, a total of 39,385 new residential buildings were started. In 1992, the total number of housing units was 24,847,000.

31 EDUCATION

In 1990, 97.1% of adults were literate (males, 97.8% and females, 96.4%). Education is free and compulsory for eight years. In the academic year 1991, there were 22,911 public and private elementary schools providing education for 3,004,264 pupils. Also, 5,010,467 students were enrolled in secondary schools.

Higher education had a total enrollment of 1,533,202 in 1991 with 57,283 teaching staff. There are 41 state universities and 15 other universities, colleges, and higher learning institutes, including the University of Bologna (founded in the 11th century), the oldest in Italy.

Selected Social Indicators

These statistics are estimates for the period 1988 to 1993. For comparison purposes, data for the United States and averages for low-income countries and high-income countries are also given.

Indicator	Italy	Low-income countries	High-income countries	United States
Per capita gross national product†	$19,840	$380	$23,680	$24,740
Population growth rate	0.1%	1.9%	0.6%	1.0%
Population growth rate in urban areas	0.0%	3.9%	0.8%	1.3%
Population per square kilometer of land	190	78	25	26
Life expectancy in years	77	62	77	76
Number of people per physician	211	>3,300	453	419
Number of pupils per teacher (primary school)	12	39	<18	20
Illiteracy rate (15 years and older)	<3%	41%	<5%	<3%
Energy consumed per capita (kg of oil equivalent)	2,697	364	5,203	7,918

† The gross national product (GNP) is the total dollar value of all goods and services produced by a country in a year. The per capita GNP is calculated by dividing a country's GNP by its population. The World Bank defines low-income countries as those with a per capita GNP of $695 or less. High-income countries have a per capita GNP of $8,626 or more. Less than 14% of the world's 5.5 billion people live in high-income countries, while almost 60% live in low-income countries.

> = greater than   < = less than

Sources: World Bank, *Social Indicators of Development 1995,* Baltimore: Johns Hopkins University Press, 1995. Central Intelligence Agency, *World Fact Book,* Washington, D.C.: Government Printing Office, 1994.

32 MEDIA

Radiotelevisione Italiana (RAI), a government corporation, broadcasts on three radio and three television networks. In 1991 there were 24,300,000 television sets and 45,650,000 radios licensed in Italy. In 1991 there were 30,715,940 telephones in use.

Italy enjoys a free press, with vigorous expression of all shades of opinion. In 1991 there were 73 dailies with a combined daily circulation of about six million.

The major daily newspapers (with their estimated circulations) are *La Repubblica* (882,600); and *Corriere della Sera* (715,000).

33 TOURISM AND RECREATION

Tourism is a major industry in Italy, which ranked as the world's fourth most popular tourist destination in 1991. In that year, 51,317,000 persons entered Italy as overnight tourists or same-day visitors. The greatest number of visitors (including repeaters) were from Switzerland, 10,228,678; Germany, 9,205,658;

France 9,114,554; Austria, 5,540,654; and the former Yugoslavia, 4,367,181. In 1991, revenues from the tourist industry reached $19.67 billion.

Among Italy's manifold tourist attractions are the artistic and architectural treasures of Rome and Florence; the thousands of historic churches and galleries in smaller cities; the canals and palaces of Venice; the ruins of ancient Pompeii; and the delicacies of northern Italian cooking. Tourists are also lured by Italy's many beaches and by excellent Alpine skiing.

34 FAMOUS ITALIANS

Gaius Julius Caesar (100?–44 BC) is famous as a military and political leader. The first Roman emperor was Octavian (Gaius Octavianus, 63 BC–AD 14), better known as Augustus. During the sixteenth century, the High Renaissance, Rome shared with Florence the leading position in the world of the arts. Major masters included Leonardo da Vinci (1452–1519), painter, designer, and inventor; and Michelangelo Buonarroti (1475–1564), whose paintings on the ceiling of the Sistine Chapel attract visitors from around the world.

Bartolommeo Cristofori (1655–1731) invented the piano; the violins of Antonius Stradivarius (Antonio Stradivari, 1644–1737) are still considered priceless treasures today. Enrico Caruso (1873–1921) was a renowned operatic singer. Arturo Toscanini (1867–1957) was one of the most renowned orchestra conductors.

Italian literature and literary language began with Dante Alighieri (1265–1321), author of *The Divine Comedy,* and Giovanni Boccaccio (1313–75), author of the *Decameron.* Famous film stars include Italian-born Rudolph Valentino (Rodolfo Alfonso Raffaele Pierre Philibert Guglielmi, 1895–1926), Sophia Loren (Scicoloni, b.1934); and Marcello Mastroianni (b.1924).

In philosophy, exploration, and statesmanship, Italy has produced many world-renowned figures: the traveler Marco Polo (1254?–1324); the explorers Christopher Columbus (Cristoforo Colombo, 1451–1506) and Amerigo Vespucci (1454–1512), after whom the Americas are named. Italian scientists and mathematicians of note include Galileo Galilei (1564–1642) and Nobel Prize winners Guglielmo Marconi (1874–1937) and Enrico Fermi (1901–54; Nobel Prize winner, 1938).

35 BIBLIOGRAPHY

Duggan, Christopher. *A Concise History of Italy.* New York: Cambridge University Press, 1994.

Hearder, Harry. *Italy: A Short History.* New York: Cambridge University Press, 1990.

McCarry, John. "Milan—Where Italy Gets Down to Business." *National Geographic,* December 1992, 90–122.

Nagel, Rob, and Anne Commire. "Francis of Assisi." In *World Leaders, People Who Shaped the World.* Volume II: Europe. Detroit: U*X*L, 1994.

———. "John XXIII." In *World Leaders, People Who Shaped the World.* Volume II: Europe. Detroit: U*X*L, 1994.

Stein, R. *Italy.* Chicago: Children's Press, 1986.

Vessels, Jane. "Sicily." *National Geographic,* August 1995, 2–35.

Zwingle, Erla. "Venice." *National Geographic,* February 1995, 73–99.

JAMAICA

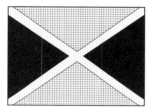

CAPITAL: Kingston.

FLAG: Two diagonal yellow gold bars forming a saltire divide the flag into four triangular panels. The two side panels are black, and the top and bottom panels are green.

ANTHEM: First line, "Eternal father, bless our land..."

MONETARY UNIT: The Jamaican dollar (J$) of 100 cents was introduced on 8 September 1969. There are coins of 1, 5, 10, and 25 cents, and 1 dollar, and notes of 2, 5, 10, 20, 50, and 100 dollars. J$1 = US$0.0302 (or US$1 = J$33.100).

WEIGHTS AND MEASURES: Both metric and imperial weights and measures are used.

HOLIDAYS: New Year's Day, 1 January; Labor Day, 23 May; Independence Day, 1st Monday in August; National Heroes' Day, 3rd Monday in October; Christmas, 25 December; Boxing Day, 26 December. Movable religious holidays include Ash Wednesday, Good Friday, and Easter Monday.

TIME: 7 AM = noon GMT.

1 LOCATION AND SIZE

Jamaica is an island in the Caribbean Sea situated about 160 kilometers (90 miles) south of Cuba. It has a total area of 10,990 square kilometers (4,243 square miles), slightly smaller than the state of Connecticut. The total coastline is 1,022 kilometers (634 miles).

Jamaica's capital city, Kingston, is located on the country's southeastern coast.

2 TOPOGRAPHY

The greater part of Jamaica is a limestone plateau, with an average elevation of about 460 meters (1,500 feet). The interior of the island is largely mountainous; the Blue Mountains dominate the eastern part of the island. The highest point on the island is Blue Mountain Peak, at 2,256 meters (7,402 feet) above sea level.

3 CLIMATE

The climate ranges from tropical at sea level to temperate in the uplands; there is relatively little seasonal variation in temperature. The average annual temperature in the coastal lowlands is 27°C (81°F); for the Blue Mountains, 13°C (55°F). The island has a mean annual rainfall of 198 centimeters (78 inches), with wide variations during the year between the north and south coasts. The rainy seasons are May to June and September to November.

4 PLANTS AND ANIMALS

In areas of heavy rainfall, bamboo, ferns, ebony, mahogany, and rosewood are found. Cactus and similar dry-area plants are found along the south and southwest

Photo credit: Susan D. Rock.

A popular beach area between St. Ann's Bay and Port Maria.

coastal area. Parts of the west and southwest consist of grassland.

The wild hog is one of the few native mammals, but there are many reptiles and lizards. Birds are abundant. The chief varieties of saltwater fish are kingfish, jack, mackerel, whiting, bonito, and tuna; freshwater varieties include snook, jewfish, gray and black snapper, and mullet.

5 ENVIRONMENT

Coastal waters have been polluted by industrial waste, sewage, and oil spills, and groundwater has suffered contamination by red mud waste from alumina processing. Over 50% of the people living in rural areas do not have pure water. In the mid-1980s, sewage systems were available to only 7% of the population. The nation's cities produce 0.3 million tons of solid waste per year.

In 1994, five of Jamaica's mammal species were endangered; two bird species and ten plant species are threatened with extinction.

6 POPULATION

Jamaica's 1991 population was 2,374,193. Population density was 218 persons per square kilometer (564 per square mile). A population of 2,677,000 was projected for the year 2000. As of 1991, 587,798 people lived in the capital city of Kingston and its suburbs.

7 MIGRATION

From 1971 through 1980, 276,200 Jamaicans left the island; 142,000 for the United States. In 1990 there were 343,000 Jamaican-born people in the United States. The great difference between rural and urban income levels has contributed to the exodus of rural dwellers to the cities, where many of these migrants remain unemployed for lack of necessary skills.

8 ETHNIC GROUPS

About 95% of the population is of partial or total African descent, with the following breakdown: 76% blacks, 15% mulattos, and 4% black-East Indians or black-Chinese. Other ethnic groups include East Indians (2%), Chinese (1%), and Europeans (2%). Nearly the whole population is native-born Jamaican.

9 LANGUAGES

Jamaica is an English-speaking country, and British usage is followed in government and the schools. Informally, a Jamaican patois (dialect) is used by most of the populace.

10 RELIGIONS

The Church of God claims the largest number of members, followed by the Baptist church. The Church of England (Anglican), formerly the dominant religion in Jamaica, now ranks third. The Roman Catholic Church is also significant. The Rastafarian movement continues to grow and is culturally influential in Jamaica and abroad. Its members, called Rastas, regard Africa (specifically Ethiopia) as Zion and consider their life outside Africa as a Babylonian captivity.

11 TRANSPORTATION

Jamaica has an extensive system of roads; in 1991 there were 18,200 kilometers (11,300 miles) of roads. In 1991 there were 97,500 licensed passenger cars and 18,000 commercial vehicles on the island. The standard-gauge rail system had 370 kilometers (230 miles) of track in 1991.

The port facilities of Kingston harbor are among the most modern in the Caribbean. The 18 other ports tend to specialize in particular commodities. Jamaica has a small merchant fleet, which included three freighters and one tanker in 1992.

Air service is the major means of passenger transport between Jamaica and outside areas. The two modern airports are Norman Manley International Air-

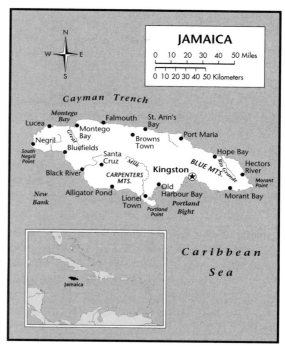

LOCATION: 17°43′ to 18°32′N; 76°11′ to 78°21′W. **TOTAL COASTLINE:** 1,022 kilometers (634 miles). **TERRITORIAL SEA LIMIT:** 12 miles.

port (Kingston) and Sangster International Airport (Montego Bay). In 1992, Air Jamaica carried 837,200 passengers.

12 HISTORY

Jamaica was discovered by Christopher Columbus in 1494 and settled by the Spanish in the early sixteenth century. The Arawak Indians, who had inhabited the island since about AD 1000, were gradually exterminated, replaced by African slaves. In 1655, the island was taken over by the English, and the Spanish were expelled five years later.

Spain formally ceded Jamaica to England in 1670 by the Treaty of Madrid.

Sugar, cocoa, and coffee plantations became the mainstay of the island's economy. With the abolition of slavery in 1834, the quarter million slaves were set free, and many became small farmers in the hill districts. The British Parliament established a crown colony government in 1866, and Jamaica's new governor, Sir John Peter Grant, introduced new programs, including development of banana cultivation and advances in education, public health, and political representation.

However, these measures did not resolve Jamaica's social and economic inequalities, and social unrest came to the surface whenever economic reverses occurred. The depression of the 1930s, coupled with a blight on the banana crop, produced serious disruption and demands for political reform. Jamaica was granted self-government and, in 1944, had its first election.

After Independence

Jamaica became an independent state on 6 August 1962, with dominion status in the Commonwealth of Nations. The Jamaica Labour Party (JLP) became the ruling party, and its leader, Sir Alexander Bustamante, became the nation's first prime minister.

The JLP held power through the 1960s. In February 1972, the rival People's National Party (PNP) gained a majority in Parliament, and Michael Manley headed a new democratic socialist government. Manley established friendly relations with Cuba, which the United States criticized.

Deteriorating economic conditions led to continuing violence in Kingston and elsewhere during the mid-1970s, discouraging tourism. By 1976, Jamaica was faced with declining exports and an unemployment rate estimated at 30–40%. Tourism suffered another blow in January 1979 with three days of rioting in Kingston at the height of the tourist season.

Manley called for elections in the fall of 1980. The opposition JLP won a landslide victory, and Edward Seaga became prime minister and minister of finance. He announced a conservative economic program that brought an immediate harvest of aid from the United States and the International Monetary Fund (IMF). In October 1981, Jamaica broke off diplomatic relations with Cuba, and two years later it participated in the US-led invasion of Grenada.

The conservative JLP under Seaga remained in power through the 1980s, but its support eroded as it carried out unpopular economic policies mandated by the IMF.

Criticizing the decline in social services under Seaga and promising to attract foreign investment, Manley and the PNP were returned to office in the 1989 elections. Manley reversed many of Seaga's policies, but by 1992, inflation was on the rise and the economy slowed. Unemployment hovered around 20%.

Manley retired in 1992, leaving the government to Percival J. Patterson, who moved politically further to the right, encouraging more reforms.

13 GOVERNMENT

The 1962 constitution provides for a governor-general appointed by the crown, a cabinet presided over by a prime minister, and a two-chamber legislature.

The Senate, the upper house, consists of 21 appointed members. The popularly elected House of Representatives consists of 60 members. The House is by far the more important of the two chambers.

The governor-general appoints both the prime minister and the leader of the opposition. The normal term of office in Parliament is five years, but elections can be called at any time. Voting is universal at age 18.

The cabinet consists of the prime minister and at least 11 additional ministers, appointed by the governor-general on the advice of the prime minister.

Responsibility for local government is vested in 12 parish councils.

14 POLITICAL PARTIES

Two political parties dominate Jamaican politics. The Jamaica Labour Party (JLP), the more conservative of the two parties, held a parliamentary majority during the first 10 years of independence, and again from 1980–89 under Edward Seaga. Seaga remains opposition leader.

The People's National Party (PNP), which was returned to power in 1989 under Norman W. Manley, its founder, holds to a moderate socialist program. Both the JLP and PNP stand for a broad program of social reform and welfare, and economic development with the participation of foreign investment.

15 JUDICIAL SYSTEM

Cases may be heard first before a lay magistrate (justice of the peace), a magistrate, or a judge in the Supreme Court, according to the seriousness of the offense or the amount of property involved. The Supreme Court also hears appeals. Final appeal rests with the seven-member Court of Appeals.

16 ARMED FORCES

The Jamaica Defense Force in 1993 numbered 4,200 personnel, including 870 reserves. Designed for minimal defense missions, the armed forces have three ground force battalions, an air wing of 170 patrol and administrative aircraft, and a coast guard of five patrol boats. In 1991, Jamaica spent US$20 million on defense.

17 ECONOMY

The structure of the Jamaican economy has undergone major changes since 1945, when it was primarily dependent on tropical agricultural products—sugar, bananas, coffee, and cocoa. The island has since become one of the world's largest producers of bauxite. It also has developed as a major tourist center for North Americans.

Between 1987 and 1991, Jamaica had the fastest growing economy in the Caribbean.

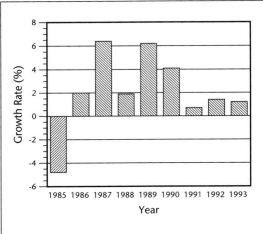

Yearly growth rate of the economy. This economic indicator tells by what percent the economy has increased or decreased when compared with the previous year.

18 INCOME

In 1992, Jamaica's gross national product (GNP) was US$3,216 million, or about US$1,440 per person. For the period 1985–92, the average inflation rate was 23.9%, resulting in a real growth rate in GNP of 2.9% per person.

19 INDUSTRY

Since 1945, when Jamaican manufacturing was confined largely to processing local agricultural products and making beer, clothing, and furniture, the industries have grown and diversified considerably. The island now produces a wide range of goods, including mineral fuels and lubricants, fertilizers, steel, cement, and agricultural machinery, along with footwear, textiles, paints, building materials, and processed foods.

20 LABOR

The labor force in 1991 was estimated at 1,069,000; the total unemployment rate at that time was 15.1%. Of those employed, 26.4% worked in agriculture, forestry, and fishing; 20.6% in industry; and 53% in services. The combined membership of unions in 1991 amounted to 16.3% of those employed.

21 AGRICULTURE

Sugar, the leading export crop, is produced mainly on plantations organized around modern sugar factories. Sugar has suffered badly from low world prices and cuts in United States buying quotas. Raw sugar production in 1992 was 221,678 tons. Banana production for export grew by 1.9% to 76,723 tons in 1992.

Other major export crops in 1992 included cocoa and coffee. Jamaica also exports coconuts, pimientos, citrus fruits, ginger, tobacco, yams, peppers, and cut flowers.

The island's food needs are met only partly by domestic production. The main food crops, grown primarily by small cultivators, are sweet potatoes and yams, rice, potatoes, manioc, tomatoes, and beans. Jamaica is a major producer of marijuana, even though it remains illegal.

22 DOMESTICATED ANIMALS

Despite increases in the livestock population and in the production of meat, milk, and poultry, increased demand has

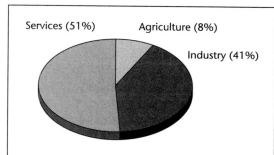

Services (51%)   Agriculture (8%)

Industry (41%)

Components of the economy. This pie chart shows how much of the country's economy is devoted to agriculture (includes forestry, hunting, and fishing), industry, or services.

resulted in continued imports of livestock products. Livestock holdings in 1992 included some 320,000 head of cattle, 440,000 goats, and 250,000 hogs. Livestock products in 1992 included 54,000 tons of poultry meat and 49,000 tons of milk.

23 FISHING

The fishing industry grew during the 1980s, primarily due to growth in inland fishing. Whereas the inland catch in 1982 was 129 tons, by 1991 it had risen to 3,230 tons. The total catch in 1991 was 10,430 tons.

24 FORESTRY

By the mid-1980s, only 184,000 hectares (455,000 acres) of Jamaica's original 1,000,000 hectares (2,500,000 acres) of forest remained. Roundwood production was 180,000 cubic meters in 1991. During the 1980s, planting of new trees averaged 1,000 hectares (2,500 acres) a year, but deforestation continued at twice that rate.

25 MINING

Jamaica is the world's third-leading producer of bauxite; in 1991, production was 11,552,000 tons, or 10% of world production. Alumina production came to 3,015,000 tons in 1991, or 6% of world production. In 1991, Jamaica produced 135,844 tons of gypsum and an estimated 95,000 tons of lime.

26 FOREIGN TRADE

In February 1991, the government implemented the new CARICOM Common External Tariff (CET), creating the first customs union in the Caribbean. At the end of 1992, the value of Jamaica's merchandise imports was US$1,500 million, while merchandise exports were valued at US$980 million.

The United States continues to be Jamaica's top trading partner, although total imports from the United States declined by 5.5% to US$882.7 million during 1992, 52% of Jamaica's total imports that year. Some of the major import categories include petroleum, grains, machinery and transport equipment, chemical, and poultry parts.

Similarly, the United States has been Jamaica's principal export market over the last two decades. In 1992, Jamaica's exports to the United States increased by 13% to US$386.3 million, or 36.7% of total exports.

27 ENERGY AND POWER

Jamaica has no coal deposits and very little hydroelectric potential. Electricity is the main source of power and is almost all

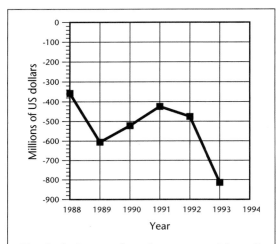

Yearly balance of trade measured in millions of US dollars. The balance of trade is the difference between what a country sells to other countries (its exports) and what it buys (its imports). If a country imports more than it exports, it has a negative balance of trade (a trade deficit). If exports exceed imports, there is a positive balance of trade (a trade surplus).

generated by steam from oil-burning plants. In 1991, the total amount of electricity generated by public and private sources was 2,735 million kilowatt hours.

28 SOCIAL DEVELOPMENT

Jamaica has pioneered in social welfare in the West Indies since 1938. Government assistance is provided to those in need, and rehabilitation grants and family allowances are made. A National Insurance Scheme (NIS) came into effect in April 1966, providing benefits in the form of old age and disability health and maternity coverage, pensions, workers' compensation, widows' and widowers' pensions, and grants.

Cultural traditions, economic discrimination, and workplace sexual harassment have prevented women from achieving full equality.

29 HEALTH

The central government provides most medical services in Jamaica through the Ministry of Health. There were 27 public hospitals in 1986, with over 5,420 beds. There were also five private hospitals with 277 beds. In 1992, 90% of the population had access to health care services.

The government conducts a broad public health program, involving epidemic control, health education, industrial health protection, and campaigns against tuberculosis, venereal diseases, yaws, and malaria. Tuberculosis, hookworm, and venereal diseases remain the most prevalent diseases. Life expectancy in 1992 averaged 74 years for both men and women.

30 HOUSING

While middle- and upper-income housing is comparable to that in neighboring areas of North America, facilities for low-income groups are poor by any standard. The problem has been aggravated by constant migration from the rural areas to the cities, causing the growth of urban slums. Most new urban housing is built of cinder block and steel on the edges of cities. Rural housing is primarily built of wood and roofed with zinc sheeting. Squatter settlements surround the major cities of Jamaica.

Selected Social Indicators

These statistics are estimates for the period 1988 to 1993. For comparison purposes, data for the United States and averages for low-income countries and high-income countries are also given.

Indicator	Jamaica	Low-income countries	High-income countries	United States
Per capita gross national product†	**$1,440**	$380	$23,680	$24,740
Population growth rate	**0.5%**	1.9%	0.6%	1.0%
Population growth rate in urban areas	**1.4%**	3.9%	0.8%	1.3%
Population per square kilometer of land	**218**	78	25	26
Life expectancy in years	**74**	62	77	76
Number of people per physician	**2,040**	>3,300	453	419
Number of pupils per teacher (primary school)	**37**	39	<18	20
Illiteracy rate (15 years and older)	**<2%**	41%	<5%	<3%
Energy consumed per capita (kg of oil equivalent)	**1,096**	364	5,203	7,918

† The gross national product (GNP) is the total dollar value of all goods and services produced by a country in a year. The per capita GNP is calculated by dividing a country's GNP by its population. The World Bank defines low-income countries as those with a per capita GNP of $695 or less. High-income countries have a per capita GNP of $8,626 or more. Less than 14% of the world's 5.5 billion people live in high-income countries, while almost 60% live in low-income countries.

> = greater than   < = less than

Sources: World Bank, *Social Indicators of Development 1995,* Baltimore: Johns Hopkins University Press, 1995. Central Intelligence Agency, *World Fact Book,* Washington, D.C.: Government Printing Office, 1994.

31 EDUCATION

Jamaica's estimated literacy rate is 98%. In 1990 there were 8,830 primary school teachers with 323,378 students. There were 225,240 secondary students. Education is compulsory for six years of primary education.

The University of the West Indies serves all British Commonwealth Caribbean territories. Higher technical education is provided at the College of Arts, Science, and Technology. At the university and higher level institutions, there were 16,018 students enrolled in 1990.

32 MEDIA

The privately owned Radio Jamaica Rediffusion broadcasts 24 hours a day. The government-owned Jamaica Broadcasting Corp., with similar transmitting facilities, broadcasts radio and television programs. In 1992 there were approximately 1,025,000 radio sets and 320,000 television receivers. In 1993, 180,000 telephones were in use.

The morning *Daily Gleaner* (circulation about 37,000 in 1986) and the evening *Daily Star* (circulation 38,000) are published by the Gleaner Co., which also publishes the *Sunday Gleaner* (81,000) and the *Weekend Star* (85,000), an overseas weekly.

33 TOURISM AND RECREATION

In recent years, Jamaica has diversified its traditional tourist market—the United States and Canada—by aggressively marketing in Europe and Japan. In 1992 European arrivals increased by 19% and Japanese arrivals increased by 50%. This positive marketing strategy helped Jamaica outperform other Caribbean destinations, registering 823,810 arrivals for the first half of 1993.

Jamaica is firmly established as a center for tourists, mainly from North America. In 1991, 844,607 tourists visited the island, 544,467 of them from the United States. Receipts from tourism in 1991 were estimated at us$764 million. There were 17,337 hotel rooms with a 57.9% occupancy rate. Major tourist areas are the resort centers of Montego Bay and Ocho Rios. Cricket is the national sport, and excellent golf and water-sports facilities are available.

34 FAMOUS JAMAICANS

Jamaica-born Marcus Garvey (1887–1940) achieved fame as the founder of the ill-fated United Negro Improvement Association. Trade unionist Sir (William) Alexander Bustamante (1894–1977) and his cousin, Norman Washington Manley (1893–1969), were rival political leaders for decades. Performer and composer

Photo credit: Jamaica Tourist Board.

Rasta Jimmy. The Rastafarian movement was founded in 1930 and is culturally influential among blacks in Jamaica and abroad.

Robert Nesta ("Bob") Marley (1945–81) became internationally famous for popularizing reggae music outside of Jamaica.

35 BIBLIOGRAPHY

Bryan, Patrick E. *The Jamaican People, 1880–1902: Race, Class and Social Control*. London: Macmillan Caribbean, 1991.

Hurwitz, Samuel J. and Edith F. *Jamaica: A Historical Portrait*. New York: Praeger, 1971.

Jamaica in Pictures. Minneapolis: Lerner, 1987.

Levi, Darrell E. *Michael Manley: The Making of a Leader*. Athens: University of Georgia Press, 1990, 1989.

JAPAN

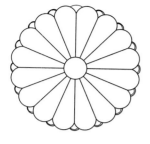

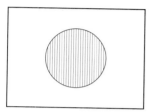

Nippon

CAPITAL: Tokyo.

FLAG: The Sun-flag (Hi-no-Maru) consists of a red circle on a white background.

ANTHEM: (de facto) *Kimigayo (The Reign of Our Emperor),* with words dating back to the ninth century.

MONETARY UNIT: The yen (¥) of 100 sen is issued in coins of 1, 5, 10, 50, 100, and 500 yen, and notes of 500, 1,000, 5,000, and 10,000 yen. ¥1 = $0.0097 (or $1 = ¥103.15).

WEIGHTS AND MEASURES: The metric system is the legal standard.

HOLIDAYS: New Year's Day, 1 January; Adults' Day, 15 January; Commemoration of the Founding of the Nation, 11 February; Vernal Equinox Day, 20 or 21 March; Emperor's Birthday, 29 April; Constitution Day, 3 May; Children's Day, 5 May; Respect for the Aged Day, 15 September; Autumnal Equinox Day, 23 or 24 September; Health-Sports Day, 10 October; Culture Day, 3 November; Labor-Thanksgiving Day, 23 November.

TIME: 9 PM = noon GMT.

1 LOCATION AND SIZE

Situated off the eastern edge of the Asian continent, the Japanese archipelago (a group of islands) has a total area of 377,835 square kilometers (145,883 square miles), slightly smaller than the state of California.

Each of Japan's five districts consists of a main island of the same name and hundreds of surrounding islands. The five districts are Honshu, 231,058 square kilometers (89,212 square miles); Hokkaido, 83,519 square kilometers (32,247 square miles); Kyushu, 42,145 square kilometers (16,272 square miles); Shikoku, 18,805 square kilometers (7,261 square miles); and Okinawa, 2,254 square kilometers (870 square miles).

Japan's principal island is Honshu, on which are located the capital city of Tokyo, the principal cities and plains, and the major industrial areas.

2 TOPOGRAPHY

Mountains cover over 71% of Japan's surface. The island of Honshu is the site of the two principal mountain ranges: the Hida (or Japan Alps) and the Akaishi mountains. These mountains are located between Tokyo and Nagoya.There are 25 mountains with peaks of over 3,000 meters (9,800 feet). The highest is the beautiful Mt. Fuji (Fuji-san), at 3,776 meters (12,388 feet). Japan has 196 volcanoes (including the dormant Mt. Fuji), of which 67 remain active. Earthquakes occur continually, with an average of 1,500 minor shocks per year.

The plains of Japan, located mostly along the seacoast, are few and small and cover only about 29% of the total land area. The largest is in the Tokyo Bay region and covers about 6,500 square kilometers (2,500 square miles).

Rivers tend to be short and swift. The longest is the Shinano (367 kilometers/228 miles) in north-central Honshu, flowing into the Sea of Japan near Niigata. The largest lake is Lake Biwa, northeast of Kyoto, with an area of 672 square kilometers (259 square miles).

3 CLIMATE

Throughout the year, there is fairly high humidity, with average rainfall ranging by area from 100 centimeters to over 300 centimeters (40–120 inches). Autumn weather is usually clear and bright. Winters tend to be warmer in the south and east of Japan than in similar latitudes. In the north and west, snowfalls are frequent and heavy. Spring is usually pleasant, and summer is hot and humid. There is a rainy season that moves from south to north during June and July.

Average temperature ranges from 17°C (63°F) in the southern portions to 9°C (48°F) in the extreme north. Hokkaido has long and severe winters with a lot of snow, while the rest of the country enjoys milder weather. The southern regions are almost subtropical. The typhoon season runs from May through October. Each year several storms sweep through the islands, accompanied by high winds and heavy rains.

4 PLANTS AND ANIMALS

Hokkaido plants include mostly conifers, or cone-bearing trees (fir, spruce, and larch), at high altitudes, and mixed northern hardwoods (oak, maple, linden, birch, ash, elm, and walnut) at lower altitudes. Honshu supports a great variety of temperate plants. Common conifers are cypress, umbrella pine, hemlock, yew, and white pine.

On the lowlands, there are live oak and camphor trees and a great mixture of bamboo with the hardwoods. Black pine and red pine make up most of the plants on the sandy lowlands and coastal areas. Shikoku and Kyushu are noted for their evergreen plants. Sugarcane and citrus fruits are found throughout the lowland areas, with broadleaf trees in the lower elevations and a mixture of evergreen and deciduous trees higher up. Throughout these islands are rich growths of bamboo.

About 140 species of animals have been identified. There are 32 carnivores, including the brown bear, ermine, mink, raccoon dog, fox, wolf, walrus, and seal. There are 450 species of birds and 30 species of reptiles. Japan's waters abound with crabs, shrimp, and great migrations of fish. There are large numbers and varieties of insects. The Japanese beetle is not very destructive in its homeland because of its many natural enemies.

5 ENVIRONMENT

The fast growth of industry has put a lot of pressure on the environment. Air pollution is a serious problem in Japan, particularly in large cities. The pollutants in the

JAPAN

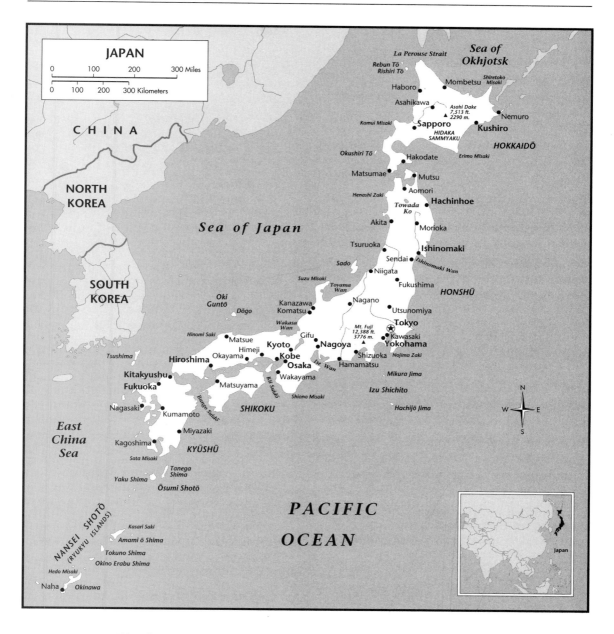

LOCATION: 122°56′ to 153°59′E; 20°25′ to 45°33′N. **TOTAL COASTLINE:** 29,751 kilometers (18,486 miles).
TERRITORIAL SEA LIMIT: 12 miles.

air have caused acid rain throughout the country. Nationwide smog alerts peaked at 328 in 1973. By 1986, after setting strict automobile emissions standards, smog alerts had declined to 85.

Water pollution is another problem in Japan. Increase in acid levels due to industrial pollutants has affected lakes, rivers, and the waters surrounding Japan. Other sources of pollution include the agricultural chemical DDT and mercury. Factory noise levels are regulated under a law of 1968. Airplanes may not take off or land after 10 PM, and the Shinkansen high-speed trains must reduce speed while traveling through large cities and their suburbs.

Of Japan's mammal species, 5 are endangered, as are 31 bird species, and 41 plants.

Photo credit: Susan D. Rock

A city street in Kyoto, Japan.

6 POPULATION

In 1990, Japan ranked seventh among the world's most populous nations, with a population of 123,612,000. The population for the year 2000 was projected to be 128,066,000. In terms of density, Japan ranks among the world leaders, with 329 persons per square kilometer (852 per square mile). The major population concentrations are found in Honshu, where 80% of Japanese live. The least densely populated major island is Hokkaido, with less than 5% of the total population.

As of 1990 there were 11 cities with populations of more than 1 million, among them Tokyo, 8,163,127; Yokohama, 3,220,350; Osaka, 2,623,831;

Kyoto, 1,461,140; Kobe, 1,477,423; and Hiroshima, 1,085,677.

7 MIGRATION

Japanese living in other countries totaled 663,074 in 1991, including 257,845 in the United States and 101,174 in Brazil. Since the early 1970s, the number of emigrants has risen sharply, reaching 82,619 in 1992.

Immigration to Japan is generally small-scale, although in recent years the illegal entry of workers from neighboring countries has become a problem. In 1992 there were 1,281,644 registered aliens, of which 688,144 were Koreans. Some

150,339 Chinese constituted the second-largest group. In 1992, 41,643 foreigners entered as permanent residents.

Internal migration of people from farm and mountain communities to the cities and suburbs has been accelerating since 1952. Most such migrants flocked to the three major population centers—the Tokyo, Osaka, and Nagoya metropolitan areas.

8 ETHNIC GROUPS

Waves of migration from the Asian continent reached Japan during the end of the Paleolithic period, blending into a complicated and diverse ethnic, linguistic, and cultural system. In physical characteristics, the Japanese belong to the Mongoloid group, mixed with traces of Malayan and Caucasoid strains.

The one remaining distinct ethnic group in Japan is the Ainu, who live on the island of Hokkaido and are physically distinct from the contemporary Japanese. The Ainu have Nordic-like features, including more facial and body hair.

9 LANGUAGES

Most linguists agree that Japanese is in a language class by itself. In vocabulary, Japanese is rich in words for abstract ideas, natural phenomena, human emotions, and ethics, but poor in words for technical and scientific expression. For these purposes, foreign words are used and written in a phonetic system (*katakana*). A distinct characteristic is the use of different forms of address to show proper respect to the listener and his or her social station.

Since the fifth century the Japanese have used Chinese characters to write with, giving them both an approximate Chinese pronunciation and a Japanese pronunciation. In addition, the Japanese invented phonetic symbols (*kana*) in the ninth century to represent grammatical devices unknown to the Chinese.

10 RELIGIONS

The principal religions in Japan are Shintoism and Buddhism. Many Japanese have ties with both a Buddhist temple and a Shinto shrine.

Shinto was originally concerned with the worship of spirits of nature. Under the influence of Chinese Confucianism, it grew to include worship of family and imperial ancestors. It is the basis of Japanese social structure. Today, Shinto exists as a private religious organization. Its membership was 109 million in 1991.

Buddhism, considered by some the most important religion in Japan, had a following of 96,255,000 in 1991. Introduced through China and Korea around AD 552, Buddhism spread rapidly throughout Japan and has had considerable influence on the nation's arts and its social institutions. There are 13 sects (*shu*) and 56 denominations, the principal *shu* being Tendai, Shingon, Jodo, Zen, Soto, Obaku, and Nichiren. Buddhism influenced the development of the great temples and gardens of Japan, the famous Japanese tea ceremony (*chanoyu*), and Japanese flower-arranging arts (*ikebana*).

In 1991 there were 1,464,000 Christians in Japan and about 1,000 Jews. After World War II, a considerable number of new religious groups sprang up. One of these, a Buddhist offshoot called the Soka-Gakkai, controlled a political party (Komeito)—at one time the third-strongest political group in Japan. Confucianism, an ethical system originating in China, has also strongly influenced Japanese society since the earliest periods.

11 TRANSPORTATION

Japan has a highly developed transportation system. In 1991, Japan had 27,327 kilometers (16,981 miles) of railways. In April 1987, the government-owned Japan National Railways (JNR) was divided into six privately owned railway companies, which had a combined total of 27,327 kilometers (16,981 miles) of lines.

In 1984, the superexpress trains of Japan's famous high-speed rail line, Shinkansen, covered the 1,069 kilometers (664 miles) between Tokyo and Fukuoka in less than seven hours, with maximum speeds of 210 kilometers/hour (130 miles/hour). By far the longest railway tunnel in the world, the 54.2-kilometer (33.7-mile) Seikan tube linking Honshu with Hokkaido was completed in 1985. Subway lines serve Tokyo and eight other cities.

Roads have become the most important means of domestic transport, carrying 65% of total passenger traffic and 90% of freight traffic in 1991. Motor vehicles in that year included 37,036,015 passenger cars and 22,838,608 commercial vehicles. There are about 1,111,874 kilometers (690,981 miles) of highways, of which about 68% are paved.

Japan is one of the world's great shipping nations. The chief ports are Yokohama (for Tokyo), Nagoya, and Kobe. In 1986, Japan ranked fifth in the world in gross tonnage of its merchant fleet. Its 944 merchant ships totaled 21,674,000 gross tons.

Japan Air Lines (JAL) is the nation's major domestic and international airline. In 1978, the new Narita International Airport, 72 kilometers (45 miles) northeast of downtown Tokyo, replaced Tokyo's Haneda International Airport as the chief international arrivals center. Environmentalists, local farmers, and others protested construction of the Narita facility, which served 18,603,000 arriving and departing passengers in 1991.

12 HISTORY

Origins

Little is known about the origins of the earliest Japanese beyond the fact that they migrated from the Asian continent. Tradition places the beginning of the Japanese nation in 660 BC when the legendary Emperor Jimmu ascended to the throne. Earlier contacts with Korea were expanded in the fifth century AD to mainland China, and the great period of cultural borrowing began: Chinese script was introduced, as well as the Chinese calendar and eventually Buddhism also. In 794, the imperial capital was removed to Heian (Kyoto), where it remained until 1868, when Tokyo became the nation's capital.

Photo credit: Susan D. Rock

A father and his son spending the afternoon fishing at a local pier.

In 1192, Yorimoto, the military leader (or *shogun*) of the Minamoto clan, established a military form of government that resulted in a feudal system that lasted for nearly 700 years. Under this system, known as the *shogunate,* all political power was in the hands of the dominant military clan, with the emperors ruling in name only. During the sixteenth century, an almost continuous civil war between rival feudal lords (*daimyos*) led to the formation of a class of professional warriors, the samurai. The first contact with the Western world took place with the arrival in 1543 of Portuguese traders, and the first guns, in southern Japan.

The Tokugawas

The Tokugawa shogunate, established in 1603 by Ieyasu Tokugawa, ruled Japan until the imperial restoration in 1868. They made Edo (modern Tokyo) their capital, closed Japan to almost all foreigners, and banned Christianity. For the next 250 years, Japan enjoyed peace, internal order, and a flowering of culture.

The arrival of Commodore Matthew C. Perry from the United States in 1853 began a decade of turmoil and confusion over the question of opening Japan. The Tokugawa shogun was forced to abdicate. In 1868, Emperor Meiji took over full sovereignty. This Meiji Restoration, as it is known, signaled the entry of Japan into the modern era.

Modern History

The Restoration leaders established a modern navy and army and universal compulsory education. In 1889, a new constitution provided for a bicameral legislature (Diet), with a civil cabinet headed by a prime minister.

By the end of the nineteenth century, a desire to expand its territory brought Japan into open conflict with its much larger western neighbors. Japan emerged victorious from wars fought with China over control of Korea (1894-95), and Russia over Manchuria and Korea (1904-05). Its victory over the Russians marked the first triumph of an Asian country over a Western power in modern times. Korea became a Japanese protectorate in 1905 and was annexed by Japan in 1910.

Japan participated in a limited way in World War I (1914–18) and was one of the Big Five powers at the Versailles Peace Conference. Its domestic economy developed rapidly, and Japan was transformed from an agricultural to an industrial nation. By the 1930s, the military became dominant. Acting independently of the central government, the military launched an invasion of Manchuria in 1931. In 1932, the prime minister was assassinated.

World War II (1939–45)

Japan withdrew from the League of Nations (which had protested the Manchurian takeover) in 1933, started a full-scale invasion of China in 1937, signed the Anti-Comintern pact with Germany in 1936, and formed a triple alliance with Germany and Italy in 1940. The military leadership signed a nonaggression pact with the Soviet Union in April 1941, setting the stage for the attack on Pearl Harbor and other Pacific targets on 7 December of that year. With its capture of the Philippines on 2 January 1942, Japan gained control of most of East Asia, including major portions of China, Indochina, and the southwest Pacific. Japan's forces, however, could not hold out against the Allied (mainly United States) military power. A series of costly sea battles brought an end to Japanese control of the Pacific.

United States leadership, headed by President Harry S. Truman, argued that a full invasion of Japan would prove too costly. They decided to bomb Japan into surrender. After four months of intense bombing with conventional weapons, the United States dropped the first atomic bomb ever used in warfare on Hiroshima on 6 August 1945. They dropped a second atomic bomb on Nagasaki three days later. An estimated 340,000 people died from the two attacks and the subsequent effects of radiation disease.

On 14 August, Japan accepted the Potsdam Declaration for unconditional surrender. During the United States occupation that followed, a series of ambitious reforms was begun: a parliamentary system of government based on the sovereignty of the people, land reform, greater local political freedom, and establishment of a free trade union movement. A new constitution was proclaimed on 3 November 1946.

The Postwar Period

With economic aid from the United States, and the determination of the Japanese people to rebuild their country, the Japanese economy rapidly recovered. The standard of living quickly surpassed the prewar level by a wide margin. In 1956 Japan was elected to United Nations membership. During the 1960s, Japan's remarkable economic expansion raised it to the level of a great trading power.

In 1968, it surpassed the Federal Republic of Germany (FRG) to stand second after the United States among non-Communist nations in total value of its gross national product (GNP). The lack of domestic petroleum resources, however, caused two separate oil crises. A second oil crisis during the 1970s led to long-range programs for energy conservation and diversification.

The yen declined in value in the early 1980s, causing Japanese exports to become cheaper in overseas markets. The United States and other leading trading partners began to demand that Japan limit certain exports and remove import barriers to Japan's domestic market.

A New Era

Emperor Hirohito died of cancer on 7 January 1989, at the age of 87. He was succeeded by the Crown Prince Akihito, who was enthroned in a formal ceremony in November 1990. The sense of entering a new era brought increased controversy over Japan's actions in the earlier part of the century, particularly during World War II. In March 1989, Prime Minister Takeshita apologized to North Korea for the suffering Japan caused over the 36 years it occupied Korea (1910–45). Emperor Akihito expressed similar regrets to President Roh Tae Woo of South Korea in May 1990. In 1992, Prime Minister Miyazawa apologized for the forced prostitution of Korean, Chinese, and Japanese women in Japanese military brothels during World War II.

The 1980s ended with a major scandal involving illegal stock trading. Scandals continued into the 1990s with stock dealings and, in 1992, contributions to politicians from a trucking company linked to organized crime. The stock market started falling in 1990. By the summer of 1992, it was at its lowest point in six years, 62% below the record high of 1989. By the end of 1993, Japan was in the midst of its worst economic downturn in at least 20 years.

Against the background of scandals and economic recession, the political landscape began a major change. After the resignation of prime minister Noboru Takeshita in April 1989, the ruling Liberal Democratic Party (LDP) lost its majority in the upper house of the Diet (parliament), its worst defeat in 34 years. The new prime minister, Mirihiro Hosokawa (JNP), was chosen on 29 July 1993, by a seven-party coalition of LDP defectors, Socialists, and conservatives. In April 1994, the LDP and the Socialist Party, traditionally opponents, allied to form a new coalition. They selected as prime minister

Tomiichi Murayama, the head of the Socialist Party and the first Socialist prime minister since 1948.

13 GOVERNMENT

Japan follows the parliamentary system in accordance with the constitution of 1947. The most significant change from the previous constitution of 1889 was the transfer of power from the emperor to the people. The emperor is now defined as "the symbol of the state and of the unity of the people." The constitution provides for the supremacy of the National Diet (parliament) as the legislative branch of the government, upholds the separation of legislative, executive, and judicial powers, and guarantees civil liberties.

The executive branch is headed by a prime minister selected from the Diet by its membership. The cabinet consists of the prime minister and 20 state ministers (as of January 1988), each heading a government ministry or agency.

The National Diet is bicameral. The House of Representatives (the lower house) has a membership of 512; the House of Councillors (the upper house) has 252 members. Anyone age 20 or older can vote.

Japan is divided into 47 prefectures containing 652 cities, 2,002 towns, and 596 villages.

14 POLITICAL PARTIES

The Liberal Democratic Party (LDP) represents much of Japanese society, but most especially the conservative elements. Formed in 1955, this party held the reins of government from its formation until July 1993. The Japan Socialist Party (JSP), Japan's principal opposition party, draws its support mainly from the working class.

In the summer of 1993, in the midst of economic recession and scandals involving corruption, sex, and organized crime, the old political order disintegrated as dozens of younger LDP members defected to form new parties. Chief among these were the Japan New Party (JNP), formed in May 1992, and the Sakigake (Harbinger Party) and the Shinseito (Renewal Party), both formed in June 1993.

15 JUDICIAL SYSTEM

The system consists of the Supreme Court, eight regional higher courts, district courts, and a number of summary courts. In addition, there are family courts, on the same level as the district courts, to rule on family conflicts and complaints such as divisions of estates, marriage annulments, and juvenile protection cases.

The Supreme Court determines the constitutionality of any law, order, regulation, or official act that is challenged during the regular hearing of a lawsuit. The Constitution affords criminal defendants a right to a speedy and public trial by an impartial judge. There is no right to a trial by jury.

16 ARMED FORCES

There has been a heated debate over the reestablishment of Japanese defense forces since Japan's participation in World War II. Laws establishing a Defense Agency and a Self-Defense Force became effective on 1 July 1954, both under firm civilian control.

The strength of Japan's armed forces in 1991 was 246,000. The Ground Self-Defense Force had 156,000 personnel, organized into 1 armored and 12 infantry divisions and 6 combined brigades. There were also 46,000 men in the reserves. The Maritime Self-Defense Force, consisting of 44,000 personnel, had 64 surface combatants, 13 combat submarines, and an air force of 99 aircraft and 72 armed helicopters. Air Self-Defense Force personnel numbered 46,000. Combat aircraft totaled 440, including jet fighters and air defense missiles supplied by the United States.

Although Japan's defense budgets—about $34 billion in 1992—rank high by world standards, they are small in relation to the size of the nation's economy. Japan relies for its military security on US conventional and nuclear forces, and the United States has repeatedly urged Japan to shoulder more of its own conventional defense burden. The United States maintains extensive military facilities and 40,000 troops in Japan.

17 ECONOMY

Japan's economy is the most advanced in Asia and the second largest in the world, behind that of the United States. Japan was the first Asian country to develop a large urban middle-class industrial society.

Since 1952, the number of farmers has fallen sharply, while industry and trade have grown rapidly. Japan relies on imports for all the raw cotton, raw wool, bauxite, and crude rubber used, as well as

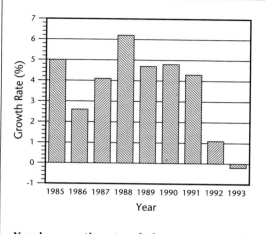

Yearly growth rate of the economy. This economic indicator tells by what percent the economy has increased or decreased when compared with the previous year.

for all oil supplies and varying proportions of other materials. To pay for these materials and for food and other import needs, Japan exports mainly manufactured products.

Real gross national product growth fell to –0.2% in 1993, its lowest level since the mid-1950s (aside from the oil crisis-related recession of 1974). In spite of the recent downturn, it is likely that Japan will maintain a healthy pace of economic development in the long term.

18 INCOME

In 1992, Japan's gross national product (GNP) was $3,507,841. For the period 1988–93, the estimated per person GNP was $31,490. For the period 1985–92 the average inflation rate was 1.4%, resulting in a real growth rate in GNP of 4.0%.

⊡19 INDUSTRY

During the 1970s and early 1980s, the rate of Japan's industrial growth surpassed that of any other non-Communist industrialized country. Of the 26 largest industrial companies in the world in the mid-1980s, four were Japanese: Toyota Motor, Matsushita Electric, Hitachi, and Nissan Motor. Despite declining profits with the economic downturn of the early 1990s, Japanese companies have continued to make large investments in new plants and equipment.

The electronics industry grew with extraordinary speed in the 1980s and now leads the world. Major electronic products in 1991 included 4.5 million facsimiles (fax machines); 18.2 million telephones; 3.0 million computers; 28 billion transistors; and 17.7 billion semiconductor integrated circuits. Also produced that year were 11.2 million radios, 15.6 million television sets, and 30.7 million videocassette recorders. Japan plays an increasingly important role in the computer industry. By 1987, Japan was fiercely competing with the United States in developing high-tech products, such as superconducting materials.

Japan is the world's leading shipbuilder. More than half the ships built are exported, including some of the world's largest oil tankers. However, rapid increases in the number of ships built by Brazil and South Korea reduced demand for Japanese-built ships from a peak of 38 million gross tons of new orders in 1973 to 7.0 million gross tons in 1991.

Photo credit: Susan D. Rock.

Toyota cars awaiting shipment to the United States.

In the early 1980s, Japan became the world's leading automobile producer, topping the United States for the first time in the history of the industry. Dominant industry giants are Nissan and Toyota, which together produced about three-fifths of all passenger cars in the mid-1980s. In 1991, a total of 10,412,000 passenger cars and vans were manufactured (up from 7,860,000 in 1985). Japan's superior technology in the design of bicycles, motorcycles, buses, and high-speed trains has been another major factor in the growth of the transport industry. In 1991, Japan produced 7.4 million bicycles and 5.0 million

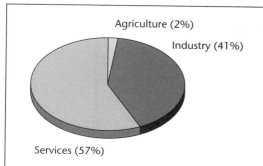

Agriculture (2%)

Industry (41%)

Services (57%)

Components of the economy. This pie chart shows how much of the country's economy is devoted to agriculture (includes forestry, hunting, and fishing), industry, or services.

[20] LABOR

The labor force in 1990 was made up of 63,840,000 people. The distribution of employed workers in 1992 was as follows: commerce and finance, 30.8%; manufacturing, 24.3%; services, 21.8%; construction, 9.6%; agriculture, forestry, fishing, aquaculture, 6.4%; transportation and communications, 6%; public utilities, 0.5%; mining, 0.1%; and unreported, 0.5%. Females comprised 41% of the work force in 1992. The minimum age for employment is 15, or 18 for dangerous work. Child labor laws are strictly enforced in Japan.

[21] AGRICULTURE

With the aid of a temperate climate, adequate rainfall, fertile soil maintained over centuries, and a large farm population, Japan has been able to develop intensive farming. In 1992, 6.2% of the labor force was engaged in agriculture.

In 1990, Japan produced much of its own food: 91% of vegetables; 63% of fruit; 15% of wheat; and 8% of beans. Almost all soybeans, feed for animals, and most of the nation's wheat are imported. In 1992, Japan produced 13.2 million tons of rice, the chief crop. In that year, rice accounted for about 92% of all cereal grain production. About 46.4% of all farmland is devoted to rice cultivation.

motorcycles, as well as 3.5 million trucks and buses.

The chemical and petrochemicals industry has been another of the economy's key growth areas since the late 1960s. Products include industrial chemicals such as sulfuric acid (7,057,000 tons in 1991), caustic soda (3,781,000 tons), and fertilizers, as well as plastics, dyestuffs, paints, and other items for domestic use. Polyethylene production increased by 10–15% annually during the late 1980s; output in 1991 was 2,982,000 tons. Output of crude steel peaked at 119.3 million tons in 1973, falling to 109.6 million tons in 1991.

Textiles and clothing, Japan's main exports during the years immediately following World War II, have steadily declined in importance. They accounted for only 2.5% of total value added in 1991 (as compared with 3.5% in 1985).

Other important crops include potatoes, sugar beets, mandarin oranges, cabbage, wheat, barley, soybeans, tobacco, and tea.

22 DOMESTICATED ANIMALS

Livestock production has been the fastest-growing area of Japanese agriculture. Meat production increased from 1.7 million tons in 1970 to 3.4 million tons in 1992. In 1992 there were 335 million chickens, 10,951,000 hogs, and 5,025,000 head of beef and dairy cattle. That year, milk production reached 8,300,000 tons (up from 1,886,997 tons in 1960); eggs, 2,586,000 tons; pork, 1,446,000 tons (147,318 tons in 1960); and beef, 594,000 tons (142,450 tons in 1960). Japan is the largest recipient of United States agricultural exports, importing about two-thirds of all US pork and beef exports in 1991.

23 FISHING

Japan is the world's foremost fishing nation, accounting on average for about 15% of the world's catch. The average annual catch is 12 million tons (excluding whaling). In 1989, per person daily consumption of fish and shellfish was among the world's highest.

Whales have been prized in Japan as a source of both food and a variety of by-products. Japanese whalers caught 2,769 whales in 1986. Japan ended commercial whaling in 1987, following a worldwide ban by the International Whaling Commission on the hunting of endangered species of whales.

24 FORESTRY

Forests cover nearly 67% of the total land area of Japan and in 1991 supplied about half the domestic demand for lumber and wood pulp. Japan was the world's second leading producer of paper and paperboard in 1991, after the United States.

In 1991, roundwood production totaled 28.3 million cubic meters, as compared with 49.1 million cubic meters in 1965. Throughout the 1980s and early 1990s, Japan has become more reliant on imported wood to satisfy domestic demand. Japan is the world's largest importer of softwood and tropical hardwood logs, and has become one of the largest importers of softwood lumber.

25 MINING

Japan is not rich in minerals, and mining is a relatively unimportant economic activity. For the last century, Japan has had to import nearly all of its petroleum, iron ore, copper, aluminum, and nickel. Coal is the most important mineral product, accounting for slightly more than half of all mineral production by value. Japan is self-sufficient in limestone production, in which it also ranks third highest globally.

26 FOREIGN TRADE

Foreign trade remains essential to the Japanese economy. Imports consist mostly of fuel, foodstuffs, industrial raw materials, and industrial machinery. Exports are varied, but manufactured products now account for nearly all of the total. Cars represent a leading export product, with the United States, Canada, Australia, Germany, and Britain the main markets. The export of office, scientific, and optical equipment is also important.

South Korea, China, and Taiwan are among the main buyers of Japan's iron

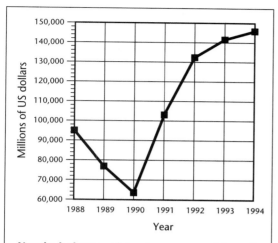

Yearly balance of trade measured in millions of US dollars. The balance of trade is the difference between what a country sells to other countries (its exports) and what it buys (its imports). If a country imports more than it exports, it has a negative balance of trade (a trade deficit). If exports exceed imports there is a positive balance of trade (a trade surplus).

and steel. Plastic materials and fertilizers are shipped primarily to South Korea and the Southeast Asian countries. Woven fabrics are supplied to China, the United States, Hong Kong, and Saudi Arabia.

In 1992 Japan ranked third in the world in total trade, after the United States and Germany. While the United States retained its position as Japan's single most important trade partner through the early 1990s, its share of the export market has declined considerably since the mid-1980s. In 1992, the United States accounted for only 28.1% of Japan's exports and 22.4% of its imports. Other leading partners in 1992 included Germany, South Korea, Taiwan, China, and Australia.

27 ENERGY AND POWER

Japan's primary 1992 energy needs were supplied by oil (57%), coal (17%), liquefied natural gas (11%), nuclear power (13%), and hydroelectricity (2%). For many years, Japan has been second only to the United States in oil imports, buying 5.3 million barrels of oil a day from overseas in 1992.

Japan ranked third in the world, behind the United States and former Soviet Union, in production of electricity in 1991, with an output of 837.7 billion kilowatt hours. Nuclear power plants accounted for 16.7% of the total; thermal (oil, natural gas, coal) plants, 63.6%; hydroelectric plants, 19.6%; and other plants (geothermal and other renewable resources), 0.1%.

28 SOCIAL DEVELOPMENT

The social stability of Japan is due largely to the strong sense of family solidarity among the Japanese. Virtually every home has its *butsudan*, or altar of the ancestors, and most elderly people are cared for in the homes of their grown children.

The social insurance system includes national health insurance, maternity coverage, unemployment insurance, and workers' accident compensation insurance. It also provides pension plans designed to maintain living standards for the elderly and for families of deceased workers.

Selected Social Indicators

These statistics are estimates for the period 1988 to 1993. For comparison purposes, data for the United States and averages for low-income countries and high-income countries are also given.

Indicator	Japan	Low-income countries	High-income countries	United States
Per capita gross national product†	**$31,490**	$380	$23,680	$24,740
Population growth rate	**0.3%**	1.9%	0.6%	1.0%
Population growth rate in urban areas	**0.4%**	3.9%	0.8%	1.3%
Population per square kilometer of land	**329**	78	25	26
Life expectancy in years	**79**	62	77	76
Number of people per physician	**607**	>3,300	453	419
Number of pupils per teacher (primary school)	**20**	39	<18	20
Illiteracy rate (15 years and older)	**<1%**	41%	<5%	<3%
Energy consumed per capita (kg of oil equivalent)	**3,642**	364	5,203	7,918

† The gross national product (GNP) is the total dollar value of all goods and services produced by a country in a year. The per capita GNP is calculated by dividing a country's GNP by its population. The World Bank defines low-income countries as those with a per capita GNP of $695 or less. High-income countries have a per capita GNP of $8,626 or more. Less than 14% of the world's 5.5 billion people live in high-income countries, while almost 60% live in low-income countries.

> = greater than   < = less than

Sources: World Bank, Social Indicators of Development 1995, Baltimore: Johns Hopkins University Press, 1995. Central Intelligence Agency, World Fact Book, Washington, D.C.: Government Printing Office, 1994.

Nearly the entire population receives benefits in one form or another from the health insurance system. Those not covered at work are insured through the National Health Insurance program.

Change is evident in the fact that women now make up 40% of Japan's employed workers. Marriages arranged by a go-between, or o-miai (half of all marriages in 1966) had declined dramatically by the 1990s.

29 HEALTH

Death rates from cancer and heart disease have risen considerably and now rank among the leading causes of death, trailing cerebrovascular diseases (high blood pressure and strokes). In 1990, the number of cancer patients increased 60% (to 810,000) from 1985. Average life expectancy was estimated to be 79 for the period 1988–93, among the highest rates in the world.

30 HOUSING

Construction of new housing slowed down in the 1980s, falling to between 1.1 million and 1.5 million units. This is due to a rapid rise in land and construction costs, which has put new housing out of the reach of many potential buyers. Condominiums and prefabricated homes provided much of the nation's new housing in the 1980s. New housing starts fell to 1.343 million in 1991 with the start of the recession. There were a total of 47.6 million housing units in 1992.

31 EDUCATION

Japan's entire educational system was reorganized and made similar to the United States system after World War II, with six years of primary school, three years of lower secondary school, three years of upper secondary school—full-time, part-time or correspondence—and four years of college. Education is available to both males and females. Virtually the entire adult population is literate.

Enrollment at the compulsory elementary and junior high school levels is very high, approaching 100%. About 95.1% continued into more advanced levels as of 1990. In that year, 9,373,295 students were enrolled in the 24,827 elementary schools; 5,369,162 students in the 11,275 lower secondary schools; and 5,623,336 students in the 5,506 upper secondary schools. The 593 junior colleges had 479,389 students and 507 universities had 2,133,362 students.

32 MEDIA

In 1991, Japan had 66,636,000 telephones. Telex, fax, and international telegram services are provided by Kokusai Denshin–Denwa (KDD).

The Japan Broadcasting Corporation (Nihon Hoso Kyokai—NHK) plays a large role in Japan's radio and television communications. As of 1991, the total number of NHK-operated and commercial radio stations reached 1,134. In 1992, Japan had 16,275 television stations. In 1991, there were 112.5 million radios and 76 million television sets in Japan.

The Japanese press is among the world's largest in terms of newspaper circulation. In 1991, daily newspapers numbered 158, with a total circulation of 71,228,000. The Japanese press is one of the most vigorous and outspoken in the world. The leading Japanese dailies, with their 1991 circulations, are *Yomiuri Shimbun* (9,722,000); *Asahi Shimbun* (8,197,600); *Mainichi Shimbun* (4,169,600); and *Nihon Keizai Shimbun* (1,719,200).

33 TOURISM AND RECREATION

Tourism in Japan is regarded as a major industry. In 1991, Japan had an estimated 3.53 million foreign visitors. Roughly half a million were American and approximately the same number were European. Nearly 1.7 million came from Japan's neighbors in northeast Asia. Almost one third (921,000) were business travelers. Tourist expenditures for 1991 totaled approximately $3.43 billion, and Japan's 217,016 hotel rooms had a 75% rate of occupancy.

Japan's chief sightseeing attractions are in the ancient former capital of Kyoto: Nijo Castle, Heian Shrine, the thirteenth-century Sanjusangendo temple, the Kinkaku-ji (Temple of the Golden Pavilion), the Ryoan-ji (Temple of the Peaceful Dragon), famed for its garden of stones and raked sand, and numerous other ancient Buddhist temples and Shinto shrines. Nearby sights in the vicinity of Nara (southeast of Osaka) include the Great Buddha, a huge bronze statue originally cast in the 8th century; the Kofuku-ji pagoda; and Horyu-ji, the 7th-century temple from which Buddhism spread throughout Japan.

Baseball is Japan's national pastime; there are two professional leagues, each with six teams. Sumo, a Japanese form of wrestling, is also popular, with tournaments held six times a year. Golf, an expensive sport because of the lack of open space, is used mainly as a means of entertaining business clients. Other pastimes include judo, karate, table tennis, fishing, and volleyball. Gardening is the most popular hobby among men and women alike.

34 FAMOUS JAPANESE

Murasaki Shikibu (late 10th–early 11th century) wrote *The Tale of Genji*, probably the best-known Japanese literary classic in English since it was first translated in the 1920s. Prominent modern novelists include Yasunari Kawabata (1899–1972), winner of the 1968 Nobel Prize for literature.

In art, the leader of the naturalist school was Maruyama Okyo (1733–95). The best-known painters and wood-block artists of the *ukiyo-e* style included Kitagawa Utamaro (1754–1806) and Ando Hiroshige (1797–1858).

Noted Japanese film directors include Yasujiro Ozu (1903–63) and Akira Kuro-sawa (b.1910). Toshiro Mifune (b.1920) is the best-known film star abroad. Contemporary composers include Toshiro Mayuzumi (b.1929) and Toru Takemitsu (b.1930). Seiji Ozawa (b.1935) is a world-famous orchestral conductor.

The leading home-run hitter in Japanese baseball history is Sadaharu Oh (b.1940), manager of the Yomiuri Giants.

Hirohito (1901–1989) became emperor of Japan in 1926. His eldest son, Crown Prince Akihito (b.1933), succeeded him in 1990.

35 BIBLIOGRAPHY

Cortazzi, Hugh. *Modern Japan: A Concise Survey.* New York: St. Martin, 1993.

Dahlby, Tracy. "Kyushu." *National Geographic,* January 1994, 88–117.

Doubilet, David. "Japan's Suruga Bay." *National Geographic,* October 1990, 2–39.

Fallows, Deborah. "Japanese Women." *National Geographic,* April 1990, 52–83.

Greene, C. *Japan.* Chicago: Children's Press, 1983.

Gup, Ted. "Hiroshima." *National Geographic,* August 1995, 78–101.

Hane, Mikiso. *Modern Japan: A Historical Survey.* 2d ed. Boulder, Colo.: Westview Press, 1992.

Nagel, Rob, and Anne Commire. "Fujiwara Michinaga." In *World Leaders, People Who Shaped the World.* Volume I: Africa and Asia. Detroit: U*X*L, 1994.

Packard, Jerrold M. *Sons of Heaven: A Portrait of the Japanese Monarchy.* New York: Scribner, 1987.

Perkins, Dorothy. *Encyclopedia of Japan: Japanese History and Culture, from Abacus to Zori.* New York: Facts on File, 1991.

Reid, T. R. "Kobe Wakes to a Nightmare." *National Geographic,* July 1995, 112–136.

Reischauer, Edwin O. *Japan: The Story of a Nation.* 4th ed. New York: Knopf, 1989.

Smith, Patrick. "Inner Japan." *National Geographic,* September 1994, 65–95.

Zich, Arthur. "Japan's Sun Rises Over the Pacific." *National Geographic,* November 1991, 36–67.

JORDAN

The Hashemite Kingdom of Jordan

Al-Mamlaka al-Urdunniyya al-Hashimiyya

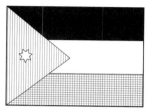

CAPITAL: 'Ammān.

FLAG: The national flag is a tricolor of black, white, and green horizontal stripes with a seven-pointed white star on a red triangle at the hoist.

ANTHEM: *As-Salam al-Maliki (Long Live the King).*

MONETARY UNIT: The Jordanian dinar (JD) is a paper currency of 1,000 fils. There are coins of 1, 5, 10, 20, 25, 50, 100, and 250 fils and notes of ½, 1, 5, 10, and 20 dinars. JD1 = $1.4286 (or $1 = JD0.7000).

WEIGHTS AND MEASURES: The metric system is the legal standard, but some local and Syrian units are still widely used, especially in the villages.

HOLIDAYS: Arbor Day, 15 January; Independence Day, 25 May; Accession of King Hussein, 11 August; King Hussein's Birthday, 14 November. Muslim religious holidays include the 1st of Muharram (Islamic New Year), 'Id al-Fitr, 'Id al-'Adha', and Milad an-Nabi. Christmas and Easter are observed by sizable Christian minorities.

TIME: 2 PM = noon GMT.

1 LOCATION AND SIZE

Situated in southwest Asia, Jordan has an area of 83,335 square kilometers (32,175 square miles), slightly smaller than the state of Indiana. It has a total boundary length of 1,753 kilometers (1,089 miles).

Jordan's capital city, 'Ammān, is located in the northwestern part of the country.

2 TOPOGRAPHY

The Jordan Valley has a maximum depression of 392 meters (1,286 feet) below sea level at the Dead Sea, the lowest point on the earth's surface. To the east of the Jordan River are the Transjordanian plateaus, with hills rising to more than 1,650 meters (5,400 feet) in the south. Desert makes up 88% of the East Bank.

The Jordan River enters the country from Israel to the north and flows into the Dead Sea.

3 CLIMATE

The Jordan Valley has little rainfall, intense summer heat, and mild, pleasant winters. The desert regions are subject to great extremes of temperature and receive rainfall of less than 20 centimeters (8 inches) annually, while the rest of the country has an average rainfall of up to 58 centimeters (23 inches) a year.

Temperatures at 'Ammān range from about –4°C (25°F) in winter to more than 38°C (100°F) in summer.

Photo credit: Embassy of Jordan.

Wadi Rum. A wadi is a stream bed or valley that is usually dry except during the rainy season. Oases are generally found in wadi areas.

4 PLANTS AND ANIMALS

The vegetation ranges from semitropical plant life in the Jordan Valley and other regions to shrubs and drought-resistant bushes in the desert. Wildlife includes the jackal, hyena, fox, wildcat, gazelle, antelope, and rabbit; the vulture, skylark, partridge, quail, woodcock, and goldfinch; and the viper and Syrian black snake.

5 ENVIRONMENT

Jordan's principal environmental problems are water shortages, soil erosion caused by overgrazing of goats and sheep, and loss of forest land. Water pollution is an important issue in Jordan. Jordan has 0.2 cubic miles of water with 65% used for farming activity and 6% used for industrial purposes. One-hundred percent of all city dwellers and 97% of rural people have pure water. Current sources of pollution are sewage, herbicides, and pesticides. Jordan's cities produce 1.2 million tons of solid waste per year.

Jordan's wildlife was reduced drastically by livestock overgrazing and uncontrolled hunting between 1930 and 1960. Larger wild animals, such as the Asiatic lion, have completely disappeared. As of 1994, 5 of Jordan's mammal species, 11 bird species, and 752 plant species are endangered.

6 POPULATION

The 1992 estimated population was 4,291,000 including the West Bank's population of 1,051,500, (excluding East Jerusalem). A population of 5,624,000 was projected for the year 2000. The estimated population density for the period 1988–93 (including the West Bank) was 44 persons per square kilometer (115 per square mile). In 1991, 'Ammān, the capital, had an estimated population of 965,000. In March 1993, 1,057,342 Palestinian refugees registered with a United Nations relief agency were living on the East Bank, about 220,000 of them in the 13 refugee centers. Another 476,236 were on the West Bank.

7 MIGRATION

About one-half or more of the population consists of refugees from territory that

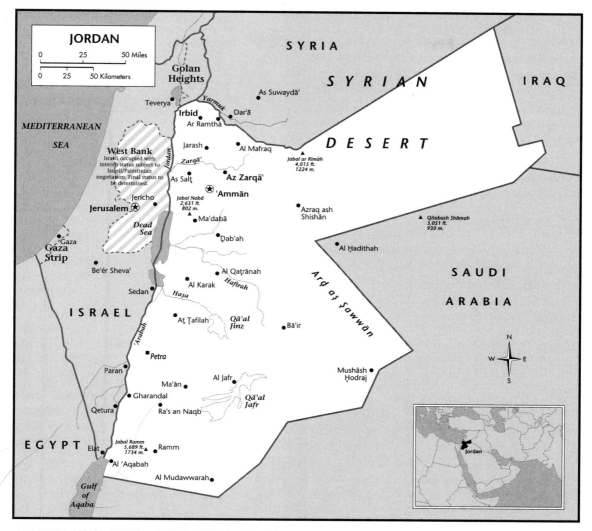

JORDAN

0 25 50 Miles
0 25 50 Kilometers

Golan Heights

SYRIA

SYRIAN

As Suwaydā'

Teverya
Yarmuk
Irbid   Dar'ā
Ar Ramthā

MEDITERRANEAN

SEA

DESERT

Jarash   Al Mafraq

Jabal ar Rimāh
4,015 ft.
1224 m.

West Bank
Israeli occupied with
interim status subject to
Israeli/Palestinian
negotiation. Final status to
be determined.

Zarqā'

As Salṭ
☪ 'Ammān
Az Zarqā'

Jericho
Jerusalem ✪

Jabal Nabā
2,631 ft.
802 m.

Azraq ash
Shishān

Qitabash Shāmah
3,051 ft.
930 m.

Dead
Sea

▲ Ma'dabā

Gaza
Gaza
Strip

Ḍab'ah

Al Ḥadithah

SAUDI

Be'ér Sheva'

Al Qaṭrānah

ARABIA

Sedan

Al Karak

Ḥafīrah

Ḥasa

Aṭ Ṭafilah

Qā'al
Jinz

Bā'ir

Ard aş Şawwān

ISRAEL

Petra

Paran

Ma'ān

Al Jafr

Mushāsh
Ḥodraj

Gharandal

Qā'al
Jafr

N
W   E
S

Qetura

Ra's an Naqb

EGYPT Elāt

Jabal Ramm
5,689 ft. ▲
1734 m.

Ramm

Al 'Aqabah

Al Mudawwarah

Gulf
of
Aqaba

Jordan

IRAQ

LOCATION: (1949): 29°17′ to 33°20′N; 34°53′ to 39°12′E. **BOUNDARY LENGTHS:** Syria, 356 kilometers (221 miles); Iraq, 146 kilometers (91 miles); Sa'udi Arabia, 744 kilometers (462 miles); Gulf of Aqaba, 27 kilometers (17 miles); Israel: 1949 armistice line, 531 kilometers (330 miles); 1967 ceasefire line, 480 kilometers (298 miles). **TERRITORIAL SEA LIMIT:** 3 miles.

became part of Israel. There is also a great deal of native-born migration by nomadic groups across the Syrian, Iraqi, and Sa'udi Arabian borders. Many Jordanians live abroad, attracted by job opportunities in the oil-rich Arab states. About 300,000 Jordanians returned from the Persian Gulf states after the 1991 war, mainly from Kuwait. About 120,000 Iraqis fled to Jordan in 1991.

8 ETHNIC GROUPS

Ethnically, the Jordanians represent a mixed stock. The Bedouin nomads of the deserts are Arab. Most of the rest of the population are Arab mixed with the numerous peoples that have been present in Jordan for thousands of years, including Greek, Egyptian, Persian, European, and Negroid inhabitants. Perhaps 1% of the population (43,000) is Armenian, and there are about 25,000 Circassians.

9 LANGUAGES

Arabic is the language of the country, spoken even by the ethnic minorities who also maintain their own languages.

10 RELIGIONS

Islam is the state religion, although all are guaranteed religious freedom. Most Jordanians (about 92%) are Sunni Muslims. Christians constitute about 5% of the population; most are Greek Orthodox or Roman Catholic. Other minority religions include Baha'is, mainly of Persian stock, and Samaritans, an unorthodox form of the ancient Jewish religion.

11 TRANSPORTATION

In 1991, of the 7,500 kilometers (4,660 miles) of road, 5,500 kilometers (3,418 miles) were paved. Passenger automobiles numbered 172,075; trucks, buses, and other commercial vehicles totaled 35,854. The rail system includes some 619 kilometers (385 miles) of narrow-gauge single track. Al 'Aqabah, Jordan's only outlet to the sea, is situated at the head of the Gulf of Aqaba, an arm of the Red Sea.

The government-owned Alia–Royal Jordanian Airline operates domestic and international flights. The major airport is the new Queen Alia International Airport.

12 HISTORY

Origins

Neolithic remains from about 7000 BC have been found in Jericho, the oldest known city in the world. In the tenth century BC, the western part of the area of Jordan formed part of the domain of the Hebrew kings David and Solomon. In the fourth century BC, Palestine and Syria were conquered by Alexander the Great, beginning about 1,000 years of on-and-off European rule.

After the second century AD, Palestine and areas east of the Jordan came under direct Roman rule. Christianity spread rapidly in Jordan and for 300 years was the dominant religion. However, when Muslim invaders appeared, little resistance was offered, and in 636, Arab rule was firmly established. The area became thoroughly Arabized and Islamized, remaining so to this day despite a century-long domination by the Crusaders (twelfth century). It was controlled by the Ottoman Turks from 1517 to 1917.

1917–1958

During World War I (1914–18), the British persuaded Sharif Hussein ibn-'Ali, the Hashemite ruler of Mecca, to start an Arab revolt against the Turks. After the defeat of the Turks, Palestine and Transjordan were placed under British administration. In 1923, the independence of

Transjordan was proclaimed under British supervision, and by 1946, Transjordan attained full independence.

After the Arab-Israeli war of 1948, King 'Abdallah annexed the area of Palestine now known as the West Bank. It was incorporated into the Hashemite Kingdom of Jordan in 1950. Meanwhile, since the 1948 war, Jordan had absorbed about 500,000 of some 1,000,000 Palestinian Arab refugees, mostly sheltered in United Nations-administered camps. On 20 July 1951, 'Abdallah was assassinated in Jerusalem by a Palestinian Arab, and the throne passed to his grandson Hussein I, who was formally enthroned on 2 May 1953.

Following the overthrow of Egypt's King Faruk in July 1952, the Arab countries were strongly influenced by the movement for Arab unity. Jordan, however, maintained a close association with Britain in an effort to preserve the kingdom as a separate, independent country. British intervention during the 1956 war in the Suez hurt their relations with Jordan. But Hussein turned again to the West for support after his cousin King Faisal II (Faysal) of Iraq was assassinated in a July 1958 coup. British troops were flown to Jordan from Cyprus.

1959–1967

Hussein, while retaining Jordan's Western ties, gradually steadied his relations with other Arab states (except Syria). But even in years of comparative peace, relations with Israel remained the focus of tensions in the region. Terrorist raids launched from within Jordan drew strong Israeli reprisals. In addition, the activities of the Palestine Liberation Organization (PLO) often violated Jordan's borders, leading Hussein in July 1966, and again in early 1967, to withdraw support for the PLO, again angering the Arab world.

In the 1967 Six-Day War with Israel, Israel took over the Jordanian West Bank (including all of Jerusalem). Jordan suffered heavy casualties, and over 300,000 Palestinians fled across the Jordan River to the East Bank. Jordan's refugee population swelled from 700,000 in 1966 to over 1,000,000, adding to the severe economic problems caused by the war.

1970–1979

After Hussein's acceptance of a cease-fire with Israel in August 1970, he tried to suppress various Palestinian guerrilla organizations, finally driving them out in July 1971. In the following September, Premier Wasfi al-Tal was assassinated by guerrilla commandos. Coup attempts, in which Libya was said to have been involved, were defeated in November 1972 and February 1973.

Jordan did not actively participate in the "Yom Kippur War" against Israel in October 1973, but it sent an armored brigade of about 2,500 men to assist Syria. After the Egyptian-Israeli Peace Treaty of 1979, Jordan joined other Arab states in trying to isolate Egypt diplomatically. Hussein refused to join further Egyptian-Israeli talks on the future of the West Bank.

Photo credit: Embassy of Jordan.

Desert police making coffee.

1980–1995

In the 1980s, Hussein followed policies of gradually liberalized internal politics. In 1988, Jordan cut its ties with the Israeli occupied West Bank. In 1989, for the first time since 1956, Jordan held relatively free parliamentary elections. New parliamentary elections were held in 1993.

In 1990, Jordan was critical of the Gulf War led by the United States. This hurt Jordan's relations with the United States and the Gulf states. Jordan lost its subsidies from the latter while having to support hundreds of thousands of refugees from the war and its aftermath.

Jordan's willingness to participate in peace talks with Israel in late 1991 helped repair relations with Western countries. In June 1994, Jordan and Israel began meetings to work out practical steps on water, borders, and energy which would lead to normal relations. In July of 1994, Jordan and Israel signed a peace treaty that officially ended their state of war. In September of 1995, Israel agreed to give administrative control of the West Bank to the Palestinians.

13 GOVERNMENT

Jordan is a constitutional monarchy. The king has wide powers over all branches of government. The constitution gives legislative power to the National Assembly, composed of a 40-member Senate and an 80-member lower house, the Chamber of Deputies. There is universal suffrage at age 18, women having received the right to vote in April 1973.

14 POLITICAL PARTIES

Political parties were abolished on 25 April 1957, following an alleged attempted coup by Arab militants. In 1992, parties were again permitted and 20 were allowed to take part in elections. The main opposition group has been the Islamic Action Front, the political arm of the Moslem (Muslim) Brotherhood.

Jordan (outside the West Bank) is divided into eight governorates, each under a governor appointed by the king.

15 JUDICIAL SYSTEM

There are four levels of civil and criminal courts, religious courts, and tribal courts.

The Supreme Court and the courts of appeals deal with appeals from lower courts. Courts of First Instance hear major civil and criminal cases. Religious courts, such as the Muslim Shari'ah courts, have authority over matters such as marriage, divorce, wills and testaments, and orphans.

16 ARMED FORCES

In 1993, the Jordanian army had some 85,000 men. The air force had 14,000 men and 113 combat aircraft. The navy had only about 400 men and 3 patrol craft. Reserve manpower was estimated at 35,000. Defense expenditures for 1990 were $404 million. Jordan has 875 peacekeepers abroad.

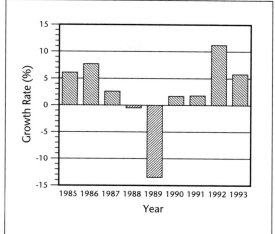

Yearly growth rate of the economy. This economic indicator tells by what percent the economy has increased or decreased when compared with the previous year.

17 ECONOMY

Jordan's economy has been greatly affected by the Arab-Israeli conflict. The loss of the West Bank in 1967 resulted in the loss of most of Jordan's richest agricultural land and a decline in the growing tourist industry. An estimated 80% of annual national income in the early 1980s came from direct grants from and exports to oil-rich Arab countries. Other sources of income included tax payments and money being sent home by Jordanians working in other Arab countries. Western economic aid, notably from the United States, Britain, and Germany, has also been important to the economy.

The start of the recession in Jordan in the mid-1980s followed by the economic collapse of 1988–89 and the Gulf War in 1990 left the country with an unemployment rate of approximately 30–35% and high inflation. About 25–30% of the population fell below the poverty line.

18 INCOME

In 1992, Jordan's gross national product (GNP) was $4,406 million or about $1,190 per person. For the period 1985–92 the average inflation rate was 7.2%, resulting in a real growth rate in per person GNP of –7.0%.

19 INDUSTRY

Most industrial income comes from four industries: cement, oil refining, phosphates, and potash. Cement production rose to 2,746,000 tons in 1992. Output of the oil refinery at Az Zarqa' rose to 2,839,000 tons in 1992. Phosphate production was 4,295,900 that same year.

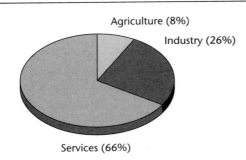

Agriculture (8%)

Industry (26%)

Services (66%)

Components of the economy. This pie chart shows how much of the country's economy is devoted to agriculture (includes forestry, hunting, and fishing), industry, or services.

21 AGRICULTURE

Although 40% of the farmable land was in the West Bank, which Israel took over in 1967, agriculture still plays a role in the economy. As of 1991, an estimated 63,000 hectares (155,600 acres) were irrigated. The main crops are wheat and barley, vegetables, fruits, and olives. In 1992, production (in tons) was as follows: tomatoes, 300,000; tangerines, 80,000; wheat, 80,000; barley, 65,000; olives, 60,000; lemons and limes, 50,000; grapes, 44,000; bananas, 27,000; and tobacco, 3,000.

Jordan's Dead Sea potash extraction plant produced over 1.26 million tons in 1992. Manufacturing output fell by 2.9% in 1991 due to the impact of the Gulf War. It grew again by 6.2% in 1992.

20 LABOR

Jordan's labor shortage of the early 1980s changed to a serious labor surplus a decade later. A high population growth rate combined with the return of Jordanians who had been living in the Persian Gulf created a situation where there were more workers than jobs.

Of the 237,060 nonagriculturally employed persons in Jordan at the start of 1991, services and government employed an estimated 62.7%, construction 1.3%, industry 21.4%, trade 5.5%, and transportation and communications 9.1%. Labor disputes are mediated by the Ministry of Labor. The minimum age for employment is 16, except for apprentices who can start at 13.

22 DOMESTICATED ANIMALS

The care and management of domesticated animals is practiced primarily by Bedouin nomads. Camels provide transportation, food (milk and meat), shelter, and clothing (hair). The sale of surplus camels is a source of cash. Sheep and goats are also maintained.

Animal products account for about one-third of agricultural output. In 1992, estimates of Jordan's livestock on the East Bank were 2,000,000 sheep, 600,000 goats, 32,000 head of cattle, and 18,000 camels. Jordan had an estimated 55,000,000 chickens in 1992.

23 FISHING

The rivers support few fish. There are no fish in the Dead Sea, and the short Gulf of Aqaba shoreline has only recently been developed for fishing. The total fish catch was only 22 tons in 1992.

24 FORESTRY

The olive, characteristic of the Mediterranean basin, is widely cultivated. By 1976, some 3,800 hectares (9,400 acres) had been newly planted as part of a government reforestation program. From 1976 to 1991, an additional 10,000 hectares (24,700 acres) also was reforested. Roundwood production was 9,000 tons in 1991.

25 MINING

Jordan's mineral resources consist chiefly of phosphate, potash, and limited manganese, copper, kaolin, and gypsum deposits. Phosphate deposits are estimated at about 1 billion tons. Production of phosphates fell to 4,433,000 tons in 1991, the lowest amount in nine years. However, Jordan still maintained its rank of fourth place globally in mined tonnage of phosphate rock.

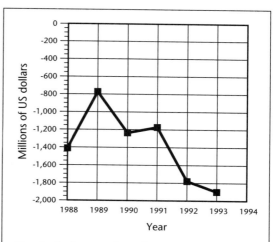

Yearly balance of trade measured in millions of US dollars. The balance of trade is the difference between what a country sells to other countries (its exports) and what it buys (its imports). If a country imports more than it exports, it has a negative balance of trade (a trade deficit). If exports exceed imports there is a positive balance of trade (a trade surplus).

26 FOREIGN TRADE

Jordan exports mainly phosphates, manufactured products, and fruits and vegetables. Imports consist mainly of machinery, manufactured products, petroleum, and foodstuffs. Exports rose to about $1.2 billion in 1992; imports increased to about $3 billion. The trade deficit soared to about $1.8 billion in 1992.

Until 1990 when the oil embargo against Iraq went into effect, Jordan bought the bulk of its crude oil from Iraq. Iraq has also been a key market for Jordanian exports. The next most important markets for Jordan were India, which purchased mainly mineral fertilizers in 1992, and Saudi Arabia, which topped the $100 million mark. The United States sold Jordan goods worth over $351 million and Germany supplied goods worth $267 million in 1992.

27 ENERGY AND POWER

Jordan does not have petroleum deposits. Its imports of oil from Sa'udi Arabia via the Trans-Arabian pipeline (Tapline) and its refinery at Az Zarqa', with an annual productive capacity of 22 million barrels, supply virtually all the country's energy needs. At the end of 1991, electricity generated totaled 3,723 million kilowatt hours. A major new thermal station at Al 'Aqabah had added 130 megawatts of generating capacity by the mid-1980s.

Selected Social Indicators

These statistics are estimates for the period 1988 to 1993. For comparison purposes, data for the United States and averages for low-income countries and high-income countries are also given.

Indicator	Jordan	Low-income countries	High-income countries	United States
Per capita gross national product†	**$1,190**	$380	$23,680	$24,740
Population growth rate	**3.8%**	1.9%	0.6%	1.0%
Population growth rate in urban areas	**4.8%**	3.9%	0.8%	1.3%
Population per square kilometer of land	**44**	78	25	26
Life expectancy in years	**70**	62	77	76
Number of people per physician	**767**	>3,300	453	419
Number of pupils per teacher (primary school)	**24**	39	<18	20
Illiteracy rate (15 years and older)	**20%**	41%	<5%	<3%
Energy consumed per capita (kg of oil equivalent)	**922**	364	5,203	7,918

† The gross national product (GNP) is the total dollar value of all goods and services produced by a country in a year. The per capita GNP is calculated by dividing a country's GNP by its population. The World Bank defines low-income countries as those with a per capita GNP of $695 or less. High-income countries have a per capita GNP of $8,626 or more. Less than 14% of the world's 5.5 billion people live in high-income countries, while almost 60% live in low-income countries.

> = greater than   < = less than

Sources: World Bank, Social Indicators of Development 1995, Baltimore: Johns Hopkins University Press, 1995. Central Intelligence Agency, World Fact Book, Washington, D.C.: Government Printing Office, 1994.

28 SOCIAL DEVELOPMENT

The social insurance system provides old-age, disability, and survivor benefits, as well as workers' compensation. The United Nations Relief and Works Agency conducts an extensive welfare program for Palestinian refugees. Many Christian sects maintain hospitals, orphanages, and schools, financed mainly by foreign sources.

Women experience legal discrimination regarding pension and social security benefits, inheritance, and divorce. Under Islamic law, a female heir's inheritance is half that of a male, and in court, a woman's testimony has only half the value of a man's. However, in 1992, Parliament effectively blocked Islamists from enacting further legislation discriminating against women.

29 HEALTH

In 1990, Jordan had 1.9 hospital beds per 1,000 people, and, in 1991, 6,395 physicians and 6,466 nurses. Total health care expenditures for 1990 were $149 million. In 1992, 97% of the population had access to health care services.

Trachoma, hepatitis, typhoid fever, intestinal parasites, acute skin inflammations, and some other conditions remain common, however. In 1991, 99% of the population had access to safe water and 100% of the population had adequate sanitation. The average life expectancy is 70 years.

30 HOUSING

Jordan still lacked adequate housing in the early 1980s. During 1981–86, some 42,300 new residential building permits were issued. According to the latest available information for 1980–88, the total number of dwellings was 660,000 with 4.1 people per dwelling.

31 EDUCATION

The literacy rate rose from only 32% of the population in 1961 to 80% in 1990, with male literacy estimated at 89.3% and female at 70.3%. Education is compulsory for nine years. A further three years prepares students for university education. In 1991, Jordan had 2,424 primary schools with 40,694 teachers and 981,255 pupils. Secondary schools had a total of 109,429 pupils the same year.

Besides the University of Jordan at 'Ammān, Jordan has universities at Irbid, at Biz Zeit, and in Al Karak. In 1991, a total of 84,226 students were enrolled at all higher level institutions. Higher education teaching staff numbered 3,753.

32 MEDIA

Jordan's four daily newspapers with 1991 estimated daily circulations are *Al-Dustur* ("Constitution"; 90,000), *Al-Rai* ("Opinion"; 120,000), *Ash-Sha'ab* ("People"; 30,000), and the *Jordan Times* (13,000).

Photo credit: Susan D. Rock

Busy downtown street corner in 'Ammān.

Al-Rai is a government-controlled paper. The government–owned television station broadcasts programs in English, Arabic, French, and Hebrew on two channels. In 1991 there were more than 1,060,000 radios and about 330,000 television sets.

33 TOURISM AND RECREATION

The Gulf War caused a decline in tourism; 2,227,688 visitors arrived in Jordan in 1991, compared with 2,633,262 the year before. Of these arrivals, 28% were from Egypt, 25% from Syria, and 13% from Iraq. There were 7,733 hotel rooms with a

40% occupancy rate, and tourism receipts totaled $317 million.

Jordan is an area of immense historical interest, with some 800 archaeological sites, including 224 in the Jordan Valley. Jordan's notable tourist attractions include the Greco-Roman remains at Jarash (ancient Garasi), one of the best-preserved cities of its time in the Middle East. Petra (Batra), carved out of the red rock by the Nabataeans, is probably the most famous historical site. Natural attractions include the Jordan Valley and the Dead Sea, which—at 392 meters (1,286 feet) below sea level—is the lowest spot on Earth.

Eastern Jordan has modern hotel facilities in 'Ammān and Al 'Aqabah. The beaches on the Gulf of Aqaba offer holiday relaxation for Jordanians as well as tourists. Sports facilities include swimming pools, tennis and squash courts, and bowling alleys.

34 FAMOUS JORDANIANS

The founder of Jordan's Hashemite dynasty was Hussein ibn-'Ali (Husayn bin 'Ali, 1856–1931). The founder of the kingdom, 'Abdallah ibn-Husayn (1882–1951), was recognized as emir in 1921 and as king in 1946. His grandson, King Hussein I (Husayn ibn-Talal, b. 1935), has ruled since 1953.

35 BIBLIOGRAPHY

Foster, L. *Jordan*. Chicago: Children's Press, 1991.

Hussein, King, of Jordan. *My War with Israel*. New York: Morrow, 1969.

Jordan in Pictures. Minneapolis: Lerner, 1988.

Lawrence, T. E. *The Seven Pillars of Wisdom*. New York: Penguin, 1976 (orig. 1926).

Salibi, Kamal S. *The Modern History of Jordan*. New York: I.B. Tauris, 1993.

KAZAKHSTAN

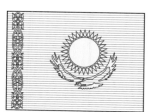

Republic of Kazakhstan
Kazakhstan Respublikasy

CAPITAL: Almaty (Alma-Ata).

FLAG: Light blue with a yellow sun and soaring eagle in the center and a yellow vertical ornamentation in the hoist.

ANTHEM: National Anthem of Kazakhstan.

MONETARY UNIT: The tenge, issued in 15 November 1993, is the national currency, replacing the ruble (R). There is a coin, the tyin. One hundred tyin equal one tenge. As of fall 1994, 50 tenge = US$1, but exchange rates fluctuate widely.

WEIGHTS AND MEASURES: The metric system is in force.

HOLIDAYS: New Year, 31 December–1 January; International Women's Day, 8 March; Nauryz (Kazakh New Year), 28 March; Solidarity Day, 1 May; Victory Day, 9 May; Independence Day, 25 October.

TIME: 5 PM = noon GMT.

1 LOCATION AND SIZE

Kazakhstan is located in southern Asia between Russia and Uzbekistan, bordering on the Caspian Sea and the Aral Sea, with a total area of 2,717,300 square kilometers (1,049,155 square miles). Kazakhstan's boundary length totals 12,012 kilometers (7,466 miles). Its capital currently is Almaty (Alma-Ata). There are plans to shift the capital to the north central part of the nation.

2 TOPOGRAPHY

The topography of Kazakhstan is varied, as it extends from the Volga River to the Altai Mountains, and from plains in western Siberia to central Asian oasis and desert.

3 CLIMATE

The country has a dry continental climate. In Almaty the mean temperature is 27°C (81°F) in July and –5°C (23°F) in January. Rainfall averages between 25 centimeters (9.8 inches) and 38 centimeters (15 inches).

4 PLANTS AND ANIMALS

Kazakhstan has typically sparse desert plant covering. Animals include the antelope, sand cat, and jerboa.

5 ENVIRONMENT

As the site of the former Soviet Union's nuclear testing programs, areas of the nation have been exposed to high levels of nuclear radiation, creating a great deal of radioactive pollution.

Badly run irrigation projects have decreased the size of the Aral Sea by 50%, eroding 3 million hectares (7.4 million acres) of land. Acid rain damages the environment within Kazakhstan and the surrounding countries. Pollution from industrial and agricultural sources has also damaged the nation's water supply.

As of 1994, Kazakhstan's wildlife was in danger of extinction due to the overall level of pollution. In the most polluted areas, 11 species of mammals and 19 species of birds and insects are already extinct.

6 POPULATION

The population of Kazakhstan was estimated at 17,035,000 at the end of 1992. The projection for 2000 was 18,332,000. The estimated population density for the period 1988–93 was 6 persons per square kilometer (16 per square mile). Almaty, the capital, had an estimated population of 1,147,000 at the beginning of 1990.

7 MIGRATION

Kazakhs abroad (in China, Mongolia, and other former Soviet republics) are encouraged to return. Emigration to other Soviet republics exceeded immigration by 301,800 during 1979–90.

8 ETHNIC GROUPS

Kazakhs constituted 40% of the population in 1989 and Russians, 38%. Germans accounted for 6%, Ukrainians for 5%, and Uzbeks and Tatars, 2% each.

9 LANGUAGES

Kazakh, the national language, is a Turkic language written in Cyrillic script with many special letters. However, no more than half of all Kazakhs can speak the language effectively, so Russian is the language commonly used to communicate.

10 RELIGIONS

Ethnic Kazakhs are primarily Sunni Muslims of the Hanafi persuasion. The other ethnic groups are Christian, mostly Eastern Orthodox. In 1993 there was also a small but significant population of 500,000 Roman Catholics.

11 TRANSPORTATION

About 14,460 kilometers (8,985 miles) of railroad tracks traverse Kazakhstan. Highways totaled 189,000 kilometers (117,000 miles) in 1990, almost entirely hard-surfaced. The primary port is Atyrau (Guryev), on the Caspian Sea.

12 HISTORY

Early History

There is evidence of humans living in present-day Kazakhstan from the earliest Stone Age, more than 300,000 years ago. The first well-established state was that of the Turkic Kaganate, in the sixth century AD. Part of the region fell under Arab influence in the eighth to ninth centuries, and Islam was introduced. For several centuries, the area was controlled by a series of warring tribes.

The present-day Kazakhs formed in the mid-fifteenth century. Russian traders

KAZAKHSTAN

0 125 250 375 500 Miles
0 125 250 375 500 Kilometers

LOCATION: 48°N; 60°E. **BOUNDARY LENGTHS:** China, 1,533 kilometers (954 miles); Kyrgyzstan, 1,051 kilometers (653 miles); Russia, 6,846 kilometers (4,254 miles); Turkmenistan, 379 kilometers (236 miles); Uzbekistan, 2,203 kilometers (1,369 miles).

and soldiers began to appear on the northwestern edge of Kazakh territory in the seventeenth century. In 1726, a Kazakh leader requested Russian military assistance against his enemies, and by the 1820s all of Kazakhstan was under Russian control. Starting in 1863, Russian troops began the conquest of Central Asia. Most of Kazakhstan was made part of the

Steppe district of the Russian empire; the rest was in Turkestan.

Beginning in the 1890s, Russian settlers moved into fertile lands in northern and eastern Kazakhstan, displacing the nomadic Kazakhs. In 1916, the Kazakhs, broken and starving, revolted. Despite a strong effort against the Russians, however, they were defeated. At the time of the

KAZAKHSTAN

1917 Russian revolution, a group of nationalists called the Alash Orda attempted to create a Kazakh government. It lasted less than two years (1918–20) before surrendering to the Bolsheviks.

Modern History

The Kazakh Autonomous Soviet Socialist Republic was declared in 1920. In the period 1929–34, Joseph Stalin abolished private agriculture and established huge collective farms. During the transition, Kazakhstan suffered repeated famines which killed at least 1.5 million Kazakhs.

In World War II (1939–45) much Russian industry was moved to Kazakhstan. This was followed in 1953–65 by the so-called Virgin Lands campaign, which converted huge tracts of Kazakh grazing land to wheat and other grain production. This brought thousands more Russians and other non-Kazakhs to Kazakhstan. As a result, Kazakhstan became the only Soviet republic in which the native people were not a majority of the population.

The first public nationalist protest in the Soviet Union before its breakup occurred in Kazakhstan in 1986. In June 1989, more civil disturbances brought about the appointment of Nursultan Nazarbaev as republic leader. Nazarbaev, who later became president, strongly promoted Kazakh participation in the formation of the Commonwealth of Independent States.

13 GOVERNMENT

The constitution of the Republic of Kazakhstan, adopted 28 January 1993, mandates three separate branches of government: a president and vice-president; a parliament, called the Majlis or Supreme Soviet; and a judiciary, appointed by the president. The president's executive powers also include appointment of a prime minister and cabinet. Elections to the new 177-seat parliament were held 7 March 1994.

Kazakhstan is divided into 19 *oblasts*, or provinces, which are, in turn, divided into *rayons*, or regions.

14 POLITICAL PARTIES

The Socialist Party is the successor to the Communist Party. The People's Congress, or Social-Democratic Party, has both Kazakh and Russian members. A third party, the Party for National Unity (SNEK), was registered in October 1992.

15 JUDICIAL SYSTEM

A Constitutional Court established in 1992 is responsible for interpreting the constitution, resolving conflicts between provinces (*oblasts*), and inter-ethnic problems. The courts are arranged in three tiers: local level, province (*oblast*) level, and Supreme Court. Local level courts provide initial hearings for less serious crimes. Oblast level courts hear more serious criminal cases and also hear cases in rural areas where no local courts have been established. Judgment of local courts may be appealed to the oblast level. The Supreme Court hears appeals from the oblast courts.

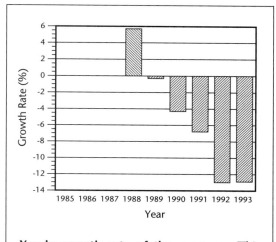

Yearly growth rate of the economy. This economic indicator tells by what percent the economy has increased or decreased when compared with the previous year.

16 ARMED FORCES

Without an independent national military establishment, Kazakhstan shares control of Commonwealth of Independent States (CIS) forces within its borders: an army corps of 6 divisions and 6 special brigades, a tactical air force of 200 fighter-bombers, an air defense force of 60 interceptors and 150 missiles, and a strategic nuclear force of 104 SS–18s and 40 bombers.

17 ECONOMY

Like other countries of the former Soviet Union, Kazakhstan has faced serious economic adjustments since 1991, resulting from the disruption of trade with other post-Soviet republics, an end to the flow of money from the Soviet central government, the decline in state production

orders, and the need for sudden currency adjustments.

Legislation adopted in 1992 has promoted the spread of private ownership in business and housing, and the inflow of large foreign investments. In 1991 per person income was $1,560. Inflation reached a staggering 2,000% in 1993, causing a severe drop in real income for much of the population, 20% of whom are feared to be facing serious poverty.

18 INCOME

In 1992, Kazakhstan's gross national product (GNP) was $28,584 million or about $1,560 per person.

19 INDUSTRY

Processing of agricultural products accounted for 23.6% of industrial output in 1991. Metallurgy and mining accounted for 14.6% of industrial output in that same year. Food processing activities yielded 840,831 tons of meat, 302,900 tons of sugar, and 101,000 tons of vegetable oil. Metal processing output in 1991 included crude steel, 6,377 thousand tons; and finished rolled ferrous metals, 4,660 thousand tons.

In 1991, textile and leather production included knitted wear, 111,820 pieces; fabrics (wool, cotton, and silk), 248,708 square meters (207,950 square yards); and shoes, 35,410 pairs. Goods produced by light industry enterprises included 535,000 electric irons, 391,000 washing machines, 130,674 tape recorders, and 86,300 radios. Machine-building is also among the largest of Kazakhstan's industries. Production in 1991 included bull-dozers, 10,278 units; metal-cutting equipment, 2,414 units; and excavators, 577 units.

20 LABOR

The labor force consists of some 8.2 million persons, with the service sector engaging 23%; agriculture, 19%; manufacturing and mining, 21%; construction, 12%; transportation and communications, 11%; trade, 8%; utilities, 4%; with finance, public administration, and defense accounting for the remaining 2%.

All workers are allowed to join or form unions of their choosing. The minimum age for employment is 16. There is no minimum wage that covers all types of work. The legal maximum workweek is 48 hours, although most businesses have a 40-hour workweek.

21 AGRICULTURE

Before the breakup of the Soviet Union, Kazakhstan reportedly had 35,698,000 hectares (88,210,000 acres) of fertile land, one-third of all agricultural land of the Soviet Union. A record wheat harvest in 1992 (32 million tons) provided 10 million tons for export. A smaller 1993 harvest (25 million tons), caused by poor weather, deteriorating equipment, and financial problems, severely reduced exports. Rice production amounted to 500,000 tons in 1992. Potatoes, fruits, and vegetables are other significant food crops.

22 DOMESTICATED ANIMALS

About 60% of Kazakhstan's total land area is permanent pastureland. In 1992, the livestock population included 58 million chickens, 33.9 million sheep, 3 million pigs, 1.5 million horses, and about 0.7 million goats. Total meat production in 1992 amounted to 1,510,000 tons, of which 48% was beef, 18% pork, 16% mutton and lamb, 13% chicken, and 5% other meat. In 1992, 168,000 tons of greasy and scoured wool were produced. That year, fresh cow milk production totaled 4,948,000 tons, and 190,800 tons of hen eggs were laid.

23 FISHING

Fisheries are concentrated around the Caspian Sea and are of some importance to the local economy.

24 FORESTRY

Only 3% of Kazakhstan is covered by forests and woodlands; forestry is of little commercial importance.

25 MINING

The eastern region of Kazakhstan is rich in many metallic minerals, including alumina, arsenic, bauxite, beryllium, bismuth, cadmium, chrome, copper, gold, iron ore, lead-zinc, manganese, molybdenum, rhenium, silver, titanium, and tungsten. Copper is mined at six facilities. Kazakhstan had supplied more than 95% of chromite production for the former Soviet Union. Asbestos, barite, and phosphate are also mined.

26 FOREIGN TRADE

In 1990, about 89% of Kazakhstan's exports and 88% of its imports came from trade with other former Soviet republics. The value of exports to countries beyond the former Soviet Union fell to $1.3 billion, and imports dropped to $1.4 billion. Exports were dominated by petroleum products (26% of the total), followed by nonferrous and ferrous metals. Kazakhstan's largest imports were machinery and oil and gas products.

Russia dominated Kazakhstan's inter-republic trade, accounting for 63% of the total in 1990. Germany, Poland, Bulgaria, the Czech Republic, and Slovakia are the largest of its international trading partners.

27 ENERGY AND POWER

Kazakhstan is richly endowed with energy reserves. The country's oil reserves alone are estimated to be equal to those of Kuwait; 470,000 barrels a day are currently produced.

Production of oil in 1992 totaled 26.7 million tons (540,000 barrels per day). Liquid natural gas production in 1992 amounted to 93,000 barrels per day. Total hard coal production in 1992 was 122.5 million tons; lignite and brown coal, 2.5 million tons. In 1992, Kazakhstan's total electric power production amounted to 79,100 million kilowatt hours.

28 SOCIAL DEVELOPMENT

Kazakh families averaged 4 members in 1989. There were 11.4 drug-related crimes and 3.1 alcohol-related deaths per 100,000 persons. Women generally have access to higher education but are still channeled into mostly low-level, low-paid jobs. The constitution provides for the upkeep and education of orphans.

29 HEALTH

The average life expectancy for the period 1988–93 was 70 years. Major causes of death in 1990 were noncommunicable diseases and injuries. In 1992, there were 253 people for each physician. There were 13.6 hospital beds per 1,000 inhabitants. Total health care expenditures in 1990 were $2.6 million.

30 HOUSING

In 1990, Kazakhstan had 14.2 square meters (107 square feet) of housing space per person. As of 1 January 1991, 520,000 households (or 18.8%) were on waiting lists for housing in urban areas.

31 EDUCATION

In the early 1990s, the adult literacy rate was estimated at 97% with males at 99% and females at 96%. There are 8,064 secondary schools in which 3,021,070 students are enrolled. Included in the 55 institutions of higher education are three universities with 285,600 pupils.

32 MEDIA

There are only 6 phones per every 100 residents. Kazakh Television was established in 1959. In 1989, there were 453 state-registered newspapers, 160 published in Kazakh, and 91 periodicals, with 31 in Kazakh. Major Kazakh newspapers were *Leninshil Zhas* and *Sotsialistik Kazakhstan*.

Selected Social Indicators

These statistics are estimates for the period 1988 to 1993. For comparison purposes, data for the United States and averages for low-income countries and high-income countries are also given.

Indicator	Kazakhstan	Low-income countries	High-income countries	United States
Per capita gross national product†	$1,560	$380	$23,680	$24,740
Population growth rate	0.6%	1.9%	0.6%	1.0%
Population growth rate in urban areas	1.4%	3.9%	0.8%	1.3%
Population per square kilometer of land	6	78	25	26
Life expectancy in years	70	62	77	76
Number of people per physician	253	>3,300	453	419
Number of pupils per teacher (primary school)	n.a.	39	<18	20
Illiteracy rate (15 years and older)	3%	41%	<5%	<3%
Energy consumed per capita (kg of oil equivalent)	4,435	364	5,203	7,918

† The gross national product (GNP) is the total dollar value of all goods and services produced by a country in a year. The per capita GNP is calculated by dividing a country's GNP by its population. The World Bank defines low-income countries as those with a per capita GNP of $695 or less. High-income countries have a per capita GNP of $8,626 or more. Less than 14% of the world's 5.5 billion people live in high-income countries, while almost 60% live in low-income countries.

n.a. = data not available   > = greater than   < = less than

Sources: World Bank, *Social Indicators of Development 1995*, Baltimore: Johns Hopkins University Press, 1995. Central Intelligence Agency, *World Fact Book*, Washington, D.C.: Government Printing Office, 1994.

33 TOURISM AND RECREATION

The principal accommodations are hotels that formerly belonged to the Soviet Intourist system. However, foreign chains are currently developing a number of projects in Central Asia.

Kazakhstan offers a wide variety of natural landscapes, ranging from forests and mountain ranges to the vast steppes where Kazakh nomads live in tents called yurts and race thoroughbred horses and camels. The capital, Almaty, has no historic attractions but is an attractive city where tree-lined streets, parks, fountains, and canals give it a European flavor.

34 FAMOUS KAZAKHS

Nursultan A. Nazarbaev and Sergey Tereshchenko have been president and prime minister of Kazakhstan since December 1991. The novelist Kaltay Muhamedjanov is from Kazakhstan.

35 BIBLIOGRAPHY

Edwards-Jones, Imogen. *The Taming of Eagles: Exploring the New Russia.* London: Weidenfeld & Nicolson, 1993.

Kazakhstan. Minneapolis: Lerner, 1993.

KENYA

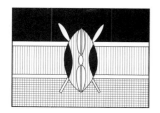

Republic of Kenya
Jamhuri ya Kenya

CAPITAL: Nairobi.

FLAG: The flag is a horizontal tricolor of black, red, and green stripes separated by narrow white bars. At the center is a red shield with black and white markings superimposed on two crossed white spears.

ANTHEM: *Wimbo Wa Taifa (National Anthem)*, beginning "Ee Mungu nguvu yetu, ilete baraka Kwetu" ("O God of all creation, bless this our land and nation").

MONETARY UNIT: The Kenya shilling (Sh) is a paper currency of 100 cents; the Kenya pound (к£) is a unit of account equivalent to 20 shillings. There are coins of 5, 10, and 50 cents, and 1 and 5 shillings; and notes of 5, 10, 20, 50, 100, and 200 shillings. Sh1 = $0.0154 (or $1 = Sh64.858).

WEIGHTS AND MEASURES: The metric system is used.

HOLIDAYS: New Year's Day, 1 January; Labor Day, 1 May; Madaraka Day, 1 June; Kenyatta Day, 20 October; Uhuru (Independence) Day, 12 December; Christmas, 25 December; Boxing Day, 26 December. Movable holidays include Good Friday, Easter Monday, 'Id al-Fitr, and 'Id al-'Adha'.

TIME: 3 PM = noon GMT.

1 LOCATION AND SIZE

Situated on the eastern coast of Africa, Kenya lies astride the equator. Its total area, including 11,230 square kilometers (4,336 square miles) of water, is 582,650 square kilometers (224,962 square miles). Comparatively, the area occupied by Kenya is slightly more than twice the size of the state of Nevada. It has a total boundary length of 3,969 kilometers (2,467 miles). Kenya's capital city, Nairobi, is located in the southcentral part of the country.

2 TOPOGRAPHY

Kenya is notable for its topographical variety. The low-lying, fertile coastal region is backed by a gradually rising coastal plain. The plain gives way in the southwest to a high plateau, rising in parts to more than 3,050 meters (10,000 feet). The northern section and most of the southeastern quarter of Kenya are semidesert. In the high plateau area, known as the Kenya Highlands, lies Mt. Kenya (5,199 meters/17,058 feet). The principal rivers are the Tana, the Athi, and the Ngiro.

3 CLIMATE

The climate of Kenya is as varied as its topography. The coastal temperature averages 27°C (81°F), and the temperature decreases as the altitude increases. The capital, Nairobi, at 1,661 meters (5,449 feet), has a mean annual temperature of 19°C (66°F); at 2,740 meters (9,000 feet) the average is 13°C (55°F). Seasonal variations are distinguished by amount of rainfall rather than by changes of temperature. Average annual rainfall varies from 13 centimeters (5 inches) a year in the driest regions of the northern plains to 193 centimeters (76 inches) near Lake Victoria.

4 PLANTS AND ANIMALS

The plant and animal life of Kenya reflect the variety of its topography and climate. In the coastal region coconut trees flourish, with occasional mangrove swamps and rain forest. The vast plains of the inland and northern regions are covered with grass, low bush, and scrub. The high-lying plains are typical savanna country of open grass dotted with thorn trees. The drier regions have only bare earth and stunted scrub. Parts of the highland areas are densely forested with bamboo and valuable timber, such as African camphor, African olive, podo, and pencil cedar.

Wildlife of great variety is to be found in Kenya. Elephant, rhinoceros, lion, zebra, giraffe, buffalo, hippopotamus, wildebeest, and many kinds of buck are among the large mammals that live on the plains and along the rivers. Kenya's many bird species include cranes, flamingos, ostriches, and vultures.

5 ENVIRONMENT

Increasing population has created demands for more food and firewood. Overfarming and overharvesting of trees has led to a loss of forests and soil erosion.

Drought and desertification also threaten fertile farm lands. The majority of people living in rural areas (85%) as well as 15% of city dwellers do not have pure water. In an effort to preserve wildlife, the government has set aside more than 2.5 million hectares (6.2 million acres) as national parks and game preserves. Game hunting and trade in ivory and skins have been banned, but poaching threatens leopards, cheetahs, lions, elephants, rhinoceroses, and other species. It is illegal to kill an animal even if it attacks. Endangered species include the Sokoke scops owl, Taita blue-banded papilio, Tana River mangabey, Tana River red colobus, green sea turtle, and hawksbill turtle.

6 POPULATION

From 1975 through 1980, Kenya registered an average annual population increase of 3.82%, not only the highest of any nation in the world during that period but also the highest ever recorded for a single country. The estimated annual growth rate was 2.7% during 1988–93, and 3.35% during 1990–95. According to United Nations estimates, the national total rose by 36% from 16,466,000 in 1980 to 22,400,000 in 1987, and by 24% to an estimated 27,885,000 in 1995. There are about 43 people per square kilometer (11 per square mile). The United Nations projected a population of 32,818,000 in the year 2000—more than five times the 1950 total. In 1990, Nairobi, the capital and principal city, had an estimated population of 1,518,000.

KENYA

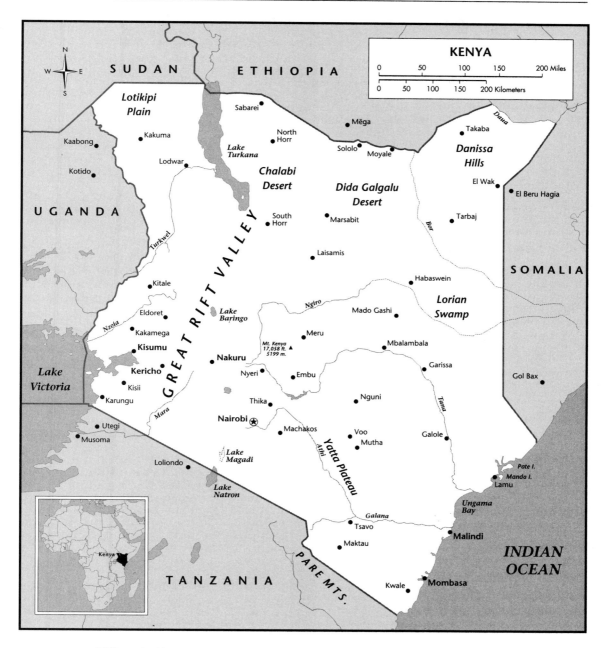

KENYA

0	50	100	150	200 Miles
0	50	100	150	200 Kilometers

SUDAN   ETHIOPIA

Lotikipi Plain

Sabarei

Mēga   Takaba

North Horr

Kakuma

Lake Turkana

Sololo   Moyale

Kaabong

Danissa Hills

Kotido

Lodwar

Chalabi Desert

El Wak

El Beru Hagia

Dida Galgalu Desert

UGANDA

South Horr

Marsabit

Tarbaj

Laisamis

SOMALIA

Kitale

Habaswein

Ngiro

Lorian Swamp

Eldoret

Lake Baringo

Mado Gashi

Kakamega

Mt. Kenya 17,058 ft. 5199 m.

Meru

Mbalambala

Kisumu

Nakuru

Garissa

Kericho

Nyeri

Embu

Gol Bax

Kisii

Karungu

Nguni

Lake Victoria

Thika

Voo

Galole

Utegi

Nairobi

Machakos

Mutha

Musoma

Lake Magadi

Yatta Plateau

Pate I.

Manda I.

Lamu

Loliondo

Lake Natron

Athi

Ungama Bay

Kenya

Galana

Tsavo

Malindi

TANZANIA

Maktau

INDIAN OCEAN

PARE MTS.

Kwale   Mombasa

GREAT RIFT VALLEY

Turkwel

Nzoia

Mara

Tana

Bor

Daua

LOCATION: 4°30′N to 4°30′S; 34° to 42°E. **BOUNDARY LENGTHS:** Sudan, 306 kilometers (190 miles); Ethiopia, 779 kilometers (484 miles); Somalia, 682 kilometers (424 miles); Indian Ocean, 523 kilometers (325 miles); Tanzania, 769 kilometers (478 miles); Lake Victoria, 138 kilometers (86 miles); Uganda, 772 kilometers (480 miles). **TERRITORIAL SEA LIMIT:** 12 miles.

7 MIGRATION

Throughout Kenya there is a slow but steady movement of the rural population to the cities in search of employment. Some Kenyans have moved to Uganda, and ethnic Somalis are present in significant numbers in Kenya's North-Eastern Province. At the end of 1992 there were 401,900 documented refugees in Kenya. Some 285,600 were Somalis, 68,600 Ethiopians, 21,800 Sudanese, and 3,600 Ugandans.

8 ETHNIC GROUPS

African peoples native to Kenya, who now form 98% of the population, fall into three major cultural and linguistic groups: Bantu, Nilotic, and Cushitic. Although most of the land area is occupied by Cushitic and Nilotic peoples, over 70% of the population is Bantu. The estimated proportions of the main tribal groups are Kikuyu 21%, Luhya 14%, Luo 13%, Kamba 11%, Kalenjin 11%, Kisii 6%, and Meru 5%.

Kenya is also home to an Arab population centered on the Indian Ocean coast. Swahilis, a group of mixed Arab-Africans, also live in the coastal region. Asians with origins traceable to India and the surrounding countries live primarily in urban centers. There is also a European community, which is primarily of British origin.

9 LANGUAGES

Nearly all the African ethnic groups have their own distinct languages. Swahili, however, has become increasingly a common language in East Africa. In 1974 it became Kenya's official language, along with English. English is used in business and government, and parliamentary bills must be drafted and presented in that language. Both Gujarati and Punjabi are widely used among the Asian community.

10 RELIGIONS

Many different religions are practiced in Kenya. As of 1987, an estimated 73% of the population was Christian: 27% was Roman Catholic, and 46% belonged to traditional Protestant groups. Those following tribal religions accounted for another 19% of the total population, and Muslims 6%.

11 TRANSPORTATION

The Kenya Railways Corporation maintains 2,040 kilometers (1,260 miles) of rail, more than half making up the main line between the Ugandan border and Mombasa, the chief port. In 1991, the road system comprised some 64,950 kilometers (40,340 miles). The major road from Nairobi to Mombasa is well paved, and the government has begun to widen and resurface secondary roads. In 1992 there were 291,134 motor vehicles, including 157,166 private passenger automobiles.

There are major international airports at Nairobi and Mombasa. Kenya Airways flies to other nations of East Africa, the Middle East, Europe, and the Indian subcontinent. It carried 759,900 passengers in 1991. That year, Nairobi handled 1,516,000 passengers and 52,200 tons of freight; Mombasa, 704,000 passengers and 1,400 tons of freight.

Photo credit: Corel Corporation.

Street scene in the village of Baragoi, Kenya, south of Lake Turkana.

12 HISTORY

Origins

During the Iron Age (c. AD 1000), the first Bantu speakers arrived from the north in what is now Kenya. Nilotic speakers entered at the end of the sixteenth century from the north or northwest, and the Somali entered northeastern Kenya in significant numbers in the late nineteenth and early twentieth centuries.

Meanwhile, another set of migrants settled on the Indian Ocean coast. As in the interior, the newcomers replaced the original hunter-gatherer inhabitants. By the tenth century the Bantu had settled the coastal region. The mixed population there of Arabs and Africans combined to create the Swahili culture, a culture marked by its own language, a devotion to Islam, and the development of numerous coastal trade centers.

1498–1920

Vasco da Gama landed at Malindi in 1498. The coastal cities then struggled for the next century to remain independent of the external threats posed first by the Portuguese and then by the Omani Arabs, who eventually drove out the Portuguese and reestablished Arab authority in 1740. Independent Arab settlements persisted for almost a century until unity was established during the rule (1806–56) of Sayyid

Sa'id. Arab control was confined to the coastal region, however.

Meanwhile, in the decades before and after the turn of the nineteenth century, Europeans began to assert their influence in East Africa. In 1886, Britain and Germany agreed on which areas of East Africa they would each control. The Imperial British East African Company began establishing its authority in the interior two years later. In December 1901, the railway linking Mombasa with Lake Victoria was completed. In the following year the boundary between Kenya and Uganda was shifted some 320 kilometers (200 miles) westward to its present position. European and Asian settlement followed the building of the railway, and by World War I (1914–18) the modern development of Kenya was clearly evident. In 1920, Kenya was declared a colony of the British crown.

Independence

Africans made use of both legal and nonlegal methods in their struggle for power against the Europeans. The Mau Mau revolutionary movement led to the declaration of a state of emergency in October 1952 that lasted until late 1959. The 1960 "Macleod" constitution mandated an African-elected majority in the Legislative Council. This marked a decisive shift in the direction of African control. On 12 December 1963, Kenya became independent. Exactly one year later it became a republic within the Commonwealth of Nations, with Jomo Kenyatta as the country's first president. His political party, the Kenya African National Union (KANU),

dominated the government. Leaders of a rival party, banned in 1969, were arrested.

Kenyatta died on 22 August 1978 and was succeeded by his vice-president, Daniel arap Moi, who was elected president without opposition a month later. In June 1982, the National Assembly voted unanimously to make Kenya formally a one-party state. President Moi ran unopposed in the elections of September 1983. In 1986, Moi declared that KANU was above government, the parliament, and the judiciary. Critics of Moi were expelled from KANU, and government repression increased. In July 1990, clashes between pro-democracy demonstrators and police left five dead. In 1991, riot police dispersed thousands of protesters.

In December 1991, in response to growing pressure by the United States and other donors of foreign aid, Moi proposed dropping the 1982 constitutional amendment legalizing one-party rule. KANU agreed to it, but opposition to Moi and civil unrest continued. In Nairobi in January 1992, more than 100,000 attended the first legal antigovernment rally in 22 years. The following year Moi delayed elections until his opposition, divided into eight parties, fell apart. In the late December elections, Moi was reelected with 37% of the vote. Foreign aid has been reduced as Moi continues to pressure the opposition in and out of parliament. In 1993, Africa Watch, a US-based human rights group, reported that as many as 1,500 Kenyans have been killed and over 300,000 displaced as a result of ethnic violence triggered by Moi's regime.

13 GOVERNMENT

According to the constitution of 1963, as later amended, the government of Kenya is led by a president who is chief of state, head of government, and commander-in-chief of the armed forces. The president appoints the members of the cabinet (the vice-president and the heads of the various ministries) from among members of the National Assembly. The unicameral National Assembly was established when the Senate and House of Representatives were merged by constitutional amendment in 1967. A constitutional amendment in 1986 increased the number of elected seats (beginning with the next election) to 188.

14 POLITICAL PARTIES

Since 1964, the Kenya African National Union (KANU) has dominated Kenyan politics. All parliamentary candidates also were KANU members in 1974 and 1979. On 9 June 1982, following reports that former vice-president Oginga Odinga was planning to form a new, Socialist-oriented party, the National Assembly declared Kenya a one-party state.

A clandestine dissident group known as Mwakenya was founded in 1981. In 1986, 44 persons were being held prisoner because of their connection with this group, 37 of whom were convicted of sedition (rebellion against the government). Other underground opposition groups emerged in the 1980s. In 1987 many of them joined to form the United Movement for Democracy (UMOJA, Swahili for unity).

In December 1991, the Moi government decided to end KANU's monopoly on legal political activity. A grand coalition known as the Forum for the Restoration of Democracy (FORD) was formed. Before the December 1992 election, it fragmented into two factions—FORD-Kenya, headed by Oginga Odinga, and FORD-Asili, led by Kenneth Matiba. The KANU-led government has not reconciled itself to the new era of multiparty politics; in 1993 alone, it arrested 36 of the 85 members of the opposition.

15 JUDICIAL SYSTEM

The judicial system consists of the Court of Appeal and subordinate courts. The High Court consists of a chief justice and 24 associate judges, who are appointed by the president of the republic. Lower courts are presided over by resident magistrates and district magistrates. Questions of Islamic law are determined by *qadis'* courts. Military courts handle court martials of military personnel.

16 ARMED FORCES

Military service is voluntary. In 1993 the army had 20,500 men in 16 specialized battalions. The navy had 650 men and 10 patrol craft. The air force had 40 combat aircraft and 38 armed helicopters. The 5,000-member national police has general service, air, and naval paramilitary units.

17 ECONOMY

Kenya's is an agricultural economy supported by a manufacturing sector and a tourism sector, which is an important foreign exchange earner. Financial difficulties

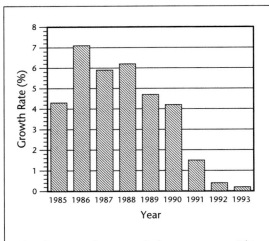

Yearly growth rate of the economy. This economic indicator tells by what percent the economy has increased or decreased when compared with the previous year.

and disagreements over the direction of future investments led to a withholding of foreign aid in 1992.

18 INCOME

In 1992 Kenya's gross national product (GNP) was $8,453 million or about $270 per person.

19 INDUSTRY

Petroleum refining accounted for 10.9% of export earnings in 1990. The transformation of agricultural raw materials, particularly of coffee and tea, remains the principal industrial activity. Meat and fruit canning, wheat flour and cornmeal milling, and sugar refining are also important. Electronics production, vehicle assembly, publishing, and soda ash processing are all significant parts of the sector. Assembly of computer components began in 1987. Kenya also manufactures chemicals, textiles, ceramics, shoes, beer and soft drinks, cigarettes, soap, machinery, metal products, cement, aluminum, steel, glass, rubber, wood, cork, and leather goods.

20 LABOR

In 1992, Kenya had 1,441,800 wage earners, 19% of whom worked in agriculture and forestry, and 13% in manufacturing. Unemployment was estimated in 1992 at over 25% of the work force. Poverty is widespread, and the working poor, who put in long hours of labor for little return, greatly outnumber the unemployed. Women constituted 60% of the work force in 1992.

The trade union movement is strong in Kenya and continues to pressure the government for better wages and improved living standards. There were some 33 unions in Kenya with approximately 350,000–385,000 workers in 1992, or about 25% of the country's industrialized work force.

21 AGRICULTURE

Agriculture remains the most important economic activity in Kenya, although less than 5% of the land is used for crop and feed production. About 80% of the work force engages in subsistence agriculture. Although there are still important European-owned coffee, tea, and sisal plantations, an increasing number of peasant farmers grow cash crops. Kenya can produce nearly all of its own basic foodstuffs.

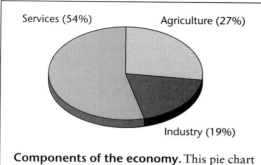

Services (54%)   Agriculture (27%)

Industry (19%)

Components of the economy. This pie chart shows how much of the country's economy is devoted to agriculture (includes forestry, hunting, and fishing), industry, or services.

To some extent, Kenya also helps feed neighboring countries.

Coffee is Kenya's leading cash crop. Production in 1992 amounted to 70,000 tons. Tea exports, and production for sale were 188,000 tons in 1992. Kenya is Africa's leading tea producer, and was third in the world in 1992, behind India and China. Other important crops in 1992 were sugarcane, 4,430,000 tons; corn, 2,561,000 tons; wheat, 200,000 tons; rice, 58,000 tons; sisal, 35,000 tons; and seed cotton, 28,000 tons.

Small farmers grow most of the corn and also produce significant quantities of potatoes, beans, peas, sorghum, sweet potatoes, cassava, bananas, and oilseeds. Other grain crops in 1992 included 55,000 tons of millet and 107,000 tons of sorghum. During the same year, Kenya harvested an estimated 770,000 tons of cassava, 600,000 tons of sweet potatoes and 240,000 tons of potatoes. Production of fruits and vegetables included plantains,

360,000 tons; pineapples, 270,000 tons; and bananas, 220,000 tons.

22 DOMESTICATED ANIMALS

In 1992 there were an estimated 11 million head of cattle, 7.5 million goats, and 6 million sheep. Milk production is adequate for domestic needs; in 1992, fresh whole cow milk production amounted to 1,810,000 tons. Some 1,600,000 cattle were delivered for slaughter in 1992. The number of chickens was estimated at 25 million.

23 FISHING

Commercial fishing takes place on the coast of the Indian Ocean and on the shores of lakes Baringo and Victoria. Fish farms have been established in various parts of Kenya. The total fish catch for 1991 was 198,637 tons. Most were freshwater fish, particularly from Lake Victoria; the inland catch was 191,218 tons.

24 FORESTRY

Both hardwoods and softwoods are produced in Kenya. The chief hardwoods are musheragi, muiri, mukeo, camphor, and musaise. The chief softwoods are podo, cedar, and cypress. Wattle, grown mainly on small African plantations, provides the base of an important industry. Kenya maintains some 2,320,000 hectares (5,733,000 acres) in indigenous forests, mangroves, and forest plantations, about 4% of the total land area. Roundwood production in 1991 was an estimated 36.8 million cubic meters, of which 95% went for fuel.

25 MINING

Although mining has declined steadily in importance since the end of World War II, it still contributes to the economy. The main products are soda ash, limestone, soapstone, fluorspar, salt, and gemstones.

26 FOREIGN TRADE

Tea (accounting for 26.4% of export income) and coffee (18.1%) were Kenya's leading exports in 1990. Petroleum products (10.9%) have emerged as the main industrial export in recent years. Trade balances have been unfavorable since 1970. Principal imports are industrial machinery, crude petroleum, motor vehicles and chassis, and iron and steel. Britain takes 19.6% of Kenya's exports, while Germany purchased 12.1%. Of Kenya's imports, 18.9% came from Britain, 12.3% from Japan, and 11.4% from the United Arab Emirates.

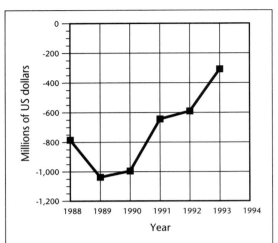

Yearly balance of trade measured in millions of US dollars. The balance of trade is the difference between what a country sells to other countries (its exports) and what it buys (its imports). If a country imports more than it exports, it has a negative balance of trade (a trade deficit). If exports exceed imports there is a positive balance of trade (a trade surplus).

27 ENERGY AND POWER

Since 1950, hydroelectric capacity has been dramatically increased, and new hydroelectric schemes have been developed. Nevertheless, the power supply is still insufficient to meet demand. About 5% of Kenya's electricity was imported in 1991 from Uganda's Owen Falls Dam project. Wood accounts for about 90% of total energy consumption. All of Kenya's crude petroleum is imported.

28 SOCIAL DEVELOPMENT

There is no nationwide social insurance system, but private and voluntary agencies are highly developed. There are societies that care for the blind, the deaf and mute, and the physically disabled, and voluntary organizations that care for the poor and destitute. Homes and hostels have been established throughout the country for the care of orphans, young offenders, and juvenile prostitutes. In the mid-1980s there were more than 10,000 community development self-help projects. A government Women's Bureau assists women's development programs. In 1967, Kenya became the first sub-Saharan African country to launch a national family planning program.

29 HEALTH

Among Kenya's major health problems are tuberculosis and protein deficiency,

Selected Social Indicators

These statistics are estimates for the period 1988 to 1993. For comparison purposes, data for the United States and averages for low-income countries and high-income countries are also given.

Indicator	Kenya	Low-income countries	High-income countries	United States
Per capita gross national product†	$270	$380	$23,680	$24,740
Population growth rate	2.7%	1.9%	0.6%	1.0%
Population growth rate in urban areas	5.9%	3.9%	0.8%	1.3%
Population per square kilometer of land	43	78	25	26
Life expectancy in years	58	62	77	76
Number of people per physician	9,851	>3,300	453	419
Number of pupils per teacher (primary school)	31	39	<18	20
Illiteracy rate (15 years and older)	31%	41%	<5%	<3%
Energy consumed per capita (kg of oil equivalent)	99	364	5,203	7,918

† The gross national product (GNP) is the total dollar value of all goods and services produced by a country in a year. The per capita GNP is calculated by dividing a country's GNP by its population. The World Bank defines low-income countries as those with a per capita GNP of $695 or less. High-income countries have a per capita GNP of $8,626 or more. Less than 14% of the world's 5.5 billion people live in high-income countries, while almost 60% live in low-income countries.

> = greater than   < = less than

Sources: World Bank, *Social Indicators of Development 1995,* Baltimore: Johns Hopkins University Press, 1995. Central Intelligence Agency, *World Fact Book,* Washington, D.C.: Government Printing Office, 1994.

the latter especially among young children. Although the incidence of malaria has been reduced, it still accounted for over 20% of outpatient deaths in 1990. Water supply, sanitation, and sleeping sickness also pose major problems. Diseases caused by parasites are widespread in some areas. In 1991, only 49% of the population had access to safe water, and only 43% had adequate sanitation. There was an average life expectancy of 58 years for the period 1988–93.

30 HOUSING

Housing in rural areas is privately owned. Most of these homes, built with tradi-

tional materials, fall apart in a relatively short time. An increasing number of people now build their homes with more permanent materials. The central government is responsible for all housing projects and works closely with local authorities.

31 EDUCATION

Although education is not compulsory, primary education is free. Children start school at the age of five or six and spend eight years at primary school, five years at secondary school, and a further four years at the university. In 1990, there were 15,196 primary schools with 5,392,319 students. In general secondary schools, there were 614,161 students, and teacher training programs had 17,914 students. In the same year, adult literacy rate was 69%, an estimated 79.8% for men and 58.5% for women. The main universities in Kenya are the Kenyatta University in Nairobi, the University of Nairobi, and the Moi University at Eldoret. The language of instruction in all the universities is English.

32 MEDIA

There were 357,251 telephones in 1991. The Voice of Kenya, broadcasting in English, Swahili, and local languages, operates one radio station and one television channel. In 1990, Channel 62, an independently owned television station, made its debut. It was estimated in 1991 that Kenya had 2.1 million radio receivers and 234,000 television sets.

In 1991, Kenya had five daily newspapers, all published in Nairobi. *The Nation*, founded in 1960, had a daily circulation of 178,700; the *Taifa Leo*, a Swahili newspaper, 48,600; the *Standard* (established in 1902), 55,000; the *Kenya Times*, 30,000; and the *Kenya Leo*, 40,000.

33 TOURISM AND RECREATION

Since Kenya became independent, tourism has become the leading source of foreign exchange revenue. In 1991, 817,550 tourists visited Kenya, 57% from Europe and 27% from Africa.

Photo safaris to the 19 national parks and game preserves are the chief attraction. The largest game preserve is Tsavo National Park, home of the world's greatest concentration of elephants. Covering an area of about 21,343 square kilometers (8,241 square miles), it is one of the world's largest wildlife sanctuaries.

Kenyan track stars have excelled in international competition, especially distance running. Kenyans won a total of six gold medals in track at the 1968, 1972, and 1984 Olympic Games.

34 FAMOUS KENYANS

The leading African figure in the modern history of Kenya is Jomo Kenyatta (1893?–1978). Imprisoned and restricted during the Mau Mau revolt, he was released in August 1961 and was president of independent Kenya from 1964 until his death. Richard Leakey (b.1944) is a leading paleoanthropologist.

35 BIBLIOGRAPHY

Arnold, Gay. *Modern Kenya.* New York: Longman, 1981.

Dinesen, Isak. *Out of Africa.* New York: Random House, 1972.

Kenya in Pictures. Minneapolis: Lerner, 1988.

Nagel, Rob, and Anne Commire. "Jomo Kenyatta." In *World Leaders, People Who Shaped the World.* Volume I: Africa and Asia. Detroit: U*X*L, 1994.

Stein, R. *Kenya.* Chicago: Children's Press, 1985.

Themes in Kenyan History. Athens: Ohio University Press, 1990.

KIRIBATI

Republic of Kiribati

CAPITAL: Tarawa.

FLAG: Above a blue and white heraldic representation of Pacific waters, a golden sun rises against a red background, with a golden frigate bird at the top.

ANTHEM: *Troika kain Kiribati (Stand Kiribati).*

MONETARY UNIT: The Australian dollar is the national currency. A$1 = US$0.7008 (or US$1 = A$1.4269).

WEIGHTS AND MEASURES: Kiribati is in transition from imperial to metric standards.

HOLIDAYS: New Year's Day, 1 January; Independence Day, 12 July; Youth Day, 4 August; Christmas Day, 25 December; Boxing Day, 26 December. Movable holidays include Good Friday, Easter Monday, Queen's Birthday (June), Bank Holiday (August), and Prince of Wales's Birthday (November).

TIME: Midnight = noon GMT.

1 LOCATION AND SIZE

Kiribati (pronounced "Kiribass") consists of 33 islands in the central Pacific, situated around the point where the International Date Line intersects the equator. Scattered over more than 5 million square kilometers (2 million square miles) of ocean, Kiribati's total land area is 717 square kilometers (277 square miles), and its total coastline is 1,143 kilometers (710 miles).

Kiribati's capital city, Tarawa, is located on the small island of Tarawa (between Abiang and Maiana).

2 TOPOGRAPHY

With the exception of Banaba, the westernmost island, the islands are coral atolls built on a submerged volcanic chain. Kirit-imati (Christmas Island) is the largest atoll in the world, with an area of 481 square kilometers (186 square miles).

3 CLIMATE

Rainfall varies from an average of 102 centimeters (40 inches) near the equator to 305 centimeters (120 inches) in the extreme north and south. Daily temperatures range from 25°C (77°F) to 32°C (90°F), with an annual mean temperature of 27°C (81°F).

4 PLANTS AND ANIMALS

Only babai (a kind of taro root), coconut palms, and pandanus trees grow easily on most islands. Pigs and poultry were probably introduced by Europeans.

5 ENVIRONMENT

The principle environmental problems facing nations in this region are global warming and the rise of sea levels. Kiribati's environment has also been damaged by mining, and agricultural chemicals have polluted coastal waters. The United Nations Report describes the wildlife in these areas as "among the most critically threatened in the world."

6 POPULATION

According to the census of November 1990, the population totaled 72,298. In 1990, Tarawa had a population of 29,028, or 40% of the total, while some islands were uninhabited. The capital, Tarawa, had an estimated population of 2,000 in the mid-1980s.

7 MIGRATION

Fiji, Nauru, and the Solomon Islands are popular places for western Kiribatians in search of work. Internal migration is mainly to copra (dried coconut meat) plantations in the Line Islands.

8 ETHNIC GROUPS

About 99% of the people are Gilbertese of Micronesian extraction. Polynesians (mainly from Tuvalu) make up 0.5% of the total; Europeans and people of mixed races, 0.6%.

9 LANGUAGES

The principal languages spoken are Kiribati and English. The official language is English, but it is seldom used on the outer islands.

10 RELIGIONS

Virtually the entire population is Christian. According to the 1990 census, 39.1% belonged to the Kiribati Protestant Church, and 53.5% were Roman Catholics. Religious minorities include the Seventh-Day Adventists, the Church of God, Assemblies of God, Mormons, and Baha'is.

11 TRANSPORTATION

There are only about 640 kilometers (400 miles) of roads, mostly on Tarawa Island. There is no rail, river, or lake transport. The port near Tarawa is equipped for handling containers. The airports on Kiritimati (Christmas Island) and at Tarawa are used for scheduled overseas flights. Bonriki International (Tarawa) serviced 51,000 passengers in 1991, including 16,000 international passengers.

12 HISTORY

Early History

European discovery dates from 1537, when Kiritimati (Christmas Island) was sighted by Spanish explorers. Commercial activities (by the British) began early in the nineteenth century. Trading ships stopped there regularly by the 1850s, and a flourishing copra (dried coconut meat) and coconut trade was established by the 1860s, as well as an illegal slave trade. In the late nineteenth century, the British set up local native governments on the annexed Kiritimati (Christmas Island), Fanning, Washington, Phoenix, Gilbert, and Ellice islands (now Tuvalu), and a period of stability followed.

Ocean Island was annexed by Britain in 1900, following Sir Albert Ellis's discovery of its valuable phosphate deposits. The British declared colonies on Ellice Island (now Tuvalu) in 1916, Kiritimati (Christmas Island) in 1919, and the uninhabited Phoenix group in 1937. During World War II (1939–45), the same islands were occupied by Japanese forces. In 1943, the Japanese were driven out by United States forces, with heavy casualties on both sides. Ocean Island was liberated by the Australians in 1945.

Independence

In a 1974 referendum, the Ellice Islands voted for separation, becoming the independent nation of Tuvalu. The Gilbert Islands became the independent Republic of Kiribati on 12 July 1979. Ieremia Tabai, chief minister at the time of independence, became president of the new republic in 1979 and was reelected in May 1982 and February 1983.

The Banabans, who had been resettled in 1946 on Rabi (Fiji) so that strip mining could be pursued on their native island, sued for damages in 1975. After a lengthy legal battle, a settlement was reached in 1981, providing for creation of a trust fund of nearly US$10.5 million for Banaban development.

Kiribati began resettling more than 4,700 people on outlying atolls in August 1988 to relieve overcrowded conditions on the Tarawa atolls. In September 1988 Kiribati ratified the South Pacific Regional Fisheries Treaty, which permits US tuna ships to operate within its 200-mile exclu-

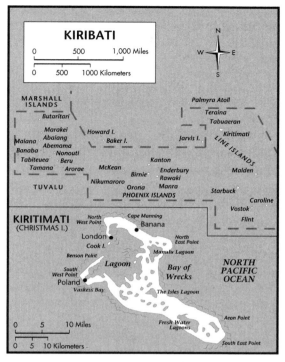

LOCATION: 4°N to 3°S; 168° to 176°E. **TOTAL COASTLINE:** 1,143 kilometers (710 miles). **TERRITORIAL SEA LIMIT:** 12 miles.

sive zone. In early 1992 the House of Assembly told the government to seek payment from the United States for damage done to the country during World War II.

13 GOVERNMENT

Kiribati is a democratic republic within the Commonwealth of Nations. It has a single-chamber legislature, the House of Assembly (*Maneaba ni Maungatabu*). The president (*beretitenti*), who is both head of state and head of government, is elected directly by popular vote from among members of the Assembly. The islands are divided into 6 districts, further divided into 21 island councils.

14 POLITICAL PARTIES

In 1985, opponents of a Soviet fishing agreement founded the Christian Democratic party. Since 1991 the Liberal Party, the Maneaba Party, the New Movement Party, and the Health Peace and Honour Party have been formed.

15 JUDICIAL SYSTEM

The 1979 constitution provides for a High Court to act as the supreme court and court of appeal. Island courts were established in 1965 to deal with civil and criminal offenses. Native land courts handle property claims.

16 ARMED FORCES

There have been no armed forces in Kiribati since legislation providing for the establishment of a defense force of 170 men was repealed in 1978.

17 ECONOMY

The nation relies on fishing, subsistence agriculture, and exports of copra (dried coconut meat) and is heavily dependent on aid from Britain and New Zealand and investment by Australia.

18 INCOME

In 1992, Kiribati's gross national product (GNP) was US$52 million, or about US$710 per person. For the period 1985–92 the average inflation rate was 5.1%, resulting in a real growth rate in per person GNP of about −1.1%.

19 INDUSTRY

Several small industries have been established, including a soft-drink plant, a biscuit factory, boat-building shops, construction companies, furniture plants, repair garages, and bakeries. The government also promotes local handicrafts.

20 LABOR

As of 1990, nearly three-quarters of the labor force was engaged in agriculture or fishing. Overseas workers sent most of their wages home to Kiribati. The minimum age for employment is 14, or 15 for industrial labor or work on board ships.

21 AGRICULTURE

Agriculture is limited chiefly to coconut and pandanus (a tropical plant) production. Overseas technical aid has allowed some islands to cultivate bananas and papaws (yellow edible fruit). About 8,000 tons of copra (dried coconut meat), 65,000 tons of coconuts, and 4,000 tons of bananas were produced in 1992.

22 DOMESTICATED ANIMALS

There were 9,000 pigs in Kiribati in 1992.

23 FISHING

Sea fishing is excellent, particularly for skipjack tuna around the Phoenix Islands. The total sea catch in 1991 was 30,001 tons.

24 FORESTRY

There is little useful timber on the islands.

Selected Social Indicators

These statistics are estimates for the period 1988 to 1993. For comparison purposes, data for the United States and averages for low-income countries and high-income countries are also given.

Indicator	Kiribati	Low-income countries	High-income countries	United States
Per capita gross national product†	$710	$380	$23,680	$24,740
Population growth rate	1.7%	1.9%	0.6%	1.0%
Population growth rate in urban areas	2.3%	3.9%	0.8%	1.3%
Population per square kilometer of land	102	78	25	26
Life expectancy in years	54	62	77	76
Number of people per physician	5,143	>3,300	453	419
Number of pupils per teacher (primary school)	30	39	<18	20
Illiteracy rate (15 years and older)	10%	41%	<5%	<3%
Energy consumed per capita (kg of oil equivalent)	105	364	5,203	7,918

† The gross national product (GNP) is the total dollar value of all goods and services produced by a country in a year. The per capita GNP is calculated by dividing a country's GNP by its population. The World Bank defines low-income countries as those with a per capita GNP of $695 or less. High-income countries have a per capita GNP of $8,626 or more. Less than 14% of the world's 5.5 billion people live in high-income countries, while almost 60% live in low-income countries.

> = greater than   < = less than

Sources: World Bank, *Social Indicators of Development 1995,* Baltimore: Johns Hopkins University Press, 1995. Central Intelligence Agency, *World Fact Book,* Washington, D.C.: Government Printing Office, 1994.

25 MINING

There has been no mining in Kiribati since the closing in 1979 of the Banaba phosphate industry.

26 FOREIGN TRADE

Copra (dried coconut meat) accounted for 77% of total domestic exports in 1992. Imports totaled US$24.1 million in 1990 (US$15.1 million in 1985), and exports were valued at US$2.6 million. Australia, New Zealand, and Britain are the major export destinations. Imports come chiefly from these countries, along with Fiji and Japan.

27 ENERGY AND POWER

The government maintains electricity generating plants on Tarawa Island and Kiritimati (Christmas Island). In 1991, electric power generating capacity was 2,000 kilowatts; production of electricity totaled 7 million kilowatt hours that year.

28 SOCIAL DEVELOPMENT

The majority of the population still lives a traditional village life with an extended family system. This makes state welfare largely unnecessary. Problems exist mainly in the south Tarawa Island area, where cities have grown rapidly. Some juvenile delinquency has developed there.

29 HEALTH

Tuberculosis remains the most serious public health problem. Other widespread diseases are leprosy, filariasis, and dysentery. Average life expectancy is 54 years.

All health services are free. Each inhabited island has a health clinic, and there is a medical radio network linking all the islands.

30 HOUSING

Most Kiribatians live in small villages of 10 to 150 houses. They construct their own dwellings from local materials. The use of more permanent building materials, such as concrete with corrugated aluminum roofing, is becoming common in urban areas.

31 EDUCATION

In 1992, Kiribati had 95 primary schools with a teaching staff of 545 and 16,020 students enrolled. At the secondary level, there were 237 teachers and 3,357 students. Kiribati has a teacher-training college, a technical institute, and a marine training school. Higher education courses are available at the Kiribati Extension Centre of the University of the South Pacific (Fiji) in Tarawa.

32 MEDIA

Radio Kiribati transmits daily in Kiribati and English. There is no commercial press; all publications are government- or church-sponsored. There were an estimated 12,000 telephones in use in 1991 in the Tarawa area.

33 TOURISM AND RECREATION

Tourism is undeveloped because of a lack of regular transport. A visitors' bureau at Tarawa makes fishing, swimming, and boating facilities available on Tarawa Island and arranges trips by sea or air to other islands.

Traditional dancing and singing styles have survived, and modern forms of recreation are developing, especially soccer. In 1991, 2,935 visitors arrived in Kiribati, 75% from Eastern Asia and the Pacific. There were 102 hotel rooms, and tourism receipts totaled US$2 million.

34 FAMOUS KIRIBATIANS

Ieremia Tabai (b.1950) was president from Kiribati independence until 1991.

35 BIBLIOGRAPHY

Grimble, Arthur Francis. *Migrations, Myth, and Magic from the Gilbert Islands.* London: Routledge & K. Paul, 1972.

Mason, Leonard (ed.). *Kiribati: A Changing Atoll Culture.* Suva: University of the South Pacific, 1985.

KOREA, DEMOCRATIC PEOPLE'S REPUBLIC OF (DPRK)

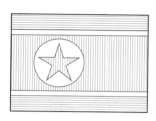

Democratic People's Republic of Korea
Choson Minjujuui Inmin Konghwa-guk

CAPITAL: P'yŏngyang.

FLAG: A wide horizontal red stripe is bordered on top and bottom by narrow blue stripes, separated from the red by thin white stripes. The left half of the red stripe contains a red five-pointed star on a circular white field.

ANTHEM: *The Song of General Kim Il-sung.*

MONETARY UNIT: The won (w) of 100 ch'on (or jeon) is the national currency. There are coins of 1, 5, 10, and 50 ch'on, and 1 won, and notes of 1, 5, 10, 50, and 100 won. w1 = $1.06 (or $1 = w0.94).

WEIGHTS AND MEASURES: The metric system and native Korean units of measurement are used.

HOLIDAYS: New Year's Day, 1 January; Kim Jong Il's Birthday, 16 February; International Women's Day, 8 March; Kim Il-sung's Birthday, 15 April; May Day, 1 May; Liberation Day, 15 August; National Foundation Day, 9 September; Founding of the Korean Workers' Party, 10 October; Anniversary of the Constitution, 27 December.

TIME: 9 PM = noon GMT.

1 LOCATION AND SIZE

The Democratic People's Republic of Korea (DPRK), often called North Korea, occupies the northern 55% of the Korean Peninsula in East Asia. It has an area of 120,540 square kilometers (46,541 square miles), slightly smaller than the state of Mississippi. It has a total boundary length of 2,309 kilometers (1,435 miles).

The DPRK's capital city, P'yŏngyang, is located in the southwestern part of the country.

2 TOPOGRAPHY

The DPRK is mostly mountainous. Mt. Paektu (Paektu San), an extinct volcano with a scenic crater lake, is the highest point at 2,744 meters (9,003 feet). Only about 20% of the country consists of lowlands and plains, but it is in these areas that the population is concentrated. The principal rivers are the Tumen, Yalu, and Taedong.

3 CLIMATE

The climate ranges widely on the small peninsula. The average January temperature is −17°C (1°F) on the north-central border and −8°C (18°F) at P'yŏngyang. In the hottest part of the summer, temperatures range only from 24°C (75°F) in P'yŏngyang to 21°C (70°F) along the northeast coast. Precipitation is around 50 centimeters (20 inches) along the upper reaches of the Tumen, but more than half of the peninsula receives 75–100 centimeters (30–40 inches) per year.

4 PLANTS AND ANIMALS

Plant life is made up mostly of evergreens in mountainous areas of the DPRK. The hilly terrain of Mt. Paektu (Paektu San) is believed to be the peninsula's last remaining habitat for Siberian tigers. It is also the home of bears, wild boar, deer, snow leopards, and lynx. At lower elevations roe deer, Amur goral, wolf, water shrew, and muskrat are common. Birds include the black Manchurian ring-necked pheasant, black grouse, and three-toed woodpecker.

5 ENVIRONMENT

Water in the DPRK has been polluted by agricultural and industrial sources. The nation has 16.1 cubic miles of water with 73% used for farming activity and 16% for industrial purposes. Korea's cities produce 2.6 million tons of solid waste per year. In 1994, 5 of Korea's mammal species and 25 of its bird species were endangered.

6 POPULATION

The population of the DPRK in 1992 was estimated at 22,618,000, about half that of South Korea (ROK). The projected population for the year 2000 was 25,934,000. The average population density for the period 1988–93 was 188 persons per square kilometer (486 per square mile). The largest urban area in 1986 was P'yŏngyang, which had an estimated population of 2 million.

7 MIGRATION

The DPRK encourages the return of overseas Koreans who migrated as refugees either from Communism or the Korean War. These people are needed to relieve the nation's chronic labor shortages. Between 1945 and 1950, an estimated 300,000 Koreans returned from Manchuria and Siberia. Over 93,000 out of about 600,000 Koreans in Japan returned to the DPRK between December 1959 and the end of 1974.

8 ETHNIC GROUPS

The Koreans are believed to be descended primarily from Tungusic peoples of the Mongoloid race, who originated in the cold northern regions of Central Asia. The DPRK has no sizable ethnic minority.

9 LANGUAGES

The Korean language is usually held to be a member of the Altaic family. Korean is written with a largely phonetic alphabet called Han'gul, whose letters resemble Chinese characters. In 1964, Kim Il-sung called for purification of Korean by replacing borrowings from English and Japanese with native Korean or familiar Chinese terms. Some Chinese (Mandarin dialect) and Russian are spoken in border areas.

10 RELIGIONS

According to current estimates most North Koreans practice no religion or are avowed atheists (deny the existence of God). Native religion is practiced by an estimated 16% of the population, mostly in rural areas. Followers of Ch'ondogyo (Religion of the Heavenly Way), which incorporates both Christian and Buddhist elements, account for about another 14%. Almost 2% of the population continues to practice Buddhism. Most of the nation's Christians fled to South Korea (ROK) to escape persecution between 1945 and 1953. Christians now make up less than 1% of the population.

11 TRANSPORTATION

The rail network is the principal means of transportation, carrying approximately 90% of the nation's freight and 70% of all passenger traffic. In 1986, railways in use comprised 8,533 kilometers (5,302 miles) of track. In 1991, highways totaled some 30,000 kilometers (18,600 miles). About 180,000 automobiles were in use in 1982.

Rivers used for freight transportation are the Yalu and Taedong. The main ports are Namp'o, Ch'ŏngjin, and Hŭngnam. In 1991, there were 71 ships in the merchant fleet with a capacity of 474,000 gross registered tons. Limited air services connect P'yŏngyang with other cities within the DPRK and in China and the former Soviet Union.

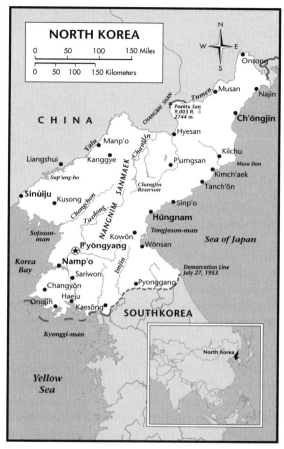

LOCATION: 37°38′ to 43°1′N; 124°13′ to 130°39′E.
BOUNDARY LENGTHS: China, 1,025 kilometers (637 miles); Russia, 16 kilometers (10 miles); ROK, 240 kilometers (149 miles); total coastline, 1,028 kilometers (639 miles). **TERRITORIAL SEA LIMIT:** 12 miles.

12 HISTORY

Early History

The history of the Korean people begins with the migration into the Korean Peninsula of Tungusic tribes from northern China and Manchuria about 3,000 BC. The recorded history of Korea begins around 194 BC, when the ancient kingdom of Choson ("Land of Morning Calm") in northwestern Korea was seized by Wiman, a military figure from China.

Wiman's successors fell victim to expanding Chinese power in 108 BC, and there followed more than four centuries of Chinese colonial rule. During this period, the advanced Chinese culture slowly spread into nearly every corner of Korea, helping unite the loosely knit Korean tribes. By AD 313, when Chinese power was ended in the region, three Korean kingdoms had emerged: Paekche, in the southwest; Silla, in the southeast; and Koguryo, in the northwest. During this period, Buddhism was introduced into Korea, from which it was later taken to Japan.

Over the following centuries, periods of division among the kingdoms alternated with three periods of unity: the Silla Unification (668–900); the reunification under the Koryo Dynasty (936–1231); and, finally, the rule of the long-lived Yi (or Li) Dynasty (1392-1910). Korea was invaded by the Manchus in 1636, eventually falling under the control of the Qing (Ch'ing), or Manchu, Dynasty in China.

Nineteenth Century

The first six decades of the nineteenth century were marked by a succession of natural disasters, and by increasing peasant unrest and rebellion. The Kanghwa Treaty of 1876 with Japan opened Korea both to Japan and to the Western nations. During the last quarter of the nineteenth century, Korea was the prize in a contest among Japan, China, Western imperialist powers, and domestic political forces. After defeating first the Chinese (1894–95) and then the Russians (1904–05), Japan formally annexed Korea in 1910, bringing to an end the Yi Dynasty.

For 35 years, Korea (renamed Choson) remained under Japanese rule, until liberated by American and Soviet troops at the end of World War II (1945).

The Korean War

After Japan surrendered on 14 August 1945, the 38th parallel was chosen as a line of demarcation between Soviet occupation forces in the North and American occupation forces in the South. The Americans set up a military government allied with conservative Korean political forces. The Soviets allied their government with leftist and Communist Korean forces led by Kim Il-sung, who had been an anti-Japanese guerrilla leader in Manchuria. The two governments were unable to agree on terms for the reunification of the country. They proclaimed two separate republics in 1948: the Republic of Korea (ROK) in the South and the Democratic People's Republic of Korea (DPRK) in the North.

On 25 June 1950, the People's Army of the DPRK invaded the ROK to unify the country under Communist control. The DPRK forces advanced rapidly, and the destruction of the ROK seemed near. However, US and UN multinational forces came to the aid of the South Koreans. A military campaign led by US General Douglas MacArthur brought about the total defeat of the DPRK's forces.

MacArthur then made a fateful decision to attack the North. China entered the fighting, forcing MacArthur into a costly retreat. The battle line stabilized near the 38th parallel, where it remained for two years. On 27 July 1953, a peace agreement finally was signed by all parties. The war killed an estimated 415,000 South Koreans, 23,300 Americans, 3,100 UN allies, and, according to official numbers, 50,000 North Koreans and Chinese (although this number is thought to be as high as 2 million).

Post-War History

The DPRK, with the aid of China and the former Soviet Union, began to restore its war-damaged economy. By the end of the 1950s, Kim Il-sung had emerged as the unchallenged leader of the DPRK. Throughout the 1970s and 1980s, the DPRK extended its diplomatic relations to over 100 countries. In the 1980s, Korea's basic divisions remained unresolved, but there was some improvement in relations between the North and South. The DPRK provided aid to the ROK after a flood in 1984. Talks under Red Cross sponsorship led to a brief reunion of separated families in 1985. The DPRK did not participate, however, in the 1988 summer Olympic Games, officially hosted by the ROK, since it was not named as cohost.

The collapse of the Soviet Union cut off an important source of economic and political support for the DPRK. In 1990, China and the ROK began to encourage mutual trade and in 1992 established formal diplomatic relations. Beginning in 1993, China demanded that all its exports to the DPRK be paid for with cash instead of through barter. The DPRK found itself increasingly isolated and in severe economic difficulty.

In the first half of the 1990s, the DPRK's foreign relations revolved around the issue of nuclear capabilities. It was suspected that the DPRK was developing the technology to build nuclear weapons. Tensions were defused with an agreement for high-level talks between the United States and the DPRK. These talks were to be followed by a summit in P'yŏngyang between the presidents of the two Koreas, the first such summit since Korea was divided in 1945.

On 8 July 1994, just as the United States-DPRK talks were beginning, President Kim Il-sung died. The talks were held off until after Kim's funeral on 17 July. Kim Jong-il replaced his father as President following an election by the Supreme People's Assembly on 11 July 1994.

13 GOVERNMENT

In theory, the highest state power is the Supreme People's Assembly (SPA), with 687 members in 1993. In practice, however, governmental control rests with the leadership of the Korean Workers' (Communist) Party. The SPA elects the president of the DPRK, the Central People's Committee, and the Administrative Council (cabinet). The state ideology is self-reliance (*Chuch'e* or *Juch'e*), the Korean version of Marxism-Leninism. Suffrage extends to all men and women 17 years of age or older. Elections are on a single slate of Communist-approved candidates, on a yes or no basis. There are 9 provinces in the DPRK, plus 3 provincial-level cities. The provinces are divided into 20 cities (*si*) and 152 counties (*kun*) each.

14 POLITICAL PARTIES

On 10 October 1945, the Communist Party merged with the New Democratic Party to form the Korean Workers' (Communist) Party, now the ruling party of the DPRK. The National Party Congress adopts the party program and approves the political line set by its Central People's Committee. Officially, there are two non-Communist political parties: the Korean Social Democratic Party, and the Friends Party, founded in 1946 for adherents of the Ch'ondogyo faith.

15 JUDICIAL SYSTEM

The DPRK's judicial system consists of the Central Court, formerly called the Supreme Court; the courts of provinces, cities, and counties; and special courts (courts-martial and transport courts). Most cases are first tried by people's courts at the city or county level. Provincial courts try important cases and examine appeals of lower court judgments. Prosecution of alleged crimes against the state is conducted in secret outside the judicial system.

16 ARMED FORCES

The DPRK has one of the world's largest and best-equipped armed forces. Out of a total of 1.1 million personnel on active duty in 1993, one million were in the army, 40,000 in the navy, and 92,000 in the air force (with 732 combat aircraft). An additional 540,000 were in the

reserves, and there was a civilian militia of 3–5 million. Defense expenditures in 1993 totaled about $5 billion. Concern has been raised abroad about the DPRK's growing capacity to produce weapons-grade nuclear material and its refusal to submit to inspections.

17 ECONOMY

The Korean War devastated much of the DPRK's economy, but postwar reconstruction helped repair it rapidly. The Communist regime has used its rich mineral resources to promote industry, especially heavy industry. Available information suggests that since the early 1990s, the country has suffered serious economic problems. A drop in oil imports from Russia has limited production in many key areas of the economy. Reports by the Bank of Korea in Seoul suggest a decline in the DPRK's gross national product (GNP) of 3.7% in 1990, followed by another 5.2% drop in 1991.

18 INCOME

The United States government estimated the DPRK's gross national product (GNP) at $22 billion in 1992, with a declining growth rate of between –10 and –15%. The per person GNP was estimated at $1,000.

19 INDUSTRY

The Communist regime has emphasized the development of manufacturing. By the late 1980s, heavy industry accounted for 50% of total industrial production.

Iron and steel manufacturing amounted to 3.7 million tons of pig iron and conver-

Photo credit: AP/Wide World Photos

Women and children wash their clothes dirtied from long, hard work in the field in the North Korean countryside along the main railway lines. In the countryside, life appears much tougher than in the capital.

sion pig iron and 7.7 million tons of steel (including rolled steel) in 1990. Industrial plants produced cement (7.6 million tons in 1990), magnesia clinker (1 million tons), zinc (170,000 tons), lead (84,000 tons), aluminum (21,000 tons), metal cutting lathes (28,000), tractors (23,000), and trucks (10,000).

The chemical industry produced an estimated 3.9 million tons of chemical fertilizers and 92,000 tons of synthetic resins in 1990, and 74,000 tons of chemical fibers in 1989. About 2.3 million tons of oil products were produced in 1990.

20 LABOR

The DPRK faces a chronic labor shortage. The civilian labor force is estimated at more than 6.1 million, about 43% of whom are engaged in agriculture, forestry, and fishing. Women are believed to constitute about 46% of the labor force. The eight-hour workday is standard but most laborers work 12–16 hours daily during production campaigns.

21 AGRICULTURE

Rice is the principal crop, occupying about 30% of all farmland in 1992. Total rice production was 5 million tons in 1992. The use of "miracle" rice strains, fertilizer, and mechanization has improved rice yields. The DPRK claims to be self-sufficient in grain products, with total production (including rice) amounting to 9.8 million tons in 1992. According to other sources, heavy imports of wheat and flour are needed. The leading grains after rice are corn, wheat, millet, and barley. Other important crops include soybeans, potatoes, sweet potatoes, pulses (peas and beans), oats, sorghum, rye, tobacco, and cotton.

22 DOMESTICATED ANIMALS

In 1992, livestock totals were estimated as follows: hogs, 3,300,000; cattle, 1,300,000; sheep, 390,000; goats, 300,000; and horses, 46,000. Livestock raising is generally associated with the state farms. Meat produced in 1992 totaled 258,000 tons; milk, 93,000; and eggs, 160,000. The DPRK was the world's third leading producer of silk in 1992 (after China and India), with 4,500 tons.

23 FISHING

The ocean and freshwater catches include mackerel, anchovy, tuna, mullet, rainbow trout, squid, kelp, sea urchin eggs, pollack eggs, and shrimp. Estimated production for 1992 was 1.7 million tons.

24 FORESTRY

Forests and woodland comprised about 8,970,000 hectares (22,165,000 acres) in the early 1990s. Predominant trees include oak, alder, larch, pine, spruce, and fir. Timber production was estimated at 4.7 million cubic meters in 1991. An estimated 4.1 million cubic meters were used for fuel, and only 875,000 cubic meters in industry.

25 MINING

Coal deposits include anthracite and lignite. The government reported a total coal production in 1991 of 90 million tons. Iron ore production was over 10 million tons. Other mineral products include gold, magnesite, tungsten, phosphate, sulfur, zinc, lead, silver, and copper.

26 FOREIGN TRADE

The DPRK's principal exports include rice, pig iron, rolled steel, cement, machinery of various types, chemicals, magnesite, textiles, weapons, and gold. Imports include petroleum, coking coal, wheat, cotton, and machinery.

China took the lead as the DPRK's largest trading partner in 1992, followed by Japan and Russia. Total trade with China amounted to almost $700 million, about 77% of which consisted of imports (mainly oil and related products). By 1992, South Korea was the DPRK's fourth largest trading partner, behind China and Japan.

27 ENERGY AND POWER

Coal, oil, and natural gas provided 40% of the DPRK's electricity generation in 1991. Hydroelectricity accounted for the rest. Coal is by far the most important part of energy production. Estimated coal production in 1991 was 90 million tons, 35 million tons more than domestic consumption that year. Production of electricity in 1991 totaled 51.9 billion kilowatt hours.

The International Atomic Energy Agency (IAEA) began inspections of DPRK nuclear facilities in March 1991, in order to determine whether or not the DPRK was reprocessing old nuclear reactor fuel, which could be used to make a nuclear weapon.

28 SOCIAL DEVELOPMENT

All citizens are entitled to free medical care, disability benefits, and retirement allowances. There are also programs allowing paid vacations and paid maternity leaves, with the state making up the rest of the cost. Retirement pensions are roughly one-half of the annual average wage. Those who continue working after retirement age receive both their salary and their pension.

Selected Social Indicators

These statistics are estimates for the period 1988 to 1993. For comparison purposes, data for the United States and averages for low-income countries and high-income countries are also given.

Indicator	DPRK	Low-income countries	High-income countries	United States
Per capita gross national product†	**$1,000**	$380	$23,680	$24,740
Population growth rate	**1.9%**	1.9%	0.6%	1.0%
Population growth rate in urban areas	**2.4%**	3.9%	0.8%	1.3%
Population per square kilometer of land	**188**	78	25	26
Life expectancy in years	**71**	62	77	76
Number of people per physician	**426**	>3,300	453	419
Number of pupils per teacher (primary school)	**n.a.**	39	<18	20
Illiteracy rate (15 years and older)	**<1%**	41%	<5%	<3%
Energy consumed per capita (kg of oil equivalent)	**1,701**	364	5,203	7,918

† The gross national product (GNP) is the total dollar value of all goods and services produced by a country in a year. The per capita GNP is calculated by dividing a country's GNP by its population. The World Bank defines low-income countries as those with a per capita GNP of $695 or less. High-income countries have a per capita GNP of $8,626 or more. Less than 14% of the world's 5.5 billion people live in high-income countries, while almost 60% live in low-income countries.

n.a. = data not available   > = greater than   < = less than

Sources: World Bank, *Social Indicators of Development 1995,* Baltimore: Johns Hopkins University Press, 1995. Central Intelligence Agency, *World Fact Book,* Washington, D.C.: Government Printing Office, 1994.

The 1972 constitution guarantees equal rights for women. The state provides nurseries and day-care centers, and large families are encouraged.

29 HEALTH

For the period 1988–93, the average number of people per doctor was 426.

Western medicine is used alongside traditional Eastern medicine (*tonguihak*). Cancer is now the leading cause of death, followed by heart disease and high blood pressure. Average life expectancy in 1992 was 71 years for both men and women.

30 HOUSING

The Korean War destroyed about one-third of the country's housing. A construction level of 150,000–200,000 units a year was projected for 1987–93. Available figures for 1980–88 show a total housing stock of 4,566,000 with 4.5 people per dwelling.

31 EDUCATION

Both primary and secondary education are free and compulsory for eleven years, beginning at age 6. The adult literacy rate was estimated to be over 99% in 1991. In 1986, there were an estimated 4,792 primary institutions with 1,466,000 students enrolled. In the 4,738 secondary institutions, 2,842,000 students were enrolled. Kim Il-sung University (founded in 1946) in P'yŏngyang is the only university, with about 12,000 students and 2,000 teachers. In 1986 there were 473 colleges with a total of 215,000 students enrolled.

32 MEDIA

There are two radio networks (Korean Central Radio and Radio P'yŏngyang) and two television networks, (Korean Central TV and Mansudae TV). In 1991 there were about 2.6 million radios and 338,000 television sets.

All newspapers and periodicals in the DPRK are published by government or party organizations. The leading national newspapers are: *Rodong Sinmun* (1991 circulation 1,500,000); *Minju Choson* (circulation 200,000); *P'yŏngyang Shinmun*; and *Radong Changuyon*.

33 TOURISM AND RECREATION

Most sightseeing takes place in the capital city of P'yŏngyang. Travel outside P'yŏngyang is closed to individual tourists but available to groups. The two most outstanding tourist sites outside the capital are the mountains in the southwest and Mt. Paektu (Paektu San) on the Chinese border. All tourism from the United States, Israel, the ROK, and South Africa, is banned without invitation.

Wrestling, tug-of-war, chess (with pieces different from the European form), and kite fighting are traditional sports.

34 FAMOUS KOREANS

Among the many historical figures of united Korea are Kim Yosin (595–673), a warrior and folk hero in Silla's struggle to unify the peninsula, and Yi Ha-ung (1820–98), known as the Taewon'gun (Prince Regent), the central political figure of the late 19th century. The dominant political figure of the DPRK is Kim Il-sung (1912–94), the leader of the nation from 1948 until his death. His son, Kim Jong-il (b. 1941), succeeded him.

35 BIBLIOGRAPHY

Eckert, Carter J. *Korea, Old and New: A History*. Cambridge, Mass.: Harvard University Press, 1990.

Hoare, James. *Korea: An Introduction*. New York: Kegan Paul International, 1988.

Olsen, Edward A. *US Policy and the Two Koreas*. Boulder, Colo.: Westview Press, 1988.

KOREA, REPUBLIC OF (ROK)

Republic of Korea
Taehan Min-guk

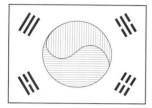

CAPITAL: Seoul.

FLAG: The flag, called the T'aegukki, shows, on a white field, a central circle divided into two parts, red on top and deep blue below, in the shape of Chinese yin and yang symbols. Broken and unbroken black bars in each of the four corners are variously arranged in sets of three, representing divination diagrams.

ANTHEM: *Aegukka (The Song of Patriotism)*, officially adopted on 15 August 1948.

MONETARY UNIT: The won (w) is the national currency. There are notes of 500, 1,000, 5,000, and 10,000 won. w1 = $0.0012 (or $1 = w806.50).

WEIGHTS AND MEASURES: Both the metric system and ancient Korean units of measurement are used.

HOLIDAYS: New Year's Days, 1–3 January; Independence Movement Day, 1 March; Labor Day, 10 March; Arbor Day, 5 April; Children's Day, 5 May; Memorial Day, 6 June; Constitution Day, 17 July; Liberation Day, 15 August; Armed Forces Day, 1 October; National Foundation Day, 3 October; Han'gul (Korean Alphabet) Day, 9 October; Christmas, 25 December.

TIME: 9 PM = noon GMT.

1 LOCATION AND SIZE

The Republic of Korea (ROK), also known as South Korea, occupies the southern 45% of the Korean Peninsula in East Asia and has an area of 98,480 square kilometers (38,023 square miles), slightly larger than the state of Indiana. The ROK has a total boundary length of 1,558 kilometers (968 miles). Over 3,000 islands, most of them off the southern and western coasts, belong to the ROK.

The ROK's capital city, Seoul, is located in the northwestern part of the country.

2 TOPOGRAPHY

Elevations in the southern part of the Korean Peninsula are generally lower than those in the north. The principal lowlands border the Yellow Sea along the west coast. Halla Mountain (1,950 meters/6,398 feet) is the nation's highest point. Principal rivers of the ROK include the

Han and Kŭm. The longest river in the ROK is the Naktong (521 kilometers/324 miles).

3 CLIMATE

The average January temperature ranges from −5°C (23°F) at Seoul to 4°C (39°F) on Cheju Island (Cheju Do). In the hottest part of the summer, average temperatures range only from 25°C to 27°C (77°–81°F) in most lowland areas. Most of the nation receives between 75 and 100 centimeters (30 and 40 inches) of rain a year.

4 PLANTS AND ANIMALS

More than 3,000 varieties of plant life, some 500 of them unique to Korea, have been noted by botanists. Zoologists have identified more than 130 freshwater fishes, 371 birds, 78 mammals, and 39 reptiles and amphibians on the peninsula. Bear, wild boar, deer, and lynx are still found in the highlands, but in fewer numbers in recent years. Migratory water fowl, cranes, herons, and other birds are found on the plains.

5 ENVIRONMENT

The purity of the nation's water is threatened by agricultural chemicals. The nation has 15.1 cubic miles of water with 75% used for agriculture and 14% used for industrial purposes; 24% of the people living in rural areas do not have pure water. In 1990, the nation dumped 10 million tons of sewage and 7 million tons of industrial chemicals into its water sources. Air pollution, associated mainly with the use of coal briquettes for home heating and the increase in automobile traffic, is also severe, with smog a common problem in Seoul.

The Naktong River delta, a marshland where thousands of birds spend the winter, is threatened by environmental pollution and by plans to dam the mouth of the river. In 1994, six of Korea's mammal species and 22 bird species were endangered, as were 33 plant species.

6 POPULATION

The 1990 census for the ROK reported a total population of 43,520,199, or nearly twice the estimated population of the DPRK. A total of 46,897,000 was projected for the year 2000. The estimated population density for the period 1988–93 was 441 persons per square kilometer (1,144 per square mile), making the ROK one of the world's most densely populated nations. Seoul, the largest city, had a population of 10,627,790 in 1990.

7 MIGRATION

From 1945 through 1949, at least 1.2 million Koreans crossed the 38th parallel into the ROK, refugees from Communism or the Korean War. Most of the emigrants are workers who send earnings back home. Emigration peaked at 48,270 in 1976, declining to 27,163 in 1990. In addition, Koreans have emigrated permanently to the United States in large numbers since 1971. The population of Korean origin in the United States was 798,849 as of 1990. In all, more than 2 million South Koreans were living abroad in 1994. Many South Koreans continue to move within the ROK from the rural areas to the cities, despite government efforts to improve village living conditions.

8 ETHNIC GROUPS

The Koreans are believed to be descended primarily from Tungusic peoples of the Mongoloid race, who originated in the cold northern regions of Central Asia. The ROK has no sizable ethnic minority.

9 LANGUAGES

The Korean language is usually held to be a member of the Altaic family. Korean is written in a largely phonetic alphabet called Han'gul, whose letters resemble Chinese characters. More than half of the vocabulary consists of words derived from Chinese.

10 RELIGIONS

Most South Koreans are quite varied in their religious beliefs, the majority following different mixtures of Taoism, Confucianism, Buddhism, Christianity, Ch'ondogyo (Religion of the Heavenly Way, which combines Buddhism and Christianity), and local tribal religions.

In 1989, Mahayana Buddhism was the principal religion, with 8,059,000 followers. Traditional Protestant groups had 6,489,010; Roman Catholicism, 1,865,000; and Confucianism, 483,009.

Ch'ondogyo, the most widespread of more than 250 new religions, had 27,000 followers. Wonbulgyo (Round Buddhism), founded in 1924, had 92,000. There were also about 20,000 Muslims in 1986.

LOCATION: 33°7' to 38°38'N; 124°36' to 130°56'E.
BOUNDARY LENGTHS: DPRK, 240 kilometers (149 miles); total coastline, 1,318 kilometers (819 miles). **TERRITORIAL SEA LIMIT:** 12 miles.

11 TRANSPORTATION

The bulk of ROK railroads, totaling 3,106 kilometers (1,930 miles) of track in 1991, are government-owned. In 1988, the railroads carried 556 million passengers. The

ROK had 62,936 kilometers (39,108 miles) of roadway in 1991, of which 21% was national highway. There were 2,727,862 passenger automobiles, 1,092,304 trucks, and 427,650 buses.

Maritime shipping expanded rapidly during the 1970s. Pusan is the chief port; other major ports include Inch'on (the port for Seoul), Kunsan, and Mokp'o.

Major airports are Kimpo International Airport at Seoul and Kimhae International Airport west of Pusan. In 1990, Kimpo International handled 113,200 flights and 16,821,000 passengers.

12 HISTORY

[For Korean history before 1948, see Korea, Democratic People's Republic of.]

The Korean War

The Republic of Korea, headed by President Syngman Rhee, was proclaimed on 15 August 1948 in the southern portion of the Korean Peninsula, which had been under United States military administration since 1945. Like the Democratic People's Republic of Korea (DPRK), established in the north with Soviet backing, the ROK claimed to be the legitimate government of all Korea. The ROK was recognized as the legitimate government by the United Nations General Assembly.

On 25 June 1950, the People's Army of the DPRK invaded the ROK to unify the country under Communist control. The DPRK forces advanced rapidly, and the destruction of the ROK seemed near. However, US and UN multinational forces came to the aid of the South Koreans. A military campaign led by US General Douglas MacArthur brought about the total defeat of the DPRK's forces.

MacArthur then made a fateful decision to attack the North. China entered the fighting, forcing MacArthur into a costly retreat. The battle line stabilized near the 38th parallel, where it remained for two years. On 27 July 1953, a peace agreement finally was signed by all parties. The war killed an estimated 415,000 South Koreans, 23,300 Americans, 3,100 United Nations allies, and, according to official numbers, 50,000 North Koreans and Chinese (although this number is thought to be as high as two million).

Post-War History

In 1954, the US and the ROK signed a mutual defense treaty, under which United States troops remained in the country. Financial assistance throughout the 1950s was provided by the United States, averaging $270 million annually between 1953 and 1958. Syngman Rhee ran the government until 1960, when his authoritarian rule provoked violent student demonstrations that finally brought about his downfall. In May 1961, the Second Korean Republic was overthrown in a military coup headed by Major General Park Chung-hee.

For the next 18 years, Park ruled South Korea, periodically resorting to martial law in response to student demonstrations and other forms of opposition. On 26 October 1979, Park was assassinated by the director of the Korean intelligence

Photo credit: AP/Wide World Photos

Korean children carry pickets calling for environmental protection in Seoul as the country marks Earth Day.

agency (KCIA), Kim Jae-gyu, who was later executed.

The Chun and Roh Regimes

In December 1979, Major General Chun Doo Hwan led a coup against Park's successor. Demonstrations by university students spread through the spring of 1980 and by mid-May the government once more declared martial law. In the 1981 elections, Chun was elected to a seven-year presidential term by a new electoral college. His Democratic Justice Party (DJP) secured a majority in the reorganized National Assembly. In June 1987, the DJP nominated its chairman, Roh Tae Woo, a former general and a close friend

of Chun, as its candidate for his successor. Roh defeated the two major opposition candidates, Kim Young Sam and Kim Dae Jung, and was inaugurated as president in February 1988.

Following a revision of the constitution in 1987, South Koreans enjoyed greater freedoms of expression and assembly and freedom of the press. In 1988, several hundred political dissidents were released from prison. The United States agreed to withdraw its nuclear weapons from the ROK in November 1991. And, on the last day of the year, the ROK and the DPRK signed an agreement to ban nuclear weapons from the entire Korean peninsula.

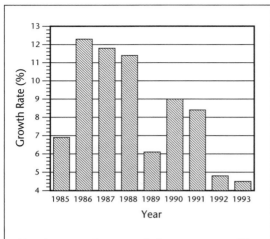

Yearly growth rate of the economy. This economic indicator tells by what percent the economy has increased or decreased when compared with the previous year.

In the presidential election on 19 December 1992, Kim Young Sam, now leader of the majority DLP, was elected president. President Kim granted amnesty to 41,000 prisoners and fired many high-ranking military officials. Kim also cleaned up the government and business sector by arresting, firing, or publicly scolding several thousand government officials and business people.

13 GOVERNMENT

Under the new constitution, which took effect in February 1988, the president is elected by direct popular vote for a single term of five years. There are also a prime minister and two deputy prime ministers, who head the State Council (the cabinet). The ROK legislature is the 299-seat National Assembly (Kuk Hoe). Suffrage is universal at age 20. The ROK is divided into nine provinces (*do*), which are further divided into cities (*si*), counties (*kun*), townships (*myon*), and villages (*i*).

14 POLITICAL PARTIES

Since the revised 1987 constitution took effect, political parties have had a greater governmental role. In 1994, the majority party was the Democratic Liberal Party (DLP) with Kim Young Sam as its president. The opposition parties were the Democratic Party (DP) and the United People's Party (UPP), along with several smaller parties.

15 JUDICIAL SYSTEM

The highest judicial court is the Supreme Court. Under the Supreme Court are three intermediate appeals courts, located in Seoul, Taegu, and Kwangju. Lower courts include district and family courts. The Constitution provides for a presumption of innocence, protection from self-incrimination, the right to a speedy trial, protection from double jeopardy, and other due process safeguards.

16 ARMED FORCES

The ROK has one of the world's largest and best-equipped armed forces. Defense spending accounted for $12.6 billion in 1992. Of a total of 633,000 personnel on active duty, 520,000 were in the army; 60,000 in the navy and marines; and 53,000 in the air force (with 403 combat aircraft). An additional 4.5 million were in the reserves. All males age 19 must serve 26 to 30 months in the military.

17 ECONOMY

The ROK has been one of the fastest-developing countries in the post-war period, shifting from an agricultural to an industrial economy in the course of only a few decades. Much of this industrialization involves heavy industry, notably steel, construction, shipbuilding, and technologically advanced goods such as electronics.

18 INCOME

In 1992, Korea's gross national product (GNP) was $296,349 million or about $7,660 per person. For the period 1985–92 the average inflation rate was 6.8%, resulting in a real growth rate in per person GNP of 8.5%.

19 INDUSTRY

The ROK ranks as a major Asian producer of steel, chemicals, ships, machinery, nonferrous metals, and electronic equipment. In the 1980s, the manufacture of metals, machinery, electronic, and other equipment overtook textile production as the country's leading industry. Production of merchant vessels in 1991 totaled 3,674,000 gross tons.

Output from major industries in 1991 included: pig iron, 18,546,000 tons; compound fertilizers, 1,823,000 tons; steel ingots, 1,059,000 tons; and cotton yarn, 569,000 tons. There were large production increases in the manufacture of a number of goods, including passenger cars (1,132,000), motorcycles (334,113), trucks (232,937), color television sets (13,353,000), and video cassette recorders (9,221,000).

20 LABOR

Of the total of 18,921,000 workers employed in 1992, 3,025,000 (16%) were engaged in agriculture, forestry, and fishing; another 4,768,000 (25.2%) in manufacturing; and 11,128,000 (58.8%) in other occupations, mostly government employment. The unemployment rate in 1992 averaged 2.4%.

21 AGRICULTURE

Rice is the chief crop of the ROK. The rice harvest in 1992 was 7,361,000 tons. Barley production in 1992 stood at 400,000 tons; potatoes, 416,000 tons; and soybeans, 180,000 tons.

Hemp, hops, and tobacco are the leading industrial crops. The ROK was the world's second leading producer (after China) of chestnuts in 1992. The orchards in the Taegu area are famous for their apples, the prime fruit crop. About two-thirds of vegetable production is made up of the mu (a large white radish) and Chinese cabbage, the main ingredients of the year-round staple *kimchi*, or "Korean pickle."

22 DOMESTICATED ANIMALS

In 1992, 75 million chickens, 5,505,000 pigs, and 2,517,449 cattle were raised. The silkworm industry has declined radically since the mid-1970s. The raw silk output of 8,000 tons in 1992 was less than one-quarter of the 1979–81 annual average. The ROK is self-sufficient in the production of milk.

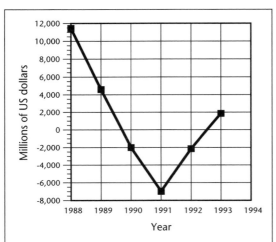

Yearly balance of trade measured in millions of US dollars. The balance of trade is the difference between what a country sells to other countries (its exports) and what it buys (its imports). If a country imports more than it exports, it has a negative balance of trade (a trade deficit). If exports exceed imports there is a positive balance of trade (a trade surplus).

23 FISHING

Korean waters have some of the best fishing in the world. The total catch in 1991 was 2,515,305 tons. Deep-sea fishing has shown remarkable growth, with marine output totaling 2,484,843 tons in 1992. Tuna provided much of the deep-sea catch.

24 FORESTRY

Forests covered 6,480,000 hectares (16,012,000 acres) in 1991, or about two-thirds of the ROK's total area. Wood supplies, however, still cannot meet the needs of the fast-growing plywood and paper industries.

25 MINING

The ROK has limited supplies of iron ore, coal, copper, lead, and zinc. Among mineral ores produced in 1991, iron totaled 134,000 tons; zinc, 22,039 tons; lead, 12,633 tons; and tungsten ore, 780 tons. In addition, the ROK produced 292 tons of silver and 23 tons of gold.

26 FOREIGN TRADE

The ROK has the eleventh largest volume of trade in the world. Ships, textiles, clothing, electronics equipment, electrical machinery, and iron and steel are its leading exports. Oil and related products, chemicals, and raw materials are major imports.

The United States and Japan have continued to be the ROK's chief trading partners, although potential new markets in Eastern Europe and the rest of Asia are being explored. Saudi Arabia and Indonesia have been major providers of oil and liquefied natural gas. Australia is a leading supplier of iron ore, coal, and grains.

27 ENERGY AND POWER

Coal is the chief fuel mined, with production totaling 14,850,000 tons in 1991. In 1992, crude oil provided 62.4% of all primary energy consumed; coal, 20.4%; nuclear energy, 12.8%; natural gas, 4%; and hydroelectricity, about 0.4%. The output of electricity in 1991 totaled 112.3 billion kilowatt hours.

28 SOCIAL DEVELOPMENT

The government passed legislation in 1988 that included old age, disability, and survi-

Selected Social Indicators

These statistics are estimates for the period 1988 to 1993. For comparison purposes, data for the United States and averages for low-income countries and high-income countries are also given.

Indicator	ROK	Low-income countries	High-income countries	United States
Per capita gross national product†	**$7,660**	$380	$23,680	$24,740
Population growth rate	**1.0%**	1.9%	0.6%	1.0%
Population growth rate in urban areas	**2.9%**	3.9%	0.8%	1.3% .
Population per square kilometer of land	**441**	78	25	26
Life expectancy in years	**71**	62	77	76
Number of people per physician	**951**	>3,300	453	419
Number of pupils per teacher (primary school)	**31**	39	<18	20
Illiteracy rate (15 years and older)	**5%**	41%	<5%	<3%
Energy consumed per capita (kg of oil equivalent)	**2,863**	364	5,203	7,918

† The gross national product (GNP) is the total dollar value of all goods and services produced by a country in a year. The per capita GNP is calculated by dividing a country's GNP by its population. The World Bank defines low-income countries as those with a per capita GNP of $695 or less. High-income countries have a per capita GNP of $8,626 or more. Less than 14% of the world's 5.5 billion people live in high-income countries, while almost 60% live in low-income countries.

> = greater than   < = less than

Sources: World Bank, *Social Indicators of Development 1995,* Baltimore: Johns Hopkins University Press, 1995. Central Intelligence Agency, *World Fact Book,* Washington, D.C.: Government Printing Office, 1994.

vors' pensions. It passed health insurance legislation in 1989.

The wage of the average female worker is roughly half of that of the average male worker. The Amended Family Law of 1991 recognizes women heads of households.

29 HEALTH

Health care has improved greatly due to improvement of diet, the rise in living standards, and the development of health and medical programs. In 1992, 100% of the population had access to health care services. Life expectancy is 71 years. Total health care expenditures in 1990 were $16.1 million. In 1992, there were 236 general hospitals. In 1990, there were three hospital beds per 1,000 people. For the period 1988–93, there were an average of 951 people per physician.

30 HOUSING

A housing shortage continues to plague the nation, especially in large cities. As of 1992, the per person housing space was 9.6 square meters (103 square feet). The government plans to construct 500,000 to 600,000 housing units per year from 1993 to 1998, increasing the rate of home ownership to 90%.

31 EDUCATION

Six-year elementary schools are free and compulsory for children between 6 and 12 years of age. Secondary education begins at 12 years of age and lasts for up to six years. Nearly 87% of children in this age group were enrolled in the secondary schools in 1990. In 1992 there were 4,560,128 students in primary schools, 2,336,284 in middle schools, 2,125,573 in high schools, 1,491,669 in colleges and universities, and 96,577 in graduate schools. The leading government university is Seoul National University.

32 MEDIA

In 1991, the number of telephone lines totaled 14,194,862. There were 125 radio stations in 1992. Koreans owned 43,850,000 radios and 9.1 million television sets in 1991.

The ROK press has been severely censored since the early 1970s. In 1991, 39 daily newspapers were published. Leading Korean-language newspapers, with their estimated daily circulations (in 1991), include *Joong-ang Ilbo*, 1,650,000; *Hankook Ilbo*, 2,000,000; *Dong-A Ilbo*, 1,095,000; and *Choson Ilbo*, 1,800,000.

33 TOURISM AND RECREATION

The tourist industry has grown rapidly. There were 3,196,000 foreign visitors in 1991, of whom 2,088,000 came from Eastern or Southeast Asia. Major tourist attractions are Seoul, the former royal capital of the Yi (or Li) Dynasty, and the city of Kyŏngju, with its treasures from the ancient kingdom of Silla.

Soccer and baseball are the most popular modern sports. Traditional sports for men are wrestling, archery, kite fighting, and *t'aekwondo* (a martial art). Popular games include *changgi*, or Korean chess, with pieces different from the European form; and *yut*, or Korean dice, played with four wooden sticks.

34 FAMOUS KOREANS (ROK)

The dominant political figures of the contemporary period in the ROK have been Syngman Rhee (1875–1965), president from 1948 to 1960; and Park Chung-hee (1917–79), president from 1963 until his assassination in 1979. The Reverend Sun Myung Moon (Mun Son-myong, b.1920), the controversial founder of the Tong-il (Unification) Church, and Kyung Wha Chung (Chung Kyung-wha, b.1943), a violinist, have both become internationally known.

35 BIBLIOGRAPHY

Hoare, James. *Korea: An Introduction*. New York: Kegan Paul International, 1988.

McNair, S. *Korea*. Chicago: Children's Press, 1986.

Oliver, Robert Tarbell. *A History of the Korean People in Modern Times: 1800 to the Present*. Newark: Univ. of Delaware Press, 1993.

Olsen, Edward A. *US Policy and the Two Koreas*. Boulder, Colo.: Westview Press, 1988.

KUWAIT

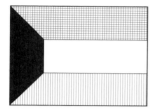

State of Kuwait
Dawlat al-Kuwayt

CAPITAL: Kuwait (Al-Kuwayt).

FLAG: The flag adopted in 1961 is a rectangle divided equally into green, white, and red horizontal stripes, with a black trapezoid whose longer base is against the staff and is equal to the breadth of the flag, and whose shorter base is equal to the breadth of the white stripe.

ANTHEM: National Anthem, melody only; no words.

MONETARY UNIT: The Kuwaiti dinar (KD) has 1,000 fils. There are coins of 1, 5, 10, 20, 50, and 100 fils, and notes of 250 and 500 fils and of 1, 5, 10, and 20 Kuwaiti dinars. KD1 = $3.3661 (or $1 = KD0.2971).

WEIGHTS AND MEASURES: The metric system is the legal standard, but imperial weights and measures also are in use, and some US measures are recognized.

HOLIDAYS: New Year's Day, 1 January; Emir's Accession Day, 25 February. Movable religious holidays include Muslim New Year (1st of Muharram); Laylat al-Miraj; Milad an-Nabi; 'Id al-Fitr; and 'Id al-'Adha'.

TIME: 3 PM = noon GMT.

1 LOCATION AND SIZE

Kuwait is situated at the western head of the Persian Gulf. Its area is estimated at about 17,820 square kilometers (6,880 square miles), slightly smaller than the state of New Jersey. Of the islands that form part of Kuwait, only Faylakah is inhabited. Kuwait has a total boundary length of 963 kilometers (602 miles).

Kuwait's capital, Kuwait city, is located on the Persian Gulf coast.

2 TOPOGRAPHY

Kuwait consists almost entirely of flat rolling desert and mud flats. There is a 120-meter (400-foot) ridge at Mina' Al-Ahmadi. There are no rivers or streams.

3 CLIMATE

Between November and April, the climate is pleasant, with cool nights and warm sunny days. In December and January, night temperatures occasionally reach the freezing point. Summer temperatures range from 29°C (84°F) in the morning to more than 49°C (120°F) in the shade at noon. Annual rainfall, which averages less than 10 centimeters (4 inches), comes in the form of showers or storms between October and April.

4 PLANTS AND ANIMALS

During the dry season, there is little vegetation. Between October and March, however, when enough rain falls, grass and foliage are plentiful, flowers and plants appear in great variety, and in the spring truffles and mushrooms can be found. Fox and jackal populations have decreased in recent years. Fish are plentiful. Among the species of migratory birds are swallows, wagtails, chiffchaff, skylarks, and wrens.

5 ENVIRONMENT

The Persian Gulf War of 1991 and its aftermath caused severe environmental problems for Kuwait. The nation's water supply has been threatened by large quantities of oil released into the environment. Kuwait has no reusable water supply and must rely on wells and desalinization of sea water. In 1994, five of Kuwait's mammal species and seven of its bird species were endangered; one plant species was also endangered.

6 POPULATION

According to the 1985 census, Kuwait had a total population of 1,697,301, but it was estimated at only 1,468,902 in mid-1994. The United Nations projection for the year 2000 was 1,718,000. Metropolitan Kuwait, the national capital, had an estimated population of 1,090,000 in 1990. The average population density is estimated at 106 persons per square kilometer (214 per square mile).

7 MIGRATION

With the discovery of oil, Kuwait acquired a large immigrant population. In 1994, foreign residents accounted for an estimated 56.4% of the population. Of the estimated 400,000 Palestinians living in Kuwait before the 1990–91 Gulf War, reportedly only about one-sixth were allowed to remain, as most were suspected of collaborating with the occupying Iraqis.

8 ETHNIC GROUPS

Ethnic Kuwaitis are mostly descendants of the tribes of Najd (central Arabia) but some descend from Iraqi Arabs. Still others are of Iranian origin. The number of non-Kuwaitis was estimated at 812,000 in 1993 (about 55% of the total), divided roughly in half between Arabs and non-Arabs.

9 LANGUAGES

Arabic is the official language. English is used generally by business people, employees of oil companies, foreign residents, and students, and it is the second language taught in the schools.

10 RELIGIONS

In 1986, Muslims comprised 90% of the population. Of these, 63% were Sunni, with a substantial (27%) Shi'ite minority. Other religious groups—primarily foreign workers—include Roman Catholics and Anglicans.

11 TRANSPORTATION

Main roads extended 3,900 kilometers (2,400 miles) in 1991. In the same year, there were some 500,000 passenger cars, and 150,000 commercial taxis, trucks, and buses in use. There are no railways. Kuwait has five ports, including a cargo port at Ash Shuaybah. In 1991, Kuwait had 28 merchant ships in service with a capacity of 1,326,000 gross registered tons.

Air transportation is highly advanced, with Kuwait Airways providing service to and from the major Middle Eastern and European cities. There were an estimated 501,000 passenger arrivals and departures at Kuwait International Airport in 1991, only 35% of the 1990 total, due to the airport's closing during the Persian Gulf War.

12 HISTORY

By the sixth century BC, the Arab coast of the Persian Gulf was a principal supply route for trade with India. Its people converted to Islam in the seventh century AD, during the lifetime of Muhammad.

Kuwait's recent history starts in 1716, when members of the tribe of Aniza migrated from the Arabian Desert to a tiny Gulf coastal area, later to be called Kuwait (a form of the word *kut,* meaning "fort"). In 1756, the settled tribesmen chose as their ruler Sheikh Sabah 'Abd ar-Rahim, founder of the present ruling dynasty. During the latter part of the century, raids by land and by sea resulted in the decline of Kuwait, but after the British crackdown on piracy in the region, trading and shipbuilding prospered.

At the end of the nineteenth century, Sheikh Mubarak as-Sabah, fearing the territorial ambitions of the Ottoman Turks, asked to be taken under British protection. The British, in turn, were concerned not only by Turkish claims but also by the activities of Russia and Germany in the area. In 1899, Sheikh Mubarak agreed not to open any of his territory to foreign control. In return, the British offered their ser-

LOCATION: 28°32′ to 30°6′N; 46°33′ to 48°27′E.
BOUNDARY LENGTHS: Persian Gulf shoreline, 499 kilometers (312 miles); Sa'udi Arabia, 222 kilometers (139 miles); Iraq, 242 kilometers (151 miles). **TERRITORIAL SEA LIMIT:** 12 miles.

vices as well as an annual subsidy to support the sheikh and his heirs.

On 19 June 1961, the protective treaty with the United Kingdom was terminated by mutual consent, and Kuwait declared itself fully independent. By this time, the sheikhdom had already become a major oil producer. Iraq refused to recognize Kuwait's independence, asserting it had inherited the Ottoman claim to the territory. Baghdad's threat of an invasion was foiled by British troops and later by the support of the Arab League. Iraq then appeared to agree to Kuwait's sovereignty, although border issues were never definitely resolved. During the next two decades, Kuwait succeeded in establishing an open and prosperous economy, based in large part on foreign, especially Palestinian and Egyptian, labor.

During the Iran-Iraq War, Kuwait, although technically neutral, provided important aid to Baghdad, including shipment of goods and over $6 billion in loans. In 1987, Iranian attacks on Persian Gulf shipping led Kuwait to request US protection for its supertankers.

With the end of the war, Iraq-Kuwait relations were stable until 1990 when Saddam Hussein, president of Iraq, accused his neighbor of illegally pumping oil from the shared Rumailia field. On 2 August 1990, Iraqi forces invaded Kuwait, asserting that they were rightfully reclaiming their own territory. Kuwaiti defense forces offered little resistance and most senior officials fled the country.

The United States led an international coalition of Arab and other nations to demand the withdrawal of Iraqi forces. After a lengthy buildup of forces, Iraq was assaulted by massive air and land forces; after six weeks, its defenses collapsed and Kuwait was liberated in February 1991. Kuwait's leaders returned to find a hostile population that resented their abandonment and demanded greater political participation. Enormous physical damage had been inflicted on the country, including over 700 oil well fires that did serious ecological damage before being extinguished after almost nine months' effort.

The regime and many Kuwaitis turned harshly against those suspected of collaboration with Iraq, and much of the large Palestinian community was ejected from the country. Relations with Iraq remained tense. Kuwait's vulnerability to possible attack from Iraq or Iran drew the nation closer to the United States, which has been willing to offer enhanced security collaboration.

13 GOVERNMENT

Kuwait is an independent, sovereign Arab state, under a constitutional monarch. Executive power is vested in the emir, who exercises it through a Council of Ministers. The National Assembly (*Majlis*) consists of 50 elected representatives and 25 appointed members.

There are five governorates, but political authority is highly centralized in the capital.

14 POLITICAL PARTIES

Political parties are prohibited, but opposition groups are active in the nation's political life. Of the 50 members of the new assembly, 31 ran as opposed to the regime.

15 JUDICIAL SYSTEM

A Tribunal of First Instance has jurisdiction over matters involving personal status, civil and commercial cases, and criminal cases, except those of a religious nature. The Court of Appeals, the highest in the land, has jurisdiction over appeals involving personal status and civil cases, as well as those involving commercial and criminal cases. Ordinary criminal cases may be appealed to the High Court of Appeals. A military court handles offenses committed by members of the security forces. Religious courts, Sunni and Shi'ite, decide family law matters according to Muslim law.

16 ARMED FORCES

Kuwait's rebuilt armed forces totaled 11,700 volunteers in 1993. The army had 8,000 men and 200 tanks; the air force, 2,500 men and 73 combat aircraft; and the navy, 1,200 men and 2 patrol craft. There is a 5,000-member National Guard. United Nations observers and advisors number 400. Estimated defense expenditures in 1992 were $9.7 million.

17 ECONOMY

The Kuwaiti standard of living was among the highest in the Middle East and in the world by the early 1980s. By 1993, Kuwait had an estimated per person income of about $19,360. The government has used its oil revenues to build ports, roads, an international airport, a seawater distillation plant, and modern government and office buildings.

Kuwait's economy suffered enormously from the effects of the Gulf War and the Iraqi occupation, which ended in February 1991 with the destruction of much of Kuwait's oil production capacity and other economic resources. The damage

Photo credit: AP/Wide World Photos

Kuwaiti men read verses out of the Koran at a cemetery, mourning those who died during the Iraqi occupation of Kuwait. They are observing 'Id al-Fitr, the traditional 3-day celebration which marks the end of the Muslim fasting month Ramadan.

inflicted on the economy is estimated at $20 billion.

18 INCOME

In 1992, the gross domestic product (GDP) was $15.3 billion or about $19,360 per person.

19 INDUSTRY

Although oil extraction continues to be the economic mainstay, Kuwait has diversified its industry to give manufacturing a larger role. Small-scale manufacturing plants produce ammonia, fertilizer, paper products, processed foods, and other consumer goods. Major refinery products were fuel oil, gas oil, naphtha, kerosene, and diesel fuel. Manufacturing all but stopped during the Iraqi invasion due to shortages of raw material and looting of equipment. After liberation, industry was hard-hit by the departure of Palestinian skilled labor.

20 LABOR

In 1992, the civilian labor force amounted to 600,000 and the government continued its postwar policy of reducing the number of foreign workers, but with limited success. At the end of 1992, about 437,000 non-Kuwaitis were working in private enterprise, and approximately 50,000 in government. Also, over 100,000 non-Kuwaitis work as domestic servants. Many laborers from developing countries are willing to tolerate poor or unhealthy working conditions in order to earn a wage significantly higher than in their own countries.

21 AGRICULTURE

Agricultural output in 1992 included 31,000 tons of vegetables and melons, and 1,000 tons of fruit.

22 DOMESTICATED ANIMALS

A small number of Bedouins raise camels, goats, and sheep for meat and milk. The 1992 (and 1990 pre–Gulf War amounts shown in parentheses) livestock population included: cattle, 5,000 (25,000);

sheep, 297,000 (200,000); goats, 1,000 (25,000); and chickens, 1,000,000 (21,000,000).

23 FISHING

Small boats catch enough fish to satisfy local demand. Species caught include sardines, mackerel, tuna, shark (for the fins exported to China), barracuda, and mullet. The fish catch in 1991 totaled 1,979 tons, down from 7,653 in 1989 because of the invasion.

24 FORESTRY

There are no natural forests in Kuwait.

25 MINING

Aside from petroleum and natural gas, the only minerals and mineral products are cement and fertilizer.

26 FOREIGN TRADE

Crude oil and oil products accounted for 91% of the total value of exports in 1989. Imports included chemicals, construction materials, petroleum equipment, iron and steel commodities, cement, timber, foodstuffs, electrical apparatus, power tools, household equipment, and motor vehicles. Kuwait's major trading partners for the period 1989–91 were the United States, Japan, Germany, and the United Kingdom.

27 ENERGY AND POWER

With proved reserves of about 94 billion barrels (12.9 billion tons) in 1992, Kuwait possesses 9.3% of the known global resources of petroleum. During the occupation and Gulf War of 1990–91, oil production totally ceased, resuming in June

Selected Social Indicators

These statistics are estimates for the period 1988 to 1993. For comparison purposes, data for the United States and averages for low-income countries and high-income countries are also given.

Indicator	Kuwait	Low-income countries	High-income countries	United States
Per capita gross national product†	**$19,360**	$380	$23,680	$24,740
Population growth rate	**-6.5%**	1.9%	0.6%	1.0%
Population growth rate in urban areas	**-6.3%**	3.9%	0.8%	1.3%
Population per square kilometer of land	**106**	78	25	26
Life expectancy in years	**75**	62	77	76
Number of people per physician	**602**	>3,300	453	419
Number of pupils per teacher (primary school)	**16**	39	<18	20
Illiteracy rate (15 years and older)	**27%**	41%	<5%	<3%
Energy consumed per capita (kg of oil equivalent)	**4,217**	364	5,203	7,918

† The gross national product (GNP) is the total dollar value of all goods and services produced by a country in a year. The per capita GNP is calculated by dividing a country's GNP by its population. The World Bank defines low-income countries as those with a per capita GNP of $695 or less. High-income countries have a per capita GNP of $8,626 or more. Less than 14% of the world's 5.5 billion people live in high-income countries, while almost 60% live in low-income countries.

> = greater than   < = less than

Sources: World Bank, *Social Indicators of Development 1995*, Baltimore: Johns Hopkins University Press, 1995. Central Intelligence Agency, *World Fact Book*, Washington, D.C.: Government Printing Office, 1994.

1991. Losses during the invasion cost Kuwait $120 million per day.

In 1993, Kuwait's average daily production was estimated at 2.1 million barrels, surpassing pre-invasion levels. All electric power is produced thermally from oil or natural gas. Electric power production reached 20,610 million kilowatt hours in 1990 before falling to 9,100 million kilowatt hours in 1991, due to the Iraqi invasion.

28 SOCIAL DEVELOPMENT

Kuwait has a widespread system of social welfare, financed by government oil revenues. It offers welfare services for the poor, provides free medical service and education to all residents, and spends heavily for waterworks, public gardens, and other public facilities. Social insurance legislation provides for old age, disability, and survivor pensions. Women have the same property rights as men, although they are not permitted to vote. Kuwaiti women married to foreign men suffer legal discrimination.

29 HEALTH

In 1992, 100% of the population had access to health care services. Influenza is common, and measles has resulted in a high fatality rate among children up to age five. In 1991, 100% of the urban population had access to safe water, and 100% of the urban population had adequate sanitation.

30 HOUSING

The National Housing Authority built about 50,000 dwelling units in 1977–85. As of the 1985 census, about 50% of all housing units were apartments, 19% were detached homes, and 15% were traditional dwellings (mostly small cottages and mud huts).

31 EDUCATION

Kuwait offers its students free education, including free food, clothing, books, stationery, and transportation, from kindergarten through the fourth year of college. In 1991, Kuwait had 218 primary schools with 114,641 students and 6,967 teachers. At the secondary level, there were 167,195 students.

In 1985–86, Kuwait University had a student enrollment of 16,359. All higher-level institutions had 23,686 students in 1991.

32 MEDIA

In 1991, there were 361,989 telephones. Kuwait Television has offered color broadcasts since 1974. Radio Kuwait produces programs in English, Urdu, Persian, and Arabic. There are some 590,000 television sets, and 715,000 radios were in use in 1991. In that year, Kuwait had eight daily newspapers. Major Arabic dailies (with estimated 1991 circulations), include *Al-Seyassa* (40,000), *Al-Qabas* (60,000), *Al-Rai al-'Amm* (50,000), and *Al-Anbaa* (60,000). English-language dailies include the *Arab Times* (40,000) and *Kuwait Times* (43,000).

33 TOURISM AND RECREATION

By the second anniversary of the Iraqi invasion, the government was well on its way to restoring the country's extensive pre-war accommodations, although hotel prices have risen steeply since the war. In 1991 there were 42,318 hotel rooms with a 64% occupancy rate. In the same year, 3.19 million tourists spent an estimated $3.43 billion in Kuwait.

34 FAMOUS KUWAITIS

Emir Sir 'Abdallah as-Salim as-Sabah (1870–1965) was revered as a man of simplicity, devotion, and deep concern for his people. His successors as emir have been Sabah as-Salim as-Sabah (1913–77), from 1965 to 1977; and Jabir al-Ahmad al-Jabir as-Sabah (b. 1928), since 1977.

35 BIBLIOGRAPHY

Kuwait in Pictures. Minneapolis: Lerner, 1989.
Slot, B. *The Origins of Kuwait.* New York: E.J. Brill, 1991.

KYRGYZSTAN

Kyrgyz Republic

Kyrgyzstan Respublikasy

CAPITAL: Bishkek.

FLAG: Red field with a yellow sun in the center; in the center of the sun is a red ring crossed by two sets of three lines, a stylized representation of the vent in a Kyrgyz yurt.

ANTHEM: *Kyrgyz National Anthem.*

MONETARY UNIT: The som, established in May 1993.

WEIGHTS AND MEASURES: The metric system is in force.

HOLIDAYS: Holidays not available.

TIME: 5 PM = noon GMT.

1 LOCATION AND SIZE

Kyrgyzstan is located in southern Asia, between China and Kazakhstan. Comparatively, it is slightly smaller than the state of South Dakota, with a total area of 198,500 square kilometers (76,641 square miles). The country's boundary length totals 3,878 kilometers (2,410 miles), and its capital city, Bishkek, is located in the north central part of the country.

2 TOPOGRAPHY

The topography of Kyrgyzstan features the peaks of the Tian Shan Mountains, which rise to 7,000 meters, as well as the valleys and basins that encompass the entire nation.

3 CLIMATE

The country's climate ranges from continental to polar in the Tian Shan Mountains. In the valley the average temperature is 28°C (82°F) in July and in January is –21°C (–5°F).

4 PLANTS AND ANIMALS

Wildflowers are found in the mountain valleys. Yak and snow leopards live in the mountains.

5 ENVIRONMENT

Among Kyrgyzstan's most significant environmental issues are water pollution and soil salinity (salt content). Eighty percent of the nation's people living in rural areas do not have a publicly regulated water supply.

6 POPULATION

The population of Kyrgyzstan was 4,290,442 in 1989, and it is estimated at 4,769,877 for 1995. The projection for 2000 is 5,189,000. The estimated population density is 23 persons per square kilometer (62.2 per square mile). Bishkek (formerly Fronze), the capital, had an estimated population of 625,000 at the beginning of 1990.

7 MIGRATION

Although migration is technically open, administrative restrictions from the Soviet era persist. In 1993 about 24,000 people immigrated and 135,000 left the country. There has been a systematic out-migration of non-Kyrgyz, especially Russians, since independence.

8 ETHNIC GROUPS

Kyrgyz constituted 52% of the population in 1989. Russians accounted for 21.5%, Uzbeks for 13%, Ukrainians for 2.5%, Germans for 2.4%, and Tatars for 1.6%. About 420,000 ethnic Kyrgyz reside elsewhere in the former Soviet Union and 170,000 in China. According to some reports, one-tenth or more of Russians left Kyrgyzstan during 1991 because of ethnic tensions. Ethnic Germans, deported to Kyrgyzstan by Stalin during World War II, are also leaving Kyrgyzstan. There have been ethnic conflicts between Kyrgyz and Uzbek inhabitants of the Osh region, as well as periodic clashes between Kyrgyz and Tajiks along the border with Tajikistan.

9 LANGUAGES

A Turkic tongue, Kyrgyz, is the official language. It was written in the Arabic script until 1926, then in Roman letters until 1940 when the Cyrillic alphabet was adopted with three special characters.

10 RELIGIONS

The population of Kyrgyzstan is primarily Sunni Muslim of the Hanafi sect. Diplomatic relations with the Vatican were opened in 1992.

11 TRANSPORTATION

As of 1991, there was a single east-west rail line of 370 kilometers (230 miles) into Kazakhstan. There are some 30,300 kilometers (18,800 miles) of highways. As Kyrgyzstan is a landlocked nation, water transportation is of minor importance, although inland travel is possible on several rivers.

12 HISTORY

The area of present-day Kyrgyzstan contains evidence of human habitation from the time of the Lower Paleolithic on, approximately 300,000 years ago. By the seventh century BC, nomads inhabited the region, which was controlled by various tribal alliances for nearly a thousand years. Beginning in the sixth century AD, various Turkic tribes began to push westward, eventually settling most of Central Asia, including Kyrgyzstan.

The territory was part of the Karakhanid state from about 950–1150, during which the urban population was actively involved in trade and manufacturing along the Silk Road. Conversion to Islam also began in this period. Genghis Khan's Mongols conquered the area in the thirteenth century, destroying most of the Karakhanid culture and introducing large numbers of new peoples into the area, of Turkic, Mongol, and Tibetan stock.

LOCATION: 41°30′N; 75°0′E. **BOUNDARY LENGTHS:** Total boundary lengths, 3,878 kilometers (2, 410 miles); China, 858 kilometers (533.2 miles); Kazakhstan, 1,051 kilometers (653 miles); Tajikistan, 870 kilometers (541 miles); Uzbekistan, 1,099 kilometers (683 miles).

The resulting mix of tribes was almost certainly the basis for the present-day Kyrgyz people, who retain much of the memory of those origins in the orally preserved genealogies of their 40 clans and tribes.

In the eighteenth century the Kyrgyz began to come under renewed pressure from Mongol tribes. This prompted some of the northern Kyrgyz to ally themselves with the Russians, who had pushed into Siberia in the seventeenth century. The southern Kyrgyz, however, were conquered by the armies of the tribal leader, Kokand. Kokand's territory, known as the Khanate, was established in the late eigh-

teenth century. This split between south and north continues to the present day in Kyrgyz life.

Most of northern Kyrgyzstan was incorporated into the Russian empire by 1863; the south followed in 1876, when Russia destroyed the Kokand Khanate. Administratively, what is now Kyrgyzstan was split among four *guberniias*. Beginning in the 1890s Russia settled Russian and other European farmers into the fertile river valleys of the north, forcing Kyrgyz nomads higher into the mountains.

By 1916, Russia's livestock and land-use policies had left the Kyrgyz badly impoverished. Hostility to the Russian tsars, or emperors, meant that there was some support for the Bolshevik revolution, at least until it became clear that it would not lead to regional independence.

As Bolshevik power was consolidated, Kyrgyzstan was first made an autonomous province (*oblast*) of the Russian Federation in 1924, then upgraded in 1926 to an autonomous republic, but still within Russia. It did not become a full Soviet Republic until 1936.

The republic was regarded as one of the least developed of the Soviet states, politically and economically, making it a great surprise when, in October 1990, Kyrgyzstan became the first Soviet republic to select its own non-Communist leader, Askar Akaev. Akaev and his supporters began an ambitious program of disengaging the republic from the Communist Party, which was interrupted by the attempted coup in Moscow of August 1991. Afterwards, Kyrgyzstan declared its independence on 31 August.

On 12 October 1991, Akaev's presidency was confirmed by direct popular election. A constitution was adopted in May 1993. Akaev's presidency was reaffirmed by a popular referendum of support conducted in January 1994.

13 GOVERNMENT

Kyrgyzstan's new constitution, ratified 5 May 1993, calls for three branches of government: the *Zhogorku kenesh*, or Supreme Council, which has legislative responsibility; the ministries, appointed by the president to oversee executive respon-

sibilities, but subject to ratification by the parliament; and a judiciary, appointed by the president. The republic is divided into six *oblasts,* or administrative regions, plus the capital city of Bishkek.

14 POLITICAL PARTIES

The Communist Party of Kirgizia, which was the only legal political party during the Soviet years, was abolished at the time of independence. A successor, the Kyrgyz Communist Party, was allowed to register in September 1992. Other communist parties include the Republican People's Party, the Social-Democrats of Kyrgyzstan, and the People's Party of Kyrgyzstan.

Other parties began as unofficial civic movements. The first was Ashar, begun in 1989 to take over unused land for housing. A number of different parties and groups are joined under the umbrella of the Democratic Movement of Kyrgyzstan (DDK). Another democratically inclined party is Asaba (Banner).

15 JUDICIAL SYSTEM

The 1993 constitution instituted a Western-type judicial system. Criminal cases are heard by a judge and two people's assessors. Appeals are possible. There is a Supreme Court, which includes a Constitutional Court authorized to review legislation and administrative acts for consistency with the constitution. It also considers cases on appeal involving individual rights and liberties of citizens. Constitutional Court decisions are final.

[16] ARMED FORCES

One Russian division occupies Kyrgyzstan, supported by 55 air defense missiles and around 200 combat aircraft, all under dual control of Commonwealth of Independent States (CIS) military authorities. The new republic plans a national army of 20,000 (half active, half reserve) based on 18 months' conscription.

[17] ECONOMY

Kyrgyzstan is among the poorest of the post-Soviet countries with a per person income estimated to be roughly half that of Russia. Although coal, gold, mercury, and uranium deposits are considerable, the country boasts few of the oil and gas reserves that promise a badly needed economic windfall to other Central Asian republics. The country's post-Soviet economy remains dominated by agriculture.

Under the presidency of Askar Akaev, the transition to a free market economy has outpaced that of most other post-Soviet republics, yet it has still been extremely difficult. As inflation continued to acclerate in 1992, average wages were estimated to have declined by 35–40% by the end of the year. In mid-1993, Kyrgyzstan was the first of the Commonwealth of Independent States countries to introduce its own currency, the som.

[18] INCOME

In 1992, Kyrgyzstan's gross national product (GNP) was $3,667 million, or about $850 per person. For the period 1985–92 the average inflation rate was 11.3%, resulting in a real growth rate in GNP of 2.3% per person.

[19] INDUSTRY

In 1991, Kyrgyzstan's industrial sector was reported to be comprised of 7,500 factories, 3,000 of which were classified as medium- and large-scale enterprises. The transfer of all industrial enterprises from government to private ownership is to be completed in a three-phase process ending in 1996.

Three-quarters of Kyrgyzstan's industrial output comes from Bishkek and surrounding areas. In 1991, mechanical and electrical engineering (vehicle assembly, washing machines, electrical appliances, electronics), light industry (mainly textiles and wool processing), and food processing made up close to 75% of the country's industrial production and 80% of its industrial exports. Other important industries include chemicals, leather goods, and construction materials.

[20] LABOR

The labor force includes nearly 1.9 million persons, with agriculture engaging 33%; industry (including mining), 28%; personal services, 20%; trade, 7%; transportation and communication, 6%, finance and business services, 3%; and other sectors, 3%.

In February 1992, a comprehensive law was passed protecting the rights of all workers to form and belong to unions. Strikes are legally permitted. In most sections of the economy, however, wage levels continue to be set by government decree.

21 AGRICULTURE

Before the collapse of the Soviet Union, 1,360,000 hectares (3,361,000 acres), or 6.9% of the total land area was devoted to crops. About 50% of Kyrgyzstan's crop-producing land is used to cultivate fodder crops. Production levels (in 1,000 tons) for 1992 include: wheat, 550; barley, 550; potatoes, 325; tobacco, 56; and cotton, 18.

22 DOMESTICATED ANIMALS

About 44% of the total land area is considered permanent pastureland. Livestock in 1992 included 13,000,000 chickens, 9,200,000 sheep, 1,200,000 dairy and beef cattle, 315,000 horses, and 300,000 goats. Yaks are also bred. Meat production in 1992 totaled 210,000 tons; cow's milk, 900,000 tons; wool, 59,200 tons; and eggs, 31,000 tons.

23 FISHING

The Naryn River is the primary site of fishing activity, but fishing is of little commercial significance.

24 FORESTRY

Forests and woodlands account for only 3% of the total land area, and the forestry sector is not commercially significant.

25 MINING

Southwestern Kyrgyzstan contains most of the nation's mineral wealth, including antimony, mercury, and uranium. The mountains also contain deposits of tungsten, molybdenum, rare earth metals, indium, sulfur, and arsenic. Gold is mined in the Issy-Kul' region. A rich deposit of tin is being developed in the eastern mountains.

26 FOREIGN TRADE

Principal inter-republic exports are agricultural equipment and other machinery, wool and textiles, refined sugar and tobacco, metals, electric power, and some electronic goods. Major imports include a wide range of engineering products, chemicals and petrochemicals, oil and gas, light industry goods such as clothing, and wood and paper products.

Exports and imports outside the former Soviet Union fell sharply in 1991, reflecting the economic changes faced both by Kyrgyzstan and its key East European trading partners. Total exports beyond the union equaled $20 million in 1991, down from $86 million in 1990. Imports declined to $443 million, down from $1,268 million in 1990.

International exports are dominated by non-ferrous metallurgy and machinery, while imported goods include mainly processed foods, machinery, and clothing. The largest extra-republic trading partners in 1991 were Germany, the former Czechoslovakia, and Bulgaria.

27 ENERGY AND POWER

Kyrgyzstan's principal energy resources are its deposits of coal. As of 1991, there were twelve coal mining enterprises operating, including six open pit mines. About 50% of Kyrgyzstan's electricity comes from hydropower. In 1991, electrical production totaled 13,900 million kilowatt hours. In 1991, Kyrgyzstan produced

Selected Social Indicators

These statistics are estimates for the period 1988 to 1993. For comparison purposes, data for the United States and averages for low-income countries and high-income countries are also given.

Indicator	Kyrgyzstan	Low-income countries	High-income countries	United States
Per capita gross national product†	**$850**	$380	$23,680	$24,740
Population growth rate	**1.7%**	1.9%	0.6%	1.0%
Population growth rate in urban areas	**2.1%**	3.9%	0.8%	1.3%
Population per square kilometer of land	**23**	78	25	26
Life expectancy in years	**69**	62	77	76
Number of people per physician	**310**	>3,300	453	419
Number of pupils per teacher (primary school)	**n.a.**	39	<18	20
Illiteracy rate (15 years and older)	**3%**	41%	<5%	<3%
Energy consumed per capita (kg of oil equivalent)	**965**	364	5,203	7,918

† The gross national product (GNP) is the total dollar value of all goods and services produced by a country in a year. The per capita GNP is calculated by dividing a country's GNP by its population. The World Bank defines low-income countries as those with a per capita GNP of $695 or less. High-income countries have a per capita GNP of $8,626 or more. Less than 14% of the world's 5.5 billion people live in high-income countries, while almost 60% live in low-income countries.

n.a. = data not available   > = greater than   < = less than

Sources: World Bank, *Social Indicators of Development 1995,* Baltimore: Johns Hopkins University Press, 1995. Central Intelligence Agency, *World Fact Book,* Washington, D.C.: Government Printing Office, 1994.

100,000 tons of oil and 100,000,000 cubic meters of natural gas.

28 SOCIAL DEVELOPMENT

In 1989, the average family size in Kyrgyzstan was 4.7 members. There were 11.8 drug-related crimes and 4.1 alcohol-related deaths per 100,000 persons.

Women have equal status under the law and are well represented in the work force in urban areas.

29 HEALTH

Kyrgyzstan has one physician per 310 people, with a nurse-to-doctor ratio of 2.8.

There are approximately 12 hospital beds per 1,000 inhabitants.

Major causes of death in 1990 were communicable diseases and maternal/perinatal causes, noncommunicable diseases, and injuries. Total health care expenditures in 1990 were $517 million. Life expectancy is 69 years.

30 HOUSING

In 1989, 42.7% of all privately owned urban housing had running water, 32.4% had sewer lines, 14% had central heating, and 1.4% had hot water. In 1990, Kyrgyzstan had 12.1 square meters of housing space per person and, as of 1 January

1991, 85,000 households (or 18.6%) were on waiting lists for housing in urban areas.

31 EDUCATION

The adult literacy rate in 1990 was estimated at 97.0%, with 98.6% of men and 95.5% of women estimated as literate. During the 1988–89 school year, there were over 1,800 secondary schools enrolling approximately one million students. During the same year, over 57,000 students were enrolled at ten institutions of higher learning, including 13,000 at the State University of Kyrgyzstan. In 1990, all higher level institutions had 58,800 pupils.

32 MEDIA

Dom Radio in Bishkek broadcasts in Kyrgyz, German, Dungan, and Russian. In 1990, daily newspaper circulation totaled 1.5 million, and over 40 periodicals were published. During 1992 the press was free to publish material without prior government approval or restraint. However, while a few fully independent newspapers and magazines existed, the government continued to exert influence over most other publications.

33 TOURISM AND RECREATION

Osh, Kyrgyzstan's second-largest city, is considered a holy city by Muslim pilgrims who visit it annually to pray at its Islamic shrines. The capital city of Bishkek is surrounded by some of the highest mountain ranges in the world. The principal accommodations are hotels that formerly belonged to the Soviet Intourist system.

34 FAMOUS KYRGYZSTANIS

Askar A. Akayev has been president of Kyrgyzstan since October 1992. Chingiz Aitmatov, winner of two Lenin Prizes for literature, is a native Kyrgyzstani.

35 BIBLIOGRAPHY

Kyrgyzstan. Washington, D.C.: International Monetary Fund, 1992.

Kyrgyzstan: The Transition to a Market Economy. Washington, D.C.: World Bank, 1993.

GLOSSARY

aboriginal: The first known inhabitants of a country. A species of animals or plants which originated within a given area.

acid rain: Rain (or snow) that has become slightly acid by mixing with industrial air pollution.

adobe: A brick made from sun-dried heavy clay mixed with straw, used in building houses. A house made of adobe bricks.

adult literacy: The ability of adults to read and write.

afforestation: The act of turning arable land into forest or woodland.

agrarian economy: An economy where agriculture is the dominant form of economic activity. A society where agriculture dominates the day-to-day activities of the population is called an agrarian society.

air link: Refers to scheduled air service that allows people and goods to travel between two places on a regular basis.

airborne industrial pollutant: Pollution caused by industry that is supported or carried by the air.

allies: Groups or persons who are united in a common purpose. Typically used to describe nations that have joined together to fight a common enemy in war.

In World War I, the term Allies described the nations that fought against Germany and its allies. In World War II, Allies described the United Kingdom, United States, the USSR and their allies, who fought against the Axis Powers of Germany, Italy, and Japan.

aloe: A plant particularly abundant in the southern part of Africa, where leaves of some species are made into ropes, fishing lines, bow strings, and hammocks. It is also a symbolic plant in the Islamic world; anyone who returns from a pilgrimage to Mecca (Mekkah) hangs aloe over his door as a token that he has performed the journey.

Altaic language family: A family of languages spoken in portions of northern and eastern Europe, and nearly the whole of northern and central Asia, together with some other regions. The family is divided into five branches: the Ugrian or Finno-Hungarian, Smoyed, Turkish, Mongolian, and Tunguse.

althing: A legislative assembly.

amendment: A change or addition to a document.

Amerindian: A contraction of the two words, American Indian. It describes native peoples of North, South, or Central America.

amnesty: An act of forgiveness or pardon, usually taken by a government, toward persons for crimes they may have committed.

Anglican: Pertaining to or connected with the Church of England.

animism: The belief that natural objects and phenomena have souls or innate spiritual powers.

annual growth rate: The rate at which something grows over a period of 12 months.

annual inflation rate: The rate of inflation in prices over the course of a year.

anthracite coal: Also called hard coal, it is usually 90 to 95 percent carbon, and burns cleanly, almost without a flame.

anti-Semitism: Agitation, persecution, or discrimination (physical, emotional, economic, political, or otherwise) directed against the Jews.

apartheid: The past governmental policy in the Republic of South Africa of separating the races in society.

appeasement: To bring to a state of peace.

appellate: Refers to an appeal of a court decision to a high authority.

applied science: Scientific techniques employed to achieve results that solve practical problems.

aquaculture: The culture or "farming" of aquatic plants or other natural produce, as in the raising of catfish in "farms."

aquatic resources: Resources that come from, grow in, or live in water, including fish and plants.

aquifer: An underground layer of porous rock, sand, or gravel that holds water.

arable land: Land that can be cultivated by plowing and used for growing crops.

arbitration: A process whereby disputes are settled by a designated person, called the arbitrator, instead of by a court of law.

archipelago: Any body of water abounding with islands, or the islands themselves collectively.

archives: A place where records or a collection of important documents are kept.

arctic climate: Cold, frigid weather similar to that experienced at or near the north pole.

aristocracy: A small minority that controls the government of a nation, typically on the basis of inherited wealth.

armistice: An agreement or truce which ends military conflict in anticipation of a peace treaty.

artesian well: A type of well where the water rises to the surface and overflows.

ASEAN *see* Association of Southeast Asian Nations

Association of Southeast Asian Nations: ASEAN was established in 1967 to promote political, economic, and social cooperation among its six member countries: Indonesia, Malaysia, the Philippines, Singapore, Thailand, and Brunei. ASEAN headquarters are in Jakarta, Indonesia. In January 1992, ASEAN agreed to create the ASEAN Free Trade Area (AFTA).

atheist: A person who denies the existence of God or of a supreme intelligent being.

atoll: A coral island, consisting of a strip or ring of coral surrounding a central lagoon.

atomic weapons: Weapons whose extremely violent explosive power comes from the splitting of the nuclei of atoms (usually uranium or plutonium) by neutrons in a rapid chain reaction. These weapons may be referred to as atom bombs, hydrogen bombs, or H-bombs.

austerity measures: Steps taken by a government to conserve money or resources during an economically difficult time, such as cutting back on federally funded programs.

Australoid: Pertains to the type of aborigines, or earliest inhabitants, of Australia.

Austronesian language: A family of languages which includes practically all the languages of the Pacific Islands—Indonesian, Melanesian, Polynesian, and Micronesian sub-families. Does not include Australian or Papuan languages.

authoritarianism: A form of government in which a person or group attempts to rule with absolute authority without the representation of the citizens.

autonomous state: A country which is completely self-governing, as opposed to being a dependency or part of another country.

autonomy: The state of existing as a self-governing entity. For instance, when a country gains its independence from another country, it gains autonomy.

average inflation rate: The average rate at which the general prices of goods and services increase over the period of a year.

average life expectancy: In any given society, the average age attained by persons at the time of death.

Axis Powers: The countries aligned against the Allied Nations in World War II, originally applied to Nazi Germany and Fascist Italy (Rome-Berlin Axis), and later extended to include Japan.

bagasse: Plant residue left after a product, such as juice, has been extracted.

Baha'i: The follower of a religious sect founded by Mirza Husayn Ali in Iran in 1863.

Baltic states. The three formerly communist countries of Estonia, Latvia, and Lithuania that border on the Baltic Sea.

Bantu language group: A name applied to the languages spoken in central and south Africa.

banyan tree: An East Indian fig tree. Individual trees develop roots from the branches that descend to the ground and become trunks. These roots support and nourish the crown of the tree.

Baptist: A member of a Protestant denomination that practices adult baptism by complete immersion in water.

barren land: Unproductive land, partly or entirely treeless.

barter: Trade practice where merchandise is exchanged directly for other merchandise or services without use of money.

bedrock: Solid rock lying under loose earth.

bicameral legislature: A legislative body consisting of two chambers, such as the U.S. House of Representatives and the U.S. Senate.

bill of rights: A written statement containing the list of privileges and powers to be granted to a body of people, usually introduced when a government or other organization is forming.

bituminous coal: Soft coal; coal which burns with a bright-yellow flame.

black market: A system of trade where goods are sold illegally, often for excessively inflated prices. This type of trade usually develops to avoid paying taxes or tariffs levied by the government, or to get around import or export restrictions on products.

bloodless coup: The sudden takeover of a country's government by hostile means but without killing anyone in the process.

boat people: Used to describe individuals (refugees) who attempt to flee their country by boat.

bog: Wet, soft, and spongy ground where the soil is composed mainly of decayed or decaying vegetable matter.

Bolshevik Revolution. A revolution in 1917 in Russia when a wing of the Russian Social Democratic party seized power. The Bolsheviks advocated the violent overthrow of capitalism.

bonded labor: Workers bound to service without pay; slaves.

border dispute: A disagreement between two countries as to the exact location or length of the dividing line between them.

Brahman: A member (by heredity) of the highest caste among the Hindus, usually assigned to the priesthood.

broadleaf forest: A forest composed mainly of broadleaf (deciduous) trees.

Buddhism: A religious system common in India and eastern Asia. Founded by and based upon the teachings of Siddhartha Gautama, Buddhism asserts that suffering is an inescapable part of life. Deliverance can only be achieved through the practice of charity, temperance, justice, honesty, and truth.

buffer state: A small country that lies between two larger, possibly hostile countries, considered to be a neutralizing force between them.

bureaucracy: A system of government that is characterized by division into bureaus of administration with their own divisional heads. Also refers to the inflexible procedures of such a system that often result in delay.

Byzantine Empire: An empire centered in the city of Byzantium, now Istanbul in present-day Turkey.

CACM *see* Central American Common Market.

candlewood: A name given to several species of trees and shrubs found in the British West Indies, northern Mexico, and the southwestern United States. The plants are characterized by a very resinous wood.

canton: A territory or small division or state within a country.

capital punishment: The ultimate act of punishment for a crime, the death penalty.

capitalism: An economic system in which goods and services and the means to produce and sell them are privately owned, and prices and wages are determined by market forces.

Caribbean Community and Common Market (CARICOM): Founded in 1973 and with its headquarters in Georgetown, Guyana, CARICOM seeks the establishment of a common trade policy and increased cooperation in the Caribbean region. Includes 13 English-speaking Caribbean nations: Antigua and Barbuda, the Bahamas, Barbados, Belize, Dominica, Grenada, Guyana, Jamaica, Montserrat, Saint Kitts-Nevis, Saint Lucia, St. Vincent/Grenadines, and Trinidad and Tobago.

CARICOM *see* Caribbean Community and Common Market.

carnivore: Flesh-eating animal or plant.

carob: The common English name for a plant that is similar to and sometimes used as a substitute for chocolate.

cartel: An organization of independent producers formed to regulate the production, pricing, or marketing practices of its members in order to limit competition and maximize their market power.

cash crop: A crop that is grown to be sold rather than kept for private use.

cassation: The reversal or annulling of a final judgment by the supreme authority.

cassava: The name of several species of stout herbs, extensively cultivated for food.

caste system: One of the artificial divisions or social classes into which the Hindus are rigidly separated according to the religious law of Brahmanism. Membership in a caste is hereditary, and the privileges and disabilities of each caste are transmitted by inheritance.

Caucasian: The white race of human beings, as determined by genealogy and physical features.

Caucasoid: Belonging to the racial group characterized by light skin pigmentation. Commonly called the "white race."

cease-fire: An official declaration of the end to the use of military force or active hostilities, even if only temporary.

CEMA *see* Council for Mutual Economic Assistance.

censorship: The practice of withholding certain items of news that may cast a country in an unfavorable light or give away secrets to the enemy.

census: An official counting of the inhabitants of a state or country with details of sex and age, family, occupation, possessions, etc.

Central American Common Market (CACM): Established in 1962, a trade alliance of five Central American nations. Participating are Costa Rica, El Salvador, Guatemala, Honduras, and Nicaragua.

Central Powers: In World War I, Germany and Austria-Hungary, and their allies, Turkey and Bulgaria.

centrally planned economy: An economic system all aspects of which are supervised and regulated by the government.

centrist position: Refers to opinions held by members of a moderate political group; that is, views that are somewhere in the middle of popular thought between conservative and liberal.

cession: Withdrawal from or yielding to physical force.

chancellor: A high-ranking government official. In some countries it is the prime minister.

cholera: An acute infectious disease characterized by severe diarrhea, vomiting, and, often, death.

Christianity: The religion founded by Jesus Christ, based on the Bible as holy scripture.

Church of England: The national and established church in England. The Church of England claims continuity with the branch of the Catholic Church that existed in England before the Reformation. Under Henry VIII, the spiritual supremacy and jurisdiction of the Pope were abolished, and the sovereign (king or queen) was declared head of the church.

circuit court: A court that convenes in two or more locations within its appointed district.

CIS *see* Commonwealth of Independent States

city-state: An independent state consisting of a city and its surrounding territory.

civil court: A court whose proceedings include determinations of rights of individual citizens, in contrast to criminal proceedings regarding individuals or the public.

civil jurisdiction: The authority to enforce the laws in civil matters brought before the court.

civil law: The law developed by a nation or state for the conduct of daily life of its own people.

civil rights: The privileges of all individuals to be treated as equals under the laws of their country; specifically, the rights given by certain amendments to the U.S. Constitution.

civil unrest: The feeling of uneasiness due to an unstable political climate, or actions taken as a result of it.

civil war: A war between groups of citizens of the same country who have different opinions or agendas. The Civil War of the United States was the conflict between the states of the North and South from 1861 to 1865.

climatic belt: A region or zone where a particular type of climate prevails.

Club du Sahel: The Club du Sahel is an informal coalition which seeks to reverse the effects of drought and the desertification in the eight Sahelian zone countries: Burkina Faso, Chad, Gambia, Mali, Mauritania, Niger, Senegal, and the Cape Verde Islands. Headquarters are in Ouagadougou, Burkina Faso.

CMEA see Council for Mutual Economic Assistance.

coalition government: A government combining differing factions within a country, usually temporary.

coastal belt: A coastal plain area of lowlands and somewhat higher ridges that run parallel to the coast.

coastal plain: A fairly level area of land along the coast of a land mass.

coca: A shrub native to South America, the leaves of which produce organic compounds that are used in the production of cocaine.

coke: The solid product of the carbonization of coal, bearing the same relation to coal that charcoal does to wood.

cold war: Refers to conflict over ideological differences that are carried on by words and diplomatic actions, not by military action. The term is usually used to refer to the tension that existed between the United States and the USSR from the 1950s until the breakup of the USSR in 1991.

collective bargaining: The negotiations between workers who are members of a union and their employer for the purpose of deciding work rules and policies regarding wages, hours, etc.

collective farm: A large farm formed from many small farms and supervised by the government; usually found in communist countries.

collective farming: The system of farming on a collective where all workers share in the income of the farm.

colloquial: Belonging to ordinary, everyday speech: often especially applied to common words and phrases which are not used in formal speech.

colonial period: The period of time when a country forms colonies in and extends control over a foreign area.

colonist: Any member of a colony or one who helps settle a new colony.

colony: A group of people who settle in a new area far from their original country, but still under the jurisdiction of that country. Also refers to the newly settled area itself.

COMECON see Council for Mutual Economic Assistance.

commerce: The trading of goods (buying and selling), especially on a large scale, between cities, states, and countries.

commercial catch: The amount of marketable fish, usually measured in tons, caught in a particular period of time.

commercial crop: Any marketable agricultural crop.

commission: A group of people designated to collectively do a job, including a government agency with certain law-making powers. Also, the power given to an individual or group to perform certain duties.

commodity: Any items, such as goods or services, that are bought or sold, or agricultural products that are traded or marketed.

common law: A legal system based on custom and decisions and opinions of the law courts. The basic system of law of England and the United States.

common market: An economic union among countries that is formed to remove trade barriers (tariffs) among those countries, increasing economic cooperation. The European Community is a notable example of a common market.

commonwealth: A commonwealth is a free association of sovereign independent states that has no charter, treaty, or constitution. The association promotes cooperation, consultation, and mutual assistance among members.

Commonwealth of Independent States: The CIS was established in December 1991 as an association of 11 republics of the former Soviet Union. The members include: Russia, Ukraine, Belarus (formerly Byelorussia), Moldova (formerly Moldavia), Armenia, Azerbaijan, Uzbekistan, Turkmenistan, Tajikistan, Kazakhstan, and Kirgizstan (formerly Kirghiziya). The Baltic states—Estonia, Latvia, and Lithuania—did not join. Georgia maintained observer status before joining the CIS in November 1993.

Commonwealth of Nations: Voluntary association of the United Kingdom and its present dependencies and associated states, as well as certain former dependencies and their dependent territories. The term was first used officially in 1926 and is embodied in the Statute of Westminster (1931). Within the Commonwealth, whose secretariat (established in 1965) is located in London, England, are numerous subgroups devoted to economic and technical cooperation.

commune: An organization of people living together in a community who share the ownership and use of property. Also refers to a small governmental district of a country, especially in Europe.

communism: A form of government whose system requires common ownership of property for the use of all citizens. All profits are to be equally distributed and prices on goods and services are usually set by the state. Also, communism refers directly to the official doctrine of the former U.S.S.R.

compulsory: Required by law or other regulation.

compulsory education: The mandatory requirement for children to attend school until they have reached a certain age or grade level.

conciliation: A process of bringing together opposing sides of a disagreement for the purpose of compromise. Or, a way of settling an international dispute in which the disagreement is submitted to an independent committee that will examine the facts and advise the participants of a possible solution.

concordat: An agreement, compact, or convention, especially between church and state.

confederation: An alliance or league formed for the purpose of promoting the common interests of its members.

Confucianism: The system of ethics and politics taught by the Chinese philosopher Confucius.

coniferous forest: A forest consisting mainly of pine, fir, and cypress trees.

conifers: Cone-bearing plants. Mostly evergreen trees and shrubs which produce cones.

conscription: To be required to join the military by law. Also known as the draft. Service personnel who join the military because of the legal requirement are called conscripts or draftees.

conservative party: A political group whose philosophy tends to be based on established traditions and not supportive of rapid change.

constituency: The registered voters in a governmental district, or a group of people that supports a position or a candidate.

constituent assembly: A group of people that has the power to determine the election of a political representative or create a constitution.

constitution: The written laws and basic rights of citizens of a country or members of an organized group.

constitutional monarchy: A system of government in which the hereditary sovereign (king or queen, usually) rules according to a written constitution.

constitutional republic: A system of government with an elected chief of state and elected representation, with a written constitution containing its governing principles. The United States is a constitutional republic.

consumer goods: Items that are bought to satisfy personal needs or wants of individuals.

continental climate: The climate of a part of the continent; the characteristics and peculiarities of the climate are a result of the land itself and its location.

continental shelf: A plain extending from the continental coast and varying in width that typically ends in a steep slope to the ocean floor.

copra: The dried meat of the coconut; it is frequently used as an ingredient of curry, and to produce coconut oil. Also written *cobra, coprah,* and *copperah.*

Coptic Christians: Members of the Coptic Church of Egypt, formerly of Ethiopia.

cordillera: A continuous ridge, range, or chain of mountains.

corvette: A small warship that is often used as an escort ship because it is easier to maneuver than larger ships like destroyers.

Council for Mutual Economic Assistance (CMEA): Also known as Comecon, the alliance of socialist economies was established on 25 January 1949 and abolished 1 January 1991. It included Afghanistan*, Albania, Angola*, Bulgaria, Cuba, Czechoslovakia, Ethiopia*, East Germany, Hungary, Laos*, Mongolia, Mozambique*, Nicaragua*, Poland, Romania, USSR, Vietnam, Yemen*, and Yugoslavia. Nations marked with an asterisk were observers only.

counterinsurgency operations: Organized military activity designed to stop rebellion against an established government.

county: A territorial division or administrative unit within a state or country.

coup d'ètat or coup: A sudden, violent overthrow of a government or its leader.

court of appeal: An appellate court, having the power of review after a case has been decided in a lower court.

court of first appeal: The next highest court to the court which has decided a case, to which that case may be presented for review.

court of last appeal: The highest court, in which a decision is not subject to review by any higher court. In the United States, it could be the Supreme Court of an individual state or the U.S. Supreme Court.

cricket (sport): A game played by two teams with a ball and bat, with two wickets (staked target) being defended by a batsman. Common in the United Kingdom and Commonwealth of Nations countries.

criminal law: The branch of law that deals primarily with crimes and their punishments.

crown colony: A colony established by a commonwealth over which the monarch has some control, as in colonies established by the United Kingdom's Commonwealth of Nations.

Crusades: Military expeditions by European Christian armies in the eleventh, twelfth, and thirteenth centuries to win land controlled by the Muslims in the middle east.

cultivable land: Land that can be prepared for the production of crops.

Cultural Revolution: An extreme reform movement in China from 1966 to 1976; its goal was to combat liberalization by restoring the ideas of Mao Zedong.

Cushitic language group: A group of Hamitic languages that are spoken in Ethiopia and other areas of eastern Africa.

customs union: An agreement between two or more countries to remove trade barriers with each other and to establish common tariff and nontariff policies with respect to imports from countries outside of the agreement.

cyclone: Any atmospheric movement, general or local, in which the wind blows spirally around and in towards a center. In the northern hemisphere, the cyclonic movement is usually counter-clockwise, and in the southern hemisphere, it is clockwise.

Cyrillic alphabet: An alphabet adopted by the Slavic people and invented by Cyril and Methodius in the ninth century as an alphabet that was easier for the copyist to write. The Russian alphabet is a slight modification of it.

decentralization: The redistribution of power in a government from one large central authority to a wider range of smaller local authorities.

deciduous species: Any species that sheds or casts off a part of itself after a definite period of time. More commonly used in reference to plants that shed their leaves on a yearly basis as opposed to those (evergreens) that retain them.

declaration of independence: A formal written document stating the intent of a group of persons to become fully self-governing.

deficit: The amount of money that is in excess between spending and income.

deficit spending: The process in which a government spends money on goods and services in excess of its income.

deforestation: The removal or clearing of a forest.

deity: A being with the attributes, nature, and essence of a god; a divinity.

delta: Triangular-shaped deposits of soil formed at the mouths of large rivers.

demarcate: To mark off from adjoining land or territory; set the limits or boundaries of.

demilitarized zone (DMZ): An area surrounded by a combat zone that has had military troops and weapons removed.

demobilize: To disband or discharge military troops.

democracy: A form of government in which the power lies in the hands of the people, who can govern directly, or can be governed indirectly by representatives elected by its citizens.

denationalize: To remove from government ownership or control.

deportation: To carry away or remove from one country to another, or to a distant place.

depression: A hollow; a surface that has sunken or fallen in.

deregulation: The act of reversing controls and restrictions on prices of goods, bank interest, and the like.

desalinization plant: A facility that produces freshwater by removing the salt from saltwater.

desegregation: The act of removing restrictions on people of a particular race that keep them socially, economically, and, sometimes, physically, separate from other groups.

desertification: The process of becoming a desert as a result of climatic changes, land mismanagement, or both.

détente: The official lessening of tension between countries in conflict.

devaluation: The official lowering of the value of a country's currency in relation to the value of gold or the currencies of other countries.

developed countries: Countries which have a high standard of living and a well-developed industrial base.

development assistance: Government programs intended to finance and promote the growth of new industries.

dialect: One of a number of regional or related modes of speech regarded as descending from a common origin.

dictatorship: A form of government in which all the power is retained by an absolute leader or tyrant. There are no rights granted to the people to elect their own representatives.

diplomatic relations: The relationship between countries as conducted by representatives of each government.

direct election: The process of selecting a representative to the government by balloting of the voting public, in contrast to selection by an elected representative of the people.

disarmament: The reduction or depletion of the number of weapons or the size of armed forces.

dissident: A person whose political opinions differ from the majority to the point of rejection.

dogma: A principle, maxim, or tenet held as being firmly established.

domain: The area of land governed by a particular ruler or government, sometimes referring to the ultimate control of that territory.

domestic spending: Money spent by a country's government on goods used, investments, running of the government, and exports and imports.

dominion: A self-governing nation that recognizes the British monarch as chief of state.

dormant volcano: A volcano that has not exhibited any signs of activity for an extended period of time.

dowry: The sum of the property or money that a bride brings to her groom at their marriage.

draft constitution: The preliminary written plans for the new constitution of a country forming a new government.

Druze: A member of a Muslim sect based in Syria, living chiefly in the mountain regions of Lebanon.

dual nationality: The status of an individual who can claim citizenship in two or more countries.

duchy: Any territory under the rule of a duke or duchess.

due process: In law, the application of the legal process to which every citizen has a right, which cannot be denied.

durable goods: Goods or products which are expected to last and perform for several years, such as cars and washing machines.

duty: A tax imposed on imports by the customs authority of a country. Duties are generally based on the value of the goods (*ad valorem* duties), some other factors such as weight or quantity (specific duties), or a combination of value and other factors (compound duties).

dyewoods: Any wood from which dye is extracted.

dynasty: A family line of sovereigns who rule in succession, and the time during which they reign.

earned income: The money paid to an individual in wages or salary.

Eastern Orthodox: The outgrowth of the original Eastern Church of the Eastern Roman Empire, consisting of eastern Europe, western Asia, and Egypt.

EC *see* European Community

ecclesiastical: Pertaining or relating to the church.

echidna: A spiny, toothless anteater of Australia, Tasmania, and New Guinea.

ecological balance: The condition of a healthy, well-functioning ecosystem, which includes all the plants and animals in a natural community together with their environment.

ecology: The branch of science that studies organisms in relationship to other organisms and to their environment.

economic depression: A prolonged period in which there is high unemployment, low production, falling prices, and general business failure.

economically active population: That portion of the people who are employed for wages and are consumers of goods and services.

ecotourism: Broad term that encompasses nature, adventure, and ethnic tourism; responsible or wilderness-sensitive tourism; soft-path or small-scale tourism; low-impact tourism; and sustainable tourism. Scientific, educational, or academic tourism (such as biotourism, archetourism, and geotourism) are also forms of ecotourism.

elected assembly: The persons that comprise a legislative body of a government who received their positions by direct election.

electoral system: A system of choosing government officials by votes cast by qualified citizens.

electoral vote: The votes of the members of the electoral college.

electorate: The people who are qualified to vote in an election.

emancipation: The freeing of persons from any kind of bondage or slavery.

embargo: A legal restriction on commercial ships to enter a country's ports, or any legal restriction of trade.

emigration: Moving from one country or region to another for the purpose of residence.

empire: A group of territories ruled by one sovereign or supreme ruler. Also, the period of time under that rule.

enclave: A territory belonging to one nation that is surrounded by that of another nation.

encroachment: The act of intruding, trespassing, or entering on the rights or possessions of another.

endangered species: A plant or animal species whose existence as a whole is threatened with extinction.

endemic: Anything that is peculiar to and characteristic of a locality or region.

Enlightenment: An intellectual movement of the late seventeenth and eighteenth centuries in which scientific thinking gained a strong foothold and old beliefs were challenged. The idea of absolute monarchy was questioned and people were gradually given more individual rights.

enteric disease: An intestinal disease.

epidemic: As applied to disease, any disease that is temporarily prevalent among people in one place at the same time.

Episcopal: Belonging to or vested in bishops or prelates; characteristic of or pertaining to a bishop or bishops.

ethnolinguistic group: A classification of related languages based on common ethnic origin.

EU *see* European Union

European Community: A regional organization created in 1958. Its purpose is to eliminate customs duties and other trade barriers in Europe. It promotes a common external tariff against other countries, a Common Agricultural Policy (CAP), and guarantees of free movement of labor and capital. The original six members were Belgium, France, West Germany, Italy, Luxembourg, and the Netherlands. Denmark, Ireland, and the United Kingdom became members in 1973; Greece joined in 1981; Spain and Portugal in 1986. Other nations continue to join.

European Union: The EU is an umbrella reference to the European Community (EC) and to two European integration efforts introduced by the Maastricht Treaty: Common Foreign and Security Policy (including defense) and Justice and Home Affairs (principally cooperation between police and other authorities on crime, terrorism, and immigration issues).

exports: Goods sold to foreign buyers.

external migration: The movement of people from their native country to another country, as opposed to internal migration, which is the movement of people from one area of a country to another in the same country.

fallout: The precipitation of particles from the atmosphere, often the result of a ground disturbance by volcanic activity or a nuclear explosion.

family planning: The use of birth control to determine the number of children a married couple will have.

Fascism: A political philosophy that holds the good of the nation as more important than the needs of the individual. Fascism also stands for a dictatorial leader and strong oppression of opposition or dissent.

federal: Pertaining to a union of states whose governments are subordinate to a central government.

federation: A union of states or other groups under the authority of a central government.

fetishism: The practice of worshipping a material object that is believed to have mysterious powers residing in it, or is the representation of a deity to which worship may be paid and from which supernatural aid is expected.

feudal estate: The property owned by a lord in medieval Europe under the feudal system.

feudal society: In medieval times, an economic and social structure in which persons could hold land given to them by a lord (nobleman) in return for service to that lord.

final jurisdiction: The final authority in the decision of a legal matter. In the United States, the Supreme Court would have final jurisdiction.

Finno-Ugric language group: A subfamily of languages spoken in northeastern Europe, including Finnish, Hungarian, Estonian, and Lapp.

fiscal year: The twelve months between the settling of financial accounts, not necessarily corresponding to a calendar year beginning on January 1.

fjord: A deep indentation of the land forming a comparatively narrow arm of the sea with more or less steep slopes or cliffs on each side.

fly: The part of a flag opposite and parallel to the one nearest the flagpole.

fodder: Food for cattle, horses, and sheep, such as hay, straw, and other kinds of vegetables.

folk religion: A religion with origins and traditions among the common people of a nation or region that is relevant to their particular life-style.

foreign exchange: Foreign currency that allows foreign countries to conduct financial transactions or settle debts with one another.

foreign policy: The course of action that one government chooses to adopt in relation to a foreign country.

Former Soviet Union: The FSU is a collective reference to republics comprising the former Soviet Union. The term, which has been used as both including and excluding the Baltic republics (Estonia, Latvia, and Lithuania), includes the other 12 republics: Russia, Ukraine, Belarus, Moldova, Armenia, Azerbaijan, Uzbekistan, Turkmenistan, Tajikistan, Kazakhstan, Kyrgizstan, and Georgia.

fossil fuels: Any mineral or mineral substance formed by the decomposition of organic matter buried beneath the earth's surface and used as a fuel.

free enterprise: The system of economics in which private business may be conducted with minimum interference by the government.

free-market economy: An economic system that relies on the market, as opposed to government planners, to set the prices for wages and products.

frigate. A medium-sized warship.

fundamentalist: A person who holds religious beliefs based on the complete acceptance of the words of the Bible or other holy scripture as the truth. For instance, a fundamentalist would believe the story of creation exactly as it is told in the Bible and would reject the idea of evolution.

game reserve: An area of land reserved for wild animals that are hunted for sport or for food.

GDP *see* gross domestic product.

Germanic language group: A large branch of the Indo-European family of languages including German itself, the Scandinavian languages, Dutch, Yiddish, Modern English, Modern Scottish, Afrikaans, and others. The group also includes extinct languages such as Gothic, Old High German, Old Saxon, Old English, Middle English, and the like.

glasnost: President Mikhail Gorbachev's frank revelations in the 1980s about the state of the economy and politics in the Soviet Union; his policy of openness.

global greenhouse gas emissions: Gases released into the atmosphere that contribute to the greenhouse effect, a condition in which the earth's excess heat cannot escape.

global warming: Also called the greenhouse effect. The theorized gradual warming of the earth's climate as a result of the burning of fossil fuels, the use of man-made chemicals, deforestation, etc.

GMT *see* Greenwich Mean Time.

GNP *see* gross national product.

grand duchy: A territory ruled by a nobleman, called a grand duke, who ranks just below a king.

Greek Catholic: A person who is a member of an Orthodox Eastern Church.

Greek Orthodox: The official church of Greece, a self-governing branch of the Orthodox Eastern Church.

Greenwich (Mean) Time: Mean solar time of the meridian at Greenwich, England, used as the basis for standard time throughout most of the world. The world is divided into 24 time zones, and all are related to the prime, or Greenwich mean, zone.

gross domestic product: A measure of the market value of all goods and services produced within the boundaries of a nation, regardless of asset ownership. Unlike gross national product, GDP excludes receipts from that nation's business operations in foreign countries.

gross national product: A measure of the market value of goods and services produced by the labor and property of a nation. Includes receipts from that nation's business operation in foreign countries

groundwater: Water located below the earth's surface, the source from which wells and springs draw their water.

guano: The excrement of seabirds and bats found in various areas around the world. Gathered commercially and sold as a fertilizer.

guerrilla: A member of a small radical military organization that uses unconventional tactics to take their enemies by surprise.

gymnasium: A secondary school, primarily in Europe, that prepares students for university.

hardwoods: The name given to deciduous trees, such as cherry, oak, maple, and mahogany.

harem: In a Muslim household, refers to the women (wives, concubines, and servants in ancient times) who live there and also to the area of the home they live in.

harmattan: An intensely dry, dusty wind felt along the coast of Africa between Cape Verde and Cape Lopez. It prevails at intervals during the months of December, January, and February.

heavy industry: Industries that use heavy or large machinery to produce goods, such as automobile manufacturing.

hoist: The part of a flag nearest the flagpole.

Holocaust: The mass slaughter of European civilians, the vast majority Jews, by the Nazis during World War II.

Holy Roman Empire: A kingdom consisting of a loose union of German and Italian territories that existed from around the ninth century until 1806.

home rule: The governing of a territory by the citizens who inhabit it.

homeland: A region or area set aside to be a state for a people of a particular national, cultural, or racial origin.

homogeneous: Of the same kind or nature, often used in reference to a whole.

Horn of Africa: The Horn of Africa comprises Djibouti, Eritrea, Ethiopia, Somalia, and Sudan.

housing starts: The initiation of new housing construction.

human rights activist: A person who vigorously pursues the attainment of basic rights for all people.

human rights issues: Any matters involving people's basic rights which are in question or thought to be abused.

humanist: A person who centers on human needs and values, and stresses dignity of the individual.

humanitarian aid: Money or supplies given to a persecuted group or people of a country at war, or those devastated by a natural disaster, to provide for basic human needs.

hydrocarbon: A compound of hydrogen and carbon, often occurring in organic substances or derivatives of organic substances such as coal, petroleum, natural gas, etc.

hydrocarbon emissions: Organic compounds containing only carbon and hydrogen, often occurring in petroleum, natural gas, coal, and bitumens, and which contribute to the greenhouse effect.

hydroelectric potential: The potential amount of electricity that can be produced hydroelectrically. Usually used in reference to a given area and how many hydroelectric power plants that area can sustain.

hydroelectric power plant: A factory that produces electrical power through the application of waterpower.

IBRD *see* World Bank.

illegal alien: Any foreign-born individual who has unlawfully entered another country.

immigration: The act or process of passing or entering into another country for the purpose of permanent residence.

imports: Goods purchased from foreign suppliers.

indigenous: Born or originating in a particular place or country; native to a particular region or area.

Indo-Aryan language group: The group that includes the languages of India; also called Indo-European language group.

Indo-European language family: The group that includes the languages of India and much of Europe and southwestern Asia.

industrialized nation: A nation whose economy is based on industry.

infanticide: The act of murdering a baby.

infidel: One who is without faith or belief; particularly, one who rejects the distinctive doctrines of a particular religion.

inflation: The general rise of prices, as measured by a consumer price index. Results in a fall in value of currency.

installed capacity: The maximum possible output of electric power at any given time.

insurgency: The state or condition in which one rises against lawful authority or established government; rebellion.

insurrectionist: One who participates in an unorganized revolt against an authority.

interim government: A temporary or provisional government.

interim president: One who is appointed to perform temporarily the duties of president during a transitional period in a government.

internal migration: Term used to describe the relocation of individuals from one region to another without leaving the confines of the country or of a specified area.

International Date Line: An arbitrary line at about the 180th meridian that designates where one day begins and another ends.

Islam: The religious system of Mohammed, practiced by Moslims and based on a belief in Allah as the supreme being and Mohammed as his prophet. The spelling variations, Muslim and Muhammed, are also used, primarily by Islamic people. Islam also refers to those nations in which it is the primary religion.

isthmus: A narrow strip of land bordered by water and connecting two larger bodies of land, such as two continents, a continent and a peninsula, or two parts of an island.

Judaism: The religious system of the Jews, based on the Old Testament as revealed to Moses and characterized by a belief in one God and adherence to the laws of scripture and rabbinic traditions.

Judeo-Christian: The dominant traditional religious makeup of the United States and other countries based on the worship of the Old and New Testaments of the Bible.

junta: A small military group in power of a country, especially after a coup.

khan: A sovereign, or ruler, in central Asia.

khanate: A kingdom ruled by a khan, or man of rank.

kwashiorkor: Severe malnutrition in infants and children caused by a diet high in carbohydrates and lacking in protein.

kwh: The abbreviation for kilowatt-hour.

labor force: The number of people in a population available for work, whether actually employed or not.

labor movement: A movement in the early to mid-1800s to organize workers in groups according to profession to give them certain rights as a group, including bargaining power for better wages, working conditions, and benefits.

land reforms: Steps taken to create a fair distribution of farmland, especially by governmental action.

landlocked country: A country that does not have direct access to the sea; it is completely surrounded by other countries.

least developed countries: A subgroup of the United Nations designation of "less developed countries;" these countries generally have no significant economic growth, low literacy rates, and per person gross national product of less than $500. Also known as undeveloped countries.

leeward: The direction identical to that of the wind. For example, a *leeward tide* is a tide that runs in the same direction that the wind blows.

leftist: A person with a liberal or radical political affiliation.

legislative branch: The branch of government which makes or enacts the laws.

leprosy: A disease that can effect the skin and/or the nerves and can cause ulcers of the skin, loss of feeling, or loss of fingers and toes.

less developed countries (LDC): Designated by the United Nations to include countries with low levels of output, living standards, and per person gross national product generally below $5,000.

literacy: The ability to read and write.

Maastricht Treaty: The Maastricht Treaty (named for the Dutch town in which the treaty was signed) is also known as the Treaty of European Union. The treaty creates a European Union by: (a) committing the member states of the European Economic Community to both European Monetary Union (EMU) and political union; (b) introducing a single currency (European Currency Unit, ECU); (c) establishing a European System of Central Banks (ESCB); (d) creating a European Central Bank (ECB); and (e) broadening EC integration by including both a common foreign and security policy (CFSP) and cooperation in justice and home affairs (CJHA). The treaty entered into force on November 1, 1993.

Maghreb states: The Maghreb states include the three nations of Algeria, Morocco, and Tunisia; sometimes includes Libya and Mauritania.

maize: Another name (Spanish or British) for corn or the color of ripe corn.

majority party: The party with the largest number of votes and the controlling political party in a government.

mangrove: A tree which abounds on tropical shores in both hemispheres. Characterized by its numerous roots which arch out from its trunk and descend from its branches, mangroves form thick, dense growths along the tidal muds, reaching lengths hundreds of miles long.

manioc: The cassava plant or its product. Manioc is a very important food-staple in tropical America.

maquis. Scrubby, thick underbrush found along the coast of the Mediterranean Sea.

marginal land: Land that could produce an economic profit, but is so poor that it is only used when better land is no longer available.

marine life: The life that exists in, or is formed by the sea.

maritime climate: The climate and weather conditions typical of areas bordering the sea.

maritime rights: The rights that protect navigation and shipping.

market access: Market access refers to the openness of a national market to foreign products. Market access reflects a government's willingness to permit imports to compete relatively unimpeded with similar domestically produced goods.

market economy: A form of society which runs by the law of supply and demand. Goods are produced by firms to be sold to consumers, who determine the demand for them. Price levels vary according to the demand for certain goods and how much of them is produced.

market price: The price a commodity will bring when sold on the open market. The price is determined by the amount of demand for the commodity by buyers.

Marshall Plan: Formally known as the European Recovery Program, a joint project between the United States and most Western European nations under which $12.5 billion in U.S. loans and grants was expended to aid European recovery after World War II.

Marxism *see* Marxist-Leninist principles.

Marxist-Leninist principles: The doctrines of Karl Marx, built upon by Nikolai Lenin, on which communism was founded. They predicted the fall of capitalism, due to its own internal faults and the resulting oppression of workers.

Marxist: A follower of Karl Marx, a German socialist and revolutionary leader of the late 1800s, who contributed to Marxist-Leninist principles.

massif: A central mountain-mass or the dominant part of a range of mountains.

matrilineal (descent): Descending from, or tracing descent through, the maternal, or mother's, family line.

Mayan language family: The languages of the Central American Indians, further divided into two subgroups: the Maya and the Huastek.

mean temperature: The air temperature unit measured by the National Weather Service by adding the maximum and minimum daily temperatures together and diving the sum by 2.

Mecca (Mekkah): A city in Saudi Arabia; a destination of pilgrims in the Islamic world.

Mediterranean climate: A wet-winter, dry-summer climate with a moderate annual temperature range.

mestizo: The offspring of a person of mixed blood; especially, a person of mixed Spanish and American Indian parentage.

migratory birds: Those birds whose instincts prompt them to move from one place to another at the regularly recurring changes of season.

migratory workers: Usually agricultural workers who move from place to place for employment depending on the growing and harvesting seasons of various crops.

military coup: A sudden, violent overthrow of a government by military forces.

military junta: The small military group in power in a country, especially after a coup.

military regime: Government conducted by a military force.

military takeover: The seizure of control of a government by the military forces.

militia: The group of citizens of a country who are either serving in the reserve military forces or are eligible to be called up in time of emergency.

millet: A cereal grass whose small grain is used for food in Europe and Asia.

minority party: The political group that comprises the smaller part of the large overall group it belongs to; the party that is not in control.

missionary: A person sent by authority of a church or religious organization to spread his religious faith in a community where his church has no self-supporting organization.

Mohammed (or Muhammedor Mahomet): An Arabian prophet, known as the "Prophet of Allah" who founded the religion of Islam in 622, and wrote *The Koran,* the scripture of Islam. Also commonly spelled Muhammed, especially by Islamic people.

monarchy: Government by a sovereign, such as a king or queen.

money economy: A system or stage of economic development in which money replaces barter in the exchange of goods and services.

Mongol: One of an Asiatic race chiefly resident in Mongolia, a region north of China proper and south of Siberia.

Mongoloid: Having physical characteristics like those of the typical Mongols (Chinese, Japanese, Turks, Eskimos, etc.).

Moors: One of the Arab tribes that conquered Spain in the eighth century.

Moslem (Muslim): A follower of Mohammed (spelled Muhammed by many Islamic people), in the religion of Islam.

mosque: An Islam place of worship and the organization with which it is connected.

mouflon: A type of wild sheep characterized by curling horns.

mujahideen (mujahedin or mujahedeen): Rebel fighters in Islamic countries, especially those supporting the cause of Islam.

mulatto: One who is the offspring of parents one of whom is white and the other is black.

municipality: A district such as a city or town having its own incorporated government.

Muslim: A frequently used variation of the spelling of Moslem, to describe a follower of the prophet Mohammed (also spelled Muhammed), the founder of the religion of Islam.

Muslim New Year: A Muslim holiday. Although in some countries 1 Muharram, which is the first month of the Islamic year, is observed as a holiday, in other places the new year is observed on Sha'ban, the eighth month of the year. This practice apparently stems from pagan Arab times. Shab-i-Bharat, a national holiday in Bangladesh on this day, is held by many to be the occasion when God ordains all actions in the coming year.

NAFTA (North American Free Trade Agreement): NAFTA, which entered into force in January 1994, is a free trade agreement between Canada, the United States, and Mexico. The agreement progressively eliminates almost all U.S.-Mexico tariffs over a 10–15 year period.

nationalism: National spirit or aspirations; desire for national unity, independence, or prosperity.

nationalization: To transfer the control or ownership of land or industries to the nation from private owners.

native tongue: One's natural language. The language that is indigenous to an area.

NATO *see* North Atlantic Treaty Organization

natural gas: A combustible gas formed naturally in the earth and generally obtained by boring a well. The chemical makeup of natural gas is principally methane, hydrogen, ethylene compounds, and nitrogen.

natural harbor: A protected portion of a sea or lake along the shore resulting from the natural formations of the land.

naturalize: To confer the rights and privileges of a native-born subject or citizen upon someone who lives in the country by choice.

nature preserve: An area where one or more species of plant and/or animal are protected from harm, injury, or destruction.

neutrality: The policy of not taking sides with any countries during a war or dispute among them.

Newly Independent States: The NIS is a collective reference to 12 republics of the former Soviet Union: Russia, Ukraine, Belarus (formerly Byelorussia), Moldova (formerly Moldavia), Armenia, Azerbaijan, Uzbekistan, Turkmenistan, Tajikistan, Kazakhstan, and Kirgizstan (formerly Kirghiziya), and Georgia. Following dissolution of the Soviet Union, the distinction between the NIS and the Commonwealth of Independent States (CIS) was that Georgia was not a member of the CIS. That distinction dissolved when Georgia joined the CIS in November 1993.

news censorship *see* censorship

Nonaligned Movement: The NAM is an alliance of third world states that aims to promote the political and economic interests of developing countries. NAM interests have included ending colonialism/neo-colonialism, supporting the integrity of independent countries, and seeking a new international economic order.

Nordic Council: The Nordic Council, established in 1952, is directed toward supporting cooperation among Nordic countries. Members include Denmark, Finland, Iceland, Norway, and Sweden. Headquarters are in Stockholm, Sweden.

North Atlantic Treaty Organization (NATO): A mutual defense organization. Members include Belgium, Canada, Denmark, France (which has only partial membership), Greece, Iceland, Italy, Luxembourg, Netherlands, Norway, Portugal, Spain, Turkey, United Kingdom, United States, and Germany.

nuclear power plant: A factory that produces electrical power through the application of the nuclear reaction known as nuclear fission.

nuclear reactor: A device used to control the rate of nuclear fission in uranium. Used in commercial applications, nuclear reactors can maintain temperatures high enough to generate sufficient quantities of steam which can then be used to produce electricity.

OAPEC (Organization of Arab Petroleum Exporting countries): OAPEC was created in 1968; members include: Algeria, Bahrain, Egypt, Iraq, Kuwait, Libya, Qatar, Saudi Arabia, Syria, and the United Arab Emirates. Headquarters are in Cairo, Egypt.

OAS (Organization of American States): The OAS (Spanish: Organización de los Estados Americanos, OEA), or the Pan American Union, is a regional organization which promotes Latin American economic and social development. Members include the United States, Mexico, and most Central American, South American, and Caribbean nations.

OAS *see* Organization of American States

oasis: Originally, a fertile spot in the Libyan desert where there is a natural spring or well and vegetation; now refers to any fertile tract in the midst of a wasteland.

occupied territory: A territory that has an enemy's military forces present.

official language: The language in which the business of a country and its government is conducted.

oligarchy: A form of government in which a few people possess the power to rule as opposed to a monarchy which is ruled by one.

OPEC *see* OAPEC

open economy: An economy that imports and exports goods.

open market: Open market operations are the actions of the central bank to influence or control the money supply by buying or selling government bonds.

opposition party: A minority political party that is opposed to the party in power.

Organization of Arab Petroleum Exporting Countries *see* OAPEC

organized labor: The body of workers who belong to labor unions.

Ottoman Empire: An Turkish empire founded by Osman I in about 1603, that variously controlled large areas of land around the Mediterranean, Black, and Caspian Seas until it was dissolved in 1918.

overfishing: To deplete the quantity of fish in an area by removing more fish than can be naturally replaced.

overgrazing: Allowing animals to graze in an area to the point that the ground vegetation is damaged or destroyed.

overseas dependencies: A distant and physically separate territory that belongs to another country and is subject to its laws and government.

Pacific Rim: The Pacific Rim, referring to countries and economies bordering the Pacific Ocean.

pact: An international agreement.

Paleolithic: The early period of the Stone Age, when rough, chipped stone implements were used.

panhandle: A long narrow strip of land projecting like the handle of a frying pan.

papyrus: The paper-reed or -rush which grows on marshy river banks in the southeastern area of the Mediterranean, but more notably in the Nile valley.

paramilitary group: A supplementary organization to the military.

parasitic diseases: A group of diseases caused by parasitic organisms which feed off the host organism.

parliamentary republic: A system of government in which a president and prime minister, plus other ministers of departments, constitute the executive branch of the government and the parliament constitutes the legislative branch.

parliamentary rule: Government by a legislative body similar to that of Great Britain, which is composed of two houses—one elected and one hereditary.

parochial: Refers to matters of a church parish or something within narrow limits.

patriarchal system: A social system in which the head of the family or tribe is the father or oldest male. Kinship is determined and traced through the male members of the tribe.

patrilineal (descent): Descending from, or tracing descent through, the paternal or father's line.

pellagra: A disease marked by skin, intestinal, and central nervous system disorders, caused by a diet deficient in niacin, one of the B vitamins.

per capita: Literally, per person; for each person counted.

perestroika: The reorganization of the political and economic structures of the Soviet Union by president Mikhail Gorbachev.

periodical: A publication whose issues appear at regular intervals, such as weekly, monthly, or yearly.

petrochemical: A chemical derived from petroleum or from natural gas.

pharmaceutical plants: Any plant that is used in the preparation of medicinal drugs.

plantain: The name of a common weed that has often been used for medicinal purposes, as a folk remedy and in modern medicine. *Plaintain* is also the name of a tropical plant producing a type of banana.

poaching: To intrude or encroach upon another's preserves for the purpose of stealing animals, especially wild game.

polar climate: Also called tundra climate. A humid, severely cold climate controlled by arctic air masses, with no warm or summer season.

political climate: The prevailing political attitude of a particular time or place.

political refugee: A person forced to flee his or her native country for political reasons.

potable water: Water that is safe for drinking.

pound sterling: The monetary unit of Great Britain, otherwise known as the pound.

prefect: An administrative official; in France, the head of a particular department.

prefecture: The territory over which a prefect has authority.

prime meridian: Zero degrees in longitude that runs through Greenwich, England, site of the Royal Observatory. All other longitudes are measured from this point.

prime minister: The premier or chief administrative official in certain countries.

private sector: The division of an economy in which production of goods and services is privately owned.

privatization: To change from public to private control or ownership.

protectorate: A state or territory controlled by a stronger state, or the relationship of the stronger country toward the lesser one it protects.

Protestant Reformation: In 1529, a Christian religious movement begun in Germany to deny the universal authority of the Pope, and to establish the Bible as the only source of truth. (*Also see* Protestant)

Protestant: A member or an adherent of one of those Christian bodies which descended from the Reformation of the sixteenth century. Originally applied to those who opposed or protested the Roman Catholic Church.

proved reserves: The quantity of a recoverable mineral resource (such as oil or natural gas) that is still in the ground.

province: An administrative territory of a country.

provisional government: A temporary government set up during time of unrest or transition in a country.

pulses: Beans, peas, or lentils.

purge: The act of ridding a society of "undesirable" or unloyal persons by banishment or murder.

Rastafarian: A member of a Jamaican cult begun in 1930 as a semi-religious, semi-political movement.

rate of literacy: The percentage of people in a society who can read and write.

recession. A period of reduced economic activity in a country or region.

referendum: The practice of submitting legislation directly to the people for a popular vote.

Reformation *see* Protestant Reformation.

refugee: One who flees to a refuge or shelter or place of safety. One who in times of persecution or political commotion flees to a foreign country for safety.

revolution: A complete change in a government or society, such as in an overthrow of the government by the people.

right-wing party: The more conservative political party.

Roman alphabet: The alphabet of the ancient Romans from which the alphabets of most modern western European languages, including English, are derived.

Roman Catholic Church: The designation of the church of which the pope or Bishop of Rome is the head, and that holds him as the successor of St. Peter and heir of his spiritual authority, privileges, and gifts.

romance language: The group of languages derived from Latin: French, Spanish, Italian, Portuguese, and other related languages.

roundwood: Timber used as poles or in similar ways without being sawn or shaped.

runoff election: A deciding election put to the voters in case of a tie between candidates.

Russian Orthodox: The arm of the Orthodox Eastern Church that was the official church of Russia under the czars.

sack: To strip of valuables, especially after capture.

Sahelian zone: Eight countries make up this dry desert zone in Africa: Burkina Faso, Chad, Gambia, Mali, Mauritania, Niger, Senegal, and the Cape Verde Islands. *Also see* Club du Sahel.

salinization: An accumulation of soluble salts in soil. This condition is common in desert climates, where water evaporates quickly in poorly drained soil due to high temperatures.

Samaritans: A native or an inhabitant of Samaria; specifically, one of a race settled in the cities of Samaria by the king of Assyria after the removal of the Israelites from the country.

savanna: A treeless or near treeless plain of a tropical or subtropical region dominated by drought-resistant grasses.

schistosomiasis: A tropical disease that is chronic and characterized by disorders of the liver, urinary bladder, lungs, or central nervous system.

secession: The act of withdrawal, such as a state withdrawing from the Union in the Civil War in the United States.

sect: A religious denomination or group, often a dissenting one with extreme views.

segregation: The enforced separation of a racial or religious group from other groups, compelling them to live and go to school separately from the rest of society.

seismic activity: Relating to or connected with an earthquake or earthquakes in general.

self-sufficient: Able to function alone without help.

separation of power: The division of power in the government among the executive, legislative, and judicial branches and the checks and balances employed to keep them separate and independent of each other.

separatism: The policy of dissenters withdrawing from a larger political or religious group.

serfdom: In the feudal system of the Middle Ages, the condition of being attached to the land owned by a lord and being transferable to a new owner.

Seventh-day Adventist: One who believes in the second coming of Christ to establish a personal reign upon the earth.

shamanism: A religion of some Asians and Amerindians in which shamans, who are priests or medicine men, are believed to influence good and evil spirits.

shantytown: An urban settlement of people in flimsy, inadequate houses.

Shia Muslim: Members of one of two great sects of Islam. Shia Muslims believe that Ali and the Imams are the rightful successors of Mohammed (also commonly spelled Muhammed). They also believe that the last recognized Imam will return as a messiah. Also known as Shiites. (*Also see* Sunnis.)

Shiites *see* Shia Muslims.

Shintoism: The system of nature- and hero-worship which forms the indigenous religion of Japan.

shoal: A place where the water of a stream, lake, or sea is of little depth. Especially, a sand-bank which shows at low water.

sierra: A chain of hills or mountains.

Sikh: A member of a politico-religious community of India, founded as a sect around 1500 and based on the principles of monotheism (belief in one god) and human brotherhood.

Sino-Tibetan language family: The family of languages spoken in eastern Asia, including China, Thailand, Tibet, and Burma.

slash-and-burn agriculture: A hasty and sometimes temporary way of clearing land to make it available for agriculture by cutting down trees and burning them.

slave trade: The transportation of black Africans beginning in the 1700s to other countries to be sold as slaves—people owned as property and compelled to work for their owners at no pay.

Slavic languages: A major subgroup of the Indo-European language family. It is further subdivided into West Slavic (including Polish, Czech, Slovak and Serbian), South Slavic (including Bulgarian, Serbo-Croatian, Slovene, and Old Church Slavonic), and East Slavic (including Russian Ukrainian and Byelorussian).

social insurance: A government plan to protect low-income people, such as health and accident insurance, pension plans, etc.

social security: A form of social insurance, including life, disability, and old-age pension for workers. It is paid for by employers, employees, and the government.

socialism: An economic system in which ownership of land and other property is distributed among the community as a whole, and every member of the community shares in the work and products of the work.

socialist: A person who advocates socialism.

softwoods: The coniferous trees, whose wood density as a whole is relatively softer than the wood of those trees referred to as hardwoods.

sorghum (also known as Syrian Grass): Plant grown in various parts of the world for its valuable uses, such as for grain, syrup, or fodder.

Southeast Asia: The region in Asia that consists of the Malay Archipelago, the Malay Peninsula, and Indochina.

staple crop: A crop that is the chief commodity or product of a place, and which has widespread and constant use or value.

state: The politically organized body of people living under one government or one of the territorial units that make up a federal government, such as in the United States.

steppe: A level tract of land more or less devoid of trees, in certain parts of European and Asiatic Russia.

student demonstration: A public gathering of students to express strong feelings about a certain situation, usually taking place near the location of the people in power to change the situation.

subarctic climate: A high latitude climate of two types: *continental subarctic*, which has very cold winters, short, cool summers, light precipitation and moist air; and *marine subarctic*, a coastal and island climate with polar air masses causing large precipitation and extreme cold.

subcontinent: A land mass of great size, but smaller than any of the continents; a large subdivision of a continent.

subsistence economy: The part of a national economy in which money plays little or no role, trade is by barter, and living standards are minimal.

subsistence farming: Farming that provides the minimum food goods necessary for the continuation of the farm family.

subtropical climate: A middle latitude climate dominated by humid, warm temperatures and heavy rainfall in summer, with cool winters and frequent cyclonic storms.

subversion: The act of attempting to overthrow or ruin a government or organization by stealthy or deceitful means.

Sudanic language group: A related group of languages spoken in various areas of northern Africa, including Yoruba, Mandingo, and Tshi.

suffrage: The right to vote.

Sufi: A Muslim mystic who believes that God alone exists, there can be no real difference between good and evil, that the soul exists within the body as in a cage, so death should be the chief object of desire, and sufism is the only true philosophy.

sultan: A king of a Muslim state.

Sunni Muslim: Members of one of two major sects of the religion of Islam. Sunni Muslims adhere to strict orthodox traditions, and believe that the four caliphs are the rightful successors to Mohammed, founder of Islam. (Mohammed is commonly spelled Muhammed, especially by Islamic people.) (*Also see* Shia Muslim.)

Taoism: The doctrine of Lao-Tzu, an ancient Chinese philosopher (about 500 B.C.) as laid down by him in the *Tao-te-ching*.

tariff: A tax assessed by a government on goods as they enter (or leave) a country. May be imposed to protect domestic industries from imported goods and/or to generate revenue.

temperate zone: The parts of the earth lying between the tropics and the polar circles. The *northern temperate zone* is the area between the tropic of Cancer and the Arctic Circle. The *southern temperate zone* is the area between the tropic of Capricorn and the Antarctic Circle.

terracing: A form of agriculture that involves cultivating crops in raised banks of earth.

terrorism: Systematic acts of violence designed to frighten or intimidate.

thermal power plant: A facility that produces electric energy from heat energy released by combustion of fuel or nuclear reactions.

Third World: A term used to describe less developed countries; as of the mid-1990s, it is being replaced by the United Nations designation Less Developed Countries, or LDC.

topography: The physical or natural features of the land.

torrid zone: The part of the earth's surface that lies between the tropics, so named for the character of its climate.

totalitarian party: The single political party in complete authoritarian control of a government or state.

trachoma: A contagious bacterial disease that affects the eye.

treaty: A negotiated agreement between two governments.

tribal system: A social community in which people are organized into groups or clans descended from common ancestors and sharing customs and languages.

tropical monsoon climate: One of the tropical rainy climates; it is sufficiently warm and rainy to produce tropical rainforest vegetation, but also has a winter dry season.

tsetse fly: Any of the several African insects which can transmit a variety of parasitic organisms through its bite. Some of these organisms can prove fatal to both human and animal victims.

tundra: A nearly level treeless area whose climate and vegetation are characteristically arctic due to its northern position; the subsoil is permanently frozen.

undeveloped countries *see* least developed countries.

unemployment rate: The overall unemployment rate is the percentage of the work force (both employed and unemployed) who claim to be unemployed.

UNICEF: An international fund set-up for children's emergency relief: United Nations Children's Fund (formerly United Nations International Children's Emergency Fund).

universal adult suffrage: The policy of giving every adult in a nation the right to vote.

untouchables: In India, members of the lowest caste in the caste system, a hereditary social class system. They were considered unworthy to touch members of higher castes.

urban guerrilla: A rebel fighter operating in an urban area.

urbanization: The process of changing from country to city.

USSR: An abbreviation of Union of Soviet Socialist Republics.

veldt: In South Africa, an unforested or thinly forested tract of land or region, a grassland.

Warsaw Pact: Agreement made 14 May 1955 (and dissolved 1 July 1991) to promote mutual defense between Albania, Bulgaria, Czechoslovakia, East Germany, Hungary, Poland, Romania, and the USSR.

Western nations: Blanket term used to describe mostly democratic, capitalist countries, including the United States, Canada, and western European countries.

wildlife sanctuary: An area of land set aside for the protection and preservation of animals and plants.

workers' compensation: A series of regular payments by an employer to a person injured on the job.

World Bank: The World Bank is a group of international institutions which provides financial and technical assistance to developing countries.

world oil crisis: The severe shortage of oil in the 1970s precipitated by the Arab oil embargo.

wormwood: A woody perennial herb native to Europe and Asiatic Russia, valued for its medicinal uses.

yaws: A tropical disease caused by a bacteria which produces raspberry-like sores on the skin.

yellow fever: A tropical viral disease caused by the bite of an infected mosquito, characterized by jaundice.

Zoroastrianism: The system of religious doctrine taught by Zoroaster and his followers in the Avesta; the religion prevalent in Persia until its overthrow by the Muslims in the seventh century.